FLASH!

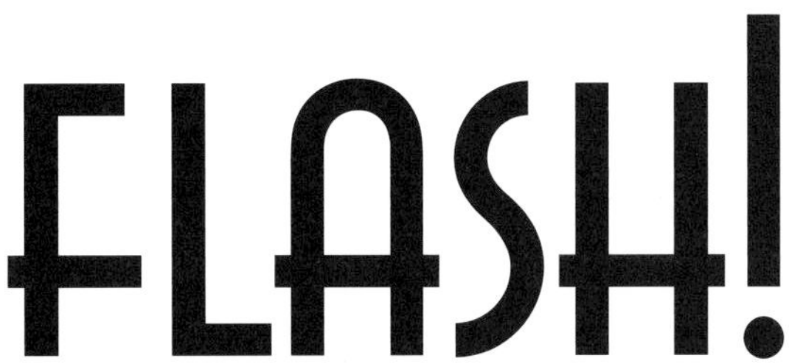

FLASH!

PHOTOGRAPHY, WRITING, & SURPRISING ILLUMINATION

KATE FLINT

OXFORD
UNIVERSITY PRESS

Great Clarendon Street, Oxford, OX2 6DP,
United Kingdom

Oxford University Press is a department of the University of Oxford. It furthers the University's objective of excellence in research, scholarship, and education by publishing worldwide. Oxford is a registered trade mark of Oxford University Press in the UK and in certain other countries

First Edition published in 2017

Impression: 1

Published in the United States of America by Oxford University Press
198 Madison Avenue, New York, NY 10016, United States of America

British Library Cataloguing in Publication Data
Data available

Library of Congress Control Number: 2017940297

ISBN 978–0–19–880826–8

Printed and bound by
CPI Group (UK) Ltd, Croydon, CR0 4YY

Lightning symbol: © kulyk/Shutterstock

To my parents,
Joy and Ray Flint

ACKNOWLEDGEMENTS

The inspiration for this book came to me—how else?—in a flash. Miles Orvell extended an invitation to me, asking me if I'd be interested in participating in an interdisciplinary colloquium at Temple University on the topic of 'Reproduction'. Specifically, he suggested that I speak on Light. My co-panelist was to be Chris Otter; our respondent Alan Trachtenberg. It was not an invitation that I would have dreamed of turning down, and during the summer of 2006, I chased around various topics in my head. And then, standing one evening at our back door in New Mexico, looking out at a spectacular thunderstorm on the Cerrillos Hills, and trying—with various degrees of success—to photograph it, I started to wonder what connections one might make between flashes of lightning and flash photography. From there, it was an easy jump to start thinking about the history of flash photography itself, and its relationship to the broader cultural histories of photography.

For some time before that, I'd been thinking, and teaching, about the relationship between photography and writing. I'd been considering the presence of photographs and photographers within literature, and the parallels and differences between telling narratives in photographs and in words. I had started to explore the ekphrastic aspects of photography—the language of its practice, and the forms used to describe and discuss its images. Asking what was distinct about flash photography and its accompanying verbal rhetoric breathed new life into this project, and although I put it to one side for a while to focus on completing other things, I owe a huge debt to Miles for this invitation, and to Chris and Alan for their generous, provocative comments and questions during the colloquium and the dinner that followed. I should note, incidentally, that as a photographer I've never been enamoured of flash photography itself, but the research that this book has entailed, and the countless flash photographs that I've examined, have given me a huge respect for its many possibilities.

My gratitude to many other people and institutions is deep and heartfelt. The project was completed thanks to a Fellowship from the American Council of Learned Societies, a Fellowship from the National Humanities Center (NHC), a Fellowship at the Georgia O'Keeffe Museum Research Center in Santa Fe, and a semester's sabbatical leave from the University of Southern California (USC). At the NHC, I benefited from the indefatigable work of the extraordinary librarians—Brooke Andrade, Sarah Harris, and Sam Schuth—who truly managed to achieve the impossible—as well as from the leadership of Robert Newman, the help of all the staff, and the stimulating company of my fellow Fellows. At the O'Keeffe Center, special thanks to Eumie Stroukoff, and to all who made me so comfortable and welcome. Again, my fellow Fellows asked great, provocative questions that helped to shape my argument as it moved into its very final stages. Benefiting from these fellowships—and much more besides—would not have been possible without the support of many at USC, and I especially thank Provost Michael Quick, Dean Steve Kay, Acting Dean Dani Byrd, Vice-Dean Peter Mancall, and my wonderful department chairs, Amy Ogata (in Art History) and David St John (in English). USC doesn't just pay lip service to supporting interdisciplinary study, it facilitates it in many practical and supportive ways. I deeply regret that Beth Garrett, former USC Provost, didn't live to see this book. The early work for it was carried out whilst I was still teaching at Rutgers University, and I'm grateful to the institutional support offered by Dean Douglas Greenberg and Dean of Humanities Ann Fabian (who asked the best kind of searching questions), and to my Chair, Carolyn Williams (who's been an enthusiastic cheerleader for this book all along). Librarians and staff at the British Library, the George Eastman House, the Getty Research Institute, the Huntington Library, the Schlesinger Library, Radcliffe Institute, Harvard University, and the USC have uniformly been helpful and resourceful. In the final stages of picture research, I've been helped by the staff of numerous galleries and museums, and by the kindness of individual artists. I'd like to offer a special thanks to Malcolm Collier for sharing memories of his father's working practices.

Flash!—or at least, many parts of it—has been aired and interrogated in many venues over the past few years. At Rutgers, members of the British Studies Center offered some acute and helpful criticism in the book's raw stages—Seth Koven was especially influential there. At USC, I've gained a great deal from sharing it publically with members of the English Department—Jack Halberstam formulated a question about race that proved especially fruitful—and with people in Art History and the Visual Studies Research Institute. Vanessa Schwartz's invitation to workshop a chapter with her seminar on News Pictures provided me with some terrific feedback, and her input has also been invaluable on other issues. Jennifer Greenhill and Megan Luke have been particularly engaged with some of the areas that I discuss, and their comments have helped me clarify certain ideas. My thanks to Jenny for her thoughts about Gordon Parks, in particular.

Further afield, I have given papers about flash photography at several conferences held by the North American Victorian Studies Association, the Modern Languages Association, and the College Art Association. Invitations to speak came—in roughly chronological order—from the Institute of English Studies, London; the Bread Loaf School of English; the University of New Mexico; the University of Virginia; the University of York Centre for Modern Studies; the University of Minnesota-Morris; Texas Christian University; Goldsmith's College, London; Rice University; the Museum of Contemporary Art, Los Angeles; the North American Studies in Romanticism Annual Conference; Brigham Young University; the Birkbeck Centre for the History and Theory of Photography, University of London; George Washington University; the Rethinking Early Photography Conference held in Lincoln, UK; University of North

Carolina; Duke University; the University of New Mexico Art Museum; and the Georgia O'Keeffe Research Center. These were wonderful, responsive audiences who came up with provocative points that never failed to help me sharpen my argument. For their conversation, hospitality, and kindnesses on these occasions, I'd especially like to mention Jesse Aleman, Alison Booth, Owen Clayton, David Peters Corbett, Hilary Fraser, Jennifer Green-Lewis, Jamie Horrocks, Linda Hughes, Isobel Hurst, Lynda Nead, Bob Patten, and Dan Sherman.

An early version of Chapter 2 was published as '"More rapid than the lightning's flash": Photography, Suddenness, and the Afterlife of Romantic Illumination', *European Romantic Review* 24/3 (2013), 369–83, and some sections of Chapter 3 appeared, in different and expanded form, in 'Photographic Memory', *Romanticism and Victorianism on the Net* 53 (February 2009), https://www.erudit.org/fr/revues/ravon/2009-n53-ravon2916/029898ar/.

Numerous other friends have sustained me through the writing of *Flash!* In England, Dinah Birch, Clare Pettitt, and Helen Small continue to give continuity to my transatlantic life, both academic and otherwise—as do Lynn and Hilary. Clare, in particular, has probably heard more about flash photography than she ever anticipated in the course of our hugely stimulating conversations about interdisciplinary scholarship (and much more besides). She's been with this book from the beginning, right through to the last words, written at her kitchen table. This book has also been kept afloat through talking to Joe Boone, Hollis Clayson, Jay Clayton, Anne Helmreich, Meredith McGill, Cassie Mansfield, Nancy Rose Marshall, Beth Meyerowitz, Dan Novak, Barry Qualls, Torrey Reade, Connie Samaras, Merry Scully, Tanya Sheehan, Jonah Siegel, Nigel Smith, Matthew Sweet—greatly expanding my knowledge of films that feature flash!—Carla Yanni, Ruth Yeazell, and very many other friends. Graduate students at USC and at Rutgers have been invaluable to me during this book's gestation, and have generously allowed me to try out ideas on them, particularly concerning the nature of the type of scholarship I—and often they—are undertaking: Nadya Bair, Lauren Dodds, Amanda Kotch, Karen Huang, Ryan Linkof, Chris McGeorge, Avigail Moss, MacKenzie Stevens, and Mimi Winick deserve special mention. Robin Coste Lewis has helped me in a variety of imaginative ways (and supplied the image of the Mammoth Cave!). I'm so happy that I can now count Devin Griffiths, once a Rutgers graduate student, as a friend and colleague here in Los Angeles.

For less academically tangible benefits, I'm enormously indebted to my cousins, Jon, Peter, and Gaynor, and their families; to David and Melanie McPherson, in Santa Fe; to Harry's Roadhouse, also in Santa Fe, for their burritos and margaritas; to the USC women's volleyball community, and to the cats who at various times have rearranged the wording of this book through sprawling on the keyboard, especially LucyFur, Moth, and Walter Gomez.

Everyone with whom I've worked at Oxford University Press has been extraordinary in the interest and care that they've shown towards this book. I'm greatly indebted to them. Jacqueline Norton has been warmly enthusiastic about the project since we first talked about it over a glass or two of wine in Austin, TX. Aimee Wright has done a terrific job in shepherding *Flash!*—and me—along. Deborah Protheroe, Senior Picture Researcher, has helped me with what at times seemed the impossible. My profound thanks to the team responsible for making the book look so good. Rowena Anketell has been a model copy-editor—intelligent and eagle-eyed. Kavya Ramu, in charge of the production team, has ensured that everything has run smoothly and efficiently. Finally, Sophie Goldsworthy's passion for photography (together with her many other qualities) has been an all-important motivating factor! I'm very grateful indeed to the book's anonymous readers, who offered great encouragement and also made some excellent suggestions.

My parents, Joy and Ray Flint, have been great friends to this book, valiantly taking an interest in it even though, I strongly suspect, their interest in flash photography is not enormously strong. I realized, to my dismay, that I've never dedicated a 'real book' to them, and make amends here.

Alice Echols has lived with *Flash!* from its earliest, hesitant incarnation. The book (or at least, boxes of notes and books) has moved with us many times, from New Jersey to California, and back and forth from Los Angeles to Santa Fe. During these years, Alice has read and reread it, and has been hugely generous with her ideas, her time, and her tolerance for the strange pieces of historical flash equipment that arrive via eBay. Her suggestions about how I could improve things have always been spot on. Words are completely inadequate for all that she's given to this book, and to me.

Every effort has been made to trace and contact copyright holders prior to publication. If notified, the publisher will be pleased to rectify any errors or omissions at the earliest opportunity.

CONTENTS

LIST OF FIGURES

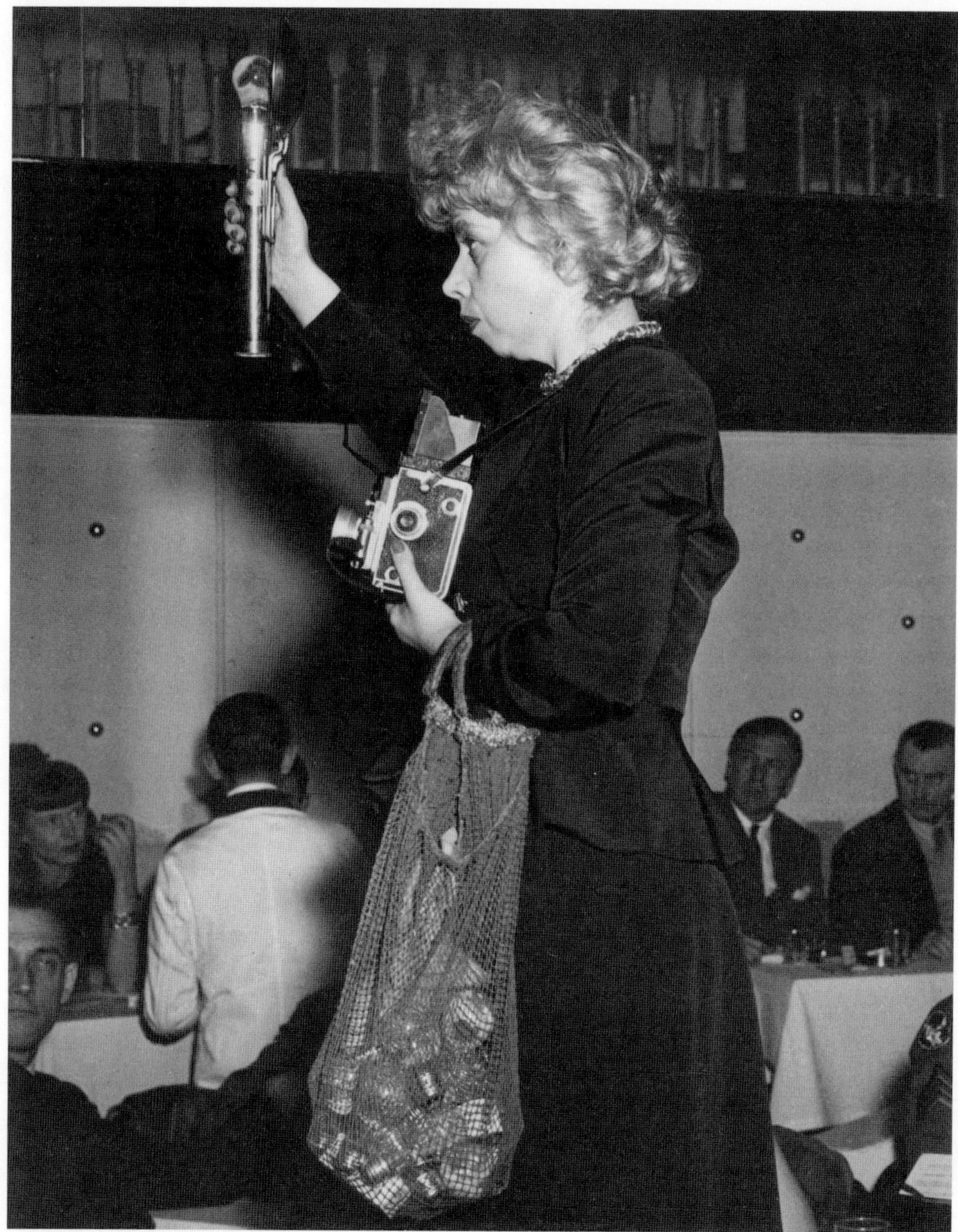

Figure 0.1 Weegee (Arthur Fellig), 'Lisette Model', *c.*1946. © Weegee (Arthur Fellig)/International Center of Photography/Getty Images.

Prologue

ALL PHOTOGRAPHY requires light, but the light of flash photography is unique—sudden, shocking, intrusive, and abrupt. It's quite unlike the light that comes from the sun, or even from ambient illumination. Looking at flash breaks down familiar categories and hierarchies of photography, since it's employed across the board: for fine art work, news photography, and amateur snapshots. Flash has revealed appalling social conditions and has burnished models on the covers of glossy magazines. Paparazzi chase celebrities with flash; large public social events and intimate family events are recorded through flash; flash puts crimes and their aftermath on display; flash lights up the most ordinary, mundane corners. Flash not only illuminates darkness, but also 'stops time'—the rapidly flashing strobe enables the depiction of rapidly moving objects.

So *Flash!* is about several things. It tackles the challenge of writing the history of light—or, at the very least, of a particular and quite distinctive form of artificial light. This is a light that functions in complete contradiction of philosopher Merleau-Ponty's assertion that 'lighting and reflection ... play their part only if they remain in the background as discreet intermediaries, and lead our gaze instead of arresting it'.[1] Nothing startles and disrupts the gaze so much as a sudden flash of light, and the effect of that flash, when captured in a photograph, is to direct that gaze quite differently from how it plays on a non-illuminated world.

Yet there is no photographic flash without the chemistry of ignited compounds, or without the channelling of electrical forces. This book, therefore, is also about the successive pieces of technological apparatus used to provide enough illumination to take an effective photograph in a particular place, at a particular time, when there would not otherwise be enough light to do so. Flash is what we might term a 'dependent technology'. There are other types of useful human-made flashes—think of the lighthouse that sends out its warning beams; or the heliograph, a wireless solar telegraph that sent messages through flashing sun off a mirror. There are the decorative flashes of exploding fireworks, and the terrifying flashes of firearms. There are natural flashes, too—I'll have plenty to say about lightning later on, but consider the tiny pulses of light emitted by fireflies, or the eerie emissions of bioluminescent creatures in the deep. And then there are what we might term accidental flashes—the sun's sudden flare off the chrome of a passing car; the little eruption of a smoker's match, lighting up, for Arthur Symons, 'then, in the dark, | Sudden, a flash, a glow, | And a hand and a ring I know'.[2] But the flash that I discuss in this book is, essentially, a by-product of photography, born out of necessity—the need to provide enough light to record an image on a plate, film, or digital chip when such light is otherwise absent.

Writing *Flash!* has meant thinking freshly about how to approach photographic history. Although some of the obvious flash photographers are here—Jacob Riis, Weegee, Brassaï—I don't foreground particular photographers or movements, although the book certainly looks at flash in relation to distinct usages—to portraiture, for example, and to documentary work, and to the fine art careers of those who wished to hold themselves aloof from the brash impulses of commercial photography. Above all, I think about the photographic flash as a particular type of illumination, as a strategy, as an event. I offer, to be sure, a history of the creative technologies that allowed highly combustible materials to be ignited and to produce a sudden, dramatic explosion of hard light, but my interest repeatedly comes back to three areas of inquiry.

First, how do we understand the experience of witnessing, or being subject to, this sudden, brief illumination and this interruption of time: what, I ask, is it like to be at the receiving end of flashlight? It may be to feel exposed; it almost certainly entails somatic discomfort—Edward Henry Machin, in Arnold Bennett's 1913 comic novella *The Regent*, suffers 'the sudden flash of the photographer's magnesium light, plainly felt by him through his closed lids'—a striking example of flash's physiological impact on the body.[3] Accounts of dazzled, temporarily blinded retinas are even more common, for flash makes the body pay attention to the properties of visual technology. And how might we think about that suddenness? How long *is* a flash—or rather, has its length been differently understood at different times in its history? Since flash photography is unlike any other form of the practice, shattering the light environment that precedes and follows it (and, indeed, disturbing our visual perception for a short while), how has it provided a vocabulary for us to talk about certain forms of recollection (the cinematic flashback; the concept of flashbulb memories)?

Second, I ask what distinguishes flash's aesthetic effects—whether these are deployed deliberately, or are a by-product of the pragmatic uses to which it's been put in lighting up darkness—and how might these affect our interpretation of a photograph's subject? How do we respond to the exaggerated rendition of darkness, and the deep shadows that it so often makes? What is the effect of having details, especially of the detritus of the everyday, suddenly made visible—often giving very ordinary things an unplanned prominence that they did not normally hold? And although light very often carries highly positive connotations, what does it mean to have 'too much' light—whether flash is held too close, and bleaches its subject, or whether we consider the biggest, most destructive flash of all: that of the atomic bomb?

Finally, and informing all these other questions, my interest has been in the cultural connotations of flash photography, and in asking what part might flash have played in popular responses to the activity of photography more broadly. To understand why flash photography was treated first with awe and amazement, then with amusement, and then with increasing resentment for its intrusive effects; to recognize the role that flash has played in contributing to a popular denigration, or at least suspicion, of the photographer, has meant going well beyond the traditional sources of the photographic historian. So as well as consulting photographic journals and manuals, photographers' memoirs and interviews, exhibition reviews, advertisements, and a whole range of other archival material, I've paid particular attention to those moments when flash erupts—sometimes quite literally—into novels and poems, TV shows and films. Sometimes the flaring of flashbulbs signals celebrity and exposure, whether sought-after or dreaded. Flash is a useful shorthand: in the first seconds of *Notting Hill* (1999), flashes alternate with the face of a beautiful woman—so that we're instantly assured of the status of the film star we've just heard announced. Sometimes this shattering of darkness is used to build, or break, suspense. What this demonstrates, unquestionably, is the inseparability of photographic history from the wider cultural and social contexts of which it is a part, and which photography has done so much to form. It is a version of media history that displays the necessity of talking about technological methods and devices, forms of communication and distribution, modes of perception, and cultural beliefs—all taken together.[4]

Take two very different examples: one American and one British. William Faulkner's short story 'All the Dead Pilots' (written 1930; published 1931) opens with the materiality of photographs, 'the snapshots hurriedly made, a little faded, a little dog-eared with the thirteen years' that commemorate First World War pilots—all now dead. They may not, literally, have fallen out of the skies or been killed in battle, but the brief flaring of bravery, of extraordinary spirit that these swaggering young men embodied is no more:

> that's all. That's it. The courage, the recklessness, call it what you will, is the flash, the instant of sublimation; then flick! the old darkness again. That's why. It's too strong for steady diet. And if it were a steady diet, it would not be a flash, a glare. And so, being momentary, it can be preserved only on paper: a picture, a few written words.[5]

Flash might have helped take these photographs of young men—but it seems more as if Faulkner sees that brief instant of their youth, their camaraderie, that's represented in the photographs as brief flashes of time in their own right; sudden insights into what was, and what (in terms of the human spirit) might be—but that only can shine out briefly with full intensity. This association of the flash with brevity, fragmentation, and with what stands either side of it is consolidated by the language in which the narrator describes this story, which does not flow easily: it falls into seven brief parts. 'That's why this story is composite: a series of brief glares in which, instantaneous and without depth or perspective, there stood into sight the portent and the threat of what the race could bear and become, in an instant between dark and dark.'[6]

If the implications of flash in Faulkner's tale—whether this flash is literal or translated into narrative form—are broad and metaphysical, flash's eruption into *The Lonely Londoners* (1956)—Trinidadian Sam Selvon's novel of post-Windrush immigration—is highly localized, both textually and in terms of Selvon's fictional location. At the centre of the novel is a Joyce-like eight-page sentence describing how, on summer nights, the large public parks are full of couples having sex in the limpid darkness. The narrator tells how 'two sports catch a fellar hiding behind some bushes with a flash camera in his hand', and beat him up.[7] One moment in Hyde Park, before the flash is even fired, encapsulates the association of flash photography with voyeurism and seediness, with the invasion of privacy. But it also tacitly suggests a whole history of race relations—one that crosses national boundaries, with Selvon's narrator pushing back against the assumptions, all too familiar in the visual annals of lynching, that black people can be exposed and demeaned though flash's intrusive, bleaching properties. The 'two sports' reverse the direction of violence, punishing the imminent photographic aggression of the peeping Tom.

But this study pushes beyond a consideration of flash's representation, and the powers that flash brings *to* representation. As well as exploring flash's sudden appearances in literature or on the screen, I look at the very language in which it was discussed and described—especially the figurative vocabulary that was attached to it. From its early days in the mid-nineteenth century to the very late 1920s, the dominant simile was that of lightning—bright, shocking, startling, unpredictable. As we shall see, finding safer and more reliable ways to explode magnesium and its compounds dominated innovation in the field for over forty years—years in which the metaphor of lightning, and the language of danger and unpredictability, gradually declined in relation to images made by flash, and then fell off rapidly after the invention of the flashbulb. All the same, a tiny atavistic sign of flash photography's more idealistic history remains, in the form in which it is indicated on a camera or cell phone—a little jagged lightning bolt.

Distinct, more violent associations grew up around this new form of flash technology, both because of its identification with scenes of crime, and—coupled with a highly portable camera—its ability to capture a supposedly private moment with an instant and invasive shard of light, or to give dazzling but completely unsubtle illumination to a scene. When the noir thriller writer Ross Macdonald described police investigators at work at a Los Angeles crime scene in *The Drowning Pool* (1950), there is no thrill of the metaphysical, just the glaring splash of harsh light as, from the kitchen door, 'I saw a white flash splatter the darkness below the garages like a brushful of whitewash'.[8] Situating the paraphernalia of flash photography in relation to the particular contexts in which it was most frequently used, as well as alongside the drive towards safety, predictability, and ease of execution that determined its changing aesthetic properties, helps one enormously in understanding how it came to take on a changing set of cultural relations.

My examples in this prologue have been drawn from both British and American sources. In the book, I primarily consider flash in a northern transatlantic context, but I touch on flash's presence in a whole range of other countries as well, from France to South Africa, Argentina to Japan. I see *Flash!* as opening up possibilities for detailed research in many other parts of the world, for exploring flash brings home the fact that photography's history is a global history—and an extremely diffuse one at that. In the nineteenth century, news of innovations (and disasters) related to flash photography spread rapidly through the press—both the specialist journals read by photographers, and more mainstream papers eager to report on scientific advances, novelty, and sensation. From the late nineteenth century onwards, the development of flash's technology has been inseparable from large-scale commercial enterprises, often with international plants, offices, advertising, and distribution networks. Whilst its use by fine art photographers is very frequently linked to the gallery system and hence to major urban cultural centres—London, New York, Los Angeles, Berlin, Paris, Tokyo, etc.—photographers themselves, whether professionals or amateurs, work worldwide. So although there have been very many local variations in the use of flash—based on economic factors, the availability of luxury goods such as cameras and their accessories, access to photographic studios and to processing facilities, and so on—and despite differences in local and national conventions and grammars of photography, the actual *experience* of flash is, potentially, highly similar everywhere. The major factor in considering flash's geographical inequalities is whether flash photography is a complete novelty—even seen as linked to quasi-magical powers of producing light from darkness—or whether it's become an often irritating commonplace. Context is everything, even as the properties of light shattering darkness remain the same.

It's understandable, therefore, that the relatively small number of works that have, to date, sought to conceptualize the use of flash, and to place it within a broader cultural matrix, do so with reference to a whole range of specific times and locales. Ulrich Baer concentrates on Jean-Martin Charcot's use of magnesium to take photographs of 'hysterics' in Paris's psychiatric hospital, the Saltpetrière, in the 1870s, and considers flash's interruptive powers insofar as they disrupt our notions about the continuity of time.[9] Alexander Nemerov argues that Frederic Remington's paintings of wild animals, hunting, and campfire life borrow their effects from flash photography, and places them in the context of developments in flash photography and electric lighting in the late nineteenth and early twentieth century.[10] Marilyn Ivy discusses how images produced by Japanese photographer Naitō Masatoshi between 1970 and 1985 visually announce that they have been produced by the artificial light of flash, which obliterates that which it would normally seek to illuminate. She sees in the powers of flash an allegory for 'modernity's aporia, nowhere more so than in Japan of the postwar period'.[11] *Blitzlicht* (2012), containing four valuable essays on the history of flash photography, was published in Switzerland and emphasizes German-language contexts and photographic scholarship.[12]

To examine flash photography is to be made very aware of photography's complex imbrication in the world—as social and artistic practice; as individual image and as expansive collections of pictures; as a series of overlapping technologies; as profession and as hobby; as something that can be breathtaking or ordinary; and as giving rise to, and requiring, specific vocabulary in which to describe its effects, its aesthetics, its associations. What distinguishes flash photography from all other forms, however, is its suddenness; its creation of momentary, intense artificial light that shatters the continuity of darkness, of shadow, or dim illumination that precedes and follows this shocking interruption. Flash's light connects us to very many varied facets of photography—and yet its properties are, unquestionably, its own.

CHAPTER ONE

Flashes of Light

The Soul's distinct connection
With immortality
Is best disclosed by Danger
Or quick Calamity—

As Lightning on a Landscape
Exhibits Sheets of Place—
Not yet suspected—but for Flash—
And Click—and Suddenness.

Emily Dickinson, Fragment 901 (1865)

A SUDDEN flash can startle, shock, illuminate. Such a flash may come from the lightning that rips apart a sky, or a photographer might set off a dazzle of magnesium powder or explode a flashbulb in order to throw bright light on a scene or subject. A flash, in other words, may be unpredictable in its origins and preternatural in its impact; or it may be the product of more or less controlled technology. This tension between the metaphysical and the human-made lies at the heart of this book.

Flashes of light have long been associated with sudden inspiration and clarity, whether divinely produced or internally generated—that is, whether seen as a bolt of illumination coming from heaven, typified by the revelation Saul received on the road to Damascus; or as Ralph Waldo Emerson's command to follow one's unique inner prompting—that 'gleam of light which flashes across [the writer's] mind from within'—rather than relying on the ideas and standards of others.[1] Such insights may be marked by the awe associated with transcendental knowledge. Yet the concept can rapidly become a cliché. Explaining how creativity works in *Proust Was a Neuroscientist* (2008), Jonah Lehrer notes that 'when people think about creative breakthroughs, they tend to imagine them as incandescent flashes, like a light bulb going on inside the brain'—a popular fiction that he is keen to debunk.[2] In this, he follows in the tradition of Nietzsche, who in his 1878 *Human, All Too Human* wrote how 'artists have an interest in the existence of a belief in the sudden occurrence of ideas, in so-called inspirations; as though the idea of a work of art, a poem, the basic proposition of a philosophy flashed down from heaven like a ray of divine grace'—when in fact what a creative person needs, above all, is the quality of judgement to reject, sift, transform, and order.[3]

The appeal of the flash as an instrument of sudden revelation—one that is powerful, surprising, somehow out of the ordinary, and also disruptive of temporal flow—has slid relatively seamlessly from its natural and human contexts to the optical and chemical processes that are employed to capture an image, to stop time. In the decades that followed the invention of photography, to write about the new medium often entailed employing vocabulary in a way that evoked the novelty and strangeness of both process and product. At the centre of this discourse lay the language of light. The narrative of photographic technology in the nineteenth century is, for the most part, one of light's relationship to motion, considering how to make the best use of natural light as it entered the camera's aperture and fell for a moment or more onto a prepared surface within. In this fashion, even 'the most transitory of things, a shadow,' claimed Henry Fox Talbot, 'the proverbial emblem of all that is fleeting and momentary, may be fettered by the spells of our "*natural magic*" and may be fixed for ever in the position which it seemed only destined for a single instant to occupy'.[4]

However extraordinary a phenomenon photography's quasi-magical powers seemed at first, those who wrote about it in its early years drew readily on two pre-existing linguistic strands: those that described the presence and operations of natural light, and those that were habitually applied to well-established aesthetic practices for recording appearances: 'the pencil of nature', Fox Talbot called the agency behind the photographic image when titling his 1844 photo book of the same name; 'the rectilineal pencils of light' did the work, according to David Brewster, writing in the *Edinburgh Review* the preceding year.[5] Elizabeth Eastlake maintained 'every form which is traced by light is the impress of one moment, or one hour, or one age in the great passage of time'.[6] This language of light was deployed on both sides of the Atlantic. In 1872 the Connecticut photographer H. J. Rodgers published his memoir, *Twenty-Three Years Under A Sky-Light, or Life and Experiences of a Photographer*. He sets up this chronicle as the record of a period of pleasures and enjoyments interspersed with an inordinate number of 'soul-trying perplexities and discouragements' resulting from the constant technological experimentations that his new practice demanded. He described this emotional oscillation between achievement and disappointment—whether technological, aesthetic, or social—in terms drawn directly from light sources in the natural world:

> As the most vivid lightning flashes proceed from the most dreary and dismal cloud, and the twinkling glimmer of the diamond penetrates the darkness, so have the heliographers' minds been made gloomy and dark at times with new projects and phases for experimental research; and through unremitting toil and incessant study, the clear and brilliant light of crowning success has all the more vividly broken away the darkness of disparagement...The shadows of stigma and disrespect which at times fell heavily and with all their somberness upon the art, by soul-inspiring and warm rays of purity, loveliness, and exaltation are, as a mist under the melting sun, dispelled.[7]

This search for technical improvement took place in relation to several parts of the photographic apparatus. It involved experimenting with using iodine or bromine or chlorine vapours to deposit particles of silver halide on the mirror-polished silver surface of the daguerreotype, or learning how to coat glass plates with an emulsion (first wet, then dry). These plates were then positioned to receive an image of the person or scene to which each had been exposed for an increasingly short period of time. The demand that one makes the best possible use of the natural light available rapidly prompted the manufacture of lenses with a fast aperture—like Joseph Petzval's 1841 portrait lens that allowed pictures to be taken ten times faster than previously. Even so, their use demanded quality light. The 'Sky-Light' of Rodgers's title is shorthand for the necessarily transparent architecture of the photographer's studio, whether a conversion or a planned construction—the 'glazed fowl house' of Julia Margaret Cameron's centre of operations;[8] or the 'fair-sized glass structure' that attracts the Lorimer sisters to rent their Baker Street accommodation in Amy Levy's 1888 novel *The Romance of a Shop*.[9] Even the highly portable Kodak or Brownie camera, which, introduced in the final decades of the century, heralded the true democratization of the medium, required good daylight by which to operate.[10]

Yet the questions of how to take photographs in complete darkness—say, in a cave or coal mine—or of how to capture a subject indoors, or by dim natural lighting, raised a very different set of technical challenges: ones that demanded the deployment of artificial sources of light. This brings us to the development of flash photography: a practice that overturns some of the most commonly rehearsed ideas about photography's characteristics, and that demands an alternative vocabulary through which to describe its operations and effects. For flash photography differs from other forms of the medium since the exposure is based on the brief flaring of an intense light, not on the opening and closing of a shutter according to the strength of a continuously available light source. Flash photography's technology depends, entirely or in part, on artificial, not natural, illumination.

Flash thus complicates considerably Roland Barthes's well-known definition of the 'noeme' of photography as 'an emanation of *past reality*: a *magic*, not an art': something resulting from the way in which a photographic plate's sensitive surface—or the sensitive surface of a film—is touched by the same rays of light that had touched the world, leaving the 'lacerating emphasis' of the '*that has been*'.[11] Although this is still true in some respects—the image will be that of a person or place, a cat or a cavern that was once there, and that never can exist again precisely as it was at that particular moment that has been filleted from time—the rays of light that fall upon the plate or film are not the natural ones that give continuity to the morning or afternoon from which a photographic moment has been taken and frozen. Rather, they are rays of light that caused a sudden interruption, an invasion; that broke into darkness; that were human made; that provided a discrete moment of light quite distinct from the darkness that preceded and followed it.

Flash photography announces its distinctive technology in other ways, too. If, as can so easily happen, the use of the flash results in a reflection of the light source on windowpane or polished surface, one is directly reminded of the artifice, the crucial technology involved in the illumination. The same intrusion of the medium is apparent in the bleached-out foreground that often results from the explosive force of the flash. This display of flash instantly qualifies the fiction that in some way the lens of the camera functions as the photographer's eye. Indeed, at the moment of taking the photograph, the photographer, if she is close to her instrument, will have her vision momentarily blinded just as dramatically and uncomfortably as her subject.

The eruption of flash disorients subject and photographer alike—and not just because of the dangers it brought with it in the early decades of its use. A camera exaggerates one's awareness of the sense of sight: both because one actively chooses to use it and because, as an apparatus, it entails the separation of viewer and world. For sight, as Hans Jonas puts it, is, unlike taste or touch or smell (on most occasions) or even hearing, the only sense 'in which the advantage lies not in proximity but in distance: the best view is by no means the closest view; to get a proper view we take the proper distance, which may vary for different objects and different purposes, but is always realised as a positive and not a defective feature in the phenomenal presence of the object'.[12] To view something properly, in Chris Otter's words, building on Jonas's comment, 'involves disembedding oneself from the viewed world'.[13] But the effect of the flash is to eliminate, even if only for a very brief burst of time, this apparent distinction between viewer and world. Although it facilitates the recording of one's material surroundings, it does not enable the sight of the spectator—in the same way that a microscope or telescope acts as a prosthesis to the eye—at the moment that the mechanical analogue to human vision does its work. Its shock to the eye obliterates, not illuminates.

The development of flash photography needs to be traced alongside the development of an adequate vocabulary for these new and alarming effects—or rather, as we shall see, alongside somewhat awkward and imperfect efforts to develop a language for this new type of illumination. The metaphor of sunlight was, on occasion, borrowed by those who wrote about the subgenre. 'The story of flash photography', John Tennant and H. Snowden Ward's 1912 *Flashlight Portraiture* opens, 'tells how the photographer, chafing under the limitations of an art largely dependent on sunlight for its successful working, devised a means of bottling the sunlight, so that he might be free to use his camera when and where he pleased—as at night, in dark interiors, in underground places, or wherever the light of day proved insufficient for his purposes.'[14] But to compare sunlight with flashlight is inaccurate and ultimately unproductive: the former suggests warmth, duration, and the diffusion of light, whereas the latter is cold and abrupt. The most readily available nature-based model for the new technology was, instead, the phenomenon of lightning, which startles, shocks, interrupts the moment—or isolates it, rather, in a sudden instant of illumination, rendering everything around it preternaturally clear by contrast to the surrounding darkness. So, too, does flash photography, deploying various combustible materials and techniques to light up—vividly and often momentarily—a scene that the camera would otherwise be unable to capture. It is no surprise that Adolf Miethe and Johannes Gaedicke, the German chemists who invented the first relatively safe, practical, and economical flash powder in 1887, called it *blitzlichtpulver*, or 'lightning light powder'. And when, in the twentieth century, Walter Benjamin famously appropriated the vocabulary of the flash to describe how memory functions, writing that 'The past can be seized only as an image which flashes up at the instant when it can be recognized and is never seen again',[15] it is far from clear whether he had in mind nature's momentary startling irradiation of that which is otherwise dark and obscure, or that capacity of the camera to seize the moment, to freeze an instant. The two phenomena seem very close—indeed, they are compressed and amalgamated in a deliberately brief poem by Bill Knott, entitled 'Flash', which, in its entirety, flares up and reads:

> Photographs—
> lightningbolts which,
> their shadows having caught up with them,
> perish.[16]

However, as we will see in Chapter 2, lightning and the photographic flash are very different in their effects upon those who experience them, in ways that go far beyond the obvious distinctions between natural and human causation. They raise quite oppositional questions about visual representation and suggestiveness. In examining these differences, I will be opening up ideas about the connections, both actual and metaphoric, between sudden visibility, imagination, and understanding—those temporal breaks that constitute 'flashes of illumination'. To explore the aesthetics of flash, I maintain, is to interrogate the connections between light and revelation, the fragility of the borderlines between awe and destruction, and the limitations of the technological sublime.

Yet the shocks delivered by flash's eruption into darkness can be of a very different kind from those delivered by lightning, and this is where the natural and the technological dramatically diverge. For as it became more commonplace and lost its wonder, flash photography became increasingly associated with irritating, aggressive intrusiveness—even as metaphysical language continues, on occasion, to be used to signal its impact and effects. This is the blinding flash world of the paparazzi; the barrage of bulbs that popped, or speedguns that flare, at the sight of a celebrity. Or this is the ritual that must be endured at weddings and formal celebrations, or the miniature assault launched by millions of family photographers, or even the bright jagged pinpricks that pepper the darkness at a rock concert. This is trespass into personal space, voyeurism in the dark, shooting the victim unawares. Flash photography accentuates the diagonal strips of dark and light that focus the hostile glare of Greta Garbo, seen in Figure 1.1, an image shot by Georges Dudognon in the Club St Germain in the 1950s; it bleaches the hand that the notoriously reclusive film star stretches towards the camera lens, her refusal of flash's properties standing for everyone who resents its intrusion.

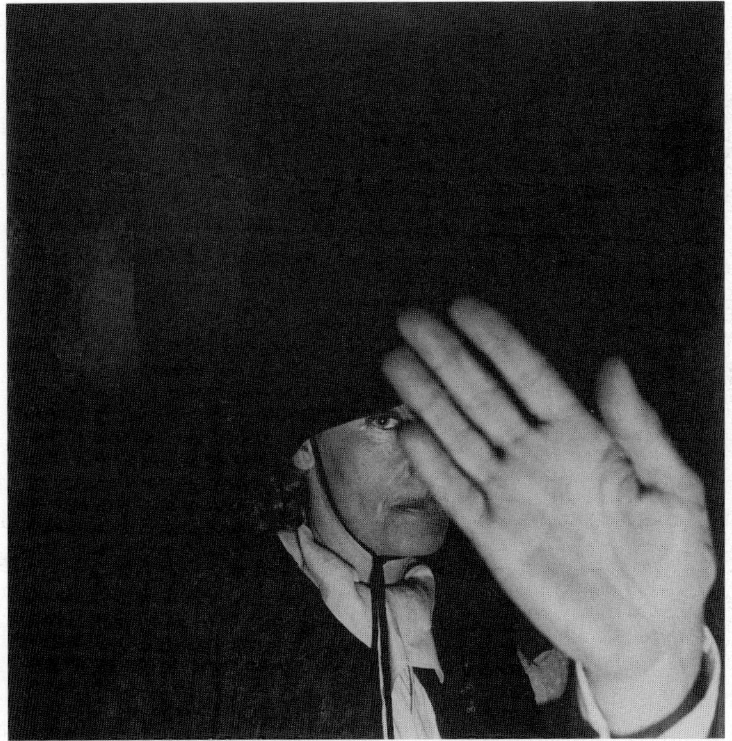

Figure 1.1 George Dudognon, 'Greta Garbo in the Club St Germain', 1950s. Gelatin silver print; 7 1/16 × 7 1/8 in. (17.94 × 18.1 cm). San Francisco Museum of Modern Art, Foto Forum purchase. © Estate of Georges Dudognon. Photograph: Don Ross.

Not only the famous are vulnerable to flash's invasive properties. Some of the Farm Security Administration (FSA) photographers who documented American social conditions in the later part of the 1930s felt very uneasy in allowing their light bulbs to illuminate the dark, private corners of domestic spaces, even if others felt no such compunction. Weegee, in his relentless pursuit of New York crime scenes in the 1940s, needed his flash equipment to capture the murders, the arrests, and the emotional aftermaths that were his trademark, but he also employed infrared bulbs and film to show courting couples kissing in cinemas or, as in Figure 1.2, pairs of lovers entwined on the beach at Coney Island.

More sensational still is the work of Kohei Yoshiyuki. This deliberately focuses on the allure of voyeuristic pursuit in a way that self-referentially calls into question the motives of both the photographer and the eventual consumer of an image. Yoshiyuki employed infrared flash in his 1971 series, *The Park*, an example of which is found in Figure 1.3. The photographer quietly followed men who creep around and get their kicks from watching others have sex in Chuo Park, Shinjuku, and in two more Tokyo parks. The tiny flash that can be seen momentarily when infrared equipment is used, Yoshiyuki said, was easily confused with beams from the headlights of passing cars.

Figure 1.2 Weegee, 'Lovers on the Beach', *c.*1955. © Weegee (Arthur Fellig)/International Center of Photography/Getty Images.

In other words, flash's invasiveness is not invariably made instantly visible. When Yoshiyuki first exhibited the photographs, in Tokyo's Komai Gallery, visitors to the show found themselves as much implicated in the act of voyeurism as the peeping Toms and as the photographer. The images were blown up to life-size, the room darkened, and the visitors issued with a torch: 'I wanted people to look at the bodies an inch at a time', he said.[17]

Flash photography feeds off a desire for knowledge, for information, for a peep at that which is usually private, secret, invisible. It removes control from the person photographed, especially if they don't know that the shock of blinding light is on its way. The work of Philip-Lorca diCorcia provides a particularly strong case in point. DiCorcia belongs to a long tradition of street photographers who have taken pictures of individuals without their knowledge or consent—think Walker Evans's or Robert Frank's available-light images of riders on the New York subway, courtesy of a hidden camera and a shutter release button hidden in the sleeve;[18] or Helen Levitt, using a right-angle viewfinder on her Leica in order to photograph unguarded individuals in the streets of Yorkville and Harlem. As with this work, the subject matter of diCorcia's *Heads* series relies on the randomness and serendipity of the urban street, the photographer

Figure 1.3 Kohei Yoshiyuki. From the series *The Park*. 'Untitled', 1971. Gelatin Silver Print © Kohei Yoshiyuki, Courtesy Yossi Milo Gallery, New York.

seizing the face from the Manhattan crowd, and allowing the spectator to read character, story, interiority. The viewer cannot help but project cultural and social expectations onto the image, but we also find our customary tools for 'reading' the face of a stranger disrupted, not least because these heads are also representative of types. This is one reason why, despite being singled out by lens and flash, their individuality is also somewhat resistant. As diCorcia remarked of his project, Times Square—where he made the series between 1999 and 2001—had become

> a kind of like touristic crossroads and I would try to predict who was an American and who wasn't and I couldn't after awhile. Everybody starts to look the same and all young people have the same piercings and you know, whatever fad, whether its a wool cap, or Converse, you know, you start to see it and you know, everybody all over the world has the same thing on. It actually turns out that the only people who are the individuals are the nuts[19]

—who, in their turn, are not quite as puzzlingly interesting as the quotidian face.

DiCorcia's *modus operandi* was somewhat different from that of other street photographers (including Harry Callahan, whose work around 1949–50 *Heads* in many way resembles). DiCorcia set up a strobe flashlight on scaffolding in Times Square—a method he'd already used in his earlier *Streetwise* series, shot in New York, Tokyo,

Paris, Calcutta, and Rome—but this time stood well back, using a long lens, a camera mounted on a tripod, and triggering the flash remotely once he sighted his prey. From hundreds of images, he selected seventeen heads for exhibition in 2001: individuals who stand out from the darkness, but who appear remote, preoccupied: a modern rendering of Wordsworth's observation in *The Prelude*, of how 'oft, amid those overflowing streets, | Have I gone forward with the crowd, and said | Unto myself, "The face of every one | That passes by me is a mystery!"'[20] Wordsworth compared the undifferentiated mass of the city to a black storm cloud against which the sharp details of individual lives could be made out. At the same time, each of these individuals was, for him, metonymic of other urban types with histories similar to those he recounts. Whether each of diCorcia's heads is read as wearing an expression that works as a blasé defence against city life—Georg Simmel's 1903 description of the self-protective mask that is worn by people in an urban setting, expressive of their need to desensitize themselves from the city's nerve-jangling affects[21]—or whether (as Luc Sante suggests, in the essay that prefaced the show's catalogue) their preoccupied and somewhat troubled faces are simply the result of moving through a chaotic city, these heads, severed from their environment, appear as anonymous types. As Sante writes:

> They are not performing; they are unaware of the light. They are illuminated at that instant because they have been selected. They may not have been selected the way bugs are, to represent their genus or phylum in a display case, but it seems more likely that they have been chosen to stand only for themselves, in all their exquisite specificity... They have no idea that the inspection is not a private matter. They do not know that they are exposed, as it were, on a laboratory slide, and lit up by the bulb of a vast and incomprehensible microscope.[22]

Except that it didn't always work that way. One of the individuals, Erno Nussenzweig, an Orthodox Hasidic Jew, learned that his image—which we see in Figure 1.4—had been taken, exhibited, and sold. Becoming a talking head, he sued diCorcia and the Pace/MacGill Gallery for violating both his right to privacy and his religious beliefs (that is, he considered that what had become a multiply reproduced image broke the part of the second commandment forbidding the making of graven images). On 8 February 2006, New York State Supreme Court Justice Judith J. Gische dismissed Nussenzweig's complaint on the grounds that whereas an individual might feel that their personal privacy has been violated under certain circumstances, the law does not necessarily agree. Civil Rights Laws sections 50 and 51 forbid the use of a plaintiff's 'name, portraits, picture, or voice' for 'advertising purposes or for trade'. But selling a work of art is not trade.[23] Any person might feel that she or he is violated by having a flashgun going off in their face, in other words, but unless that image is subsequently turned into an advertisement, their privacy has not legally been infringed upon. Nussenzweig was walking through a busy city: no trespassing on private property was involved. Whether or not someone might feel as though flash violently invades their personal privacy is another matter altogether.

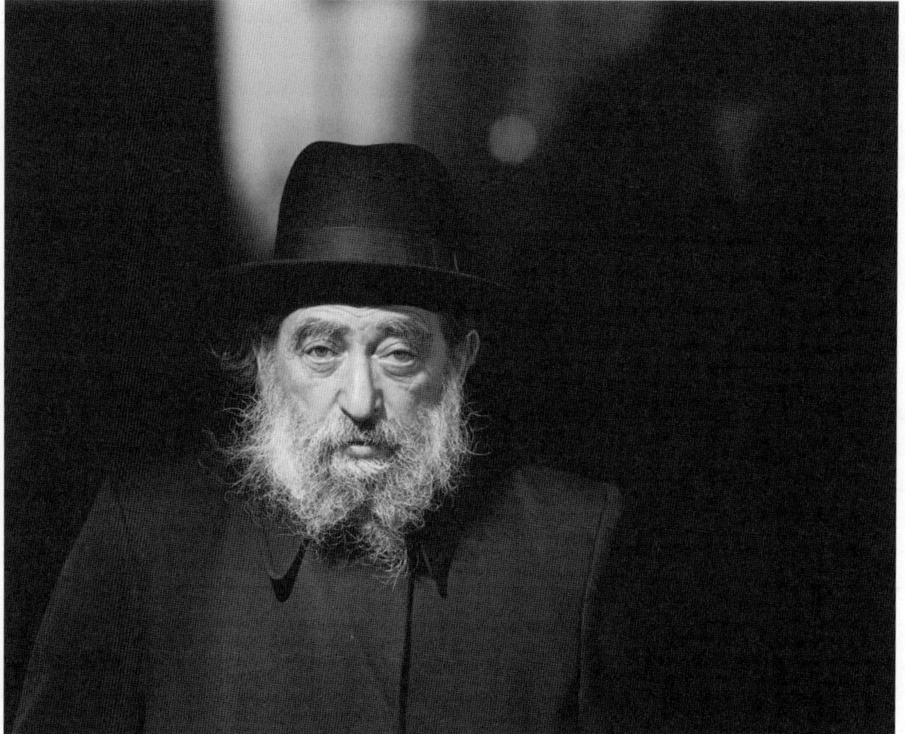

Figure 1.4 Philip-Lorca diCorcia, 'Head #13', 2001. Fujicolor Crystal Archive print. Original image in colour. 48 × 60 in. (121.9 × 152.4 cm). Copyright the artist.

Courtesy the artist and David Zwirner, New York/London.

This book traces the development of flash photography from the earliest attempts to illuminate darkness using magnesium powder or magnesium ribbon, through to today's use of the flash. It is nowadays an indispensable weapon in the armoury of the press photographer; a quotidian and built-in part of many cameras, and a tool that allows the art photographer to obtain particular kinds of illumination—whether she or he is searching for subtle effects, deliberately playing on the medium's whole sleazy set of associations with voyeurism, or singling out individuals in the metropolitan crowd. I use flash photography as a means of telling one particular version of the cultural history of photography—a version that sees the medium initially producing wonder because of its power to capture the transient and to allow one to see hitherto unobserved and unremarked-upon detail, and then becoming so ubiquitous that it's all too easy to take it for granted, possessing in its own right a form of invisibility through its very commonplaceness. But the book also tells a story about the language in which photography is described and discussed, whether by practitioners, critics, or imaginative writers. In this version, the vocabulary attached to flash photography regularly, even if not consistently, seeks to associate the medium with illumination and inspiration, with shock and awe and surprise. Even after flash became a very familiar photographic tool, it continues to be used to literary effect, signifying sudden, startling interruption.

Of course, discussing the use of the flash means examining the photographs that it makes possible. My interest is less in these, however, than it is in the experience of the flash: as something that unsettles one's sense of duration and of one's continuous habitation of space, and as something far more invasive and actively troublesome to the human (and animal) subject than are most types of photography. An unobtrusive surveillance camera is much more insidious in its operation, for with a flash, one can rarely escape knowing that one *has* been photographed. What's more, one's often been dazzled, temporarily blinded in the process. The overstimulated retina can produce a temporary reduction in vision lasting as long as twenty minutes. The flash may be an instrument to the photographer; to the subject, it causes a brief, unpleasant, somatic reaction.

The experience of being at the receiving end of a photographer's flash—indeed, the whole experience of being photographed—is completely bound up with the technological innovations made that allowed one to photograph in the dark, or in dull and diminished light, and with the developments necessary, as well, for certain types of flash to be used to freeze very rapid movement. The story of flash photography—like that of photography more generally—is one of chemical substances and specialist apparatus; of gaining control over the amount of light necessary to record an image on a light-sensitive surface. But we're not initially talking about the fine-tuning of lenses and shutters to synchronize with explosions of light—at least, not until the era of the flashbulb and the built-in flash—but of far more hit-and-miss forms of invention.

In its early decades, flash photography required a certain expertise with chemical ingredients and ancillary equipment that went beyond the technological knowledge involved in operating a camera. It thus offers an excellent opportunity to examine the overlap between amateur and professional activity among photographic practitioners, as reflected in countless manuals, 'how-to' books, photographic contests, and photography magazines. The development of flash photography offers up testimony to the active inventiveness and technical explorations of enthusiastic amateur and professional photographer alike.

The flash itself, caught in a mirror or window or other shiny surface, or leaving a record of its presence in bleached-out portions of an image, or described by someone who has witnessed or imagined it, may be said to be an object of scientific knowledge of a certain type, belonging to the category that Lorraine Daston specifies in her introduction to *Biographies of Scientific Objects*: a category that consists, she writes, of things that belong to the category of applied metaphysics. Her interest lies in 'how whole domains of phenomena—dreams, atoms, monsters, culture, mortality, centers of gravity, value, cytoplasmic particles, the self, tuberculosis—come into being and pass away as objects of scientific inquiry'.[24] As we have already seen, and as Chapter 2 will explore in more detail, flash was written about in ways that constantly drew on the terms of the natural sublime. But flashguns and flashcubes and flash units, the means to the end, stimulate no such metaphysical associations. They are just incontrovertibly, prosaically *there*. Whatever the metaphysical associations of light, writing the cultural history of flash photography cannot be carried on without an understanding of the technological apparatuses that brought it about. In this chapter, I concentrate on the earlier decades of flash technology, since they were responsible for establishing so many of the tropes and associations that I go on to discuss. Later innovations, although touched upon briefly here, are treated in more detail later in the book in relation to the new associations to which they gave rise.

There exist two reasonably thorough treatments of flash's technical development: Chris Howes's *To Photograph Darkness: The History of Underground and Flash Photography* (1990), and Pierre Bron and Philip L. Condax's *The Photographic Flash: A Concise Illustrated History* (1998). There are also some useful and well-illustrated websites, indicating a contemporary network of photo-technology historians whose contribution to the minutiae of photography's history helps to reveal the tiny variations that demonstrate the multiplicity of individuals and firms working simultaneously towards similar ends.[25] As the title of Howes's book suggests, he is largely concerned with those who explored underground caverns—sometimes out of sheer curiosity and adventure, sometimes as tourists, sometimes prospecting for potential commercial uses (a site for the development of hydroelectric power; the source of massive amounts of bat guano). The photography of mines, and those who worked within them, constitutes a small but important subfield of flash photography's history, helping show the role of industrial and commercial (and later, military) needs in furthering research in flash technology. Howes gives a good account of the constant trial by error involved in illuminating subterranean spaces for the purposes of photography—and the dangers that were also often encountered, and *To Photograph Darkness* is also particularly effective at bringing home quite how uneven was the circulation of information concerning flash technology, despite the fact of its global reach. Bron and Condax's volume is likewise extremely informative by way of social history, although containing many fewer memorable anecdotes. They give far more weight to the electric spark as a light source than I do, fascinated, as well they might be, with its power to catch a splash or a bullet's trajectory in a way that's invisible to the human eye. They emphasize, too, the development of the electronic flash, something that takes up almost two-thirds of their book. Theirs is a chronological and teleological history, looking at the technological improvements and inventions that have led to the increasing ease, for different types of photographers, of using artificial means of illuminating their subjects.

In both of these books, the emphasis falls on the importance of perfecting combustible materials, and igniting them in a safe and reliable manner. As early as 1840–1, photographers were achieving shorter exposure times by the use of limelight, but this proved far too harsh for satisfactory portrait photography. Limelight, developed in the 1820s, was created by directing an oxyhydrogen flame at a cylinder of quicklime, or calcium oxide. It was employed in the later 1830s to illuminate both outdoor and indoor performances, and first used for indoor stage lighting at London's Covent Garden Theatre in 1837. It also provided a bright light source for magic lanterns, lasting 'long enough to see service in the early years of film projection'.[26]

In 1839–40 the London-based geologist Captain Levett Ibbetson, working at the Royal Polytechnic Institute, was using limelight to shorten exposure times when making daguerreotypes of fossils. Inventor Alexander Bain, writing in the *Westminster Review* about Ibbetson's experiments, reported, 'For some reason which we are unable to explain, an impression can be obtained by the hydro-oxygen light in less than five minutes, which would require five-and-twenty with the camera and the light of the sun.'[27] The article was illustrated by a transverse section of a madrepore—a species of coral magnified twelve and a half times (Figure 1.5). To be sure, the length of a flash is a relative thing. A five-minute burst of intense brightness is hardly the same as an explosion lasting a fraction of a second. But when one compares these few minutes with the duration of an exposure that would have been required by the original source of illumination,

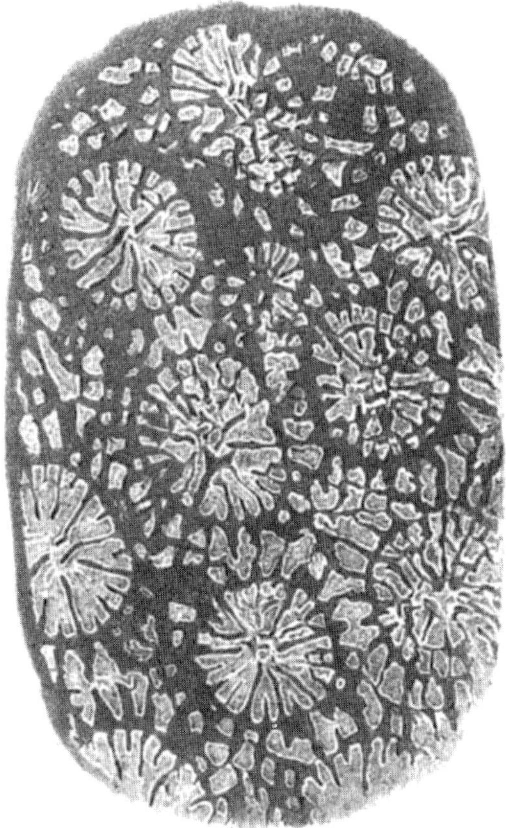

Figure 1.5 Captain Levett Ibbetson, Transverse section of madrepore, *Westminster Review* 34 (September 1840), between 460 and 461.

the sun, then this daguerreotype of a cross-section of coral has a strong claim to be considered the first flash photograph.

But something more promising than limelight was at hand—magnesium. Magnesium, although the eighth most abundant element in the earth's crust, and the fourth most common in the earth itself, is not something that can be quarried or mined in isolation: it has to be extracted from the other elements with which it is found in combination. In 1808 Humphrey Davy was the first scientist to isolate it, but a commercial means of producing it was not developed until the early 1860s, and even then it was very costly. William Crookes, then editor of the *Photographic News*, wrote in 1859 of the brilliant but terrifically expensive light that could be made by holding one end of a piece of magnesium wire and sticking the other end in a candle: 'It then burns away of its own accord evolving a light insupportably brilliant to the unprotected eye and possessing powerful actinic properties.' He was answering a correspondent who planned to visit the Great Mammoth Cave in Kentucky, and was wondering if photogen would provide sufficient light for photographing underground. Crookes recommended burning phosphorus in oxygen, pointing out that Michael Faraday 'has called this light the "sun in a bottle", and it well deserves its cognomen'.[28]

Magnesium, however, became the preferred form of bottled sunlight for photographers working in dark places (although in France, Nadar [Gaspard-Félix Tournachon] created some striking images of the Paris catacombs after lugging electric batteries underground). Professor Robert Bunsen, of Heidelberg, and Henry Roscoe, of Owen's College, Manchester, both saw considerable potential in the brightness of burning magnesium, stimulating considerable interest in the metal. This led to Edward Sonstradt's creation of a greatly improved method of extracting and purifying it.[29] Magnesium remained extremely expensive, however. In England, it cost £6 a pound, which worked out at 2*s.* 6*d.* a foot. It also took a good deal of time—up to a day—for the magnesium oxide fumes to subside.[30]

Manchester professional photographer Alfred Brothers took the earliest underground photos in England in Derbyshire on 27 January 1864, of the Blue John Cavern, and on 22 February of the same year made the first magnesium-lit portrait—of Roscoe—during a demonstration at Manchester's Literary and Philosophical Society. One should note, incidentally, the role played by public demonstrations and lectures in spreading the news about flash in its early forms—Figure 1.6 shows a demonstration of magnesium-lit photography at a meeting of the British Association for the Advancement of Science in Birmingham in September 1865.[31] In 1865 Charles Piazzi Smyth, Scotland's Astronomer Royal, lit the inside of the Grand Pyramid in Egypt, using magnesium flares, so that he might record its dimensions (it's disappointing that Smyth's dying wish was ignored: he wanted to be buried with a camera, so that he could photograph souls arising on the Day of Judgement—something for which he presumably would not have needed his lighting apparatus).[32]

In 1865 the photographic journalist, editor, writer, and photographer J. Traill Taylor introduced his new flash powder, a mixture of powdered magnesium and an oxidizing

Figure 1.6 Demonstration of magnesium for making photographs by flash for members of the British Association for the Advancement of Science at Birmingham Town Hall in 1865. Pictorial Press Ltd/Alamy Stock Photo.

agent, but since magnesium was still so expensive (and his compound apparently gave off a horrible smell), it was not widely adopted. What we witness around this time, though, is an example of English manufacturing entrepreneurship expanding into the United States, with its larger and geographically growing market. Brothers and Smyth worked closely with the Magnesium Metal Company, in Salford, Manchester, which made both magnesium wire and a lamp in which to burn it; they supplied Brothers with the material for his cave photographs, and used Smyth's images of Egypt to help publicize the new metal. Magnesium ribbon was coiled upon a wheel, 'and unwound by means of clockwork as fast as the metal was consumed', which allowed for a steady, consistent light.[33] By late 1865, an offshoot of this company, the American Magnesium Company, was putting the same materials into production in Boston: 'How Americans delight in what is good and new!' exclaimed an article in the *British Journal of Photography* in December of that year, anticipating future success for lighting materials based around this mineral.[34] In 1866 Cincinnatti photographer Charles Waldack went 7 miles underground to record the Mammoth Caves in Kentucky, with a commission to make some

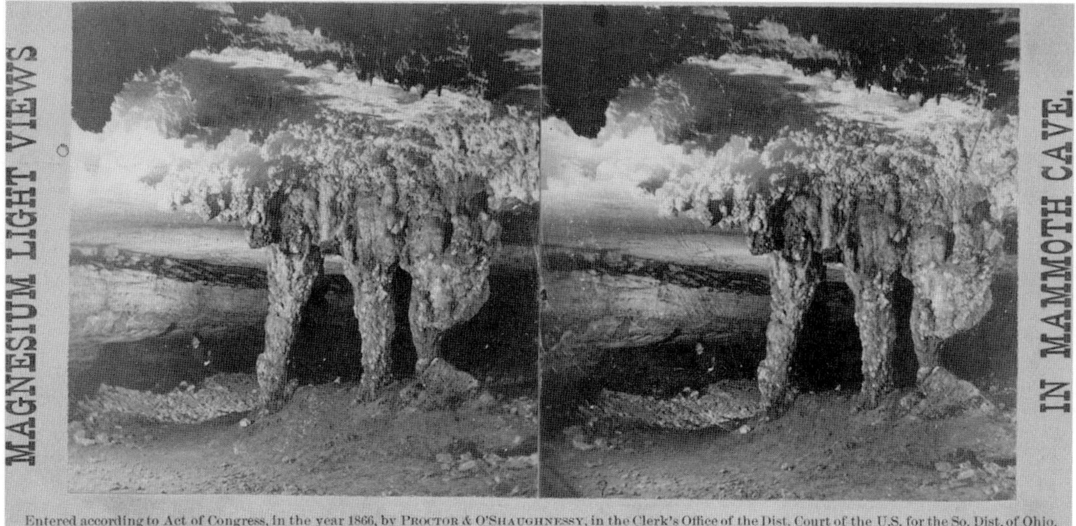

Figure 1.7 Charles Waldack, 'Mammoth Cave Views. No. 9. The Altar. In the foreground is a cluster of columns called the altar, at which a romantic marriage took place between two parties whose union on the face of the earth was prevented by family interference.' Stereoscopic card, published by E. and T. T. Anthony, 1866 (author's image).

stereoscopic slides aimed at reigniting the post-Civil War tourist industry there (Figure 1.7). He used a compound of magnesium filings and pulverized gunpowder exploded in reflectors to provide his light source. Because wet plate collodion was still being used to cover the plates, its fast evaporation time meant that he had to carry all his equipment for preparation and development down into the caves, warming the plates on fires made by burning bourbon in the reflectors. The editor of the *Philadelphia Photographer*, to whom Waldack sent his work, could hardly contain his vocabulary of awe in responding to the letter in which Waldack recounts his methods:

> These pictures now lie before us, and are the *most wonderful* ones we have ever seen. We can scarcely remove our eyes from the instrument, or lay them down to write, for perfect wonder. Oh! Is not photography a great power? What else could creep into the bowels of the earth, and bring forth such pictures therefrom, as these?[35]

Photographic journals registered the fact that something new was happening through deploying photography's earliest and most useful metaphor, the 'sun picture'. 'Mr Waldack', wrote a correspondent in the British *Photographic News*, reviewing the stereoscopic views produced by the American, and echoing Faraday's language, has 'stored sunlight in the shape of magnesium'.[36]

During the next twenty or so years, devices were introduced that allowed powdered magnesium to be ignited safely—usually these involved blowing it through an alcohol flame, which resulted in a brief bright flash, its duration very much dependent on the skill of the operator. The rapidly falling price for magnesium in the 1880s, following the introduction of new and much cheaper methods for its extraction, meant that there was a notable push to try and manufacture a more stable and less smoky compound that could be widely and easily used by photographers. In 1887, as mentioned earlier, the German chemists Adolf Miethe and Johannes Gaedicke invented the first easily manufactured flash powder. They mixed magnesium powder with potassium sulphate and antimony chlorate, and called it *blitzlichtpulver*, or 'lightning light powder'. The chlorate compound worked as an oxidizer; the sulphide added to the brilliance of the flash. News of its effectiveness spread rapidly through the specialist press and through news media—indeed, this speedy circulation of technological information brings home the transhemispheric history of photography. This internationalism is made manifest in volume 2 of the *American Annual of Photography*, appearing in 1887: the volume that covers Miethe and Gaedicke's invention. It contains details of photographic societies not just in the United States and the United Kingdom, but also in Australia, New Zealand, India, Germany, Austria, Hungary, Bohemia, France, Russia, and Norway. Similarly, it lists photographic periodicals published in some twelve countries, and a list of photographic books appearing that year in English, French, and German. It also carries a short piece about *blitzpulver* by Gaedicke himself that concludes by saying that it may, perhaps, 'take a good while yet before the photographers of the old continent will adopt this new method of lighting. Let us hope, then, Americans will speedily select it for their practical work, to cultivate its advantages and earn benefits from its use.'[37] Even if photography is demonstrably global, the United States is singled out for its exemplary modernity when it comes to its eager adoption of new inventions.

Gaedicke may have been flattering his immediate readership by commending the energy of American enterprise and the embrace of the new. The many early enthusiastic references to the use of *blitzlichtpulver* in the British photographic press hardly suggest that Britain lagged behind in this respect. What's more, by the time the volume containing Gaedicke's remarks had been published, the news of *blitzlichtpulver* had already spread rapidly in America by means of both the photographic and the general media. Most famously, the police reporter, Danish-born Jacob Riis, tells us how he was alerted to its existence:

> One morning, scanning my newspaper at the breakfast table, I put it down with an outcry that startled my wife, sitting opposite. There it was, the thing I had been looking for all those years. A four-line despatch from somewhere in Germany, if I remember right, had it all. A way had been discovered, it ran, to take pictures by flashlight. The darkest corner might be photographed that way.[38]

This is a hard story to prove—I can find no such four-line account in the New York press at the time, and certainly not in the papers that he was most likely to have been reading, the *New York Tribune* (for which he wrote) and *The Sun* (in which he published the next year). On the other hand, *The Sun* on 16 October 1887 described a flashlight demonstration by H. G. Piffard at the Society of Amateur Photographers five days earlier, at which he sprinkled 10–15 grains of magnesium on about 6 grains of guncotton. 'There was a flash of light that made the entire room as bright as noonday for a second.' 'All manner of dark places can be photographed by this method', we learn a little later, in language highly similar to Riis's.[39] We should also note that Piffard was one of the photographers who first worked with Riis to take pictures of slum dwellings, and in fact, the earliest evidence of these expeditions is unclear whether *blitzlichtpulver* itself, or magnesium and guncotton, was in fact employed—very typical of the experimentation with means and equipment at this highly transitional moment in flash's history.

Flash allowed for the creation of the photographs that were, Riis judged, just what he needed to make vivid for his readers and lecture audiences the squalor of living and working conditions on Manhattan's Lower East Side. As he recounts, his images—of tenement living and working conditions, overcrowded and filthy—carried evidential weight that 'mere words' failed to provide.[40] Exposure time had, in general, been speeded up by this stage of the century: gelatin dry plates, invented in 1874, came to replace wet collodion plates. Factory-produced, these plates were almost universally in use a decade later, and allowed an exposure time that was six times speedier than previously: they were, too, far easier to transport. But it was the bright light given off by the explosion of the *blitzlichtpulver*—or at least, by some form of ignited magnesium—that allowed Riis to take his pictures in dimly lit rooms and cellars and stairwells.[41]

Riis rapidly discovered that photographers in New York, Philadelphia, and further afield had been alert to this invention since the end of the summer of 1887. When the *Photographic Times* gave Gaedicke and Miethe's formula—60 parts chlorate of potassium, 30 parts powdered metallic magnesium, 10 parts sulphide of antimony—in August 1887, it clearly assumed that at least some of its readers were quite familiar with the idea.[42] *Blitzlichtpulver* itself was publicized in various ways, from advertisements to public demonstrations, and these continued throughout the autumn. The American *Photographic Times* reported on Gaedicke's son displaying the compound to the Society of Amateur Photographers of New York in December of 1887, where he 'lighted what appeared to be a fuse, and quickly closed a small slide; in about two seconds a most intense blinding blue flash, nearly as quick as lightning, appeared in the box, and the exposure was made'.[43] The analogy with lightning's sudden, strange burst of illumination reinforces, once again, the desire to connect new technology with the awe-inducing power of the natural world.

But the history of flash photography's technology—the experience of those who used it, the experience of those who were photographed through its means—involves a lot more than the development of the flashy compounds themselves. As we shall see, Riis's significant intervention was to lie in the uses to which he put them. Exploding them safely was a matter of considerable concern. Riis initially went off into the tenements and dark alleys of New York at night in the company of Piffard, the keen amateur photographer Richard Hoe Lawrence—plus, very often, a couple of policemen. 'It was not too much to say', he recounts (of an episode illustrated by Thomas Fogarty, in Figure 1.8),

"The tenants bolted through the windows."

Figure 1.8 Thomas Fogarty, illustration to Jacob Riis, *The Making of an American* (New York: Macmillan, 1901), 269. Bodleian Library, University of Oxford. 24724 e. 80.

> that our party carried terror wherever it went...The flashlight of those days was contained in cartridges fired from a revolver. The spectacle of half a dozen strange men invading a house in the midnight hour armed with big pistols which they shot off recklessly was hardly reassuring, however sugary our speech, and it was not to be wondered at if the tenants bolted through windows and down fire-escapes wherever we went.[44]

The pistol method of firing *blitzlichtpulver* (fill brass chamber with powder, use cap to ignite) never became all that widely used, even though a refinement, using magnesium cartridges, was subsequently produced (see Figure 1.9). Riis, who soon began taking the photographs himself, improvised using a frying pan—with nearly disastrous results—destroying a camera, setting a building on fire, setting his clothes alight...at which point, several of his friends clubbed together to buy him something more reliable. Nonetheless, the label 'flashgun', with its associations of aggression and violence, stuck, even when the equipment bore no obvious resemblance to a firearm. 'Flashlight' was used too—but that also referred to the whole process of taking a photograph by artificial means. 'Flash lamp' was a further alternative.

What characterizes the multiple but very similar objects that were quickly put on the market is that they were continually being modified, transformed, and tinkered with.

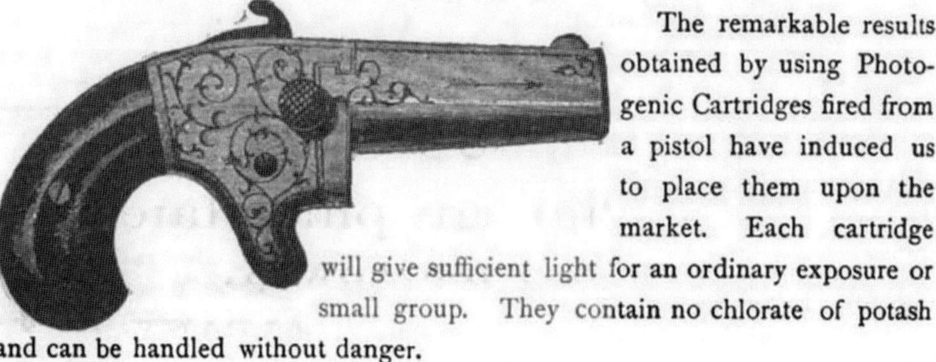

Figure 1.9 Advertisement for a photogenic pistol and magnesium cartridges, *Anthony's Photographic Bulletin* 20 (12 January 1889), p. xxiv.

Numerous new patents were filed; advertisements regularly claimed superiority—or better value for money—over other named examples of the type. Nor was *blitzlichtpulver* the only compound on the market. Around the same time that Miethe and Gaedecke launched their product, William Harrison combined magnesium with lycopodium, a very light fine yellow powder made from the spores of a clubmoss, and used in theatres to produce flashes of lightning.[45] What remained constant, however, were the dangers of flash powder. As photography manuals were quick to remind their readers, one absolutely couldn't use the new compound in the old kind of blow-lamp, or it would explode in one's face. Indeed, since the mixture that constituted flash powder was, effectively, an explosive, it had to be used and stored very carefully. It could be ignited just by friction. Johnson, the premier British manufacturer, sold it ready to be mixed rather than as a compound—which certainly made storage and transportation easier, but introduced some rather scary home chemistry. For the next forty years, the press reported many accidents—often fatal, certainly disfiguring—to people who worked in warehouses for photographic chemicals, and were careless with their stock, or to photographers themselves—who came to lose eyebrows, fingers, and worse. In 1930 William Randolph Hearst banned flash powder's use by any of his fifty-odd photographers after one of his staffers lost an arm in an accident.

Although the language of improvement is de rigueur in most brief accounts of the history of flash photography, the introduction of *blitzlichtpulver* didn't signal some overnight switch in the method of taking flash photographs. Rather, methods of illumination overlapped in their use. One reason that *blitzlichtpulver* often seems to appear in photographic histories as though its invention caused some rapid and absolute shift in practice is surely to be found in the highly quotable nature of Riis's account. The eureka-like moment in which he presents his personal discovery of *blitzlichtpulver* has, in turn, been greatly responsible for historians of photography seeing its arrival as if it were some startling meteorite—rather than part of the more diverse and simultaneous experiments that were being made more broadly in the late 1880s with newly affordable magnesium.

In fact, flash powder's adoption was a far more gradual and piecemeal process. As both advertisements and photography manuals tell us, the use of pure magnesium—the powder puffed into the air, and then ignited by a tiny burst from a gas flame—continued well into the twentieth century. F. J. Mortimer's *Magnesium Light Photography* gives a particularly detailed account of how to blow air through a flame using pneumatic pressure—the 'rubber tube, ball, and accumulator [are] similar to the familiar scent spray', he helpfully explains (such an apparatus is illustrated in Figure 1.10)—or one could use an oxyhydrogen light for the lantern and attach a cylinder of oxygen, regulating the oxygen flow by means of a chemist's spring clip or a small double-ended stopcock.[46] At this point, *blitzlichtpulver*, even if dangerous, starts to look not just simpler, but indeed decidedly more portable.

Photographers shifted towards its use, as well, in large part because of the greater amount of control that it offered over exposures. Mortimer, who might not have been too cautious in his approach, suggests applying a lighted taper, or spreading it on a train of guncotton (an adaptation of a common technique used with pure magnesium)

Figure 1.10 The Todd-Foret Magnesium Flash Lamp, in Paul N. Hasluck (ed.), *The Book of Photography: Practical, Theoretic, and Applied* (London: Cassell and Co., 1907), 476.

or—scarily combustible—on a strip of thin celluloid. But most people preferred the method of placing it in a small iron tray, and then striking a spark at arm's length—say, by a string attached to a mechanical striker, or, more commonly, by another air-bulb that would activate the striker flint. How much light do you want? Around one twenty-fifth of a second? Use 10 grains. Three twenty-fifths? Use 60. By around 1910, faster plates and films made it possible to use less powder, as did refinements to its formula: adding the nitrates of zirconium, cerium, and thorium made it burn much brighter, so that one could achieve a flash as fast as a hundredth of a second. That precise speed was important—obviously people tend to blink if a flash goes off in their eyes, and that speed is faster than a blink. Other innovations were designed to facilitate greater precision. In 1890, for example, Lincoln photographer Robert Slingsby (long a practitioner of using artificial light to take photographs) filed patent #3,571 for a device designed to synchronize a flashbulb with the release of the camera shutter (the apparatus involved bellows, rubber tubes, and an India-rubber ball),[47] and later in the 1890s, patents were issued for battery-operated flash devices that performed the same function.

One of the things that is very obvious about the process—apart from the need to be careful about ceilings, draperies, and things of that sort—is how much smoke was produced. The development of the flashgun went hand in hand with that of its accessories, such as smoke condensers that an assistant could sweep through the air catching stray particles that were often made from old crinoline hoops; or, later, the large white canvas bags that were used for exploding the powder—set off electrically—which also had the effect of diffusing the light. Indeed, electricity was increasingly used as a means of ignition: the perfection of one technology is dependent, in the case of the flashlight, on the innovative deployment of another. A photographer could set up their studio so as to be able to set off four—or more—flashlights at once. If photographing a big scene—a banquet, say—one could connect fifty flashlights with rubber tubing—ensuring that every piece of tubing was exactly the same length. Or, if less technically ambitious, one could just put the powder in a long trough. Innovators tweaked the design of the flashlight for their own purposes. The renowned animal photographer George Shiras, for example, worked out how to mount his on the front of a boat, as we see in Figure 1.11.

Each differently constructed flashlight, each example of the paraphernalia surrounding the practice of flash photography, needs to be understood as a strong example of what social anthropologist Alfred Gell has called 'a concrete product of human ingenuity'.[48] It's this continual but multiply sited drive towards adaptation that makes it so very hard to generalize when writing a history of flash technology. At one end of the spectrum, one can have the amateur's biscuit-tin contraption, and at the other, the increasing commercialization of photographic equipment.

It was the task of a flashgun to be an efficiently functional object. It existed to hold the explosive powder that, ignited, was responsible for an effective flash of light, and it usually incorporated the means of ignition—a metal wheel and a flint to be struck, or the holder for a percussive cap. Over and beyond that, its shape was dictated by the

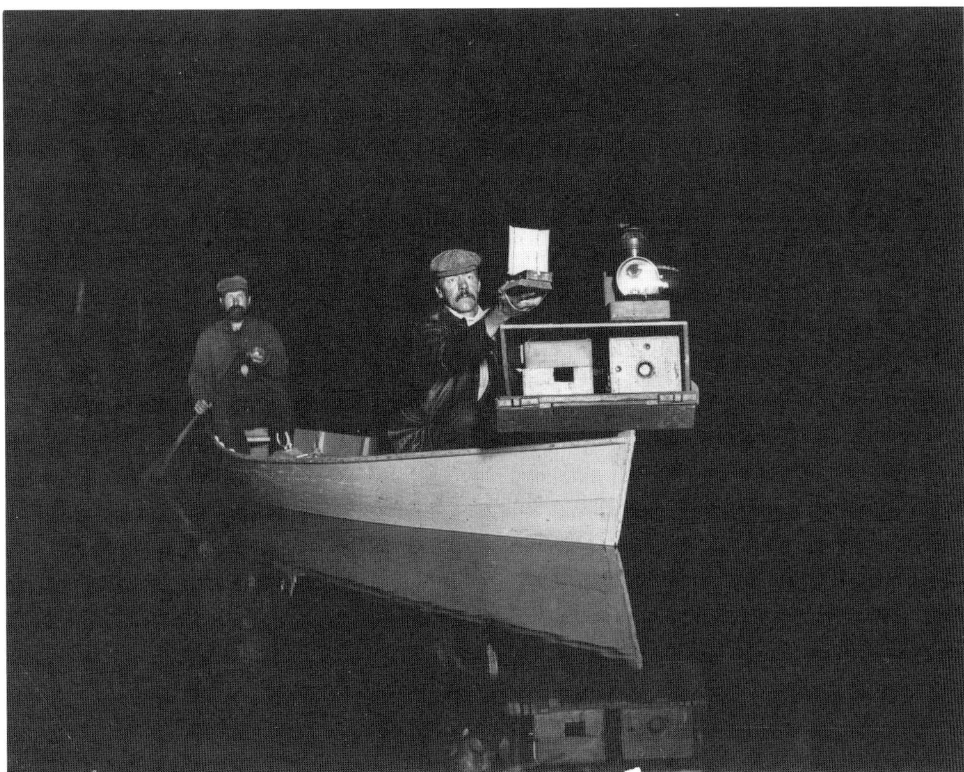

Figure 1.11 George Shiras, 'George Shiras and his assistant John Hammer aboard their jacklighting-equipped canoe, Whitefish Lake, Lake Superior region, Michigan', 1893.
National Geographic Society.

necessity of igniting the powder at a safe distance from the photographer or the photographer's assistant. This technology was very much a means to an end—the real end, the objective of the photographer—and the customary object of study in photographic history—being an image that could be achieved through no other means than through the projection of artificial light onto its subject matter. During the first half-century of flash photography, this might mean taking a portrait indoors on a dull day, or recording the opulent interiors of the residences of the wealthy, or the revelation of slum living conditions, or the interior of an opium den; it might mean capturing children at play; it might involve the fabrication of an artificial but aesthetically pleasing intersection of light and shade. In all of this—even the drama of flaring magnesium and its compounds—the flashgun plays but an ancillary role to the chemistry of photographic emulsions, the manipulations of the darkroom, the type of paper used for printing, the reproduction and distribution of the image—let alone, of course, to improvements in camera technology, whether relating to shutter release or the perfecting of lenses.

It is, in fact, impossible to separate out the development of flash equipment from the general economic consolidation that supported the development of photography. In particular, after the rapid growth in amateur photography brought about by the exponential growth in relatively cheap, easy-to-use cameras from the late 1880s onwards, manufacturers sized up the potential for allegedly simple flash-related products aimed at the amateur. Smith put their flash powder into Actino flash cartridges, which were calibrated according to the size of exposure that the purchaser wanted, and Eastman made a very similar product. In 1914 these would cost between 25 and 50 cents for a can of six, and the cartridge holder was another 50 cents—hardly out of reach of the average middle-class photographer.[49] Manufacturers of flash products published their own guides aimed at those who were unfamiliar with the new technology. For example, Smith-Victor's 1912 pamphlet *Flashlight Photography* emphasizes the usefulness of the design of the flashlight when it comes to catching one's domestic subject more or less unawares:

> The cartridge is supported on a small detachable shelf having a polished aluminum reflecting surface behind it. The cartridge fuse passes through a small hole in this surface to the back of reflector. It is thus concealed from subjects. Their inability to see it burn enables you to catch more pleasing poses and expressions of subjects than when they know the exact moment the flash is to take place.[50]

In *The Social Life of Things*, Arjun Appadurai suggests that 'even though from a *theoretical* point of view human actors encode things with significance, from a *methodological* point of view it is the things-in-motion that illuminate their human and social context'.[51] The word 'illuminate' is peculiarly apt when one considers the work that this particular—but representative—pamphlet envisages being done by the object-combination of flashgun and flash cartridge. It publishes a selection of images, each 'made by an amateur', that show precisely how domestic flash photography may be used to celebrate particular versions of social activity: a small boy on a rocking horse; two small children playing with toys under a decorated Christmas tree; a group of friends seated around a fireplace—with the flash being set off *within* the fireplace; an amateur dramatics group, dressed perhaps as early colonists; a portrait of a rather sultry young woman; a silhouette of a young girl; and two unbearably cute kittens perched in the top of a pair of rubber boots.

The Eastman Company were even more proactive when it came to catering to a domestic market than were Smith-Victor. They too sold flash cartridges, but their real innovation—around 1900—was the introduction of the flash sheet: films of collodion in which magnesium was incorporated. These could be affixed to a wooden rod, like a walking stick; or pinned to the edge of a shelf—and set off by means of a match—or placed in a more solid-looking holder that Kodak also sold. In both France and Germany, one could also buy flash sachets, rather like large explosive teabags (Figure 1.12). By the mid-1920s, the Eastman Company were offering a more technically sophisticated 'Electric Flashlight Outfit', which, as another advertisement in a British publication explains,

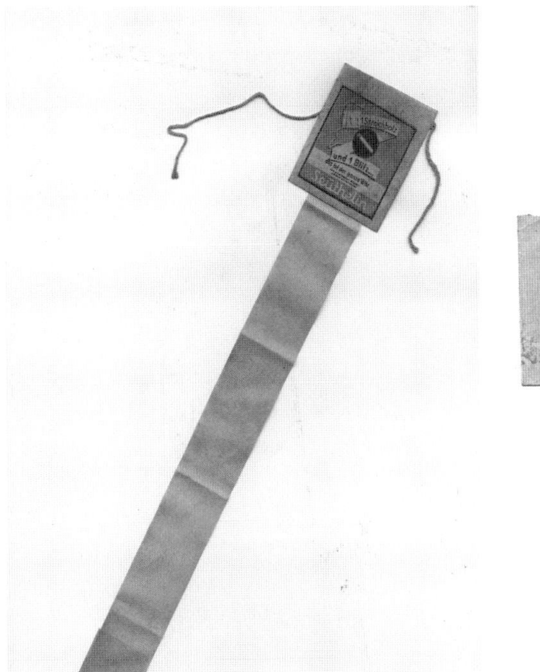

Figure 1.12 Seüthelin flash sachet and envelope ('1 Streichholz und 1 Blitz' (one match and one flash)), early 1900s (photo: Kate Flint).

consists of a porcelain tray, a metal holder, a dry battery and sufficient flash powder for 18–20 flashes. It is necessary only to pull the metal arms over the wire, pour on the required quantity of flash powder and press the spring handle into contact with the metal holder to make a quick, brilliant flash of actinic light. No mess, no smoke, no danger.[52]

The development of the flashbulb in the late 1920s was to render the flashgun and other means of igniting flash powder pretty much obsolete—although advertisements in photographic magazines show that implements designed to explode what came to be known as 'combustible flash' were still being advertised well into the 1950s. Indeed, for certain purposes, such as illuminating a night-time crime scene, where police evidence demanded that a relatively deep field be made visible, flash powder continued to be used into the 1960s.[53] Strictly speaking, the original flashbulb was the apparatus invented by a M. Chauffour in 1893, in which magnesium ribbon was fired inside a glass bulb: it was used by Louis Boutan to make the first underwater photographs by photoflash (Figure 1.13).[54]

The first version of the expendable flashbulb was created by Dr Paul Vierkötter in 1925, and then, based on his design, the first commercial flashbulb—the Vacublitz—was manufactured by Hauser, the German company, in 1929. Vierkötter used a coated magnesium wire inside a glass bulb which contained a low-pressure oxygen atmosphere: the first commercial bulbs—which were then manufactured in England and the

Figure 1.13 Louis Boutan, *La Photographie sous-marine et les progrès de la photographie* (Paris: Schleicher Frères, 1900), 234.

United States by General Electric—held lightly crushed aluminum foil inside the same kind of vacuum. In 1934 Philips, in Holland, made the first wire-filled flashbulbs, which gave out more light, burned much more steadily, and were generally more reliable—and throughout the rest of the 1930s, flashbulbs became safer, as a tough lacquer was manufactured that, applied inside and out, made them much less liable to explode—or, should they blow up, allowed for the shards of debris to be contained. Initially, these flashbulbs were only a little bit smaller than a regular household light bulb, but in 1939 a #5 'midget' flashbulb was introduced—about the size of a small egg.

Indeed, so consistent did the operation of flashbulbs become that the American Standards Association was able to introduce three categories that determined which bulb one should use for which lighting conditions. In 1935 the Ihagee Exacta Model B was the first camera to be produced with built-in flash synchronization; in 1939 synchronizers for inexpensive cameras were introduced. In 1963 the Flashcube—which had four separate flashbulbs, each with its own reflector—was marketed, and so on. Smaller and more convenient flash devices were introduced, notably that four-square Flashcube in 1963, the Sylvania Magicube in 1969, the Flash Bar 10 in 1972, the Flip Flash I (1975)—a two-row arrangement of bulbs that could be flipped around halfway through that was copied by other companies, including Philips and Polaroid. Flash technology was introduced into point-and-shoot cameras, and now cell phones can emit a short burst of vivid light that mimics the electronic flash. In other words, flash photography has become entirely commonplace—indeed, it might well be said that it has lost almost all of its mystique, and almost all of its power to shock.

But in the 1960s and 1970s, we find the final explicit burst of enthusiasm for flash technology in terms that link it to the new, to the modern. 'It's new, it's now, it's—Flashcube!' proclaims a TV advertisement from the 1960s for this attachment to the Instamatic camera, linking it to the dance floor and the Swinging Sixties.[55] The Sylvania publicity emphasized women (as snappers) and children (as subjects), and even offered the homemaker (for $3 and a coupon) a foam-rubber Sylvania Pop-art pillow, seen in Figure 1.14 ('You can make your home swing now for practically no money at all'). Hovering uncertainly between glamour and convenience, the promise offered by the flash devices of this period drew from, and helped to document, the labour-saving ethos of contemporary domestic life. Flash photography, it was intimated, was so easy to execute that it would make both the photographer and their subject happy, and would ensure their position as truly modern members of their consumerist society.

Yet at the same time that flashbulbs enormously simplified things for amateur photographers wanting to take pictures indoors or at night, so the lighting tools available to professional photographers continued to improve in terms of availability and sophistication. Indeed, 'almost as soon as photography was born', photo-technology

Figure 1.14 Sylvania Pop-art pillow, advertising Sylvania Blue Dot flashcubes, 1969 (photo: Kate Flint).

expert T. D. Towers tells us, 'experiments began to use electricity for artificial lighting'.[56] Leon Foucault in 1844 used a carbon-arc lamp (invented by Humphry Davy is 1809) to take daguerreotypes of medical specimens. By 1857, Russian photographer Sergei Lvovich Levistsky was taking portraits using a battery-powered arc lamp, and as already noted, Nadar employed portable—loosely speaking—battery-powered illumination. In 1877 Henry Van Der Weyde set up a London studio that used gas-dynamo-driven arc lamps. In 1913 American chemist Irving Langmuir developed a gas-filled tungsten filament lamp, and by the 1930s, the steady spread of mains electricity meant that the tungsten lamp was the major source of artificial light used by photographers. Another type of gas and vapour discharge lamp was also sometimes

Figure 1.15 Malick Sidibé. 'Nuit de Noel (Happy-Club)', 1963/2008. Gelatin silver print. Dimensions variable © Malick Sidibé. Courtesy of the artist and Jack Shainman Gallery, New York.

used, the xenon mercury vapour type (developed by Cooper Hewitt in 1901). By 1920, lighting innovators discovered that they could overrun tungsten filament lamps, creating 'photofloods'. These had very high light outputs, and were to become the standard for studio/professional photographers.

The adoption of these steady light sources meant that flash photography became increasingly associated with particular groups of users. There was a very large group of amateurs who were delighted to welcome the less messy, less dangerous, more easily regulated flashbulb. There were those photographers who needed the portability of the flashbulb—which meant that flash became especially identified with news photographers, crime photographers, paparazzi, and certain types of documentarians—photographers who needed to move relatively rapidly in the field, or under circumstances where cumbersome equipment would be thoroughly impractical. Sometimes, those who combined their flash with a lightweight camera were especially advantaged. The renowned Malian photographer Malick Sidibé recounted how, in the mid-1950s, he bought his first camera (a Brownie Flash), and became much in demand photographing parties. 'The early photographers like Seydou Keita worked with plate cameras and were not able to get out and use a flash. So I was much in demand by the local youth. Everywhere... in town, everywhere! Whenever there was a dance, I was invited.'[57]

Sidibé's images of young people dancing, as seen in Figure 1.15, encapsulate flash's aesthetic at its best. Without doubt, flash has been used to take a photograph where darkness would have otherwise made it impossible. In 'Nuit de Noel (Happy-Club)', the bright light bounces back off light suit and striped dress, which helps makes the dancers stand out against the deep night behind them; simultaneously, it records the everyday in the form of chairs, bottles, and what looks like a speaker nestling in the branches of a plastic palm tree. But there is also something revelatory in Sidibé's use of a flash that illuminates the faces of the couple completely, blissfully caught up in each other's presence and in their synchronized dance steps. This is non-invasive (Sidibé's own recollections help us understand this), yet it is a shared private moment, made available to us not just by technology, but also by the cooperation of the dancing pair. Flash is not aggressively interrupting them, not intruding on their experience, but suspending it in time. Flash allows us, we might say, a privileged moment of witnessing.

CHAPTER TWO

Lightning Flashes

In 1839 poet, writer, and traveller Emmeline Stuart-Wortley witnessed a spectacular Italian thunderstorm. In her 'Sonnet: A Night Storm at Venice', she puts before the reader two of lightning's most obvious aesthetic characteristics: suddenness and defamiliarization:

> The Lightnings flash upon St Mark's great dome,
> Which starts to proud pale Beauty suddenly!—
> And seems itself a Lightning to the eye;
> White, clear, and dazzling-bright—while the after gloom
> Closes upon it, like a swallowing tomb![1]

Although Stuart-Wortley was writing some eighty years after Burke published his treatise on the *Sublime and the Beautiful* in 1757, she still seems very much under the sway of his conviction that light, to be considered sublime, needs to be examined along with its opposite, darkness. 'Lightning', says Burke, 'is certainly productive of grandeur, which it owes chiefly to the extreme velocity of its motion', to the rapidity with which it effects a transition from dark to brilliant light and back again. With the force of Milton's inky-black hell behind his theorizing, Burke proclaims 'darkness is more productive of sublime ideas than light'.[2] There is something of this in Stuart-Wortley's terminology when she calls the medium from which the lightning emanates 'darkness startling'[3]—not quite as unsettling as Milton's 'darkness visible',[4] but similarly pointing to the fact that sudden dazzling illumination renders its surroundings more resonantly dark than before.

Up until the final quatrain, the poet is doing little more than buying into the long-standing and enduring use—from Longinus through Burke to Kant and beyond—of lightning as a recurrent image of the natural sublime.[5] As such, it was readily adopted by Romantic artists to signal the capacity wielded by the natural world for provoking pleasurable fear in the spectator—consider, for example, Théodore Géricault and Eugène Delacroix's studies of horses terrified by lightning, or J. M. W. Turner's *c.*1835 watercolour of the Piazzetta in Venice, shown in Figure 2.1. This recorded a beauty that Ruskin was to wish, a couple of years later, that he himself could capture:

> A heavy thunder cloud came over the Doge's palace in the twilight, and rapid limitless flashes of silent lightning showed first behind its ridges, as the rockets rose behind the smoke of St Angelo

Figure 2.1 Joseph Mallord William Turner, *The Piazzetta, Venice*, *c.*1835. Watercolour, bodycolour, pen and ink and scraping on paper. 8.7 × 12.63 in. (22.1 × 32.1 cm) Scottish National Gallery. Henry Vaughan Bequest 1900.

[that is, like the fireworks he had seen in Rome]; then retired over Lido, lighting the whole noble group of the Salute with a bluish spectral white, as every flash touched on it with vague, mysterious gracefulness—Turner's own—the edges of the dome dark against the reflected lighting on the ground of sky. I must try if I cannot give the effect some time.[6]

Through its connection to the Kantian sublime, and hence to the human capacity for registering our power to experience and enjoy intense moments that take us out of ourselves; and through, too, the scientific experiments of Benjamin Franklin and others,[7] lightning became increasingly less associated with images of divine wrath (Zeus/Jupiter's angry thunderbolts, God's power to smite the sinful)—although its role as punisher lingered on in pictures like John Martin's 1852 *The Destruction of Sodom and Gomorrah* (Figure 2.2), in which a thick jagged bolt shoots down the sky behind Lot and his family as they make their escape from the brimstone and fire destroying the urban landscape behind them.

But the effect of lightning in all its scary immediacy is hard to represent, whether in paint or language. John Martin's and Turner's bolts are moments of sudden illumination frozen in time. Although Turner's scurrying crowds suggest something of the panic that a violent thunderstorm can induce, these images fail to transmit lightning's

Figure 2.2 John Martin, *The Destruction of Sodom and Gomorrah*, 1852. Oil on canvas. 53.7 × 83.6 in. (136.3 × 212.3 cm.) Laing Art Gallery, Newcastle-upon-Tyne, UK © Tyne & Wear.

visceral terror. Indeed, Stuart-Wortley follows up her rather laboured attempts at a verbal rendition of chiaroscuro with four lines of ekphrastic defeat:

> Can pen or pencil e'er bepaint such scene?
> Nay! it is stamped and written on the brain:
> It flashes through the soul, with triumph keen,
> And there must long, unlocked by words remain![8]

However conventional this expression of inadequacy may be, these words importantly call attention to how lightning affects not just the eye, but also the body, its shock inhabiting the nervous system. In 1792 the body's electric circuitry had been conclusively demonstrated by Luigi Galvani and Alessandro Volta. Tennyson celebrated this idea in *In Memoriam*, with his reference to the body's 'electric force, that keeps | A thousand pulses dancing';[9] in 1855 Alexander Bain was to extend this physiological logic to the brain, with his widely circulated, if contentious claim of 'no currents, no mind'.[10] Even if lightning is, as we shall see later in this chapter, customarily represented as the object of observation, removed from the spectator, its energies obey the same laws as do the impulses that animate Walt Whitman's 'body electric'.[11] And even if the presence of static electricity within the atmosphere is not often explicitly remarked upon by literary commentators, lightning's impact is more than visual: it potentially offers an energizing transmission of highly charged particles.[12] Later in the century, Mark Twain was to remark in his *Autobiography* how lightning worked somatically upon him. As in Stuart-Wortley's sonnet, light is transformed from the medium by which we see, into something which affects us physically and emotionally:

> a prodigious storm of thunder and lightning accompanied by a deluging rain that turned the streets and lanes into rivers caused me to repent and resolve to lead a better life. I can remember those awful thunder-bursts and the white glare of the lightning yet and the wild lashing of the rain against the windowpanes... With every glare of lightning I shriveled and shrank together in mortal terror, and in the interval of black darkness that followed I poured out my lamentings over my lost condition, and my supplications for just one more chance, with an energy and feeling of sincerity quite foreign to my nature.
>
> But in the morning I saw that it was a false alarm and concluded to resume business at the old stand and wait for another reminder.[13]

Despite Twain's customary rhetoric of self-deflation, his sense of the personal revelation that lightning can bring is, like its association with the sublime, a recurrent aspect of the poetics of lightning. Take Randall Jarrell's famous declaration, in relation to his own craft, that 'A poet is a man who manages, in a lifetime of standing out in thunderstorms, to be struck by lightning five or six times'.[14] The essential aspects of this revelation lie, first, in its immediacy: its accidental and unbidden quality (for it is not the product of disciplined or rational human inquiry), its capacity to take one by surprise—a characteristic readily extendable as simile. Consider, for example, the occasion when John Baptist Cavalletto mimics the sinister Rigaud/Blandois to Arthur Clennam in Dickens's *Little Dorrit*, and 'he indicated a very remarkable and sinister smile. The whole change passed over him like a flash of light', causing Clennam to wonder at the transformative power of this momentary impersonation, the mimicry the more frightening because its very evanescence was like a flare of memory.[15]

Additionally, the revelation produced by lightning seems to have, at least in the moment of its occurrence, unarguable authority, whether divine or human. Voiceless, flaming, alive, sublime: lightning flashes frequently throughout Percy Shelley's writing, its force co-opted to celebrate the dangerous power of poetry, 'a sword of lightning, ever unsheathed, which consumes the scabbard that would contain it'.[16] Wordsworth, in the episode of *The Prelude* (1805) in which he describes crossing the Alps, compares the way in which the imagination shoots out from us and allows us to see further into the world to lightning's sudden and supernal revelations that surpass the workings of our reason, writing of 'when the light of sense | Goes out in flashes that have shewn to us | The invisible world'.[17] But that didn't quite seem to nail it for him: reason was still, somehow, too determinate an agent in this process, and by the 1850 version, 'sense' is obliterated, exploded, rather than having a more exploratory role: 'the light of sense | Goes out, but with a flash that has revealed | The invisible world'.[18] His uncertainty about how to phrase the arrival of sudden and startling insight encapsulates a continuing uncertainty about the effects of lightning itself: does the impression of revelation come from the light itself, or from the contrast with the surrounding dark?

When Nietszche invokes 'the lightning bolt of truth' at the end of *Ecce Homo*,[19] he is, of course, setting up this form of revelation as human-generated, coming from within, in direct opposition to the hypocrisy of Christian theology. But the phenomenon had long been appropriated by those seeking to demonstrate the power of divine illumination: being 'blinded by the light', from the Book of Revelation to Bruce Springsteen, is a concept very readily melded with lightning's shocking, surprising force. This conceit—the condensation of natural electricity and God's power—was energetically exploited by Gerard Manley Hopkins. Notably, the opening lines of his 1877 sonnet, 'The world is charged with the grandeur of God | It will flame out, like shining from shook foil',[20] were, unlike so many of his celebratory meditations on God's presence within nature, generated not from the experience, or loss, of a particular place or moment of observation, but from the force of a simile. In an 1883 letter to Robert Bridges (one that clearly demonstrates how assiduously he continued to follow Ruskin's advice to observe nature as accurately as possible), Hopkins claims that the poem was written 'expressly for the image's sake'. He explains that he used '"foil" in its sense of leaf or tinsel, and no other word whatever will give the effect I want. Shaken goldfoil gives off broad glares like sheet lightning and also, and this is true of nothing else, owing to its zigzag dents and creasings and network of small many cornered facets, a sort of fork lightning too.'[21] If he changed his original choice of word, 'lightning', to 'shining', it was to achieve his own compression of verbal energy through alliteration, rather than because of any weakness in signification. This remains, after all, in the word 'charged', which has carried the implications of 'full of electricity' since 1750, when Benjamin Franklin employed it in this context. In a journal entry, Hopkins glosses the opening phrase of the next line, 'gathers to a greatness', as 'a force…gathered before it was discharged'.[22]

In other poems, Hopkins uses lightning as a metaphor for the awe experienced in the face of God's potency. The eighteenth-century philosophical theologian Jonathan Edwards had written bluntly that 'The extreme fierceness and extraordinary power of the heat of lightning is an intimation of the exceeding power and terribleness of the wrath of God',[23] and in 'The Wreck of the Deutschland' (written 1875–6; published 1918), 'lightning' is likewise equated with the threatening, potentially punishing 'lashed rod' of God, the 'lightning of fire hard-hurled', like one of Jupiter's thunderbolts, to be contrasted with the mercy of Christ, who exhibits no 'dooms-day dazzle in his coming'.[24] But usually, Hopkins is far more nuanced in his response to lightning, allowing for the simultaneity of beauty and terror. 'The shepherd's brow, fronting forked lightning, owns | The horror and the havoc and the glory | Of it', he wrote.[25] Hopkins connects biblical and classical writing: underpinning his reference to Jupiter is his interest in the fragmented writings of Heraclitus, and the Greek philosopher's belief not just that fire is the underlying element of nature, but also that the 'thunderbolt steers all things'.[26] Yet as his frequent and deliberate employment of electrical vocabulary suggests, Hopkins also knew his contemporary science, and when he was writing about how God's compelling, dangerous power not only demonstrates itself within nature, but may also safely be conducted to earth, he was implicitly drawing on discussions concerning the material, rather than spiritual, connotations of electricity.[27]

These dual currents—of mythology on the one hand, and of contemporary physics and the physical sciences on the other—animate nineteenth-century representations and discussions of lightning.[28] Notwithstanding the advances in the understanding, channelling, and harnessing of electrical energy that took place throughout the nineteenth century, lightning always—and despite its beauty—carries with it a raw edge of imminent danger, of proximity to a destructive force. Milton's Christ, one might recollect, 'Saw Satan fall like lightning down from heaven'.[29] This danger, however, was not just figured in terms inherited from two millennia of religious and folkloric belief. As we shall see, technological developments in artificial lighting produced their own, new forms of the sublime, but the elemental power of lightning itself was co-opted to critique and dramatize a range of highly contemporary issues. For example, in Mary Shelley's *Frankenstein* (1818; revised 1831), the risky enterprise of meddling with galvanic forces in nature is anticipated quite early in the novel, when we are shown their inherent violence through the image of lightning destroying an 'old and beautiful' oak, causing fire to stream from its blasted trunk.[30] When the scientist first encounters the monster he created, it is within an Alpine scene where he watches lightning 'play on the summit of Mont Blanc in the most beautiful figures'.[31] By the shores of Lake Geneva, he is dazzled by 'vivid flashes of lightning' which light up the lake, 'making it appear like a vast sheet of fire'.[32] Ostensibly beautiful, the earlier storm scene hardly renders this a propitious location when the Monster emerges from the gloom: 'A flash of lightning illuminated the object and discovered its shape plainly to me; its gigantic stature, and the deformity of its aspect, more hideous than belongs to humanity.'[33] Mary Shelley's lightning is more than a Gothic prop. It mocks the association of illumination with scientific advance and the Enlightenment, and transforms it instead into an instrument that reveals the horrific distortions of human presumption, whilst at the same time it offers a practical demonstration of nature's independent forces.

Likewise, a critique of contemporary 'advancement', especially when linked to the temptations of personal gain, is a powerful motivating force behind Herman Melville's 1854 short story 'The Lightning-Rod Man'. During a violent thunderstorm, the narrator is interrupted in his rural cottage by an itinerant salesman. The sole ware that the peddler offers is a copper lightning conductor, which he tries to terrify his potential customer into buying through a rapid-fire patter drawn from the folklore of lightning. Does he not know that to stand by the fireplace—especially since this is decorated with 'immense iron fire-dogs'—is to place himself in the most potentially lethal spot in the house?[34] The soot and hot air would act as conductors; the floor is of oak, notorious for attracting lightning; he should even beware of the phenomenon of reverse lightning, which passes not from clouds to earth, but from earth to clouds. He is taunted with his physical vulnerability: '"Think of being a heap of charred offal, like a haltered horse burnt in his stall; and all in one flash!"'[35] Yet the thunderstorm passes away, leaving house and human unharmed; the angry stranger tries to spear the defiant narrator with his pitchfork-like rod, and is finally expelled, to continue his wanderings round the country, driving 'a brave trade with the fears of man'.[36] In this brief but multivalent tale, Melville, on the surface, tells a story of stoic virtue expelling alarmist evil: the peddler is a pale version of the forces of the storm; his 'sunken pitfalls of eyes ... played with an innocuous sort of lightning: the gleam without the bolt'.[37] Behind this, of course, lies a Puritan allegory of faith not just casting out fear but also refusing idolatory, putting one's trust in superstitious trappings designed to ward off harm.[38] The tale is an indictment, too, of a particular form of evangelical proselytizing as exemplified in 'one manifestation of nineteenth-century American Christianity, the fire-and-brimstone salvation salesman'.[39] Furthermore, despite the fact that the story derives much of its force from implying that we are dealing with more complex forces than are ever made explicit, it is also a satire on a burgeoning consumer market, and on the shameless manipulation of human insecurities by fast-talking salespeople.

But, except in so far as it creates a Gothic frisson, there is little that is aesthetically tempting about Melville's lightning, whether described zigzagging across the sky, or personified in the figure he baits with the jocular title of 'Jupiter Tonans'.[40] However, more generally, and as we saw in relation to Hopkins, it was the tension created by lightning's combination of beauty and danger that was most amenable to metaphoric appropriation. Charlotte Brontë, explaining why she dedicated the second edition of *Jane Eyre* to Thackeray, refutes the common comparison of him to Fielding by saying that despite the attractiveness of his humour and the brightness of his wit, 'both bear the same relation to his serious genius that the mere lambent sheet-lightning playing under the edge of the summer-cloud does to the electric death-spark hid in its womb'.[41] Within the novel itself, lightning's danger is inextricable from a particular kind of peril—that of sexual attraction (the remark about Thackeray serves to link lightning with generative reproductive powers, too). In chapter 12, Jane reminds herself, and by extension her readers, that it is as well to be extremely cautious of attractive men, remarking that she 'should have known instinctively that they neither had nor could have sympathy with anything in me, and should have shunned them as one would fire, lightning, or anything else that is bright but antipathetic'.[42] This caution sets one up, of course, for the implications of one of Victorian literature's most famous storms where, just after Rochester proposes to Jane, the elements intervene: 'a livid, vivid spark leapt out of a cloud at which I was looking, and there was a crack, a crash, and a close rattling peal; and I thought only of hiding my dazzled eyes against Mr. Rochester's shoulder'.[43] When Adele tells Jane, the next morning, that the chestnut tree under which they had been talking had been cleft in two by a lightning strike during the night, it does not take a particularly prescient reader to realize that Jane's confidence in her employer's ability to take care of her against externally produced revelations is decidedly misplaced, and that responding to sexual magnetism may be equally perilous.

Yet it was by no means invariably the case that when lightning was invoked to signify the power of sexuality, it was simultaneously regarded as a potentially lethal force.

Rather, it could be loaded with unstoppable energy, following natural laws of attraction. Walt Whitman asks, in 'A Song of Myself',

> Is this then a touch? quivering me to a new identity,
> Flames and ether making a rush for my veins,
> Treacherous tip of me reaching and crowding to help them,
> My flesh and blood playing out lightning to strike what is hardly
> different from myself...[44]

Engaging with lightning, here, suggests the compelling riskiness of new sexual contact: one thinks forward to Foucault (writing of Bataille) comparing transgression to a lightning bolt.[45] In *Middlemarch*, a novel that crackles with electrical discharge when Will and Dorothea approach one another, the current of connection that runs between them is Eliot's primary means of signifying the mutuality of their physical attraction.[46] The scene in which they finally acknowledge their feelings is dramatically illuminated by a violent storm. 'The light was more and more sombre, but there came a flash of lightning which made them start and look at each other, and then smile'—an acknowledgement shortly followed by another 'vivid flash of lightning which lit each of them up for the other—and the light seemed to be the terror of a hopeless love'.[47] The illumination here is multifunctional: a literal making visible of each other's expression; a moment of heightened awareness of the other one's appeal; an externalization both of attraction and of the dangers of not acting upon it.

The stagy melodrama of Eliot's scene is as nothing, though, when placed alongside a novel that appeared the previous year, Thomas Hardy's *Desperate Remedies*. Here, the heroine, Cytherea, takes refuge in the house of the estate manager during a thunderstorm. Manston is a self-consciously sexy, diabolic modern villain, highly attuned to the backdrop against which he manifests himself: 'The clouds, from which darts, forks, zigzags, and balls of fire continually sprang, did not appear to be more than a hundred yards above their heads, and every now and then a flash and a peal made gaps in the steward's descriptions.'[48] So what does he do, as well as asking her in? He starts to extemporize a harmony on his organ. The ensuing scene is worth quoting in full:

> Presently he ceased, and began searching for some music-book.
>
> 'What a splendid flash!' he said, as the lightning again shone in through the mullioned window...The thunder pealed again. Cytherea, in spite of herself, was frightened, not only at the weather, but at the general unearthly weirdness which seemed to surround her there.
>
> 'I wish I—the lightning wasn't so bright. Do you think it will last long?' she said, timidly.
>
> 'It can't last much longer,' he murmured, without turning, running his fingers again over the keys. 'But this is nothing,' he continued, suddenly stopping and regarding her. 'It seems brighter because of the deep shadow under those trees yonder. Don't mind it; now look at me—look in my face—now.'
>
> He had faced the window, looking fixedly at the sky with his dark strong eyes. She seemed compelled to do as she was bidden, and looked in the too-delicately beautiful face.
>
> The flash came; but he did not turn or blink, keeping his eyes fixed as firmly as before. 'There,' he said, turning to her, 'that's the way to look at lightning.'

'O, it might have blinded you!' she exclaimed.

'Nonsense—not lightning of this sort—I shouldn't have stared at it if there had been danger. It is only sheet-lightning now. Now, will you have another piece? Something from an oratorio this time?'[49]

What is remarkable about this passage is how Hardy takes agency away from the lightning, and gives it to Manston. Figured throughout the novel as a prototype of a modern man who will stop at nothing to achieve his ends, the steward co-opts nature for his sexually predatory ambitions, using the physical attributes of lightning as a form of emotional manipulation, forcing Cytherea to observe him as he resolutely fails to flinch at what she, at least, fears must be a blindingly intense momentary glare. And, of course, she's made to look intently at his illuminated features, as though, indeed, he were having his photograph taken by flash.

This comparison may not be as far-fetched as it sounds. By 1871, when *Desperate Remedies* was published, a number of photographers had experimented with substances that would allow them to take photographs on dull days, or of interiors without recourse to stand lamps, or of people or places that were in complete or quasi-darkness. Limelight, although useful for capturing static objects, dramatically bleached out the features of individuals and created exaggerated shadows, so photographers experimented with other forms of lighting. Closest to Manston's sadistic play with lightning was the work of John Moule,[50] who on 8 February 1857 patented a pyrotechnic compound that he termed 'photogen', a mixture of nitrate of potash, flowers of sulphur, antimony sulphide, and powdered red orpiment. These ingredients were very like those used to produce Bengal Lights—lit as fireworks, and used as flares to signal at sea.[51] Ignited within a hexagonal lamp and burning with a brilliant blue-white light—quite similar to the illumination produced by lightning—it was relatively cheap (around 2*d*. an exposure), and was rapidly adopted by portrait studios in London, despite its unreliability in igniting, and the noxious and toxic fumes that it often gave off. An advertisement for this new compound published in the *Photographic News* early in 1859 indicates that Moule demonstrated its effectiveness at the Royal Polytechnic Institution, in Regent Street: he boasts that his is 'the only invention whereby Portraits can be produced at night quite equal to those taken by daylight', and moreover, that 'it can be used in the drawing room without the slightest danger'—an early indication of the desire to domesticate flash photography.[52] The composition burned for about twenty seconds, and exposures could be made in fifteen seconds or less—a long flash, to be sure, but certainly a brilliant interruption of darkness, and equivalent in its duration to the illumination provided by sheet lightning.

Admittedly, the brightness of the light, even when shielded by a square of blue glass positioned between lamp and sitter, caused problems.[53] The effects—again like those of lightning's glare—were harsh and contrasty: a carrying to extremes of Ruskin's complaint against photography in general, that it 'either exaggerates shadows, or loses detail in the lights'.[54] 'Hideous portraits...ghastly and gravelike', one critic called them, reviewing the fifth annual exhibition of the Photographic Society at which Moule showed five examples, adding that if they are all that one might expect from this process, 'we should advise the practitioner at once to abandon photogenic light for the more cheering and inspiring light of old Sol himself'.[55] On the other side of the Atlantic, on the eve of the Civil War, Oliver Wendell Holmes speculated that 'the time is perhaps at hand when a flash of light, as sudden and brief as that of the lightning which shows a whirling wheel standing stock still, shall preserve the very instant of the shock of contact of the mighty armies that are even now gathering'.[56]

The new lighting method had instant novelty value and practical application as well as giving rise to speculation about future uses. It was estimated that in the winter of 1860, some 30,000 portraits were taken by this means in London alone.[57] It's almost certain that Hardy would have become aware of this means of illuminating darkness (he lived in London from 1862 to 1867): his interest in photography provides, after all, an important hinge in the plot of *Desperate Remedies,* as Manston changes out the photographic backing on a couple of cartes de visite in order to prove that his murdered first wife indeed lives—only to be foiled by Cytherea realizing that azure eyes (however imperfect the photographic technology) would surely never show up as black.[58] Where this leads us, however (apart from demonstrating a growing popular interest in photography), is to ask how, and why, the aesthetics of lightning and flash photography start to diverge.

This certainly did not happen for some while. As well as the metaphorical appropriation of lightning to describe experiments with artificial illumination, direct connections between lightning and the mechanical ability to capture the image were being drawn throughout the nineteenth century through accounts of 'keraunography', the study of what was believed to be lightning's power to imprint an image onto a receptive surface—whether it be the replica of a landscape found on the fleece of sheep struck by lightning, or the profile of a girl caught on a tin tray, or the outlines of a frizzled cat—whiskers, tail fur, and all—supposedly imprinted on a bald man's head. These are accounts in which the apparent magic of nature and of new technology drew anecdotally close together.[59] Nor are these occurrences merely ones that appear and circulate as newspaper fillers. T. L. Phipson, well established as a scientist in both Belgium and London, devoted a whole chapter in his *Familiar Letters on Some Mysteries of Nature and Discoveries in Science* (1876) to the phenomenon, opening his discussion with some examples about which he expresses a good deal of scepticism (figures of crosses being imprinted on the workmen rebuilding the Temple of Jerusalem in 360 CE; crosses appearing on the bodies of those who were worshipping when Wells Cathedral was struck by lightning in 1595), but then proceeds to assert that, in his opinion, lightning prints do occur.

> Doubtless, when images are produced, they indicate ofttimes with nearly photographic precision the objects from which the electric discharge emanated towards the body of the person—the objects whose image is reproduced upon the skin forms part of the electric circuit. The extraordinary velocity with which electricity travels renders it of little importance whether

the object printed be in contact with the body which receives the impression, or at some considerable distance from it. The same remark holds good for the action of light in photography. As to the molecular change induced in the tissue upon which the image is impressed, it may be assimilated to what takes place upon a photographic plate; and when we can explain how the forms, and even the *colours*, of objects placed at a distance print their images upon certain chemical compounds, we shall have made a step towards the solution of the problem of lightning-prints.[60]

Confident, too, in making the connection with photographic methods were the French doctor M. Boudin, in his *Histoire physique et médicale de la foudre*, and Andreas Poey, director of the Observatory in Havana, in a memoir, *The Photographic Effects of Lightning* (2nd edn. 1861). Boudin coined the word 'keraunography' (or 'writing with thunder'); both he and Poey saw the human skin as the light-sensitive surface, the tree—or coin or cat—as the object photographed, and the lightning as the agent that records the form.

Understandably, the popular press jumped at accounts of the inexplicably impressed image, which persisted into the twentieth century—accounts that regularly attributed extraordinary, even supernatural, powers to lightning itself, authorizing them through the association of photography with scientific proof. Take the case of Abbott Parker, struck in the back by lightning in Morristown, NJ, in 1904.

Upon being removed to the Catholic Hospital, Parker was placed on a cot over which hung a large crucifix. While the patient's back was being bathed with alcohol and water the physicians and nuns were astonished to see a picture of the crucifixion on the flesh, whereas a few minutes before no picture was there. The nuns believed that it was a miracle, and the doctors were mystified, as they declared that the picture was not the result of tattooing. An expert tattooer, after an examination, also decided that the picture was not tattooed. A theory which seems generally accepted is that Parker's skin had become sensitized by the effect of lightning, and acted as a photographic plate for the crucifix hanging over his cot.[61]

Lightning and photography maintained a less sensationalist relationship as well. As Jennifer Tucker has described, nineteenth-century meteorology and photography worked hand in hand in their attempt to describe and understand the phenomenon of severe weather.[62] Photography proved crucial in demonstrating that lightning does not take the zigzag path beloved of classical and neoclassical artists, and, later, of cartoonists. Turner, as we saw in his Venice lightning picture (Figure 2.1), was one of the very few artists who had understood this—testimony to his extraordinarily observant eye—but from the first daguerreotype of a streak of lightning, taken in St Louis on 18 June 1847, through the picture taken by William Jennings of Philadelphia, *c.*1885 and confidently labelled by him 'First Photograph of Lightning' (as seen in Figure 2.3), to the collection of images of lightning accumulated in 1887 by the Royal Meteorological Society of London, it became easier to classify different types of lightning, to recognize that lightning discharges are often composed of multiple flashes, and to counter that inaccurate and jagged stereotype.[63]

But this relationship between lightning and photography could be turned around. An A. J. Jarman wrote to the *Photographic News* in 1877 about a severe thunderstorm

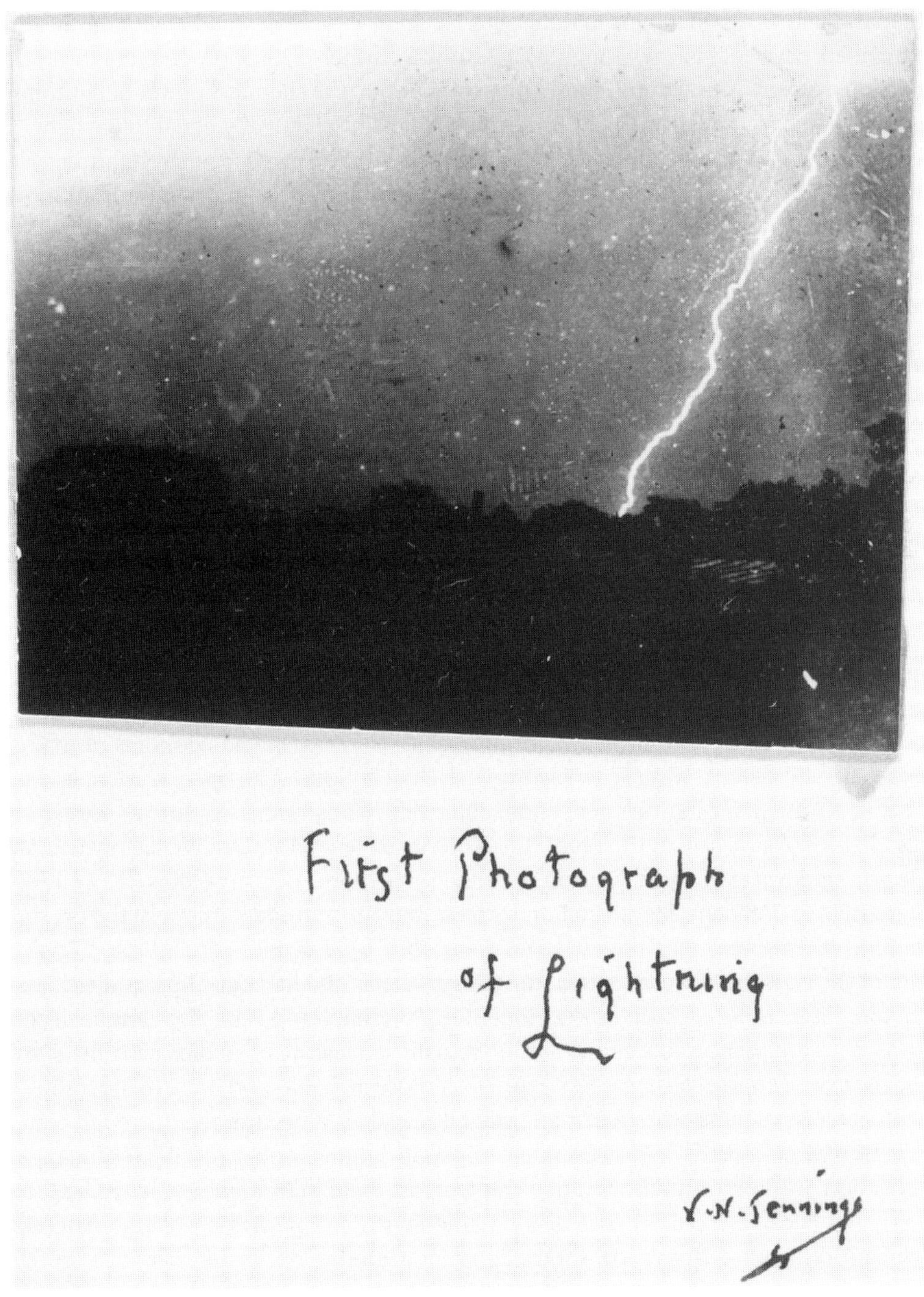

Figure 2.3 William N. Jennings, 'First Photograph of Lightning', *c.*1885. Gelatin silver print. Image: 4.1 × 5.3 cm (1 ⅝ × 2 1/16 in.). Mount: 15.2 × 8.9 cm (6 × 3 ½ in.) George Eastman Museum. Gift of the 3M Foundation, ex-collection Louis Walton Sipley. 1983.0679.0003.

that he'd witnessed on 10 June in Ramsgate. He set up his camera, and—with the aid, he estimated, of twenty flashes of lightning—took a quarter-plate photograph of the back of Queen Street. 'This, I think, shows most clearly that the chemical power of lightning is quite equal to the electric light produced artificially, and nearly equal to daylight.'[64] This was, he said, the first time he'd heard of a photograph being taken by lightning. He wasn't, however, correct. According to a note by Phipson in his 1875 translation of Wilfrid de Fonvielle's wonderfully comprehensive *Éclairs et tonnerre*, a recent number of the *Moniteur de photographie* mentions that this has just been done in New York.[65] But certainly, by 1898 this was a known practice, even if something of a novelty: the *Photo-Beacon* (published in Chicago—prime thunderstorm territory) suggested that this was something well worth a try, 'now that the thunderstorm season is again with us', and remarked on an especially effective image the writer had seen of hundreds of people huddled together under the portico of a building for shelter—one that had been taken by the lightning of a violent storm.[66]

This last note appeared beside a short feature on 'flat pictures', prompted by a reader's inquiry about the disappointing image he'd recently made by flashlight. By the time this note appeared, artificial lightning, in the form of *blitzlichtpulver*, had been available for a decade. Moule's photogen had too many disadvantages to take off commercially, in the long run: the couple of decades that followed its short flare of popularity witnessed further experiments with magnesium powder and magnesium wire, and also with non-flash forms of illuminating the photographic subject, made possible by new developments in electric and gas lighting.[67] Until the widespread adoption of mains electricity, however, it was extremely expensive to employ it—an establishment had to be able to maintain its own generator (and even mains electricity proved costly to install, too). As we saw in Chapter 1, the American Henry Van Der Weyde opened an electric studio at 182 Regent Street in 1877, and three more London studios (the London Stereoscopic Company, Mayall (in Bond Street), and Negretti and Zambra (at the Crystal Palace)) had electricity by the early 1880s, but they were rarities at that time.[68] By the end of the century, however, much more mains electricity had been laid, and cheaper equipment introduced, such as the Houghton Portable Hand Feed Arc Lamp. All the same, the employment of electric lighting remained a feature of studios patronized by the more well-to-do. Flash was less expensive, more portable, and more democratic—both in terms of those who used it and what it revealed. When the breakthrough compound was discovered and distributed, the associations with lightning—brilliance, revelation, inspiration, authority, power—were all there in its name, which at least in Germany became a crucial part of its marketing. Agfa's packaging of the material, which it distributed from 1903, shows lightning shooting out in all directions on the packaging of the flash powder, ready to be ignited, as we see in Figure 2.4, in one of their own flash lamps.

A piece that Johannes Gaedicke published in the *American Annual of Photography* sounded as though he was trying to coin a new term that would permanently meld his invention with the natural phenomenon. Called 'The Lightning Photographer', it

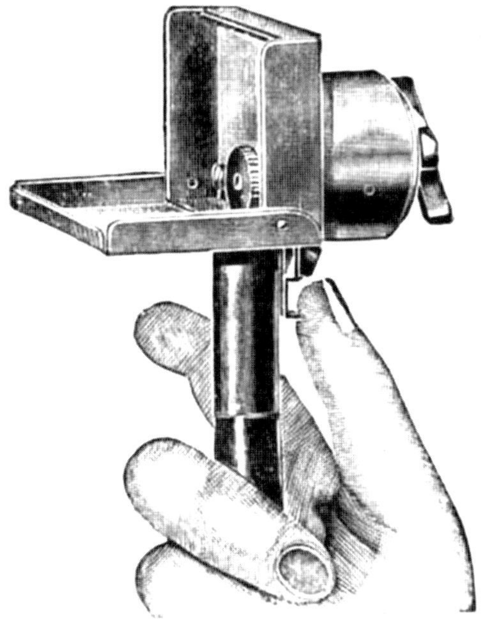

"AGFA" BLITZLICHT

(Flash Powder)

Minimum smoke development. Maximum light. The most rapid flash. Silent discharge. No danger of explosion. Great durability. Convenient packing. Economy in use.

No. 1 size, (10 grams).... $ .35
No. 2 size (25 grams)..... .70
No. 3 size (50 grams)..... 1.20
No. 4 size (100 grams).... 1.90

Figure 2.4 'Agfa' flash lamp and *blitzlicht*, in George L. Barrows (ed.), *The 'Agfa' Book of Photography by Flashlight* (2nd edn., New York: Berlin Aniline Works, *c.*1910), 72 and 73.

postulated a future in which a couple of cousins, wanting a picture taken of themselves at midnight, would

> just have to send round the corner to the 'lightning photographer' who lives there... A group of the two friends is posed near the chimney-piece, focus taken by lamplight, and while they are still engaged in pleasant conversation—flash—a momentary light illumines the room, to give place again to the former relative darkness.[69]

Certainly, *blitz* was to take off, in German, as the generic term for the 'flash' in flash photography from this point.

As we have seen, the news of *blitzlichtpulver*'s invention travelled widely and speedily. Let us return to the case of Jacob Riis. At first, the images produced by Riis's collaborators were translated into line drawings—published, with the journalist's text, as 'Flashes from the Slums', in the *New York Sun* in February 1888. He subsequently incorporated them as lantern slides in his lectures; produced them as evidence against slum landlords; published them in his December 1889 *Scribner's Magazine* article 'How the Other Half Lives: Studies Among the Tenements'; and used them as illustrations for his books, including *How the Other Half Lives* (1890) and *Children of the Poor* (1892). Riis's commitment to publicizing these conditions was a timely one. Coupled with rapidly growing concerns about public health, epidemiology, and social reform, and sharing in the interest excited by the publication of William Booth's *In Darkest England and the Way Out* (1890)—preceded by Booth's popular American lecture tour—this meant that, as Peter Bacon

Hales claims in his excellent reading of Riis's career, 'probably more than any other single individual in the history of the genre [of urban photography, he] brought together the technological, philosophical, and stylistic strands of his time and his culture'.[70]

Riis celebrates himself as a pioneering campaigner, tending to underplay the work of several decades of reformers–particularly those who approached social problems from a more radical perspective than he did. But he did not present flash as testimony to the modernity of electricity that was changing cityscapes, interiors, and social practices. Rather, harking back to earlier associations of light with Christian revelation, he saw flash illuminating darkness as if delivering a spiritual blessing, heralding a bright dawn: 'Light ahead!' he promises.[71] But Riis's enterprise of literal and figurative enlightenment was not carried out without considerable personal risk—not at the hands of the slum dwellers themselves, but because of the highly flammable nature of his equipment. When he took over the photography himself, he abandoned, as we have already seen, the apparatus that had earlier occasioned understandable terror: 'I substituted a frying-pan for the revolver, and flashed the light on that. It seemed more homelike. But, as I said, I am clumsy. Twice I set fire to the house with the apparatus, and once to myself.'[72] In *How the Other Half Lives*, he recalls how, 'with unpractised hands', he managed to ignite a tenement house where he'd been photographing a room of blind beggars: 'When the blinding effect of the flash had passed away and I could see once more, I discovered that a lot of paper and rags that hung on the wall were ablaze.'[73] Luckily, he managed to smother the conflagration himself.

Illumination and terror: the effects of Riis's flash photography were, indeed, much like those of lightning. Although in some cases it would seem that he positioned his subjects so as to mimic the sentimental postures of genre painting, in others their startled faces look straight out at the camera. And something else is strikingly apparent in some of these photographs. The material effects of flash photography not only involve the production of exaggerated contrasts, and the laying bare of detail and texture, but they also show something of the means by which they were taken. As we have seen, some of Riis's earlier photographs fog out the arc of vision that is close to the flash itself—something that Riis had to learn to avoid, by standing further back from his subjects. One of them clearly shows the device that was used to ignite the flash, too. The explosion of the powder, as well, on occasion gets caught on the photographic plate; bounces back from a glass window or another shiny surface; is made manifest through the bleaching of faces, the extreme whitening of shirts and collars, as we see in Figure 2.5. Rather than photographic technology operating as an apparently transparent recording device, flash displays itself and its eruption in the darkness.

Those glaring windowpanes are significant, because in them is reflected a major distinction between lightning and flash photography. This is a distinction that is connected to, but reaches beyond, the most fundamental difference of all: the fact that the former is an unpredictable natural display, the latter a more or less controlled product of human technology, deliberately directed towards a chosen subject. The difference that Riis's photography allows one to perceive clearly is one of representation. To represent

Figure 2.5 Jacob Riis, 'Bohemian Cigar Makers at Work in Their Tenement', *c.*1890. Jacob A. (Jacob August) Riis (1849–1914)/Museum of the City of New York. 2008.1.15.

lightning inevitably means being at some kind of a distance from it. Lightning's presence in a painting may call attention to the practice of scientific inquiry, as with the jagged bolt in Januarius Zick's *Newton's Contribution to Optics* (*c.*1790). It may be the thin silver thread that pulls together the composition, highlighting the melodramatic effect of stormy light on a landscape in the American luminist Martin Johnson Heade's *Thunder Storm on Narragansett Bay* (1868). Or it may bring home to us the beauty that a lightning show reflected on a calm sea can produce—in, for example, Albert Moore's *Lightning and Light* (1892), seen in Figure 2.6, a work that is also an occasion for the painter to show off his skills at painting light and tonality, producing a study in greys and silvers and whites, set off by the palest of greens and yellows. In *Lightning and Light*, both the watchers within the painting and the spectators of the art work itself are put in an analogous position, watching a formidable natural spectacle at a distance. The woman who looks towards the spectator may, in the most literal of terms, be averting her eyes from the overwhelming brightness of the lightning, but she also functions as an intermediary figure, inviting us in to look at the light show that holds her companions in

Figure 2.6 Albert Moore, *Lightning and Light*, 1892. Oil on canvas, 31 ½ × 54 ½ in. (87.6 × 145.6 cm). Private collection. © The FORBES Magazine Collection, New York/Bridgeman Images.

thrall. Only occasionally, in painting, do we see lightning's illuminatory power without the depiction of its flash in the sky. Chevalier Féréol de Bonnemaison's *Young Woman Overtaken by a Storm* (1799), shown in Figure 2.7, is an exception in this respect. Scantily clad, to say the least, she clasps herself tight as she unadvisedly shelters under a tree, lit up by lightning's blue-white glare as if exposed to flash.

For Kant, this distance between the witness and the lightning's flash was crucial to the sublimity of the storm scene he evokes:

> Bold, overhanging, and as it were threatening, rocks; clouds piled up in the sky, moving with lightning flashes and thunder peals; volcanoes in all their violence of destruction; hurricanes with their track of devastation; the boundless ocean in a state of tumult; the lofty waterfall of a mighty river, and such like; these exhibit our faculty of resistance as insignificantly small in comparison with their might. But the sight of them is the more attractive, the more fearful it is, provided only that we are in security.[74]

Flash photography gives us no such distance—and not just because it isn't accompanied by dramatic sound, that crash or rumble that is at once a further emblem of wrath and destruction, and also a marker of time and space, of separation between observer and storm. Rousseau reminds us in *Émile* (1762): 'The distance from which thunder is coming can be judged by the time from the lightning to the clap.'[75] The presence of the flash in Riis's photographs is an accidental by-product of the means used to take the

Figure 2.7 Chevalier Féréol de Bonnemaison (French, *c.*1770–1827), *Young Woman Overtaken by a Storm* (*Une jeune femme s'étant avancée dans la campagne se trouve surprise par l'orage*), 1799. Oil on canvas, 39 3/8 × 31 11/16 in. (100 × 80.5 cm). Brooklyn Museum, Gift of Louis Thomas, 71.138.1 (Photo: Brooklyn Museum).

image. It might be compared to the shadow of the photographer and camera that falls across an image—except this is usually avoidable, and, if prominently apparent, is likely to be a chosen part of the composition. It could be paralleled with the inveterate self-portraitist Lee Friedlander's inclusion of himself and camera in the driver's side mirror in several images in his *America by Car* (2010)—but this constitutes, of course, a deliberate and repeated insertion of the active photographer into the image. Ben Shahn's 'Street Scene, Circleville, Ohio' (1938) perhaps forms a closer point of comparison—it's impossible to gauge whether or not he intended to show himself holding up his Leica 35-millimetre camera with its right-angle viewfinder, although this provides a wonderful example of some deceptive technology effectively deployed in street photography—the kind of surreptitious approach to one's subject that's only possible for the flash photographer who adopts infrared technology.

All these images share the capacity to debunk any belief that photography provides some transparent window onto the world. However, they differ in one important respect: the three examples that I've just cited alert one to the presence of human agency, whilst the bright reflection of flash powder reminds one, first and foremost, of the technology that makes representation possible. Even if lightning may be the imagined source of illumination within a painting, it is powerfully present as a subject. But in a flash photograph, the thing that causes the shock, that blinds both photographer and subject alike through excess of light, that disorients, is part of the technology of representation. It is not—except inadvertently—its subject. Furthermore, this is not light that illuminates things for those who experience its sudden over-bright glare: rather, it dazzles, bleaches the world, temporarily blinds, causes distorting after-images.

Here, I believe, are some of the major reasons why the aesthetics of flash photography start to veer away from those of lightning, however much its nineteenth-century practitioners repeatedly called on a shared rhetoric of illumination and terror. But other factors come into play as well. It's not that electricity loses its power to create awe and terror when deployed by humans. Nor was it the case that artificial light was debarred from association with the category of the sublime. As David Nye has shown, electricity became one of the most notable elements in this late nineteenth-century category of wonder, alongside bridges, skyscrapers, railroad engineering, and factories. It was used to enhance natural features, as with the Niagara Falls illuminations that helped dissolve any clear distinction between natural and artificial sites;[76] its lighting was 'a visual representation of the new force'[77] that powered factories, communication systems, and urban living, and it featured prominently in the great expositions of the late nineteenth and early twentieth centuries, where again lines between nature and technology were deliberately blurred. In 1904, at the St Louis World's Fair, artificial lightning was made to flash out from a central point and flicker along the man-made horizon.

It goes without saying that the limited range of a pan of ignited *blitzlichtpulver* could not compete with the overwhelming quality of these displays, let alone with the force of nature's demonstrations. But more was at stake than scale. As photographic practitioners and journalists started to drop the parallel between lightning and flash photography (at least outside the German-speaking world), after the turn from the nineteenth to the twentieth century, two things were happening. First, flash photography—due to the success of *blitzlichtpulver* and its spin-offs—was becoming much less of a media sensation, even as its shocks necessarily continued to register on individual subjects. Regular comparisons between technology and lightning only returned, as we shall see, with the really big flash of the atomic bomb. But what also needs to be taken into account is the increasing separation between art photography and photography as a means to a representational end. While news photographers quickly lost sight of the spiritual implications of throwing light on current conditions that was so important to Riis, for many of the photographers who wanted to see themselves as artists rather than as mere recorders of the circumstantial, the distinction between the natural and artificial origins of light became crucial. Even though some Secessionist photographers employed flash, later art photography practitioners, attempting to distance themselves from the utilitarian, and insisting on the aesthetic qualities of their photography, came to repudiate flash and its effects. Following Henri Cartier-Bresson, who in the 1950s made clear his vehement preference for making use only of available lighting, in 1982 André Kertesz claimed 'Flash killed the original ethic'.[78] Such luminary purists were not going to harm their cause by drawing parallels between the despised flash and the sublime grandeur of lightning.

The violence of Kertesz's verb is telling. Lightning, of course, is deadly if one gets too close: consider the laconic way in which Humbert Humbert describes his mother's death in *Lolita*: 'My very photogenic mother died in a freak accident (picnic, lightning) when I was three.'[79] There's a hint here, though, that—according to HH's typically allusive and perverse logic—Mrs Humbert's beauty may have had a hand in her demise, attracting lightning as she would have attracted an intrusive photographer armed with a flashgun. It is, indeed, in literary texts—fiction, poetry, and essays—that the metaphor of lightning continues to be evoked, or hinted at, in relation to flash photography. It is, perhaps, at its most useful when it's used in passing, as a momentarily startling parallel or allusion, much in keeping with the sudden eruption of a flashgun or flashbulb itself, dazzling—even blinding—for a moment, and then gone.

These fleeting, if striking, occurrences are of different types. Almost always the hierarchical distinction between the grandeur of lightning and the relative puniness of the photographic flash is preserved. Sometimes, however, it's hard to prise apart the lightning bolt from the camera's aide. Both, after all, carry an association with instantaneousness, with the suddenness of an isolated moment. They come together, for example, in Susan Sontag's maxim: 'Life is not about significant details, illuminated in a flash, fixed forever. Photographs are.'[80] I mentioned in Chapter 1 how Walter Benjamin's image of the past as 'an image which flashes up at the instant when it can be recognized and is never seen again' may be interpreted as the flash of lightning or the flash of a flashgun. Elsewhere, though, Benjamin is explicit in referring to the present moment as a flash of lightning. Rather than the past throwing light on the present, or the present throwing light on the past, the momentary, ever-changing present is equated, in the Arcades Project, to a flash—that instant when 'what has been comes together in a flash with the now to form a constellation'.[81] This represents a caesura in the moment of thought, a moment when the dialectic—here the continual oscillation between past and present—is held in suspension. 'The dialectical image', he proclaims, 'is an image that emerges suddenly, in a flash. What has been is to be held fast—as an image flashing up in the now of its recognizability.'[82]

Lightning may be implied here, but the point that Benjamin is making holds equally true in relation to chemically produced flashes. When one experiences a flash at close hand—a moment in which there is no time for reflection, and in which, in any case, one is dazzled, shocked, removed from the ordinary—one is catapulted into a sense of immediacy, of self-presence, where thought, recollection, and distance are all rendered impossible. This is as true if a lightning storm is upon one as it is of the instant or so when a photographic flash goes off. Context might tell one to be more afraid of the former, but the sense of suspended time is the same in both cases. Only in representation—of the silver streak down the sky, of the detail-less bounce-back from a shiny surface—is there the opportunity to hold the flash still for contemplation—and at the same time eviscerate it of its essence.

Eduardo Cadava, in his extended analysis and meditation upon the ways in which Walter Benjamin articulated his ideas about the fragmented nature of history through the language of photography, notes how 'Benjamin's vocabulary of lightning helps register what comes to pass in the opening and closing of vision. It tells us what brings sight to writing.'[83] But it only seems to be within writing that is at one remove from the visual medium, that imagines rather than describes or analyses photography, that one can still locate that original and explicit yearning to claim some of the startling characteristics of lightning for the photographic flash. In Anne Carson's *Autobiography of Red*, for example, her protagonist Geryon is a modern-day incarnation of Stesichorus' mythic red-winged monster—tormented, gifted, queer contemporary boy, trying to understand his passion for Herakles by visiting the terrestial sublime of a volcano—and, crucially, he is a photographer. For Carson, the camera's technology is both the enabler of his image-taking and an instrument of a deeper revelation, allowing her to write of 'the flashes in which a man possesses himself'.[84]

Like Emily Dickinson, whose poetry she cites at one point in *Autobiography of Red*—and unlike much flash photography—Carson's writing is elliptical, allusive, and demands interpretative effort. Back around 1870, Dickinson wrote,

> The Lightning is a yellow Fork
> From Tables in the sky
> By inadvertent fingers dropt
> The awful Cutlery
>
> Of mansions never quite disclosed
> And never quite concealed
> The Apparatus of the Dark
> To ignorance revealed.[85]

Here, she suggests the promise that a sudden streak of lightning holds out—one of a revelation that nonetheless is past before one can possibly know it in its entirety; which diminishes one's sense of a secure grasp on the world; which hints that one is part of a bigger scheme of things than one can understand or verbalize.

This sense of wonder was possessed, too, by the pioneers of flash photography. But as it turned out, their wonder was not so much derived from the external world as it was a product of their own power to reveal it. The technology of visibility that they offered was one that lit up surfaces, but hinted at neither human nor metaphysical depths. It was light that dazzled, rather than providing illumination in any deeper sense. Despite the desires that were originally projected onto it, and which continue to be invoked in imaginative writing, the actual practice of flash photography fell well short, in the end, of playing a role in the technological sublime. It is precisely Dickinson's sense of the startling revelation that occurs in the moment; that is ephemeral; that cannot be fully retained; that is wanting. When Ken Kesey, in his second novel *Sometimes a Great Notion* (1964), writes that 'Far off a fever of lightning takes a flash picture of Mary's Peak', the metaphor is one that tames and reduces the natural force.[86] For lightning has shocked us, and then disappeared, before we can fully take on board what we have seen.

An exploration of flash's aesthetics must involve an examination of the connections between light and revelation—how much light is too much? But it also demonstrates the difficulty of finding a language for certain of technology's shocks. These may not be spectacular and lasting shocks, but in this case, they are shocks that disrupt temporal perception in a quite new way, and that proved to have no effective analogue in the natural world. What looked to be a readily available figurative vocabulary for the narrative of technological development—the language of lightning, and all the attendant associations of awe, grandeur, and the sublime—was illuminating, in the end, only through what we learn when we examine the disruptive logic created by an analogy that does not quite work.[87] It is as though a metaphor had been optimistically projected onto a new phenomenon and not quite reached it. All the same, exploring this failed or incomplete analogy serves to clarify the distinctive features and effects of this particular photographic technology.

CHAPTER THREE

Flash Memory

In Amy Levy's 1888 novel *The Romance of a Shop*, four orphaned sisters establish a commercial photography business in London. Late one night, the doorbell rings in their Baker Street studio. Gertrude, the most courageous, practical, and pragmatic of the girls, goes to investigate, and 're-appeared with a grave face'.

> 'Well?'
>
> They all questioned her, with lips and eyes.
>
> 'Some one has been here about work', she said, slowly; 'but it's rather a dismal sort of job. It is to photograph a dead person.'
>
> 'Gerty, what *do* you mean?'
>
> 'Oh, I believe it is quite usual. A lady—Lady Watergate—died to-day, and her husband wishes the body to be photographed to-morrow morning.'[1]

The circumstances generate a discussion about the kind of photographic work that is, and is not, considered proper for women to undertake. The consensus of opinion is that this is an unpleasantly morbid commission, but the next morning, Gertrude nonetheless goes round to Lord Watergate's grand but gloomy house overlooking Regent's Park. After all, as she puts it, '"we cannot afford to refuse work"'.[2] The fact that the corpse of this lady, with her shining masses of golden hair, 'haggard with sickness, pale with the last strange pallor, but beautiful withal, exquisitely, astonishingly beautiful', was lying 'well within the light from the windows' makes the photographer's task easier than it might otherwise have been.[3] Nineteenth-century photographic magazines on both sides of the Atlantic contain detailed instructions about how, respectfully, to direct light from windows onto the deceased's face, using such techniques as white reflecting screens and mirrors. But on this occasion, Gertrude did not need any manipulation of the natural light in order to achieve the photographic memorialization that had been commissioned. Although the rest of Lord Watergate's house was darkened by blinds, its gloomy corners illuminated only by gas globes supported by pseudo-classical figures, the large room in which the dead woman lay had had its blinds raised to such a degree that the photographer was 'dazzled' by natural light on her entrance.[4]

The end result 'represented a woman lying dead or asleep, with her hair spread out on the pillow',[5] an image that positions Gertrude's photograph in a long tradition of representing the deceased. These pictures appeared to offer material evidence to substantiate the consolatory thought that death is a peaceful process, and that the beloved relative lies at rest. This was a topic that was treated both in painting—Philadelphia artist George Lambdin's *The Last Sleep* (1859), showing a beautiful, ethereal woman lying in a darkened chamber, is a notable mid-century canvas—and in the sentimental genre photograph. For example, Roger Fenton's 'Study of Mother and Daughter Mourning over Deceased Child' (1856–7) depicts three women—one possibly a nursemaid—grouped around a small wicker crib, the daughter turned away in deep grief and burying her head in the lap of the older woman. There is just enough ambiguity in the ages of these women for us to be uncertain who, exactly, gave birth to the dead child. What is unmistakable, though, is Fenton's ability to stage grief within a studio setting: one that gains extra pathos from drab and skimpy furnishings that are, in turn, aesthetically deployed so that light reflects back off the baby's white bed clothing, off the cloth that is draped over a meagre dresser, and from a small mirror.

From Gertrude's perspective, something was not quite right, quite sufficient, about her deathbed photographs. Although the prints show her to have '"succeeded better than I expected"'—she lacked experience in carrying out such a task—she notes regretfully that '"the light was not all that could be wished"'.[6] It is not at all clear whether the tone of regret in Gertrude's voice emanates from an aesthetic disappointment at the fact that she has failed to do visual justice to her impression of the 'exquisitely, astonishingly beautiful' late Lady Watergate[7]—whether, to put it in more general terms, she is like others at this time voicing a lament at the slippage between the affect of a scene itself and its captured simulacrum—or whether something else is at stake. The problem does not exactly seem to be a technical one. Her regret may, it is hinted, come from the fact that she has failed to do justice to the desire of the living, rather than to the appearance of the dead. Because despite the striking nature of the corpse, and the novelty of the commission, the material images that Gertrude captured with her camera that day are not what lodged most vividly in her memory. For in the room with the dead body was the woman's widower, Lord Watergate, who had loved his dead wife passionately, been broken-hearted when she betrayed him, and had taken her back when she was dying of consumption, forgiving everything. As Gertrude gathers up her apparatus to leave,

> For one brief, but vivid moment, her eyes encountered the glance of two miserable grey eyes, looking out with a sort of dazed wonder from a pale and sunken face. The broad forehead, projecting over the eyes; the fine, but rough-hewn features; the brown hair and beard; the tall, stooping, sinewy figure: these together formed a picture which imprinted itself as by a flash on Gertrude's overwrought consciousness, and was destined not to fade for many days to come.[8]

There was a close relationship between photography and the material manifestations of mourning and memorialization in the nineteenth century, whether one considers deathbed photographs themselves, or the commemoration found in mourning jewellery, such as lockets and bracelets and rings, or the display of images of the deceased in portraits of the living.[9] Both the deathbed photograph and the presence of a photograph within a family group, or in the hands of a single (and by associative presumption, bereaved) figure, offer a poignant and pointed illustration of Christian Metz's characterization of the photograph as fetish, as signifying both loss and protection against loss.[10]

But my concern in this chapter is not with photographs' capacity to prompt memory and to keep memory alive. Nor am I dealing with the memorializing use of photographs to record vanishing buildings and views—rather than people—and their incorporation into a new literary culture of nostalgia and belatedness.[11] Rather, I want to examine the phrase 'photographic memory' and see how it, and the language in which memory was described and discussed in the mid- and late nineteenth century, is related to the popular understanding of the potential, and the limitations, of photography's material attributes and functioning. From my point of view, what is especially striking about this is the incorporation of the vocabulary of 'flash' into the workings of memory, bringing with it connotations of instantaneity and surprise. This is an exploration, in other words, of how—and how far—technological innovation impacts on the formulation of human perception.

Levy's wording in *The Romance of a Shop* points, whether wittingly or otherwise, to the potential that flash and photography, working together, brought to the formulation of ideas about how memory functions—ideas that become encapsulated in the cinematographic flashback, that technique by which the past is introduced into the rolling present in which we experience a film. For Romantic writers, in a pre-photographic era, the language of flash was the language both of revelation and of recollection. This is how Wordsworth's daffodils appeared to him subsequent to his encounter with their dancing yellow forms:

> For oft, when on my couch I lie
> In vacant or in pensive mood,
> They flash upon that inward eye
> Which is the bliss of solitude ...[12]

Memory, in other words, is experienced in terms of an illuminating vision, however brief: it is here firmly identified with the act of recall. But by the later nineteenth century, the emphasis on the association of flash and memory comes to stress rapidity as much as—even, perhaps, more than—image making. This is very apparent in some of the twentieth-century compound words that draw upon the vocabulary of flash: flashbacks, flash drives, and, indeed 'flash memory' itself. Chapter 2 concentrated on the element of light that is one of flash's crucial components; here, and in Chapter 4, I explore the associations of flash with speed and suddenness.

To speak of having a 'photographic memory' is to imply that someone can recall something with preternatural clarity. The term was first used, however, in a much more generalized sense. In *The Convalescent* (1859), Nathaniel Parker Willis asks, 'Why should not the Fairfaxes...give us, from their family records, the many photographic memories they must contain of Washington?'[13] The context does not make it clear whether he has in mind actual views of the city—engraved or lithographic reproductions of the daguerreotypes made by John Plumbe Jr, say[14]—or, more probably, whether the narrator is referring to detailed written accounts in letters or journals, or, even less tangibly, a whole mental archive of precise recollections. An indication of how 'photographic memories' might be envisaged in general terms is given by the narrator's recollection, in *Life, Here and There,* of one particular location on the Chemung River, where the road parallels the water, and a spring gushes from the rock above, allowing a deep green patch of wild mint to flourish: it is

> one of those exquisite spots which paint their own picture insensibly in the memory, even while you look on them—natural 'Daguerreotypes', as it were; and you are surprised, years afterward, to find yourself remembering every leaf and stone, and the song of every bird that sung in the pine-trees overhead, while you were watching the curve of the spring leap.[15]

Notably, photographic memories, at this young stage in the history of the medium, are seen as emanating from the qualities of the objects observed, not from any activity on the part of the perceiver. Whether consciously or not, Willis's language echoes that of Daguerre and William Henry Fox Talbot in their early writings, claiming—as Fox Talbot put it in a paper read to the Royal Society in 1839—that photography is 'the Process by which Natural Objects May be Made to Delineate Themselves Without Aid of the Artist's Pencil'. In other words, it presents unmediated, faithful, documentary authority. At the same time, the word 'paint' suggests a slow accretion of detail: this is not a rapid process.

Even by the time Willis was writing in 1859, however, the image was being turned back on itself, and human memory itself was starting to be described as a photographic plate. Photography, still a relatively slow process, even with the advent of faster lenses, and later with the substitution in the 1880s of the gelatin-based dry collodion process for that using wet collodion plates, meant that what was suggested was a gradual deposit of visual information, layer after layer. Douwe Draaisma, in *Metaphors of Memory* (2000), provides a rich account of the evolution of this metaphor in the latter half of the nineteenth century, placing it, in turn, within a long history of attempts to find analogues within the material world for how the mind records experience and perceptions. The American physiologist, chemist, and pioneer of photography John William Draper published his *Human Physiology* in 1856, with its theory that the human nervous system receives 'relics or traces of impressions', memory traces that Draper saw as even more indelibly inscribed than the 'photographic drawing' that allows images that have fallen on an inorganic surface to be preserved (he went so far as to believe that a shadow never falls upon a wall without leaving its permanent trace there).[16] The German physician Adolf Kussmaul, in the early 1880s, likewise wrote of how sensory impressions are like 'the invisible images, which the sun makes on a prepared silver surface'.[17]

Jennifer Green-Lewis has written eloquently about the impact of photography on the nineteenth century, persuasively arguing for its symbiotic connection to what she terms 'a crisis of memory, a heightened fear of forgetting in the Victorian period, stimulated... by the emergence onto the plate of the mind of too many things to remember'.[18] This created, she maintains, anxiety about the mind's capacity to remember detail, and concomitant admiration for the power of the daguerreotype (notable for its capacity to record minute detail) and the photograph to capture and retain images of the material world. Photographs, she explains, acted both as substitutes and as prompts for human memory, helping one set up 'a kind of resistance to the oblivion that surrounds life and into which the better part of it disappears'.[19]

But, of course, the memory doesn't normally work like a daguerreotype, or a wet plate left in a camera with an open lens, and nor—except for particular uses—would we particularly want it to. 'If someone could retain in his memory everything he had experienced,' writes Milan Kundera in *Ignorance*, 'if he could at any time call up any fragment of his past, he would be nothing like human beings: neither his love nor his friendship would resemble ours.'[20] People who possess 'photographic memory'—what is now termed 'eidetic memory'—the power to recollect numbers or words or images with extraordinary exactitude—may be considered as burdened as they are gifted, as Borges memorably dramatized in his fantastical 1944 short story 'Funes, His Memory'.

Moreover, anthropologist and eugenicist Francis Galton in the late 1870s tacitly acknowledged the inadequacies of the metaphor of the mind as a single photographic plate when he used the principle of the compound photograph to suggest the way in which the memory in fact overlays and blurs the images it contains. 'Our general impressions', Galton told the Royal Institution on 25 April 1879, 'are founded upon blended memories.' He illustrated his point by projecting three separate portraits by means of three separate magic lanterns upon the same screen, then by showing actual composite photographs, and also a camera with six converging lenses and an attached screen on which six separate pictures might be adjusted and brilliantly illuminated by means of artificial light.[21]

Alternatively, rather than hypothesizing a 'blended memory', analogous to the production of a composite photograph in which individual distinguishing marks are, as it were, averaged out, the memory's receptive surface could be figured as something much more akin to that idea of the mind as palimpsest put forward by Thomas De Quincey in 1845, in which—in an image remarkably evocative of the new practice of photography—'everlasting ideas, images and feelings, have fallen upon your brain softly as light', with each seeming to bury that which precedes it, without that initial impression having been extinguished.[22] Such a figuration of the photographic operations of memory feeds into the way that Proust (who, via Baudelaire, was strongly influenced by De Quincey's concept) describes the difference between the real and the imagined Albertine:

> since memory begins at once to record photographs independent of one another, eliminates every link, any kind of sequence between the scenes portrayed in the collections which it exposes to our view, the most recent does not necessarily destroy or cancel those that came before. Confronted with the commonplace and touching Albertine to whom I had spoken that afternoon, I still saw the other mysterious Albertine outlined against the sea.[23]

Proust's account, superimposing experience upon recollection and idealized projection, brings home how the idea of the memory as a photographic device functions best when it is used in a suggestive fashion, when it depends upon an injection of subjectivity, rather than when its employer is attempting to find a metaphor that will explain physiological process. Clare Dillon has termed De Quincey's palimpsest a 'psychological fantasy', and notes that it thus 'shares in the undecidable fate of all fantasies. It is somehow real and not real, both internal and external to the mind. It has a psychical reality that, however, does not preclude its material reality.'[24] The photographic plate still receives an impression of the light rays that have fallen on some person or object at a given moment, just as the individual's memory holds sensory impressions that—as is now thought—stay there through the synaptic connections that take place in the brain between one neuron and another. Yet one's sensation of *having* a memory—often simultaneously visually vivid, emotionally intense, and frustratingly evanescent—that is something else altogether.

Late nineteenth-century psychologists started to object to the fact that comparisons between the workings of the memory and the recording processes of the camera took no account of the means by which memories lodge themselves in the unconscious. Nor do they account for the mobile, and often exceedingly rapid, nature of many of these recollections—the phenomenon that people refer to when they remember things 'in a flash'. Siegfried Kracauer, heir to these objectors, came up in 1927 with a couple of paragraphs that succinctly destabilize the comparison between memory and photography. Memory's records are full of gaps, he wrote: 'it skips years or stretches temporal distance'.[25] Compared with a photograph, memory collects and arranges details in an arbitrary fashion. More allusively, as though using language to mimic the affect of memory itself rather than the qualities of a photograph, he sees memories as being 'opaque, like frosted glass which scarcely a ray of light can penetrate', embedded in 'the uncontrolled life of the drives'. What is recollected is that which one's consciousness recognizes as 'true'. But at least such memories are potentially recoverable: in the surface existence of a photograph, 'a person's history is buried as if under a layer of snow'.[26]

Kracauer's remarks help to reinforce the fact that those writers who attempted to explain memory through the metaphor of the photograph fell firmly into the camp of those who sought to understand it primarily through physiological terms, rather than concentrating on the wayward, unpredictable, mutable features that were more readily explained through the developing theories of subjectivity and the unconscious. Frances Power Cobbe, in her 1866 piece entitled 'The Fallacies of Memory', drew a clear distinction between the two ways of looking at the faculty, pronouncing firmly that

> Memory is neither an impression made, once for all, like an engraving on a tablet, nor yet safe for an hour from obliteration or modification, after being formed. Rather is memory a finger-mark traced on shifting sand, ever exposed to obliteration when left unrenewed; and if renewed, then modified, and made, not the same, but a fresh and different mark.[27]

Her language echoes not the vocabulary of photography's successes in capturing traces of the material world, but the long-standing trope used to express apprehension about any form of representation ever being able to capture the essence of anything and hold it still. It reworks Edmund Spenser's sixteenth-century lament at writing's inability to stay human transience ('One day I wrote her name upon the strand, | But came the waves and washèd it away |...| Vain man (said she) that dost in vain assay | A mortal thing so to immortalize'[28]), a trope that Oscar Rejlander employed when recollecting his horrified dismay, early in his career as a photographer, that his early prints faded. 'I felt', he said, 'as if I were only writing on sand', and was tempted to give up.[29]

Rejlander was one of the few nineteenth-century photographers to attempt photographing a memory. His composite print of 1859, 'Hard Times', seen in Figure 3.1, shows a gaunt labourer—probably a carpenter, since one of Rejlander's photographic studies shows him holding a saw—sitting on the edge of a bed. On the bed, a sick-looking woman and child; the spent candle and empty mug suggest an all-night vigil. In the background we see the man and woman in what we presume were better times: at least, the woman is gazing up at her partner with an adoring expression. Alternatively, the strange outstretched man's arm, whilst compositionally functioning to direct our attention to the woman's face, could also be understood as an act of releasing her to a future, heavenly existence. Rejlander has overprinted the negatives so that the woman's beautiful face now blends into the head of the dejected and desperate man: consumed with exhaustion and worry, we're led to assume that thoughts of the past, and memories of his wife when healthy and happy—or thoughts of her ascendancy to heaven—fill his brain. Possibilities for readings that point backwards and forwards are signalled through the blurred and obscured representation of a time that—whenever it is—is not the present of the photograph. The fact that Rejlander labelled the photograph a 'spiritualistic' exercise might seem to look forward to the departure of the woman's soul—on the other hand, it could signal that the man is haunted by his memories, as well as saddened by what he fears will happen. The translucent form of the couple certainly has much in common with the representation of ghosts of the dead that became so popular later in the century, and was often achieved through forms of combination printing.

One reason why these photographs were so convincing is surely because the shadowy image of transparent individuals corresponded to a sense that it is somehow natural to present that which belongs to the memory as having a hazy existence.[30] As Robin Kelsey writes:

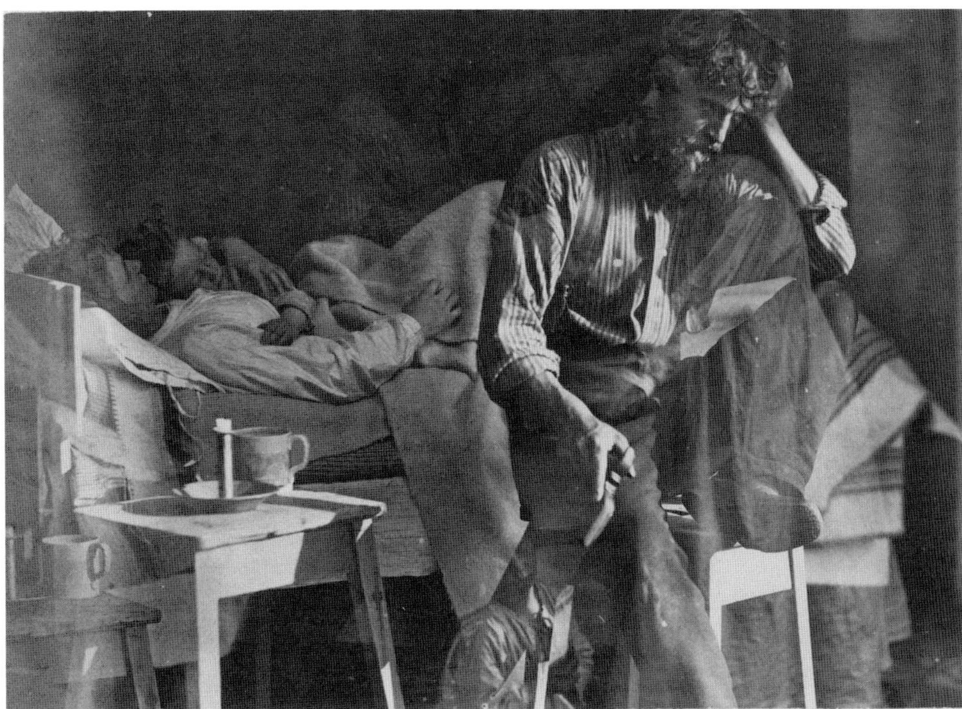

Figure 3.1 Oscar Rejlander, 'Hard Times', *c.*1860. Albumen silver print. Image: 14 × 20 cm. Mount: 22 × 28 cm. George Eastman Museum. Purchase, ex-collection A. E. Marshall. 1972.0249.0042.

In response to the acceleration of science and mechanization in the nineteenth century, error and imprecision had taken on a new power to signify human uniqueness. Mists and fog had become predominant Victorian metaphors for the ineffable mediations of human experience and the compensatory balm of sentiment. They signified the filtering effects of emotion, communication or memory.[31]

However, this is not how Gertrude, in *The Romance of a Shop*, remembers the death room scene that she memorialized. Some six months later, she is puzzled when, photographing an artist's work in a studio, she knows that she has previously encountered the tall, sunburned man who enters. The face that his appearance called to mind was, however, 'pale, haggard, worn with watching and sorrow. Then, as by a flash, she saw it all again before her eyes; the dainty room flooded with October sunlight; the dead woman lying there with her golden hair spread on the pillow; the bearded, averted face, and stooping form of the figure that crouched by the window.'[32] This mention of the 'flash' is highly significant, recalling the 'picture which imprinted itself as by a flash on Gertrude's overwrought consciousness'.[33]

There is no textual evidence that suggests that Levy envisaged the Lorimer sisters as using flash: their glass studio would have provided the necessary light for their bread-and-butter portrait photography. But it is of note that it was in 1887, the year before the novel was published, that the German pair of Miethe and Gaedicke invented *blitzlichtpulver*. This substance, its effects, and the facility of its use were enthusiastically written up in the photographic press with which Levy certainly seems to have been familiar, in language that, like earlier writing about flash illumination, drew parallels between the science of photography and the sudden, awe-inspiring shock of illumination produced by natural lightning. Flash powder was, for that matter, readily appreciated as an explosive substance that would greatly aid the practice of post-mortem photography, which had long been challenged by difficulties of indoor lighting. In 1865 Valentine Blanchard claimed to have used magnesium wire for the purpose of taking a post-mortem portrait 'in a private house late on a dull day'.[34] By 1891, the *British Journal of Photography*, in an untitled news item, noted that

> The difficulty of taking the photograph of a corpse is generally great, owing to the position in which it is placed as regard illumination, and the objection to any alteration, and often even to the window-blinds being raised. However, these difficulties are now easily overcome, or rather avoided, by the employment of the flash-light. We were recently shown some very satisfactory results—of their kind—obtained by this means.[35]

Flash photography of the dead found a place in more institutional settings, as well. As early as April 1888, the *Chicago News* reported that at the New York City Morgue, it was customary to take a photograph of every body that was brought in, so as to aid with later identification. 'There are often imperative reasons for not keeping bodies over night, and in these cases the photographs are made by the magnesium flash light. This process is also used at the New York hospital for photographing surgical patients, both before and after operations.'[36]

Significantly, the vocabulary of flash is re-employed by Levy not in reference to deathbed lighting problems, but in a scene that blends reminiscence, the workings of memory, and the shock of a sudden, illuminating realization. Towards the end of the novel, Gertrude's wayward sister Phyllis lies in her coffin, dead of consumption—a death that implants itself in the memory through olfactory rather than the visual senses, through the overpowering smell of tuberose from the dead girl's lover that imposes itself on the delicate perfume of roses and violets left by family and friends. Then Gertrude realizes why Lord Watergate had taken such a concerned interest in her sister: 'It was explained now, she thought, as the image of another dead face floated before her vision. That also was the face of a woman, beautiful and frail; of a woman who had sinned. She had never seen the resemblance before; it was clear enough now.'[37] Memory of the departed has started to become visually fragile, an impression, rather than something vivid. But the linguistic pattern that was established earlier breaks out one more time, when, a month or so later, the widower—of course—proposes to Gertrude. Even though, the first time round, she refuses—or at least postpones—him ('"too soon, too soon"'), it is at this moment that 'By a lightning flash her own heart stood revealed to her', and she realizes that love has been slowly building and growing within her.[38]

In Virginia Woolf's first novel, *The Voyage Out* (1915), she describes some guests watching out a storm in their tropical hotel. 'The flashes now came frequently, lighting up faces as if they were going to be photographed.'[39] Something significant has happened here. Rather than flash photography being described in terms of lightning, it becomes a metaphor for the effects of lightning itself. The simile is borrowed from the modern world that in many ways Rachel, Woolf's heroine, finds herself uncomfortably unfit to enter.

The Romance of the Shop demonstrates how the vocabulary that links flashlight and memory might—although not provably so—be connected to the latest developments in the technology of photographic lighting. In the 1890s the associations of flash photography with other forms of electrically charged modernity—indeed, with modernity itself—becomes unmistakable. In his autobiographical novel *Jean Santeuil*, unpublished during his lifetime but written between 1895 and 1899, Proust does not specifically mention photographic illumination, but he aligns the operation of memory with the rapidity of electronic transmission:

> The presiding genius of memory which, more quickly than any electric flash can make the circuit of the globe and, no less quickly, that of Time, had set [Jean] back in the past without his noticing that so much as a second had elapsed. Electricity does not take less time to bring to the ear pressed to the telephone receiver the sound of a voice which, in fact, is many miles distant, than does memory, that other powerful element in nature which, like light or electricity, moving at a speed so vertiginous that it seems almost to be its opposite, an absence of all speed, a sort of omnipresence.[40]

It is certainly tempting to see this as synonymous with the capacity of the photographic flash to freeze a moment of time. If 'photographic memory' has endured as a layperson's term for 'eidetic memory'—that power to recall, with extraordinary accuracy, strings of words or numbers, or the tiny details of an imaged scene—this popular usage was soon coupled with the language of the developing technology of illumination. This is brought home by Fred White's 1901 short story 'The Black Narcissus', which describes Inspector Darch of Scotland Yard as 'a man with a gliding step and a moist grey eye, that took the whole room and the trim garden beyond and eke the novelist in like the flash of a camera, and held the picture on the mental gelatine for all time'.[41] Perception is characterized as something that has the clarity, efficiency, and speed of a flash's light.

What is more, flashes could be used to induce memory—something allied to their broader deployment within psychological experiments in the later nineteenth century, most notably at the hands of Freud's mentor, Jean-Martin Charcot, at the Parisian psychiatric hospital, the Salpêtrière.[42] In the United States, Hugo Münsterberg, from Berlin, who was invited by William James to teach at Harvard from 1892 to 1895 and returned on a more permanent basis in 1897, and who is now thought of as the founder of applied psychology, recorded and explored cases where flashes of light induced both a trance and an altered memory.[43]

In fiction, nowhere is the link between flash technology and memory brought out more clearly than in Grant Allen's short novel *Recalled to Life*, published on both sides of the Atlantic in 1891. Allen, a British science writer, journalist, and popular novelist, had an unerring talent for sniffing out subject matter of highly current and slightly sensational interest—women's sexual relationships outside marriage, the employment of middle-class women, race relations in Britain and America, the future destruction of London by a volcano. The drama of new developments in photographic technology, combined with an interest in how memory may be revived and recovered, and the phenomenon of dual and divided consciousness, are used to structure this story.[44] Despite the date of the novel, he does not write directly about the new *blitzpulver*, however, but ostensibly invokes flash's other major experimental form at this time: the use of the electrical spark in time-lapse photography. Yet, the language in which the illumination of the subject is described is surely far more suited to the blinding impact of this recently invented compound than it is to the methods of Étienne-Jules Marey or Eadward Muybridge, which are also clearly evoked.

Marey, like Jules Janssen, used a *fusil photographique*, a gun-shaped contraption, as seen in Figure 3.2, in which a light-sensitive plate was made to rotate—using a clockwork mechanism—behind a lens, stopping just long enough for part of it to be exposed to light. As the next, unexposed part of the plate moved round, so a slotted disk stopped the light, until the moment came for the plate to stop, and the shutter was reopened in order to allow the exposure. The central axis of this mechanism operated relatively speedily, at twelve revolutions a second.[45]

By contrast, Eadweard Muybridge used not a single camera, but an array—in the case of his famous series of 1878, twelve of them, set 21 inches apart—the electronic shutter of each one triggered by a thin thread (or, on occasion, underground tripwire) that, in turn, was attached to an eight-jar battery.[46] Bright flashes certainly became associated with time-lapse photography in the twentieth century, as we shall see, and quite possibly Allen knew of Arthur Mason Worthington's pioneering work in observing—and drawing, not photographing—mercury droplets falling on a glass plate using the illumination of a spark produced by connecting two oppositely charged Leyden jars, since accounts of this experiment had been published in the *Proceedings of the Royal Society* in 1876 and 1877.[47] As Worthington describes it, when the inner coats of these jars are connected, 'the positive and negative charges unite with a dazzling flash and a simultaneous discharge and flash takes place between the two outer coats across the spark-gap in the dark room'.[48] Allen, inventively, combines elements of such experimental studies of motion with the far more domestic associations of *blitzlichtpulver*'s use, effectively writing a very low-key form of science fiction in order to construct a sensational story that focuses on the topical subject of traumatic memory loss and recovery.

When the novel opens, Una can remember nothing before a terrible scene that took place—so she's been told—in her nineteenth year. 'My babyhood, my childhood, my girlhood, my school-days were all utterly blotted out by that one strange shock of

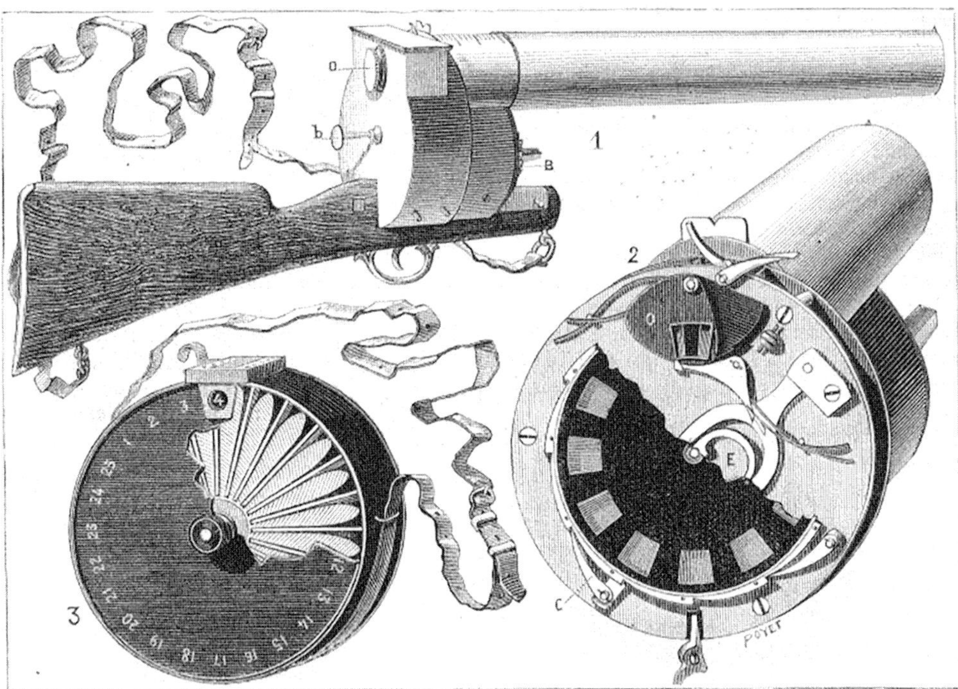

Figure 3.2 Étienne-Jules Marey, 'Fusil photographique', engraving, *La Nature* 464 (22 April 1882), 329.

horror.'[49] Unable to remember her name—even to remember language—she was 'examined and reported upon as a Psychological Curiosity'.[50] As for the event itself, the first-person narrator teases the audience with the drama of it all:

> I remember it all even now with horrible distinctness. Each item in it photographed itself vividly on my mind's eye. I saw it as in a picture—just as clearly, just as visually. And the effect, now I look back on it with a mature judgment, was precisely like a photograph in another way too. It was wholly unrelated in time and space: it stood alone by itself, lighted up by a single spark, without rational connection before or after it.[51]

This mental impression is both *like* an image taken by flash, and, it quickly emerges, is *of* a flash photograph—or rather, not of the photograph itself, but of the moment of its taking. It is a memory of an event, not a memory that has been encapsulated in, or produced by, a material image.

> I saw myself standing in a large, square room—a very handsome old room, filled with book-shelves like a library. On one side stood a table, and on the table a box. A flash of light rendered the whole scene visible. But it wasn't light that came in through the window. It was rather like lightning, so quick it was, and clear, and short-lived, and terrible.[52]

By the side of the box are wires, and the bottles and baths and plates of an amateur photographer's kit. Halfway to the door is the body of a dead man, lying in a little pool of blood that's still gurgling out of a wound on his left breast. Una subsequently learned—through the testimony of others—to call him her father (just as she's had to learn the words, and purpose, of all the other elements in the room—even books).

What's more, the murderer is in the recollected scene, as well as the dead man: a tall man, in his later twenties, who appears to be a gentleman, is ready to leap through the window. She, puzzlingly, has the impression that he's no common burglar, but there's no hint as to why he might have committed murder. And there's a further indecipherable element: 'I also saw, like an instantaneous flash, one hand pushed behind him, waving me off, I almost thought, with the gesture of one warning.'[53] Una keeps puzzling over this man's identity—she's sure that she must have seen him before—

> But the blank that came over my memory, came over it with the fatal shot, All that went before, was to me as though it were not. I recollect vaguely, as the first point in my life, that my eyes were shut hard, and darkness came over me. While they were so shut, I heard an explosion. Next moment, I believe, I opened them, and saw this Picture. No sensitive-plate could have photographed it more instantaneously, as by an electric spark, than did my retina that evening, as for months after I saw it all. In another moment, I shut my lids again, and all was over.[54]

Allen here borrows, wholesale, the metaphor of the memory as a photographic plate. Moreover, and given the construction of the mechanical apparatus on the table, it's significant that Allen elsewhere described the mind as a largely mechanical device, 'a thinking machine…minutely constructed, inscrutable in all its cranks and wheels, composed of numberless cells and batteries, all connected together by microscopically tiny telegraph wires'.[55]

Four years later, once Una learns to talk—as if for the first time—and learns to comprehend the world around her, she is interviewed by a Scotland Yard detective. Her imprinted memory is as strong as ever; the metaphor, one now sees, may have been suggested to her by her recuperative surroundings on the east coast of England. '"I could describe to you exactly all the objects in the room,"' she assures the Inspector.

> 'The Picture it left behind has burned itself into my brain like a flash of lightning!'
>
> The Inspector drew his chair nearer. 'Now, Miss Callingham,' he said in a very serious voice, 'that's a remarkable expression—like a flash of lightning.'[56]

Her interlocutor has a photograph with him, which he consults, and uses to verify her statements, but does not initially share. He asks some pointed questions—was there just one great flash of light alone, or had there been several?—and then inquires if this is the picture that haunts her?—before showing her a photograph that depicts the scene she so vividly recollects. It shows her standing there, and the Inspector explains that it was itself taken by a new process that her father had invented

> for taking instantaneous photographs by the electric light, with a clock-work mechanism. It was an apparatus that let sensitive-plates revolve one after another opposite the lens of a camera; and as each was exposed, the clock-work that moved it produced an electric spark, so as to represent such a series of effects as the successive positions of a horse in trotting.

The visual allusion to Muybridge is very marked in this explanatory example.[57] Clearly *something* by way of memory is stirred in Una, here, as 'the Inspector could tell by the answering flash in my eye'.[58] Whilst it's impossible to tell whether that particular vocabulary of illumination is completely intentional, it certainly consolidates our attention to the literal and metaphorical workings of flash. Alas, Una cannot remember any more, whereas, as the disappointed Inspector practically points out, there must originally have been six plates in this apparatus, but only one—the one left inside it—was recovered. Both memory and plate, at this point in the story, reflect the singularity implicit in Una's name.

Una learns the facts of the case, so far as they were known—and indeed, the circumstances of her previous life—from newspaper reports. The Inspector tells her that it would seem that the murderer had returned to the scene of the crime to retrieve the exposed plates, thus alerting the police to the fact that the whole train of events leading up to that final scene of escape must very likely have been recorded. Energized, she determines to go back to the house where the murder happened, and slowly, perplexing further elements emerge. It seems that she feared, rather than loved, her father; it looks like a woman's hand that was gesturing a warning, not a man's; it seems as though Una may have had a beloved suitor in her past. In a dream—or rather, 'with a sudden burst of intuition, the truth flashed upon me all at once. My dream was no mere dream, but a revelation in my sleep'[59]—a strong happy memory of her childhood in Australia comes to her, and she starts to suspect that the answer to all the mysteries may lie right back in her early years—a suspicion that's underscored by the particular vocabulary of illumination with which this novel is saturated.

Narrated at breakneck speed, *Recalled to Life* moves from the east coast of England, to Devon, to Canada, where Una goes to pursue Dr Ivor—with whom she was once, apparently, in love; and whom, as a result of what she takes to be photographic evidence, she believes to be her father's murderer. Slowly, more early memories—many of them puzzling and contradictory—start to return. And then—'a crash, a fierce grating, a dull hiss, a clatter',[60] and the Canadian train in which she's travelling is wrecked in a collision. Una is unconscious for maybe half an hour, despite the fact that the 'actual crash came and went like lightning'[61]—the further traumatic event, perhaps, which allows her memory to return when shown the missing photographic plates, and that connects her experience to the use of flash in psychologists' memory experiments. For she was escorted across Canada by Dr Ivor and his sister (who concealed their identities from her for a while, for obvious reasons); convalesces in their house; and only when she is about to turn Dr Ivor in to the police does he reveal the actual perpetrator—by means of a print taken from one of the plates he had liberated:

> It represented a scene just before the one the Inspector gave me. And there, in its midst, I saw myself as a girl, with a pistol in my hand. The muzzle flashed and smoked. I knew the whole truth. It was I myself who held the pistol and fired at my father![62]

Needless to say, all is explained by Jack Ivor: the man Una shot was *not* her actual father (who had been abandoned on a rocky Pacific islet by Callingham, who had then returned to Australia, married the man's supposed widow for her money, and claimed Una for his own). A long chain of events had led to Dr Ivor—in love with Una back in England, and (most coincidentally) confided in by her actual father—confronting Callingham about his past, at a moment when Una happened to be concealed behind a curtain in an alcove in his study. 'I remember all, at last. It comes back to me like a flash',[63] she—inevitably—exclaims. She remembers, too, that her not-father suddenly pinned him to the spot with the handles of electric apparatus, and wired him up, whilst also threatening to chloroform him, stifle him—and shoot him if he moved. No wonder Una dashed forward to release her lover—simultaneously and accidentally pressing the knob that set the photographic machine to work—and set off an indoor lightning show: 'flash came fast after flash. There was a sudden illumination. The room was lighter than day. It grew alternately bright as noon and then as dark as pitch again by contrast.'[64] Soon, there's another flash, as she grabs the revolver from Callingham's grasp, and shoots him dead—just as Dr Ivor, still half-dazed, 'took it all in, like a flash of lightning', and 'saw how impossible it would ever be to convince anybody else of the truth of our story', and fled.[65] Although he managed, a few days later, to retrieve the incriminating plates, Una's condition prevented him from reconnecting with her, until she arrived in Canada—in order, he rightly intuited, to try and hunt him down as the murderer. With everything clarified, the couple, of course, fall—engaged—into each other's arms.

Recalled by Life is a breathtakingly improbable novel, and as a review in the *American Journal of Photography* put it: 'we fear that Mr Grant Allen would find it difficult to answer the questions which a practical photographer would be inclined to ask'.[66] But it is also, as Anne Stiles has brilliantly shown, a serious engagement with contemporary theories of body and mind, as well as a demonstration that 'knowing a photograph's context is crucial to understanding its contents'.[67] For my purpose, it's significant not just as that very rare thing—a sustained piece of fictional writing that maintains a material and metaphorical concern with the phenomenon of the flash throughout the whole text—but also as a powerful confirmation of a late nineteenth-century association of flash photography and the imprinting of memory. The recurrent language of the flash-illuminated scene 'burning' itself into Una's consciousness and memory ties together both the external and artificial source of brightness, and the physiological workings of her brain.

The technology of flash photography—the very shock that it delivers—emphasizes suddenness, surprise, interruption. Indeed, as Grant Allen himself wrote in *Physiological Aesthetics*, 'any violent and sudden sense stimulant, such as the roar of a cannon, a flash of lightning, a shooting pain, or an unexpected shaking... forcibly interrupts the regular course of consciousness'.[68] These interruptive characteristics, one might fairly say, characterize an important type of memory: the unprepared-for eruption of the past into the present—just as Gertrude's impressions of Lord Warburton sprang out with peculiar brilliancy. This is the type of frequently involuntary, and certainly very powerful, memory that has come to be termed a 'flashback', the term taken from the language of film.

A film, of course, animates and gives temporality, through sequencing, to photograph after photograph, frame after frame. It consists of a sequence of flashes—something that for Vladimir Nabokov closely resembled the working of memory. 'I see the awakening of consciousness as a series of spaced flashes, with the intervals between them gradually diminishing until bright blocks of perception are formed, affording memory a slippery hold', he wrote in *Speak, Memory* (1966).[69] We have already encountered Hugo Münsterberg's interest in flashes as an experimental psychologist: his enthusiasm for the new genre of the cinema, and his interest in perception, attention, emotion, imagination, and memory, coalesce in a pioneering work of film theory, *The Photoplay* (1916). Here, he carefully explains how the illusion of movement works, discounting earlier theories about the persistence of an image on the retina.[70] As later media historians have extensively documented, there is a clear historical progression between those images made by Marey, Muybridge, and others, mediated through devices such as the zoopraxiscope, and the motion picture. Phillip Prodger succinctly explains:

> Even though films are made out of thousands of individual frames, when these frames are projected in quick succession, they appear animated. The reasons for this are physiological. When people are exposed to a quick flash of an image, they briefly hold it in mind. If another similar image is flashed during the retention period, the brain smoothes the transition from one to the next. If the process is repeated, the result is an optical illusion of continuous movement.[71]

The intrusion of memories into the present was often signalled, in early film, by the use of slow fades in and out, or the use of blurred definition. But a snap recollection, an unbidden image or sequence from the past, an image that carries with it a highly emotional or vivid memory, a memory that arrives with the violent effect of a sudden bright light—such is the true flashback.

The narrative concept of the flashback within film is usually credited to a 1916 *Variety* magazine review—although early film-makers certainly employed sequences depicting dreams, or visions, or series of 'dissolves' that set up past events, trying out various means of translating to the screen fiction's capacity to narrate past events during the course of a forward-moving narrative, and it would seem that the term was coming into use before this review.[72] Maureen Turim explains, 'Literature and theater certainly used techniques similar to the flashback before cinema, but the etymology of this term for a return to a narrative past inserted into a narrative present is apparently derived from the speed with which cinematic editing was able to cut decisively to another space and time.'[73] The word 'flash' was already in use by 1913 to signify the 3 to 10 feet or so (some scripts specified the precise length) of film necessary for the briefest of filmic moments—with 'cutback' or 'switchback' employed to describe a film's temporal backward glance.[74] In 1914 Catherine Carr provided the definition 'FLASH—A brief glimpse of a scene, just enough to account for the presence of some character in a particular place'.[75] Evidence that the phrase 'flashback' itself was in circulation by the mid-1910s, albeit with a slightly different spin from what was to become its customary usage, comes from Leslie T. Peacocke's *Hints on Photoplay Writing* (1916)—reprinted from *Photoplay* magazine in 1915–16—where two definitions are offered to the budding screenwriter:

> FLASH—The throwing upon the screen for a fragment of a moment of a scene or character or other component part of the plot, to heighten the effect of the immediate scene.
>
> FLASH-BACK—A fragment of a previous scene reflashed on the screen to intensify or clarify the scene being shown.[76]

Having become standard usage to indicate a segment inserted into a film that takes one back to a previous time, the phrase has also, by extension, come to describe those moments in ordinary life. Within a movie, a flashback might take just an instant or a couple of minutes—the elaborately framed biographical reconstructions in *Citizen Kane* (1941) provide the paradigmatic example here—or even longer. In Frank Capra's *It's a Wonderful Life* (1946), for example, Angel Joseph, briefing George Bailey's guardian angel Clarence for his mission to save George's life, plays him a kind of film (he even pauses it in freeze-frame at one moment) to bring him up to speed about the despairing man's past. However, although this (hour-long) part of the film fulfils one of the characteristics of the flashback in that it fills in history for both Clarence and viewer, it diverges from convention in that it is presented with heavenly omniscience, rather than representing the mind of an individual momentarily darting back to a previous instant in their lives.[77] It does not carry the disruptive impact of flash's intrusion.

The cinematic flashback is not just a convenient narrative device; it is also a means of representing the physiological phenomenon that Roger Brown and James Kulik were, in 1977—drawing on later developments in the technology of flash photography—to term the 'flashbulb memory'.[78] Their central example was the fact that almost everyone remembers what they were doing when they heard of the assassination of John F. Kennedy (a more contemporary example might be the Ancient Mariner-like tendencies with which people narrate, and create a bond over, what they were doing on 11 September 2001). These flashbulb memories blend together sharply recalled detail that might not necessarily be in any way exceptional in its own right—indeed, perhaps more often mundane than not—with a sense of shock: shock at the unexpected. Brown and Kulik emphasize, too, that flashbulb memories also entail a high awareness of consequentiality, and/or a significant amount of emotional arousal. But the details recollected may have everything to do with the narrator's immediate environment at the moment of emotional impact, and need not have anything whatsoever to do with the ostensible source of the shock. Such memories, indeed, often contain quite arbitrary components, just as a flash that's set off without aesthetic pre-planning can illuminate the accidental and the ordinary objects within the environment that form the backdrop to the photographer's intended subject. They are, indeed, 'very like a photograph that indiscriminately preserves the scene'.[79] Moreover, these involuntary subjective memories don't have to be visual, but often involve smells, sounds, bodily sensations. In her memoir *The Place You Love Is Gone*, Melissa Holbrook Pierson explains,

> Your mind is a strange album full of what they call flashbulb memories, images printed on a chemically sensitive brain by a sudden shock of light. Thus you recall where you were standing in the living room within reach of the walnut hi-fi announcing urgent news of a president's violent death—not because this news stunned you but because your mother's reaction did. Her stricken expression was the light that momentarily blinded you, leaving yellow blankness where the world should be, the quick blinking finally bringing a grey shape into existence on top of that lemony background: the frozen image in negative of her face.[80]

As much research has demonstrated, such flashbulb memories are not necessarily factually accurate, although it is a consistent feature of them that their holders are absolutely confident about what they recall. The supposed memories may burn themselves into our consciousness not just because of the rareness or significance of the occasion remembered, but also, as Ulric Neisser has hypothesized, because they recall 'an occasion when two narratives that we ordinarily keep separate—the course of history and the course of our life—were momentarily put in alignment'.[81] Brown and Kulik were drawing on what is now an outmoded understanding of neurobiology, 'according to which the brain, stimulated by the exciting event, sends a "Print now!" command to encode everything into the memory'.[82] And of course, flashbulbs themselves are rarely seen these days. But the vocabulary itself has stuck, both in ongoing scientific research on this particular mode of retrieving the past, and in popular speech.

Some flashbulb memories may be acutely personal—being in an accident, being attacked, experiencing a moment of mortifying embarrassment. But the term is most frequently linked to the sudden impact of a public, widely shared news event—the kind of happening about which one typically learns through a *newsflash*. Media historian Barbie Zeliger has noted, 'visual work often involves catching the sequence of events or issues midstream, strategically freezing it at its potentially strongest moment of meaningful representation. This point is crucial for explaining the role of images in memory. It suggests that images help us remember the past by freezing its representation at a powerful moment already known to us.'[83]

I'll have more to say about the association of flash with speed, and with freezing time. But there is one further—and obvious—concept to invoke here, and that is the concept of 'flash memory' itself. Flash memory is the name given to an electronic data storage device. It is non-volatile, meaning that it continues to store information even when it is not powered. It's most frequently encountered in memory cards, USB flash drives, solid state drives, and other products that are used for transfer as well as for storage. Invented in 1984 by Dr Fujio Masuoka, who was working for Toshiba in the early 1980s, and first fully commercialized in 2000, when IBM and Trek Technology began selling the first USB flash drives, the name 'flash' is said to have been suggested by his colleague Shōji Ariizumi, because the *erasure* process of the memory card or stick was so rapid that it reminded him of a camera's flash.[84]

What is so strange about this nomenclature is that 'flash' here signifies not instantaneous, vivid recall, but obliteration. This is not the flash of illumination or revelation, but the blinding light that sears the retina and makes sight—or retrieval—impossible. The terminology for the memory cards—the flash cards—that sit inside our cameras, onto which we electronically record images that may come to stand in for actual memories, turns out to be somewhat ironic. By analogy, we may see this blank slate of deleted data as related to Roland Barthes's anxiety, voiced in *Camera Lucida*, about what photography ultimately does to memory: 'not only is the Photograph never, in essence, a memory', he writes, 'but it actually blocks memory, quickly becomes a counter-memory'.[85] The connection of flash with violence and destruction—a connection embodied within the concept of flash memory—is one that is present in Allen's *Recalled to Life*, and it's one to which we'll return in Chapter 7 when we explore the connection between flash, violence, and crime. The effacement that's referenced in the phrase 'flash memory', however, is also akin to memory's repression of the traumatic: flash as blast, flash as ripping apart continuity, flash as producing a flare of light too painful to bear.

Victorian commentators on memory and photography were quick to see the unarguable metaphoric connection between the recording processes of the mind and the way in which certain prepared surfaces could be made to record, whether permanently or semi-permanently, the material surface of the world. But this was a comparison that soon ran up against the limitations and inadequacies of such an understanding of memory. Nonetheless, other developments in photographic technology—developments designed to throw light on that which was dark, obscure, and otherwise very difficult to record—started to offer up a more specialized vocabulary: one that could be appropriated to suggest particular types of striking recollection. The techniques of flash photography, and the vocabulary in which human recollection is described, come together strikingly when attempting to describe the tendency of the human mind to flash back, whether deliberately or not, to the memories impressed within it.

CHAPTER FOUR

Stopping Time

ON SATURDAY 14 June 1851, Henry Fox Talbot conducted an experiment at the Royal Institution, London. As he described it the next day, in a letter to the eminent physicist, chemist, and scientific philosopher Michael Faraday,

> A printed paper was fastened to a disk, which was then made to revolve as rapidly as possible. The [electrical] battery was discharged, and on opening ye Camera it was found to have received an impression. The image of the printed letters was just as sharp as if the disk had been motionless. I am not aware of this experiment having ever been made before.[1]

Fox Talbot had just taken a flash photograph. As the letter indicates, he wished that he could improve the brightness of the electrical discharge—he hypothesized that one might discharge the battery through a tube lined spirally with pieces of tinfoil, or place a flat coil of copper ribbons in the circuit. But he had also achieved another photographic challenge: he had recorded, with some success, the image of a rapidly moving object.

Most of the rest of this book concentrates on a combustible chemical process that seeks to illuminate that which is dark or obscure. Even if, in this context, the vocabulary of flash was often connected with that of speed, the technology used by early flash photographers—their lenses, the plates on which images were recorded, early film—did not provide the conditions that allowed rapid motion to be captured as anything other than a blur. In *The Children of the Poor* (1908), Jacob Riis recollected

> Little Susie, whose picture I took while she was pasting linen on tin covers for pocket-flasks—one of the hundred odd trades, wholly impossible of classification, one meets with in the tenements of the poor—with hands so deft and swift that even the flash could not catch her moving arm, but lost it altogether.[2]

The blur, indeed, adds to the painful poignancy of this image, shown in Figure 4.1, refusing a comparison of this interior to, say, a Dutch interior with women peacefully occupied in domestic work. This may be home labour, but it is conducted with the speed of economic necessity that animates piecework.

But rather than throwing the light of social investigation onto the dwellings of the poor, on tenement workplaces, police station lodging rooms, or children at prayer in

Figure 4.1 Jacob Riis, 'Little Susie at her Work', Gotham Court, *c.*1890. Jacob A. (Jacob August) Riis (1849–1914)/Museum of the City of New York. 90.13.4.133.

the Five Points House of Industry, as Riis was to do; or even recording the material substance of his own possessions, one of the ends to which he turned the camera in the plates collected in *The Pencil of Nature* (1844–6), Fox Talbot was launching an alternative form of flash photography from that discussed in most of this book. He saw the potential for flashes of electricity to freeze motion. He was building on a long-observed property of lightning: that a flash, at night, could appear to suspend, motionless, falling rain or the water playing in a fountain. One of his scientific contemporaries, Charles Wheatstone (inventor of, among other things, the stereoscope), had conducted an experiment at the Royal Society in 1833, in which he used an electrical spark as a means, as he put it,

> of observing rapidly changing phenomena during a single instance of their continued action, and of making a variety of experiments relating to the motions of bodies when their successive positions follow each other too quickly to be seen under ordinary circumstances.
>
> A few obvious instances will at present suffice. A rapidly moving wheel, or a revolving disc on which any object is painted, seems perfectly stationary when illuminated by the explosion of a charged jar. Insects on the wing appear, by the same means, fixed in the air. Vibrating strings are

seen at rest in their deflected positions. A rapid succession of drops of water, appearing to the eye in a continuous stream, is seen to be what it really is, not what it ordinarily appears to be.[3]

The goal of distinguishing what something 'really is' from what it 'appears to be' was to inform innovations in photographing moving bodies and objects for the remainder of the nineteenth century, and beyond. This was an enterprise closely related to the confident belief that photographs themselves offered objective scientific evidence.[4] As Philip Brookman concisely puts it, in the context of Eadweard Muybridge's imaging of twisting summersaulters and speedily trotting horses,

Like the introduction of the microscope and telescope, the institutionalization of the camera as a research tool provided scientists with unprecedented methodologies based on direct observation. The emergent disciplines of biology, chemistry, geology, and astronomy, for example, were each rooted in the analysis and interpretation of observed facts. What had been invisible to the eye became more evident with photography, and what was made visible by the camera could be recorded, categorized, and structured for analytical study within a topological framework.[5]

The history of high-speed photography offers an ideal place at which to pause and consider what, in fact, constitutes a 'flash'—or rather, what distinctions, and what continuities, there may be between the 'flash' as an interval of startlingly bright light, where the emphasis falls on the act of illumination, and the 'flash' as a very brief but temporally definable moment, where the sense of distinct but decidedly ephemeral duration is paramount. There is no etymological distinction, according to the *Oxford English Dictionary* (OED), when it comes to the word's origins. Even though it's tempting to suggest a link with the French *flèche*, or arrow, which would propel one straight into the inexorable effects of 'time's arrow', the *OED*'s editors more prosaically suggest that the word is onomatopoeic, analogous to 'splash'—although quite what it's supposed to sound like (an arrow whizzing through the air? a sizzling bolt of lightning?) isn't specified under the entry for 'flash' itself. The two meanings of flash are spliced together when we consider on the one hand the very rapid bursts of light that permit the capture of movement, and on the other, the quick succession of static images that, when run together at a sufficient speed, flash by one in order to create the illusion of movement.

'Flash' is a word that signals modernity, too, through its relationship to two significant by-products of large-scale industrialization that have been identified and discussed by Sue Zemka: 'a wider distribution of abstract time' (that is, time that is quantifiable, homogenous, accurate, and standardized) and 'a more widespread and precise attention to small intervals of abstract time'—for example, a flash.[6] The extended association with modernity does not necessarily carry positive connotations along with it. Martha Rosler can readily condemn 'neoliberal art'—the 'bling' produced by Jeff Koons serves as an example—through this one word. '"Neoliberal art is art that appeals to neoliberals,"' she says in an interview. '"It's art that asserts pure individualism and doesn't try to hide that it's about flash."'[7] To be 'flashy' is to be superficial, showy, here today and gone tomorrow. The origins of this usage, however, do not lie within the attractions of gleam and glitter, but themselves go back to the onomatopoeic. In the late sixteenth and early seventeenth century, in a now obsolete deployment of the word, to be 'flashy' was to be over-moist, watery, frothy. From this meaning developed its connection with that which was insipid, vapid, and empty of substance. By the time that it was used—a few decades later—in connection with sparkling brilliance, it became associated, almost simultaneously, with that which is transitory or momentary (as in the Puritan William Prynne's censorious reminder that 'Reprobates haue oft times many sodaine, transitory, and flashy ioyes'[8]).

In Chapter 3, we encountered the relationship of flashes to the prehistory of the cinema: a prehistory, including an inventive proliferation of optical toys and devices, that has recently become a narrative as familiar as it is compelling. It is a narrative that understands such devices as part of what Leo Charney has called an 'environment of fleeting sensations and ephemeral distractions'; described by Georg Simmel in 1903 as consisting of 'the rapid crowding of changing images, the sharp discontinuity in the grasp of a single glance'.[9] It goes back to a cluster of inventions in the early 1830s, constructed around the time that Wheatstone was experimenting with electric sparks. In 1832 Michael Faraday published in the *Journal of Physics and Mathematics* details of a series of experiments in which he demonstrated the optical illusion caused by rapidly rotating gears, which moved too quickly for the human eye to detect movement. Building on this work, the Belgian scientist Joseph Plateau produced in 1832–3 a disk that rotated at high speeds, with fourteen to sixteen drawings showing different phases of the animation separated by slots, giving the viewer the illusion of movement when its reflection was observed in a mirror—the Phenakistoscope. The device, as the illustration reproduced in Figure 4.2 from an 1884 compendium of amusements for 'young ladies' shows, was one that endured the century as a source of amusement.

Working at the same time as Plateau, Simon von Stampfer in Salzburg developed a similar, two-disk device. One disk had slits round its circumference; the other showed successive images of progressive movement—turn the slitted disk on the same axis as the image disk, and the view through these slits allows one to have the impression of a continuously moving image. As with the Phenakistoscope, and William George Horner's 1834 invention of a rotating drum, holding pictures on the inner rim, that he called a Daedaleum (later renamed the Zoetrope, the 'wheel of the devil' giving way to the 'wheel of life'), this effect was thought to be dependent on a property of the human retina known as 'persistence of vision'—that is, the idea that an after-image remains on the retina for somewhere between a fourteenth and a twenty-fifth of a second. This theory was challenged by Max Wertheimer in 1912, who, in putting forward his theory of the 'phi phenomenon' and the 'beta phenomenon', argued that the reason that we see movement in the case of such apparatuses as the zoetrope and the motion picture is that we don't register the blank spaces between the frames, which are changed faster than the eye can see.[10] Both theories remain in circulation, and are still contested. What, however, is certainly true is that when a film is projected at anything slower than around sixteen frames a minute, we see not continuity in movement, but a noticeable flicker. Is a flicker, however, a flash? How strong does a burst of light have to be to be termed a flash?

The Phenakistoscope.

Figure 4.2 The Phenakistoscope, *The Young Ladies' Treasure Book: A Complete Cyclopedia of Practical Instruction and Direction for all Indoor and Outdoor Occupations and Amusements Suitable to Young Ladies* (London: Ward Lock & Co., 1884), 807.

Simon von Stampfer called his invention the Stroboscope, from the Greek *στρόβος* (*strobos*), 'whirlpool' and *σκοπεῖν* (*skopein*), 'to look at'. In both name and basic principles, it was the ancestor of later machines that produce an intermittent source of very brief flashes that are both strong enough to overpower any other existing light source and synchronized to the movement of the object in question—something that may mean that anything from just a few flashes to many thousand a second are emitted. The effect is to make the moving object appear completely still—a stillness that may be captured by a very rapid camera exposure.

As with so many developments in photographic technology, advances in the electronic means of producing and deploying flash resulted from the experimental work of a number of people, taking place across national boundaries. In Moravia in the 1860s, Ernst Mach managed to use a very brief spark to create photographs of a bullet in flight—the fastest moving object he could find—in order to explore the shock waves it created: his subsequent collaboration with Professor Peter Salcher at the Imperial

Austrian Naval Academy in Fiume consolidated the relationship between high-speed flash photography and the development of military hardware. In Riga, and also in the mid-1860s, August Toeppler used an electric generator to produce a spark for the same end.[11] Photographing the rapidly moving became easier with the invention of dry-plate photography. In 1890 Lord Rayleigh (John William Strutt) photographed soap bubbles by putting a sparking condenser inside an ordinary projection lantern. This in turn condensed the electric sparks onto a camera lens, and exposed a plate, thus taking a photograph of the bubble in front of the lens at the moment when its viscous surface is shattered—the spark and bursting bubble were each caused by very carefully synchronized falling balls.[12] In 1892 C. Vernon Boys (a regular correspondent of Mach's) gave an illustrated talk at the Edinburgh Meeting of the British Association about his experiments showing a bullet piercing various objects (a sheet of cardboard, a plate of glass), using 'instantaneous illumination—a flash of light. It is of course obvious', he reminds his audience, 'that it depends entirely upon the speed of the object and the sharpness required, whether any particular flash is instantaneous enough. No flash is absolutely instantaneous, though some may last a very short time.'[13] Conducted in a pitch-dark passage of the Royal College of Science, no camera was used. The bullet itself produced the spark through piercing a lead wire and thus completing an electronic circuit, allowing the motion to be recorded on a photographic plate—as we see in Figure 4.3. This plate, when developed, revealed what Walter Benjamin was famously to term the 'optical unconscious'—in other words, information that has been received by the retina, but is too rapid to be processed, except when captured by technology.[14] In Boys's own words, 'if…the first wish of the experimentalist is to see what he is doing, then in these cases surely, where in general people would not think of attempting to look with their natural eyes, it may be worth while to take advantage of this electro-photographic eye'.[15]

Potentially, all kinds of knowledge and explanation might be forthcoming. Boys spoke about F. J. Smith, who had been taking sequential photographs on one plate in order to elucidate one particular conundrum:

> I had hoped to show one of these series of an intentional character, to wit, a series of a cat held by its four legs in an inverted position and allowed to drop. The cat, as everyone is aware, seems to do that which is known to be dynamically impossible, namely, on being dropped upside down to turn round after being let go and to come down the right way up. The process can be followed by one of Mr Smith's multiple spark photographs. However, his cats do not seem to like the experiments, and he has had in consequence had so much trouble with them that his results, while they are of interest, are not, up to the present, suitable for exhibition.[16]

But C. Vernon Boys's images offer more than information. They feed and stimulate curiosity, and, like so much scientific photography, are aesthetically compelling in their own right—illustrating the premise of Kelley Wilder's *Photography and Science* that the dividing line between 'art' and the scientific photograph is, and always has been, a highly artificial one, dependent on context, not on intrinsic qualities.[17] These images reveal abstract designs that are both beautiful and at the same time directly connected to

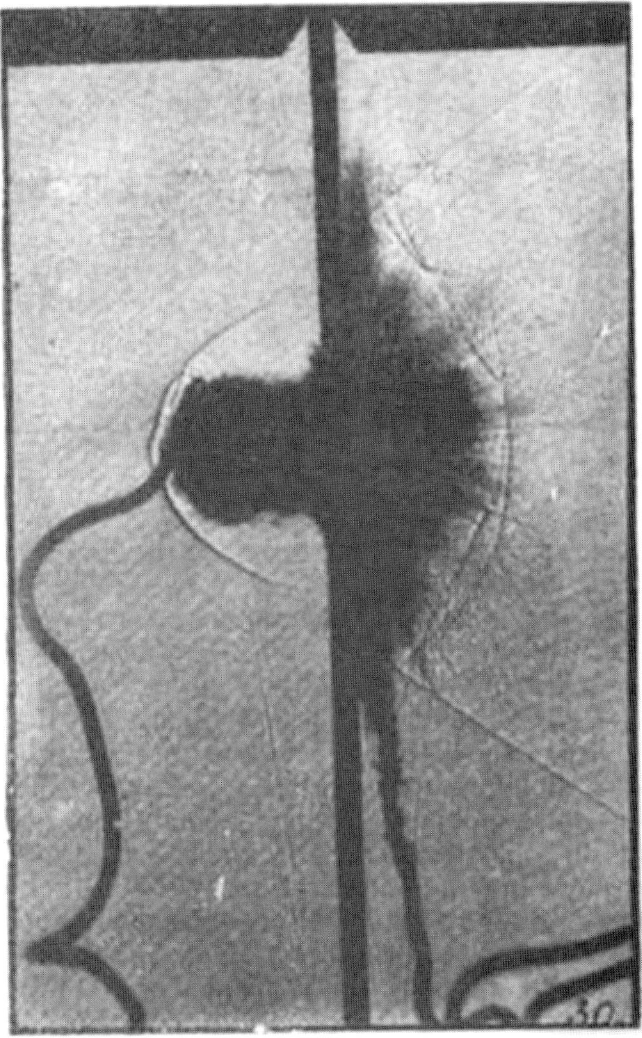

Figure 4.3 C. Vernon Boys, 'Bullet piercing a glass plate', *Nature* (9 March 1893), 445.

the invisible dynamics to be found in the material world, achieved through mechanical rather than human objectivity. Arthur Worthington's images of splashing droplets, first drawn by hand as a result of careful ocular observation, and beautifully symmetrical, were revealed as ideal projections of what he believed that he was seeing in the split second that he saw a falling drop of fluid illuminated by a spark. They gave way to the irregular, unruly coronets and droplets that were made visible in 1894 (Figure 4.4), when using spark photography to capture the 'evanescent morphology of nature' displayed in the spreading mobility of a mercury or milk-drop splash.[18]

The name most commonly associated with bridging the scientific–aesthetic imagery divide—certainly the name that is also indivisibly associated with flash photography—is that of Harold Edgerton. As a graduate student at MIT, Edgerton combined the camera

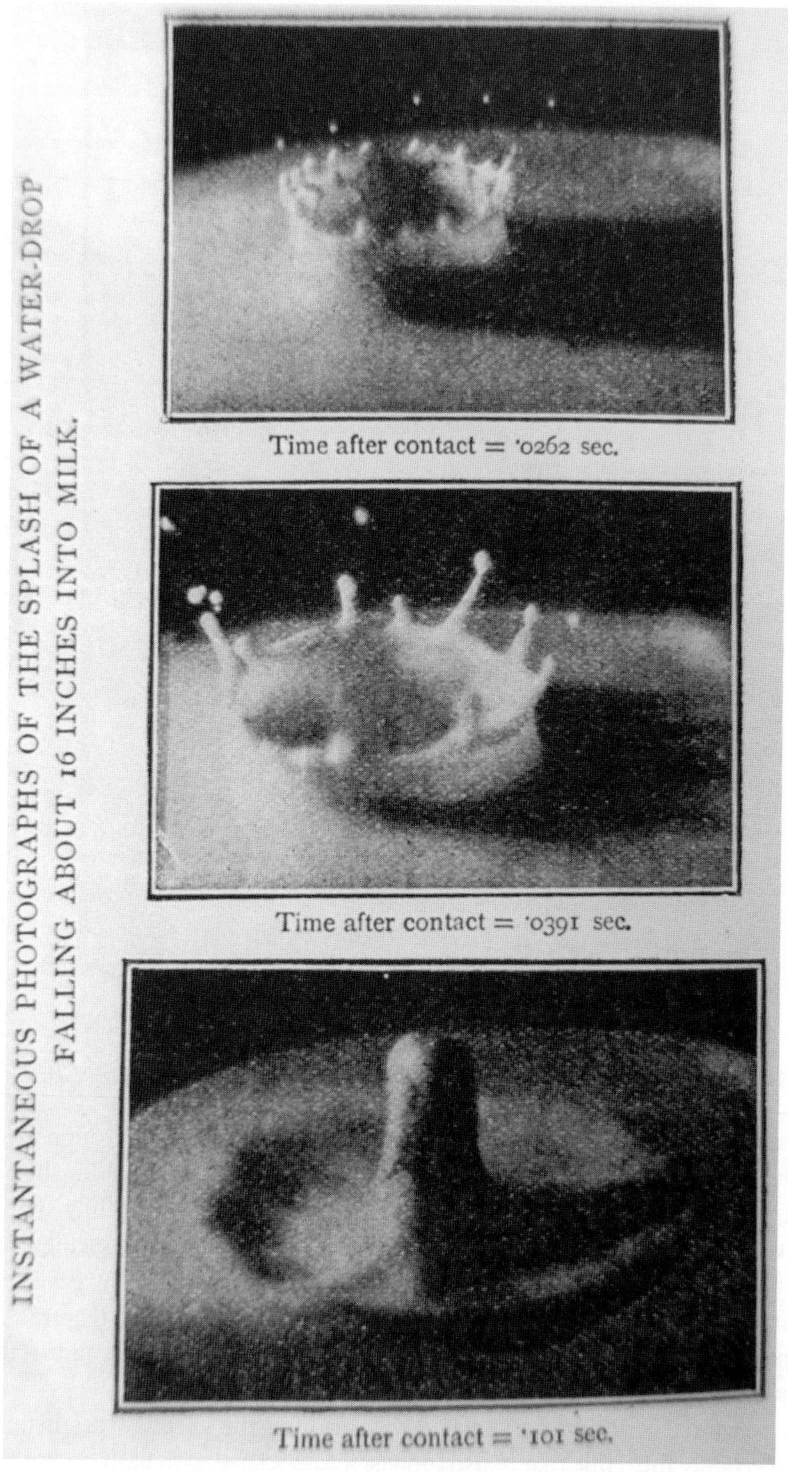

INSTANTANEOUS PHOTOGRAPHS OF THE SPLASH OF A WATER-DROP FALLING ABOUT 16 INCHES INTO MILK.
Time after contact = ·0262 sec.
Time after contact = ·0391 sec.
Time after contact = ·101 sec.

Figure 4.4 Arthur Worthington (1894), frontispiece to *The Story of a Splash* (London: Society for the Propagation of Christian Knowledge, 1895).

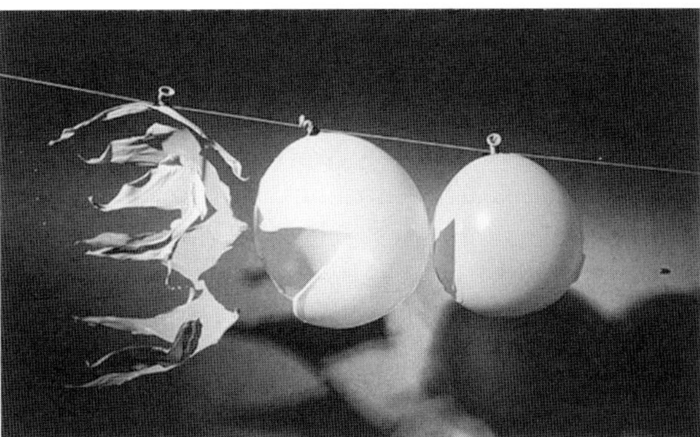

Figure 4.5 Dr Harold E. Edgerton, 'Bullet Through Balloons', 1959.

with the stroboscope in order to study synchronous motors—that is, motors that operate at the same speed as the electrical current running them—and incorporated recent advances in the knowledge and techniques of combustible gases in order to make a device that would produce very high-speed bursts of light from electrically controlled neon tubes. From 1931, the year in which he obtained his PhD, Edgerton conceived and improved strobes that allowed him to photograph events as unthinkably brief as a millionth of a second,[19] creating the illusion of stopped motion: milk drops falling and humming birds in flight; bullets piercing playing cards, balloons—as we see in Figure 4.5—light bulbs, or bananas; golfers and tennis players swinging at balls, and dancers whirling in elegant parabolas; gymnasts floating through the air 'as if seen in a levitation dream'.[20]

Much of Edgerton's initial work was on behalf of commercial organizations: the stroboscopic flash could allow engineers to detect challenges, and think up solutions, for mechanical instruments and processes ranging from ships' propellers to shot-making. High-speed flash photography provided clinching legal evidence—for example, proving that the methods of making soap powder practised by Lever Brothers and by Procter & Gamble differed from one another. During the Second World War, Edgerton was employed by the Army to develop equipment that would take effective night-time aerial reconnaissance shots; he, and his colleagues, created the 'rapatronic'—rapid electronic—camera that used the far more powerful flash emitted by the atomic bomb itself to take photographs of such bombs being tested in the South Pacific.[21] In the last three decades of his life, he was chiefly occupied with sonar and with underwater photography: the undersea explorer Jacques Cousteau, with whom he worked closely, called his good friend 'Papa Flash'.[22]

Edgerton's work was widely visible: first in specialist publications, like *Electronics* and *Review of Scientific Instruments*, then in the more popular *Technology Review*, and subsequently in a range of journals, including *American Golfer, Fortune, Life* (his collaboration with Gjon Mili led to some spectacular stroboscopic images of dancers and theatre performers), and *National Geographic*—starting with his rigid-winged

'Hummingbirds in Action' of 1947. Despite his disclaimer ('Don't make me out to be an artist. I am after the facts. Only the facts'[23]), his work was exhibited alongside photography that was created solely with an aesthetic purpose in mind. 'Milk Drop, Coronet' (1936) was chosen by Beaumont Newhall for his controversial show of the history of photography at New York's Museum of Modern Art in 1937.[24] If by now its viscous surface and spattering tentacles, echoing Worthington's earlier work, have become what Geoffrey Batchen has rather sneeringly termed a 'quintessential cliché of the photographic',[25] it brought home, in the exhibition context, how the high-speed flash could produce an image of uncanny and slightly unsettling beauty. Here was a moment from the past, held still for an everlasting instant, but with the next falling drop about to disrupt, or repeat, the symmetry. Edgerton was fascinated by the way the ordinary could become strange, and beautiful, as a result of stroboscopic flash, showing the elegance of water falling into a tin can, a soda siphon splashing into a glass. Edward Steichen, the photographer, and director of MOMA's Department of Photography from 1947 to 1962, wrote of how excited he was 'on seeing'—as we do in Figure 4.6—'the succession of exposures of a man swinging a golf ball...It

Figure 4.6 Dr Harold E. Edgerton, 'Bobby Jones with a Driver', 1938.

not only opened a new vista from a scientific standpoint, but [it was] also a new art form.'[26]

Steichen was writing, of course, when the status of photography in relation to its presence within major art museums was still uncertain, but Edgerton's parabola, with the whirling shaft of the golf club looking like the seats flung out in some fairground ride, conveys unsuspected elegance in the trajectory of the rapid swish. What's more, Edgerton's photography revealed something of the lines of force that the pre-war Italian Futurists had depicted in their painting—the lines of energy that they saw as holding matter together. Edgerton's 'Fan and Smoke', shown at London's Royal Photographic Society in 1934, depicts a whirling fan spinning titanium tetrachloride smoke into vortices: again, a significant modernist figure, the vortex, is photographically consolidated by means of the flash. Mili himself (with, for example, the complex curves and spokes of a conductor's hand and baton in action) and Berenice Abbott (notably with the elegant simplicity of the declining curves of a bouncing golf ball that we see in Figure 4.7) were among the other photographers of the 1940s who used the strobe's flash to record very rapid sequential movement, as well as to 'stop time',[27] and in doing so created compositions that blurred the line between abstract art and photographic documentation.

Even the briefest of flashes involves an interval of time. As Kris Belden-Adams suggests, although 'our existing discourses tend to examine Edgerton's stroboscopy biographically, as an extension of late-nineteenth-century motion studies, his work... presents the opportunity to take a closer look at the complex nature of expressing and

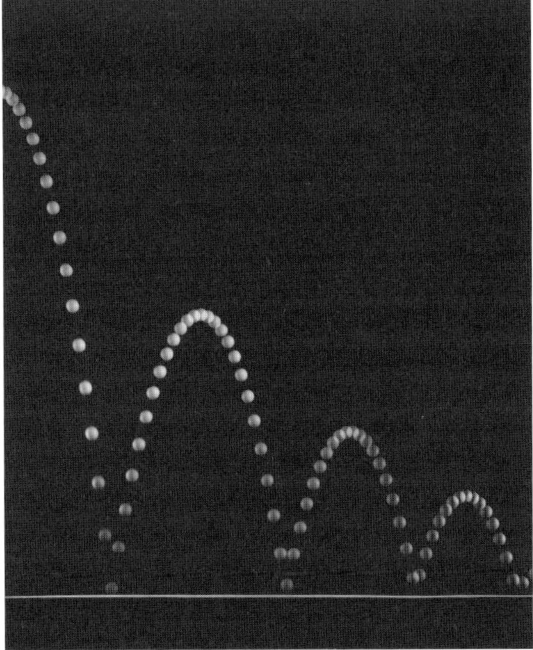

Figure 4.7 Berenice Abbott, 'Bouncing Ball Time Exposure', 1958–61. © Berenice Abbott/Getty Images.

interpreting time in photography'.[28] However infinitesimal the stroboscopic flash used to take an image, its emission may still be thought of in terms of duration. Belden-Adams borrows an image from mathematical philosopher Charles Sanders Peirce to bring this home: 'Even what is called an "instantaneous photograph" ', Peirce writes, 'is a composite of the effects of intervals of exposure more numerous by far than the sands of the sea.'[29] Yet at the same time, the photograph captures—to follow Thierry de Duve's reasoning—a moment that does not in fact exist, since 'reality is not made out of singular events; it is made out of the continuous happening of things'. What we experience with the instantaneous photograph is the sense of being 'too late'—the action is already completed; the tennis ball has been hit; the bullet has lodged in some safe end-point out of view—and also too soon, since the event that is being recorded shows an action arrested before its completion. This results, as de Duve would have it, in the 'sudden vanishing of the present tense, splitting into the contradiction of being simultaneously too late and too early'.[30]

If these comments about the artificiality of 'stopped time' apply to any photograph that records action, and that hence implies temporal flow, they also point to what distinguishes the temporality of the flash. When one considers a flash that illuminates the dark and obscure, that pierces the night or suddenly lays bare a dingy interior, one thinks more in terms of extreme contrasts of light and dark: darkness bracketing an intense explosion of luminosity. But focusing on the flash as a temporal phenomenon, rather than one that derives its importance from illumination, returns one to considering it primarily as an interruption—a very brief interruption, that one hardly has time to register before that moment has passed, recorded only through a photographic exposure, the record of which shows how things were during a split second that passed too quickly for one to observe anything oneself—other, maybe, than a rapid moving blur.

For the experimental scientist and scientific photographer, the event of the flash is, however, not what matters. It's crucial that it's of a measurable duration, that one can accurately fix the intervals between flashes, and that it's extraordinarily bright. But the event of the flash itself, its effect on the spectator—this is immaterial. The flash in these cases is purely instrumental, a means to an end.

But under other circumstances, the effect of the flash on its perceiver is of central importance. The existence of what have come to be called 'flicker effects' has been noted for a couple of centuries. The physiologist Jan Purkinje in 1823 drew the patterns that he saw when waving his fingers across one eye and staring at the sun; the Scottish scientist David Brewster published an article in 1834 'on the influences of successive impulses of light upon the retina', having experienced a dazzling, dizzying response whilst walking beside high iron railings in the sunshine.[31] As Jimena Canales has discussed, interest in what actually happens in the brain when one experiences a series of intense flashes intensified at the end of the 1950s, when scientists

> adopted high-power electronic stroboscopes, which became available after the war and which were used in scientific, military, and industrial settings to observe fast events. But they used them in an entirely different way. Instead of illuminating the phenomena under investigation, they stared directly into the strobe, sometimes with their eyes only a few centimeters from the source of light.[32]

They built on work by Lord E. D. Adrian, B. H. C. Matthews, and William Grey Walter, who confirmed not only that rapidly flickering light could produce epileptic fits—as had been known since at least Roman times—but also that 'the flashes changed the electrical rhythmic patterns emitted by the brain'.[33] In 1957–8 the British neuroscientist John R. Smythies combined light with a known hallucinogenic, having his subjects stare into the stroboscope while taking mescaline. This research led not only to Carl Jung's interest in his work (because the quality of mescaline visions seemed to have nothing to do with the personality of the person experiencing them, Jung saw this as evidence of the collective unconscious), but also to Aldous Huxley's experiments with mescaline, lysergic acid, and the strobe. Huxley noted how the colours that are seen change with the speed of the strobe's flashes, from orange and red, and then—with the lamp flashing faster than fifteen flashes a second—to green and blue, and at yet higher speeds, to white and grey.[34]

Another person eager to try out LSD and who was to combine its effects with those of the strobe was Ken Kesey, who volunteered as a subject at Menlo Park Veterans' Hospital, the site of government-sponsored research on the drug.[35] Tom Wolfe's *The Electric Kool-Aid Acid Test* (1968), which, in a breathless, exhilarating, swirling, Walt Whitman-esque rush of prose, recreates 'the mental atmosphere or subjective reality'[36] as well as the activities of Kesey and the Merry Pranksters in the mid-1960s (a remarkable achievement for a writer who claims that he never took acid himself),[37] is saturated with language that links the vocabulary of flash to the Acid Tests. These events—parties, happenings, forerunners of raves, held largely in California with a couple in Oregon—were a 'mix of music, liquid light projections, and weird sound effects, filtered through hallucinogenic drugs'.[38] The flashes are both internal and external. The flash is the revelation, especially the revelation that occurs in the first stages of an acid trip: the revelation that one is entering into one's self, into the world set bare by one's senses. '"Cosmo," Kesey called the flash of a higher order lying behind the riot of color and form that marked the first stage of the psychedelic journey. Cosmo was a superior intelligence, to which the rest of the world remained blind.'[39] It gave the feeling of enhanced communication: 'Speaking of the flash, Lesh [Phil Lesh, of the Grateful Dead] thought it was "as close as you could come to being someone else".'[40] And then flashes come from outside, fusing with whatever is happening in the brain, producing an 'awareness that flashed deeper than cerebration'.[41] Kesey explains to the British reporter Gary Goldhill that on one occasion in Mexico, he took acid, went outside, 'and there was an electrical storm, and there was lightning everywhere and I pointed to the sky and lightning flashes and all of a sudden I had a second skin, of lightning, electricity, like a suit of electricity, and I knew it was in us to be superheroes'.[42] A superhero: Kesey, at that time, was touched not by the old myths and heroes (Hercules, Orpheus, Ulysses), but by the new ones: Superman, Captain Marvel, and—of course—he 'began traveling and thinking at the speed of light as…The Flash…the current fantasy'.[43] Wolfe retrospectively parallels this new knowledge to mystical revelation, finding that this helps him grasp the experience that all the Merry Pranksters went through:

an *ecstasy*, in short. In most cases, according to scriptures and legend, it happened in a flash. Mohammed fasting and meditating on a mountainside near Mecca and—*flash!*—ecstasy, vast revelation and the beginning of Islam. Zoroaster hauling haoma water along the road and—*flash!*—he runs into the flaming form of Ahura Mazda, and the beginning of Zoroastrianism. Saul of Tarsus walking along the road to Damascus and—*flash!*—he hears the voice of the Lord and becomes a Christian…Sounds like an acid head, of course. What they all saw in…a flash was the solution to the basic predicament of being *human*, the personal *I, Me*, trapped, mortal and helpless, in a vast impersonal *It*, the world around me.[44]

Wolfe describes the busload of Pranksters who go to a Beatles concert at San Francisco's Cow Palace at the end of August 1965, and are mesmerized, fascinated, by the hundreds of exploding lights in the audience that appear during the set by Martha and the Vandellas. These create a display that adds to and complements the set lighting, accompanies the escalating screaming hysteria that rises in anticipation of the Fab Four's emergence on stage: 'they are flashbulbs, hundreds, thousands of teeny freaks with flashbulb cameras, aimed at the stage or just shot off in optic orgasm. Sheets of screams, rock 'n' roll, *blam blam*, a sea of flashbulbs.'[45]

But these camera flashbulbs (signs of a new consumer toy—the Instamatic 100, with a pop-up flash unit that held one peanut flashbulb at a time, had been introduced in 1963) were nothing compared with the elaborate light shows that accompanied the Acid Tests themselves. Here, the use of the strobe was notable. Wolfe describes how the strobe was employed as an instrument for studying motion, explains that at certain speeds strobe lights are so synched that they can throw epileptics into seizures, and that it was being discovered that strobes could project an individual 'into many of the sensations of an LSD experience without taking LSD'.[46] In the field of experimental art, this knowledge had already been developed in 1963 by Brion Gysin, inventor of the 'Dream Machine', a 1-metre-tall cylinder with slots cut in it, a 100-watt light bulb inside, that rotated on a turntable. Looking at this, Gysin said, was 'Like hallucinating without drugs'.[47] Combined with acid, the strobe light was sensational.

To people standing under the mighty strobe everything seemed to fragment. Ecstatic dancers—their hands flew off their arms, frozen in the air—their glistening faces came apart—a gleaming ellipse of teeth here, a pair of buffered highlit cheekbones there—all flacking and fragmenting into images as in an old flicker movie—a man in slices!—all of history pinned up on a butterfly board; the *experience*, of course.[48]

Wolfe's prose—fragmented and staccato, and then swooping forward in a glittering rush of words; sentences often lacking main verbs and reluctant to close; holding the reader in the present tense for very many of his 400 pages; chaotic on the surface, though with an underlying if hazy sense of progression from one (historical) state to the next—works as a verbal surrogate for these visual effects. If people's perceptual experiences whilst in a state of altered consciousness found many outlets in visual art,[49] how to get at the nature of the experience through photography was a challenge that faced anyone documenting these Acid Tests. The answer? Use a strobe light oneself! Wolfe describes the team from *Life* magazine that turned up in Los Angeles early in 1966, interviewing the Pranksters, and photographing them in a studio. Albert Rosenfeld, *Life*'s science editor, then wrote this into a solemn warning against the drug's effects—'an LSD trip is not always a round trip. What the LSD user may be buying is a one-way ticket to an asylum, a prison or a grave.'[50] His piece was accompanied by a number of Lawrence Schiller's photographs showing a young woman in San Francisco staring enraptured at a bare light bulb, and a sculptor in Chicago so transfixed by the pattern on a dingy armchair that he spent half an hour trying to take a photo of it. But Schiller—whom Timothy Leary had put into contact with Kesey—also took an iconic image of Neal Cassady staring at his own shadow, and, shown in Figure 4.8, one of him

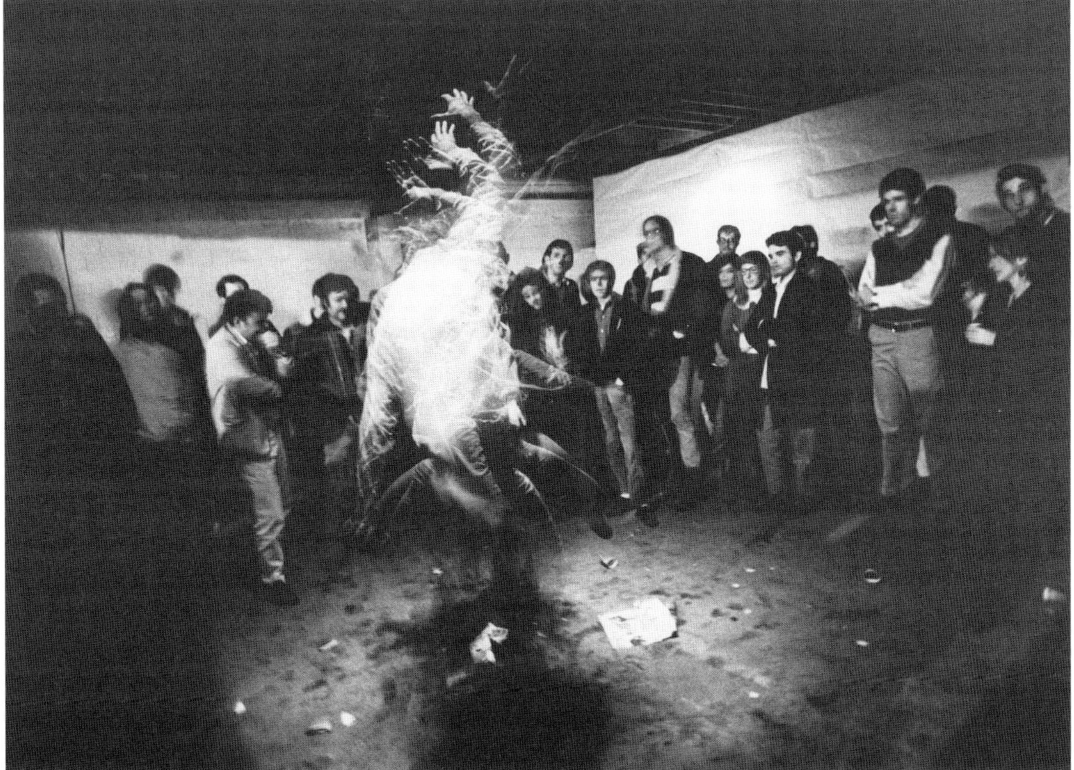

Figure 4.8 Lawrence Schiller, 'Dancer at an "Acid Test"'. © Lawrence Schiller/Getty Images.

waving his arms up and down—making him 'look like he had multi-arms, like the great god Shiva'.[51] Set against a row of standing spectators, this blur of limbs, this dervish-like figure, appears as an externalization of someone caught in acid's effects, thanks to the deployment of the photographic strobe.

Wolfe describes Kesey's sensation of his brain on acid in terms that closely parallel the workings of the strobe. 'Thousands of thoughts per second were rapping around between synapses, fractions of a second, so what the hell is a minute.'[52] The ideas here are curiously reminiscent of Walter Pater, whose comments, in the Conclusion to *The Renaissance* (1873), were to be extraordinarily influential on modernist conceptions of consciousness. In this Conclusion, Pater writes about how each impression received by the individual mind is 'limited by time, and that as time is infinitely divisible, each of them is infinitely divisible also; all that is actual in it being a single moment, gone while we try to apprehend it, of which it may ever be more truly said that it has ceased to be than that it is'. The onus is on us to expand each interval of all the intervals that go to make up our life, and to get in 'as many pulsations as possible into the given time', so as to give us 'a quickened sense of life…a quickened, multiplied consciousness'.[53] For Pater, this expansion of the sense of the now is something that may come from any kind of heightened experience, including being in the presence of a beautiful work of art. The shared ground lies in the language of pulsations—like a quickened, urgent heart-beat—that is both the sign of passing time and yet can be turned into a device—mental or optical—that fools us into thinking that time's passing can, indeed, be halted.

In his writings on the principles of Futurist sculpture, published in 1914, Umberto Boccioni claimed, 'We must try to find a form which is the expression of this new absolute—*speed*—which a true modern spirit cannot neglect.'[54] He achieved this himself through the interpenetration of blurred forms irradiated with shafts of light, which mimicked the human eye's confusion and limitations when confronted with rapid movement. Edgerton's technological inventions, by contrast, froze this rapidity in order to show what the human eye can never see unaided. Flash, in his hands, created something of extraordinary precision and clarity. But the underlying message of the resulting images—of shards of apple or banana pulp or those ragged ribbons of pierced balloons, even the delicate parabola of the golfer's swing—is one of speed. When flashes were repeated over and over again, as with the stroboscopic light show, or the dance floor strobe, the effect is slightly different: one of being held, however manically, in a slowed-down, estranged version of the continual present. These oscillating, nervous, exhausting flickers are, moreover, like an exaggeration of modernity's capacity to disrupt and scatter one's attention.

The vocabulary of flash has long attached itself to notions of speed and ephemerality—to see or possess something for a flash; to experience a flash of hope. From the middle of the twentieth century, the bestowal of 'Flash' as a proper name acts as a very clear signifier of energy and motion. The shift in connotation from the mid-nineteenth century's much less savoury meanings can be traced through the associations that cluster around the names of two popular fictional characters. Harry Flashman, the (anti-)hero Victorian soldier of George MacDonald Fraser's series of novels *The Flashman Papers* (1969–2005), took his origins from an unpleasant drunken bully—called Flashman—in Thomas Hughes's *Tom Brown's School Days* (1857), published when the association of 'flash' with everything that is showy, dishonest, and dishonourable was uppermost.[55] As a British *Slang Dictionary* of 1874 spelt out,

> *Flash*, showy, smart, knowing; a word with various meanings. A person is said to be dressed FLASH when his garb is showy, and after a fashion, but without taste. A person is said to be FLASH when he apes the appearance or manners of his betters, or when he is trying to be superior to his friends and relations. FLASH also means 'fast', roguish, and sometimes infers counterfeit or deceptive—and this, perhaps, is its general signification.[56]

The American Alex Raymond, who launched the *Flash Gordon* comic strip in 1934, had no problems with his hero's name in the United States or in Britain, but he had to be renamed 'Speed Gordon' in Australia, where the earlier connotations of 'flash' were still dominant.[57] In France, where his adventures appeared in *Le Journal de Mickey*, he was known as 'Guy l'éclair'—Guy Lightning. Flash Gordon, however, has become a nickname synonymous with speediness. Hip-hop artist and DJ Grandmaster Flash (born Joseph Saddler in 1958) was given the nickname Flash 'by my friend Gordon Upshaw…Because we both liked Flash Gordon cartoons—and he was already Gordon—and because I could run real fast'.[58]

As we learned from Ken Kesey's self-identification, the same associations hang around 'The Flash', created for DC Comics by writer Gardner Fox and graphic artist Harry Lampert, and first appearing in *Flash Comics #1* in January 1940. Indeed, there are four different superheroes who have assumed the super-speedy mantle of the Flash. Perhaps the most notable is Barry Allen, who came into being in 1956: a police scientist who obtained his special speedy powers (able to run extraordinarily fast, and having matching reflexes; sometimes speaking very quickly indeed; occasionally able to control lightning) after being bathed in chemicals after a shelf of them was shattered by a lightning bolt. He was the version of the Flash featured in a TV action series of 1990; he is continually up to date. 'High-speed Internet, 4G wireless, the latest operating system for the industry's most souped-up laptop…and it's all still a snail's pace to The Flash', proclaims the DC Comics website.[59] This is the Flash of 'the Pranksters' ubiquitous comic books, [who] caught speeding bullets by streaking at precisely their speed and reaching out and picking them up like eggs'.[60]

Suddenly appearing and disappearing, the Flash exemplifies the idea of the 'flash' as constituting a distinct but very brief intervention. This usage continues—indeed, has proliferated in recent years, with the brief flarings of flash sales, and flash mobs, and flash restaurants, and food that's flash-fried, and flash fiction, and flash poetry. Flash can be dangerous—think of 'flash floods'. There's a sense of edginess, an association with being at the vanguard, the cutting edge, that accompanies the most recent of these flashy coinings. There is, too, an aura of urgency, consolidated by the concept of the 'news flash', that brief announcement of a happening of considerable significance that's condensed into a terse statement. Right-wing columnist Westbrook Pegler succinctly defined it:

> Flash is the highest rating in news value...The flash is a newspaper and press association signal to get ready for a story which will dominate page one...the old method required the telephone operator to yelp 'Flash!' But the mechanization of the telegraph business abolished this dramatic note and flashes are now [he was writing in 1941] signaled by alarm bells on the mechanical telegraph printers.[61]

Likewise, the very twenty-first-century phenomenon of the 'flash mob' is propelled by the latest technology. A group of people, usually largely unknown to each other, 'assemble suddenly in a public place, perform such unusual or notable activity according to predetermined instructions, and then quickly disperse'.[62] The meeting place and other details are disseminated via email or text message. They might, for example, bring umbrellas and walk two city blocks singing songs from *Mary Poppins*; or each carry a book to swap with another mobber. A significant number of mob activities play with time, doing things in slow motion as though under strobe lights. An Austin flash mob staged slow-motion sword fighting with rolled-up newspapers,[63] and the perennially inventive New York-based group, Improv Everywhere (motto: 'we cause scenes'), in 2006 held an event in the 23rd Street Home Depot, in Manhattan—five minutes of slow-motion shopping, followed by five minutes at an ordinary pace, followed by five minutes of freezing in place. As the website on which this particular occasion was chronicled notes, it was deliberately planned so as to play with time, creating the illusion that different people, within the same physical space, were living in different time frames.[64] If such an event is pretty much impossible to capture in a photograph (although there's video footage of its synchronized phases), that's not true of a follow-up event, when for five minutes in January 2008, an Improv Everywhere flash mob froze in place on the concourse of Grand Central Station—as though nailed in time by a camera's shutter.[65] The group's chief photographer, Chad Nicholson, could only capture the sense of time passing through a long exposure that showed regular pedestrians as a blur, and the participants turned into statuary.

The idea that a short story could possess the power of a sudden shaft of illumination existed way before the coining of the phrase 'flash fiction'. Reviewing Rudyard Kipling's *Plain Tales from the Hills* in the *Edinburgh Review* in 1891, Rowland E. Prothero wrote of the author's 'pictorial treatment, of which daring directness, sharpness of outline, and naked reality, are the characteristics...The picture is given as it were in a flash of lightning'—and then the comparison is made between the materiality of the genre and its mode of consumption in the modern world—'he who travels by express train may read it at a glance'.[66] Like a flash mob event, flash fiction most certainly has duration—it's a piece of fiction clocking in at under a thousand words, for some; under five hundred, for others. But compared to a conventional novel, even a short story, it's startlingly brief. 'Intense, urgent and a little explosive', Declan Burke called it in the *Irish Times*;[67]

and Irish fiction writer Alison Wells, in an online piece entitled 'Why Flash Fiction Will Last', spells out some of its salient features: its immediacy, its distillation of experience, the precision of language that it demands, its deliberate deployment of pauses. It's 'a way of telling humanity about itself, a burst of recognition, a "flash" (if you'll pardon the pun) of realization'. She notes, too, how this mini-genre has been regarded as something that 'suits our society, fast moving, fast thinking, short, good to go, available in consumable bites or bytes', and honed to our short attention spans.[68] If the same observation had also been made in the late nineteenth century about that railway form, now, over a century later, flash fiction operates as a symptom of how life has speeded up.

The very short-term restaurant—called simply 'Flash'—that was open at London's Royal Academy of Arts for three months (November 2008 to January 2009) was part place to eat, part art installation. The whole construction—walls, reception desk, door—was designed by architect David Kohn from 190 art storage crates, each of which was inlaid with water-jet cut felt and computer-cut vinyl, with some panels decorated by Rory Crichton, showing octopi and other aquarium creatures.[69] From the roof hung a strange object, made in collaboration with Swarovski and Giles Deacon—a 2-metre-wide glass chandelier, studded with peridot crystals and clear lights, looking like an exploded disco ball—or a disco ball seen under the influence of psychedelic drugs during a light show, caught static in the strobe.[70]

Given the restaurant's pedigree, as well as its name, this comparison is not a far-fetched one, since Flash was operated by Pablo Flack and David Waddington. They were not just pioneers of London's pop-up dining scene, but operators of a restaurant with a wonderfully cringe-making punning name, the Bistrotheque. Strobe lighting—let alone the flashing of the strobe off the glitter ball—has become a cliché of both disco and rave decor. In the aptly named *Energy Flash*, his study of the rave scene, Simon Reynolds notes the ubiquity of strobes at rave venues, from those that lit the 'peasouper, strawberry-flavoured smoke' of London's Shoom, in the late 1980s, to the 'strobe-strafed catacombs' of Berlin's The Bunker.[71] Strobes are still commonplace within dance culture's lighting effects—seen at their dizzying best with the swooping travelling coloured strobe spotlights accompanying a performance of Deadmau5's 2010 ten-minute electronic number, 'Strobe'. But no one is going to be surprised into a state of wonder by the strobe on a dance floor today, unlike the early days of disco. Tim Lawrence, in *Love Saves the Day*, describes the skills of early disco DJ Francis Grasso, who worked lights as well as spinning the forty-fives, and

> operated the discotheque's state-of-the-art strobes, which generated a profoundly disorienting environment. 'When the strobe lights went on they really *strobed*,' says DePino. 'They made it look like people were dancing in slow motion. It was intense, surreal.' Frank Crapanzano was similarly spellbound. 'The Sanctuary was the first place I ever saw a strobe light. The effect was so overwhelming I had to stop dancing—*and I'm a dancer*. Everyone looked ominous and satanic. It was just beyond.'[72]

Yet within a few decades, the shocking novelty of disco's lighting effects had become commonplace. 'And now', proclaims Samson Young, the American narrator of Martin

Amis's 1989 novel *London Fields*, 'at dusk, outside my window, the trees shake their heads like disco dancers in the strobe lights of nightlife long ago.'[73]

The rapid flashes of high-speed photography, like other forms of flash, offer revelation—revelation of movement and forces invisible to the human eye; revelation of the beauty of an everyday occurrence; revelations of time-suspended intensity. Its techniques continue to be used by commercial and art photographers to create eye-catching, arresting effects. All three of these forms of revelation may be found at once. Japanese photographer Shinichi Maruyama, for example, has produced various series of images created by throwing ink or water in the air, and capturing the forms as they fall, as seen in Figure 4.9. This process, for him, is like creating moving sculpture that he then freezes in place. There's something of the performance to this work, and he also—particularly with his *Gardens* series—has likened his work to Zen meditation:

I have tried to represent this feeling I get from Zen gardens in my artwork. Although I am still far from those enlightened monks who labor in nature, my actions of repeatedly throwing liquid

Figure 4.9 Shinichi Maruyama, 'Water Sculpture #7', 2009. © Shinichi Maruyama, courtesy of Bruce Silverstein Gallery, NY.

into the air and photographing the resulting shapes and sculptural formations over and over—endlessly—could be considered a form of spiritual practice to find personal enlightenment.[74]

Or one could think of Ori Gersht, whose combination of high-speed photography and video simultaneously references old master painting and Harold Edgerton's work, as with his short piece showing a freeze-dried pomegranate that's exploded in an airy ball of shards by a bullet that passes through it: work that shows beauty and destruction combined, and that is exhibited both as slow-motion video and as still photographic images.[75] Or there's Olafur Eliasson's spectacular 2011 installation, *Model for a Timeless Garden*, in which he used strobe lighting to immobilize fountain sprays of water. Eliasson's other-worldly creation returns us to the origins of the earliest experiments with flash in the mid-nineteenth century.[76]

But in conclusion, I want to elaborate on a body of work by a photographer who has worked with flash's antithesis—an antithesis that I'll term 'slow photography'. Like Gersht, Hiroshi Sugimoto has been fascinated with the intersections of light and time throughout his career, perhaps most notably in his long exposures of seascapes, with no land or vessel to give any human scale, and, often, the horizon so hazy that any distinction between sea and land is rendered obscure through watery haze. He uses photographic technology to obliterate any sense of interruption, drawing the spectator, however briefly, into a temporal flow. This sense of fluid duration is what Norman Bryson has termed the 'metabolism' of Sugimoto's work, a fluidity that exists both within the relationship between image and viewer's body through the act of perception, and between each image in the series and the next. It functions as a rebuttal of the 'high-velocity systems' that we continually encounter in the modern world.[77] Bryson relates it to the Japanese concept of *ukiyo-e*, roughly translatable as 'the world in flux', but 'without ontological ground. Sugimoto's photographs may be', he says, 'the *ukiyo-e* of our time'.[78]

In Sugimoto's *Theatres* series, light is both instrument and subject, as exemplified in the Ohio movie house interior seen in Figure 4.10. An ongoing series, begun in 1978, it consists of long-exposure photographs taken in cinemas, which produce an image of a plain, extremely bright white light on the screen: 'one evening', Sugimoto claims,

> I had a near-hallucinatory vision. The question-and-answer session that led up to this vision went something like this: *Suppose you shoot a whole movie in a single frame?* And the answer: *You get a shining screen.* Immediately I sprang into action, experimenting toward realizing this vision. Dressed up as a tourist, I walked into a cheap cinema in the East Village with a large-format camera. As soon as the movie started, I fixed the shutter at a wide-open aperture, and two hours later when the movie finished, I clicked the shutter closed. That evening, I developed the film, and the vision exploded behind my eyes.[79]

From New York to Ohio to Los Angeles, there are subtle differences between each movie theatre when it comes to the proscenium arch, the pillars flanking the stage, the rows of seats, the Egyptian or art deco designs—all of them framing the screen, and just shadowily visible. But one element remains constant, even when an outdoor movie

Figure 4.10 Hiroshi Sugimoto, 'Ohio Theater, Ohio', 1980. © Hiroshi Sugimoto, courtesy Fraenkel Gallery, San Francisco.

theatre is being shot: that gleaming, blank rectangle. Some critics have seen in this startlingly white screen a strong element of social critique, reading it as an Adorno-like reference to the emptiness of mass consumption, the lack of content in mass culture.[80] Others find an expression of transience that goes far beyond the time that has passed both in the playing of the movie and in the imagined time that passes on the screen, for the theatres and drive-ins that he photographs are the sites of cinema's heyday, and are decorated extravagantly, 'evocative symbols of the glory days of the silver screen…If these images have a certain poignant quietude about them, it is because they speak so eloquently about the passage of time.'[81] This point is made even more forcefully by some of the 2015 additions to the series, which show films projected onto screens in decayed, ruined movie theatres. Hans Belting, one of Sugimoto's most perceptive critics, writes of how his images expose the cinema as 'the place of illusions. It is resistant to the flow of time in the films shown there and waits in the dark for the next film.' If we ourselves are watching a film, our eyes follow 'the images that are produced in the light and at the same time swallow the light', writes Belting—but in Sugimoto's work, the 'camera's rigid mechanics annul all of the images that have been run through before our eyes during the length of the film and produce only a "photograph" in its etymological sense, an image of pure light'.[82]

Each one of Sugimoto's brightly gleaming screens represents not a continuous light—whatever the impression made by the final image—but is a composite image: a record of the many, many flashes that go to make up the motion picture—two and a half hours of light passing. Yet in its final, static form, it's also a film distilled into a flash. This luminous blank screen, Sugimoto himself has said, was in part the result of wanting to make a simple form visible. But this is no ordinary bright light: it represents the accumulation of frame after frame flashing onto the screen. Indeed, that apparent shiny blank space contains 'too much information and too much information means emptiness'.[83] This last phrase reads as a rebuff of various kinds: to a modern world hungry for visual evidence; to the speed with which we are invited to view, to experience, to consume, and not to reflect; and to the continual demands on our attention made by the rapid interruptions of technological modernity.

Yet Sugimoto has also laid the ground for his pure white screens to be read in a different way. Flash photography's relationship to time has been a double-edged one. It has allowed us to see the beauties of a moment that we could never visually process without mechanical aids (and this technology has had many utilitarian benefits as well). But its deployment has also been continually associated, particularly in the second half of the twentieth century and beyond, with the here-today, gone-tomorrow speediness of a superficial consumer culture. Somehow, it's never quite thrown off its more dubious associations with flashiness and superficiality. It is the light of revelation, but it's also the light of bling. Sugimoto, in his movie theatre images, has managed to capture both of these aspects. He celebrates, commemorates, and mourns the extravagant nature of movie theatre architecture. But he also gives us a transcendental generalization, showing us how time passing—formed by a rapid sequence of frames that certainly owes something to the original principles of the stroboscope, even the Phenakistoscope—may ultimately be represented as one huge flash of light.

CHAPTER FIVE

Throwing Light

WRITING TO the art critic and educator Elizabeth McCausland in 1938, excavating some 'fossil fragments of early memories', Lewis Hine vividly described the experience of using flash to photograph 'the surge of bewildered beings' who had just landed at Ellis Island. First, a small group had to be isolated, and have it explained to them in pantomime that it 'would be lovely if they would only stick around just a moment'.

We get the focus, on the ground glass, of course, then, hoping they will stay put, get the flash lamp ready. A horizontal pan on a vertical narrow road with a plunger into which a small paper cap was inserted and then the powder was poured across the pan in what seemed, at the time, to be enough to cover the situation. Meantime, the group had strayed around a little and you had to give a quick focal adjustment, while someone held the lamp. The shutter was closed, of course, plate holder inserted and cover slide removed, usually, the lamp retrieved and then the real work began. By that time most of the group were either silly or stony or weeping with hysteria because the bystanders had been busy pelting them with advice and comments, and the climax came when you raised the flash pan aloft over them and they waited, rigidly, for the blast. It took all the resources of a hypnotist, a supersalesman, and a ball pitcher to prepare them to play the game and then to outguess them so most were not either wincing or shutting eyes when the time came to shoot. Naturally, everyone shut his eyes when the flash went off but the fact that their reactions were a little slower than the optics of the flash saved the day, usually.

As he concluded, laconically, 'The smoke, by the way, was a big drawback if you wanted to take a second exposure or if you had any regard for the people who had to stay in the room after you left.'[1]

The elaborate procedures demanded by flash photography prior to the invention of the flashbulb—and when the professional photographer was still using a heavy camera and tripod—qualify its associations with speed. Hine's account also brings home quite how invasive the practice could be. Flash photography has been indispensable to documentary photography, and it is in relation to this genre that we encounter most starkly its most singular and most contradictory aspects: on the one hand, its impetus towards revelation and its capacity to render visible that which would otherwise remain in darkness, and, on the other, its associations with unwelcome intrusion. At the same time, documentary photography brings out a further notable characteristic of flash photography: its drive towards the democratic. Whilst all photography is democratic to some extent, in that it reveals every detail, chosen or otherwise, that can be captured by a particular combination of lens and light, flash photography is exceptional in this respect. Especially in the early decades of its use, it could not be carefully controlled, and this means that work tools or crockery or tattered lace curtains often take on unplanned prominence. A sudden flare of light reveals, with clarity, each dent on a kitchen utensil and the label on each carefully stored can; each photograph on a mantelshelf or image on the walls; each cherished ornament; each little heap of waste paper or discarded rag; each piece of polished furniture or stained floor or scratched banister or accumulation of dust; each shiny button; each wrinkle. Flash can make plain, can bring out of obscurity, the appearance of things that may never have been seen before with such clarity, let alone recorded with such precision.

The prose of 'Flashes from the Slums', Jacob Riis's first published account of his project to photograph New York's darkest corners by night, tells of these nocturnal expeditions as though they are photographic smash-and-grab raids:

> Somnolent policemen on the street, denizens of the dives in their dens, tramps and bummers in their so-called lodgings, and all the wild and wonderful variety of the New York night life have in their turn marveled at and been frightened by the phenomenon. What they saw was three or four figures in the gloom, a ghostly tripod, some weird and uncanny movements, the blinding flash, and then they heard the patter of retreating footsteps, and the mysterious visitors were gone before they could select their scattered thoughts and try to find out what it was all about.[2]

Elsewhere, Riis employs a Gothic register not so much to vivify the drama of the flashlight as to press home his point about the awfulness of the conditions he encountered, as when he wrote of three peddlers who slept among decaying fruit and wreckage of all sorts in the cellar of a tenement at the lower end of Ludlow Street—a tenement that contained 297 tenants. The water was ankle-deep on the floor; 'the feeblest ray of light never found its way down there, the hatches having been carefully covered with rags and matting…It was an awful place, and by the light of my candle the three, with their unkempt beards and hair and sallow faces, looked more like hideous ghosts than living men.'[3]

Notably, Riis is not describing here the detailed disclosure of dank living conditions that the flash revealed: rather, the scene about which he writes is that of his original impression, lit by a tentatively flickering candle. One cannot tell exactly what a bright flaring flash will show: the photographer is literally taking a shot in the dark. These are the dark circumstances in which Riis would have had to have envisaged (and on occasion stage-managed) all of the plates that he exposed by flashlight. Riis's writing and images, read together, show a mismatch between the murky surroundings—in which touch and smell, rather than sight, reveal the viscerally unpleasant nature of what lies to hand or underfoot—and the eventual image provided by the photograph. The latter may, indeed, provide a detailed visual record of what that sudden burst of light put on show: Riis's prose, however, works to stimulate preliminary or supplementary sensory affect.

The concept of descending into the underworld, of bringing light to dark places—or, more exactly, of using light to make dark places visible—was, for Riis, infused with spiritual associations. Although he rarely belabours his religious motivation in his prose, it is clear that for him, flash powder was much more than a timely technological innovation, and the Christian equation of light with goodness repeatedly inflects his writing. He often loops back to the image of his work figuratively, as well as literally, illuminating slum conditions. 'I hate darkness and dirt anywhere', he wrote in his autobiography, 'and naturally want to let in the light'; and again, two pages before he concludes his account, he optimistically prophesies 'Light ahead!'[4] The literal language of illumination melded, for Riis, with biblical overtones: he saw himself, as he took up this new technology, as providing revelation, and the transcendental overtones of his vocabulary—like the sublime associations with lightning that hung around the language of *blitzlicht*—helped to underscore its significance as an instrument of quasi-divine intervention and purgation. In this, of course, he was building on a familiar trope of social reform. Literary historian Lewis Fried, in *Makers of the City* (1990), explains how 'American letters, often drawing upon biblical images of the fallen city or upon the hope of a New Jerusalem, made it possible and popular to see the city as divided. One half was dark, resistant to Christian virtue and not amenable to social control and order; the other half dwelt in light and was propertied, stable, virtuous, and domestic.'[5] The moral resonances carried by the language of dark and light could be found in the titles of such works as Helen Campbell's *Darkness and Daylight, or, Lights and Shadows of New York Life* (1891).[6]

As Bonnie Yochelson has pointed out, 'Although the technology of the flashlight was new, Riis's imagery was not.'[7] Since the 1860s, *Harper's Weekly* and *Frank Leslie's Illustrated Weekly*, in particular, had been publishing line engravings of tenements, lodging houses, sweatshops, and so on to illustrate their exposés of social conditions. For example, in the engraving reproduced in Figure 5.1, Paul Frenzeny's 'Underground Lodgings for the Poor, Greenwich Street, New York', light falls tenderly on the vulnerable faces of the sleeping poor, as well as on the large snowflakes that swirl in through the door.

Maren Stange uses the similarities between C. A. Keetel's 'Bottle Alley' (*Harper's Weekly*, 1880) and Richard Hoe Lawrence's 'A Downtown Morgue'—one of those early flash photographs taken at Riis's direction—to draw attention to photographers' 'reliance on pictorial conventions governing the representation of such scenes'.[8] Yet there are some substantial differences between the photographs and the line drawings. For the most part, features are softened and sentimentalized in the illustrations—especially when they are most strongly illuminated. The poor, especially the women, sleep the sleep of the weary. If awake, they often seem lost in contemplation, as if wondering about the chain of events that brought them there: artists play up sensibility and misery in a visual claim on our compassion. Only occasionally do we encounter an actively expressive gaze. A man looks ruefully at the artist-spectator in Winslow Homer's 'Station House Lodgers' (*Harper's Weekly*, 7 February 1874); at the bottom of the elaborate frontispiece of Campbell's *Darkness and Daylight*, shown in Figure 5.2, a couple of women

Figure 5.1 Paul Frenzeny, 'Underground Lodgings for the Poor, Greenwich Street, New York', *Harper's Weekly* (20 February 1869), 116.

at the top of a heap of slumbering humans cower with apprehension in the strong beam of a hand-held torch.

But a considerable number of Riis's subjects display indignation, resentment, or fear, as displayed in Figure 5.3. It's hard to tell whether this is related to the fact that—as the *Darkness and Daylight* illustration reminds us—the apparatus of urban surveillance had long shone unwelcome light on destitute people, or whether it's a somatic response to the shock of the flash. It is the flash, however, that captures the moment of unbidden intrusion. Moreover, assumptions about photography's capacity to supply incontrovertible evidence—assumptions about photography's evidentiary role that underpinned Riis's campaigning deployment of his materials, in lectures and publications—mean that we tend to accept the idea that this is a direct record of what it was like to be suddenly, and resentfully, at the receiving end of exploded *blitzlichtpulver*. In a broader framework, it was this belief in the evidentiary forcefulness of illumination and photographic record that gave weight not just to Riis's image production and its deployment, to its use by others who borrowed it for their own reformist ends, and to the similar

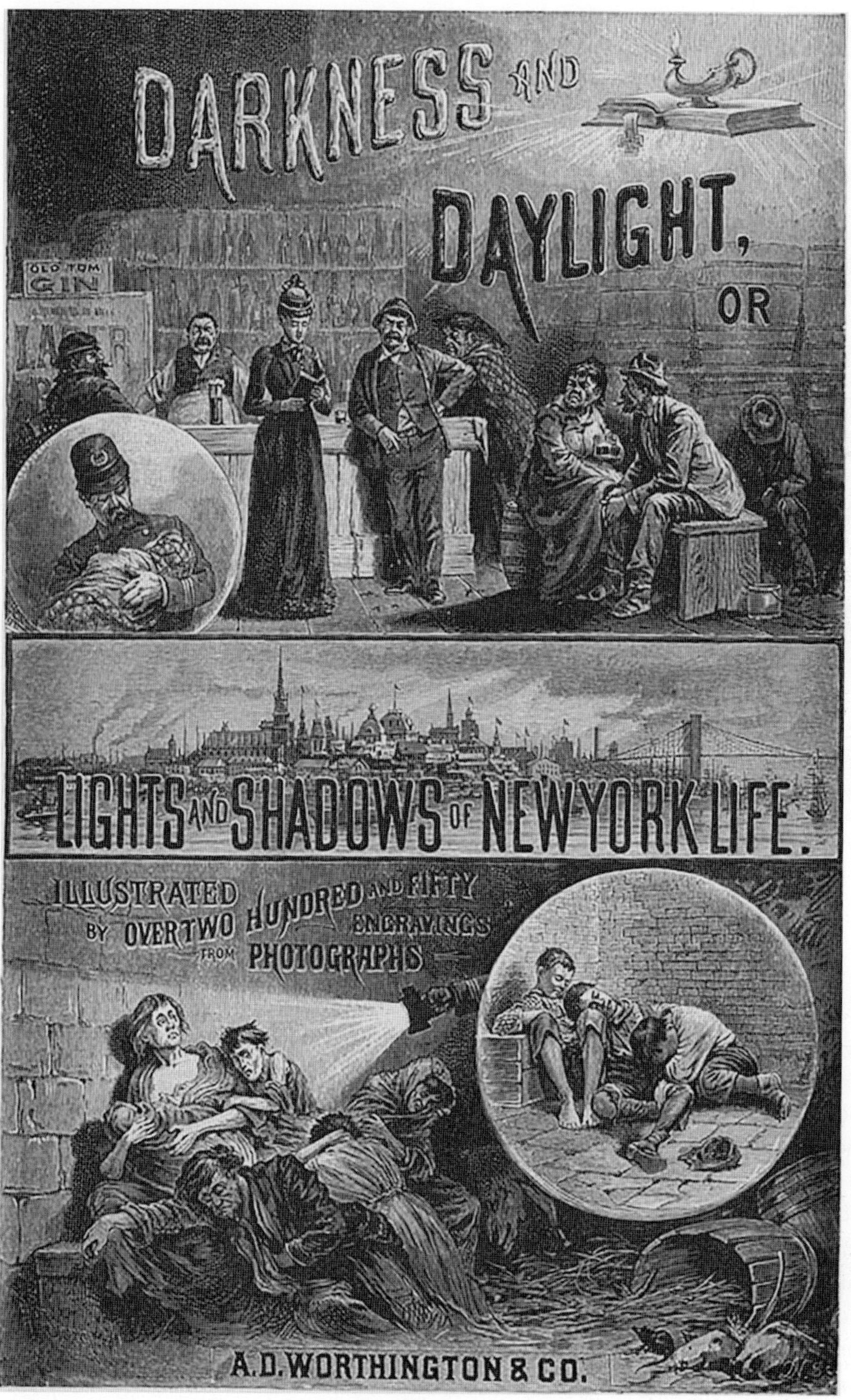

Figure 5.2 Helen Campbell, Frontispiece, *Darkness and Daylight; or Lights and Shadows of New York Life* (Hartford, CT: A. D. Worthington & Co., 1891).

Figure 5.3 Richard Hoe Lawrence and Henry G. Piffard, 'A Cellar Dive in the Bend', *c.*1895. Richard Hoe Lawrence and Henry G. (Henry Granger) Piffard (1842–1910) for Jacob A. (Jacob August) Riis (1849–1914)/Museum of the City of New York. 90.13.4.329.

work of others.[9] In February 1888 the *Photographic Times* tells of a well-known (but unnamed) temperance orator's plans to present a series of lantern slides of New York locations 'to illustrate a story to be called "The Prodigal Son"... by the new instantaneous flash process, we can get views of the interiors by day or night and in a manner to give every feature of the pictures taken with a lifelike vividness and accuracy away ahead of the ordinary photographs'.[10]

The Publishers' Preface to *Darkness and Daylight* explains how 'Recent developments in photography have rendered it possible to catch instantaneously'—again, the emphasis on speed and the moment—

> all the details of a scene with the utmost fidelity. The publishers and their photographer explored the city together for months, by day and by night, seeking for living material on the streets, up narrow alleys and in tenement houses, in missions and charitable institutions, in low lodging-houses and cellars, in underground resorts and stale-beer dives, in haunts of criminals and training-schools of crime, and in nooks and corners known only to the police and rarely visited by any one else. These two hundred and fifty remarkable pictures were selected from upwards of a thousand photographs taken at all hours of the day and night. Many of them were taken at moments when the people portrayed would rather have been anywhere else than before the

lens' eye. By far the greater part was made by flash-light, without the aid of which much of the life herein shown so truthfully could not have been presented at all. Some of them were made under circumstances of great difficulty, in dimly-lighted holes and in underground places, literally 'in darkest New York', where the light of day never penetrates.[11]

Most of these photographs were taken by Oscar G. Mason, a pioneer of clinical medical photography who directed the photographic department of Bellevue Hospital in New York. One engraving, shown in Figure 5.4, 'A Sly Opium Smoker', was after Riis, and bears a caption suggesting that those who *appear* to be unconscious of photographic activity may not be as unknowing as it seems.

All the same, none of these images were snatched rapidly with the opportunism of a street photographer. Few could have been completely unaware of the arrival of several people together with a cumbersome camera, tripod, and flash equipment. And Riis's figures were by no means always as arbitrarily and candidly posed as might at first glance appear. Writer and photographer Jack London, a great admirer of Riis's work, was well

A SLY OPIUM SMOKER.

(This photograph was made by flash-light in a Chinese opium den on Pell street when the smoker was supposed to be fast asleep. Subsequently the photograph disclosed the fact that he had at least one eye open when the picture was made.)

Figure 5.4 'A Sly Opium Smoker', engraving after Jacob Riis, in Helen Campbell, *Darkness and Daylight; or Lights and Shadows of New York Life* (Hartford, CT: A. D. Worthington & Co., 1891), 571.

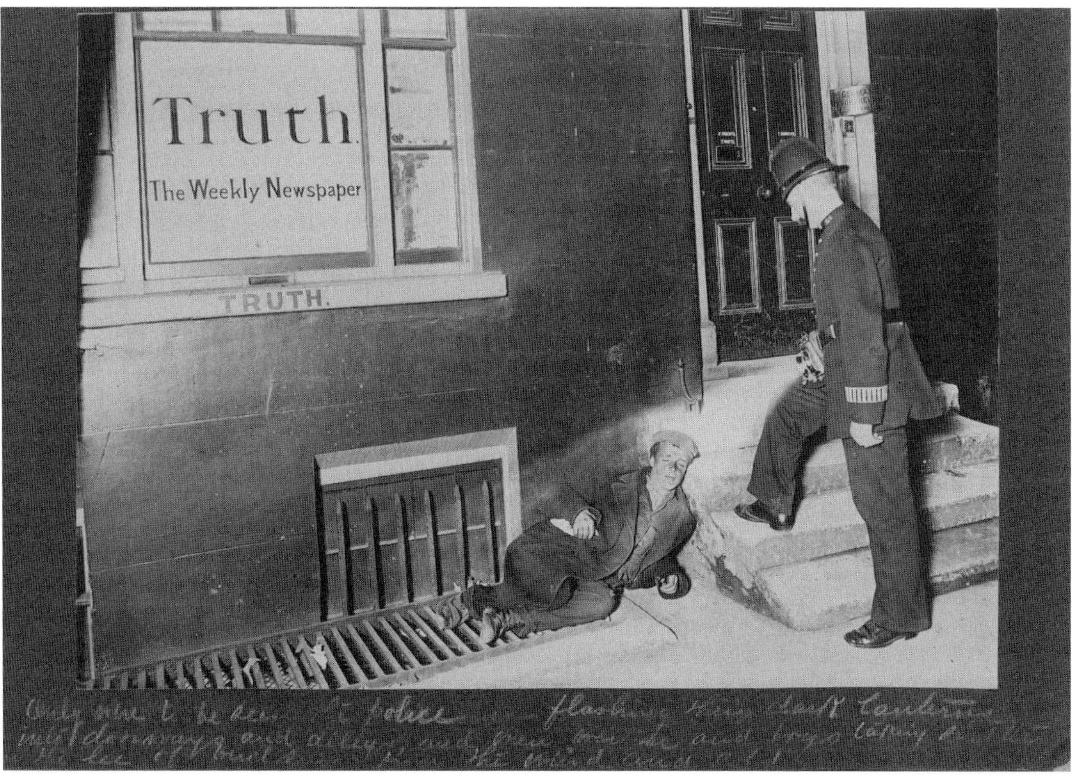

Figure 5.5 Jack London, '*Truth*: The Weekly Newspaper', 1902. JLP 466 Alb. 28 #03565. The Huntington Library, San Marino, California.

aware of the dualities that could be at play in documentary photography. '*Truth*: The Weekly Newspaper'—a photograph that he included in *People of the Abyss* (1903)—draws attention to its own staginess through positioning the disturbed sleeper under the newspaper's boastful title. The policeman with his flashlight and the street person seen in Figure 5.5 are shown up as representative icons, performing a ritual in which authority and exposed subject play their familiar roles, rather than appearing as individuals with their own particular histories. It's a tension—should documentary focus on the typical or on the specific?—that still animates discussions of socially engaged photography.[12]

Riis's predilection for the typical is well brought out by Peter Hales, who has done so much to make us aware of Riis's careful framing and staging, explaining how Riis often arranged not only his human subjects, but also the props that accompany them. An Italian woman and her baby sit in the traditional posture of Madonna and Child, eyes raised heavenwards in supplication, a straw hat hanging above her positioned like a loosely floating halo. Another halo-like hat and cross-like joist are found above the head of the Hebrew Master ready for the Sabbath eve, depicted in Figure 5.6. Like the religious weight carried by the loaf of bread on the table, these have readily legible iconographic traction, linking this man—as a Pre-Raphaelite painter like Holman

Figure 5.6 Jacob Riis, 'Ready for Sabbath Eve in a Coal Cellar—A Cobbler in Ludlow Street', *c.*1890. Jacob A. (Jacob August) Riis (1849–1914)/Museum of the City of New York. 90.13.4.291.

Hunt might—to the symbols of Christianity. The emotional affect of these typological symbols is underscored by the poverty inherent in the peeling paint and worn tablecloth and scratched table legs. The dirt and grime that is engrained into wood and cloth seem, like the archetypal figure, enduring and eternal—or at least depressingly hard to budge. The revelatory work performed by the flash is twofold: it brings out the textures of poverty, to be sure, but it also assists in the recording of what was possibly never meant to be seen, and what is ultimately entirely illegible—the two hands holding what appears to be a spade, or shovel, on the right side of the frame.

Or *is* this arbitrary? Hales would have it otherwise:

> In fact, this picture is so carefully composed and utterly purposeful that it demands that ill-formed appearance. That shovel *must* be in the picture, for it signals the inappropriateness of the coal cellar as a dwelling. We are, apparently, watching a devout Jew interrupted from his devotions by the rude work around him. To include more than the hands of the shoveler, however, might detract from the presence of that lone human figure; it would also decrease the symbolic force of that shovel.[13]

It's certainly tempting to believe in this level of intentionality, and in some cases, including the two photographs mentioned here, his subjects can be seen as collaborators in helping him achieve his desired effect—but did Riis really possess as much artistic control over the fake-arbitrary as, say, Jeff Wall? Elsewhere, other stray hands (as in the sets of fingers caught by the flash in 'An All-Night Two-Cent Restaurant, in "The Bend"', or the seemingly ownerless black hand in 'A Black-and-Tan Dive in "Africa"') are disconcerting through their apparently disembodied qualities, rendering the scenes less than entirely legible.

Rather like the unexpected appearance of part of a flashgun, or the depiction of *blitzlichtpulver*'s reflection that I discussed in Chapter 2, these hands raise the topic of chance's relationship to flash photography. Robin Kelsey, in *Photography and the Art of Chance*, makes the useful claim that 'In photographs, accidents appear in two related but divergent forms: the glitch and the inadvertently recorded detail'.[14] The light that blazes back from a windowpane, the product of the technology used to make enough illumination to take a picture, might, like the appearance of a surface blemish on a negative when it is printed out, be said to fall into the first category, and many of those arbitrarily appearing hands into the second. What is more, in appearing to be accidental, these visible tokens can bring their own kind of guilty pleasures, as though we have been given privileged access to the spontaneous, and to that which would normally be hidden from us. In turn, this can consolidate spectators' sense of distance, difference, and, thereby, relative privilege—however compassionate the response may also be.[15]

But much of the detail revealed by Riis's flash, and by that of his documentarian successors, complicates Kelsey's definition. A great deal of the dirt and the grime, the peeling wallpaper, the rickety furniture, the broken balustrades, the scratched woodwork, the filthy bedclothes, the pewter jugs, the battered tin boxes, the incongruously pretty calendar hung on a beam (as we see in 'An Italian Home Under a Dump', reproduced in Figure 5.7) might never previously have been made as visible as they were by the light of the flash. To be sure, flash creates its own aesthetic. It accentuates the shadows, making the dark appear truly Stygian, and it brings out all the marks to be found on the surfaces of the material objects that it illuminates. In *What Photography Is*, James Elkins invites us to imagine photographs without the people they contain; to replace the ostensible subject of human-in-environment with the foregrounding of objects alone. If we did this, we would be left, he says, with a mass of 'overlooked, un-needed and unwanted details'. Yet these parts are 'actually the majority of the photograph...Judged by the square inch, photographs of people—that is, most photographs—are not mainly photographs of people. In terms of square inches, they are mainly photographs of other things.' Elkins then invokes a word to establish a categorical distinction between photography and painting: 'The *surround*, as I like to call it, is not the same as the *background* that painters know, because backgrounds are put in mark by mark and are therefore always noticed, always intended.'[16] It is the unintended surround, one might say, that the flash is especially adept at revealing.

Figure 5.7 Jacob Riis, 'An Italian Home Under a Dump', *c*.1892. Jacob A. (Jacob August) Riis (1849–1914)/Museum of the City of New York. 2008.1.28.

Yet however inadvertent, even surprising, a stray hand or frying pan might be, the overall effect of such revelation was quite deliberate. In other words, an individual detail might be the product of chance, but this is deliberative chance, deployed towards a reformist end. Riis's photographs, as William Chapman Sharpe puts it,

> were literally exposures—exposures of greasy wallpaper and grimy skin, filthy bedding and soot-caked stoves that never saw the light of day. It was a vision created only for an instant by the flash camera. Displaying what even the poor themselves were unable to see, the full degradation of their environment, Riis hoped to destroy the world his flash fell on. Photography is often thought of as a form of preservation; for Riis it was an agent of demolition.[17]

On the other hand, there is no absolute guarantee that Riis photographed even an interior exactly as he found it. We can assume, as we've already seen, that he posed some of his subjects. Consider, again, that image of Little Susie pasting linen onto tin covers (Figure 4.1). Were the room's inhabitants aware that the picture was crooked? Were they working too hard to notice? Or did Riis himself tilt the frame, giving a compositional unity through this diagonal? These photographs promise revelations of daily life, but the revelation may have been staged in the interest of creating an effective impression.

Depicting material facts, Riis's, like so many documentary images, are very frequently designed to work on spectators' emotions and associations. Virginia Woolf, writing in 1938 about pictures of atrocities—dead children killed by bombs—circulated by the Spanish Government in 1936–7, was misleading when she claimed that such 'photographs are not an argument; they are simply a crude statement of facts addressed to the eye', since even strikingly graphic news images have their own visual language in which they communicate. Yet she is spot on when she recognizes the visceral, affective impact of much documentary work. As she puts it, 'the eye is connected with the brain; the brain with the nervous system. That system sends its messages in a flash through every past memory and present feeling.'[18]

Jacob Riis was not the only early flash photographer to employ a religion-inflected choice of words to describe his documentary practice. In a lecture he gave in 1909, Riis's admirer Lewis Hine spoke of the 'great social peril' of 'darkness and ignorance', against which 'light is required. Light! Light in floods... in this campaign for light we have for our advance agent the light writer—the photograph.'[19] However, Hine employed a different style of flash photography than did Riis. Rather than swoop into a location, ignite his flash, and expose the plate, Hine was, as Kate Sampsell-Willmann has shown us, 'a disciple of Deweyist experiential learning and Jamesian democratic Pragmatism'.[20] He spent time among his subjects, sharing their surroundings, communicating with them, more concerned with character than with material facts. Even when he was taking photographs in busy, less than ideal conditions, when his subjects' minds were surely elsewhere, he took the trouble—as the quotation that opens this chapter shows—to explain to them what he was up to.

Dedicated, at least in the first part of his career, to producing images that provide valuable information to aid campaigns of social reform, Hine was actively engaged not just in the taking, but also in the cropping, sizing, and captioning of these photographs.[21] Whether he was depicting a crowd of newsboys waiting in an Indianapolis newspaper office for the 'Base Ball edition' to come off the presses (as seen in Figure 5.8)—the flash glinting back off their pupils—or recording the activities of child labourers in the South: spinning and spooling, warping, sweeping and doffing, picking up bobbins, ravelling and looping in cotton mills; cigar making; shrimp picking; canning; and oyster shucking—his emphasis habitually falls on the individuality of his subjects.

To be sure, in Hine's post-1921 work, when he was trying less to serve reformist interests, and was more concerned to make workers conceive of themselves as heroes, working in tandem with the machines that powered American industry, it is not so much the eyes of people that shine back at one; rather, flash's glare bounces off the surfaces of industrial machinery.[22] These were photographs taken very much for propagandist ends, whether that propaganda was in the service of social reform or in the celebration of labour. Extraneous detail certainly appears, in the textures of planks and beams and

Figure 5.8 Lewis Hine, 'Indianapolis Newsboys waiting for the Base Ball edition, in a Newspaper Office', 1908. Library of Congress: National Child Labor Committee Collection. LC-US Z 62-30456.

barrels, but the photographs do not invite the same kind of investigative, detail-oriented scrutiny as do Riis's. Most probably, this is because they are so frequently of workplaces, and these tend not to be as marked by signs of everyday living as are domestic spaces, where even the poorest dwellings—like the hovel under the Rivington Street dump shown in Figure 5.7—can bear traces of their occupants' pasts, habits, and attempts to decorate and personalize.

So rather than looking further at Hine, visually striking though many of his images made by flash may be, I want to turn to another American photographer who made significant use of flash: Jessie Tarbox Beals. Beals was remarkable for her enterprise and energy at a time when relatively few women worked, as she did, on commission as photographers for newspapers and magazines, whilst also maintaining a flourishing private studio. She is probably best known for the images of native peoples who were on display at the St Louis World's Fair in 1904, and which foreground a sympathetic domesticity.[23] In general, her photographic presence in St Louis, which helped to launch the New York phase of her career, was publicized by means of photographs celebrating her daredevil ingenuity—climbing ladders or riding in hot-air balloons to get the best shots. Tracing her commercial career not only helps us understand the degree to which she was a photographic pioneer—including in her adoption of flash—but it also shows some of the reasons why flash photography came through association to occupy a rather low place in the aesthetic hierarchy. In turn, this has led to one of its most noticeable attributes, the surprising illumination of the everyday, being underemphasized, undervalued, and under-noticed.

As a commercial photographer, Beals had an eclectic repertoire. She used flash not just for newsworthy events (on one noteworthy occasion climbing up on a transom to take a photo of a murder trial through a Buffalo courthouse window),[24] but also in making portraits of individuals, of cats, of babies—sometimes in combination—images that were her bread and butter. Her account books show the numerous magazines and papers for which she worked (often uncredited)—from the *Herald Tribune* to *Vogue, Town and Country*, and *American Golfer*; she had a particularly strong reputation as a photographer of upper-middle-class interiors, in which the shining light that beams back from polished furniture speaks both to inherent opulence and to the hidden labour of those who keep these surfaces so sparkling. She also made images that fell within the parameters of Photo

Figure 5.9 Jessie Tarbox Beals, 'Four Children in a Tenement Room', *c*.1916. CSS Photography Archives. Courtesy of Community Service Society of New York and the Rare Book and Manuscript Library, Columbia University.

Figure 5.10 Jessie Tarbox Beals, 'Tenement Families', *c.*1916. CSS Photography Archives. Courtesy of Community Service Society of New York and the Rare Book and Manuscript Library, Columbia University.

Secession, Stieglitzian aesthetics, relying on the muted light of urban illumination and smoky, misty, snowy air.

And Beals was a participant in the early American documentary movement. Like Riis—and like some other women photographers of the time, including Frances Benjamin Johnson—she made photographs on assignment for contemporary charitable organizations and for publications like the journal *Charities and the Commons* that drew attention to substandard housing and working conditions. Like Riis, again, she took these photographs—many of which are datable to the 1910–12 period—primarily with a view to their informational content. As the labelling in photographic archives shows, there has, indeed, often been confusion between Beals's and Riis's work, both because of the subject matter and because of basic compositional parallels. Commonly attributed to Riis, certain images by Beals were in fact acquired by Riis for New York's Charity Organization Society. Enjoying a relatively brief career as a photographer himself, he continued to collect images with which to illustrate his lectures and articles on the topic of social reform.

Figure 5.11 Jessie Tarbox Beals, 'Two Children in Tenement Rooms', *c.*1910. CSS Photography Archives. Courtesy of Community Service Society of New York and the Rare Book and Manuscript Library, Columbia University.

Yet if we consider Beals's work alongside Riis's, we can see that there is much more variety in her photographs, even when it comes to recording tenement life. His reforming drive emphasizes the bareness, raggedness, desperation of poverty: his subjects are presented as victims. By contrast, the carefully arranged possessions in some of the interiors that Beals shows us, plus the fact that the inhabitants are smiling, restores a sense of dignity, even cheerfulness, to some of these settings and their occupants—as we see in Figures 5.9 and 5.10. On the other hand, she is no idealist when it comes to the homes of the poor. She also depicts rooms where, despite a modicum of material goods, the inhabitants have let everything slide into grubby chaos—and note the reflection of Beals's heavy camera and her flash in the mirror in Figure 5.11. Especially in photographs where there are no humans present at all, like Figures 5.12 and 5.13, she demonstrates that whilst poverty may indeed consist in an absence of material goods and comfort, it can also inhere within a psyche that has just given up when it comes to trying to organize material stuff; that has no time or inclination to do so. She dramatizes the two-way interaction between environment and state of mind. Beals's interest in human psychology cannot be separated from her depiction of urban interiors, but the range of

Figure 5.12 Jessie Tarbox Beals, 'Bedroom, Tenement', 1910s. CSS Photography Archives. Courtesy of Community Service Society of New York and the Rare Book and Manuscript Library, Columbia University.

emotions and different degrees of pride in one's surroundings that materializes in her work displays her understanding of this interaction's complexity.

Like these images by Beals, 'Child with Cat and Two Women'—Figure 5.14—is held in the archives of the Community Service Society, in New York. The photographer is unknown, although its style is certainly very close to that of Beals, and the engagement of the people in the room implies that a certain rapport had been achieved with them. Almost certainly a flash device was used to take it—the shadows and reflections suggest that it was held high and off to the left. But what is going on? Is this a visit to the woman's home by a 'friendly visitor', as turn-of-the-century social workers were called? If so, why does the little girl wear outdoor clothes? Does her expression suggest mistrust of the photographer, or of the woman in a hat, or bewilderment at the whole set of circumstances? Is the younger woman sad to see her leave, or happy to have her home? Is she saying goodbye to the kitten? Does the array of pill bottles on the mantelshelf suggest that someone—mother, child, absent family member—is sick? Why the flag on the same mantelshelf? What of the mismatch—surely flash makes this suddenly apparent—between the untidy newspapers shoved into the grubby area behind the

Figure 5.13 Jessie Tarbox Beals, 'Tenement Interior Falzone Family', *c.*1910. CSS Photography Archives. Courtesy of Community Service Society of New York and the Rare Book and Manuscript Library, Columbia University.

stove and the mess of papers on the table behind, and the china and trinkets that display a desire to decorate and beautify these shabby surroundings? What does the image say about the intersection of human resilience and charitable intervention? What happens next? The photograph may have stopped life's daily flow for a moment, and even brought out and fixed details that are not normally readily apparent. But very often, the most provocative images are those that suggest tensions, stories, circumstances, and inner lives that the camera can hint at, but never fully reveal.

Very different in subject matter from her tenement photographs, although not in technique, are the pictures of Greenwich Village that Beals made in the later 1910s and 1920s. Beals moved to this bohemian milieu in 1917: the artistically and socially progressive corner of New York that Christine Stansell describes in *American Moderns*—with the significant qualification that Stansell's book ends in 1916, just at the time that Beals arrived downtown.[25] For by 1917, the locations that Beals records had started to become—to put it bluntly—tourist destinations. She herself played a role in this commercialization: some of her images illustrated an article entitled 'America's Bohemia' that appeared in

Figure 5.14 Unknown Photographer, 'Child with Cat and Two Women', *c.*1910. CSS Photography Archives. Courtesy of Community Service Society of New York and the Rare Book and Manuscript Library, Columbia University.

McCall's Magazine in July 1917, including 'The Treasure Box, with its destinies carefully guided by two men', a portrait of Persis Kirmse, the British painter of dogs and cats, in her studio, and 'Miss Florence Gough's shop [which] was originally a stable; but now the stalls, newly painted and adorned, are occupied by queer manikins who show off hats and smocks with Fifth Avenue assurance'.[26] She moved with a friend to a three-bedroom apartment with up-to-the-minute decor—'The walls of the larger room, converted into a salon', *The Villager* reported, 'were painted turquoise blue, and the furniture orange and black'[27]—and she opened a Tea Room and Art Gallery, where, among other things, she sold postcards of local stores and cafes and tea rooms and restaurants—where she was clearly a regular: a lot of her bad poems were written on the backs of their menus. She documented the 1920s equivalents of restaurant pop-ups, like 'A Spaghetti Bar at Grace Godwin's Garrett', as seen in the postcard reproduced as Figure 5.15. Politically eclectic—she joined the Liberal Club, attended Republican meetings—she had very little connection to the rapidly waning political radicalism of the pre-war village. Notwithstanding her own heterosexuality, she was closely connected, through her friendships and through the people and styles that she recorded, with the growth of the Village as a gay and lesbian centre—or what C. Grand Pierre, in a volume in Beals's personal

Figure 5.15 Jessie Tarbox Beals, 'A Spaghetti Bar at Grace Godwin's Garrett', *c.*1917–18. Beals No. A9399; from Jessie Tarbox Beals Photograph Collection (PR004), box 4, folder 39, New York Historical Society.

collection, called 'noisy hangouts where congregated "Lesbians" and "Fairies"—unfortunates who might be charitably condoned had they not been inclined to parade their peculiarities'.[28] What she records is precisely the shift that Stansell addresses in her conclusion when she remarks that 'Bohemia has always been susceptible to *embourgeoisement*...Initially devoted to criticizing, even opposing, bourgeois culture, bohemia turned out to be a reserve of inspiration for renovating middle-class life in the great shift from a nineteenth-century work-oriented ethic to a consumerist, leisured society.'[29] The surfaces, the superficiality suggested here is coterminous with the proliferation of objects, the material constitution of Beals's images of bohemia.

In all of Beals's image-making, the flash was a necessary tool; in her writing, radio broadcasts, and interviews, it went unmentioned.[30] It determined visibility, it doubtless caused a momentary blinding shock to the eyeball of both photographer and subject when it was discharged but, causing no recorded accidents in her hands, it had become, in a sense, invisible, ordinary. Moreover, flash's growing association with mass-produced images and with the illustrated press rapidly reduced the novelty value that attached to its use—at least to those who moved in circles where photography was a regular accompaniment to leisure activities or part of public life. Yet if the making manifest of everyday material objects is something found in representations of tenement rooms and bohemian studios alike, the power dynamics between observer and observed is hardly the same. In the case of the latter, the subjects seem cheerful participants, even performers; Beals is their social peer and, in some cases, their friend. Indeed, it's precisely *because* many of her Greenwich Village subjects seem so comfortable performing for the camera that the relationships between them often are less intriguing than the juxtaposition of heterogeneous objects in the rooms behind them.

The uneasy boundary line between exposure and intrusion was something troubling to a number of the Farm Security Administration photographers. The Farm Security Administration (FSA) was set up in 1935 as part of the New Deal. Originally called the Resettlement Administration, it was concerned with the improvement of the lives of sharecroppers, tenant farmers, and poor landowners. It carried out various forms of relief work, gave educational aid, and built camps for migrant workers. The FSA's photography programme, active 1935–44, under the direction of Roy Stryker, initially aimed to document the lives of the poor of rural America, but its remit widened, especially after Stryker adopted a wider policy of 'introducing America to Americans', with the additional goal of assembling a historical record of a changing country. As Miles Orvell reminds us, 'The FSA project was a crucial part of the pivotal turn of American twentieth-century culture—toward a central government's vision of re-shaping habits of individualism through agricultural engineering and technocratic control, through social intervention and the rational employment of philanthropic surveillance.'[31]

Many of these photographers—but, as we shall see, by no means all—used flash extensively. Looking through the huge FSA–Office of War Information photo file trying to identify images taken by flash is not an unchallenging exercise.[32] The labelling and indexing of the archive puts the emphasis on content and location, not on technical knowledge—indeed, there's no notation at all about the type of camera used, or about exposure, or, indeed, about whether flash was or was not employed. Only very rarely, as with the appearance of the off-camera flash in the top left-hand corner of John Collier's image of the Romero grandfather, in Figure 5.16, does the apparatus itself appear. We have to rely on first-hand, circumstantial information given in autobiographical testimony (including the invaluable series of interviews with former FSA photographers given to Richard Doud between 1963 and 1965); and then on the information provided by photographs themselves: the brilliant flare that's caught in a mirror or on a glass pane; a telltale bleaching of faces and garments in an image's foreground; or suspiciously bright reflections that bounce back from car chassis or polished furniture or cans of vegetables or bales of cotton. Sometimes, as with the Community Service Society archives, one can go hunting for possible images through exploring the results of a very generic search for 'interior', say, or 'store'. But even so, it's not always possible to be certain: an image might have been taken by the light of a couple of well-positioned kerosene lamps, say, or even by one of the portable photo flood lamps that were starting to come into use, although few photographers travelled with these in the field.

Alan Trachtenberg calls attention to the 'unresolved tension between "objectivity" and "subjectivity"' in the FSA work,[33] and this tension is apparent between the attitudes of photographers who very noticeably incorporated effects achieved through the use of flash in their work—like Russell Lee, John Collier, Marion Post Wolcott, John Vachon, and Jack Delano—and those who repudiated it, disliking both the aesthetically harsh contrasts that it achieved and, particularly, its invasive properties. Both Dorothea

Figure 5.16 John Collier Jr., 'Trampas, New Mexico. The Lopez children often call on their grandfather in the evenings to hear tales of the old days when Trampas was a thriving sheep town', January 1943. Library of Congress Prints and Photographs Division, Washington DC. LC-DIG-fsa-8d25856.

Lange and Ben Shahn spoke especially strongly about their distaste at using flash, and how it broke down the privacy and self-respect of those whom they photographed. Others occasionally used it, but recognized that its effects could be aesthetically disruptive. Walker Evans, for example, with his penchant for simplicity and for tranquil light in his interior scenes of the Burroughs' home that is visually and verbally described (as the 'Gudger' household) in *Let Us Now Praise Famous Men* (1941), seems to have reversed the 'small bright mirror in a wire stand' that Agee notes on the bedroom mantelshelf, so that the flash was not reflected back, as we see in Figure 5.17.[34]

Figure 5.17 Walker Evans, 'Fireplace in bedroom of Floyd Burroughs' cabin. Hale County, Alabama', summer 1936. Library of Congress Prints and Photographs Division, Washington DC. LC-USF342-T01-008136-A.

By the time that the FSA photographers went to work, the technology of flash photography had changed beyond all recognition from the clumsy apparatus used by Riis and, in the earlier parts of their careers, by Hine and Beals. The invention of the flashbulb at the end of the 1920s meant that photographers no longer had to wait for the air to clear—literally—before taking their next shot: all they had to do was change the bulb, being careful not to burn their fingers in the process. It was now much easier to carry around the light-making equipment, even if the Graflex Speed Graphic (invented 1898, and the camera most frequently provided by the FSA for their photographers) remained a heavy and cumbersome tool, weighing over six pounds, even as it had other advantages: photographers could see the image that they were shooting the right way up, not inverted in the viewfinder; they could choose between using plates or film, and the camera could be held either horizontally or vertically. For some, the mere mention of using flashbulbs was synonymous with enthusiastic information gathering. Arthur Rothstein wrote back to Roy Stryker in September 1939 that he was sitting with Duane B. Wilson of the local FSA office in Denver, 'ready to take off. We expect to cover the state thoroughly and have already left a trail of flash bulbs in Weld County.'[35]

The supply of flashbulbs, like film, was mailed off from the FSA headquarters in Washington DC to their travelling photographers, the uncertainties of the supply chain causing anxiety at both ends. Stryker telegrammed Wolcott on 18 May 1939 'WHY HAVEN'T YOU PICKED UP FLASHBULBS GENERAL DELIVERY ATLANTA? CAPTION AND RETURN IMMEDIATELY PRINTS MADE GREENSBORO GEORGIA TODAY.'[36] John Vachon, whose letters home to his wife Penny give a vivid sense of what it was like being on the road for months at a time, clearly monitored his stock quite closely, since the availability of flashbulbs determined how many indoor shots he would be able to take. On 29 October 1938 he was relatively profligate when shooting images of Mildred Irwin, a retired sex worker who was an entertainer in a saloon bar in North Platte, Nebraska (he was perhaps lucky to have any photographic equipment at all—a mishap with bags when changing buses en route meant that he was surprised, when opening up, to see a box of Kotex, several dresses, and some 'Underpretties' instead of bulbs, an exposure meter, film, and his Speed Graphic).[37] Then a week later in Omaha (his equipment having been retrieved), he calculated, when going to photograph an ornate bar, 'I'm going to use 3 flash bulbs in that place, which will leave me 4'.[38] However, his letter the next day recounts that one bulb was wasted when the shutter failed to trip, and the second two shots were taken in haste because he was being hassled by drunks.[39] A couple of years later, Vachon wrote from Benton Harbor, Michigan that 'My flash bulbs are flashing away to the pt, where I won't have many in Milwaukee'.[40]

The question of whether or not to use flash, however, fundamentally had very little to do with convenience. For a number of the photographers, their relationship to flash was an ethical one, illustrating perfectly the remark made by Susan Sontag, in the context of the FSA's work, that 'even when photographers are most concerned with mirroring reality, they are still haunted by tacit imperatives of taste and conscience'.[41] Dorothea Lange's best known images are taken outdoors, showing migratory workers from

Oklahoma on the road, say, or life in the tent cities of California. In part, this is due to the fact that she disliked intruding into people's private spaces at all—unless invited to do so—but also because she hated how flashbulbs disturbed her subjects. Linda Gordon, Lange's biographer, recounts Stryker recalling how Lange was once 'in a sharecropper's home; they had no light in there. Yet Russell [Lee] went in and flashed the damned thing, and got lousy pictures. They were lousy pictures, because the woman was sick.' Lange, he recollects, explained that she wouldn't intrude in this way: '"even though we could hardly see what was going on in there because I didn't want to spoil that...I wouldn't dare; it would have been an insult to that woman; it would have been unfair to her"'.[42]

Ben Shahn shared a similar stance. It was not that he completely objected to letting the camera intrude into people's lives: he did, after all, famously use a Leica with an angle finder, which allowed him to look in one direction, and shoot in another.[43] However, he repudiated the flash. 'When some of the people came in and began to use flash I thought it was immoral,' he said. 'You know, you come into a sharecropper's cabin and it's dark. But a flash destroyed that darkness. It is true that a flash would actually illuminate the comic papers that they used to paste on their walls'—and here one thinks of the redeployed newsprint that is made visible in his 'Interior of Negro tenant farmer's home' (Figure 5.18), taken in Little Rock, Arkansas in 1935, that not only throws together comic strips but also underscores the visual irony inherent in this decoration—images of successful jockeys, women in fur coats, and, indeed, white working-class poverty.

Yet, says Shahn, what made the biggest impact on him was not the barren quality of the papered walls, but something less tangible, less an easy matter of record.

> It was the darkness, the glistening of the eyes, the glistening of a brass ornament on top of a big bed, you know, a glass, a mirror that would catch light. I wanted very much to hold on to this, you see. Now, that's a matter of personal judgement about this thing whether you divulge everything or whether things are kept mysterious as they are viewed.[44]

Given the documentary imperative of the FSA, Shahn's position (even if in practical terms he went against it on occasion) can be seen as an act of resistance, both in aesthetic and humanitarian terms, refusing to tear away people's privacy through exposing them to a sudden flare of light. His other photographs of what look like the same boy, his brother, and their mother are taken outside their home, in bright sunlight. What caught his eye was not necessarily what eventually made it onto his favourite slow, fine-grained Perritzbromena film. There are very few interiors among Shahn's 1,609 FSA photographs, and even fewer depicting extreme poverty. Only one other image shows newspapers being used to paper a wall, in a strawberry grower's house in Hammond, Louisiana,[45] and here it is obviously the jokey surrealism of the juxtaposed images that caught his eye. Several other interior shots show the anxious, respectable, yet penny-pinching lifestyle of a farmhouse near Mechanicsburg, Ohio; and several more again make use of natural light to create still-life compositions. The 'Interior of

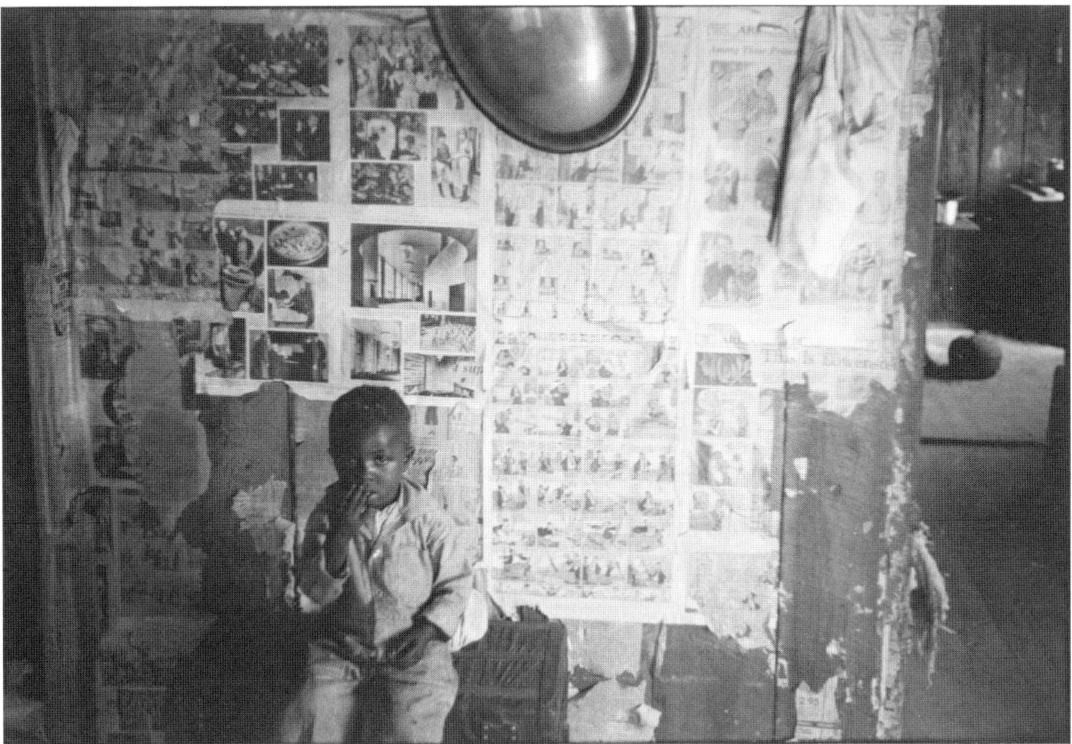

Figure 5.18 Ben Shahn, 'Interior of Negro tenant farmer's home. Little Rock, Arkansas', October 1935. Library of Congress Prints and Photographs Division, Washington DC. LC-DIG-fsa-8a16140.

Negro tenant farmer's home' is an anomaly, and not one with which Shahn felt personally comfortable.

In *The Disciplinary Frame* (2009), John Tagg makes a convincing case for how documentary photography may work in the service of a state—not as an instrument of blatant upbeat propaganda, as with Soviet photography (or, indeed, with a certain number of those FSA images that emphasized harvests and orchards and the good works carried out by the Resettlement Commission), but in the formation of a concerned, politically responsible subject, invested both in social reform and in a particular version of the liberal democratic state.[46] Shahn's decision to grant the people whom he photographs a measure of privacy is a different kind of gesture. It recognizes their pre-existing self-respect and need to be respected. If the credentials of any liberal subject are consolidated by his work, they are those of the photographer himself, not those of the viewer of an ultimately non-existent image.

But other documentary photographers of the 1930s knew that their use of flash was disruptive to certain individuals, and carried on regardless. This does not mean that they were necessarily unaffected by the impact caused by their lighting technology. John Vachon wrote home in touched wonderment in 1942 from Bismarck, North

Dakota, where he had spent the day taking photographs in tiny, rural schools set off Highway 10, deep in the snowy landscape:

Two little kids—boy and girl—out of class of about 10, in rural school this morning, began to *cry* when I shot off first flash bulb. And sobbed piteously for the next 20 minutes. Scared I guess. There is really something very remote and touching about these schools and farm kids. It all seems so far away from civilization and education I mean education in the frilly sense of your damn nursery schools. These are so human. The teachers are all timid little farm girls themselves. But the kids crying about the flashbulbs, that got me at the heart.[47]

No such compassionate compunction was shown by Margaret Bourke-White when looking back to her use of the flash in her role as a documentary photographer in the American South. Bourke-White did not work for Stryker's FSA office: according to Arthur Rothstein, Stryker greatly respected her work, but 'thought her style a little theatrical for an essay on southern tenant farmers'.[48] It was a style honed on advertising photography and on industrial subjects. In 1934 she made a turn towards human interest stories, photographing hardship in the Dust Bowl; in July and August 1936, and March 1937, she made two trips to the South with her writer collaborator Erskine Caldwell, and later in 1937, they published *You Have Seen Their Faces*—instantly controversial for its exposure and condemnation of, as Robert Snyder puts it, 'a variety of Southern shortcomings: illiteracy, disease, and malnutrition; racial prejudice; religious bigotry; a worn-out agricultural system based on sharecropping and peonage; and cultural sterility'.[49] These themes were accentuated by the tendency towards eye-catching angles and dramatic lighting that Bourke-White had used as a commercial photographer.

Bourke-White was quick to adopt the new technology that developed around the flashbulb. As the 'Notes on photographs' at the back of *You Have Seen Their Faces* tells us, she primarily used a 3 ¼ × 4 ¼ Linhof camera in taking the images for this book, with a synchronized flash, using several extensions so that she could engage more than one bulb at a time, and a remote control.[50] Vicki Goldberg explains the visual implications of her choices.

A single flash tends to flatten the subject, and Margaret always sought a sculptural representation, even speaking of photography as a kind of sculpture in which the photographer chips away the inessentials. Light thrown from several angles produces a more three-dimensional effect. Margaret was an early exponent of the 'master-slave' lighting arrangement, where several lights are set out, all responsive to the master and the shutter release.[51]

She and Caldwell worked very much as a team. Caldwell would engage people in conversation—his own Southern accent helped here—and Bourke-White would, to some extent, direct the visual aspects of the scenario. As she explained in the technical notes:

Flash bulbs provide the best means I know, under poor light conditions, of letting your subject talk away until just that expression which you want to capture crosses his face. Sometimes I would set up the camera in a corner of the room, sit some distance away from it with a remote control in my hand, and watch our people while Mr. Caldwell talked with them. It might be an hour before their faces or gestures gave us what we were trying to express, but the instant it occurred the scene was imprisoned on a sheet of film before they knew what had happened.[52]

But Bourke-White's autobiography is uncomfortably lacking in self-awareness when she considers the impact that flashlight might have made on her subjects. She describes the trip that she and Erskine Caldwell took to South Carolina. In Exminster,[53] they came upon the Pentecostal Holiness church at worship, with a small, all-white congregation in full religious fervour. Finding the door locked, they jumped through the open window, Bourke-White shooting away, and Caldwell replenishing her supply of flashbulbs from the stash he carried in his pockets. She credits the effects of technology with her success in obtaining these pictures: 'Certainly the backwoods congregation had never seen flashbulbs,' she remarks, in a somewhat patronizing tone. 'Under the sway of the sermon with its fearful warnings of hell to all who did not mend their sinful ways, these worshipers must have thought we were avenging angels come down in a blaze of light in direct response to their preacher's fiery words.'[54] How naïve to believe that a small if startling electrical explosion could be confused with divine illumination, is the unvoiced, but very obvious, subtext.

These images of women caught up in holy rapture are accompanied by captions that do nothing to dispel our impression of Bourke-White's retrospective condescension. If many of her photographs evoke compassion through a deliberate deployment of sentimentalism—a brave smile, a stoical gaze, a baby sucking a thin and worn mother's breast, a barefoot toddler rubbing his eye—an evocation that is consolidated through Caldwell's commentary, these church shots operate through something closer to ridicule. Figure 5.19 shows a woman standing between preacher and harmonium, stretching her hands high to heaven, and is labelled 'Mildred has on a new pair of shoes today',[55] two pictures of a woman happily dancing in a dark sprigged dress, with the congregation seemingly singing away in the background—seen in Figure 5.20—bear the caption 'Mrs. Peterson is growing thinner'.[56] Despite the women's respectable clothing, they are surely celebrating inward illumination, not demonstrating vanity. The worship of the Foot Washers, Shouters, and Holy Rollers is derided by Caldwell in the text as the product of the placebo offered up by preachers to those who live in poverty, promising plenitude in an afterlife rather than this one, a form of dishonesty that he rails against as strongly as he attacks the merciless policies of landlords. Yet he also pours scorn on congregations themselves, who, he writes, 'intoxicate themselves with a primitive form of religious frenzy that has its closest counterpart in alcoholic drunkenness'[57]—as though the folly of their deluded escapism makes them an unobjectionable target for being duped by flash's blinding light, and absolves them from subsequently being treated with respect.

A distinction needs to be drawn here between Bourke-White's attitude, and perhaps her practice, and that of the FSA photographers. Roy Stryker boasted that one of his greatest sources of pride was that he could 'think of no time that [any of them] ever showed any disrespect [for their subjects], ever looked down upon anyone, ever ridicule[d] . . . anything that looked funny'.[58] This claim needs to be taken with a grain of

Exminster, South Carolina
"Mildred has on a new pair of shoes today."

Figure 5.19 Margaret Bourke-White, 'Mildred has on a new pair of shoes today', Bourke-White and Erskine Caldwell, *You Have Seen Their Faces* (New York: Modern Age Books, 1937), [133]. Photo © Estate of Margaret Bourke-White/Licensed by VAGA, New York, NY.

salt, since certainly Marion Post Wolcott, among others, had no problem with mocking self-importance. Post Wolcott had an adept eye for composition when it came to making photographs that accentuated the difference between the privileged and the poor within the society of the late 1930s and early 1940s. This is made very evident in the formally dressed women (and one obscured man), with their picnic table and beach rugs, who are shown in 'Winter visitors picnic on running board of car on beach. Sarasota, Florida, 1941', or in the surely satiric tweedy 'Judge at the horse races. Warrenton, Virginia, 1941', heavily perched on a small and apparently nasty-tempered horse.[59]

Post Wolcott appreciated the control over light that the flash attachment gave her.[60] She made considerable use of the off-camera technique—that is, holding the flashgun in her hand, away from the camera, and angling it to determine the direction of light that she wanted. This allowed her to use flash for polemical ends, calling attention to particular aspects of living environments and to the attitudes of those who inhabit them. Like Riis and Beals, she employed it to put the grimy side of poverty on display,[61] as with her images of a pair of grubby children on an untidy bed in a house in Charleston West Virginia in 1938, the walls entirely papered with the collapsed cardboard packaging

Exminster, South Carolina
"Mrs. Peterson is growing thinner."

Figure 5.20 Margaret Bourke-White, 'Mrs. Peterson is growing thinner', Bourke-White and Erskine Caldwell, *You Have Seen Their Faces* (New York: Modern Age Books, 1937), [135]. Photo © Estate of Margaret Bourke-White/Licensed by VAGA, New York, NY.

of Post Toasties cornflakes cartons, as seen in Figure 5.21. Hanging from the ceiling like two little corpses are the flash-illuminated bodies of two large dolls, their ankles bound with white cord—the cleanest things in sight.[62] But while flash readily makes visible every last stain, smudge, and scratch, it can also work (especially if the negative is printed so as to bring out contrasts) to emphasize cleanliness, respectability, and the fact that considerable effort has gone into someone's appearance. Take, for example, the shots that she made of dancers in juke joints, as seen in Figure 5.22, and the glaring white of their best clothes; or the small African American boy's white shirt as he gathers up some canned beans from the plentifully stocked shelves of the family pantry in 'Child of an FSA Client: La Delta Project, Thomastown, Louisiana, 1940'.[63] The point made through the flash's bleaching properties is the same in each case: that spruceness and spotlessness are not incommensurate with a relatively low income.[64]

What is even more striking, however, is not the fact that she, like other documentary photographers of her time, uses flash to make visible the telling details of the textures of everyday life, but that on occasion, she also uses its highlighting powers to reinforce an individual's assumed superiority. Nowhere is this more apparent than in a sequence of images from 1940 of Mr Whitley in his General Store in Wendell, North Carolina.

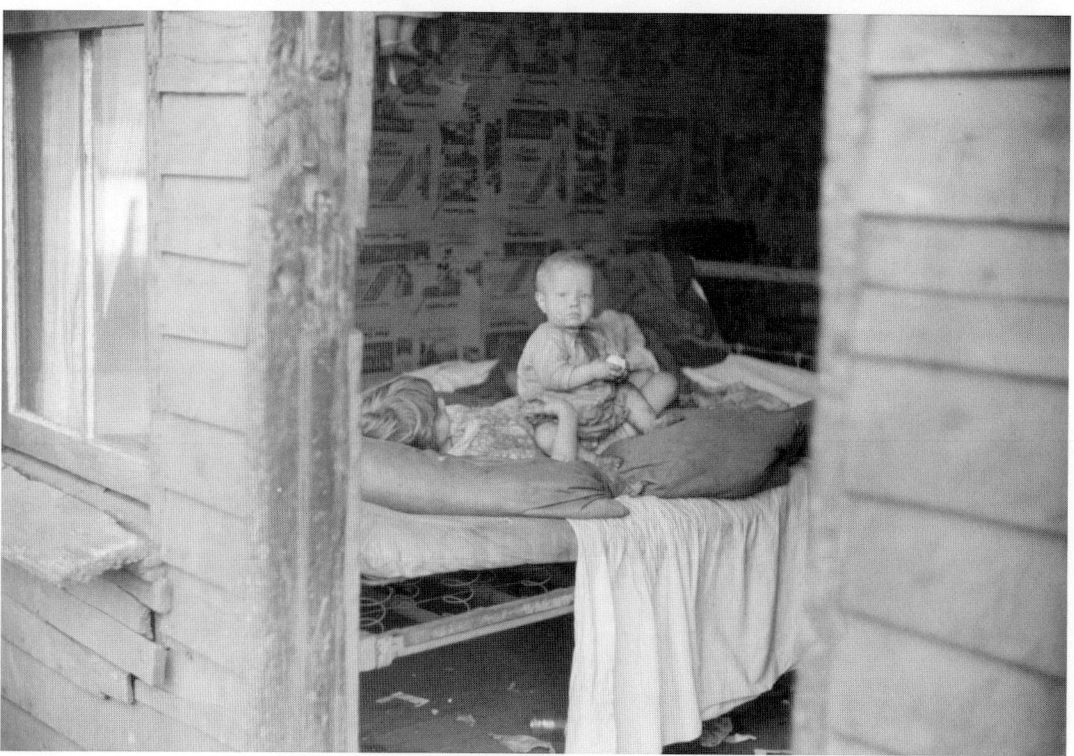

Figure 5.21 Marion Post Wolcott, 'Children in bedroom of their home. Mother has TB, father is on WPA (Works Progress Administration), Charleston, West Virginia', September 1938. Library of Congress Prints and Photographs Division, Washington DC. LC-DIG-fsa-8a38892.

Figure 5.22 Marion Post Wolcott, 'Negroes jitterbugging in a juke joint on Saturday afternoon. Clarksdale, Mississippi Delta', November 1939. Library of Congress Prints and Photographs Division, Washington DC. LC-DIG-fsa-8c10917.

Post Wolcott's captions fill in some biographical detail: he also owns a bank, cotton exchange, and real estate. He was the first man to settle in town; he cut down trees and pulled out stumps for "main" street. Or—as his tombstone, erected five years later, put it, 'Mr R. B. Whitley, Mr Rayford Bryant Whitley, Pioneer Citizen, Builder, Man of God, Friend to Man'.[65] Mr Whitley does not appear to have an opulent lifestyle—at least, that's the conclusion that one draws from his ill-fitting and slightly grubby suit (the flash brings out its stains beautifully well, as shown in Figure 5.23), and from the ratty armchair in which he sits—sits, in another photograph, despite the spare chair available beside him, whilst 'A Negro who is president of an industrial school' stands in front of him asking for a donation.[66] But in making the light bounce off his pale face and off the hand that holds a cigar to his lips, and off his silver dollar watch fob, and off the cane that he grasps with confidence, it's as though Post Wolcott shows him not so much as a set of shiny surfaces as basking in the inner glow of his internalized civic, racial, and masculine self-importance.

Figure 5.23 Marion Post Wolcott, 'R. B. Whitley, who was one of the first citizens of the town and is one of its leading citizens, owner of the general store, president of the bank, and owns a cotton mill nearby and a farm. He is a big land owner, owns Whitley-Davis farm and a cotton mill in Clayton. He said he cut down the trees and pulled the stumps out of the main street, and was the first man in that town of Wendell, Wake County, North Carolina', September 1939. Library of Congress Prints and Photographs Division, Washington DC. LC-DIG-fsa-8c30356.

Marion Post Wolcott was a knowing as well as a technically skilled photographer, using her flash to interpret the scene in front of her, and thereby to direct the viewer's response. Russell Lee was no less technically expert—as evidenced by his ability to freeze time and motion as a soda fountain server in Corpus Christi, Texas flips a ball of ice cream into a malted milkshake, the flashbulb brightly reflected behind him (shown in Figure 5.24). Despite Dorothea Lange's accusations about his insensitive style of shooting, those who reminisce about Lee time and again stress his affability, the trouble that he took to sit down with them and chat, and to tell them, directly, things like '"You're having a tough time here and the rest of the country needs to see pictures of it so they can appreciate what you're going through". Or he might say, "You've got old pictures here of your family and that's part of your history. Pictures of what you're going through will be part of our country's history."'[67] F. Jack Hurley wrote that

Figure 5.24 Russell Lee, 'Soda jerker flipping ice cream into malted milk shakes. Corpus Christi, Texas', February 1939. Library of Congress Prints and Photographs Division, Washington DC. LC-DIG-fsa-8b37302.

> when he would go into a room with a camera, though it might be a tenant farmer's room or a poor southern sharecropper's room and the occupant might not be worth $25 total, Russell Lee could look with great love and perhaps even envy at the photographs on the mantelpiece or at the cherished old radio—at whatever said to him, 'This is a home; somebody lives here; this is somebody's place.'[68]

Among all the FSA photographers, Lee was the one most strongly identified with the use of flash. John Szarkowski, the photo historian, curator, and critic sums up:

> I can think of no other photographer of the time, except newspaper photographers, who was so committed to the flash gun on the camera, which fired a blinding ton of light on the camera's line of sight into the dark. From a formal point of view one might describe Lee's most distinctive pictures of this time as those of a sweeter-tempered Weegee, working in the country.[69]

Lee's interiors, showing home and community life—most notably in the tiny settlement of Pie Town in New Mexico (as seen in Figures 5.25 and 5.26), where he and his wife Jean spent a couple of weeks in 1940[70]—have on occasion been accused of idealizing a presumed frontier mentality and way of existence—what Lee himself called, in relation to this location, 'that combination of self-reliance and community aid that you always hear about as having existed on the frontier'.[71] But in taking his photographs, Lee was

Figure 5.25 Russell Lee, 'Jack Whinery and his family, homesteaders, Pie Town, New Mexico', September 1940. Original in colour. Library of Congress Prints and Photographs Division, Washington DC. LC-DIG-fsac-1a34169.

representative less of the FSA mission to document some particular objective or issue than of its other form of activity, 'the wandering field trips that went on for months and months,' as John Collier put it, 'to gather what Stryker used to like to call the "feel of the land"'.[72] Certainly, Lee could produce some harrowing pictures of poverty—his images of Chicago, some of which appear in Richard Wright's *12 Million Black Voices*—will be discussed in Chapter 6. Yet even in these, he was always fascinated with the minute, individualizing details of everyday life, and relished the information that he could obtain with a sharp lens on a good camera, and direct flash.

> I became concerned with details in a place. I'd go into a bedroom and there might be something on a dresser that would interest me. It might be on a bedside table. Sometimes there would be mementos of their travels; sometimes photographs; sometimes objects of art. It could be a religious symbol or a portrait of their parents. The things people kept around them could tell you an awful lot about the antecedents of these people.[73]

Because of his fondness for collecting such detail, Roy Stryker called him 'a taxonomist with a camera'.[74]

Figure 5.26 Russell Lee, 'Mrs Caudill and her daughter in their dugout, Pie Town, New Mexico. The Caudills have one of the few radios in their neighborhood, and many farmers and their families visit the Caudills on winter nights to listen to music and news and play Forty Two,' June 1940. Library of Congress Prints and Photographs Division, Washington DC. LC-DIG-fsa-8a28253.

Stryker's phrase returns one to the value that the flash holds for recording the everyday. Flash allows photographs to be taken that can subsequently be studied at leisure, and employed to analyse social and cultural tendencies. We see this not just in Lee's interest in domestic living spaces, but also in the work of John Collier. Collier joined the FSA in 1941, relatively late in its existence, and his early work was proficient if unremarkable, photographing the Amish in Pennsylvania, a shipyard in Newport where a battleship was being built, and coal mines in Pittsburgh, where he worked underground, setting off as many as eight synchronized flashbulbs at once.[75] His most significant body of photographs, however, was taken when he returned to Northern New Mexico (his base since his family moved there in 1919) and photographed the Spanish-American people of Trampas and nearby Peñasco.

In spending a few chilly days with the Lopez family in January 1943, Collier exemplified—like Lee in Pie Town—how embedding oneself, however temporarily, in a community allows one access to individuals' daily activities and rituals. Although the people in some of the images, like the one supposedly showing storytelling by firelight, and like the women spinning, look somewhat stiff and staged, what stands out is the heterogeneous collection of decorative objects that are on display, and that the flash makes visible. They include family photographs—ones that look to be from the nineteenth as well as the twentieth century—and rosaries; newspaper clippings, religious prints and store advertisements; pictures of movie starlets and of La Santa Niña de Atocha. This is the iconography of a society in transition, positioned between a traditional way of life and homogenizing trends in national culture. This is sharply brought home by one of Collier's colour images of the altar in the Trampas church, shown in Figure 5.27,

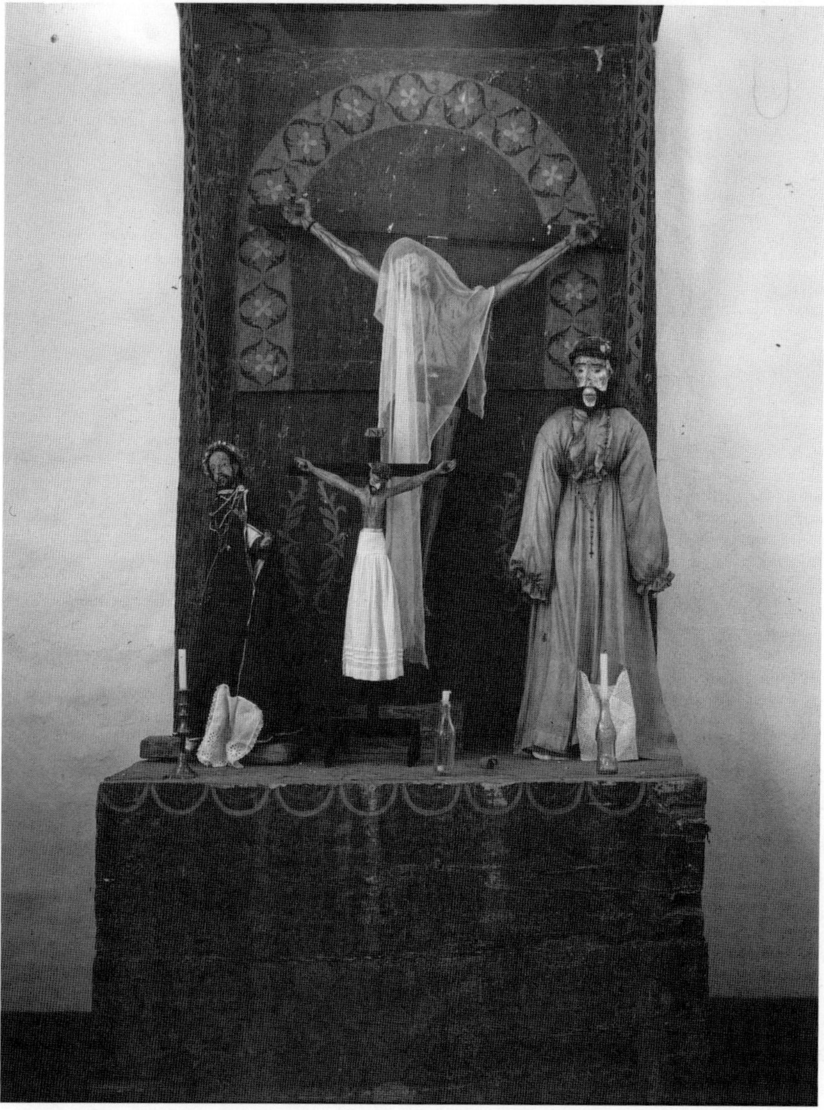

Figure 5.27 John Collier, Jr., 'Altar in the church, Trampas, New Mexico. The prevailing colors are grey and blue. A Coca-Cola bottle is used as a candle holder', spring 1943. Original in colour. Library of Congress Prints and Photographs Division Washington, DC. LC-DIG-fsac-1a34486.

complete with *bultos*—traditional carved wood devotional figures; traditional Spanish decorative painting; and (as Collier pointed out in his photo notes) two Coca Cola bottles being used as candle-holders.

Collier was to join the merchant marines, and, after the war, was again employed by Stryker, who by that time had gone to work for Standard Oil. Stryker sent him first to the Canadian Arctic, and then to photograph in South America, encouraging him to record a wide range of communities and community action. He and his wife Mary independently collaborated with an Ecuadorian anthropologist, Anibal Buitrón, documenting the indigenous community of Otavalo, Ecuador. The resulting publication, *The Awakening Valley* (1949), can be seen as a link between the FSA documentation produced by Collier and others, and Collier's more sustained theorizing of the use that photography might be to anthropologists.

Near the opening of *Visual Anthropology: Photography as Research Method* (1967; rev. edn. 1986), the book that John Collier wrote with his son Malcolm, the Colliers invoke the work done by Jacob Riis. 'Unwieldy cameras and powder flash recorded such scenes as the "Bandits' Roost", interiors of slum homes and schools. These early records of "urban anthropology" helped establish the first building codes and apartment regulations.'[76] But the Colliers had more specific claims to make for the value of flash photography than its capacity to provide material evidence that would spur people to reformist action. Photography in general, they say, 'allows one to see without fatigue; the last exposure is just as detailed as the first'.[77] One can capture one's valuable initial impressions with a camera; one can record 'materials and circumstances about which we have limited knowledge, and decode them as one's own knowledge deepens; the major problem is that one may quickly amass an unwieldy amount of experience'.[78] 'The memory of film replaces the notebook and ensures complete quotation under the most trying circumstance'[79]—and among trying circumstances, most certainly, may be counted dim lighting.

This is where flash comes in as an essential tool when it comes to making what the Colliers memorably term a 'cultural inventory'. Indeed, the chapter that bears this heading opens with a full-page image of a mirrored reflection of John Collier holding an off-camera flash to illuminate the contents of a dressing table in a New Mexican Pueblo home (shown in Figure 5.28).[80] 'A cultural inventory can go beyond the material items to become a detailing of human functions, the quality of life, and the nature of psychological well-being', the Colliers tell us on the opposite page. 'The photographic inventory can record not only the range of artifacts in a home but also their relationship to each other, the style of their placement in space'—groupings that they later term 'proxemic variables'—'all the aspects that define and express the way in which people use and order their space and possessions'.[81] Thus the dressing-table top has snapshots that seem to be of a Pueblo feast day tucked into the mirror's frame, and formal graduation photographs in separate frames below; baby photographs behind make-up; a feather in a jar next to an alarm clock and a business card; a toy plastic horse and a carved stone fetish. 'Such information', as the Colliers put it, like the images of the Lopez family interiors in Trampas, 'not only provides insight into the present character of people's lives but can also describe acculturation and track cultural continuity and change.'[82]

Figure 5.28 John Collier Jr., 'Bureau with Portraits and Mementos (and self portrait), New Mexico', *c.*1958. Gelatin silver print; 7 1/16 × 7 1/8 in. (17.94 × 18.1 cm) San Francisco Museum of Modern Art, Gift of Mary Collier in memory of John Collier, Jr. © Mary E. T. Collier Estate. Courtesy San Francisco Museum of Modern Art: photograph Don Ross.

As flash technology became an unsensational part of a photographer's equipment, it retained the power to seize the existence of things at one particular moment—not just in the sense that any photograph does, but also through a moment of illumination that rendered things temporarily, and artificially, visible. Their appearance, in place, in proximity to one another, and sometimes to the people who used them or had put them there, endured in the eventual images. In these images, we see things that most likely were never observed as clearly by those who lived alongside them every day, either because they lived in literal darkness or dim light, or because of a natural tendency to become habituated to one's environment—just as, for the anthropologist in the field, the response of even the most observant anthropologist 'may deaden through monotony'.[83] This form of exposure happens twice over. First, the revelation that is momentarily the property of everyone who happens to be present in an interior—something referred to by Louise Rosskam when she remarked on 'the stark quality of Russell Lee's photographs, where he stuck a flashbulb on the camera and went vroom, you know. And all of a sudden a little shack opened up with every little piece of grime on the wall, radio cords mixed up with the electrical cords, and what-not, was absolutely a complete blank, before he put it down, and everybody could see it'[84]—and then with the capture of these suddenly illuminated details on film. These details, in turn, can deepen our knowledge of a material environment and of the lives of those who live in it.

Much of the fascination of early flash photographs comes precisely from this privileged exposure. Whether designed to stimulate social and political conscience and intervention, to sate curiosity, or to suggest to a tourist that a hidden haunt is being revealed to them, flash, as well as being responsible for a violent interruption, allowed for the representation and preservation of the ordinary: of what Jacques Rancière, in *Aisthesis*, beautifully terms 'the apprehension of the inexhaustible historicity found at every street corner, in every skin fold, and at every moment of time'.[85] Flash, that is to say, is associated not just with a rapid explosion of light, a momentary interruption, but also with enabling a form of attentive looking: a form of looking that we are invited to turn upon everyday surroundings.

CHAPTER SIX

Light-Skinned

RALPH ELLISON was a photographer as well as a novelist; someone with a strong and interrogative interest in the visual.[1] His novel *Invisible Man* is filled with images of light, of electricity, of what the invisible man himself calls the 'darkness of lightness'.[2] 'Without light I am not only invisible, but formless as well', the narrator famously asserts.[3] Yet in his introduction to the thirtieth anniversary edition of the novel in 1982, Ellison counters the assertion—common, he says, among pseudoscientific sociologists in the early 1950s—that African Americans experienced 'high visibility'.[4] Or rather, he argues that such '"high visibility" actually rendered them *un*-visible—whether at high noon in Macy's window or illuminated by flaming torches and flashbulbs while undergoing the ritual sacrifice that was dedicated to the ideal of white supremacy'.[5]

Ellison's overall point is that to be frequently *represented* is not necessarily to be *seen*—at least, not seen in terms that go beyond renewing a white viewer's well-entrenched preconceptions. As he puts it on the opening page of the novel, the invisibility to which he refers results not from the workings of the physical eye, but from people's—white people's—'*inner* eyes, those eyes with which they look through their physical eyes upon reality'—eyes of assumptions, white privilege, prejudice, 'moral blindness'.[6] In that retrospective introduction, Ellison explicitly couples flash photography itself with aggression that stemmed from the workings of these inner eyes. Employed to record the terrible violence of lynching, murderous light erupted into the darkness in the form of Ku Klux Klan torches, with the sudden, sharp intrusion of flash then documenting the aftermath. In the final chapter of *Invisible Man*, set during the 1943 disturbances that came to be known as the Harlem Riots—events themselves that were made visible through the news media thanks to the illumination of flash[7]—the narrator, moving through the wrecked streets with their looted stores and shattered store fronts, is stopped short by a shocking sight:

> Ahead of me the body hung, white, naked, and horribly feminine from a lamppost. I felt myself spin around with horror and it was as though I had turned some nightmarish somersault. I whirled, still moving by reflex, back-tracking and stopped and now there was another and another, seven—all hanging before a gutted storefront. I stumbled, hearing the cracking of bones underfoot and saw a physician's skeleton shattered on the street, the skull rolling away from the backbone, as I steadied long enough to notice the unnatural stiffness of those hanging above me. They were mannequins—'Dummies!' I said aloud.[8]

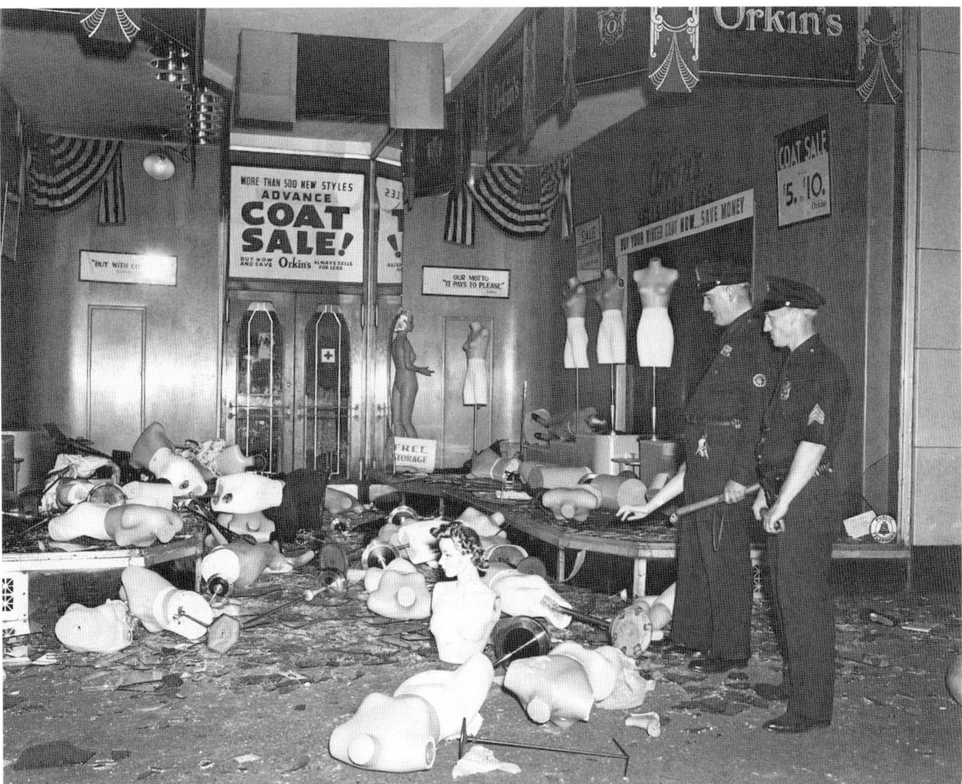

Figure 6.1 Weegee (Arthur Fellig), 'Harlem Riot of 1943'. © New York Daily News Archive / Getty Images.

These are the uncanny figures caught—as we see in Figure 6.1—by the news photographer Weegee in several of his photographs of the riots.

Ellison, as well as understanding the surreal visual power of mannequins as demonstrated in the photography of Henri Cartier-Bresson and Lisette Model, also knew all too well what these discarded simulacra of human torsos and limbs brought instantly to mind.[9] As Ken Gonzales-Day has described it, flash powder, and later flashbulbs, were instrumental to the production of lynching's imagery, rendering this illumination 'less a tool than a weapon which symbolically strips its victim of all humanity'.[10] These were the photographs, like Figure 6.2, that showed both the victims of lynchings—the flash often, and ironically, bleaching them—and those who gazed on their hanging bodies. They were taken from the end of Reconstruction to 1960, and are mostly of African American men in the Deep South (although as Gonzales-Day shows, Latinos, Native Americans, and Asian Americans were also summarily executed in this way). It is no coincidence that, as Amy Louise Wood has pointed out, there was an upturn in lynching photographs when amateur photography became easier, and more popular, during the 1890s,[11] but perhaps above all, these images circulated as

Figure 6.2 Lawrence Beitler, 'The lynching of African Americans, Thomas Shipp and Abram Smith, Marion, Indiana, 1930'. © World History Archive/age fotostock.

postcards, functioned as souvenirs, were stuck in family albums. Luc Sante writes that these lynchings were 'depicted in much the same way as carnivals and train derailments'—in other words, falling somewhere between entertainment and rubbernecking curiosity: he also, and convincingly, claims that when they circulated in postcard form, the images say more about the mindset of the sender than that of the photographer.[12] At the same time, however, that these images were certainly marketed openly—and were meant, as Dora Apel puts it, 'not only to consolidate white supremacist solidarity across class lines at a time when the gap between rich and poor whites was huge, but also to reserve a position of privilege and power for the white patriarchal elite'[13]—they circulated in a more polemical way, calling attention to the brutality of these summary executions.[14]

In lynching photographs, the use of flash becomes a chilling literalization of the trope of the white photographer 'throwing light' on the dark subject.[15] On the one hand flash could fairly be regarded as a valuable tool for recording and disseminating information about black lives. This is fully exemplified in the photographs that Edwin

Rosskam selected from the Farm Security Administration (FSA) files to illustrate Richard White's 1941 *12 Million Black Voices*, with text and images foregrounding

> those materials of Negro life identified with the countless black millions who made up the bulk of the slave population during the seventeenth, eighteenth, and nineteenth centuries; those teeming black millions who endured the physical and spiritual ravages of serfdom; those legions of nameless blacks who felt the shock and hope of sudden emancipation; those terrified black folk who withstood the brutal wrath of the Ku Klux Klan, and who fled the cotton and tobacco plantations to seek refuge in northern and southern cities coincident with the decline of the cotton culture of the Old South.[16]

The photographs that were chosen included a number that flash made possible: a child asleep in a shabby room in rural Maryland, looking small and vulnerable, and a range of Chicago interiors taken by Russell Lee, who, together with Rosskam, travelled up to the Windy City especially to shoot images for this publication. On the other hand, flash has been, as we have seen, a technology tainted not just by some of its uses, but often by the rhetoric surrounding it and aspects of its contemporary practice—rhetoric that often assumed an equation between light and revelation, and between darkness—blackness—and dirt, poverty, the abject.[17]

This chapter explores how racial difference impacts the history of flash photography—from the point of view of the subject, the photographer, and the viewer of the image. Although it concentrates on photography of, and by, African Americans in the middle of the twentieth century, it considers more broadly the aesthetic issues posed by the particular form of illumination that flashlight brings to black skins—a topic that will be taken up again in Chapter 10. Flash was, of course, used by black photographers from the beginning. It was employed by early pioneers such as the Goodridge brothers in Saginaw, MI;[18] and by studio photographers seeking likenesses for commercial and 'scientific' ends—including those people who took the striking images that appear in the albums that W. E. B. Du Bois prepared for the 1900 Paris Exposition.[19] Among these was Thomas E. Askew, Atlanta's first African American photographer, who was particularly skilled in his manipulation of artificial light. But I take up this history as it relates to the period just before Ellison published *Invisible Man*, and through three separate paths: first, the pictures published in a 1937–9 African American photo news periodical called, appropriately, *Flash!*; second, through documentary images made by Gordon Parks—another FSA photographer—a number of which were included in his 1947 how-to book simply entitled *Flash Photography*; and finally, some remarks by Roy DeCarava, a photographer who explicitly rejected the use of flash.

Flash! was published in Washington DC between June 1937 and August 1939, one of a number of short-lived periodicals aimed at a black readership that appeared between the wars, and one of the earliest black 'newspicture' magazines.[20] It made strong claims for its intentions. As it moved into 1938, the editorial 'New Year Forecast' prophesied that it would

> gain an undisputed position of establishment in the forefront of American magazine endeavor, having obtained the perspective of today's leading publishers, the insight of men and women of long and intelligent experience, the thorough organization that comes through cooperative endeavor in association with the best publications, and a fascination that is incomparable.
>
> No longer an experiment, it will represent the outstanding dynamic and satisfying weekly presentation of the significant drama of American life, with colored men and women in the title roles.

Flash! billed itself as 'A JOURNAL OF NEGRO AFFAIRS—carrying information in word and picture to all parts of the world, about the cosmopolitan Negro life in such centers as the Nation's Capital, New York and Chicago, and of the Negro metropolitan life in all the finer cities of the Western Hemisphere, including, of course, your own'; 'A NEWSPICTURE MAGAZINE—which publishes every luminary who is definitely left out of other secular publications because of reasons well known'; 'AN ART SURVEY... depicting for your edification Negro musical stars and composers of the first magnitude'; 'A SCIENTIFIC GUIDE—explaining the Negro's attack on the frontiers of the tremendous scientific fields of engineering, aviation, biochemistry, agriculture and the healing arts'; 'A MOTION PICTURE GUIDE—setting forth the leading presentations of the cinema before they are first run'; and 'A MAGAZINE OF SPORT PAR EXCELLENCE'. In short—and the editorial language exploits to the full the visual metaphor established in its title—'FLASH will herald the brilliance of Negro American life, against a back ground [*sic*] of darkness and sophisticated blues'.[21] It aimed at achieving these editorial aspirations 'by securing the assistance of a national advisory board of black educators, business men and women, military personnel, politicians, and entertainers'.[22] However, as Daniel points out, its timing was unfortunate—even if it claimed a circulation of 58,000. Despite the attraction of a magazine with so many images, it could not compete with what weekly papers published in New York, Chicago, and Pittsburgh were offering by way of editorial comment at a time when the country was gearing up for war, including their extended and animated discussion about the roles that would be played by black youth. At least initially, *Flash!* appeared to be more concerned with personalities than with political substance.

Flash! contained within its own pages self-advertisements that called attention to the editorial conviction that photography illuminates. In conceptualizing a 'flash' the magazine borrowed from the imagery of lightning's searing electric power—using its zigzag in the same way that early advertisements for *blitzlichtpulver* borrowed from this visual register. It advertised itself both through images that showed the sudden illumination of a photographic flashbulb (itself a signifier of modernity in the 1930s) and, as we see in Figure 6.3, through invoking steadier strong beams that emanated from the most up-to-date technology and machines. The editorial material couldn't

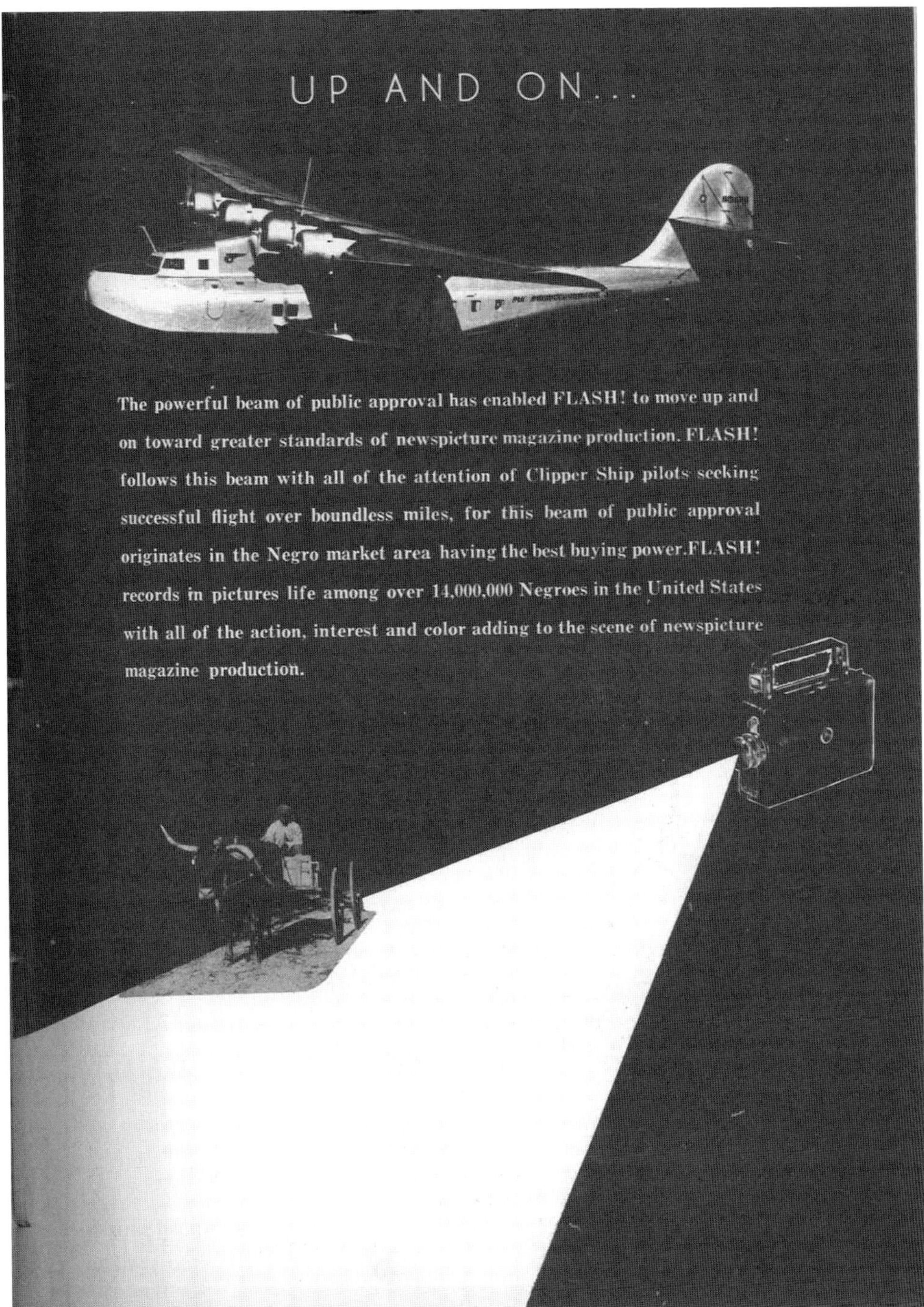

Figure 6.3 Advertisement for *Flash! Flash! Weekly Newspicture Magazine* (19 July 1937), 3.

resist playing on other associations, too, praising, for example, the notable athlete 'Jesse Owens, Ohio flash, who stood the country on its collective ear with his blinding speed and lengthy leaps at the Berlin games'.[23] It reported on occasions where flash made its presence surprisingly felt—incidentally reminding one that the reign of flash powder hadn't yet entirely ceded to the flashbulb. We read how the well-known tenor

> Roland Hayes was well received by Wash's top drawer set in his recital last Friday night…The artist's repertoire included both foreign and American offerings, but the selection, 'Dawn' with words by Paul Lawrence Dunbar, and music by Coleridge Taylor was the best received…Hayes showed exceptional control when he calmed the audience when the curtain burst into flames from the sparks of a flash light camera…However, Percival Parham, accompanist for Hayes, caused subdued laughter, when the somewhat feminine pianist placed his hands upon his hips, and assumed an air of remonstrance when the vigilant stage fireman spilled extinguisher fluid on his music.[24]

Sadly, no image was published of this particular moment of flash-induced high camp, although that number of *Flash!* included a decorous image from the Scurlock studio of patrons entering the auditorium. But in general, the magazine's eclectic content was copiously illustrated by photographs. Very many of these were by African Americans: Charles 'Teenie' Harris (shown in Figure 6.4); Larry Grymes; Ralph Vaughn; Morgan and Marvin Smith, with their striking pictures of New York swing musicians;[25] Robert Scurlock—one of the Scurlock studio family, who had been the premier chroniclers of DC middle-class black society and culture since 1911;[26] Bill Howard; Robert McNeill.[27] Nicole Fleetwood, in her chapter on 'Teenie' Harris in *Troubling Vision*, highlights his typicality as a 'picture-taking man', one who ceaselessly documented local everyday happenings within his community.[28] Fleetwood follows Deborah Willis's description of his work as showing 'the normalcy of black life'; as she puts it, a 'counterpoint to narratives of invisibility or deviant hypervisibility that circulated in mainstream media'.[29] As bell hooks has observed in more general terms, 'The camera was the central instrument by which blacks could disprove representations of us created by white folks'[30]—an observation that beautifully fits, for example, the formal portrait, shown in Figure 6.5, of Roland Hayes with his wife Alzada and daughter Afrika that had appeared in the well-established Baltimore newspaper, the *Afro-American*, the previous year, heralded 'FLASH!!! HERE IS THE FIRST PHOTO OF MR AND MRS ROLAND HAYES'.[31] The idea of normalcy may be usefully extended to much of the social life depicted in *Flash!*, even if—or maybe because—many of the images, showing dances and sororities, dinners and weddings, graduations and bridge clubs, recorded the socially privileged life of a very particular segment of black society. At the same time, as press photographer Vera Jackson (based in Los Angeles) recalled, there was an air of defiance to this material display, too:

> we had just come out of the hard luck times of the 1930s. In order to forget these bad times and to look forward to the promise of prosperity and jobs and other opportunities, there was a showiness on the part of most of us. We were most impressed with elegance, richness, or opulence in our homes, and our dress and all activities which we pursued.[32]

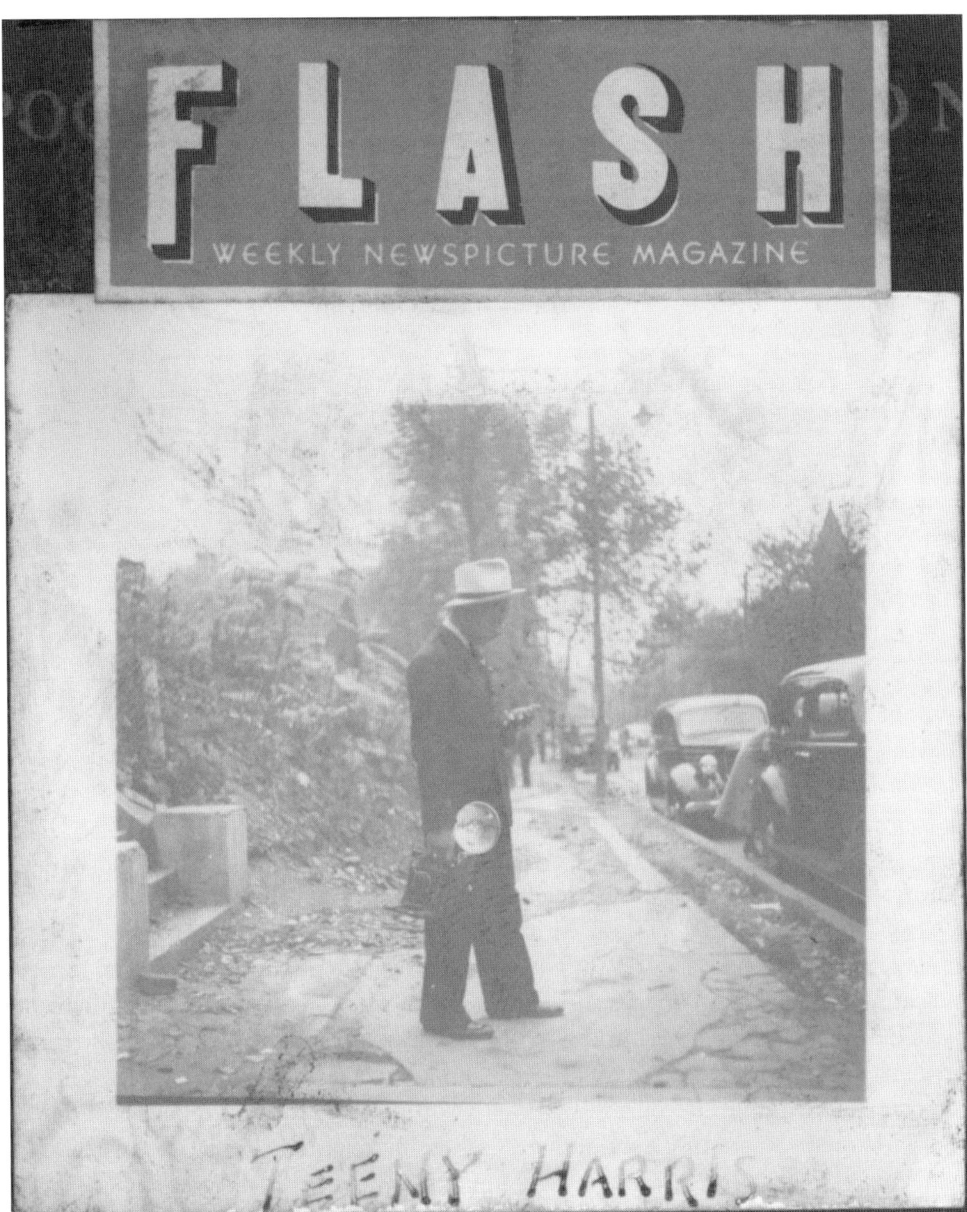

Figure 6.4 Unknown American, 'Copy of *Flash Magazine* headline with photograph of photographer Charles "Teenie" Harris holding camera and standing on sidewalk', *c.*1938–9. Gelatin silver print. H: 4 in. × W: 4 in (10.16 × 10.16 cm). Carnegie Museum of Art, Pittsburgh: Gift of the Estate of Charles 'Teenie' Harris, 1996.90.37 © Carnegie Museum of Art, Charles 'Teenie' Harris Archive.

Figure 6.5 Unknown photographer, 'Roland Hayes seated on sofa with wife Helen Alzada Mann and daughter, Afrika', mid-1930s, Courtesy of the E. Azalia Hackley Collection of African Americans in the Performing Arts, Detroit Public Library, Detroit Public Library.

Flash!'s editorial material drew attention to its role as a publication of social record, indicating that its many images were primarily means to an end, throwing light on black daily life, special events, and notables. Flash was responsible for very particular aesthetic effects that served the magazine's policy of putting a very positive spin on African American life and culture. As well as offering general illumination of diners and partygoers, a carefully used camera flash helped lighten skin tone considerably, achieving a similar effect to the skin-lightening that Harris, and others, also performed in the darkroom. Colour film notoriously had its fidelity predicated on the norm of pink Anglo skin[33]—but a different norm pertained in these images. For example, J. W. Charleston's photographs (shown in Figure 6.6) illustrating 'Welfare Head at Mu-So-Lit Club' were developed so as to ensure that all the black men were clearly visible, leaving the white people present *over*exposed. The emphasis is reinforced by the caption that uses bold typeface to emphasize the main point of human interest.[34] These darkroom choices are apparent even in advertisements, as in the publicity for Bell Clothes, showing scat singer and band leader Cab Calloway inspecting the merchandise, the blandly white shop attendant only an imperceptible tinge darker in his skin colour than

Welfare Head At Mu-So-Lit Club

Photos by J. W. Charleston

Above, THE CANDID CAMERA CAUGHT part of the audience hearing Elwood Street, welfare director, as he made a stirring address at the Mu-So-Lit Club on Friday night.

Above, J. FLIPPER DERRICOTTE LOOKS ON with a smile as Dr. Robert B. Pearson, president of the Mu-So-Lit Club, greets Mr. Street following his address touching on civic problems.

Flash! Five

Figure 6.6 J. W. Charleston, 'Welfare Head at Mu-So-Lit Club', *Flash! Weekly Newspicture Magazine* (20 March 1937), 5.

Calloway's gleaming shirt collar, whilst the already relatively light-skinned Calloway is flattered through the way the illumination sculpts and makes visible his handsome face. *Flash!* magazine turned the bleaching properties of flash photography to the advantage of its own readership.[35]

The deliberately upbeat emphasis adopted by *Flash!* during its first year was not uniformly welcomed. It caused at least one letter writer, Mrs Etheline W. Stewart, from Atlanta, to complain that she was 'keenly disappointed in FLASH's failure to project itself into the many social imperfections which make race problems for the Negro in Washington, D.C., and throughout the Nation…as long as lynching, tenant farming conditions and segregation exist to keep the colored race from being treated as human beings'. The editorial prose bristled in a self-righteous manner, proclaiming that 'FLASH! is fully aware of the conditions spoken of in Mrs. Stewart's letter. By virtue of its editorial policy, FLASH! will fight no causes'—even if it would continue to 'picturize and encourage, by means of photographs, those who carry on for the betterment of conditions for all peoples in America'.[36] This editorial policy, designedly setting itself against any tendency to present African Americans as victims or underdogs, was very similar to the upbeat stance that the far longer-lived *Ebony* took when it launched in November 1945, immediately after the war, proclaiming that it would 'try to mirror the happier side of Negro life' and 'present a true, accurate balanced picture of how the colored American fares'.[37] *Ebony* was far more ready than its news-picture predecessor *Life* (which first appeared in its photo-heavy incarnation in November 1936, and was in many respects a model for *Ebony*) to publish 'the positive, everyday achievements (of Negroes) from Hollywood to Harlem . . . about which not enough is said'.[38] Yet *Ebony*'s founding, as Daniel puts it, established an unstated magazine publishing assumption—until O?—'that the United States was, indeed, a two-society nation. There was a white life and there was a black life. The two seldom met in self-image.'[39] Nonetheless, what was so significant about many of the images that it—like *Flash!*—carried was this emphasis on ordinary black life. This ensured that flash photography did not just render African American subjects visible because of their position as entertainers or sportsmen or because they belonged to the suffering poor.[40] As Sara Blair has written,

> The New Deal camera had (however inadvertently) distorted and reified the realities of black experience in America; in its definitive images of raggedly clothed sharecroppers, shanty-dwellers, and evicted tenant farmers, it crated a new iconography of the African-American as atavistic survivor, unfit for the rigors and opportunities of the modernity it celebrated. That very fact made photography irresistible to black writers as a mode of both counter-protest and introspection.[41]

Flash! certainly celebrated swing musicians, orchestra players, and black aviators, yet alongside them flash photography was used to record such diverse scenes of ordinariness as children in preschool in Atlanta, first aid practice among boy scouts, and an Internal Revenue Service (IRS) stenographer named Etta Benson at work, as well as the birthday parties, the images of university life at Howard or Lincoln, the debutantes and the glitzy nightclubs. By contrast, as Mary Alice Sentman's detailed analysis has shown, with the exception of the first year in *Life*'s history, 'coverage of black everyday life was markedly absent' in the pages of this better-known news-picture magazine.[42]

Yet although *Flash!* might have started by tapping into its readership's aspirational inclinations and by celebrating its achievements, it increasingly, and despite its early disavowals (and contrary to Daniel's analysis), became a publication with a strong social conscience. It balanced its leisure and entertainment features with a commitment to black politics that stretched far beyond the United States. By August 1937, for example, it was carrying a piece on 'Liberia—The Land Hitler and Poland Would Annex', and in February 1938 it published shockingly graphic images of the war in Ethiopia. Internally, its news-picture article 'Bronx Slave Market', published in February 1938, called attention to the conditions of domestic workers in New York, under a deliberately blunt title.[43] Nor could all the dramatic shows that it reported upon be categorized as escapist entertainment. *Flash!* was particularly diligent in commenting on productions mounted by the Federal Theater Project—the Works Progress Administration (WPA) initiative that served to bring theatre to many people who might not otherwise experience it, and that focused on issues of grave social concern.[44] These included *Bassa Moona* ('An Original African Dance Drama' at New York's Lafayette Theater), Theodore Browne's *Natural Man* (in Seattle, where Browne led the Seattle Negro Unit of the FTP), Gus Smith in *Turpentine* ('a dramatic exposure of the harrowing conditions existing in Florida turpentine camps'),[45] and—staged in New York and ten other cities (and adapted to the specifics of housing problems in each)—Arthur

Arent's *One Third of a Nation* (1938). All of the reporting on these plays was accompanied by flash photographs taken within the theatre, and, as we see in Figure 6.7, in the case of *One Third of a Nation*, also by documentary photographs that had been made whilst researching this exposé of tenement housing in New York, using flash photography to throw light on darkness very much in the tradition of Jacob Riis. Seen in the pages of *Flash!*, these images of overcrowded rooms and filthy kitchens—the flashlight bouncing back off a colander and chipped crockery, showing heaps of trash and unsanitary plumbing—certainly served to reinforce the evils of profiteering and heartless landlords, the failure of the 1937 Housing Act, and the powerlessness of the ordinary person. Moreover, in showing that living in shocking poverty was not just a problem faced by black people, these images served to dilute the form of spectatorship associated with representing African American tenement life, illustrating how class and racial interests may offer points of intersection.

In offering commentary on living conditions and relative incomes in the US, *Flash!*'s editorial team on occasion deliberately manipulated the photographic medium, as when collaging an image of a low-income African American family (again, with flashlight reflecting back from their heavily used plates and pots and mugs) onto 'a background fashioned for the $10,000-a-year group'—complete with gleaming candle holders on the mantelpiece, drapes, a chaise longue, and fresh flowers—in order to illustrate the point that 'ENVIRONMENT DETERMINES WHAT A CHILD WILL BE' (see Figure 6.8). Although out of preference they employed black photographers, they made frequent use of FSA materials if these provided relevant visual evidence or interest, showing readers, say, Alfred Murphy, the 105-year-old former slave who was a pupil in a WPA adult literacy class, or Arthur Rothstein's FSA shots of Gee's Bend, Alabama. These Rothstein images of impoverished interiors (and their rather uneasy-seeming occupants), including the one shown in Figure 6.9, accompanied an article on the menace of the sharecropping system. Nor, in the end, did *Flash!* ignore other forms of racial prejudice and profiling, carrying a full-page article on the 'Scottsboro boys', nine young men who were falsely accused and imprisoned on a trumped-up rape charge, and reporting on the 2,000-strong protest in DC in August 1938 that demanded—unsuccessfully, of course—the removal of the 'D.C. higher-ups who condone the action of the killer cops who added their 59th victim when they shot down Wallace McKnight' on the suspicion of committing a misdemeanour. Yet this was a very watered-down coverage of race relations at the time. One has only to compare the news carried by *Flash!* with, for example, that to be found in the *Afro-American* to recognize its highly selective treatment of widespread police brutality and miscarriages of justice.

All the same—despite this selectivity, despite its initial impetus towards the uplifting—*Flash!* printed lynching photographs. To do so was to reverse the message that these images may originally have carried.[46] Shawn Michelle Smith has hypothesized about the well-known picture of Rubin Stacy's hanging body (unknown photographer, 19 July 1935) that 'the girls (and by proxy later viewers) are schooled in the threat of black men as well as the power of white men'.[47] To encounter this image in the pages

ONE THIRD OF A NATION

By A. RIVERO

UNSANITARY UTENSILS ARE A CONSTANT MENACE TO LIFE.

ONE THIRD OF A NATION. a fast moving drama written by Arthur Arent from material collected by a trained staff of research workers, and directed by Lem Ward, exposes the problem of slum clearance. "The living newspaper" technique, created by the WPA Federal Theatre and used in such successful productions as, "Injunction Granted" and "Power," is employed in ONE THIRD OF A NATION. The process may be described as a newspaper on the stage with living characters enacting news stories, features and editorials.

OVER SEVENTY-FIVE THESPIANS make up the cast of this realistic reproduction of New York's slum housing since the presentation of the Trinity Church grant, through the historical cholorea epidemic, to the present program of slum clearance. Local and national housing officials call it 'a most valuable document"—drama critics acclaim it an outstanding production. Judging from the advance ticket sale ONE THIRD OF A NATION is due for a long run.

THE ABOVE SCENE IS A REPLICA OF ANY UNDERPRIVILEGED COMMUNITY.

A DESPERATE EFFORT TO KEEP WARM AND GET LIGHT OFTEN RESULTS IN FIRE.

ADD BATES AND KERMIT AUGUSTINE IN A SCENE SHOWING SLEEPING CONDITIONS.

Flash! Twenty-one

Figure 6.7 Photographs made whilst researching the play *One Third of a Nation*, and set designs for the production (Arthur Arent, with research by members of the editorial staff of the Federal Theatre Project): *Flash! Weekly Newspicture Magazine* (7 March 1938), 20.

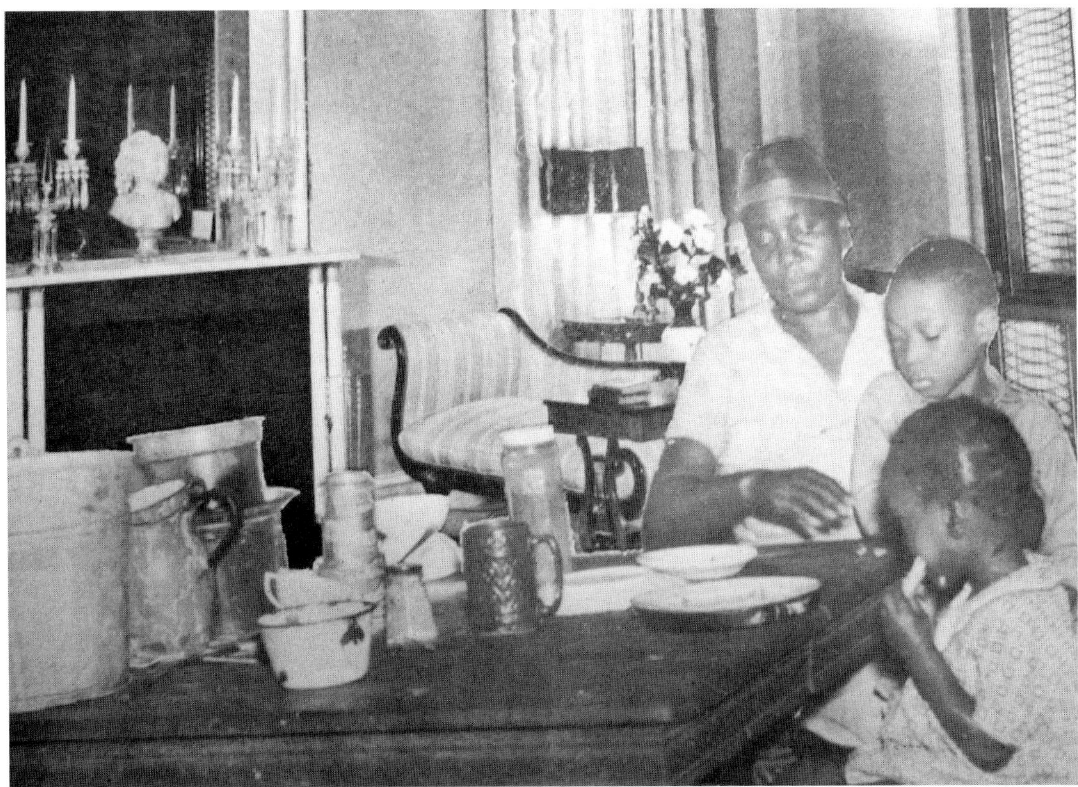

Figure 6.8 Collaged photographs, 'Environment Determines What a Child Will Be', *Flash! Weekly Newspicture Magazine* (24 January 1938), 7.

of *Flash!* is to see the expressions on these white girls' faces, in all their bland curiosity and self-righteous smiles, shockingly illuminated. If for Ralph Ellison, envisaging life as it might be seen from a white perspective, black visibility within predominantly white American society could be compared to 'flies in the milk',[48] the presence in the pages of *Flash!* of these white spectators at a lynching produces a similarly visual and visceral reaction.

Calling attention to gloating and ghoulish white spectatorship is the gesture performed even more strongly—thanks to the ability, via Photoshop, to eliminate the hanging figures—by the inclusion of Lawrence Beitler's image of lynchings in Marion (Figure 6.2), doctored by Claudia Rankine's husband John Lucas in *Citizen* (2014).[49] We know what's there, in the new darkness of that black space, of course—but the flash falls firmly on the faces of the community that condones this practice. And in Rankine and Lucas's visualization, flashes remain a weapon today: the 'flashes, a siren sounding' of police vehicles throb slowly throughout their collaborative video 'Stop and Frisk', imposing themselves from the outside over the identities of three black youths in a clothes store, image and text reinforcing the message of the racist assumptions that are upheld by today's sanctioned instruments of law.

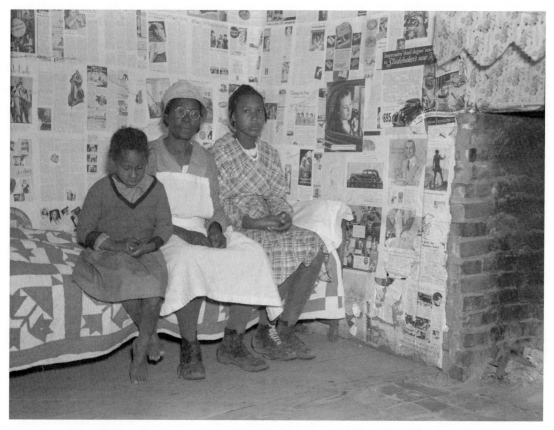

Figure 6.9 Arthur Rothstein, 'Negroes at Gees Bend, Alabama. Descendants of slaves of the Pettway plantation. They are still living very primitively on the plantation', February 1937. Library of Congress Prints & Photographs Division Washington, DC LC-DIG-fsa-8b35939.

The work of a wide range of African American photographers appears in the relatively short-lived news periodical *Flash!*. Probably the best known of these photographers is Gordon Parks—a man who loved his flash. Fellow photographer Robert McNeill reminisced: 'I remember seeing him covering a Howard University commencement, and even the other black photographers who were there were saying, "Who is that crazy [guy]?" I mean, Gordon would use four flashbulbs for a single shot, outdoors where he could have gotten away without using any.'[50] Parks's life story has been often told—most directly by himself, in several autobiographies, the most thorough of these being *Voices in the Mirror* (1990). Born in Kansas in 1912, he left school at 16, worked as a brothel pianist, a pianist for a big-band jazz troupe, a bus boy, a porter on the North Pacific Railroad, and then a waiter on the *North Coast Limited*, which is where he encountered the work of FSA photographers. One day in 1938, cleaning up a lounge car and looking at the magazines passengers had left behind, as was his custom,

> I found a portfolio of photographs that I would never forget. They were of migrant workers. Dispossessed, beaten by storms, dust and floods, they roamed the highways in caravans of battered jalopies and wagons between Oklahoma and California, scrounging for work. Some were so poor that they traveled on foot, pushing their young in baby buggies and carts. They lived in shanties with siding and roofs of cardboard boxes, the inside walls dressed with newspapers. There was a man with two children running through a dust storm to their shanty. The names of the photographers stuck in my mind—Arthur Rothstein, Russell Lee, Carl Mydans, Walker Evans, Ben Shahn, John Vachon, Jack Delano and Dorothea Lange. They all worked for the Farm Security Administration, a government agency set up by President Roosevelt to aid submarginal farmers. These stark, tragic images of human beings caught up in the confusion of poverty saddened me. I took the magazine home and studied it for weeks.[51]

More than studying the images, he bought his first camera, a Voightlander Brilliant, for $7.50 in a Seattle pawnshop.

Although all of these photographers were white, much of their work was not just sympathetic towards black people, but was put to active use in contexts aimed at reforming the conditions under which black people lived and worked. Of no one's imagery was this more true than Russell Lee. Notably, nineteen of his photographs appear in *12 Million Black Voices*. This is a book that Parks said 'became my Bible…a powerful statement against bigotry'. 'In Washington during 1942 that book had become my catechism, telling me that I was at the crossroads; that voices were rising and black men were moving forward—and that I should be moving with them.'[52] During the two weeks that Rosskam and Lee spent on Chicago's South Side in April 1941, Lee took over 1,000 shots, the biggest group of urban subjects in the FSA's archives. Many are of interiors, and necessarily use flash in a way that once again accentuates peeling lath and plaster walls, broken and filthy toilets, battered kitchen utensils and washing hanging in the cramped, crowded kitchenettes that Wright described as 'our prison, our death sentence without a trial'.[53]

Rather than being printed in a way that lightens skin tones, the plates in *12 Million Black Voices* are designed to emphasize darkness, seeking a low tonal register that provides a visual counterpart to the text's message of current gloom and despair, the dark backdrop to the call of the final paragraph to which Parks responded so energetically.[54] Maren Stange has called attention, moreover, to the deployment of a full-page bleed that 'dissociates the images from the status of mere illustration, or specimenlike evidence, and the suggestion of indefinite extension, rather than specific containment, in the images' often-dark backgrounds implies the dialectics of placenessness and boundedness—the diasporic dislocations—that are posited in the verbal text'.[55]

All the same, as Nicholas Natanson has pointed out, Rosskam engaged in some careful retouching in order to play up this hardship and pathos. 'The kitchenette creates thousands of one-room houses where our black mothers sit, deserted, with their children about their knees', Wright wrote. 'The kitchenette blights the personalities of our growing children, disorganizes them, blinds them to hope.' These words accompany an image of a woman and three young children crammed into a cluttered room—but in Lee's original, the exposure did not result in quite such dark and gloomy shadows, and the irreverence created by a small boy poking out his tongue suggests

Figure 6.10 Russell Lee, 'Children of a family on relief playing. Chicago, Illinois', April 1941. Library of Congress Prints & Photographs Division Washington, DC LC-DIG-fsa-8c00887.

something besides cowed victimhood.[56] What is more, the Chicago images by Lee that appear in Wright's volume are without exception of the very worst housing: the only forms of hope and cheerfulness (other than a couple of wan smiles) are found outside the home, in a storefront church and at a roller-skating rink. The book does not contain any of the other kinds of subjects that Lee used flash to capture (a good selection of these are to be found in Stange's *Bronzeville*) and that might have been more suited to *Flash!* (by then defunct) or *Ebony* (yet to be)—images of, say, a middle-class black doctor in his airy, light, and well-polished home, or the contrasts apparent within 'Children of a family on relief' (Figure 6.10). Here flash illuminates not just the damp-warped wall paper, but also two girls playing their instruments—light falling on the sheet music on the piano, its ivory keys, the smooth wood of a violin's surface, the bright lampshade. All these details represent a poignant, determined maintenance of the family's lifestyle, even of upward mobility, even when times are tough. Even in some of the kitchenette images, like Figure 6.11, the flash brings out such details as the shine on a pair of highly polished shoes of a smartly dressed working woman. Taken as a whole, Lee's Chicago images bring into relief the precarious proximity of poverty and comfortable life.

Figure 6.11 Russell Lee, 'Kitchen of apartment occupied by Negroes, South Side of Chicago, Illinois', April 1941. Library of Congress Prints & Photographs Division Washington, DC LC-USF33-013004-M1.

As we saw in Chapter 5, Lee loved to take pictures of interiors, because he was fascinated by what they revealed of people's histories and personalities. But he didn't just dive into homes uninvited. He was notable among FSA photographers for the length of time that he took talking to his subjects, getting to know them, earning their trust, and this is reflected in the human rapport found in his pictures. Gordon Parks, too, shared this curiosity about everyday lives and their details, and this also informs his image-taking. In 1942 he worked as an intern for the FSA whilst he held the prestigious Julius Rosenfeld fellowship. This allowed him to sit and look at the materials in the archive 'day in and day out', trying to 'absorb something of the feeling and flavor of what they had captured'.[57] He and Russell Lee were to become good friends.

Very early on during Parks's time in DC, Roy Stryker sent him out to get a sense of the city, and he returned shocked by the racist hatred that he found there. His dislike of the nation's capital was to prove an enduring one, exacerbated by precisely the inter-black prejudice based on gradations of skin colour that underpinned the darkroom practices at *Flash!*

> What was so terrible about Washington, D.C., at least at that particular time and before that time, was that the lighter-skinned blacks discriminated most against their black friends. Washington was famous for it. The lighter-skinned blacks did this because a lot of them were illegitimate sons of white land owners from places like Virginia. They had been put in special kinds of 'high-place' positions. Do you understand? They had, in a sense, an attitude of superiority about them, because they were fair-skinned; they had straight hair and could pass for being white, in some instances. So they wanted their daughters to marry light-skinned black men. It was a terrible thing. Washington, D.C., was the worst place in the country for that sort of thing.[58]

Parks's problem became an interpretative one. He wanted to use his camera to fight the evils of racism and poverty—but how can one photograph a bigot? 'You could not photograph a person who turns you away from the motion picture ticket window, or someone who refuses to feed you, or someone who refuses to wait on you in a store. You could not photograph him and say, "This is a bigot", because bigots have a way of looking just like everybody else.'[59] His answer was that such evils are best exposed through showing those who suffer most from their effects—something that for him was best done through talking with individuals, visiting them in their homes. This

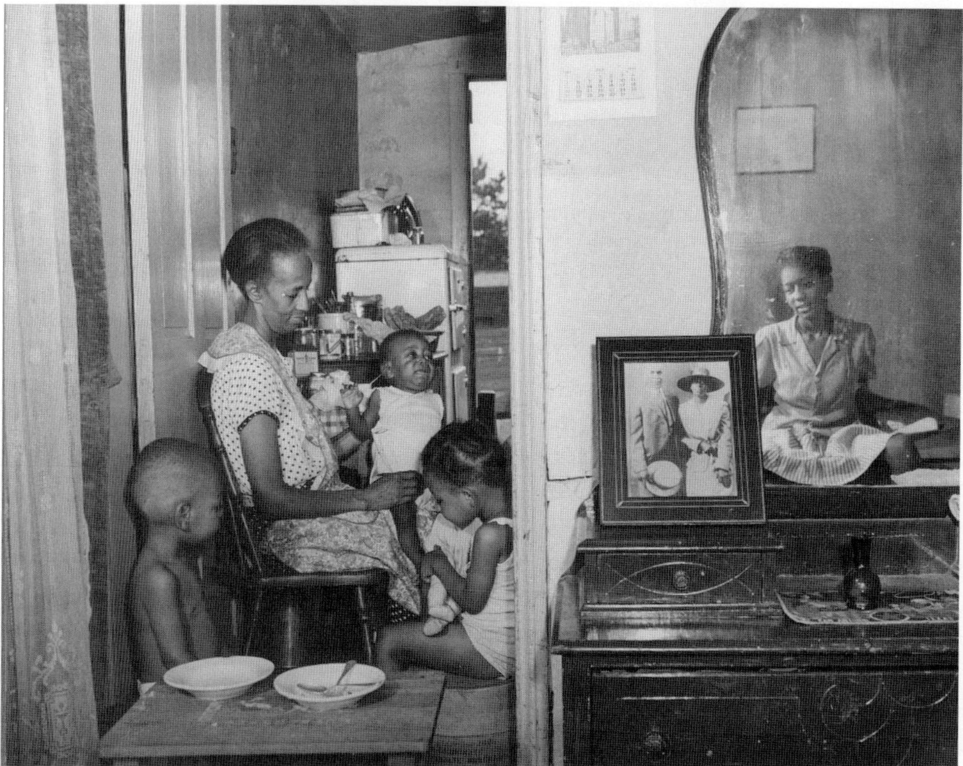

Figure 6.12 Gordon Parks, 'Washington, D.C. Mrs. Ella Watson, a government charwoman, with three grandchildren and her adopted daughter', August 1942. Library of Congress Prints & Photographs Division Washington, DC LC-DIG-ppmsca-05823.

remained a steady practice for Parks, starting with the series of documentary images that rendered visible the domestic and working life of a government cleaning woman, Ella Watson, whom he famously posed with mop and broom under the national flag (visually quoting Grant Wood's popular 1930 painting *American Gothic*)[60] and whom he subsequently followed through the metaphoric shadows of the Capitol—'to her dark house, her storefront church; to her small happinesses and daily frustrations'.[61] These flash images, like those shown in Figures 6.12–6.14, with their commitment to intimate domestic detail, have a good deal in common with Lee's work, and anticipate Collier's anthropological concerns. The photos of Ella Watson's home do not just show off domestic cleanliness—light shines off bureau and bedstead—but Parks's use of flash also calls attention to the individualism of a shrine-like dressing-table top (a couple of elephants alongside Christian figurines, with her small grandchildren on a bed in the background); shows us the importance and formality of the daily Bible reading with biblical calendar and image on the wall behind providing a continuation of the redemptive message after the reading ends; draws our eyes to a family portrait—quite probably Ella Watson with her husband, who was accidentally shot and killed two days before

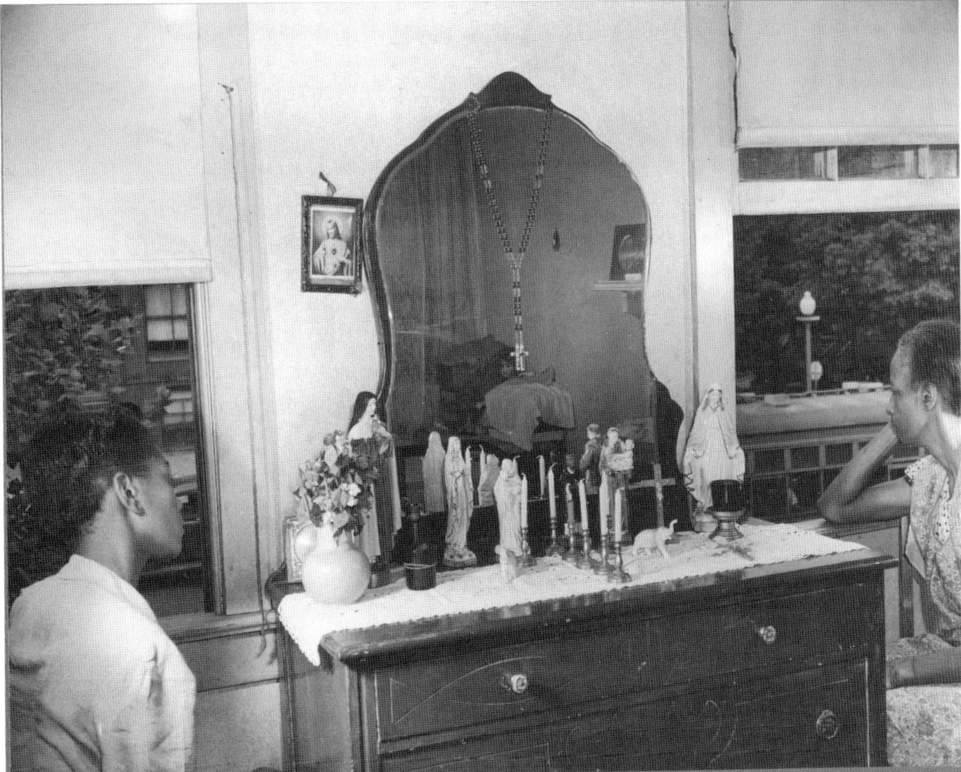

Figure 6.13 Gordon Parks, 'Washington, D.C. Mrs. Ella Watson, a government charwoman and her adopted daughter', August 1942. Library of Congress Prints & Photographs Division Washington, DC LC-USF34- 013431-C.

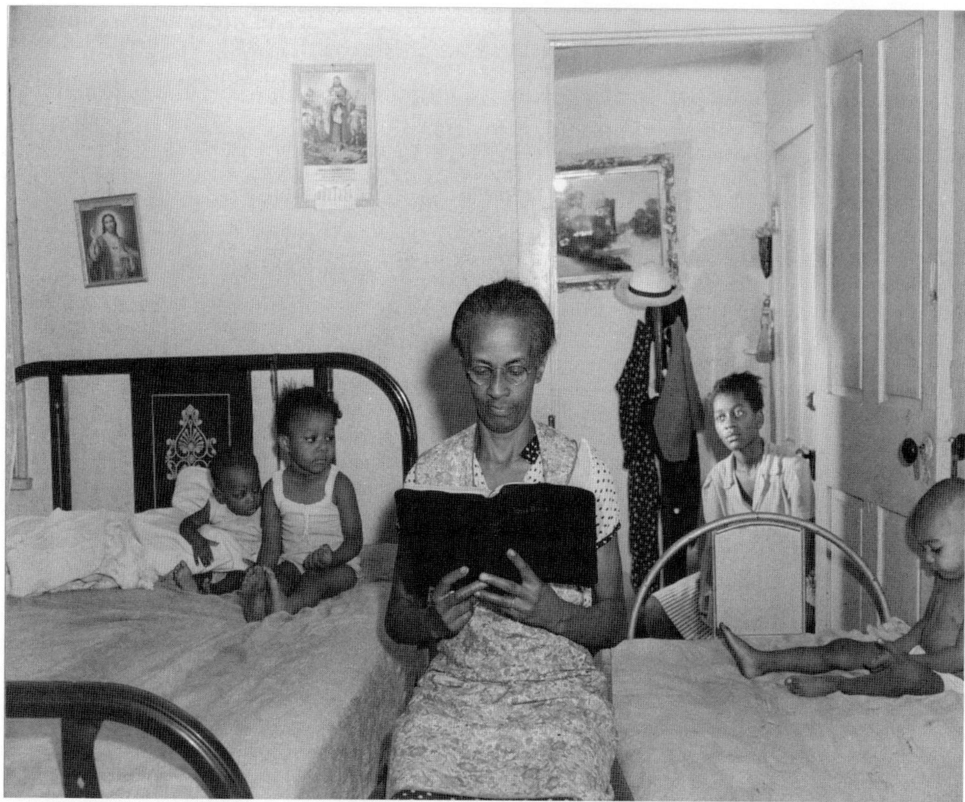

Figure 6.14 Gordon Parks, 'Washington, D.C. Mrs. Ella Watson, a government charwoman, reading the Bible to her household', August 1942. Library of Congress Prints & Photographs Division Washington, DC LC-DIG-ppmsca-05820.

her daughter was born.[62] Notably, though, despite the retrospective bleak social commentary implicit in the phrase 'dark house', in these images flash is not being used to put the grime and decay associated with poverty on display. Rather, right down to the gleam off the top of Ella Watson's spectacles, it allows Parks to foreground the pride taken in respectability; in keeping one's surroundings in shiningly clean order, and maintaining family rituals, connections, and memories.

Parks's photographing of Ella Watson was akin to a photojournalism project: subsequent series of his were to focus on the social world of individuals, including 'Flavio', a 1961 *Life* assignment under the rubric 'Poverty in America', showing the existence of a boy in a Rio de Janeiro favela, and the March 1968 *Life* feature on the Fontanelle family of Harlem. But most noticeable for his innovative use of flash was the 1948 photo essay 'Harlem Gang Leader'.[63] Parks's aim here was to show the complicated world of one young man, Leonard ('Red') Jackson, fiercely loyal and protective of both his biological family and his gang, the Midtowners—a set of intense, honour-bound emotional ties that Parks later compared to those of the Mafia.[64] Parks took intimate, tender shots of Jackson and his family at home on 99th Street—tightly embracing a girl

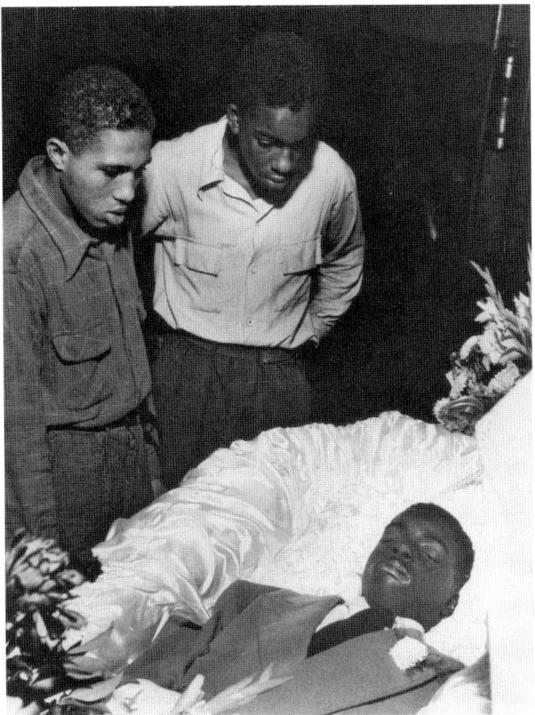

Figure 6.15 Gordon Parks, 'Red and Herbie Levi at the Funeral of Maurice Gaines, Harlem, New York', 1948. Courtesy of and copyright the Gordon Parks Foundation.

friend in a neighbourhood candy store; holding yarn whilst his mother knits a table mat, listens to the radio, and his elder brother Arthur sketches; with Herbie ('Buddy') Levi, the leader of the friendly Nomad gang, visiting the body of a 15-year-old Nomad, Maurice Gaines, in a mortuary chapel, as we see in Figure 6.15 (the flash bounces off the wounds around his mouth, wounds that confirmed their belief that this was a gang murder, not, as the police maintained, an accidental death), and on the streets.[65] As Parks recounted in an interview, he knew (or could guess) where the gangs were going to meet, knew that the atmosphere was tense in the aftermath of Gaines's death, and set up his equipment in advance. The flash he used when taking images like Figure 6.16 was not the invasive, in-your-face burst of light of the news photographer's flashbulb, but was infrared flash, used with infrared film, attached to 'a small camera the *Life* technicians had rigged up. The infrared flash, they told me, would hardly be discernible—just a small flicker of light in the darkness.'[66] 'When the infrared flash went off, it was just a little flicker, a red dot, but it gave all this light. After things started, the police came. I just left the lights and everything else. We lost a lot of stuff.'[67] The resulting image of young men grappling, arms and legs thrashing out of the darkness, is slightly blurred, with Parks's flash catching cheeks and chests, sleeves and shiny watches. It perfectly captures the fight's chaotic, impassioned immediacy.

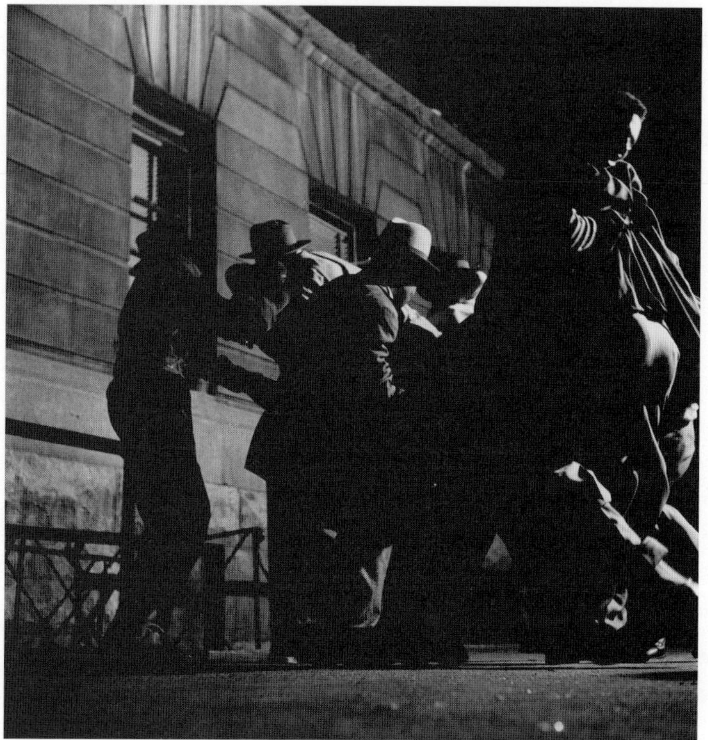

Figure 6.16 Gordon Parks, 'Untitled, Harlem, New York', 1948. Courtesy of and copyright the Gordon Parks Foundation.

As his pragmatic adoption of the infrared flash suggests, Parks was interested in the whole range of flash's technical and expressive properties, including the reflective and absorptive possibilities when it came to lighting and photographing black skin. The *Life* position came after a couple of freelancing years. Roy Stryker had laid him off from the Standard Oil Photography Project (Parks generously chose to believe that this was out of curiosity about what he would do), and most of his work was in fashion photography, especially for *Vogue*. During this time the publisher Franklin Watts invited him to publish 'a know-how book on lighting and a book of portraits' with him, for a welcome advance of around $1,000.[68] The second of these, *Camera Portraits*, is remarkable for the fact that it doesn't even mention flash: indeed, Parks had almost entirely moved to using studio lights for this genre. But its predecessor is quite different in its emphasis.

In 1947 Parks brought out *Flash Photography* in 'Grosset's Library of Practical Handbooks', aimed at increasing proficiency in flash's use by 'the Beginner and the Professional'. This is a ninety-six-page book (see Figure 6.17) in which the visual rhetoric is far more interesting than the verbal, although it gives clear instructions for how to use synchronizers and reflectors, and about which flashbulbs to buy for what purposes. It includes some classic examples of flash photography, from Weegee's flash-on-camera

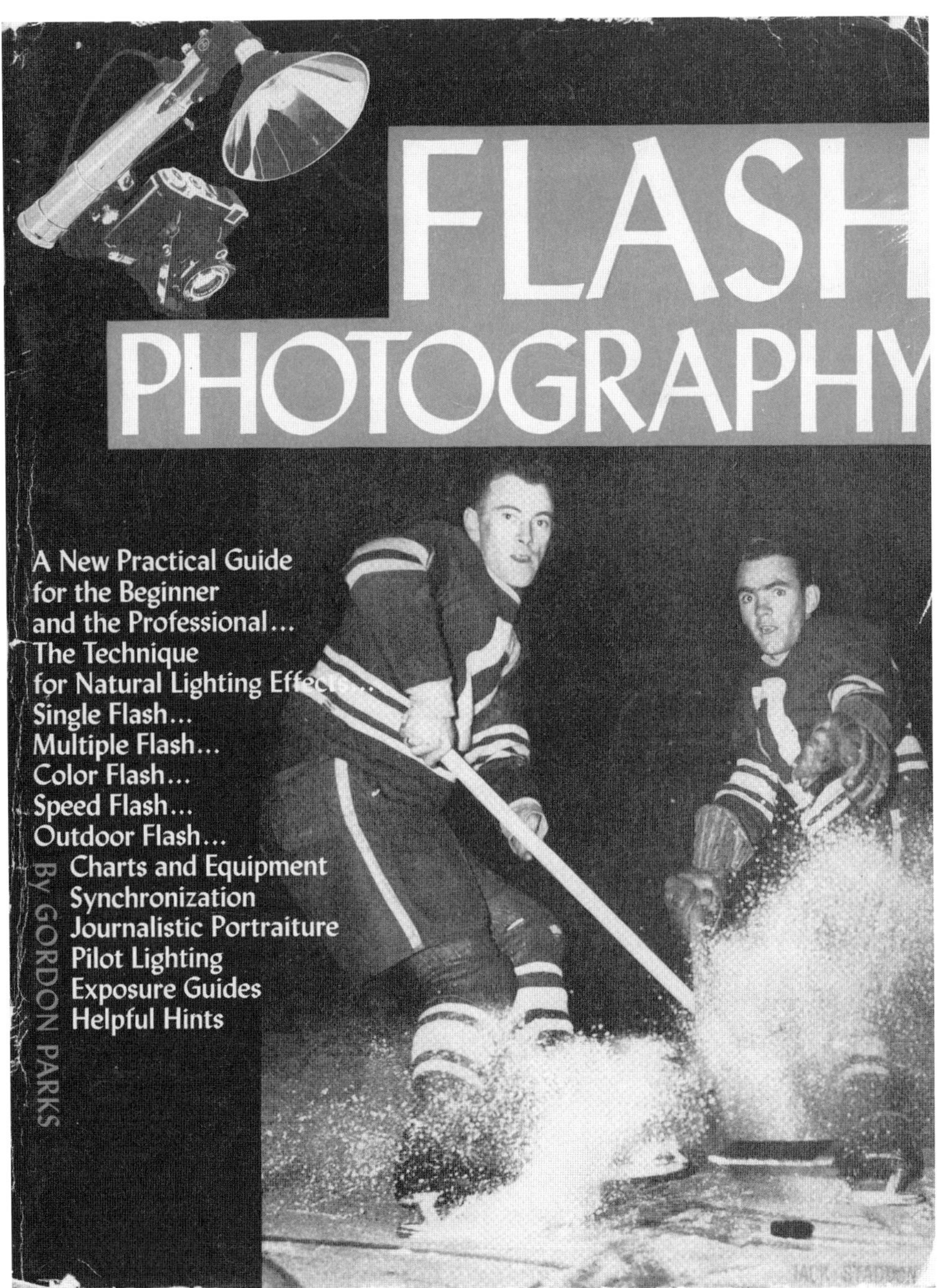

Figure 6.17 Cover, Gordon Parks, *Flash Photography* (New York: Grosset & Dunlap, 1947).

Figure 6.18 Gordon Parks, 'Grease Cooker', *Flash Photography* (New York: Grosset & Dunlap, 1947), 53.

news images, to the elaborate set-up used by Herbert Gehr in photographing Washington Market—and indeed Parks's own multiply lit Union Station. Thirty-four of the eighty-three photographs are credited to Parks himself. Whilst there isn't a single mention of skin tonality in the text—even though opposite Philippe Halsman's portrait of Marion Anderson we are told that the 'emphasis light' 'helps separate the subject from the background and brightens the hair, jewelry, or hat',[69] twelve of the images are entirely of black subjects. If around 7 per cent is still a small percentage, it offers infinitely more black visibility than do other contemporary, white-authored photo manuals. Although (unless star performers) these subjects are distinguished by archetypal labels—'Grease Cooker', 'Foundry Worker' (Figures 6.18 and 6.19)—the same is true of the white portraits—New England Farmer, Roundhouse Worker. The low camera angle offers all workers the same heroic status. In this monumentalism, Parks appears to be drawing, in both composition and sentiment, on the photographs that Lewis Hine drew together in *Men at Work* (1932).

This is not the only commentary on racial visibility offered by Parks's selection of images, however. Three other frames deserve particular comment. One is a Signals Corps photo here entitled 'Collaborator's End' (see Figure 6.20). It shows the execution of a collaborator by a French firing squad in Rennes, France, on 21 November 1944.[70]

Grease Cooker
Gordon Parks
One No. 22 was held above the subject to the side at a 15 feet distance. The exposure was 1/50 of a second at f/11 on fast panchromatic film. The camera used was a 4x5 Speed Graphic.

Figure 6.19 Gordon Parks, 'Foundry Worker', *Flash Photography* (New York: Grosset & Dunlap, 1947), 89.

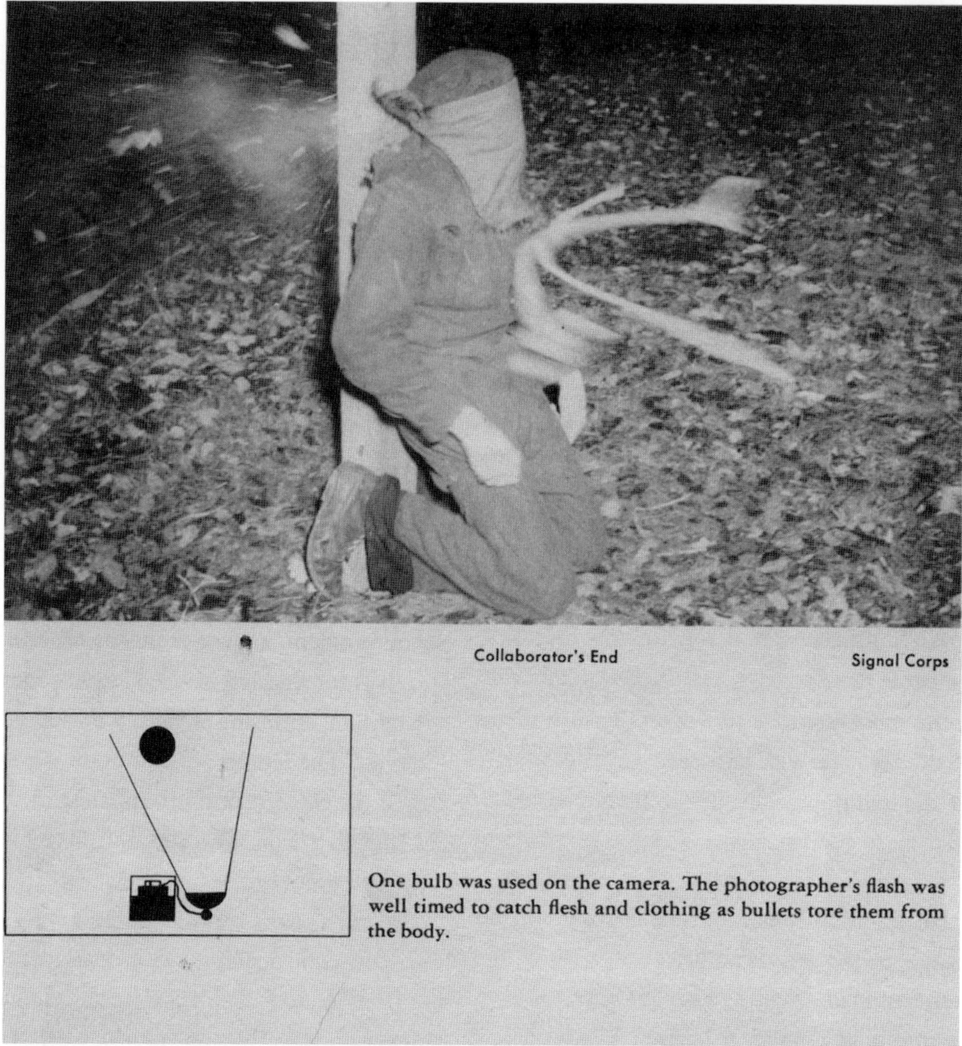
Collaborator's End
Signal Corps
One bulb was used on the camera. The photographer's flash was well timed to catch flesh and clothing as bullets tore them from the body.

Figure 6.20 Signals Corps, 'Collaborator's End', in Gordon Parks, *Flash Photography* (New York: Grosset & Dunlap, 1947), 28.

'One bulb was used on the camera. The photographer's flash was well timed to catch flesh and clothing as bullets tore them from the body', Parks commented laconically.[71] Is this image included in some kind of implicit dialogue with lynching photographs, showing the legitimate punishment of a white transgressor? Its sensationalism is certainly remarkable, even by the standard of execution photographs, since this is not a death about to happen, or that has just happened, but captured in an explosive instant. It would have been highly unlikely, given the prevalent power relations, that Parks would have addressed race relations head-on in a publication of this sort, which was likely to

Philip Sperry
This photograph is typical of those of crowds where the bulb is aimed toward the front rows. The people in the back area receive an inadequate portion of the light and those near the camera are generally overexposed. One Superflash No. 3 was exposed by open-flash at f/32.

Figure 6.21 Philip Sperry, crowd photo I, from Gordon Parks, *Flash Photography* (New York: Grosset & Dunlap, 1947), 46.

Philip Sperry
This photograph is a definite improvement over the one on page 46. The bulb was held a bit to the side and aimed toward the rear center, resulting in a more even distribution of the light. One Superflash No. 3 was exposed in the open-flash manner at f/32.

Figure 6.22 Philip Sperry, crowd photo II, from Gordon Parks, *Flash Photography* (New York: Grosset & Dunlap, 1947), 46.

have had a large white readership. But images, as the volume shows, can offer a powerful visual intervention in relation to racial differences and expectations without the need for verbal commentary.

Similarly, albeit more easy to interpret, even though again there are no words to guide us—there is a pair of images (Figures 6.21 and 6.22) that are designed to show how best to angle the flash when photographing a crowd. 'This photograph', we are told of an image of an audience at an unnamed event—'is typical of those of crowds where the bulb is aimed toward the front rows.'[72] 'And this'—the comment accompanying an almost identical view laid out on the opposite page is completely deadpan—'is a definite improvement over the one on p. 46.'[73] In terms of an even spread of light over the assembled company, yes. But something else is instantly apparent to the alert viewer. A properly angled flash renders instantly visible the presence of the African American man, otherwise swallowed up by the white mass.

Gordon Parks was nothing if not flamboyant in his use of flash, a central component in his armoury of photographic tools—and armoury is, indeed, the right word. He was quite upfront about its aggressive potential: 'I have always felt as though I needed a weapon against evil', he said in his long conversation with Martin Bush. He recounted a conversation that he'd had with one of the Black Panthers whom he photographed in the 1960s about the usefulness of a camera as opposed to a gun.

> I said, 'Well, you know, I'm in the fight the same as you are. I ride with you every night. You have chosen a gun; I have chosen a camera. I know there is a policeman following us. Every night we are trailed. They are waiting to shoot us up. Do you think their bullets are going to miss me and go to you because I'm Gordon Parks? I'm taking risks to show that you might have a voice . . . I'm risking my life just being with you. So, my weapon's here with me; your weapon is in your pocket. You've got a 45 in your pocket. But I think my weapon is stronger'. And it proved to be. The kid got killed three months later in a shootout.[74]

Parks is literalizing the connections that were famously brought out by Susan Sontag in *On Photography* when she remarked, 'There is an aggression implicit in every use of the camera . . . However hazy our awareness of this fantasy, it is named without subtlety whenever we talk about "loading" and "aiming" a camera, about "shooting" a film.'[75] This connection between flash photography and violence was present from the start, present in the pistol-like contraption that was one of the early means of exploding flash powder and that established the enduring terminology of the 'flashgun'. It is a connection that we will explore further: for now, we should just note how this vocabulary unmistakably ties Parks's view of his profession to some very obvious clichés of race and masculinity—stereotypes that, in fact, he tends to avoid in the framing and lighting of his work.

But I turn finally, in this chapter, to the work of a photographer whose attitude towards flash represents the antithesis to that of Parks, and that implicitly repudiates his aggressive approach. In 1990 Roy DeCarava gave two interviews that were published in *Callaloo*, in which he spoke both about his photographic practice and, more generally, about the concept of a black aesthetic—one characterized, for him, by a commitment to freedom, survival, humanitarianism, a realistic appraisal of life, and community.[76] More specifically, he proclaims his love of natural light, which he accords near-transcendental significance. 'I think light is a wonderful phenomenon', he said. 'If you think about it, light is the source of life. The sun is *the* light that makes all things possible.'[77] His equation of light with that which is life-giving—indeed, later in the interview he terms his work 'spiritual'[78]—spills into the aesthetic decisions that he makes. DeCarava's terminology overlaps with the metaphorically freighted language used by some of flash photography's pioneers. But for DeCarava, this sacred illumination had, if possible, to come from a natural, not artificial source. He was prepared to compromise when it came to the light provided by an electric light bulb or table lamp, say—after all, one of his mentors when it came to depicting illumination was Edward Hopper[79]—but for him, what mattered was using verisimilitudinal, ambient lighting.

Unsurprisingly, given these views about the importance of natural light, DeCarava's major role model as a photographer was Cartier-Bresson, someone who regarded flash with complete disdain.[80] Like Cartier-Bresson, DeCarava wanted to have the moment in which a photograph would be made create itself—not be made by the flash. Images taken by flash, after all, bear a quite different relationship to temporality than do those in which time is, as Barthes has it, immobilized. With non-flash photographs, we can conceptualize time as a stream that has been temporarily halted. But flash illuminates a scene that has been sliced out of darkness: the moment before the picture was taken and the moment afterwards are radically different in terms of lighting, shadow and visibility from the one that the flash lit up for us. This aesthetic of flash is one that—as we will see in Chapter 7—links it to the drama of crime scenes, whether the images be taken by police or by journalists. This is 'the white flash of a dozen silver bulbs' that blinds Bigger in Wright's *Native Son*, rendering him temporarily as sightless as the white eyes of the permanently blind Mrs Dalton; 'the silver lightning flashed in his eyes' as Mrs Dalton's big white cat leaps onto his shoulders, and the newsmen raise their cameras for the shot.[81]

Yet rather than creating and exploiting the theatrical, DeCarava makes images that invite contemplation. His style is one that—as Maren Stange has written—is formalist, expressive.[82] Some of his work can be read as offering social commentary—such as his well-known 1949 image 'Graduation', in which a young woman stands in her graduation dress in a derelict Harlem lot, a huge advertisement for a Chevrolet on a billboard in the background, and the triangular wedge of light in which she's positioned pointing equivocally towards a bright future or a dead end. More generally, however, he provides atmosphere, not a photographic form of documentary or critical race intervention.

'For me,' wrote DeCarava, 'photography must be visual, rather than intellectual or ideological.'[83] Langston Hughes, who called DeCarava 'a Rembrandt of the camera', was so moved by his images of Harlem that he desired only to 'meditate on [them] and write what came into his head', helping to affirm the value of Harlem life, not point to its trials.[84] The result was the photo book *The Sweet Flypaper of Life* (1955).

In her volume *Bellocq's Ophelia*, Natasha Trethewey takes as her speaker one of the subjects of turn-of-the-century New Orleans photographer E. J. Bellocq, best known for his images of sex workers in Storyville.[85] This fictional protagonist is not left frozen by the camera lens in a perpetual state of uncertainty, as DeCarava's shaft of sunlight holds the graduating girl in suspension, but is liberated by the darkness that follows the invasion of artificial light. At the end of the final poem, Trethewey asks us to think of her as no longer subject, but agent—seeing clearly. The flash makes an urgent and liberating interruption in her life: a rupture in time.

> Her brow furrowed
> as she looks out to the left, past all of them.
> Imagine her a moment later—after
> the flash, blinded—stepping out
> of the frame, wide-eyed, into her life.[86]

The whole sequence of poems is, indeed, about her learning to be a perceptive viewer—of her past, her surroundings, of how photography works. In an earlier poem, we find her starting to think about

> the way the camera can dissect
> the body, render it reflecting light
> or gathering darkness—surfaces
> gray as stone or steel, lifeless, flat.[87]

DeCarava's photography emphasizes the power of bodies that gather darkness, that inhabit shadows. This was a choice he made early in his career, when he turned from painting and printmaking to the camera, and learned from Homer Page, a protégé of Edward Steichen, to change from a style of printing his photographs that brought out the contrast from the brightest white to deep black to one that was softer, that emphasized slow gradation, working—to quote Peter Galassi—in a 'narrower range of deep tones, thus breathing space and life into a luxury of dark grays', insisting on 'dissolution of material form in a unified field of light and shadow'.[88] This very much suited his personal aesthetic. 'I do have an affinity for the middle tones and the dark tones because they're beautiful', he acknowledged, 'and they appeal to me on a very subjective level. I love the quality of so many different shades of dark, so many different shades of gray.'[89]

On occasion, to be sure, DeCarava played with extremes of contrast, but used only the available light, whether that came from the sun or from the pallid illumination of a dim bulb in a corridor. Take 'Hallway', an image that he described as being both very literal and psychologically provocative precisely because of the suggestivity of its darkness.

It's about a hallway that I know I must have experienced as a child. Not just one hallway; it was all the hallways that I grew up in. They were poor, poor tenements, badly lit, narrow and confining; hallways that had something to do with the economics of building for poor people. When I saw this particular hallway I went home on the subway and got my camera and tripod, which I rarely use. The ambience, the light in this hallway was so personal, so individual that any other kind of light would not have worked. It just brought back all those things that I had experienced as a child in those hallways. It was frightening, it was scary, it was spooky, as we would say when we were kids. And it was depressing. And yet, here I am as an adult, years and ages and ages later, looking at the same hallway and finding it beautiful.[90]

In a 2015 *New York Times* piece celebrating DeCarava, novelist Teju Cole writes that the photographer 'tried to think through the peculiar challenge of shooting black people at a time when black appearance, in both senses (the way black people looked and the very presence of black people) was under question'. Although this is not an article that mentions flash, Cole describes how DeCarava did not try to brighten blackness, but 'went against expectation and darkened it further'. 'What is dark', Cole says, is here 'neither blank nor empty. It is in fact full of wise light which, with patient seeing, can open up into glories.' And Cole wonderfully invokes Édouard Glissant's exploration of the word, the idea, the ideal of opacity:

Glissant defined it as a right not to have to be understood on others' terms, a right to be misunderstood if need be. The argument was rooted in linguistic considerations: It was a stance against certain expectations of transparency embodied in the French language. Glissant sought to defend the opacity, obscurity and inscrutability of Caribbean blacks and other marginalized peoples. External pressures insisted on everything being illuminated, simplified and explained. Glissant's response: No. And this gentle refusal, this suggestion that there is another way, a deeper way, holds true for DeCarava, too.[91]

DeCarava's comments about how he understands light have the same resonance as those made by Ben Shahn, when that photographer explained how he wanted to record the power of shadows. 'I don't try and alter light, which is why I never use flash', DeCarava told Miller.

I hate it with a passion because it obliterates what I saw.

When I fall in love with something I see, when something interests me it interests me in the context of the light that it's in. So why should I try to change the light and what I see, to get this 'perfect' information laden print? I don't care about that. The reason why my photographs are so dark is that I take photographs everywhere, light or not. If I can see it, I will take a picture of it. If it's dark, so be it.[92]

These remarks separate out not just natural and artificial light, but also natural vision, from that which we might, anthropomorphically, ascribe to the camera. For flash, as we have seen, blinds, at the instant of its release, both photographer and subjects. The view that's obtained of their room or workspace has a clarity that's rarely, if ever, achieved outside the photograph: details are made brightly visible. The whole spatial and sensory experience that is suggested by the resulting image in no way corresponds to that of any human participant in the scene, and their sense of atmosphere, of visibility and knowability. Poverty may be exposed by the flash: at the same time, what is so frequently lost from the final image is a sense of complexity, of mystery, of a life that resists being put into easy descriptive language.

DeCarava's comments, furthermore, significantly complicate any temptation to draw an over-neat analogy between the stark tonal contrasts achieved through flash photography—those clear distinctions between dark and light that can easily be read in metaphorical as well as literal ways—and the multiple forms of subordination produced through racial inequality, as if this consists of some simple contrast between black and white. His rhetoric, indeed, overtly repudiates such equations: it draws attention to black's power to connote, not denote in the manner of documentary photography. Yet his language also reminds one of the polarizing properties of lightness and darkness, just as surely as motifs of dark and light, of artificial versus natural light run through *Invisible Man*, ready to be taken up by its photographic illustrators, including Parks himself, insistently reminding one of the temptations as well as the fallacies of falling into binary thinking—visible versus invisible, above ground versus below, black versus white.

The vocabulary of flash photography has been an emotionally loaded one throughout its history, whether it draws on the sublime register of celestial lightning, or exploits anxieties about intrusion, voyeurism, and the rupturing of private space. So it's no surprise that African American photographers of this period, employing flash for their particular documentary, aesthetic, and quietly polemical ends, should also see it in relation to both revelation and violation. DeCarava might claim that he sees no connection between the darkness of an image and a black aesthetic. It's far less clear, however, that flash's bleaching glare did not, for some, carry additional, especially charged overtones of violence, exposure, and white racial hatred. As is shown by Ellison's remarks about the paradoxical high visbility of African Americans, the undercurrent of visual reference that linked flash, in the early and mid-twentieth century, to the imagery of lynching adds particularly potent connotations to its use. It remained a technology with a troubled history for African Americans, even though many black photographers found it—and continue to find it—a necessary tool for making race visible on their own terms.

CHAPTER SEVEN

Death by Exposure

In 1888, the year after *blitzlichtpulver*'s invention, the *Photographic News* published a comic sketch, set in a London police station.

> *Police Inspector.* What's the charge P 244?
>
> *P 244.* I was on dooty at eight o'clock to-night in Trafalgar Square when I see prisoner come along with this 'ere box in his right hand. Directly he got within three or four yards of me, something blazed up in his other hand, and suspecting as the box he'd got was an infernal masheen, and that he was one of them diameters [dynamiters], I took him into custody. I found this powder and this pice of crumpled paper in his possession.
>
> *Inspector (to prisoner).* Have you anything to say?
>
> *Prisoner.* Certainly, I have a good deal to say. In the first place, this box is a camera, and not an infernal machine, excepting when it makes people very ugly. This powder and paper, of which I have some more in my waistcoat pocket, from the new illuminating combination magnesium powder and gun paper [*sic*].
>
> *Inspector.* Most dangerous. Highly explosive. 21 Reserve, bring a pail of water at once.
>
> *Prisoner.* Excuse me, but there is not the slightest danger. I was going to say it occurred to me that I would like to take the portrait of P 244 here, and I accordingly lighted a small quantity, as I am doing now (*strikes a match and lights the compound. Before the police recover from the shock the flash is over. They rush forward and seize him).*

The prisoner—understandably angry, since the ignorant police have plunged his camera into water as a precautionary measure—tries to defend himself against their apprehensions, and against their claims that they have 'had no end of complaints from people who have been frightened by sudden flashes of light exactly the same as yours'. But he is held in a cell overnight, and only released once Colonel Majendie—Her Majesty's Chief Inspector of Explosives—confirms his story. 'MORAL. Amateur photographers must be careful how they use the magnesium flash in the street until the police get used to it.'[1]

The advice given at the end of this rather heavy-handed piece of humour seems to have been serious enough. Plenty of evidence suggests that people who were *not* accustomed to flash photography were, indeed, alarmed by it. News photographers' memoirs enjoy relating the havoc caused by their equipment. When Tammany leader Richard Croker arrived in the US to appear on a platform at Madison Square Garden alongside Democratic presidential candidate William Jennings Bryan on 17 October 1900, *Collier's Weekly*—a pioneering publication in the history of news journalism—wanted a picture of the occasion. Flash photography was not allowed in the Garden: photographer Jimmy Hare and his cousin smuggled in a portable flash lamp. 'Pandemonium stole the show from Bryan for the next five minutes. There was nearly a panic. The people in front of Jimmy got the idea a bomb had been thrown; even many behind him did not realize it was only a flashlight.'[2] Somewhat later, following the Japanese invasion of Shanghai in 1937, George M. Lacks (obliged to use very volatile and unreliable Japanese flashbulbs) had the opportunity to photograph a famous yet camera-shy warlord, 'planned his shot, focused, put in a bulb, then "Bang!"—the bulb exploded with a loud report—sentries and bodyguards ran in from all points—George felt bayonets pricking his skin on all sides'—and the warlord had to be thoroughly convinced that Lacks was not trying to assassinate him.[3] The combustible dangers of flash illumination even extended to earlier flash technologies. James Jarché recalls his first photographic assignment around 1899, when he was about 9, assisting his father, who ran a successful photographic business in London's Dockland, and who had been called out at night to photograph a young man's dead mother. The boy's task was to hold the magnesium ribbon, but he became so engrossed in what his father was doing that he set fire to the dingy lace curtain in the lodging house—the bereaved son had enough presence of mind to throw the blazing material out of the window.[4] But it was the relatively volatile nature of the flash compound that was responsible for the largest number of accidents, both to photographers and to those who were involved in its preparation or transportation or storage.

This chapter looks at the use of flash photography by news reporters, especially in the decade or so following the invention of the flashbulb. It considers the connections between photography, crime, violence, and detection, both within the press and in fictional form. It concludes with an assessment of the part played by Weegee in establishing many of flash photography's enduring associations—Weegee, the American news photographer and would-be fine art practitioner whose name and image were synonymous with flash. First, however, let us consider the years when flash photography could, itself, be news.

Flash powder was a huge boon to taking news photographs where it had previously been too dark to make a viable exposure. Francis A. Collins, writing in 1916, was typical in noting that 'the camera man no longer waits for daylight to photograph a railroad wreck, for instance, but catches his picture in the flare of a pound or more of flash powder'.[5] However, this powder was unquestionably dangerous, even deadly. It was not just the specialist photographic press that frequently carried accounts of people being maimed or killed as a result of being careless with the chemical components of flash. News items about these lethal and spectacular explosions were regularly passed around the general press—something made easy not just nationally, but also internationally, by the development of the telegraph as a means of rapidly transmitting and syndicating news, 'quicker than the sunbeam's path and the lightning's flash', to borrow the words of George Howard, 7th Earl of Carlisle, and Lord Lieutenant of Ireland in 1857, at the launch of what proved to be an unsuccessful attempt to lay a transatlantic cable.[6] A couple of examples from the early years of flash may stand for a host of other incidents that helped to establish its alarming reputation, whether as a result of its components or its effects.

In February 1888 a lady lion-tamer appearing at Dan Lowry's Music Hall, in Dublin, was badly mauled when—wanting a photograph to be taken of herself with her head inside a lion's mouth—this lion closed his jaws on Mlle Senide's head, most probably startled by the flash.[7] On 20 October 1888, a keg of flash powder exploded at the wholesale chemical house of Wiley and Wallace, in Philadelphia, killing a 16-year-old worker, John D. Cruice (who seems to have been passing the chemicals through too coarsely grained a sieve), and destroying a considerable amount of stock;[8] four days later, in San Francisco, a young employee at Samuel C. Patridge's photographic establishment was fatally wounded when a Hawkridge flash pistol with which he was experimenting exploded.[9] Cruice's father sued, citing negligence; very shortly before the case was up for trial, Joseph Wiley himself and three assistants were killed whilst attempting to remove the last of the flash powder from the chemicals. Pouring the compound down a sink, playing a hose upon it, it appears that Wiley struck the bottle against the sink in order to loosen the powder. Two other employees were injured; panicked workers jumped from the upper floors of the wrecked building.

An article in *Wilson's Photographic Magazine* in 1912 estimated that at least twelve people had been killed by flash powder's misuse in Philadelphia alone,[10] and its destructive force continued, whether destroying small-town photo studios, blinding and mutilating photographers, blowing people out of windows and onto the street, or causing large fires that spread far beyond workshops and warehouses. Von Schwartz's 1904 handbook, *Fire and Explosion Risks*, translated from the German and published in London 'for the use of fire insurance officials, fire brigade officers, members of the legal profession', and so on, has a whole chapter on the risks of storing flash powder.[11] The insurance industry was, understandably, draconian in its specifications when it came to conditions of manufacture and storage. Flash powder's known instability and riskiness ensured that for forty years, the fires and injuries that it caused provided regular sensational news fare, thus accentuating, each time, the associations of this branch of photography with bravery, or at least daring; sometimes with aggression, and sometimes with sheer folly.

Photographic manuals for both the professional and amateur photographer were full of cautionary advice about the injuries that could be sustained using flash. Animal photographers were warned against starting forest fires from sparks falling onto dry leaves.[12] There were many prescriptions about its indoor use, especially with regard to igniting it too close to curtains or other flammable materials. 'Don't place it too near curtains or wall paper or friend wife will have something to say', wryly cautioned a typical article in an amateur journal, whilst also reminding the reader not to prepare the powder whilst smoking a pipe or cigar.[13] These dangers lasted well past the introduction of the flashbulb, reminding us, once again, that the history of flash photography is not a tidily linear one. James Kinkaid, in his 1936 version of *Press Photography*, whilst noting that flashbulbs are starting to make things less dangerous and more predictable, nonetheless warns the would-be press photographer that he or she might still need to use flash powder. This should be treated 'with the same respect you would give a stick of dynamite with a percussion cap in place'.[14] He advises that it is a good thing to use an old leather glove whilst discharging it, and never to pour powder into the flashgun from the container in which it is carried, whether that container be glass or metal—'no safer than a hand grenade. More than one photographer is using a maimed hand today because he failed to heed this warning.'[15] The fact that the hazards of flash powder had become a cliché of the popular imagination, one that endured the invention of the flashbulb, is evidenced from the 1939 Mickey Mouse cartoon, *Society Dog Show*. Mickey enters Pluto into a dog show populated entirely by snooty canines and their even snootier owners. Pluto—unsurprisingly—fails to impress the judges, although he does fall soppily in love with a very cute Pekinese. Mickey and Pluto sit glumly, excluded, as the Trick Dogs are announced—balancing on balls, juggling, walking on their front paws. The photographer hired to capture this show ignites his mound of white flash powder, setting fire to all the bunting in the theatre. In the ensuing fiery melee, the Pekinese is trapped under a lamp—and Pluto becomes the hero of the hour, dramatically rescuing her on roller skates.[16]

In the autobiographies of those news photographers who employed flash, it seems almost de rigueur to include at least one anecdote testifying to its unpredictable, dangerous qualities. To write of an explosive event in which they, the perpetrator, remained more or less unscathed, but others were deafened, singed, or scared out of their skin was simultaneously the occasion for injecting a little humour and for enhancing the reckless, devil-may-care persona of the photographer, blasé about the dangers attached to their trade. For example, Harry J. Coleman, working for Hearst's *New York Journal* in 1903, set out to get a picture of the six-day bicycle racers starting out from Madison Square Garden—a picture that would show not just the cyclists, but also the crowds who were there to watch them, and their food and supplies for the week. He and his colleagues set up a contraption containing a huge quantity of flash powder, ignited by a gunpowder cap set off from 20 feet away.

> Probably there has never been such an indoor explosion recorded in the peacetime history of our country... Everyone inside the old Garden, including the racers, was blinded by the great flash of light and choked by the magnesium clouds which billowed above the scene—everyone, that is, except us cameramen, who knew enough to keep our eyes closed. The resulting pandemonium is still vivid in my memory. When the shroud lifted and vision returned to eyes wild with

panic, we were pained to discover that the force and violence of our blast had spilled all the riders

as well as blowing back the infield crowd—and the rail they were holding—some 6 feet.[17] In London, Edward J. Dean recalls taking a photograph of the royal family attending a production of R. C. Sherriff's play about the First World War, *Journey's End*, and, since the theatre lighting would not have been bright enough on its own, setting up the necessary explosive charge in the dugout on stage. This was certainly effective for photographic purposes, although apparently the King looked a little startled, but 'we were told later that our experiment had caused the actors temporary blindness, had singed their hair and eyebrows, and had scorched their clothes. The explosion had been so realistic that flashpowder was afterwards used for that particular scene, but not in the generous quantities we had provided.'[18]

The dangers of flash powder were, without a doubt, very real. If professional photographers could apparently get somewhat sanguine about the injuries that they incurred, this should be read in the light of their tendency towards a performance of masculine bravado in their self-presentation. Jimmy Hare 'had had so many burns from flashlights he had become adept at their treatment and resigned to their occurrence', we learn in his biography, its author differentiating only between the deeper injuries caused by the magnesium powder that one blew through a lamp, and the more surface wounds caused by the compound form of flash powder.[19] William Randolph Hearst was deeply dismayed when, in his role as newspaper proprietor, he learned how serious injuries to press photographers could be. Photographer Mike Rotunno took the credit for filling Hearst in about this. 'Probably the most important picture is the one I didn't get', he reminisced. He was ready to take a picture of Hearst and his family arriving at Chicago's Midway airport after their first air trip in the early 1930s, but the wind blew the flash powder out of his gun three times running. Chatting to Hearst about the 'woes of a photographer and his flash gun', the magnate was shocked to learn from Rotunno that one of his own employees, Nick McDonald of the *Chicago Herald-Examiner*, 'had lost a hand to the unstable flash powder'. Eddie McGill, another Chicago photographer who worked for the *Tribune*, had earlier suffered a skull fracture from a flash pan that bent when it was fired.[20] Hearst told Rotunno that something would have to be done, and the photographer learned the next day that 'the order went out from the "Chief" to all his newspapers to cease using flash powder in any form', with Hearst promising to sponsor research into the flashbulb, then in development.[21]

Photographers who used flash powder wrote gleefully of how they were able to flee a scene, plate in hand, under the cover of the smelly fog that exploding this substance released into the air. What was a liability in the studio could be a literal smokescreen when it came to their own practice. The flashbulbs that took its place left a much less handy trail. By the early 1950s, automatic ejectors shot flashbulbs high into the air, thus meaning that photographers avoided inadvertently burning their fingers on the hot bulb, but causing a litter of unpleasant shards. Stanley Devon recalls the aftermath of the arrival of Princess Elizabeth and the Duke of Edinburgh for a royal tour in Canada early in the 1950s, where they kept their cool as they were chased by a mob of picture-hungry photographers, who in their turn were being pursued by the Royal Canadian Mounted Police on horseback. After their departure, 'the airfield emptied. The only relic of this fantastic drive was a trail of burnt-out flash-bulbs crunched crisply underfoot by the departing Guard of Honour.'[22]

The associations of flash powder with danger and violence did not just come from its combustibility and volatility. As we have seen, original options for igniting it involved using a pistol-like contraption—the original 'flashgun'. This name—and the associations of violence and weaponry—stuck, even when a differently shaped apparatus was employed. Furthermore, the allusion is clear in the black humour of the words that are sometimes seen engraved round a gun barrel, or that appear on a military tank's placard: 'SMILE. WAIT FOR FLASH.' As Susan Sontag elaborates in *On Photography*, the latent fantasy of camera as weapon 'is named without subtlety whenever we talk about "loading" and "aiming" a camera, about shooting a film . . . Like a car, a camera is sold as a predatory weapon—one that's as automated as possible, ready to spring.' Of course, as she says, this is all hyperbole—yet, for Sontag, there is, nonetheless, 'something predatory about taking a picture . . . Just as the camera is a sublimation of the gun, to photograph someone is a sublimated murder — a soft murder, appropriate to a sad, frightened time.'[23] Or, as Danny Kean, the ex-con turned tabloid photographer, played by James Cagney in the 1933 movie *Picture Snatcher*, puts it, on receiving his camera: 'Works just like a GUN! Trigger an' all!'[24] The association of flashes of light with violence was, of course, consolidated by the flashes that came from actual firearms, as in Dashiell Hammett's hard-boiled crime novel *Red Harvest* (1929): 'From a hedge by the road, a flash of orange pointed briefly up at the man in the window. His gun flashed downward. He leaned further out. No second flash came from the hedge.'[25] The two work in consort in Alfred Hitchcock's 1940 *Foreign Correspondent*, which capitalized on the explicit identification of flash photography with aggression: a man posing as a news photographer kills a central European chancellor with a pistol fired at the same moment as he sets off his flash—the flash here functioning as cover, rather than as instrument.

The invention of the flashbulb dramatically changed the working habits of the press photographer, and exponentially increased their chances of obtaining a newsworthy shot. This was especially true if their target was opportunistic, rather than carefully planned in advance. Looking back at the previous decade in 1941, photographer and photo historian Don M. Paul wrote that

> Since 1930, almost every major development in synchronized flash has been due to the perseverance of newspaper men who have put in a plug for it on all occasions, and have hastened its

acceptance by means of homemade equipment which soon became standard, and through revolutionary usages which eventually became regular procedure. Thanks to the newsmen, flash has become indispensable. It has occasioned new trends in photography, it is the basis of a new kind of journalism.[26]

Sammy Schulman looked back to the very first time that he encountered the flashbulb. He has been on assignment in Tunisia and France, and returned to London to find a cable from Walter Howie, manager of the International News Photo organization (INP), telling him to look out for a package of something that would '"revolutionize photography"'.[27] Soon, a packet containing a dozen flashbulbs arrived, together with a device for igniting the magnesium foil inside the bulbs.

There still isn't any doubt in my mind that the flash bulb is the greatest invention since the self-starter. The flashbulb took the stiffness out of news photography. It removed the invisible clamps from behind the heads of the subjects of news pictures. It changed the news cameraman from a brandishing madman who filled places with thumping explosions of fire and smoke into a more or less undisheveled and discreetly anonymous addition to any scene. It took the tension out of the faces you see in your newspapers. It enabled the camera to get into places where it had never been before. Lastly, it reduced the life insurance premiums on photographers, some of whom had been blinded or critically burned by premature explosions of their flash powder.[28]

INP adopted the winged flashgun as a symbol of how quickly and effectively news photographs could now be delivered—photographs that had themselves been seized in an instant, their effectiveness depending on a swift coalescence of eye and apparatus, serendipity and practice. Handbooks emphasized the imperative of speed: 'Every day handsome rewards are there for the snatching. And it is snatching! There's not much time for pondering. Here's your picture—*now!*—there, it's gone. Just like that.'[29] As newspaper photographer John Floherty put it, 'the subject as seen by the cameraman was as fleeting as a flash of summer lightning caught in that same split second'.[30]

Until the 1930s, the little tray into which one placed one's powder before igniting it (usually by means of a tug on a device that struck a spark with a flint) remained the tool in trade of the press photographer. But after the widespread adoption of the flashbulb and the 'speed gun' that was used to synchronize it, everything changed. This new technology, wrote Sontheimer, enables the 'newspaper cameraman…to take hundreds of pictures he previously used to lose while fumbling to pour some flash powder out of a bottle, preparatory to a blast that would scare the pants of everyone for yards around'.[31] The flashbulb rendered powder flash pretty much obsolete, although it was not entirely replaced for a while. Advertisements in photographic magazines show that it, and its accompanying apparatus, were still being advertised as late as the early 1960s: flash powder remained especially useful if a large area needed to be illuminated. Weegee, even if his self-image was inseparable from his Speed Graphic with synchronized flashgun, continued to employ it for occasions, like fires at night, where he wanted to throw light on a relatively broad scene, and could not get too close to the action.

The flashbulb was, though, just one component in the rapid growth of this fiercely competitive industry in news pictures. It took its place alongside the development of lightweight, hand-held press cameras, especially the Speed Graphic, and the development of wire distribution in the 1930s. Whilst the wire service was in operation as a way of distributing news and news images in a very spotty way from the mid-1920s, it became easily available from the middle of the decade. 'We can flash a photograph across the world in ten minutes', claimed British photography writer T. Thorne Baker in 1934, 'so that the newspapers of other countries can publish it too.'[32] As William Hannigan has put it, 'what the wire services did was create the potential for an event to be changed from a personal or regional experience to a national cultural experience. The image now operated as a link, unifying the American culture through shared experience.'[33] It was not just the news pictures themselves that were shared, but also a certain aesthetic: one that, at least when it came to shots taken in poor or non-existent light, accentuated the contrast between dark and shadow, pinpointed the direction of a viewer's gaze, and hence increased the melodramatic possibilities inherent within a scene.

Flashbulbs had further advantages. They allowed pictures to be taken where flash powder had previously been forbidden. 'The invention of the flashbulb has removed these restrictions', noted Jack Price (who had been chief staff photographer on New York's *Morning World*) in 1935, 'with the result that photographs may now be made of steamship piers, court-rooms, below decks aboard ship, in mines and tunnels and numerous places where previously the photographer was barred.'[34] Yet despite proving to be far safer than flash powder, these new devices were initially treated with some caution. Jarché recalls an assignment to take photographs down one of the deepest coal mines in Wales: before the descent, those members of the colliery management in charge of the visit insisted on holding a flashbulb over a gas ring to see if it would ignite the fumes.[35] And since for a photographer who happened, fortuitously, to be on the scene at the time of a breaking news story, the bulbs might be in very limited supply, this photographer would have to guard their stash of artificial light—their only available opportunity for getting a picture scoop—very carefully. In February 1933 Sammy Schulman was present in Miami when a gunman tried to assassinate President-Elect Roosevelt, missing him, but hitting Mayor Cermak of Chicago—he managed to obtain a quick shot of him swaying, fatally injured. A tiny, dishevelled, wild-looking, and emaciated man, Giuseppe Zangara, was arrested. Schulman only had one bulb left, and (asked by Roosevelt to take no pictures in the hospital) the photographer raced off to the city jail, where, when Zangara was dragged out of his cell, he asked a shirt to be thrown round his naked body for decency's sake and commanded a cop to point a gun at him, setting up the picture carefully, in order to make the best use of his one remaining bulb and obtain his portrait of the tiny killer framed by the forces of the law (see Figure 7.1).

As Schulman's anecdote illustrates, the flashbulb became an indispensable tool for reporting crimes committed under the cover of darkness. This led to a consolidation of flash's association with the nefarious, the violent, the sensational. Photographers working for the tabloids—which covered crime in the most lurid detail—hanging out

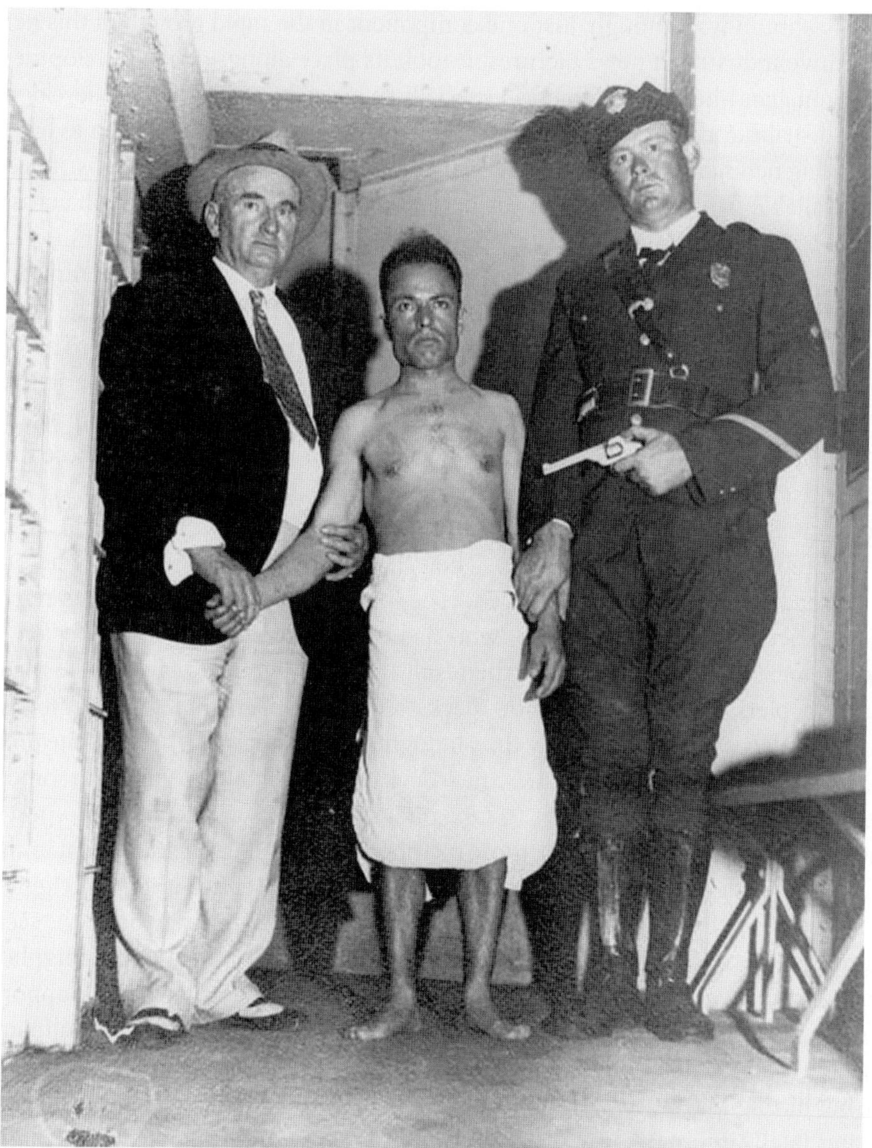

Figure 7.1 Sammy Schulman, 'Giuseppe Zangara in custody after his unsuccessful attempt on President Roosevelt's life', 1933. Courtesy of the State Archives of Florida.

around criminals and low dives, operating almost entirely at night, were quite low in the newspaper hierarchy. In David J. Krajicek's memorable phrase, crime reporters in general were considered 'the catfish of the newsroom'.[36] This cut-throat atmosphere was not just confined to New York and other major American cities. Stanley Devon writes his autobiography in language that is very close to the discourse of tabloid journalism (indeed here, and with other news photographers' life writing, one wonders, before the days of acknowledged ghostwriting, what journalistic collaboration may be happening), and he portrays London's picture-chasing world as equally savage. His style, and that of other newsmen who represented themselves as cut-throat and courageous in their determination to get the shot, familiar with every turn of a city, determinedly autonomous, and stereotypically male in their outlook and allegiances, owes a great deal to the style of hard-boiled crime fiction of the 1930s and 1940s.[37] With page space being increasingly dominated by pictures, newspapers demanded images that went with the news headlines of the day—not merely those that filled a hole.

> Agencies and papers fought other agencies and papers. Photographers fought photographers, and all who got in their way. I had landed myself in a jungle at a time when its life was at its wildest. And the newest and wildest beast was the Fleet Street cameraman...the more gentlemanly you behaved, the less likely you were to get a picture. Your only chance seemed to be to become more cunning and unscrupulous than the rest. Among the agency photographers, where competition was fiercest, it bred a race of hard-boiled, callous men who put no scruples between them and their pictures.[38]

Between the 1920s and the 1930s, the type of crime reportage—and accompanying photography—that most captivated the public's attention shifted from a fascination with murder trials and court scenes to street-level violence, and the flashbulb was a crucial piece of the technology that made this possible.[39]

The double-edged nature of flash photography—on the one hand a highly useful instrument of illumination, yet on the other, a volatile compound (and later, a potentially volatile bulb)—made it a compelling component of the literature of crime. It functions both as an instrument on the side of law and order—recording a murder or a robbery, and even facilitating in its detection—and as a potential weapon. Within imaginative works, sometimes the flash itself is used to accentuate atmosphere, to puncture darkness, to suggest sudden, dramatic danger—or to create danger in its own right. Near the opening of Raymond Chandler's *The Big Sleep* (1939), as Marlowe approaches an address in West Hollywood, 'a sudden flash of hard white light shot out of Geiger's house like a wave of summer lightning', leading him to find a dead man, a doped and naked girl, a blackened flashbulb on a tripod, and—surprise!—no plate in the camera. This scene translated perfectly to the screen, where the flash rips into the wet darkness.[40] *A Shot in the Dark* (1941, dir. William McGann) includes a reporter who gets to investigate a murder location when he distracts the police by throwing a flashbulb down a hallway so that it explodes. In *Rogues' Gallery* (1944, dir. Albert Herman), the photographer engineers the escape of the reporter heroine and himself by letting off a flashbulb in the villain's face—the indivisibility of news photographer and flashgun is signalled by their prominence on the movie's poster. This idea of the flash as a weapon—rather than as an instrument used to reveal the truth—is an enduring one, and is found across a range of genres, not least in the *Batman* comics. The Giant Flash Camera was first introduced in issue 104 (December 1956), and then reappeared in issue 108 (June 1957) as one of the trophies in the Bat Cave—having been captured from the Flash Bandits.[41] It was used for training a new recruit, Batman Jones, who shows admirable common sense about the light's damaging effects, saying if such a contraption were used against him, he'd just shield his eyes temporarily.

Flash photograph's role as a facilitator of justice was indivisible from the assumption that photography could provide reliable, factual evidence: that it carried forensic authority. When flash powder was first introduced, the press seized on its potential for catching criminal perpetrators. A much-syndicated news item in March 1889 told of a patent application that had been made by two photographers from Dubuque, Iowa, involving a wire attached to safe knob or door handle that would cause a flash to go off, resulting in the photographer's image being caught on a camera plate.[42] Fifty years later, Rus Arnold's little manual *Flash Photography* picks up on recent newspaper stories of a man who had been troubled with petty theft at his gas station.

> Finally he decided to catch the burglar. With a simple camera he had lying around, he arranged a 'burglar alarm' using a photoelectric cell. When the burglar stepped into the path of an infra-red ray, the photoelectric cell set off the flash camera and rang a bell. The intruder was frightened away, but not before the picture had been taken

—leading to the offender's arrest a couple of days later.[43]

From its inception, photography was used by police forces themselves in the course of recording crimes, criminals, and the scenes of crimes.[44] But as Don Paul, writing in 1950, put it: 'one point has always limited their utility—lighting conditions. With the perfecting of the flashbulb, the last obstacle to standard acceptance was eliminated. Bottled daylight, in the form of the flashbulb, evened up photographic conditions so that documentary records could be made under all circumstances.'[45] As a current textbook on police photography succinctly puts it, 'much of the police photographer's job requires that artificial light be created because many auto accidents and crimes occur in the dark'.[46] Like other police and law enforcement manuals, this book gives careful advice about calibrating the relationship between street lights and camera flash; about calculating how far the flash's light will reach; about avoiding intense shadows; and about avoiding glare and reflections, especially when concentrating on, say, the detail left by a footprint in the snow. Police archives provide a very comprehensive collection of images of crimes and criminals, of course, but these archives also contain a treasure trove of examples of flash's visual effects, including its characteristic power of producing dramatic chiaroscuro, its bleaching of areas that are close to the explosion of light, the unintended appearance of the flashgun's rim in the corner of a picture (as in Figure 7.2), the telltale covering of a face or eyes (as in Figure 7.3)—or even the unabashed posing for the camera, like a starlet, that's the response of the guilty and exposed to having the flash pointed in their direction (see Figure 7.4).

In imaginative works, flash is presented as an indispensable tool to the detective—especially the amateur detective. Indeed, as we saw with Grant Allen's *Recalled to Life*, flash produced some highly inventive plots in relation to criminal activity, whether in prose fiction or in film. A 1912 film melodrama, *The Girl Reporter's Big Scoop*, had the heroine going undercover as a maid to spy on a band of robbers, and learning flash photography in order to catch them in the act.[47] Anthony Sharpe's 1924 pulp thriller, *The Mystery of the Flashlight Print*, features a villain caught on camera strangling his estranged wife in a Scottish wood. He believes that he executed this crime in complete solitude, at the dead

Figure 7.2 Unknown photographer, 'Body of a woman in a print dress lying on the floor in front of a Singer treadle sewing machine', late 1930s/early 1940s.

New South Wales. Police Department. Justice and Police Museum # 31297.

of night, but he is mystified and 'tormented by the thought of that inexplicable light which had blazed so brightly, if so briefly, as the dead woman had slid from his hands'.

'In Heaven's name, what—'

His hoarse whisper broke off suddenly, and his blood chilled to the heart at the explanation that leaped into his mind.

'A flashlight, by all that's incredible!'

Although there's a momentary associative hint for the reader that divine power might have shone out a revelatory beam, implying that evil doing can never be concealed, the explanation is far more matter of fact. He wonders, of course—'But what was a flashlight doing there in that wood?'

The silent question brought him no consolation, no sense of relief. He had recently read a book by a famous naturalist, dealing with the Canadian beaver, and the book had been illustrated by unique photographs taken at night, the beavers, by simple mechanical means, having been made to fire the flashlights and to photograph themselves. Not for a moment did he doubt that

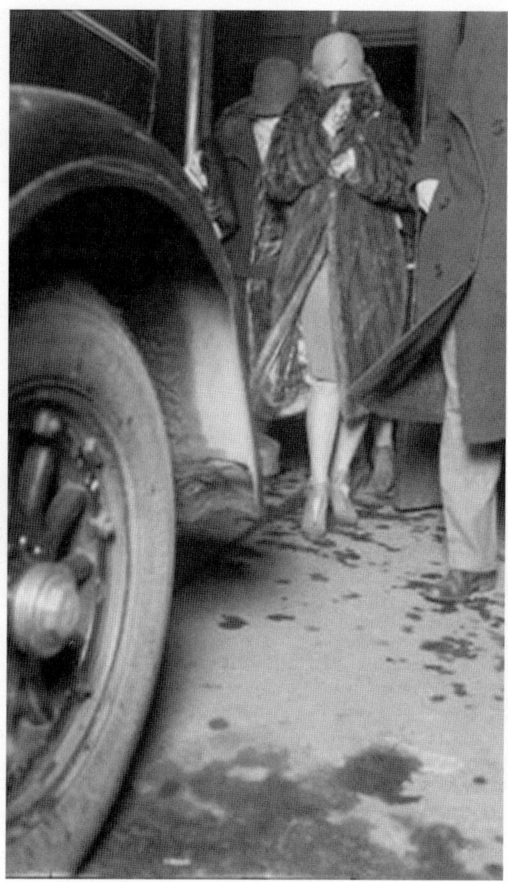

Figure 7.3 Unknown photographer, from *Chicago Tribune*, 20 February 1929. Mrs. Myrtle Gorman, of 434 Roscoe St., Common-law wife of Peter Gusenberg, who was murdered when rival gangsters mowed him and six companions down in a North Clark Street garage. Mrs Gorman denied all knowledge of Gusenberg's activities. Mrs. Gorman is leaving Gusenberg's inquest, February 19, 1929. The murders were known as the St. Valentine's Day massacre.

something akin to this was the explanation of that otherwise inexplicable light. In the struggle he or his victim had touched something, thread or wire, which had fired the light, and— [*sic*]

His heart gave a great bound of fear! The camera! There must have been a camera, else why the flashlight[?][48]

He had, indeed, set off a trigger intended to photograph owls. Arthur Ransome's children's novel, *The Big Six* (1940), has a particularly resourceful team of young detectives putting flash equipment to work to catch local villains who have been harming boats. Ransome's illustrations (Figures 7.5 and 7.6) couple the practical with the dramatic. Ransome, a keen amateur photographer himself, gives a clear diagram of the flashlight apparatus, with a shield constructed from a square biscuit tin. The resulting 'tremendous hissing flare of white light'—also illustrated—does its job.[49] In these last two

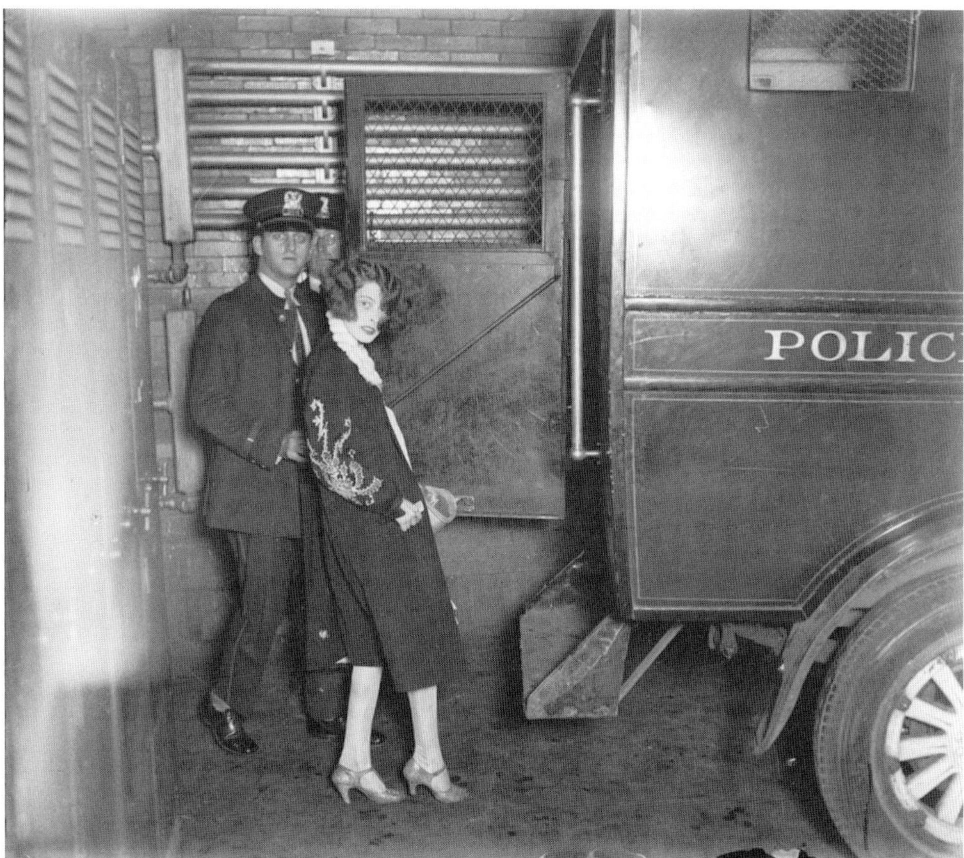

Figure 7.4 Unknown photographer, from *Chicago Tribune*, 1st July 1927. Gertrude 'Billie' Murphy, 22, is brought in for questioning in the murder case of Michael Stopec, who was shot and killed in an apartment hotel, circa July 1927. Murphy had been friends of the married Stopec and his suspected killer Henry Guardino, 31. It is said that Stopec and Guardino were 'bitter rivals for the favor of Billie' and that Murphy had tired of Guardino and was going to stay with Stopec. Murphy was also married to a man in the Joliet penitentiary.

cases, the innocent benefit from the technology of night-time wildlife photography—a type of hunting and shooting that its practitioners advanced as more rewarding, and less destructive, than that done with a rifle.[50]

The activity of wildlife hunting by camera flash takes one back to the work of the news photographer. At times, of course, these pursuits collapsed into one another. In 1933, the Associated Press decided that the Loch Ness monster story might be a world beater—especially if a picture of the elusive creature were obtained. Edward Dean, not the only press photographer to be dispatched to Scotland in pursuit of this story, thought that he had detected some promising tracks in the mud and, working in secret, set up an elaborate apparatus. 'The camera was camouflaged, and to it ran wires from

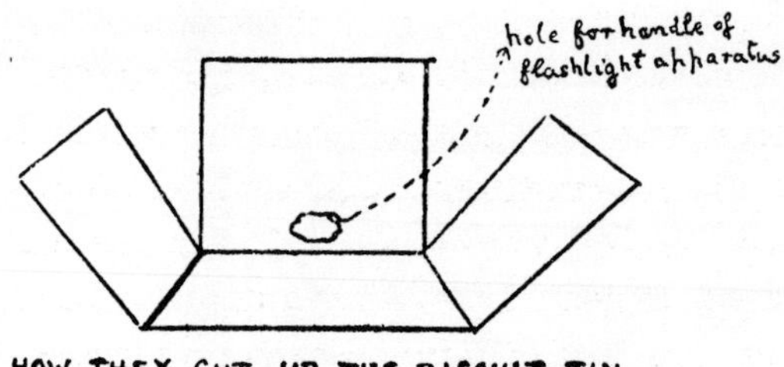

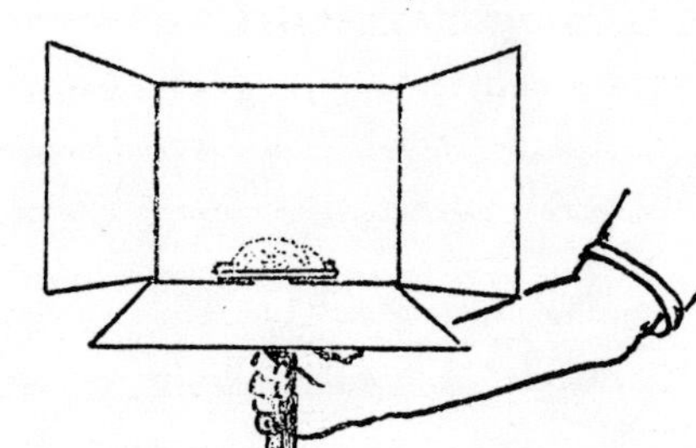

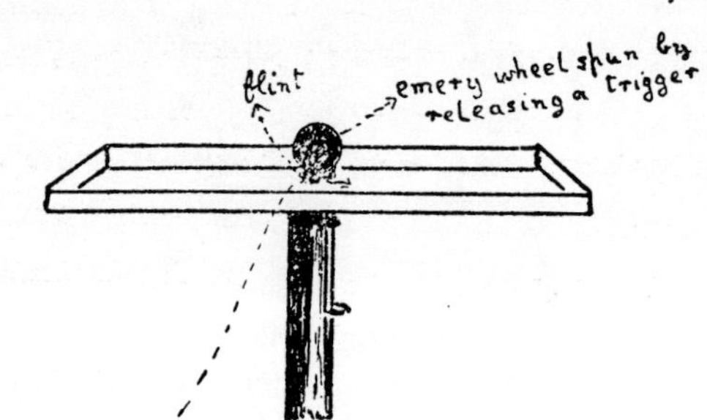

THE FLASHLIGHT AND ITS SHIELD

Figure 7.5 Arthur Ransome, 'The Flashlight and Its Shield', illustration to *The Big Six* (London: Jonathan Cape, 1940), 335. © Arthur Ransome Literary Estate.

the edge, from the water, and from various points near by. The shutter was to be left open, with flash bulbs fixed and ready, so that anything that touched one of the wires would automatically release the shutter and operate the camera.' To his great excitement, the next morning he found that the bulbs had exploded, the shutter had clicked—but alas, instead of Nessie, 'all I had for my trouble was a group of fat-legged Boy Scouts standing still in attitudes of frightened rigidness. They had been caught by the camera while engaged on a night stalking patrol.'[51]

Figure 7.6 Arthur Ransome, 'The Moment', illustration to *The Big Six* (London: Jonathan Cape, 1940), 351. © Arthur Ransome Literary Estate.

But the connection between pursuing four- and two-legged prey ran deeper. In his 1941 book *Newspaperman*, Morton Sontheimer quotes a remark of FSA photographer Edwin Rosskam. What matters, Rosskam said, is '"knowing when to snap the shutter. It is akin to marksmanship. That shutter and finger are like the trigger and sights on your rifle in a big-game hunt. The aiming must be meticulous."'[52] Like a bullet's impact, there is something irrevocable about taking a photograph, Sammy Schulman reminded his readers: 'When you pull a trigger on a news camera you are recording the unadorned

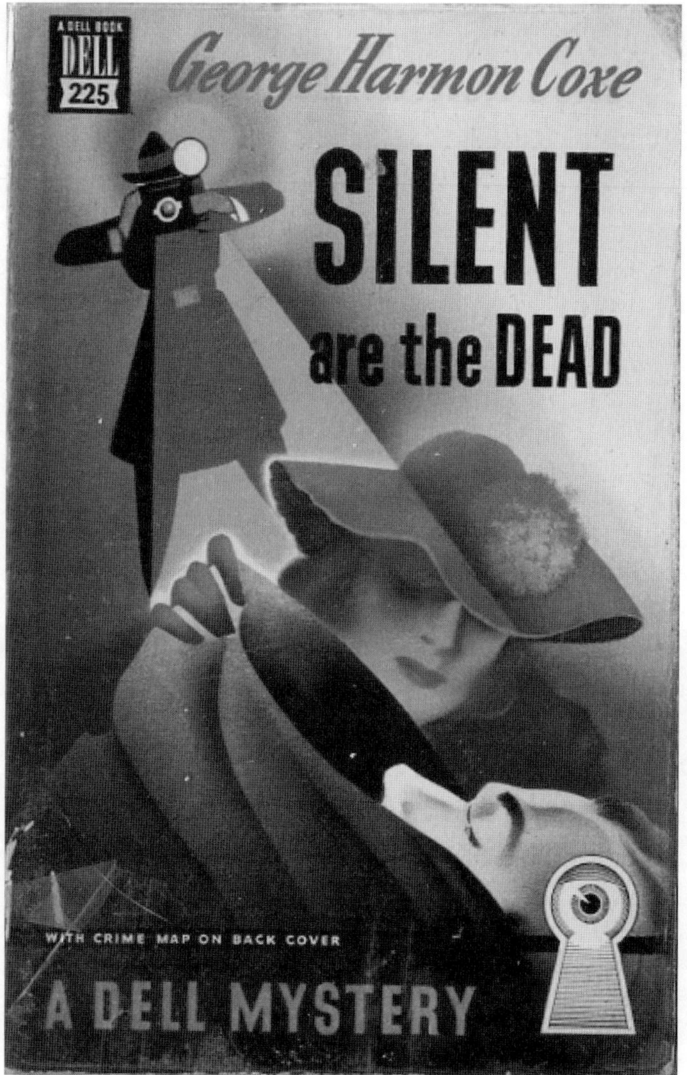

Figure 7.7 Cover, George Harmon Coxe, *Silent are the Dead* (New York: Dell, 1941).

truth. You get the works; there's no way to change things, or pretty them up or make them worse. There's no "x" key on a Speed Graphic. That black box we wield is a terribly revealing weapon.'[53]

By extension, popular culture developed the figure of the news photographer who went out to hunt in the urban jungle of the late 1930s and early 1940s as a type of hard-boiled masculinity—one very close to the simultaneously developing gumshoe detective. Both populated the pages of pulp magazines such as *Black Mask*.[54] Most notably, George Harmon Coxe's press photographer Flash Casey first appeared in a number of short stories published in *Black Mask* between 1934 and 1942. His persona expanded into novels, radio and TV performances, and film, the flash apparatus that he wields on book jackets serving to identify him (as in Figure 7.7).[55] More than 400 different radio scripts were broadcast between 1943 and 1955, and in the broadcasts, necessarily, flash becomes not so much a violent visual interruption as a *sound*. 'FLASHBULB & SHUTTER CLICK', reads a typical direction.[56] Flash Casey's expertise relied on the fact that he often worked closely alongside the police force, but was not subject to the same protocols, and did not have the same (theoretical) accountability as they did.

Coxe's stories are very much of their moment. *Murder for Two* (1943) finds Casey frustrated, unable to join the army because of a gammy knee. By way of war service, he teaches an advanced course in practical defence photography for the American Women's Voluntary Service, and finds one of his pupils, Karen Harding, accompanying him on assignment, outdoing him when it comes to deploying the latest technology. He turns round to see 'a tiny and instantaneous red glow…"Let's see," he said. "That was a blackout bulb, huh? It won't come out if you haven't got infra-red film."' The girl assures him that her camera is, indeed, appropriately loaded, thanks to her previous instruction. '"You told us all about how we could take pictures in the dark without any giveaway flash if we used these new bulbs and infra-red film."'[57] The reader is being treated to some instruction, too, about how to take flash pictures by stealth, whilst the tense conflation of explosive flash and real firearms is postponed to the conclusion where Casey himself faces down the woman whom he now knows to be the novel's main murderer, Helen MacKay, with Stanley Furness (former husband of MacKay's first victim, and set to marry MacKay) standing by, horrified. Casey

> lifted the camera as the gun muzzle angled upward. He saw her hand tighten and her lips draw back. Furness saw it too. 'Helen!' he yelled and reached for the gun and then she pulled the trigger and Casey's flashbulb went off.
>
> Furness was too far away. He couldn't reach the gun and for an instant there was only that explosion of light that stopped all motion and highlighted the woman, the man, and the gun. Then the glare was gone and there had been no sound but that of the hammer clicking emptily.[58]

Casey knew, all along, what the prose briefly conceals from the reader—that the revolver's chambers held no bullets.

When Coxe revived Casey for three more novels in the early 1960s, Jack, or Mr Casey, is barely called 'Flash' at all, however. The name is part of his past, along with—self-referentially—a radio series that had been allegedly based on him, and that formed the basis for his newspaper colleagues' teasing. In *The Man Who Died Too Soon* (1962), this past is expanded upon. Back in the days of volatile magnesium powder, 'there had been one occasion when, in his inexperience, he had used too much powder and nearly set a room on fire, and someone had tagged him with that name and it had stuck'.[59] Although there's no hard evidence to suggest that Casey's revival owed anything to a new photographer-detective, the timing is suggestive. The TV series *Man With a Camera* (1958–60) has a striking opening sequence. After two minutes' worth of plot-establishment for the twenty-four or so minutes of drama to come, a Speed Graphic with flash attachment fills the screen. The camera zooms in to focus on the flashbulb itself—flash!—cut to an intertitle with a drawn camera plus flashgun by way of illustration, and the series title in large letters (announced, too, in a voice-over)—flash!—and cut to another intertitle with the same illustration, and—again the voice-over—the information, 'starring Charles Bronson'. Mike Kovac, the protagonist, played by Bronson, was a former combat photographer in the Korean War, now working freelance for various clients, including the press, police, and insurance companies. He becomes involved (often as a private eye) in a number of criminal cases. His photographic armoury does not just include the flashgun—he uses a camera hidden in his necktie, in a cigarette lighter, and so on. But as that title sequence suggests, he is especially associated with flash, and flash turns up in a number of roles. In the very first episode, Kovac is forced to use his flash when the gangsters whom he's shadowing turn out almost all the lights in a room where they're plotting to throw a boxing match, which gives away his presence (not, perhaps, putting flash in the most positive of lights); 'Black Light' has Kovac using infrared flash with infrared film, the bulb giving away just a tiny little gleam of light in the dark as he's trying to track down corrupt cops in a New York precinct; 'The Last Portrait' uses the gun-and-its-flash-disguised-as-a-camera trope in a complicated plot involving the assassination of an Arab (country unspecified) leader who's visiting the UN.[60]

This series—instrumental in establishing Bronson's career—was sponsored by the manufacturers of Sylvania flashbulbs. This product (aimed at the domestic consumer, rather than the detective or news photographer) was advertised throughout. One series of fifteen episodes aired, and were sufficiently popular for a second series to go into production. But the programme's role as an advertising vehicle made it very vulnerable to market developments in flash photography, however, and when Polaroid brought out their new Wink-Light in 1959, which used a capacitator to fire a bulb that could be used about a hundred times without needing to be changed, Sylvania withdrew their investment in the series—only eleven of the projected fourteen second-series episodes were filmed.[61] One wonders how much Bronson regretted the axing, since he subsequently dubbed *Man With a Camera* 'the biggest "plug" show in the history of television…I was the hero, a news cameraman, but the director had to keep stopping the action to make sure the label on the equipment was visible. By the tenth week I realized I was playing second banana to a flash-bulb.'[62]

The title sequence of *Man With a Camera*, figuring Charles Bronson pointing his flash straight at the viewer, grabbing one's attention, is highly similar to the iconic image of Weegee—Arthur Fellig (1899–1968)—whose somewhat portly figure and self-burnished image was inseparable from his Speed Graphic camera and his Graflex flash synchronizer,

Figure 7.8 Weegee (Arthur Fellig), 'New York Photographer "Weegee"', 1930s. © Bettmann/ Getty Images.

as in Figure 7.8. Originally developed as a camera that could easily be carried on a bicycle, the Speed Graphic was the press camera of choice from the 1920s until the early 1950s, when it was eventually eclipsed by the ease of smaller cameras.[63] This is the Weegee everyone recognizes, the Weegee that advertises Weegee. 'Weegee and his Love—his Camera', the caption in *Naked City* reads.[64] He took self-portraits in his spartan room, the walls papered with favourite news shots, his Speed Graphic and flashgun on a bedside table improvised from cartons of flashbulbs, as we see in Figure 7.9. Weegee's career was built upon producing the kind of images that only flash photography could deliver. He opened his 1953 pamphlet, *Weegee's Secrets of Shooting with Photoflash*, by trumpeting his credentials: 'In the past twenty-two years I have taken about ninety-eight percent of all my pictures with flash.'[65] Weegee made his name with rapidly shot pictures of crime scenes, arrests, dramatic fire rescues, and catastrophic car wrecks. As his career developed, so did a kind of idiosyncratic jokiness—especially after his four-year stint in Hollywood. He even, through darkroom manipulation, squeezed his subjects inside flashbulbs. Indeed, he put himself inside one, as shown in Figure 7.10. Weegee's name was synonymous with the flash.

Weegee's early career spanned the major shift in flash technology described in the opening section of this chapter. Hired by the Ducket & Adler Photo Studio in Lower

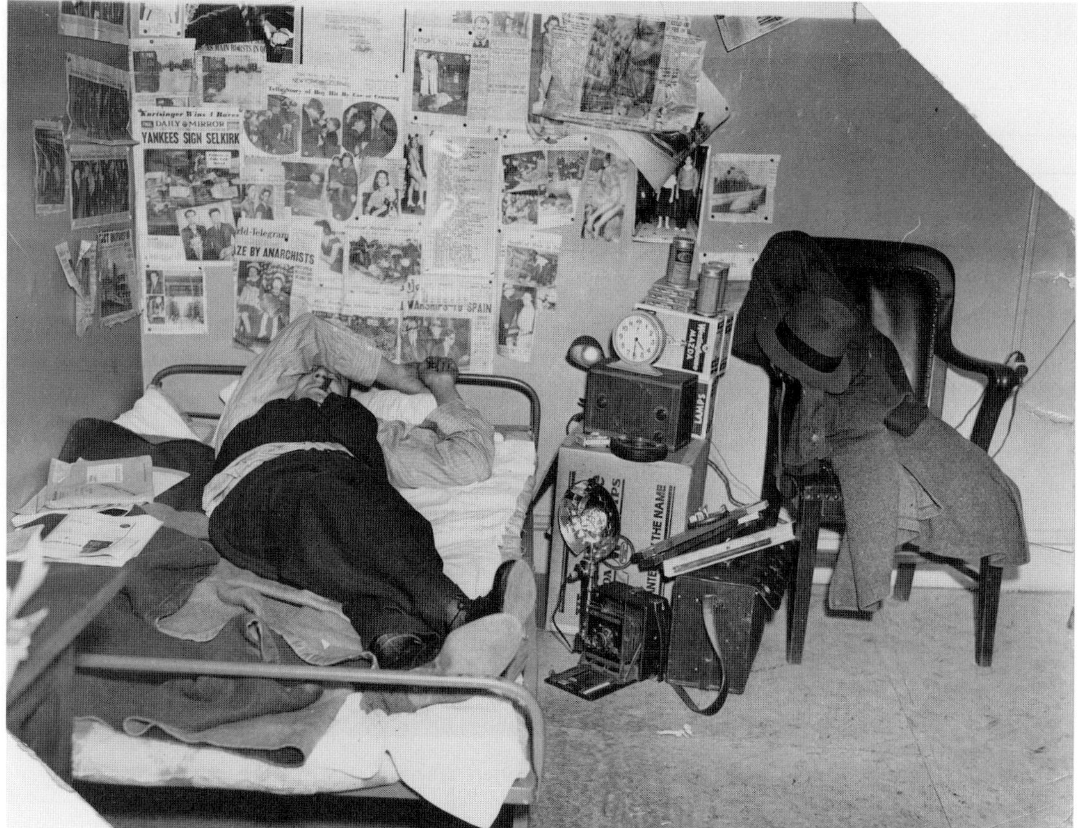

Figure 7.9 Weegee (Arthur Fellig), 'My Studio', mid-1930s. © Weegee (Arthur Fellig)/International Center of Photography/Getty Images.

Manhattan, one of the then Arthur Fellig's tasks—once he graduated from floor sweeper and errand boy to cameraman's assistant—was to prepare the magnesium flash powder. Describing his period working for Acme Newspapers between 1924 and 1935 (largely in the darkroom, he was at that time only occasionally sent out as a photographer)[66] he gives the invention of the flashbulb a transformative historical role:

> Over the developing trays in the dark room at Acme, history passed through my hands. Fires, explosions, railroad wrecks, ship collisions, prohibition gang wars, murders, kings, presidents, everybody famous and everything exciting that turned up in the Twenties. I handled the first flashbulb, produced by General Electric to take the place of the dangerous and messy flash powder. I saw the first photograph of President Coolidge transmitted over telephone wires from the White House to New York City; I processed it. Photography was growing up, and so was I.[67]

It was the invention and fine-tuning of the flashbulb that made possible Weegee's career as a press photographer specializing in those scenes that so often took place in darkness. His news pictures were published in the liberal daily newspaper *PM*, sometimes

Figure 7.10 Weegee (Arthur Fellig), 'Weegee inside a flashbulb', early to mid-1950s. © Weegee (Arthur Fellig)/International Center of Photography/Getty Images.

with a column in which he told the story that lay behind an image's making.[68] He also took a number of indoor shots of bars and clubs, his emphasis constantly falling on the offbeat and the louche—a choice of subject matter that, unlike the melodramas of street violence and disaster, he took with him when he moved temporarily to Los Angeles.

Weegee arrived in a city where flashbulbs were popping off all the time, and not just at the stars or on the screen. Officer George T. George, with the Los Angeles Police Department (LAPD), was pioneering in his use of flash photography in everyday police work, issuing kits to officers in squad cars containing either a Recomar 18 or a Speed Graphic camera, and a plentiful supply of flashbulbs. As well as recognizing its usefulness for standard police work—for example, recording a traffic accident that took place at night—this LAPD activity included such work as helping to bust indecency in vaudeville shows.

> Several police photographers took a box quite near the stage at a recent show. They let word slip back to the manager, through an usher, that they were talent scouts from the New York stage. Backstage was a beehive of activity as this information filtered through. The actors put all the 'oomph' of which they were capable into their actions. The 'talent scouts' took countless flash pictures of all the highly flavored episodes on the stage. Although normally there would have been objections from the management to flash photography during a performance, there was none because both cast and management were excited with the possibility of 'going places'.[69]

Of course, no one was going any further than a police cell.

Whilst in Los Angeles, Weegee was employed as a technical consultant to the mystery-thriller *The Sleeping City* (1950), and as a result was sent by Universal to eleven cities where he photographed local residents.[70] These are images that, like his pictures of Los Angeles's Skid Row, show off his skills as an urban documentarian, very much in the tradition of Jacob Riis: they are the successors to the very numerous photographs that he took of people sleeping in the dark doorways and stairwells of New York, in missions and flophouses and collapsed on bar tables. He was always attuned to a populist visual sensibility, however. He used his photography to undercut social pretension of all kinds. As Luc Sante puts it, as 'a populist artist, Weegee appealed to a working-class audience and reflected its outlook and concerns. Accordingly, his work was direct, blunt, wholehearted, cornball, bawdy, riotous, unapologetic, sentimental, opportunistic, and gleefully complicit with the basest instincts of all concerned.'[71] He knew what editors wanted.

> Being a free-lance photographer was not the easiest was to make a living. There had to be a good meaty story to get the editors to buy the pictures. A truck crash with the driver trapped inside, his face a crisscross of blood . . . a tenement-house fire, with the screaming people being carried down the aerial ladder clutching their babies, dogs, cats, canaries, parrots, monkeys, and even snakes . . . a just-shot gangster, lying in the gutter, well dressed in his dark suit and pearl hat, hot off the griddle, with a priest, who seemed to appear from nowhere, giving him the last rites . . . just-caught stick-up men, lady burglars, etc.
>
> These were the pictures that I took and sold. It was during the Depression, and people could forget their own troubles by reading about others.[72]

But there was, all the same, a critical bite. The instincts on which Sante remarked included voyeurism: Weegee both fed readers' curiosity about the spectacle of death and disaster, and, in turning the flash onto the self-absorbed array of expressions (as seen in Figure 7.11) of those who rubbernecked these scenes, mirrored and interrogated the print spectator's own gaze.[73]

Fellig was never one to shrink from self-aggrandizement, ceaselessly promoting and performing the human commodity that went under the one-word name of Weegee. Weegee scholar Miles Barth has caustically remarked, indeed, that he had 'an ego big enough to suck the air out of the Hollywood bowl'.[74] The cut-throat Depression atmosphere rendered self-publicity highly necessary in his profession, as new technology, making flash photography easier, collapsed the distinction between professional and amateur when it came to grabbing news images in the field. To quote again from his autobiography:

Figure 7.11 Weegee (Arthur Fellig), 'Crowd Gathers at East Side Murder Scene', c.1940. © Weegee (Arthur Fellig)/International Center of Photography/Getty Images.

the *Daily News* and *Mirror* readers, instead of calling up the tabloids with news tips, for which they got fifty cents each, had become picture conscious. They had bought themselves Brownies with flashgun attachments and had started to shoot pictures themselves. One ambitious amateur even began to set tenement houses on fire…

Cab drivers, instead of cruising for fares, went looking for spot news with loaded cameras alongside them. Ambulance drivers now rushed to answer their emergency calls so as to be the first with the pictures. Even the wreckers, who, for a fiver, used to get tipped off by the cops to the scenes of auto collisions, carried cameras.[75]

Weegee stood out from the average photographer, however. His most memorable pictures record not just the newsworthy event—the fact of a murder or fire—but also its human impact. As Susan Squiers has pointed out, his images were different from those pictures of violent crime that had become commonplace in the American tabloid press during the 1930s. Certainly in New York, these obeyed 'a standardized visual logic in representing crime. Most newspaper photographs were taken either at a further remove from the subject than were Weegee's, or so close up as to look almost clinical...the average tabloid photographer treated crime victims more as uninflected objects around which law enforcement officials might importantly gather.'[76]

By contrast, Weegee looked for human expressions that signalled the uniqueness of a moment. His work is often distinguished from that of his news photographer competitors by his practice of turning the camera to show the anguished, baffled, shocked expressions of people under extreme stress, or the exhaustion of members of the emergency services, or the merely curious and sometimes disconcertingly detached bystander. In these images, people—as William Sharpe beautifully puts it—'are flash frozen into their own watchful rigor mortis, distanced from the corpses only by their capacity to stand upright and look at something'.[77] Curiosity, shock, and complete absorption in a moment were the emotions that attracted Weegee as a photographer: the expressions that people adopt when they don't know, or don't care, that they are being watched. One of his favourite photographic moves was to shoot from behind, underscoring the fact that there's another side—invisible to us—of the public face that we put on for the world. Seen from the front, the images of flashlit faces make emotion visible at times when repression is impossible. In Hollywood, repeating an idea he had already shared in the New York press, Weegee said that autograph hunters expressed more genuine, unforced emotion than was conveyed through the conventionalized expressions of trained actors. 'A photographer is a hunter with a camera', he was to say—anticipating Sontag, shadowing the fictional detectives who used such weaponry to track their game—'alert, with his sense keen, with his mind in tune with what is going on around him ready to click the shutter on the dramatic moment...the moment that never comes back.'[78] He readily capitalized on the tough-guy, cynical, joke-cracking, womanizing image of the news photographer—the kind of persona epitomized by Flash Casey.

To be exposed to the flash is to be exposed to the world. Sometimes, this pictorial impulse verges on the voyeuristic, as Sante noted, and Weegee's images frequently exemplify the fine line between voyeurism, the humorous, and the documentary. Exposure may be linked to shame—to the desire for an anonymity that's soon to vanish, or to the face-concealing actions of those who, for whatever reason, might not want to have their presence recorded in the company of, say, the shiny gold call girl depicted in Figure 7.12. Moreover, Weegee might play with the idea of being the bad boy, the reprobate under arrest (he photographed himself in the back of a police van), but his close relationship with a cooperative police force kept circling back to the self-image of himself as detective, inspecting a body in a trunk, posing as if his photographer's base were indeed a paddy wagon. As Richard Meyer has shown in his piece 'Learning from Low Culture', Weegee's photographs have come to symbolize the violent crime of the period, whether fictional or factual, and indeed, the presence of the flash blurs the distinction between reportage—artificially illuminating a scene—and the imaginative, where, as well as being a necessary tool of photographic technology, its power to create a sudden shock can also play a significant role.[79]

Weegee's photographs, whether taken on the east or west coasts, are not just important because of the contents of his representation, whether these involve murdered bodies,

Figure 7.12 Weegee (Arthur Fellig), 'Golden Girl', *c.*1950. © Weegee (Arthur Fellig)/International Center of Photography/Getty Images.

or arrests, or car accidents, or behind-the-scenes movie theatre shots, or showgirls, or skid row. They matter because they exploit the aesthetic potential of flash photography at a certain point in its development. Flashlight, in these images, is not an invisible means to an end: it is always announcing its presence. It often leaves its distinctive visible trace—gleaming back from a car's metalwork; giving a flaring reflection off a shiny door or off an eyeball peering from the darkness, as in Figure 7.13. A flash going off in a dressing-room mirror, however unintentionally, calls attention to the camera's complicity in producing artifice. Flash's visible presence, as was the case with the inadvertent reflections in Riis's images of New York tenements, stops us from considering a photograph as offering some unmediated image of the world. In their exaggeration of the distinction between light and dark, they do not just accentuate the illuminated subject matter, they also draw out the blackness of the surrounding city. This blackness speaks in an easy metaphoric register of obscurity, hidden identities, fate, and wrongdoing to the point of evil—what Miles Orvell has called 'a simplified syntax of high contrasts'.[80] Occasionally, Weegee shines flashlight onto something more politically pointed in relation to such divisions, as we see in Figure 7.14. This image shows four black youths on one side of a cinema, and a vast array of unoccupied seats

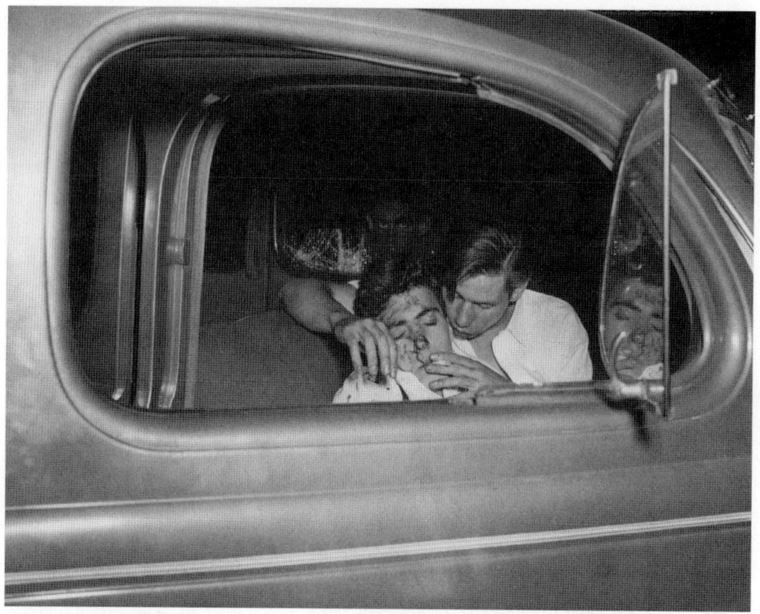

Figure 7.13 Weegee (Arthur Fellig), 'Crash Victim', 1941. © Weegee (Arthur Fellig)/International Center of Photography/Getty Images.

on the other, light reflecting back from the varnished surfaces of chair backs and, especially, the wood partition that looks like a slippery and forbidding wall.

The locations in which Weegee's photographs were published, moreover, add to the associations of flash-illuminated images with the lowbrow, even the seedy and tawdry. Many of the crime images appeared in the sensationalist New York press, and Richard Meyer has drawn attention to later dissemination that reinforced the heterosexual masculinity of the photographic world. Reminding us that 'Advanced photography and pulp sensationalism were not so far from one another as conventional accounts of each genre might lead us to believe', Meyer writes that,

> Following the publication of *Naked Hollywood* in 1953, Weegee's photographs of celebrities, strippers, and naked mannequins were frequently reproduced in popular photography and men's magazines. These magazines ranged from technical publications such as *Modern Photography* to sensationally designed pocket-sized pulps such as *Eye* and *Brief*; from Hollywood entertainment magazines like *Picture Week* and *Night and Day* to girlie magazines like *High* ('The Tall Magazine for Men') and *Ho!* ('The Long Magazine for Men').
>
> In many cases, however, the boundary between these various kinds of magazines was blurred such that photographic instruction and erotic display, technical information about new lenses and lavish photo-spreads of women appeared within the same publication.[81]

Weegee was rarely a subtle photographer, and he certainly did not possess a nuanced take on metaphor, including the absolutes of good and evil encouraged by the visual language of illumination on which his work relied. He describes an incident at the police station at East 51st Street, one of his favourite haunts.

Figure 7.14 Weegee (Arthur Fellig), 'A Washington D.C. Movie Theatre', 1941. © Weegee (Arthur Fellig)/International Center of Photography/Getty Images.

> Seated in the chair was the handcuffed burglar. The minute he saw me, he covered up. Out of the side of his mouth, he said, 'I don't want my picture took!' (Such grammar!). But this guy was a hardened criminal and knew his rights. The cops couldn't force him to pose for me. I put my camera down on a nearby desk, and said, to no one in particular, 'I'm going out to get a cup of coffee and a pastrami sandwich'. As I reached the door, I looked back. The guy was uncovered. The flash bulb went off when I pressed the remote control switch in my pocket, and I had my picture. When criminals tried to cover their faces it was a challenge to me. I literally uncovered not only their faces, but their black souls as well.[82]

When he shows people covering their faces, however—Irma Twiss Epstein, a nurse accused of killing a baby, burying her head with its respectable velvet hat in her hands,

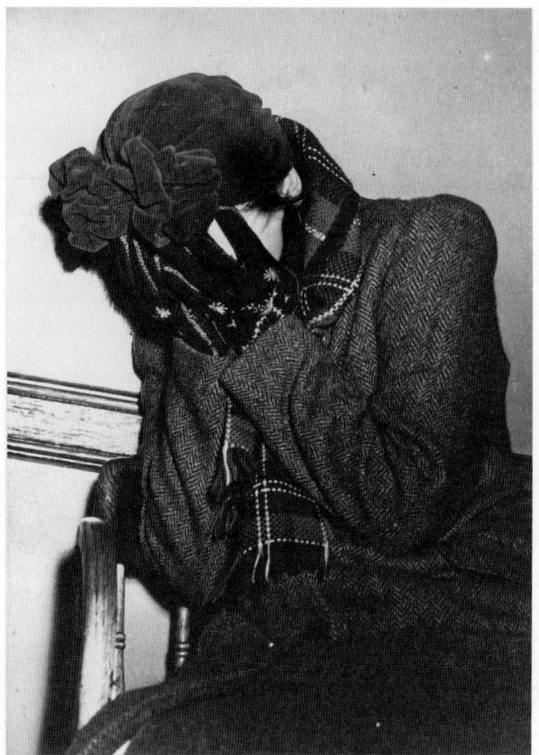

Figure 7.15 Weegee (Arthur Fellig), 'Irma Twiss Epstein', 1942. © Weegee (Arthur Fellig)/International Center of Photography/Getty Images.

as shown in Figure 7.15; an 'Ermine-Wrapped Patron Caught in a Gambling Den'; Henry Rosen and Harvey Stemmer, arrested in 1945 for bribing baseball players coming out of a police station elevator (Weegee knew where to wait) with their faces barely concealed behind large white handkerchiefs (Figure 7.16)—Weegee is not so much putting evil souls on display as he is shining a light on the shame and embarrassment that accompanies public exposure. Notably, the only people who seem consistently joyous in their arrests are transvestites—both cross-dressing performers and sex workers—who invariably beam at the camera as they stand between police officers, or stand framed by the back of a police van, as in Figure 7.17—as though Weegee is offering them a moment of celebrity fame. But with this notable exception, Weegee showed no compassion for the transgressor. A jewel thief 'pleaded with me not to take his picture . . . it would break his poor dear mother's heart. I told him that he should have thought of his mother before he went into the thieving business, and I let a big flash go off right in his face.'[83]

What stands out about Weegee's work, in addition to his play with dark and light, the disclosed and the concealed, is how it underscores flash's power to break in to the daily flow of time, just like the events themselves that Weegee—and other news photographers—so frequently recorded. The extreme contrast between illumination and darkness in the image that makes its way into the newspaper is the contrast between

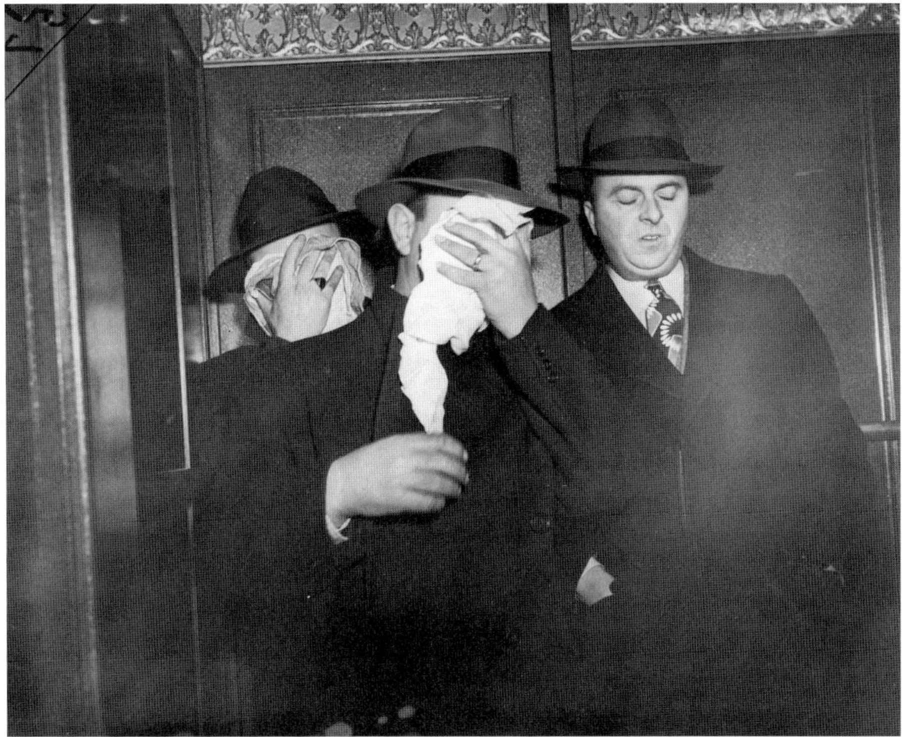

Figure 7.16 Weegee (Arthur Fellig), 'Shame of Arrest', 1945. © Weegee (Arthur Fellig)/International Center of Photography/Getty Images.

the startling immediacy of an extraordinary happening and the continuity of daily existence, which is suddenly rendered invisible. This does not just apply to murders or car accidents: those whom Weegee photographed waiting in line to see a film star were looking for some excitement and borrowed glamour in their own ordinary lives—the kind of escape from daily routines that going to a film brings with it. A strong awareness of this desire to have humdrum and routine existence interrupted by some kind of thrill informs a significant number of Weegee's Los Angeles photographs. It reveals something of a patronizing disdain for a public obsessed with manufactured fame—particularly as the tinsel of Hollywood faded in his own eyes.

Weegee used the flash to illuminate emotional response. Flash brings out the contours in people's faces – their lines and creases and five o'clock shadows and tiredness and pores and stubble and age spots as well as their shifty or frightened eyes. Flash's ability to reveal detail was an aspect that made an enormous impact on Diane Arbus's work, as well. Arbus used flash extensively in her portraits of freaks, of circus performers, of social misfits—indeed, of people in general whose expressions, quirks, and personal surroundings she captures with unflinching, unflattering realism. Weegee was a notable influence upon her: not only did she explicitly admire his work, but on at least one occasion, she went out on assignment with him in his battered Chevrolet.[84]

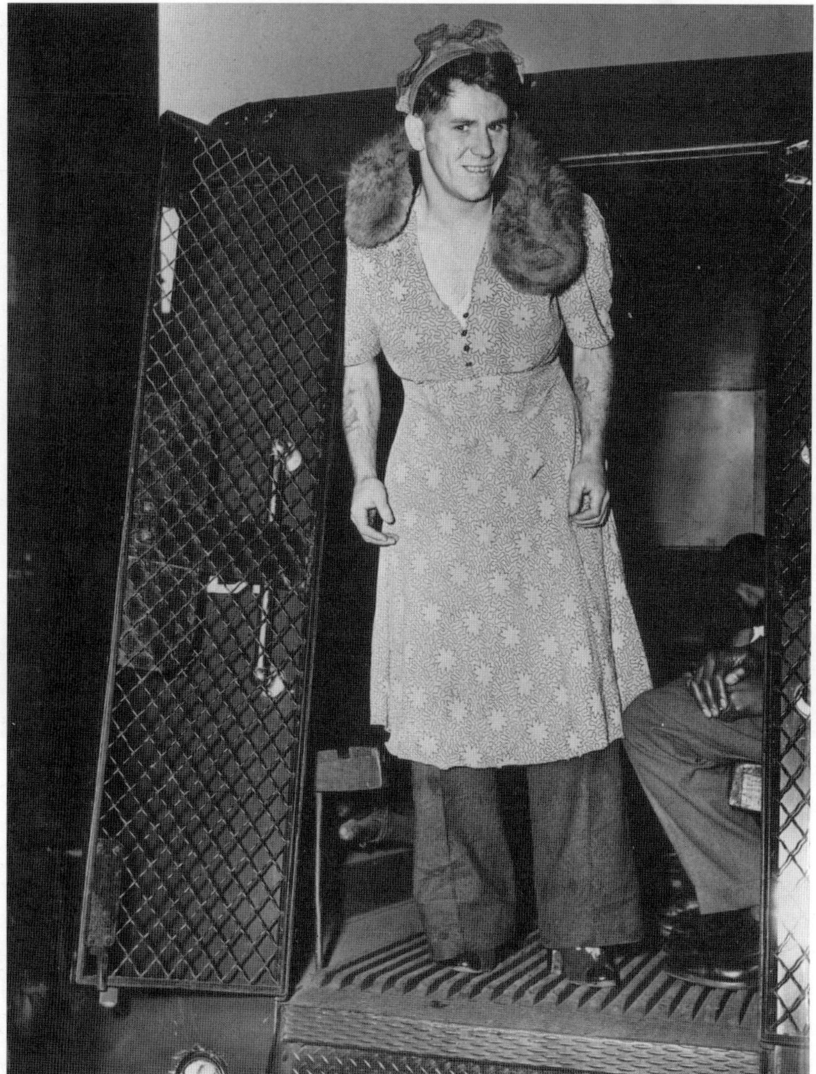

Figure 7.17 Weegee (Arthur Fellig), 'Cross Dresser (Myrtle from Myrtle Street)', 1943. © Weegee (Arthur Fellig)/International Center of Photography/Getty Images.

Like Weegee, Arbus captured performers, including female impersonators, in their dressing rooms; she photographed inside movie theatres; she took photographs of people on the city streets who fascinated her eye. But despite Weegee's influence upon her, the two photographers differed considerably in what they used their flash to emphasize. Unlike Weegee (although very much following the example of the German photographer August Sander), she very often asked people to pose for her in ways that brought out their own sense of identity, yet capturing what most fascinated her, which she terms 'the gap between intention and effect'.[85] To this end, too, she frequently used flash to illuminate private interiors, whether it bounces from the lamé dress and clutter of oriental ornaments in 'A widow in her bedroom' (1963), or the reflected light gleams off exposed flesh, wine goblet, and telephone in a quite different sort of bedroom in 'Dominatrix embracing her client' (1970). Interiors, as well as postures, testify to her anthropological curiosity.[86] If Weegee was drawn to raw emotion, Arbus very often concentrated on texture—whether of lived-in faces or hairy tattooed chests; crumpled bedclothes or the lacy patterns on pantyhose. As she put it in 1971, 'I wanted to see the real differences between things ... between flesh and material, the densities of different kinds of things: air and water and shiny'.[87] In an exhibition wall label at the 1967 *New Documents* show at the Museum of Modern Art, New York, the curator John Szarkowski commented on how Arbus, together with Lee Friedlander and Garry Winogrand, were producing a new kind of work: 'What they have in common is the belief that the commonplace is really worth looking at, and the courage to look at it with a minimum of theorizing.'[88] None of them were at all shy about using flash in their examination of the ordinary.

Yet both Arbus and Weegee put the category of the ordinary under destabilizing scrutiny. The more detail that is revealed of an individual's face, the stranger and more idiosyncratic it appears. There is considerable intrusiveness in this: light breaks into private space in a kind of emotional, rather than sexual, voyeurism. Weegee did not take the kind of portrait that suggests psychological depth, although on occasion, Arbus certainly brought out people's inner complexity. Rather, in his work, emotions shine bare on people's faces, having been startled out of them. It is both fascinating and uncomfortable to witness this shock and curiosity—we become implicated in this invasive spectatorship. And Weegee understood the compulsion *to* look: in his images, eyes sometimes peer out of the deep darkness: looking knowingly, smugly, curiously at that ducking form, say, of the 16-year-old Harold Horn cowering on the back seat of a car, recoiling from the detective who arrested him for knocking over a milk wagon with a stolen car.

Weegee did not gloss over the connection between where he poked his camera—and the fascination for witnessing privacy that he was feeding—and voyeurism of a more traditional sort. Indeed, he capitalized on it. His book titles—*Naked City*, *Naked Hollywood*—both promise to lay bare the seamy side of their locations, and play with the titillation suggested by the idea of nakedness.[89] As Weegee himself cheerfully and brazenly put it: 'Years ago, I found that there is a peculiar public fascination for the word NAKED. Try it yourself in a dull conversation about anything ... politics, somebody's operation, or camel-hunting in Algeria ... and watch the ears perk.'[90] But if Weegee is an unabashed ogler of women's legs and breasts—so much so that he wasn't afraid to caricature his own proclivities for more, more, more; if he could turn his lens with complete impunity on a couple making out, as he did on Coney Island Beach when using infrared flash and infrared film—he was in Hollywood, as in New York, repeatedly drawn to those whose gaze was completely transfixed and absorbed by something. In turning towards the photographic rat pack in 'The Stars Look Down' (Figure 7.18), the expression on the faces of these men is somewhere between adoration of the star whom

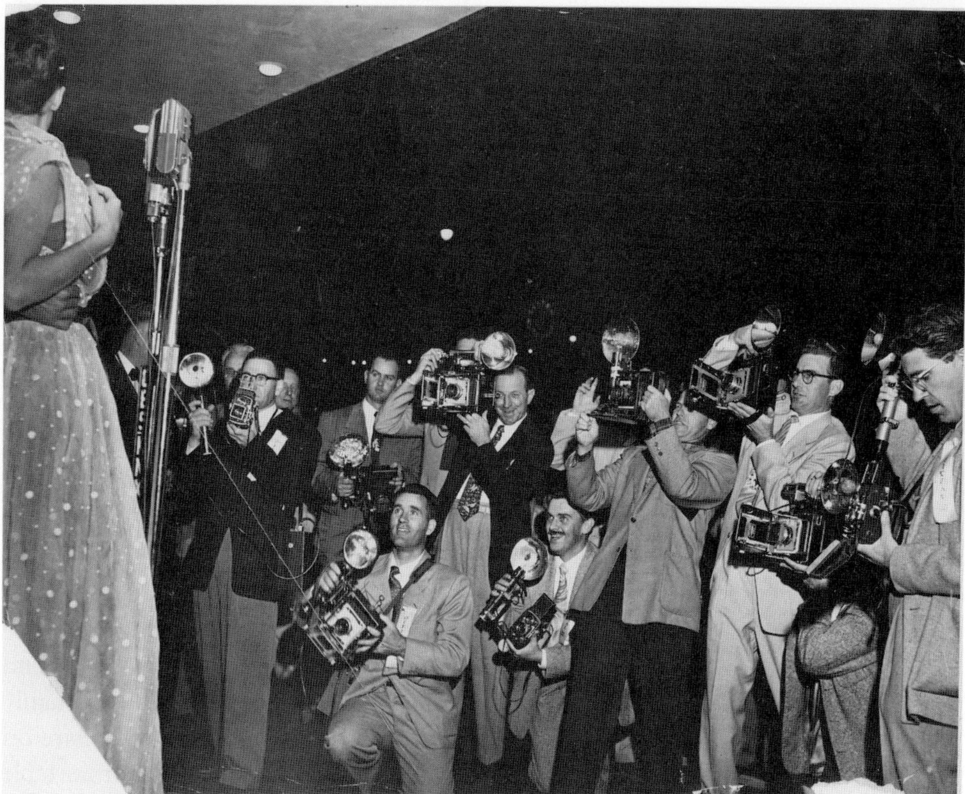

Figure 7.18 Weegee (Arthur Fellig), 'The Stars Look Down', *c.*1951. © Weegee (Arthur Fellig)/ International Center of Photography/Getty Images.

they're capturing, envy at the guy who evidently has his hand round her waist, and excitement at the shot that they are about to take. In many of these cases—just as with those who stare at the aftermath of a violent crime—the detail that is captured by the flash emphasizes humanity, individuality, vulnerability. This individuality, and the way in which, even in a crowd, people are so frequently caught up in their own intensely personal set of feelings, brings home a point that Weegee was to make—and that is accentuated by all that surrounding deep darkness in the flash-illuminated photographs—that in New York, ten and a half million people lived together in a state of isolation from one another.

Weegee's stay in Los Angeles lasted only four years. He had failed to make a breakthrough into the big time of the movie world, and had become dismayed by the phoneyness that characterized the city for him. *Naked Hollywood*, appearing in 1953, was accurately described by its editor Mel Harris as 'a pictorial satire of the film capital'.[91] As well as for its caustic juxtapositions, though, the volume is notable for its trick photographs, the distortions that Weegee admired and valued probably more than anyone else did. He felt that in them he was 'giving the camera a new dimension', as he put it in his autobiography: one that was modern and expressive, 'creative and imaginative'.[92] Another way of understanding them was that his documentary flash photography, however original its point of view, however expressive its manipulation of dark and illumination, did not carry the kudos of 'high art' that he craved.

Weegee returned to New York at the end of 1951, renting a one-room apartment, and his career never really picked up again. Helen Gee, owner of the Greenwich Village Photography Gallery and Coffeehouse (which may well be where Diane Arbus got to know him: she was a regular), paints a picture of him as brash, abrasive, and lecherous. Coming to the coffee house, 'Weegee was a pest. He didn't appear often, but when he did, there were complaints. He would roam around the room, popping off flashbulbs in customer's [*sic*] faces, and scowl and mutter when they protested. He'd go from table to table handing out greasy name cards, rubber-stamped with his logo, Weegee the Famous.'[93] She banned him for a while—he broke the ban on photographing on the premises, which he had brought upon himself after a customer threatened to smash his camera—and then, still admiring his work, resurrected the acquaintanceship and asked him to exhibit. This went nowhere—he was only interested in showing his trick photography, his women with five breasts or multiple limbs.

But Weegee could not afford to drop his trademark mode of photography entirely—not just because he still sold photographs to a variety of outlets, but also because his association with the genre could be turned to other sorts of commercial advantage. 'Weegee, the world's foremost flash photographer', runs the byline in the article-cum-advertisements that ran in such magazines as *Popular Science* and *Popular Mechanics*, alongside publicity for fishing flies and metal boats, air pistols and husky he-man knives. By the 1950s, the perfecting of the flashbulb had made the use of flash much easier for the amateur: in the hands of Weegee and Mel Harris, this becomes a crucial selling point:

> Nowadays film and cameras are manufactured to careful specifications...and thanks to the miracle of the flash bulb, you can have 'LIGHT—*where* you want it...and *when* you want it'. Yes—the mechanical aspects of photography have been perfected to such a degree that it's a cinch to take a well-exposed pleasing picture...simply load your camera with film, insert a Westinghouse flash bulb, take aim, shoot...and presto! a picture. *But* there's one more ingredient that should go into a photo—ATTITUDE...this makes the difference between an ordinary picture and a great one.[94]

Most of the tips are for shooting very everyday stuff—children, parties, publicity for clubs—with some rather anodyne comments about news photography, the 'drama of life', and about where a photographer should best position themselves at a fire—tips that are supposed to make the reader feel as though Weegee's telling them about his own special skills. But the cover photograph for *Weegee's Secrets*, shown in Figure 7.19, takes one right back to the image of the hard-bitten newshound hunting

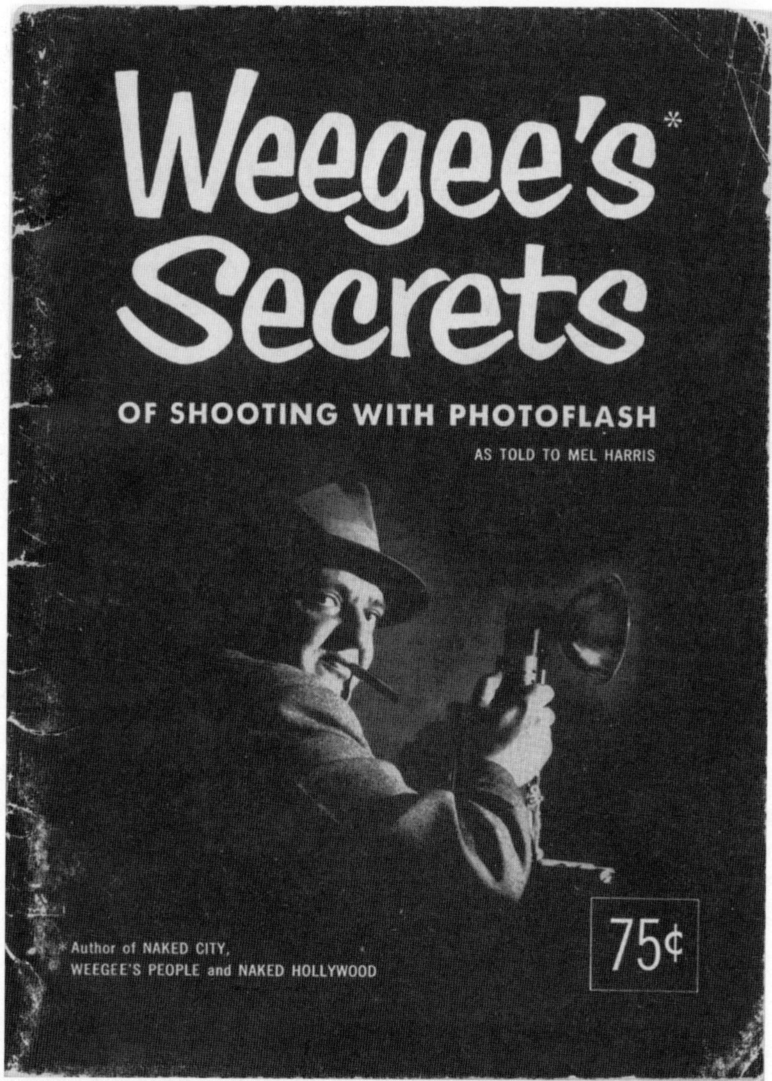

Figure 7.19 Cover: Weegee (Arthur Fellig) with Mel Harris, *Weegee's Secrets of Shooting with Photoflash* (New York: Designers 3, 1953). © Weegee (Arthur Fellig)/International Center of Photography/Getty Images.

down his prey, the flash lighting deliberately playing on its parallels to the techniques of film noir camera work. As Alan Trachtenberg puts it, simultaneously referencing the aesthetics of the pamphlet's cover and of night-time flashbulb photography far more generally, 'By illuminating darkness the flash gives it substance. And darkness revealed in turn reveals itself, as on the cover of *Weegee's Secrets*, to be the abode of the artist; it's where Weegee the crime photographer and secret artist resides, mantled in blackness.'[95]

If selling his secrets to benefit not just himself, but also the General Electric company who made Westinghouse bulbs (with deliberation, he refers in *Weegee's Secrets* to 'the miracle of the Westinghouse flashbulb[96]), was one way in which Weegee capitalized on his relationship to flash photography, another, slightly earlier one involved the flashbulb itself. Covering Hollywood premieres, he discovered, was not only repetitive in itself:

> Considering that every photographer in that crazy town was doing the same, the pictures got pretty boring. I realized [Weegee said] that to sell my pictures I would have to come up with something new. There were the stars in the middle of the fleet of cameras with the barrage of flash bulbs going off to the right, to the left.[97]

And then it hits him—he could get the mood of the premiere *and* have something unique to sell by putting the stars—in flashbulbs! So he took a #5 midget bulb, placed it inside the enlarger, made an exposure, developed the negative—and then did a double exposure using both this negative and that of—say—Trigger, or, indeed, himself. In the volume *Weegee's Candid Camera*, he gives the reader careful instructions on how to replicate this simple montage.

As with much of Weegee's work, there is a fine balance in these double light bulb exposures between the populist and the aesthetically original. In its turn, that brings home how false it can be to try and draw a distinction between the two—a distinction, in Weegee's case, that is made particularly hard because of his own love of paradox and juxtaposition. His photo books carefully double up images, so that they are in visual dialogue with one another, and individual images exploit contrasts—ones that he was not above setting up for dramatic effect. Flash photography underpinned his whole professional career in terms of how he made his reputation and how he made his living, but he always knew he was selling a product, whether a photograph to the newspapers, or, indeed, his own personality (the two coalesce in the Westinghouse campaign). Yet ever alert to the importance of self-promotion, Weegee nonetheless gave full acknowledgement to the technology that made it possible.

Indeed, flash's characteristics stand as a convenient, if unintended, metaphor for both Weegee's work and his self-image. Flash sheds light on the otherwise invisible, yet it is often brash in its illumination; it points up contrasts that we might not otherwise have seen, yet exaggerates them. It creates a bridge between documentary and drama, and between a sense of revelation and of the stagy and artificial, that disrupts the verisimilitude on which documentary is customarily thought to depend. If these are the signature features of Weegee's own work, they are also, albeit not always in such an exaggerated form, strongly present in police photography, and in many of the run-of-the-mill photographs of nocturnal crimes and disasters that were printed in the tabloids.

Yet despite his reliance on the illumination of flash, Weegee's work also reveals a certain ambiguity about its powers. The image used for *Naked City*'s frontispiece, showing the Brooklyn Bridge with a sky dramatically lit up by lightning behind it (Figure 7.20), suggests that Weegee knew that it is possible to stand back from the illumination

Figure 7.20 Weegee (Arthur Fellig), Frontispiece, *Naked City* (1945). © Weegee (Arthur Fellig)/ International Center of Photography/Getty Images.

offered by the Graflex, and to acknowledge the potential in a more sublime, dangerous electrical force.[98] His positioning of this image suggests an uncharacteristic act of self-abnegation when faced with the raw power of natural electricity. The photographic flash, despite all its promise of revelation, in the end appears as a rather insignificant form of illumination besides the unpredictable power unleashed by a thunderstorm.

This reminder of a sudden flash that is far brighter and far more destructive than the photographer's briefly flaring tool, when put together with the less than salubrious associations between crime and the use of the photographic flash—let alone with sleazy sensationalism that extends beyond the overtly criminal underworld—added up to an intensification of the negative associations that started to cluster around flash photography by the 1940s. Added to the stereotype of the rapacious and sensation-seeking news photographer, the cultural connotations of flash photography were becoming less and less positive as the twentieth century progressed.

CHAPTER EIGHT

Theatrical Light

IN *KING KONG* (dirs. Merian C. Cooper and Ernest B. Schoedsack, 1933), a wildlife filmmaker, Carl Denham (Robert Armstrong), travels to a remote jungle island, populated with ferocious atavistic monsters, and—having first stunned him with a gas bomb—returns to New York with a giant ape. In chains and shackles—and tied up in a position of crucifixion—this monstrous, hairy, pained, and angry creature is put on the stage of a Broadway theatre as 'Kong, the Eighth Wonder of the World'— 'a show, to gratify your curiosity', Denham tells the packed audience. He's joined on stage by Denham, by the movie's love interest, Ann Darrow (Fay Wray) ('there the beast, and here the beauty'), and by her fiancé and fellow expedition member, Jack Driscoll (Bruce Cabot). Press photographers crowd onto the side of the stage, 'so that the audience may have the privilege of seeing them take the first photographs of Kong and his captors'—and let fly with a barrage of shots from their flashguns—still at the technological point when the bulbs look for all the world like ordinary domestic light bulbs. Their presence enrages Kong, who growls loudly and shakes his chains—an aggressive response that only intensifies when the photographers aim their lenses and flash away at the engaged couple. 'Hold on, hold on', yells Denham, but he's too late. Kong thinks that they're attacking Ann, and, enraged, he breaks loose, and rampages through the streets of New York. In one publicity still for the movie, shown in Figure 8.1, he stands against the New York skyline with lightning shooting all around him, as if electric power is shooting from his own massive arms: it's an image that Weegee was to echo, whether consciously or not, in his frontispiece for *Naked City*. Finding Ann, Kong runs off with her onto the top of the recently completed Empire State Building where, in a barrage of plane gunfire, he meets his death.

Kong's theatre experience plays on, and reinforces, the connections between stardom, publicity, theatricality, and flash photography. The genuinely scary scene lived on in the cultural imagination. It is referenced in the 'Monty Can't Buy Me Love' episode of *The Simpsons* (aired 2 May 1999), in which Mr Burns, having captured the Loch Ness monster, warns photographers that flash might scare the adorable Nessie. Instead, he ends up as the terrified creature, running amok and causing havoc. The popping of flashbulbs, or the white light of a synchronized flash unit, has become cinema and

Figure 8.1 Ernest Bachrach, 'Primate Peril' (still from *King Kong*, 1933). Everett Collection Inc./Alamy Stock Photo.

television's visual shorthand for fame, or notoriety. In the Johnny Cash biopic *Walk the Line* (2005), we know that the big time has been reached when Cash (Joaquin Phoenix) walks onto the stage to an explosion of light: a visual reminder that if fame brings publicity, it also brings exposure. In *The Aviator*, Martin Scorsese's 2004 biopic of Howard Hughes—a film regularly punctuated, like so much of Scorsese's work, with the disruptive light of flashbulbs—Hughes is seen at the premiere of *Hell's Angels* (1930) with Jean Harlow on his arm, crunching his way down a red carpet thick with glass shards from these explosive bulbs. This is one of the most viscerally repellent representations of flash photography on film—a sequence that encapsulates all that is most aggressive and unpleasant about the medium. Hughes's face, Harlow's face, and on occasion the whole screen are scorched white. A flashbulb blows up, its sharp glass fragments adding to the wreckage underfoot. The light from these bulbs, and the spent bulbs themselves, give material form to the increasing psychological pain that Hughes is experiencing from the persistent and invasive press.[1] The TV legal and political drama series *The Good Wife* (2009–16) opens with a slow-motion shot of former Cook County Illinois State's Attorney Peter Florrick (Chris Noth) walking hand in hand down a corridor with Alicia (Julianna Margulies), his wife. As he enters a room to plead innocent to involvement in a corruption and prostitution scandal, he's met with flashes of light big and small—from reporters' flash units, from cell phones. As he starts to speak, one particularly bright and loud flash is accompanied with a sound like a whiplash; his words are uttered to a backdrop provided by an onslaught of rapid-fire explosions of photographic light. The repeated filmic association of flash with emotional distress that follows from different types of exposure to the white glare of publicity has played an important role in its denigration as a medium.

Objections to flash have always been somatic as well as having to do with protecting privacy. The earliest examples of such objections suggest that it was not just the unexpected brilliant light that prompted its subjects to remonstrate against its use, but the whole sensory experience. The photographer Paul Martin, for example, recollected attending a meeting of the Religious Tract Society, very early in the twentieth century, at Exeter Hall, one of London's most prominent venues for charitable events, where Princess Christian was due to present some monetary handouts:

> At the arranged signal my partner uncapped the lens, while I pulled the string of the flash-lamp. A flash! an explosion! and a white balloon floated to the ceiling. The lamp was recharged and a fresh plate got ready, when the Chairman shouted: 'I should like to tell the photographers that Her Royal Highness does not object to being photographed, but she does object to being frightened out of her life, so please, if you are taking any more, kindly put up your hands as a warning'.[2]

This they did, but the second explosion was even louder, and Martin and his assistant made a hasty retreat under the cover of a white fog of smoke—itself sufficient to hold up the proceedings. It was doubtless in part this kind of assault on the senses that prompted the English popular novelist and celebrity Marie Corelli (who so notoriously loathed photographers that she sent out her servants to check that the field was clear before she ventured outside) to say, when she *did* agree to sit for news photographer Bernard Grant, that it was only 'on the condition that I did not use flashlight'.[3] Extremely vain, continually having her photos retouched to conceal her ageing, she might also have been painfully aware of its ability to illuminate the least imperfections of her skin. As Ryan Linkof reminds us, the advent of the flashbulb at the end of the 1920s made it possible for candid shots to be taken in such places as nightclubs and restaurants, cafes and dance halls, and the increasing practice of dining out among the British upper classes increased their vulnerability to such exposure.[4] As he also shows, the flashbulb made capturing off-guarded expressions far easier than previously. These subjects are screwing up their eyes, or turning their heads away, in anticipation of the blinding light, or worse—this was still a time when flashbulbs could very easily blow up in the face without warning.

Many paparazzi would defend their activities on the grounds that their subjects are public figures—indeed, many celebrities, and their publicists, collude with them to provide staged but apparently spontaneous photo-ops. There is, therefore, very often an element of photographing a performance, even if the performance is one of privacy invaded. Glenn Harvey and Mark Saunders wrote of their experience pursuing Diana, Princess of Wales with a camera, claiming that 'We were an integral part of Diana's life.

The paparazzi and Diana were as one, both feeding off each other.'[5] This argument shows paparazzi in a mutual, manipulated commercial transaction. Undeniably, flash illumination has been essential to the development of the celebrity and star system, and to the publicity that keeps performers in the public eye, whether the apparent peep into their lives has been deliberately set up—fake paparazzi shots, as it were—or whether what is displayed is a more informal, perhaps unsanctioned window into their private, offstage or off-set world. Philip Waller has shown how the growth of the carte de visite and author photograph—some of these manifestly taken by flash—was important to the marketing of author as celebrity in late nineteenth-century Britain,[6] and the photograph subsequently grew yet further as a tool essential to the construction and circulation of celebrity.[7]

It was hardly as though the celebrities who appear in paparazzi pictures were unused to flash as a part of their professional lives, whether on or off set. Flash was used in theatres from the late nineteenth century to provide images of performers and productions, and flash photography became essential to promotion within the movie industry. Together with a panoply of further apparatus—gels and dome diffusers and umbrellas, standing studio lights and reflective or absorbent backcloths and strobes and remotely triggered Speedlights—flash has been essential for taking publicity photographs for the film industry. In Los Angeles, developers of flashbulbs also worked closely with the needs of the studios and with their constant demands for glamour shots and production stills—particularly during the years that the studio system retained very close control of the stars whom they employed and promoted.[8] Flashbulb companies maintained representatives in Hollywood. Taking pictures on set by flash allowed for more natural expressions to be captured, and avoided the melting of make-up that took place under the heavy spots and floods of the portrait studio. A major studio could be responsible for generating over 10,000 stills a week. Along with the needs of the tabloid press and the military, Los Angeles's demands as a centre of the movie industry helped to drive the development of flash technology in the late 1930s and 1940s.

In many ways, a still's relationship to a theatrical or filmic performance is analogous to a flash photograph's relationship to the existence that surrounds it—an aggressive extraction. Barbara Hodgdon approaches her definition of a still through reminding us of Peggy Phelan's remark that performance leaves no leftovers.[9] But 'the theatrical still is just such a left-over, the visible remains of what is no longer visible, a fragment that steals theatre, stills it—and dis-tills it'. It is both a commodity and a teaser, before and during the run of a performance; afterwards, it forms part of an archive. 'Considered as a performance in pieces, the theatre photograph undertakes a visual conversation with performance: silent, impoverished, partial, it seizes appearances, violently severs them from their original context.'[10] This severance is the more apparent when one considers that theatrical stills are not usually just taken during a dress rehearsal, still less during a public performance, but may result from a separate photocall, with key moments being restaged and held for the shot. Film stills frequently—as with that shot of King Kong with lightning shooting around him—represent instants that are not in the film itself at all.[11]

As Hodgdon remarks, the available images rarely capture the moment from a theatrical performance that one wishes that they did: rather, they serve 'as a mnemonic trace that triggers a "flashbulb memory"—that mixture of personal circumstance and public event held in memory... which radiates out from the photograph' to bring back 'sensory and intellectual joy'.[12]

The association of flash photography with intrusion and invasiveness has become synonymous with the work of paparazzi.[13] Paparazzi photography, as Carol Squiers succinctly put it,

> is a rough-edged hybrid that is patched together from the visual regimes and positivist assumptions that constitute four types of photography that are practiced and consumed as if they are distinct from one another: photojournalism; documentary; celebrity photography, which is itself a hybrid of editorial and promotional photography; and surveillance photography. The paparazzo brings these photographies together in a way that maximizes outrage and seems to blanket the entire medium in disgrace.[14]

The paparazzi's relentless use of the flashgun has ensured that their name and image has become culturally synonymous with the worst excesses of the exploitative and invasive photographer, caring for nothing other than hunting down The Shot—a dizzying, blinding profession that lends itself to the hyperbole of Lady Gaga's song and video 'Paparazzi'. They appear to be—or are, as Peter Howe's plentiful association with them revealed—notoriously hard-skinned, 'a group that seems so blissfully unconcerned about the opinions of others'. They are a group whom he is careful to distinguish from the event photographers who might, say, crowd the red carpet at a movie premiere: the paparazzi may do this from time to time, but their 'true calling requires more cunning, resourcefulness, creativity, and sheer nerve than a red carpet ever demanded'.[15] Paparazzi are, increasingly, a global phenomenon, at least within cultures where there is money to make their stake-outs and their audacity worthwhile. In the late 2000s, they were scarcely a presence within India; photographers were paid one-off fees (normally between Rs150 and Rs200 a picture, or just a few dollars)[16] and there was little demand for candid shots. Now, as one photographer, Viral Bhayani, notes, the profession has become cut-throat, with more outlets for images, more publicists working with them, and also a fierce competition to get the kind of images of informal moments that stars don't themselves post to social media.[17] Paparazzi are a relatively recent presence in China, too. Although their presence is broadly welcomed, because they feed people's appetite for access to media personalities and on occasion expose celebrities' bad behaviour, their own behaviour has also excited a good deal of debate. In January 2015 pop singer Yoa Beina died aged only 33 from breast cancer, and donated her corneas. A couple of reporters from the *Shenzhen Evening Post* dressed up as medical staff and (possibly with the collusion of the medical team) took photographs (which were not subsequently published) of these corneas being removed.[18] Although Lisa Henderson, in her lucid discussion of photography and privacy, has drawn a distinction between 'the practical emphasis... on getting the picture'—which is clearly paramount to news photographers in general, and not just to the category of paparazzi—and 'the ethical emphasis . . . on whether or not to publish it', such exploits as those of the Chinese paparazzi blur the distinction, especially in the public mind.[19]

The paparazzi's name (though not, clearly, the profession) derives from the figure of the news photographer Paparazzo in Federico Fellini's 1960 film *La dolce vita*,[20] and the image, shown in Figure 8.2, of the phalanx of photographers clustered at the foot of an airplane's steps as Sylvia, the famous Swedish-American actress (played by Anita Ekberg), emerges, has become a visual synecdoche for a press pack with their flashguns at the ready. The film was largely shot on the Via Veneto, which, as Roger Ebert explained, was *the* 'Roman street of nightclubs, sidewalk cafes and the parade of the night. His hero is a gossip columnist, Marcello, who chronicles "the sweet life" of fading aristocrats, second-rate movie stars, aging playboys and women of commerce',[21] and Paparazzo's character was based on a real-life photographer, Tazio Secchiaroli—almost inseparable, in images from the time, from his Vespa or Lamborghini scooter, ready for a quick pursuit.[22]

Secchiaroli's dramatic black-and-white work, together with that of the American Ron Galella, represents paparazzi photography at its most aesthetically striking, often

Figure 8.2 Still from *La dolce vita* (dir. Federico Fellini, 1960). Courtesy Everett Collection.

playing on the contrasts between revelation and the dark surroundings out of which a figure has emerged (or in which they are still entwined with someone else). Both the photographers and the subjects on the Via Veneto knew that photographs would sell better and bring a star more notice if it looked as though the photograph was tough to obtain—if it had, even, involved a contretemps between photographer and celebrity—and so scuffles would be staged. Howe describes how a tree or similar object might (deliberately) appear in the foreground of a picture 'so as to give it an illicit, stolen quality'.[23]

Galella's *No Pictures* provides a compelling gallery of celebrities hiding themselves from him, or, Garbo-like, raising a hand (bleached in the process by the flash) to block his intrusion. Garbo herself hides behind a handkerchief that, thanks to the flash, is bright white, the most conspicuous element of the image—as Felix Hoffmann writes, 'here, the act of veiling becomes a weapon against the exposure of privacy, resistance to the paparazzo yet at the same time a symbol of surrendering to one's destiny'.[24] Sometimes the celebrities glare at Galella, or yell at him, or give him the bird. Sometimes, indeed, they are actually about to attack him: just after he took a picture of Marlon Brando on 12 June 1973 (a picture in which, remarkably—or retouched?—Brando's dark glasses remain a deep and menacing black, accentuated by the way the flashlight bounces off forehead and cheeks), the actor swung a punch to Galella's lower jaw, breaking the bone and five teeth.[25] The next year, on 26 November, fellow photographer Paul Schmulbach took a picture of him standing with his flashgun behind Marlon Brando as the star arrived for a gala at New York's Waldorf Astoria hotel—reproduced as Figure 8.3. This time, Galella's head is safely, self-parodically

Figure 8.3 Paul Schmulbach image of Ron Galella and Marlon Brando, 1974. Entertainment Pictures/Alamy Stock Photo.

protected by a gleaming football helmet.[26] Allan Sekula's 1975 *Artforum* article on Gallela's extended photographic dance with Jacqueline Onassis brings out how his images are images of social relations: not in the sense that they present a complex of celebrities, drivers, bodyguards, and bystanders—although they do—but that, like the work of paparazzi more generally, they are 'implicated in the construction of public myth'. Sekula concludes—although he did not exactly mean it as a compliment—'his one virtue as an artist lies in the fact that what is most hidden in most photographer's work, the transaction that brought the image into the world, is painfully obvious in his'.[27] This observation works extremely well to describe that further transaction that is so often obvious in Galella's work, and in that of very many other paparazzi besides: the way in which the mechanical labour performed by the firing of a flashlight is made very visible.[28]

The growing revulsion against flash photography, especially where it is seen as being inappropriately intrusive, is tied in with a prevalent and long-standing distaste in popular writing and cinema for the figure of the photographer in general, who is often portrayed as voyeuristic, exploitative, and emotionally stunted. This image is usually heavily gendered: the fictional or filmic woman photographer is almost invariably an art photographer or a war photographer; if she's seen as traversing boundaries in other ways, it's in exposing her family to a public gaze in a way that—as with Sally Mann—might be seen as inappropriate. The professional voyeur behind a lens is epitomized by the womanizing Thomas, the central figure in Michelangelo Antonioni's *Blow-Up* (1966), wielding his camera—under strong studio lights—like a prosthetic phallus, or, six years earlier, and even more menacingly, by the character of Mark Lewis (Carl Boehm), in Michael Powell's *Peeping Tom* (1960). Although Lewis uses a portable movie camera to record the terror in the eyes of the women he tracks down and kills, he locates his second victim, Vivian, through his evening work, using flash to take soft-porn pin-up images in a seedy London studio. The film repeatedly—indeed, notoriously—makes its viewer reflect on the connections between Lewis's voyeurism, the camera lens, and our spectatorial complicity. Some complicity necessarily applies to anyone with an appetite for the published work of paparazzi.

It is the barrage of blinding light that one associates with hungry press photographers (a bevy appear in Powell's film, flashing away as Vivian's corpse is taken away in a police van)—or for that matter with the overzealous family snapper, of whom we will hear more in Chapter 9—that has helped to give photographers a particularly bad name as insensitive, flashing their bulbs or speed light when least welcome.[29] The paparazzi's use of flash photography has come to stand for the worst kind of financially motivated hunting-with-camera. Peter Howe's definition of paparazzi is a succinct one. 'It refers to those photographers who seek out and follow celebrities, or crash events to which they weren't invited, in order to photograph them in their most unguarded moments. In short, it's taking photographs you shouldn't take in places you shouldn't be.'[30] They hunt their prey only as long as that subject carries a figurative dollar sign on their back. On film, paparazzi appear at their most insatiable in Louis Malle's 1962 movie *La vie privée* (*A Very Private Affair*) starring Brigitte Bardot as a film star relentlessly pursued by photographers, and indeed by her celebrity in general: famous, visible, she is both adored and reviled. The film has been called the first 'autobiopic'—in which a film star plays a character modelled on herself: Malle loosely based *La Vie privée* on Bardot's own detestation of paparazzi and endless invasions on her privacy.[31] In it, Jill, the central figure, is presented as disconcertingly passive (very unlike Bardot herself). She is mobbed by admirers and verbally attacked by a cleaning lady in an elevator; she plays a kind of sideshow to the world of high culture in which her lover, Fabio, is a celebrated play director. The film's sensational conclusion is entirely fictional, of course. Blinded by a photographer's flashbulb, Jill falls to her death from a rooftop from which she is watching Fabio's production of Kleist's *Katherine of Heilbronn*.[32] The aggressive, incessant speediness of the modern celebrity-centred mass media—a culture condensed into the assault of the flashbulb—is replaced by the slow motion of her fall, to the strains of Verdi's *Requiem*.

In recent times, no individual has been more closely, more fatally associated with the paparazzi's flash than Diana, Princess of Wales. With an international public insatiably hungry for images of her, she was continually surrounded by the paparazzi's blinding lights. As those hard-ball British photographers Harvey and Saunders put it, on the night in March 1981 that the newly engaged Diana first emerged as a member of the royal family, stepping out of a car at Goldsmiths' Hall: 'As 1,000 camera flashes popped the greatest megastar of the 20th century was born.'[33] Even if initially, as Harvey and Saunders report, she could exclaim '"I said no flashy thingys!"',[34] she became practised at using the pack of photographers that invariably followed her around. In her authoritative and evocative biography of Diana, Tina Brown describes her as arriving at a gala fundraiser in 1985 'in a blaze of halogen', and, even more memorably, comments that 'No wonder she made such an impact at the bedsides of sick children. Arriving in a flashing cone of artificial light, she must have seemed to them like a glowing angel come to soothe the sorrow of our world below.'[35] Brown has achieved the seemingly impossible here, turning flash's cruel and invasive presence into something quasi-magical as she invokes Diana's particular aura.

Public hatred of paparazzi reached a crescendo with the death of Princess Diana. Even if the fatal crash in the fluorescent-lit tunnel under Paris's Place de l'Alma was eventually determined to be due to a driving error on the part of her speeding, drunk driver, rumour at the time insistently suggested that he was racing to get away from a pack of pursuing paparazzi and, more damning still, that he had been fatally distracted by a flash—a flash reported by a passenger in a nearby taxi. The idea that flash photographers had hounded her to her death was in part cemented by Diana's brother, Earl Spencer, when he said bitterly a few hours after her death that 'I always believed the press would kill her in the end. But not even I could imagine that they would take such a direct hand in her death as seems to be the case.'[36] Even if the paparazzi were, indeed, close behind—and the assumption that they were trying to grab shots at the scene rather than help the victims was another mark against them—it seems that they cannot be directly held responsible in any way. Yet they were quickly on the scene—as Brown puts it, a policeman, arriving a minute or so after the crash, 'fought his way to the car through at least a dozen excited paparazzi, whose flashes were going off like machine guns'. But as she points out, many of those who had spent the longest time chasing Diana were left emotionally bereft. Many also found that they were professionally tainted by having been in the tunnel that night. Moreover, what 'none of the image mercenaries expected was that the convergence of the most famous woman of the century and the horrific car crash that killed her would render the paparazzi pictures unpublishable to this day in mainstream media'.[37] This remains, nothwithstanding, the defining event that consolidated the already tarnished image of this profession.

In the twenty-first century, paparazzi photography has become an ever-more intense and crowded field. The fictional apotheosis of the type is found in Carl Hiaasen's 2010 novel *Star Island*, where the crazed, star-obsessed photographer Bang Abbott's unsavouriness is rammed home from chapter 1, as he sets off 'flash bursts' from his Nikon aimed at his prey lying unconscious in an ambulance.[38] Abbott is a central figure in the promotion of vacuous celebrity culture that Hiaasen is satirizing—even if on this occasion he's fallen for a trick, since the woman is an undercover double for the starlet whom he believes he's pursuing with his camera. In the book's conclusion, Hiaasen gives him his comeuppance, and grants him a cruel fate: today 'he rents a small studio in Culver City, where he specializes in portraits of toddlers, prom couples and small pets. He is also available for corporate functions.'[39]

Photography of celebrities relies on the concept of performance, whether this is an aspect of the public display for which the celebrity is famed in the first place, or of the varieties of pose that they put on when faced by a long lens or an imminent flash or fifty, or simply the sense on both sides that this is—as paparazzo Pascal Rostain puts it—'a game of cat and mouse, of cops and robbers'.[40] A different sort of theatricality—a large-scale dramatic aesthetics—is created through the use of multiple flashbulbs. Such a spectacular, public use of light represents the obverse of the desire to bring out every ordinary detail of the domestic space. At its most simple, this type of shooting involves an electric flash on an extension cord—or multiples—known as a slave flash—synchronized with an on-camera flash, or it entails the deployment of cordless, portable electronic flash units. Right from the inauguration of the synchronized flash, camera magazines and photographic manuals have been full of detailed instructions about how best to set up these lights in a studio, or other relatively small space. But what concerns me here is not how flash photography became a quotidian part of photographic studio practice, although it is well worth noting that some of its aesthetically most striking experimental uses have come from people exploring its potential for shooting fashion or in making eye-catching advertising images. Rather, I want to consider the role that flash has played in large-scale, dramatic illumination, both indoors and outside.

The desire to create a sensational, one-off photograph by means of a big flash has a long history. As early as 1859—and without perhaps quite knowing what they would be dealing with—the firm of Oxley and Lane placed an advertisement in *The Colonist*—a newspaper in Nelson, New Zealand—to the effect that 'Professor Moule's Photogen has not yet arrived, but when it does, it will be made known by the ILLUMINATION OF NELSON from the Church Hill; so that no one will be able to doubt its powers'.[41] At the end of the nineteenth century, Seneca Ray Stoddart produced some remarkable nocturnal photographs, including an image of the Statue of Liberty that required over a pound and a half of magnesium compound (and had a horrific accident when his flash misfired when taking a night-time photograph of an in situ model of the Washington Square Arch). The *Daily Mirror* started off 1906 with an image, taken from a first-floor window, of the 10,000 people who assembled round St Paul's Cathedral at midnight on 31 December. 'The feelings of the crowd when the flash went off are better imagined than described, especially when we learn that the flash-pan used was blown against the wall by the force of the explosion.'[42] Whilst a barrage of simultaneously fired flash sources had long been used to illuminate large gatherings, like a ballroom, in the 1930s and 1940s a number of ambitious lighting set-ups were used for the temporary brightening of outdoor environments and the creation of images that could in no way have been produced using natural light.[43] As well as being responsible for some spectacular photographs, they served a number of other functions: they were manifestations of a photographer's ingenuity; they acknowledged the aesthetic pleasure that could be given in a still photograph by the manipulation of light—in a way analogous to the inventive artificiality of stage and film lighting—and, increasingly, they became a means of commercial product promotion.

Flash photography has a long record of usefulness within the industrial and commercial world. The pages of *Abel's Photographic Weekly*—later *Professional and Amateur Photographer*, and then *Professional Photographer*—the trade journal for professional photographers—offer lots of advice about its employment, as do manuals aimed at those who photographed buildings and machinery and store windows.[44] Whereas plenty of industrial objects and commodities could be photographed using a very long exposure, since they're not going to move around, these guides draw attention to the occasions when flash can be particularly useful. For example, taking a picture of a store window is often best done at night, when it is illuminated from within (to minimize reflection), and a side-positioned flash can capture the externalities of the window during the longer exposure.[45] The biggest challenges undoubtedly came with photographing a banquet or similar large gathering such as the one taken by Rockwood, of New York, early in 1888, 'showing the interior of the Twelfth Regiment Armory. The picture, which shows 4,000 people, was taken instantaneously at night, and required the use of eight ounces of magnesium.'[46] An image such as this, at once eye-catching and publicity-attracting, helped other photographers see the commercial potential in such an enterprise. 'Many of us have seen reproductions of such pictures made at some prominent function, by one of the more progressive members of the profession, and have looked at them with awe... But for most of us it was too wonderful to be real', wrote George Wallace Hance in 1914.[47] For many freelance photographers, the biggest profits came from such occasions, even if, to get on the right side of venue managers, one had to be, as Hance explained, something of a hustler.

This genre of work was made easier by the innovation of special banquet cameras—before wide-angle lenses became available, these used 7 × 17, 8 × 20, or 12 × 20 plate sizes, so that a large assembly could be captured without too much camera tilt.[48] But the real skill came in setting up the room's illumination. Because of the inadvisability of filling the room with irritating and smelly smoke, flashbags were usually employed. James Boniface Schriever strongly recommended the use of those manufactured by Prosch (his reiteration of their name in his chapter on 'smokeless devices' in *Commercial, Press, Scientific Photography* suggests that this is a form of advertising on Prosch's part): they were carefully positioned—say, four at the side, and two in front of the group, with about ¼ oz of flash powder in each bag—and ignited by means of an electric current run from the building.[49] In expert hands, such shots could show all round a banquet room with its elaborate decorations and—most important, for sales—capture hundreds of faces at once with extraordinary clarity.

Society photographers' dependence on flash was relatively short-lived. By 1934, Baker noted that 'Flashlight has gone now'—he was a little premature—'for plates have been made of such wonderful sensitiveness to incandescent light that dinner parties, balls and even theatrical performances can be photographed in their own light, unaided by the magnesium flash.'[50] Moreover, the power of these interior flashes was nothing when compared to the large-scale productions of a few decades later. The first of these ambitious outdoor shots—certainly the first to attract a large amount of attention—was Herbert Gehr's 1942 photograph of New York's Washington Street Market at 1 a.m., shown in Figure 8.4. Gehr (born Edmund Bert Gerhard, in Berlin) joined the staff of the Black Star agency in 1938, shortly after arriving in America, and already having a reputation for taking pictures with dramatic lighting. For example, in 1937, when working in Egypt as a newsreel cameraman, he made stills of the Sphinx at night, using car headlights and flash powder.[51] Don Mohler, who became chief advertising officer at General Electric, offered a concise explanation of how Gehr's Washington Market photograph was made, saying that it is one of those 'impossible' shots that editors go for:

> Assistants with hand flash units were stationed at second floor level for four or five blocks down the street on the right. The camera, on a tripod was set for 'Time'. When ready, the shutter was opened and the lamp at the camera flashed. This was the signal for all the others to set off their flashes. The shutter was then closed. Elaborate? Yes, but well worth the effort.[52]

The image appeared in *Life* magazine (for which Gehr worked extensively) on 3 August 1942, with the boast that 'it took 12 hours and 20 men to get this shot', and proclaiming that this was 'one of the most complicated pictures LIFE ever asked any photographer to make'. It was problematic both because the city was 'dimmed out' as a wartime precaution and because the scene was filled with movement. Nineteen men from *Life*'s

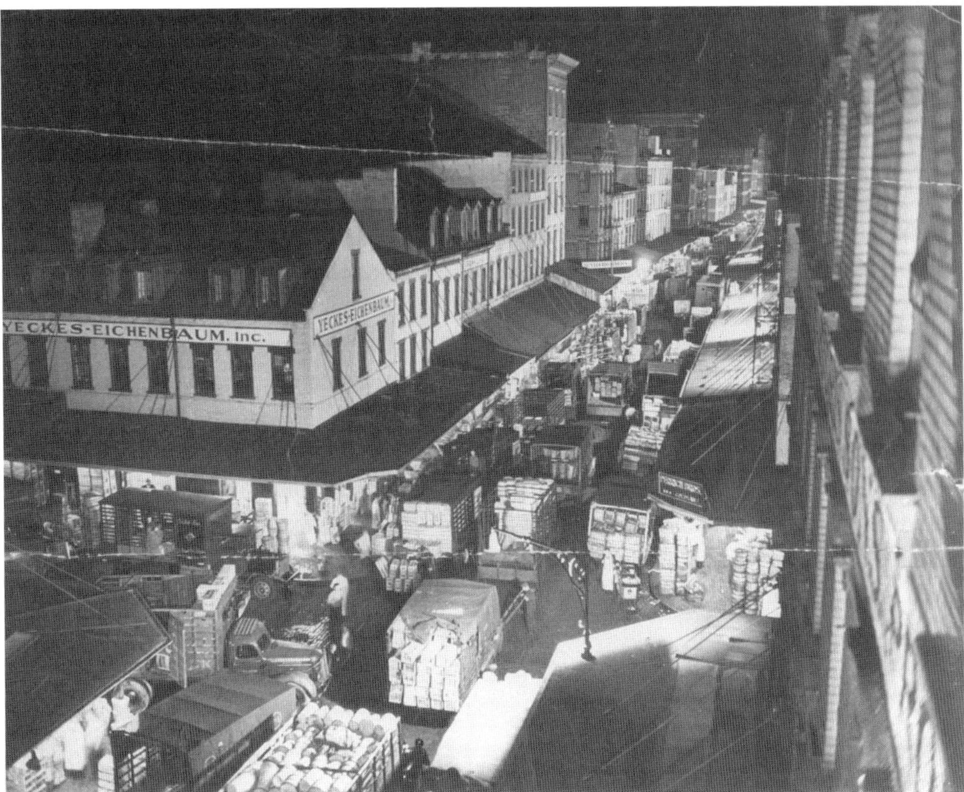

Figure 8.4 Herbert Gehr, 'Washington Street Market', 1942. © Herbert Gehr/Getty Images.

Armed Services Photo School, 'where men from Army, Navy and Marines are trained under LIFE supervision', were drafted in, and sent off to stand on fire escapes with their reflectors, each set with three big bulbs. As Geoffrey Gilbert told it in 1947,

> Telephonic communications were established and watches synchronised as carefully as for a military operation. The shooting was over in six seconds, but during this very short passage of time Washington Street was a flaming white way, light leaping from point to point like a chased animal, while salesmen dropped their books and startled truck-drivers jumped on their brakes. So sound was the organisation that a second shot was not deemed necessary, and six taxi-cabs took the photographers triumphantly home.[53]

Life's reference to the co-option of men from the Armed Services, together with the small photograph of Gehr passing out flashbulbs to them that appeared on the magazine's contents page, is a pointer to the fact that the image was more than an aesthetic tour de force. Appearing in an issue that also offered visual reporting on the Battle of the Arctic Convoy, on a US submarine sinking a Japanese submarine, and on the hardship in Greece that followed the Nazi invasion of that country, Gehr's sensational image was accompanied by three more mundane flash shots of squash, watermelon, and summer celery, and a paragraph of editorial prose reminding readers of the importance of Washington Street Market's activity to the war effort, and of the part that they themselves could play in consuming 'Victory Special' foods—that is, foods in season rather than canned food, as represented by the '12,000,000 lb. of perishable fruit and vegetables that come into Washington Market every night'.[54]

If Gehr's image of Washington Street Market was, in its way, a news photograph, emphasizing the war effort, another New York City news photographer, O. Winston Link, was to turn his camera lens to a vanishing world, that of the steam railroad. He used multiple flashbulbs to create dramatic night-time views of the Norfolk and Western trains. Starting in 1955, Link concentrated on the locomotives and personnel of the 238-mile Shenandoah Valley Line (which had reached the high point of its freight traffic during the Second World War). Using an assistant, recruiting locals—to go swimming in a creek, to smooch at a drive-in movie (as we see in Figure 8.5)—as the trains roared past, Link's set-ups were extremely elaborate. His images required imaginative visualization, with the sites measured and the light sources carefully diagrammed out well in advance. He used flash reflectors equipped with different strength flashbulbs; he created single spots of illumination—like a boy's lantern or an illuminated window—with single bulbs. Wired together, all of these lights were connected to his 'red box', the power supply that provided the huge surge necessary to set off everything at the moment when

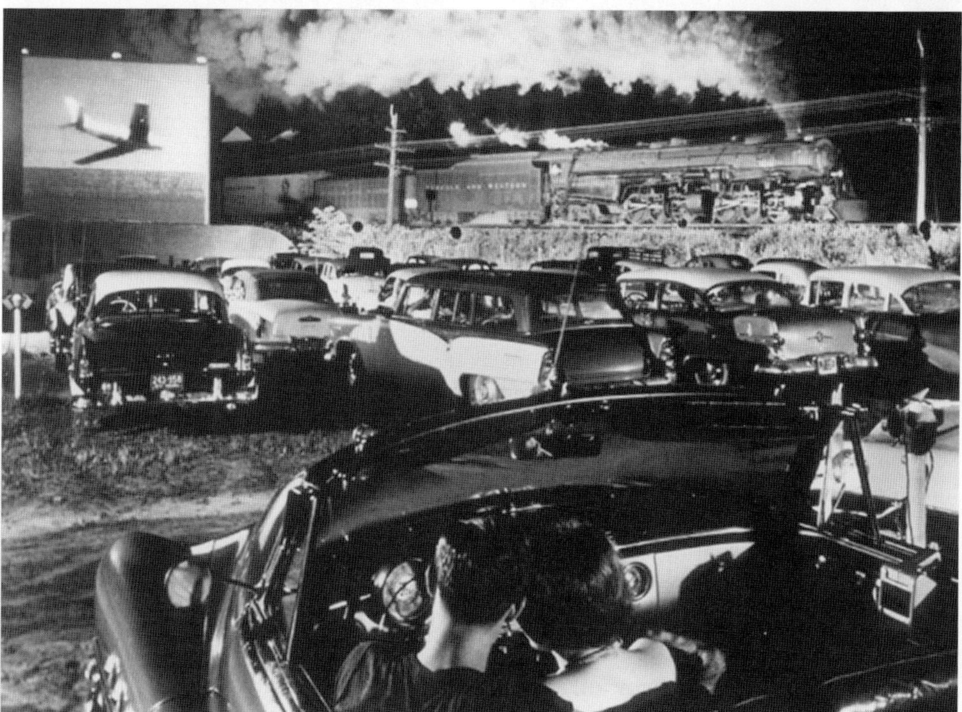

Figure 8.5 O. Winston Link, 'Hotshot Eastbound at Iaeger, West Virginia, 1956'. © O. Winston Link Museum.

a train's position would ensure the most effective picture. This box was, as his assistant Thomas Garver described it, 'a forerunner of the battery capacitator flash units just then becoming popular... About the size of a small makeup case and painted a dull red, it contained three separate battery capacitator power units capable of firing all the flash-bulbs—up to sixty of them—simultaneously with the triggering solenoids on three view cameras.'[55] The results were both dramatic and non-naturalistic. They illuminated darkness, but with the objective of creating an extraordinary image that conveyed the grandeur and magic of the steam period, documenting its atmosphere rather than its material details.

The most spectacular and varied sequence of ambitious shots employing flash were the 'Big Shot' images orchestrated by Sylvania Electric Products Inc's photoflash division to advertise its products—a set of well-publicized photographic events that began in 1951 with an image of the quintessential new suburb of Levittown, reproduced as part of a two-page spread in *Collier's* magazine under the heading 'A Town Takes Its Own Picture', together with a photograph of an aide counting the 1,500 bulbs that went into its making—an image in which the bulbs look uncannily like skulls in a catacomb.[56] This is large-scale flash, not standing in for daylight, or even for other forms of artificial lighting—it was too elaborate in its set-up for that. What appears to matter is not so much the moment of the image's taking as the final photograph, at once offering extraordinary clarity and showing a highly artificial scene, one never ordinarily visible. These subjects included the Horseshoe Curve of the Pennsylvania Railroad, just as a train was rounding it (6,000 bulbs); the Chicago Museum of Science and Industry—with fireworks reflected in Lake Michigan; Carlsbad Caverns; the St Louis Airport; the Pyramid of the Moon, north-east of Mexico City; and the floor of the New York Stock Exchange—which required only a modest seventy-six of the large #3 flashbulbs.[57] The 1966 Sylvania Big Shot taken in Lincoln Center was used as the new cover of the Metropolitan Opera's programme following their move there. Each location threw up its own particular challenges. The shot at the Met—plotted out by the photographer, Joseph Costa, using Polaroids—was especially shiny and reflective, not least because of the gold curtain. Logging the details of each shoot engaged the non-specialist newspaper reporter in a particular kind of rhetoric: one that suggested know-how about photo techno-wizardry, even if they were just repeating the statistics that were included in Sylvania's press releases, and one that by inference assumed the photographic hobbyist's engagement with such details on the one hand, and the general public's wondering response to the complexity of lighting techniques on the other. Describing Costa's positioning of the 201 Sylvania bulbs that were used on this occasion, the *Burlington Daily Times*'s reporter carefully recounted how

> The lighting for the photograph spanned a ceiling-to-orchestra floor design, which was equivalent in output to 400,000 sixty-watt standard household bulbs. Two dozen Sylvania No. 3's lit up the ceiling alone, and AGI's [Sylvania's regular Blue Dot flashbulbs, aimed very much at the amateur user] were positioned in every box, on a white 3 by 5 card which distributed the light evenly throughout.

In addition to the Sylvania flashbulbs, supplies consisted of such things as 24,000 feet of single-strand wire... red, green, white, blue... color-coded into eight circuits, to be plugged into a circuit controlbox; 100 screwbase sockets; 100 twelve-inch reflectors; 100 mounting clamps; 1,000 wire nuts. Add to these a Sinar 8 by 10 view camera; 121 mm super-angulon lens; Ektachrome B film;—set the camera at f-18—open the shutter for five seconds—and pffffffff—another Sylvania 'Big Shot' becomes history.[58]

What Sylvania produced was a mid-twentieth-century version of—to use David Nye's term—the 'American Technological Sublime', something not just measured by the display of light itself but also characterized, as evident here, by the amount of detailed planning that went into the making of each photograph. During the years that they carried out this annual self-promotion ritual, its grandiose display coincided with the period of the Cold War, and whereas a number of the Big Shot locations fell into the category of tourist destinations or sites of city pride, other subjects can be read as politically inflected, not least the choice of the aircraft carrier the USS *Antietam*, one of twenty-four Essex-class aircraft carriers built during and shortly after the Second World War for the United States Navy.

However, one notable feature of outdoor Big Shots was that they rapidly turned into a form of mass participation: amateur photographers did, after all, constitute a substantial part of Sylvania's target consumers. In 1969—for what was to prove the last Big Shot engineered by Sylvania—1,145 Sylvania flashbulbs were fired simultaneously to photograph the new West German luxury liner Hamburg. This was set up by Al Gordon, Sylvania's special projects manager, a group of Sylvania technicians, and two crew members whilst the ship travelled to New York from Cuxshaven, German, on its maiden voyage. Whilst the official photograph was taken from the twentieth floor of 17 Battery Place by Allen Little, well known as a ship photographer, using a 4 × 5 Linhoff camera with a Schneider 300-millimetre lens and Ektachrome daylight film (reportage of these events offered ample opportunity for free publicity for a range of photographic products), 'thousands of amateur camera fans, in boats and along Battery Park, also captured the big flash by timing their shots to an official countdown broadcast by WABC radio'.[59]

The association of a Big Shot with mass participation has been retained with its revival in 1987 by the Biomedical Photography Department at the Rochester Institute of Technology (RIT), who organize periodic Big Shots. But rather than these serving as a commercial publicity stunt, calling attention to one particular brand of flashbulbs, this new Big Shot is a far more democratic affair (although RIT has some corporate sponsorship for it), with individuals holding electronic flash units, flashlights, cell phones with light-emiting units, or whatever is effective and to hand. As their website explains:

When the camera shutter is opened, participants 'paint' the subject with light during a timed exposure. Lights are aimed randomly across the scene and the exposure is created over time rather than as a result of one large discharge. All exterior lights are turned off when possible, while sometimes interior lights are left on. This provides illumination from inside leading to a photograph that is both unique and a community event. The lighting is non-directional when produced this way and often results in shadowless outcomes.[60]

Recent Big Shots have included Churchill Downs, the Erie Canal, the National Museum of the American Indian, and—a particularly spectacular event in 2014—High Falls, Rochester, shown in Figure 8.6. These events require considerable planning, just as the Sylvania shots did, and community participation that goes beyond the 750 or so enthusiasts who wield the illumination. In 2014 CSX Transportation, which has a long history of involvement with the Rochester area, provided two new locomotives and a string of railcars that fill out the bridge. RG&E (Rochester Gas and Electricity) both had their hydroelectric team increase the flow of water over the falls and turned off all the dam lights for the duration of the shot—they saw this as a gesture of support for innovation, education, and the arts in the communities they served; the City of Rochester turned off more than 110 street lights.[61] The resulting image reinterprets the industrial sublime, acknowledging its relationship to raw nature, visually interleaving the power of rushing water and the spectacular beauty of ice with the solid structures of the once-flourishing rust-belt city, while showing different means of harnessing both water and electricity. Yet the lights set in the middle distance bring out a particularly pointed irony, the ruins—in this instance of the Gorsline building—that accompany this grandeur. The presence of decayed industrial buildings underscores the relevance of the setting, since Rochester had been the home of the Eastman Kodak Company since 1888. It filed for chapter 11 bankruptcy in January 2012, having failed to predict and plan for the disruptive effects of digital photography.[62] Ruins may be a conventional component of the sublime: they take on a particular poignancy here.

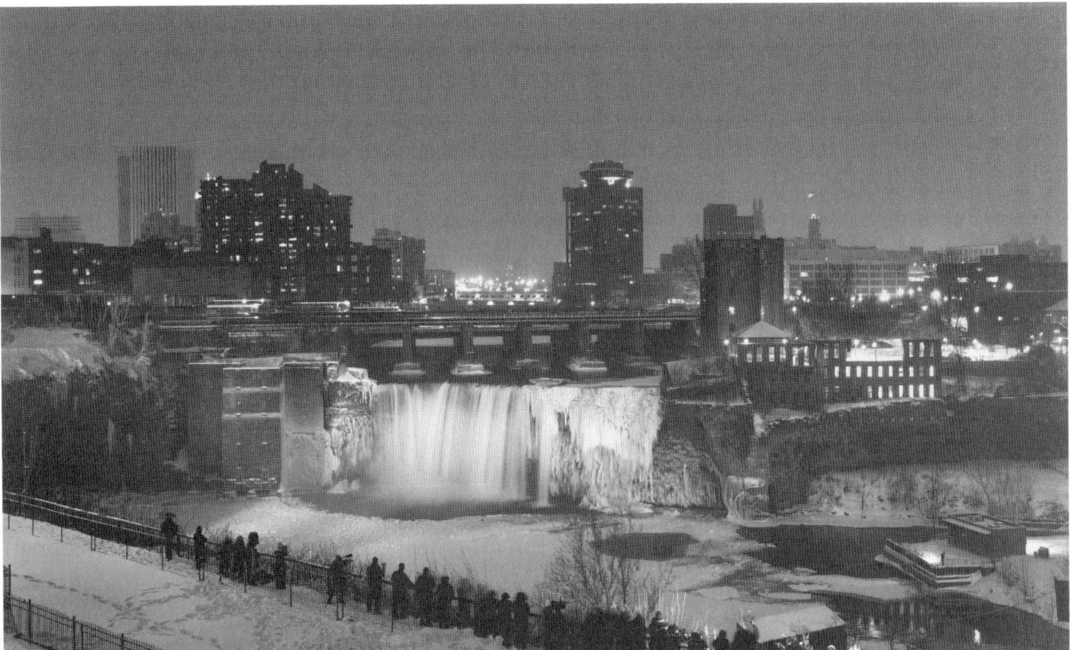

Figure 8.6 'RIT Big Shot No 29 High Falls Rochester New York', 2014. Image Courtesy of RIT Big Shot.

The Sylvania spectacles were not the biggest or the brightest visible flashes to be witnessed in the 1940s and 1950s, nor were flashbulbs the only tools of illumination that enabled photographs to be taken in the dark. For these, we need to go further afield. The searingly bright light emitted by atomic tests, and by the atomic bomb itself, made the flash of flash photography look puny, even on its grandest scale.

But let us turn, first, to one of the best-known eruptions of the photographer's flashbulb to be found on film. In Alfred Hitchcock's *Rear Window* (1954), the protagonist, L. B. 'Jeff' Jefferies (James Stewart), is a news photographer forced to rest up with a broken leg: this leads him to observe the activities taking place in the apartment building opposite his window through his telephoto lens (although not a photograph is taken). 'Sure, he's a snooper, but aren't we all?' asked Hitchcock in relation to his quintessential movie about scopophilia (in its broadest sense).[63] He becomes suspicious about the activities behind one of the sets of windows; convinced—correctly, it turns out—that one man, Lars Thorwald (Raymond Burr), has murdered his wife. Thorwald gets wind of the fact that he's being watched, and comes over to attack him. Famously, in the film's conclusion, Jeff uses his photographic flashgun as a weapon against Thorwald, flaring the flashbulb into his face. The temporary effectiveness of the assault is brought home by the film's use of reverse perspective, so that we experience the shot not only from behind the lens, but also as if it were going off in Thorwald's—and our—eyes. The screen is momentarily flooded with the red of the shocked retina. The flash, crucially, buys Jeff time—although he is ultimately unable to stop Thorwald's assault. This flash may shock, but it doesn't inflict lasting damage on the attacker, who tips Jeff out of the window—dislodging him, too, 'from the safety of his subject space...into the object space that all others have occupied with respect to the voyeur throughout the film'.[64] As John Belton has pointed out, this transfer of vision from Jeff to Thorwald is also a moment when—figuratively and literally—we witness voyeuristic pleasure become voyeuristic pain; when the distinction between appropriate and inappropriate voyeurism is consolidated through the red suffusion that fills the screen.[65] Thorwald is arrested, shortly afterwards, by the police.

The film is notable not just for the many questions that it raises about the ethics of surveillance and voyeurism—and the wobbly boundary between the two—but also for the combined work of the scriptwriter John Michael Hayes and Hitchcock's cinematographic eye, which picked up on the many visual cues in Cornell Woolrich's 1942 short story (originally entitled 'It Had to Be Murder' and published in *Dime Detective Magazine*) that provided the basis for the movie.[66] Woolrich's unnamed protagonist is not a photographer: he uses a combination of his own eyes and speculative imagination, aided by a telescope left around from a boating trip, and by the lights that are turned on and off in the rooms opposite. The 'spyglass' affords him excellent vision: looking at Thorwald's reactions, as he speaks to him on the phone, 'I was practically fluoroscoping him'—fluoroscopy involves using X-rays to obtain real-time moving images of a body's interior. More than this, however, the hints of flash's violence lie in the text awaiting appropriation. By telephone, the protagonist obliquely accuses Thorwald of murder, and observes his discomfited reaction: 'Through the window I saw him pull open the collar of his shirt as though its stricture was intolerable. Then he backed his hand over his eyes like you do when there's a light blinding you.'[67] But he takes a while to realize quite how the murder had been committed, or rather, where Mrs Thorwald's body must be concealed. When this knowledge comes to him (she's under a false floor in the apartment upstairs that's undergoing renovation), it's at a moment of tension—he hasn't quite perceived, even if the reader has, that Thorwald is at that very moment creeping up his own stairs—but 'suddenly it exploded. Why at this particular moment, I don't know. That was some mystery of the inner workings of my own mind. It flashed like waiting gunpowder which a spark has finally reached along a slow train.'[68] The literal flashes that burst into the text once Thorwald is actually inside the narrator's room do not, however, emanate from the photographer, as they do in the film, but from the murderous invader. The first time he fires his gun, 'The flash of the shot lit up the room for a second, it was so dark. Or at least the corners of it, like flickering, weak lightning.'[69] If there's a hint, here, of the long-standing comparison to the photographic flash, the blinding source of Hitchcock's visual inspiration becomes clearly evident in the simile used to narrate the second shot: 'He whirled, fired at me so close that it was like looking at sunrise in the face.'[70]

Thorwald's gun, in Woolrich's story, fails to hit the narrator: the first time it shatters the clay bust of a French eighteenth-century notable that he had draped and set up above his shoulders as a decoy; the second shot misses. But for that matter, in the film, the sudden and intense light only briefly, if dramatically, interrupts the action, and fails to fell Thorwald. We may read this as a cautionary presentation of the limits of the photographic flash, something that is further brought home by the inclusion of an image of an atomic explosion as a point of reference within the set of *Rear Window*, in the form of one of the framed news photographs (by Jeff himself?) that is on display on the sideboard.[71] On the one hand, this visual rhetoric helps to establish the Cold War context of the movie: a context that for a contemporary audience complicated ethical issues around the activities of spying and surveillance.[72] On the other, to compare, however tacitly, the flash of a nuclear explosion to the effects released by this piece of photographic equipment is a means of suggesting the ultimate puniness of a photographer's release of light.

Nuclear explosions vastly outscaled the photographic flash—or indeed, any other kind of light—even if the atom bomb tested in Nevada on 22 April 1952, almost certainly the largest yet detonated on the American continent, with a flash visible for at least 75 miles, was popularly known as 'Operation Big Shot'.[73] When Little Boy released the equivalent of 13,500 tons of TNT over the centre of Hiroshima on 6 August 1945, 'to many of the people who saw it, the fireball looked like a tremendous bluish white flash that blazed for about three seconds'—to quote the language of the Pacific War Research

Society, as they describe the factual circumstances of that devastating moment, and the content for the recollections proffered by those whom they interviewed, like Mrs Hizume, telling of the 'sudden blinding flash that seemed to sear her eyeballs'.[74] But the problem was this: if the vocabulary of flash—and this brief, searing, obliterating, terrible explosion of light could be called nothing else—was already the language used to talk about the little explosions released by a photographer, or even by, say, an exploding munitions dump, how could any language approach adequacy for this? All the same, at least one witness compared what he saw to a familiar visual experience. 'On a hillside two kilometers northwest of the city, P. Siomes, a German Jesuit missionary, was gazing out the window toward Hiroshima when "a garish light which resemble[d] the magnesium light used in photography" filled the whole vista'.[75] Joseph Kanon, in his 1997 thriller *Los Alamos*, in trying to get his readers to imagine the testing of the first atomic bomb, had to go beyond this: 'Suddenly, there was a pinprick, whiter than magnesium, a photographer's bulb, and he was blinded with light. It flashed through his body, filling all the space around them, so that even the air disappeared. Just the light.'[76]

Unlike the nearly half-million people whose ordinary day was split apart by the Hiroshima bomb, the observers at the Trinity Site on the White Sands Missile Range, New Mexico, were expecting something on 16 July 1945. They numbered both the scientists who worked alongside physicist J. Robert Oppenheimer, director of the Manhattan Project at the Los Alamos National Laboratory where the first atomic bombs were developed, and military observers. At a viewing site 20 miles to the north-west of the Trinity Site, busloads of visitors from Los Alamos and beyond waited.[77] They anticipated a light beyond anything that they had previously known; they were issued with dark glasses; at least one person, the quantum physicist Richard Feynman, climbed into the cab of his truck for the protection from ultraviolet rays that its windshield would afford him as he looked towards Alamogordo. He described what he saw with a clinical clarity, although he ducked at the moment that 'the horizon lit up with a tremendous flash'.[78] When he looked up again, he saw a white light changing into yellow and then orange: 'A big ball of orange, the center that was so bright, becomes a ball of orange that starts to rise and billow a little bit and get a little black around the edges, and then you see it's a big ball of smoke with flashes on the inside of the fire going out, the heat.'[79] Figure 8.7 depicts it shedding its light over the surrounding desert.

These, and subsequent nuclear explosions, constituted a form of flash that both challenged description and caused those who wrote of them to reach for the language of the sublime, to suggest that there was something in its magnitude that approached—however horrifically—the transcendent. Brigadier General Thomas F. Farrell, who was present alongside Oppenheimer in the shelter at the Trinity Site, described the lighting effects that he witnessed—and then said that, in fact, the 'clarity and beauty cannot be described but must be seen to be imagined. It was that, beauty the great poets dream about but describe most poorly and inadequately.' He went on to recall not just the visual impact, but also the noise that followed, a 'strong, sustained, awesome roar which warned of doomsday and made us feel that we puny things were blasphemous to dare

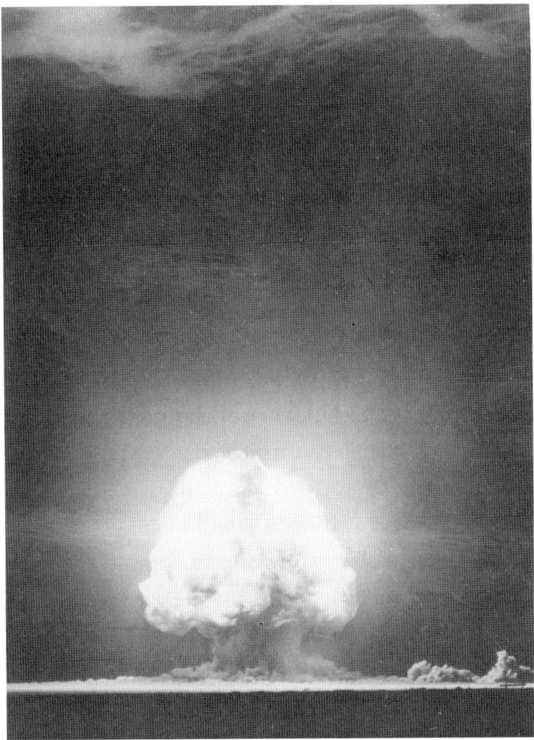

Figure 8.7 Trinity Site atomic test, 16 July 1945. Los Alamos National Laboratory T-144. Photo courtesy of the Los Alamos National Laboratory. US Government Archives.

tamper with the forces heretofore reserved to the Almighty'.[80] Isidor Rabi, who had won the Nobel Prize for physics in 1944, called the explosion 'the brightest light I have ever seen or that I think anyone has ever seen. It blasted; it pounced; it bored its way right through you. It was a vision which was seen with more than the eye.'[81]

In seeking to describe this atomic light, many observers of this and other nuclear tests—as well as those who witnessed the actual dropping of the atomic bombs in Japan—had recourse, once again, to the vocabulary of lightning—albeit this time a great deal more loaded with metaphysical potential than the language of the magnesium flash.[82] The suitability of the meteorological rhetoric of awe and destruction is underscored by the presence of actual thunderstorms at the time of the Alamogordo testing, something which understandably made many who were present extremely anxious—physicist Enrico Fermi, for example, was worried that they would all be drenched in radioactive rain.[83] Much is made of these dramatic meteorological conditions in John Adams/Peter Sellars's opera, *Doctor Atomic* (2005).[84] The ironic juxtaposition of natural and unnatural flashes is brought home by the lullaby sung by Pasqualina, the Tewa woman who babysits the Oppenheimer children: 'In the north the cloud-flower blossoms | And now the lightning flashes, | And now the thunder clashes, | And now the rain comes down!'[85] Adams and Sellars's challenge was how to display on the stage what

Oppenheimer calls, in the libretto, the flash of 'brilliant luminescence',[86] and how to find adequate musical expression. Adams decided to visualize the explosion as if from afar—'a dawn coming from entirely the wrong direction', Rhodes wrote to him in reply to a query, and to accompany this with 'a slow crescendo for trilling strings, to which is added a flash of winds and bass—a chord that dazzles and fades, like a false dawn'.[87]

In 1955 visitors to Edward Steichen's *Family of Man* exhibition in New York were presented with just one colour image among all the black-and-white photographs, isolated near the end of the show in its own room. This was a 6 × 8-foot transparency of test 'Mike', a thermonuclear explosion at Enewetak Atoll in early 1954. The implications were clear: the mushroom-shaped dome, glowing bright orange and searing white, striped with bands of dark cloud, contained the deadly power to destroy all the positive aspects of humanity that viewers had just encountered. The photograph was shocking in its impact. It was also shockingly beautiful.

Atomic explosions were photographed for a number of reasons—scientific, military, for their newsworthy qualities, and, as Julia Bryan-Wilson has pointed out, in the spirit of bearing witness, even as a kind of tourist.[88] At least 100,000 exposures were made of the first, Trinity test alone—by cameras on tripods, by film cameras, and even by a pinhole camera, the core of the explosion appearing as a searing white light—or an empty visual space. Gamma radiation produces the same photochemical effect as does visible light: an excess of it leads to fogging.[89] Bryan-Wilson pushes the connection between these explosions and photography much further than the fact of record-making. 'The flash of the bomb', she writes, 'often acts in place of the flash of the photo in these images and this substitution demonstrates how, in fact, there is a particular affinity between photography and atomic weapons, as the technology of sight and the technology of death are conjoined in an intimate marriage.'[90] This affinity is at its most stark when we see how the atomic bomb's detonation pulverized both people and buildings, leaving only what Susan Schuppli has called 'radical contact prints'—atomic shadows.[91] The comparison is brought home, wordlessly, in Barbara Norfleet's 1988 picture of Robert Oppenheimer's statue in the Bradbury Science Museum at Los Alamos (Figure 8.8), the flash overbleaching the surface, making it look as though the creator of the nuclear bomb is now caught in its invasive glare. Irreversible material effects of atomic materials were rendered instantly visible in the pockmarks that appeared on the surfaces of film used to capture nuclear explosions, the huge flash recording not just the fact of its occurrence, but also its destructive powers.

In *Atomic Light*, Akira Lippit explores the meanings that centre on this transformational, destructive, obliterating light. He draws on the words used by abstract painter Willem de Kooning in 1951 to comment on the radical visuality unleashed by the atomic bomb. In the 'sadistic metaphysics' of de Kooning's account, in its 'sacrificial logic', the witnesses of the atomic bomb

> exchanged their eyesight for a sublime visuality: the eyes of those witnesses 'who saw the light melted out of sheer ecstasy'. Ecstatic, outside, blinded. The last form of light, perhaps, that anyone needed to see. The last light of history, according to de Kooning, or the light at the end of history.[92]

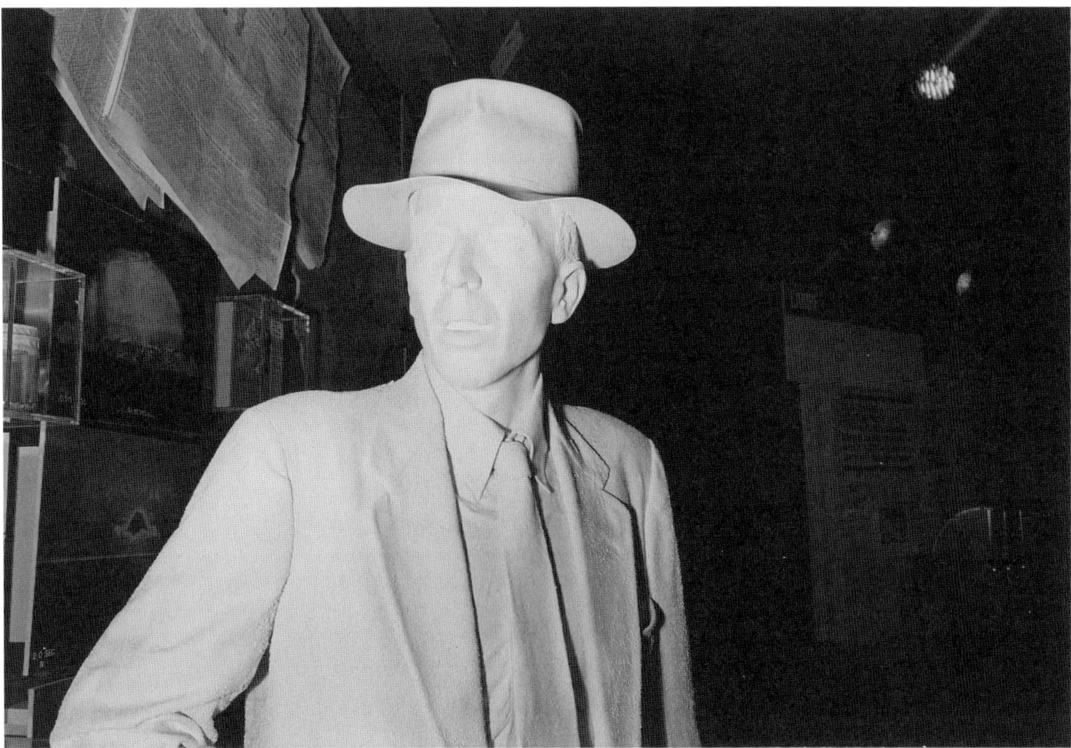

Figure 8.8 Barbara Norfleet, 'Dr. J. Robert Oppenheimer, Bradbury Science Museum Los Alamos, NM', 1988. Gelatin silver print; 16 × 20 in. (40.64 × 50.8 cm) San Francisco Museum of Modern Art, Gift of the artist. © Barbara Norfleet. Photograph: Katherine Du Tiel.

Furthermore, Lippit isolates the paradox that characterizes atomic explosions: whilst they are extremely visible—dangerously, blindingly visible—nonetheless, in their deadly effects, they are insidiously *in*visible. Radiation cannot be tasted, touched, smelt, or, indeed, seen. As Bryan-Wilson remarks, the inadequacy of nuclear photographs when it comes to registering the long-term effects of what they record reveals 'the fundamental insufficiency of photography as a document of causality'.[93] That shatteringly bright light, which forms the bleached core of the images of these explosions, is in fact too bright to print out as anything other than an absolute vacancy—a white hole. It is emptied of all detail, all visual description—a visual analogue for the inability of observers to find language for what they saw, since this was a brightness that surpassed all known forms of ocular experience. In Alain Resnais's 1959 film, *Hiroshima mon amour*, a Japanese man intones to his French lover: 'You saw nothing in Hiroshima. Nothing'. She contradicts him. 'I saw *everything. Everything.*'[94] One absolute cancels out the other, leaving a void of meaning.

Atomic photography can capture the threat, the actuality—at a distance—and the effects of atomic power. But what photography can never make manifest, even as it provokes, is the internalized fear of annihilation that accompanies each replication of the biggest flash of all.

CHAPTER NINE

The Modernity of Flash

Her Picture

He took her picture in a chair,
  With books and works of art around;
The proof, she said, was more than fair,
  But then no atmosphere was found.

He took her picture on a rock,
  A stream and rustic bridge behind.
It gave her nerves a frightful shock
  Because there was no soughing wind.

He took her picture in the sand,
  A nymph disporting by the shore.
The scene, she cried, was nice and grand;
  It only lacked the ocean's roar.

He took her picture by a wheel,
  A Grecian maid, who spins and nods.
Alas! she thought it should reveal
  The early lights of ancient gods.

He took her picture by flashlight,
  Where smoke and smell will often linger.
Her joy was boundless, out of sight;
  It showed the gem upon her finger!

Homer Fort

HOMER FORT penned this ditty at the turn of the twentieth century. It reflects the world of the professional photographer's studio, and the eclectic assortment of settings in which the young lady sitter was posed. By turn, this fussy subject was left dissatisfied by a scene designed to showcase her cultured tastes—a studio setting that was replicated time and again in the United States and in Europe, as a German image shows (Figure 9.1); her comfort in a pastoral setting; her love of the sea's wildness; and her role as a classical symbol of femininity, at once accomplished and patient. But at last she is satisfied. No

Figure 9.1 Photographic studio with magnesium flash in use, Berlin, 1887. MARKA/Alamy Stock Photo.

longer relying, one assumes, on the natural light that came through the studio's glass, the photographer resorts to flash, despite its irritant properties. This does the trick! The young woman is propitiated by the way the light flashes back from a precious stone, which by inference we read as a diamond engagement ring.[1] To be affianced; to be certified as desirable; to wear an economic status symbol—this is the role that the sitter (disappointingly) chooses. For Fort, her shallowness seems conflated with the very practice of flash photography—they are coupled in gentle, condescending mockery.

Fort's photographer is a professional—that is, someone who earns an income through their photographic practice. Whereas many of the other photographers whom we have seen employing flash did so within the public sphere—working for newspapers or the police force, recording and publicizing social conditions—his work takes place within a more vernacular context, making images that will become part of a family record, or will circulate privately among a small group of friends. Such flashlight photos may be taken in a studio, or, say, at a party or wedding, looking to convey social conventions of happiness, jollity, harmonious sociability.[2] 'Flash bang wallop | What a picture, what a photograph!' sings the exuberant ensemble in the 1963 musical *Half a Sixpence*.[3] This vehicle for the English performer Tommy Steele, loosely based on H. G. Wells's novel *Kipps*, is set in 1905, the same year that Wells's text was published. It was turned into a movie, directed by George Sidney, in 1967. For many of us now, this film provides a rare opportunity to see a flashgun in action, the photographer exploding his white powder with a flash, a puff of white smoke, as he records the wedding party on his camera's plates.

Professional photographers continued—and continue—to have an important role when it comes to commemorating important family events, or to taking formal portraits. Instructional manuals aimed at those who must consistently, reliably produce the results that flatter their sitters, together with articles in the photographic press, provide an extensive record, from the later nineteenth century onwards, of the particular challenges that are involved when using flash, when posing one's subject, when combining light from a flash with that from other sources, and when adopting or adapting specific pieces of flash equipment. Much of this advice is, to the casual photographer, extremely technical in its emphasis: it is certainly intended for those who know and understand the mechanics of their cameras well, and who have sufficient comprehension of the physics of light (and, early on, of chemistry) to be able not only to follow instructions, but also to envisage the final results.

However, my focus in this chapter is not primarily on those who practise photography for a living, but on the amateur photographer, and especially, on the person who may take photographs irregularly—on special social occasions, on vacation—and who might be attracted to flash for practical reasons, and yet be apprehensive about how to deploy it effectively or, especially in its early days, safely. I explore flash's use at four distinct periods: during its first and most combustible phase; after the invention and wide adoption of the flashbulb; following the development of the on-camera flashcube; and in today's digital age, when a built-in flash is a standard component of point-and-shoot cameras and even cell phones—probably, by now, the most frequently used tool for vernacular photography.

'Amateur' is, of course, an imprecise word to employ, not least because in the early days of photography, it was primarily those with an independent income and with control over their own time who could afford to experiment with this new art-science.[4] As photography developed as a medium, clear-cut distinctions were often drawn between 'amateurs' and 'professionals', as happened across many spheres in the latter part of the nineteenth century—distinctions that looked to denigrate the productions of 'amateurs' as lacking the grasp of skill and technique enjoyed by their professional counterparts.[5] Yet, as has been very usefully explained in both the British and American contexts, so-called amateur photographers were responsible, especially in the nineteenth and early twentieth centuries, for advancing not just the science of photography, but also its aesthetics. Without the utilitarian obligations of the studio photographer, they could devote themselves, say, to the practice of landscape photography, something that allowed them 'to assert their own agency', as Paul Spencer Sternberger puts it, and hence to help elevate photography into an art form, assisting and intensifying nature through their skill.[6] We shall later see how, by the mid-twentieth century, the terms on which photography's claims to be regarded as a fine art relied, at least for some prominent exponents, on the repudiation of flash. This unease about unnatural lighting effects had their roots in the aesthetics of this period. P. H. Emerson, in his *Naturalistic Photography*—written just after flash powder's invention—observes, in his section on studio lighting and equipment, that means 'may be arranged for taking pictures by artificial light, if necessary, though personally we do not care for them. The tonality, though true to the light, has a false, artificial appearance by day…The best of these we have seen were done by the American "blitz-pulver" '—Hamerton seems unclear about the substance's origins, although it's perhaps telling that he looks across the Atlantic as a likely source of ersatz illumination—'but the results appeared to us somewhat artificial. We think artists will always avoid these artificial lights.'[7]

It is, perhaps, more useful to draw a distinction between the 'serious' amateur and the 'casual' amateur—a distinction that follows sociologist Robert Stebbins's division between 'serious' and 'casual' leisure. He isolates a number of defining components that are very handy when it comes to identifying the 'serious' amateur photographer: (1) the investment of significant personal effort based on acquired knowledge, training, and skill—sometimes all three; (2) the achievement of recognizable, durable benefits (such as self-actualization and self-expression); (3) an engagement in a particular subculture, or what sociologists term 'idioculture', signifying people bound together by shared knowledge and practices—here, we might think of involvement in photographic societies and camera clubs, participation in competitions, reading and contributing words and images to journals; and (4) identifying strongly with one's chosen pursuit. The tendency to persevere, despite setbacks, is lauded—and is also something emphasized in periodical articles as a necessary practical and, indeed, moral quality. 'You are not likely to succeed in flashlight portraiture by trying an occasional flash just for the fun of the thing', W. S. Ritch told readers of the *American Amateur Photographer* in 1903, 'but if you put your mind and heart into this one branch of photography, studying and practicing persistently, taking advantage of your failures to do better next time, and using more brains than anything else, success will be comparatively easy. Persistent thinking on subject will accomplish anything.'[8] A further quality, turning one's leisure pursuit into an actual career, might seem less pertinent, but when one considers how a professional photographer who has, for example, developed a novel means of exploding flash powder might have it written up in the columns of the *American Amateur Photographer*, or how a studio portrait photographer might take indoor genre photographs by flash in their spare time, the division is less than clear-cut.[9] These characteristics become further complicated, moreover, by factors of gender. Middle-class women might have more leisure time than many men of their backgrounds, and hence more opportunity to pursue serious photography, but frequently had to fight for admission to the societies where information concerning scientific and technical developments was discussed.[10]

The casual amateur, however, was just the type of photographer that the *American Amateur Photographer* was setting itself up against. This monthly periodical was launched in 1889—a year after the first Kodak camera came on the market, with its mechanized mass appeal ('You press the button—we do the rest')—and two years after the invention of *blitzlichtpulver*.[11] In 1891 Kodak brought out the first camera that was reloadable in daylight. Even if these first cameras were not cheap (the first Kodak camera (1888–9) cost $25; the No. 1 Kodak (1889–95) also cost $25; the 'A' Daylight Kodak camera (1891–5) $8.50), Kodak had a breakthrough with the Brownie in 1900, which sold for just $1.[12] By making cameras affordable, and, above all, by removing the necessity of a darkroom for developing and printing, the turn of the twentieth century saw, worldwide, a huge gap develop between the committed, serious amateur who saw darkroom work as integral to their aesthetic choices and decisions, and those who just looked to record the person or scene in front of them. An unsigned piece in the journal's first number (probably penned by its editor, Frederick Converse Beach) complained that now that 'a fairly serviceable set of apparatus' may be 'purchased for a song',

> It has become a popular belief that all the difficulties have been removed, and that any one can now take pictures. Photography has been degraded to the level of a mere sport, and many take it up, as they do lawn tennis, merely for an amusement, without a thought of the grand and elevating possibilities it opens up to them. The making of pictures is fast becoming merely an episode in a day's pleasure, not the earnest and untiring search for the beautiful.

A true photographer will not just seek to appreciate nature's beauties, and learn to discriminate 'between the picturesque and the trivial', but will also 'interpret aright the grace and charm of field and forest, lane and hedge-row, brook-side and sea-shore. Technical manipulation will be to him only a means to an end, and that end the interpretation of beauty.'[13] Within this statement resides some central tenets of the American photographic pictorialist school and the articulation of what was to grow into disdain for the 'snapshooter'—that casual photographer summed up nearly forty years later by Olla Mason writing that 'the average adult snapshooter is not interested in art and will not be bothered with technical knowledge'.[14] Within it, too, lies the core of an important strand of opposition to flash photography: that not just was it unnatural, in the sense that it used artificially produced rather than natural or even ambient light, but that it also destroyed a photographer's sense of continuity and immersion—even contemplative immersion—with their world.

Yet the editors of the *American Amateur Photographer* were in no way purist about the use of flash, and the journal was no different from its counterparts on both sides of the Atlantic in offering information about the effectiveness, or otherwise, of new products designed to make the use of flash easier and safer (including the filing of patents); information about accidents involving its misuse; and advice about how to make striking and original photographs through using it with an informed knowledge of its effects. Wordy advertisements performed much the same function as editorial material when it came to describing how to employ a product and what one can, at best, hope from it:

they exude, of course, a tone of authority and expertise in their rhetoric of persuasion. Take, for example, over half a page of prose placed by the Eastman Kodak Company in October 1903, in which the reader is reminded that it is 'FLASHLIGHT TIME.—THE SEASON FOR EVENING PHOTOGRAPHY IS AT HAND.—INTERIORS AND PORTRAITS'. This is an advertisement not for powder, nor for some means of igniting it, but for a yet simpler, less messy, less unpredictable domestic-oriented commodity. The advertisement both informs and describes; it situates these pyrotechnic products in their practical and aesthetic context:

> Eastman's Flash Sheets—thin, inflammable sheets which look like gray cardboard—offer the best possible means of producing the flashlight. These sheets require no accessories. To use, simply pin to a card and light with a match. They are not instantaneous. There's their great virtue. It's the first instantaneous glare of the ordinary flash which gives the harsh contrast between light and shade and the weird effect seen in many flashlight pictures. This isn't necessary. Flashlight pictures rightly made have just as soft a lighting as daylight pictures.
>
> Eastman's Flash Sheets burn with an even, steady light for about a second. Owing to the broad surface of light (from the entire surface of the flame) the shadows are less harsh than with ordinary flash powders where the light comes from a smaller point—an important feature in portraiture. Then, too, with flash sheets the flash is not so blinding. The sudden flare of the ordinary flash cannot help startling the sitter—and the picture shows it. Portraits made with Eastman's Flash Sheets have not the staring eyes and distorted features common to most portraits made with instantaneous flashes.
>
> The sheets give a minimum of smoke and residue, and therefore are particularly adapted to parlor use. Sometimes a flash stronger than one sheet will give is needed. In such cases pin two or more sheets to the cardboard with corners slightly overlapping. Touch the lowest one with a match. Thus it is easy to regulate the amount of light.[15]

Articles that ostensibly offer objective advice also act as promotional vehicles for pieces of apparatus. An article about effective lighting in the *Photographic Times* in 1898 tells that 'artistic effects' are more easily achieved by having more than one source of light, 'and with one well forward to one side—moving them during exposure—you get modelling and relief'.[16] At this point, the author suggests the Byron Lamp, shown in Figure 9.2, just introduced by the Scovill & Adams Co.

As soon as flashlight powder was invented, its potential to transform the scope of the amateur photographer was widely registered. Often, however, this was in terms that drew on an already well-established association between photography and humour that Heinz and Bridget Henisch see, in part, as a defensive response to the impact of high technology on society: 'To some extent, the mirth is a common defense used as a mask for embarrassment in the face of perplexing problems.'[17] One could certainly count flash's ability to misfire—sometimes all too literally—among these. Mocking the craze for photography in its various phases is a form of defence, too, against the irritating social interruption caused by the individual who keeps insisting that a party or picnic momentarily freezes in order to be commemorated—something that the introduction of the flash only accentuates. Just after its invention was announced, the *Philadelphia Evening Telegram*'s reporter indulged in a mild fantasy about how the new

Figure 9.2 The Byron Lamp, *Photographic Times* 30 (April 1898), 154.

capacity for taking photographs in the dark would lead both to obsessive behaviour and to the detection of all kinds of things going on under the cover of darkness:

the amateur photographer will henceforth go a gunning in the darkness...The camera will be fitted to a pistol barrel or the pistol barrel to the camera and cocking the weapon will expose the plate. As soon as the weapon is aimed the flash from the muzzle will instantly served to photograph the object, and the game will be securely bagged in a moment. The fleeting thief, the expression of the man who treads upon the unforeseen carpet tack, as well as that of the husband out late who is trying to assume an expression of indifferent sobriety before he lights the domestic gas, will now adorn the albums, where they have hitherto been unknown. The invention [will] greatly widen the fields of amusement and experiment which have attracted some thousands to amateur photography.[18]

This account builds on the idea that a flash camera could act as a detective device, to be sure, but it also summons up the scenes of domestic comedy veering into slapstick that formed a staple of late nineteenth-century commercially circulating stereo cards.[19] What's more, it points to the licence—again, on both sides of the Atlantic—that photography in general, as a social pursuit, gave to dressing up and posing in staged comic set pieces, deliberately ridiculous, evidence of elaborate fun, and often involving cross-dressing and various forms of clowning for the camera.

The advent of the flash greatly aided the making of such photographic tableaux—as we see in an 1891 image made by the prolific Staten Island amateur photographer, Alice Austen.[20] Figure 9.3 shows Austen portraying herself hamming it up late one evening with Gertrude Eccleston, an Episcopalian minister's daughter, using Indian fabric in front of an alcove with what looks like a daybed in it to create a space that is somewhere between a small proscenium arch and a harem's inner sanctum. Austen carefully notes on the negative sleeve: 'Trude & I masked, short skirts. 11 p.m., Thursday Aug. 6th 1891. Gas on, flash. Stanley 35, Waterbury lense. 11ft.'[21] Fun and technical expertise—the flash brings out the brilliance of their undergarments, the polished shoes, the uncanny

Figure 9.3 Alice Austen, 'Trude & I Masked, Short Skirts', 1891. Courtesy of the Alice Austen House.

half-disguise of their gleaming half-masks, and their bright cigarettes, nearly, but not quite, touching.

Alice Austen was exceptional in many ways—the range of her photographs goes far beyond family scenes and records of leisure and travel. Photographically active for over forty years, she produced some notable images of New York street sellers and snow sweepers, of children selling newspapers, of immigrants in Battery Park. She was also very fortunate in having an uncle who was professor of chemistry at Rutgers University, who worked with her when it came to mastering the technical aspects of her pursuit. But for those who did not have family members to hand, for the many casual photographers who did not read the photographic press on a weekly or monthly basis, much of their advice came from small advice manuals. Flash could be covered in a chapter or two, or could command the entire book. Many of these publications were, in turn, either reprints of articles that originally appeared in specialist journals, or were published by the manufacturers of photographic equipment. This last point speaks to what Grace Lees-Maffei, writing about the historiographical challenges involved in studying manuals that engage with etiquette, homemaking, and home decoration—fields that have a considerable overlap with the world of the home-based photo-hobbyist—calls the 'often nebulous border between advice and advertising'.[22] Even manuals with no visible connection to a specific company frequently carried advertisements for relevant equipment, and, as we've just seen, press advertisements themselves were often full of useful tips.

This instructional literature affords a vivid overview of the photographic and domestic environments in which flash photography flourished—or, at least, in which its authors imagined it being conducted. It is strong on detailed technical advice, certainly, but what also stands out is the emphasis on improvisation, on the photographer him- or herself making use of whatever might handily be pressed into service in order to make a successful image. For example, photographers are often advised that they may get the best effects through reflected light. Louis Clarence Bennett, in *Flash Lights and How to Take Them* (1891), suggests that if 'the walls of the room are very dark it may be necessary to use a side reflector, which may be a Japanese screen or a common clothes-horse with a sheet thrown over it'.[23] He also suggests rubbing soap on a mirror to stop it reflecting.[24] F. J. Mortimer, in a book expanded from articles that had been published in the *Photographic Monthly*, addresses himself to the British amateur who may combine a photographic hobby with country rambles or bicycling, when it's improbable that he will be travelling with the same kind of apparatus that he enjoys at home. All the same, he may carry 'a small packet of magnesium powder' with him. 'In country districts, fine old character studies in many a chimney corner can thus be secured on the spur of the moment, especially at the village inn after the day's work is over. A clay pipe, a little whisky'—for an effective conduit for the flare, one surmises, rather than for lubricating the inhabitant of the chimney corner—'and a strip torn from a handkerchief provide all that is necessary for an efficient flashlight apparatus.'[25] D. Grant, in his 1914 *Manual of Photography: With Special Reference to Work in the Tropics*, advises that 'a newspaper is a useful adjunct' as a flashlight reflector, especially when photographing architectural detail.[26]

A number of these manuals take their authority, both verbal and visual, from the careers of their authors. The pictorialist photographer Francis James Mortimer, from Portsmouth, England, who was to go on to be editor of the *Amateur Photographer* (from 1908 to 1944) and *Photograms of the Year* (from 1912 to 1944), was a founding member of the London Salon and member of the Linked Ring, and someone who continually experimented with dramatic light effects (including ones that he achieved through combination printing). In *Magnesium Light Photography* he suggests that impressive but subtle effects can be achieved by combining daylight and flash, supplementing the daylight that comes through smaller windows and door with a flash placed on a shelf outside the main window, the window itself being covered with tissue paper. Mortimer illustrates this technique with a quietly but effectively lit scene, 'Washing Up' (Figure 9.4), which mimics Vermeer both in the subject matter—a respectable but modestly dressed woman, well covered with an apron, carefully, even contemplatively washing dishes at the kitchen sink—and in the use of light to give beauty and stillness to a very ordinary domestic occupation. The effect is naturalistic, even if the means of achieving it are not. And 'effect' is the operative word, in what is a very deliberately composed scene, especially when compared with the revelation of random and untidy detail that flash's harsh and contrastive properties gave to documentary photography. Here, the dustpan under the table is not evidence of slipshod housekeeping, but provides a subtly lit diagonal that leads the viewer's eye upwards into the image from the abstract patches of light and shade in the foreground, forming one side of a triangle that slopes back again from the far edge of the apron, and up the edge of the draining board to the tap that, in turn, is lit by the diffused flash. The diffusion of light is, moreover, accentuated through the half-tone reproduction in this particular volume.[27]

By contrast to this idealized naturalism, the St Louis studio photographer Fitz W. Guerin created scenes that no one could be duped into thinking were realistic: his tableaux involved elaborately painted backcloths, featuring bucolic pastoral landscapes, woodland glades, and crashing breakers (a feature of which Mortimer was also excessively fond, and which formed a staple of his own highly stylized combination prints). Even the supposedly living creatures hover between the real and the artificial. The exuberant children and barely clad women are surely live—even if a baby's wings are fake—but a stuffed owl with a pipe in its mouth occupies a strange hinterland, as do the people who lean out of obviously painted backgrounds to embrace living flesh. And in 'Women and Two Girls Crying Over a Dead Bird' (Figure 9.5), the bird has presumably been stuffed for some time, but it's impossible to tell the condition of the guilty cat. Guerin's *Portraits in Photography by the Aid of Flash* (1898) may not be intended for those who wanted to emulate his elaborate studio set-ups, but it inculcates the same basic principle: place the 'flash machine' where you would expect natural light to come from, or, as he puts it, 'I finally came to the conclusion that to succeed at all I must follow the same method in lighting by the aid of flashlight as I had previously done in my efforts with daylight'.[28] Sometimes, he admits, his pictures could not have been made at all except with the aid of a flash—and, indeed, with other forms of assistance. The expression

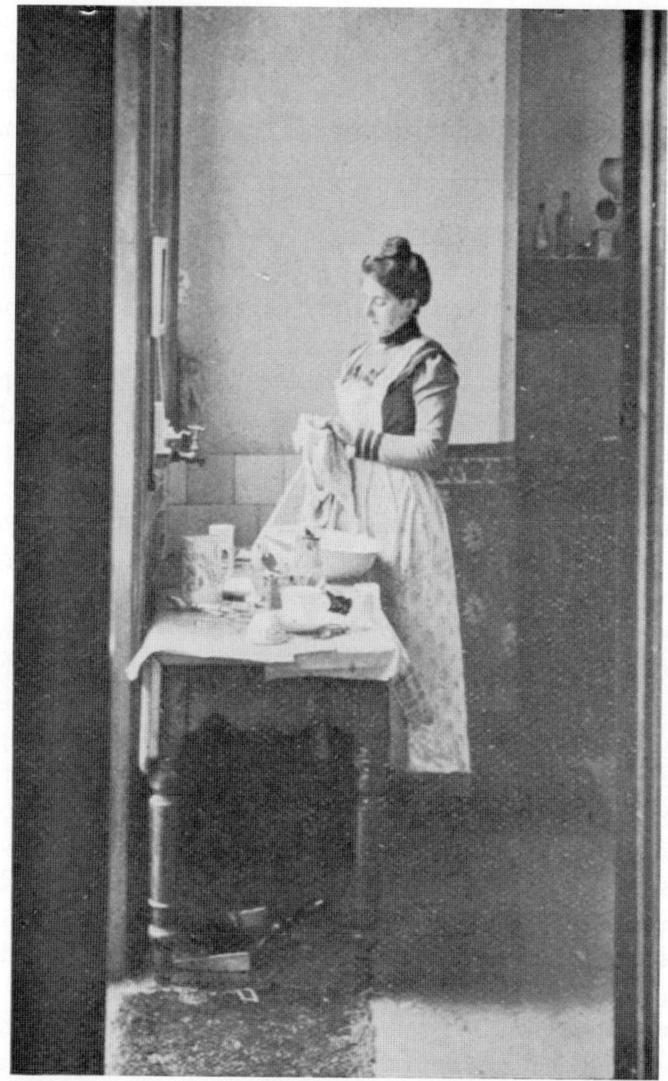

Figure 9.4 Francis James Mortimer, 'Washing Up', *Magnesium Light Photography: Being the Actual Methods of One who Has Had a Very Wide and Successful Practical Experience in the Work* (London: Dawbarn & Ward, 1906), 71.

of the child in 'Babes in the Woods', for example, reproduced in Figure 9.6, 'was not assumed for the occasion, but was perfectly natural, for when I was all ready to make the exposure, my assistant, who was on the floor behind the child, pricked the little one with a needle, consequently the expression followed by an instantaneous exposure. Light used in the usual way.'[29] That last, laconic sentence makes it hard to be sure—as is true in so many cases—whether or not the writer intends a humorous effect in his prose as well as in the accompanying image; whether photographers, indeed, laugh at themselves, or use

Figure 9.5 Fitz W. Guerin, 'Women and Two Girls Crying Over a Dead Bird; Boy Holding Cat by Scruff of Neck', *c.*1900–10. Library of Congress Prints and Photographs Division. LC-USZ62-77010.

humour as a way of establishing a rapport with their readers and fellow practitioners; or whether, indeed, they are just more clumsy writers than they are picture-takers.

This same uncertainty applies to our reading of safety instructions. By 1940, ten years after the invention of the flashbulb, it was possible for Rus Arnold to write, in one of the new wave of advice manuals, 'Today it all seems very amusing, looking back on the dirt and smoke used by the flash powder.'[30] Yet the tone in which potential disaster is discussed is far from stable. 'It seems incredible that a photographer would have his or her face over or anywhere near the flash, or that the receptacle containing the charge of powder should be placed in close proximity to lace curtains, valuable table-cloths, or on well-polished surfaces of furniture', commented John J. Curtis in 1925, his incredulous tone flattering the reader's common sense; simultaneously bestowing essential advice and confirming membership of a practised and practical group of photographers through raising a smile from those who would do nothing so ridiculous.[31] But especially

Figure 9.6 Fitz W. Guerin, 'Babes in the Woods', *Portraits in Photography by the Aid of Flash Light* (St Louis: Fitz W. Guerin, 1898), 33.

in the early days of flash photography, some of this advice is given in an unambiguously serious voice. Mortimer, again, warns that

Photographers are sometimes very reckless in letting off startling and explosive flashes in public places and without any warning to the passers-by. Even though the flash may do no damage, there is danger of shock to nervous persons, and the possibility of stampeding a horse. Photographers should, therefore, use all possible precautions and only attempt such work when a definite and important end is to be gained. Should any serious accident occur, the photographer can be held responsible, and there is no doubt it would lead to serious restrictions on the use of flashlights. Even at the present time the police have wide powers under the Explosives Act, and matters would be very unpleasant for any photographer against whom they had to be enforced.[32]

William Ritch, writing an advice pamphlet for Eastman Kodak in 1904, moves the cautionary counsel back indoors when he discusses the merits and demerits of various new proprietary means of exploding flash that were designed to make it easy for those who had no intention of becoming involved with messy and potentially dangerous chemistry. An Eastman Flash Sheet, pinned to an 8-foot-long strip of wood that's tied upright to the back of a chair, should suffice for most purposes, but the subject must possess 'enough self control to remain quiet during the burning of the sheet, which takes about one second; but for nervous people and little children, it is necessary to use the cartridges [Eastman Spreader Cartridges, used in conjunction with a special pistol] as these are practically instantaneous'.[33]

The volatile nature of flash lent itself to humorous sketches, such as the police station vignette that we encountered in Chapter 7, or scenes based on trying to photograph a terrified pet. But given the potential for drama and disaster that is so apparent in the advice literature, it is perhaps surprising that it does not appear more frequently within the narrative fiction of the time. When the narrator of H. G. Wells's *The Time Machine* (1895) goes underground into the territory of the repellent Morlocks and exclaims 'If only I had thought of a Kodak! I could have flashed that glimpse of the Underworld in a second, and examined it at leisure',[34] it seems more probable that he's talking about the speediness of this new camera than alluding to any properties of illumination. Yet there are a handful of unmistakable references to flash equipment. Charles Hyne's racy and improbable adventure story, *The Recipe for Diamonds* (1894), involves a race between two groups of men to find a formula for diamonds that was written on the wall of a Minorcan burial chamber by a twelfth-century alchemist. The (blind) rival to the story's heroes manages to reach the inscription first and photographs it by flashlight before obliterating it—however, once they catch up with him, he destroys the plate rather than share the evidence that the flash allowed him to gather.[35] In *Captain Kodak* (1899)—a novel intended to excite and to some extent instruct young people about using cameras—Allan can't wait to try out his new Kodak camera, but it arrives when daylight is fading. '"You could make a flashlight"', his friend Owen helpfully suggests, but the challenges raised by this possibility disappear when flames from a factory fire in town provide enough light to take some spectacular shots.[36] More dramatic is the moment when Rocco, the renowned head chef in Arnold Bennett's crime story burlesque *The Grand Babylon Hotel* (1902), makes use of his photographic hobby when a corpse is discovered in a hotel bedroom. After

the chef switched off the two electric lights . . . the State bedroom was in darkness. In that swift darkness Racksole heard Rocco spring on to the bed. Another half-dozen moments of suspense, and there was a blinding flash of white, which endured for several seconds, and showed Rocco standing like an evil spirit over the corpse, the black box in one hand and a burning piece of aluminium wire in the other. The aluminium wire burnt out, and darkness followed blacker than before.

Rocco had photographed the corpse by flashlight.

At the same moment, of course, 'the dazzling flare which had disclosed the features of the dead man to the insensible lens of the camera had disclosed them also' to the American millionaire Theodore Racksole, who has just purchased the hotel.[37]

The suddenly dazzling flash in the Grand Babylon serves as one more reminder of the consolidation of flash photography and crime in the popular imagination. But the realities of its use were far more prosaic, and these are reflected time and again in the growing body of advice literature. Two representative examples—one from each side of the Atlantic—give a vivid portrayal of domestic practices. *Flashlight Photography*, a small volume from the early 1920s (without author or date, but advertised in *American Photography* in 1922), offers many useful tips about placing and igniting flash, and—although a range of equipment is specifically mentioned—it effectively functions as a promotion for the easy-to-use Actino Flash Cartridges. These cartridges were sold in packets of six, came in three sizes—#12 illuminated a 12-foot room; #18 an 18-foot room; #30 a 30-foot room—and were filled with Victor Flash Powder, so that they were predictable in the amount of light that they produced, although some inventive and slightly scary uses are proposed as well: 'good camp fire scenes may be made, by wrapping the powder from a No. 30 Actino Cartridge in tissue paper and tossing it in fire after opening shutter'.[38] In England, Curtis's *Flashlight for the Amateur Photographer* (1925)—reprinted from articles that had appeared in the *New Photographer*—was a somewhat more substantial volume, which contains some discussion about commercial uses of flash—noting its increasing use within advertising, especially of furniture and clothes—and even speculates about 'the actual time occupied by a "flash"'.[39] Although recommending that one purchases pre-prepared flash powder (coming in the form of two separate powders, to be mixed just before using), some of its improvisations sound a little alarming, as when Curtis describes making a picture of a billiard game: 'the mixed powder was arranged in a heap on the saucepan lid, which was then placed on the top of a pair of household steps'.[40] What could possibly go wrong?

Two further emphases stand out from this 1925 manual. One is the equation of photography with hobbyism, and the assertion that it 'is pretty certain to assume that most amateur photographers have another hobby besides photography'. This might be wireless building, model engine or model yacht building, fretwork, designing, flower studies, stamp collecting—the flash photographer 'has the chance of making his own illustrated catalogue'—or the making of tabletop tableaux with sand and mirrors and dolls, all ready for photographing.[41] The other aligns it directly with the American pamphlet in its foregrounding of domesticity. The finest subjects for this class of work, we are told, are 'kiddies'.

Wherever there is a child in the house there is then a fruitful source of opportunity. Put that child in contact with a box of toy bricks, trains, soldiers, or Meccano, and the enthusiastic photographer can keep going all the evening. Then on another occasion enter the house when bath time is imminent, and another batch of plates will soon be exposed...Most children will lend themselves readily for this work, and I have always found them ready to act as models and to pose more naturally than when being photographed out of doors; firstly, because they are surrounded with objects that are familiar to them and are with their own parents or relations, and secondly, kiddies generally like fireworks or anything approaching fireworks.

Other subjects that serve very usefully are pets, such as dogs and cats; but once during an evening is usually sufficient for these creatures; they do not like the flash, and, as a rule, cannot be found when wanted a second time.[42]

The introduction of the flashbulb transformed the practice of domestic photography, just as it had revolutionized the careers of newspaper photographers.[43] This transformation was, however, of a somewhat different kind. It was not so much that the subject matter shifted dramatically: what changed was the *number* of people who started to take photographs using flash. Cameras themselves became far easier to use. Although the first fully automated camera—the Super Kodak Six-20 camera of 1938—was, at $225, extremely expensive, it was the forerunner of the cheap automatic cameras that came onto the market in the 1950s. Flash photography was greatly facilitated by the invention of the synchronized flash—the clicking of the shutter automatically triggering the flashbulb—in the mid-1930s. Initially this was only available on fairly advanced cameras, but it was soon added to simple cameras. The Agfa Sur-Flash appeared in 1935;[44] the Ansohe Falcon Press Flash in 1939; and the first popular Kodak flash camera, the Brownie Flash Six-20, in 1940, with a flashbulb holder that screwed into the camera, as illustrated in Figure 9.7. Its manual promises that 'You will enjoy every picture-taking moment that you spend with your Brownie Flash Six-20, because it combines simplicity of operation with dependable performance'. It is illustrated with pictures, seen in Figure 9.8, that not only show (very clearly) the operation of the camera and flash, but that, once again, illustrate supposedly typical white middle-class domestic scenes—a small boy playing with a box of wooden bricks; two girls reading demurely in front of a fireplace; another looking coy in the bath. The only warnings appear in very small print indeed: 'Caution: Under certain conditions, the lamps may crack or shatter when flashed. It is therefore recommended that a protective transparent screen be used over the front of the reflector. Do not flash the lamps in an explosive atmosphere without safety equipment.'[45]

Someone who purchased a Brownie Flash Six-20 or its close rivals was very likely to have only a rudimentary knowledge of flash photography—the ideal reader for Rus Arnold's little manual, *Flash Photography*, which also appeared in 1940. Arnold, a widely published Chicago photojournalist and expert on flash photography, is enormously informative about flash's many and growing uses in this volume, but he also takes a reassuring stance towards the complete novice. 'The first flash picture is the

Figure 9.7 Brownie Flash Six-20 camera (photo: Kate Flint).

hardest. Or, to be more exact, the first flash picture is the only hard one... The only difficulty—one experienced by most amateur and professional photographers—is getting up the courage to take that first flash picture.' He compares it to jumping off a bank into a swimming hole: terrifying the first time, and then fun.[46] He explains such elementary but crucial concepts as the Law of Intensity, whereby, knowing the strength of one's flashbulb, one knows how far its flash will reach—and then one can work out the necessary exposure according to the speed of one's film.[47] Arnold offers the practical advice to do as very many photographers did: paste the relevant table into one's camera case or on the back of the flashgun reflector. I remember that my own uncle did just this.

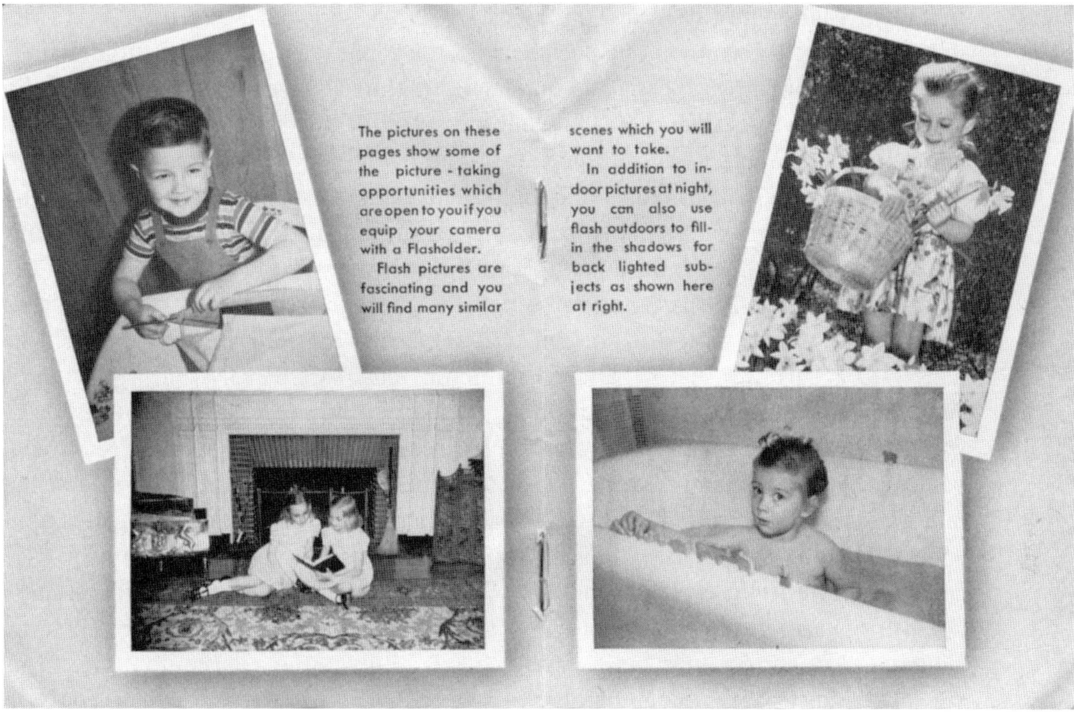

The pictures on these pages show some of the picture - taking opportunities which are open to you if you equip your camera with a Flasholder.
Flash pictures are fascinating and you will find many similar scenes which you will want to take.
In addition to indoor pictures at night, you can also use flash outdoors to fill-in the shadows for back lighted subjects as shown here at right.

Figure 9.8 *Picture-Taking with the Brownie Flash Six-20* (Rochester, NY: Eastman Kodak Co., n.d.), 14–15.

But Arnold's volume was symptomatic of the changing presentation of flash techniques to the general public in several other ways. First, although gender stereotypes were upheld in many respects—in talking the reader slowly and calmly through the taking of their first flash photograph, the example given of a subject is 'junior trying out his new toy train'[48]—the images of the open flash in use (where the flashgun is held away from the camera), of press cameras with magnetic flash synchronizers and mechanical synchronizers, and of an inexpensive camera (indeed, it looks like a Flash Brownie Six-20) with a built-in synchronized flash mechanism, all show a woman holding the apparatus. Kodak had highlighted women in their advertising since the 1890s: as Nancy West tells us, 'Unquestionably, Eastman's original reason for deploying the image of the Kodak Girl was that a "picture of a pretty girl", as he so prosaically phrased it, "sells more than a tree or a house".'[49] West acknowledges the equation, common in critiques of commodity culture, between woman's objectification and the objectification of a commercially advertised object of desire, but she uses advertising journals from the early twentieth century to suggest that something else is happening as well: that commentators believe that 'the woman's fashion sense acts as an indicator of the mechanically superior products she endorses, as if an appreciation of mechanical efficiency requires nothing more than an attention to appearance'.[50] By the time of mid-twentieth-century advertising, however, employing a woman model seems to function in a slightly different way—one far closer to the images included by Arnold of a sensible, capable, active woman (I suspect his wife, the cookery writer Lucy Arnold) who is using the equipment with ease, and underscoring the message that flash photography is not fiddly, specialized (and certainly not messy) work, but is fun.

Second, the popularity of all branches of photography by this period is reflected in Arnold's insistence that flash can—and should—work as a means for making photography fresh again, and breaking away from wearily predictable poses. Take pictures of your child that bring out their individuality. 'Forget immediately all those old standbys of the child-photographer. The flashbulb will endear itself forever to all persons of taste if it puts an end once and for all to the horrible clichés of child portraiture which confront us daily.'[51] One surmises that he reached numerous deaf ears. Finally, and significantly, Arnold stressed the fact that flash photography was not necessarily expensive. He emphasizes the democracy of it as a pastime: 'Are you a millionaire? You can very easily bankrupt yourself buying necessary flash equipment. Are you on the other side of the financial see-saw? All you need is a dollar box camera, a fifty-cent flashgun, a roll of film, and a flashbulb or two.'[52] Even if flashbulbs seem expensive at first, 'that is only by false comparison with *not* using the flashbulb'.[53] One will be far less likely to waste film if one's not using guesswork to make the right exposures through natural indoor lighting. Ultimately, the correct question to be asking about purchasing a flashbulb, 'a "bottle of sunlight" ready to obey your commands',[54] is whether or not it is a good investment. And what—Arnold makes a sentimental pitch—could be a better investment than the eventual picture of one's child, guaranteed to afford hours of pleasure?

Arnold's emphases are repeated in other manuals of the 1940s and 1950s, and in the advertising materials that promoted the equipment that he, and other authors, envisaged that their readers would be using.[55] Such advertisements, like the one in Figure 9.9, emphasized that having a camera with a flash attachment on hand meant that one was always '*READY FOR ACTION*'—the Federal Fed-Flash Camera's promotional materials from 1948 that advertised this low-price, easy-to-use Bakelite camera showed the brand name in a lightning-flash-like banner jumping off the flashgun shield, with an extra zigzag under 'Fed-Flash', and was typical in this adoption of flash's long-standing associations with natural electricity.[56] There is, of course, an echo of wartime preparedness about this slogan, and one should note that the increase in popularity of flash photography in the years following the Second World War is a reflection not just of consumer goods in general becoming more readily available than they had been, but of the circumstances that had hampered flash photography in particular. Although synchronized flash units, using a wire release, had been invented before the start of the war, as the English news photographer Lancelot Vining noted, 'Soon after the start of the 1939 war, the releases were no longer obtainable. As no suitable ones were being produced in this country, and as all flash lamps were sent to the Services, flash photography took a long holiday until peace had settled in again.'[57]

That zigzag was repeated in other advertisements, and on the manual that accompanied the outfit. Aimed at a more advanced photographer, Ilex's Acme Synchro

Figure 9.9 Federal Fed-Flash Camera advertisement, *Popular Photography* (August 1948), 41.

Shutters were advertised in 1947 with bright light shooting out all round them, like a comic book version of a meteorite. Agfalux's Foldaway Flashgun (*c.*1956) has its properties of illumination suggested by diagonal stripes of light that resemble the sun's rays more closely than they do lightning, and in a colour advertisement from 1958, Sylvania promotes its M-25 and M-5 flashbulbs with yellow bands that fan out all over the page from the white-light source of the small bulbs themselves—their diminutive size being displayed, say, by a photograph of a man's fist holding one of them between finger and thumb. 'Your sun, the flashcube', promised a 1967 ad for the Kodak Instamatic 104 camera.

The 'Ready For Action' Fed-Flash ad reproduced in Figure 9.9 was typical of much flash advertising of the late 1940s and 1950s—whether aimed at amateur or expert—in that, by showing camera and flashgun, it emphasized the innate appeal and technical specifications of the object of desire itself. Of course, it was demanded of the apparatus that it would be easy to operate and that it would give sharp and well-lit pictures, and advertisements increasingly reproduced photographs that purported to be taken by the cameras they were advertising. The presence of Christmas as a gift-giving occasion frequently serves a double role in such images: the camera might make an ideal gift, and it would also be an excellent idea to have one on hand to capture a family's supposed happiness—as exemplified in the glint in the eye of the little girl who, in an advertisement for 11-cent GE Mazda Flashbulbs, stands in her dressing gown smirking radiantly at the shiny decorations on a Christmas tree. The other constant in the publicity aimed at the casual amateur of this period was value for money. We have already encountered Arnold stressing this point; in the early 1950s, Howard Luray was saying the same thing in *Your Simple Flash Camera,* asking,

> Do you know the greatest bargain of the century?
>
> It's the simple flash camera.
>
> For a few cents per picture the flash camera indelibly records fleeting instants which could not otherwise be recaptured for all the money in the world! Moments which are with us one minute, then gone forever—a baby's first smile or step, a birthday party, wedding or graduation...all these things and more, indoors and out, are recorded easily and accurately by the flash camera.

He promises that his little book 'will help you get the most out of an inexpensive flash camera. It will help you get better pictures, with a minimum of effort'—and this emphasis on economy, as well as on family-oriented affective experience, mimics the language of advertising campaigns.[58]

Advertising also helps us tell the story of the next important shifts in flash technology: the advent of the flashcube in the early 1960s; the coming of the Magicube (or X-Flashcube) in 1970; and the flipflash (and the very similar top flash and flip bar—different manufacturers had different names, in order to circumnavigate patent issues). The flashcube (powered by low-voltage batteries) incorporated four AG1-sized bulbs on four sides of a cube, with a plastic reflector behind them: one inserted the cube into a socket on the camera, and it rotated as the film was wound. The Magicube looked very similar, but was fired mechanically by a small bar striking a pin (this made it suitable for use on even very cheap cameras). In 1972 Flash Bar was developed for the Polaroid SX-70 camera: the triggering of a built-in sensor directed the voltage to the next available bulb. Flip Flash, for Kodak Instamatic cameras, appeared in 1975 (followed by the improved Flip Flash II in 1978), and these involved eight or ten bulbs placed in a flat rectangular strip—the photographer had to invert the strip when they were halfway through.

If the details of flash's technological developments, even when recounted in their most basic and redacted form, start to sound as though one has wandered into the specialist and intense world of the obsessed hobbyist, the advertising that promoted these new lighting effects worked in quite the opposite direction. It was designed to make the purchaser believe that there was nothing more to taking a great photograph using flash than screwing in a flashcube or using a fully automatic camera with a built-in flash—or as a 1984 advertisement for the Polaroid 600 put it, this technology was designed 'to free you from all the technical gobbledygook, so that you can get on with creating the pictures'.[59] Five years earlier, an ad for the Kodak Colorburst 250 instant camera (Kodak's version of Polaroid's technology) proclaimed 'Flash without fuss. Instantly'—it makes the point that one doesn't even have to fiddle around looking for a Flip Flash: 'Just slide out the flash, aim and shoot.' The advice is illustrated by several sets of advertisements. One, reproduced in Figure 9.10 (found in such general circulation magazines as *Newsweek*), depicts a chubby, jolly middle-aged white man in a dressing gown holding a square image—which we are asked to presume was taken just a minute earlier—of him raiding the refrigerator in the middle of the night. The other (Figure 9.11) uses exactly the same storyline, but features a hunkier middle-aged black man, and appeared in *Ebony* and *Jet*. The racial difference between the two ads suggests a determined effort on Kodak's part (or on the part of J. Walter Thompson, the company who handled their account) to encourage consumer identification with the subject of their images, and presumably with the person who took them (the logic of convention would suggest a female partner, but that subject position is left entirely open). It's a way of suggesting that instant cameras—with flash—might indeed serve the function of privately recording something naughty, without spelling out the proposition any more loudly than by showing—especially with regards to the second advertisement—an attractive, fun-loving man wearing nightwear; his head, against the gleaming white refrigerator, looking remarkably as though it could be resting on a pillow.[60]

Moreover, the publicity led one to believe that in using this technology, one was being truly modern. 'Meet the Robot on the Ilford Monarch', a British advertisement invites. Jackson Lears, looking at the coming of mass production in the early twentieth century, commented that 'The agenda of national advertising was to subordinate the magic of product to the magic of process: the constant creation and recreation of new fetishes, in accordance with the imperatives of technological determinism'.[61] The process celebrated in this marketing is not just the teleology surrounding affordable artificial illumination, but also the engagement of the consumer in observing, recording, and remembering their world—most commonly at Christmas, and also on

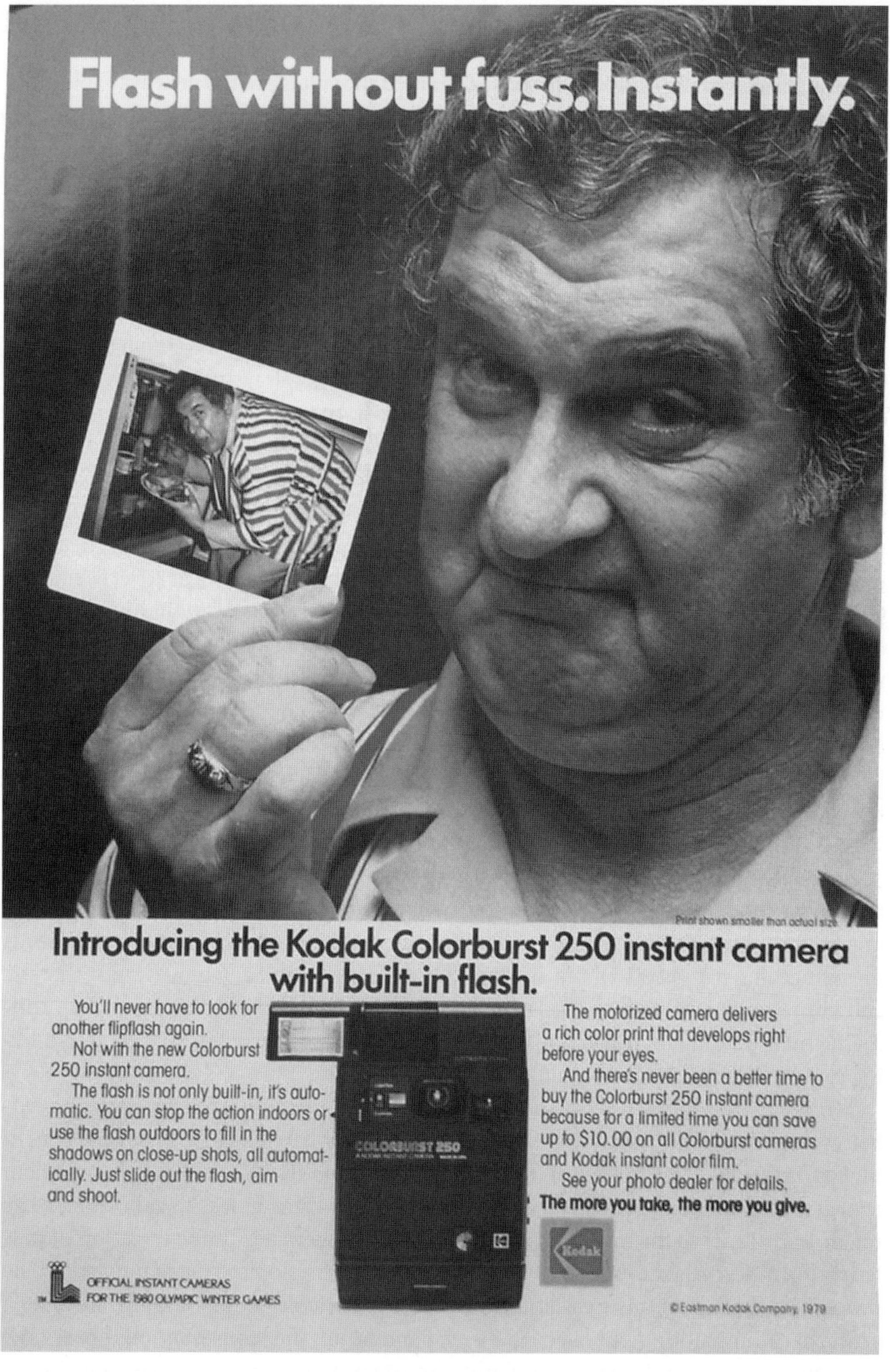

Figure 9.10 Kodak Colorburst advertisement: 'Flash without fuss. Instantly', 1979 (circulated in magazines with a primarily white readership).

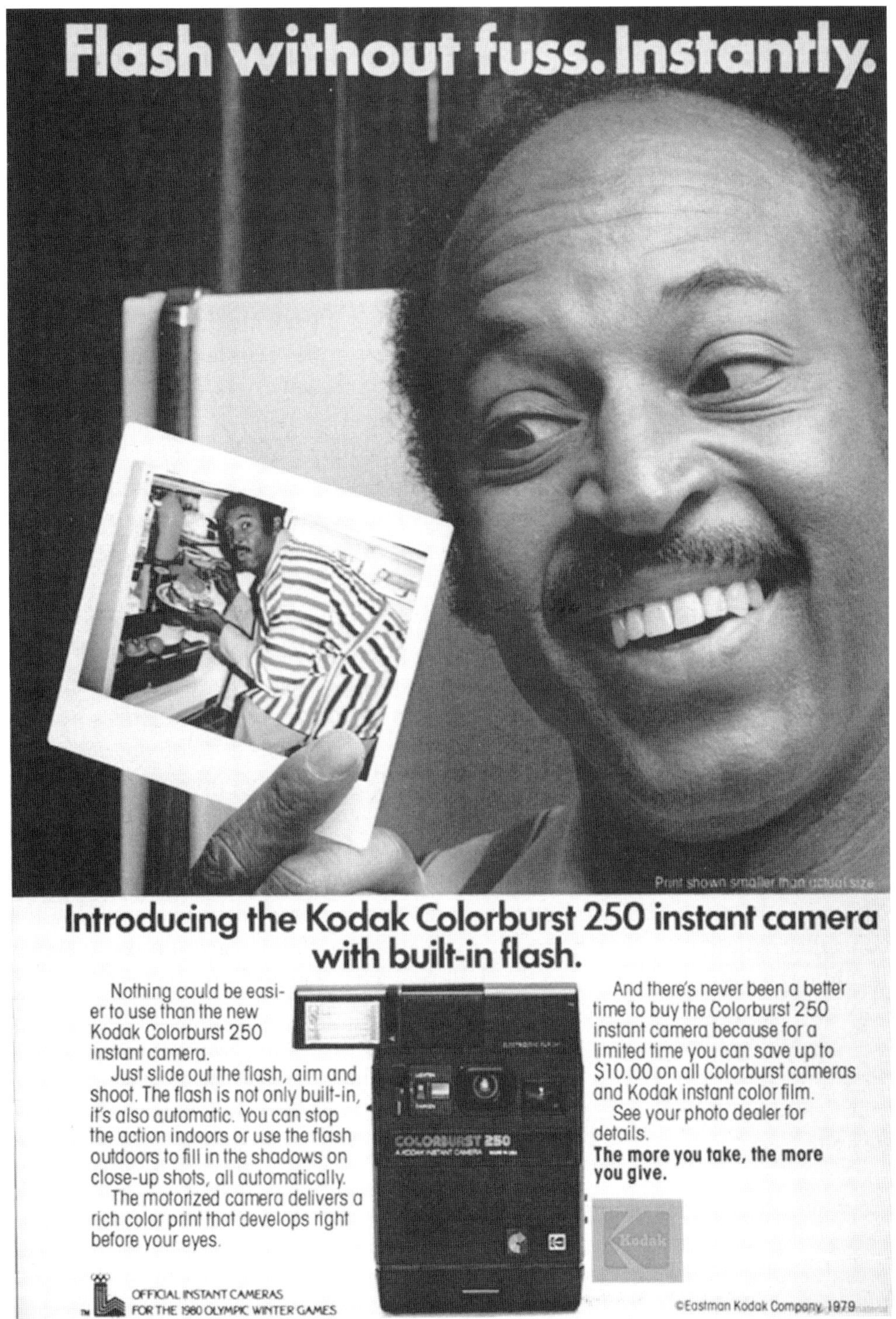

Figure 9.11 Kodak Colorburst advertisement: 'Flash without fuss. Instantly', 1979 (circulated in magazines with a primarily African American readership).

summer vacations. A 1983 Kmart ad shows 'a most EGGCITING OFFER' of Easter baskets with Magicubes, Flash Bars, and Flip Flash units nestling among the shiny shredded cellophane.[62] Although Christmas continues to be the prime time for advertising that targets the occasional photographer, there was also an emphasis on convenience—especially, once camera flashes became a built-in part of small cameras, on the convenience of having a lightweight device on hand that would illuminate even night-time scenes. A combined print and TV commercial series of advertisements for the Kodak Elektralite 10 camera in the late 1970s and early 1980s featured Michael Landon, star of the TV Western series *Bonanza* (1959–73): at least one commercial looked back to his identification with this show, with him taking Instamatic pictures of cowboys jumping off a second-floor balcony and onto their horses—or falling straight into a water trough.[63] The repeated motto, on film and on the page, was 'Ready in a Flash!' If the reprise of *Bonanza*, and the choice, for this advertisement, of a lighting style and lettering that is highly reminiscent of that used on pulp paperbacks, suggest that the consumer's nostalgia is being tweaked, the emphasis on one's convenient flash camera rendering one prepared for any fortuitous photographic opportunity is the takeaway message.

Indeed, to take flash photographs is often presented not just as being *present*, in the moment, but as being hip, forward-looking, with it—or so the advertising language and images would have one believe. This emphasis on the appeal of technological modernity in fact predates the flashcube. Sylvania's 1958 advertisement for their (relatively) tiny M-25 bulb—which appeared in such mainstream outlets as *Readers' Digest*—trumpeted that it was 'the world's first *zirconium*-filled flashbulb . . . Sylvania fills the world's tiniest flashbulb with the fantastic light-giving power of zirconium, wonder-metal of the Atomic Age'.[64] Zirconium is a hard, corrosion-resistant metal that, because it does not easily absorb neutrons, is used for cladding nuclear reactors—the major reason why it was likely to sound sensationally modern in 1958—and for space vehicle parts. This is an advertisement that is predicated on supplying the consumer with information, however: a still analogue to the television commercials that told one precisely how to fit a flashbulb and what it would do. There is a vast leap between the 1950s Sylvania commercial that moved live from a pair of game show contestants to a man stationed by the side of a little heap of flashbulb boxes—explaining that today, 'thanks to the magic of flash photography, the high moments of your holiday fun can be preserved in pictures', and reminding one to buy some extra boxes at Christmas as 'gifts for photo fans',[65]—and the advertising styles of the mid-sixties and beyond. The sharp contrast can be found by comparing the stilted Sylvania diction to a *c.*1965 Kodak Instamatic commercial shot—in colour—on an op-art dance floor, with many jump-cut, wildly angled shots of fashionably clad white young people exuberantly dancing, while in the background, a jazzy band plays a tune remarkably similar to the Beatles' 'Can't Buy Me Love' (1964). What is already a disruptive visual experience is repeatedly broken up yet more by a man taking flash pictures with his new Instamatic camera—as seen in Figure 9.12—'four powerful

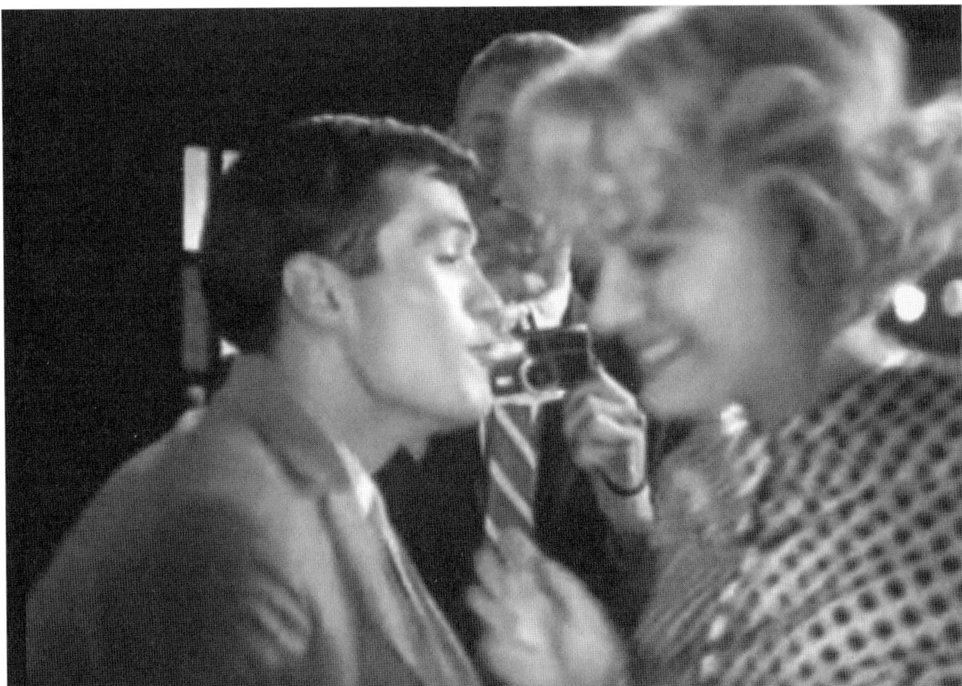

Figure 9.12 Kodak Instamatic 104 television commercial: screen grab.

Figure 9.13 Sylvania flashcubes (photo: Kate Flint).

flashes in one tiny cube'. As the voice-over announces: 'It's new. It's now. It's flash cube.'[66] Yet although the new flashcubes could be advertised as appealing to the hip and trendy, as we saw with the advertising cushion shown in Figure 1.14, the fact that they were very easy to use was also emphasized through the far more conventional domestic imagery used in much of their packaging, as Figure 9.13 demonstrates.

Not only did flash increasingly become an everyday part of point-and-shoot cameras, but it also became a regular feature of the cell phone. The first US camera phone, the clunky clamshell Sanyo SCP-5300 introduced on Sprint in 2002, had a rudimentary flash;[67] the iPhone 4, released in 2010, was the first iPhone to have an LED flash that one could choose whether to flare or not. LED technology, incidentally, running off low voltage, is far cheaper than the flashtube circuit needed to operate a xenon flash—what we see with a cell phone is an almost instantaneous on-off bright camera light, rather than true camera flash technology. Even the 'photo booth' feature of a Mac computer—the one that allows one to take one's own portrait through the little camera above the screen—flares a white light quickly in one's face, mimicking the hard sharp blue light of the photo booth. By the time almost anyone with a camera had the ability to deploy flash (or its simulacrum), more elaborate technology and techniques increasingly became the province of the serious—or the relatively serious—amateur or the professional.

The numbers who would count themselves in the former category, however, have increased enormously as a result of three factors: the introduction of small battery-powered flashes (Nikon's proprietary name, the Speedlight—first introduced in the mid-1960s, and sometimes mutated to Speedlite, has become the shorthand term for these); the widespread adoption (datable to around 1988) of digital cameras with the ability to review instantly the results of one's lighting choices on the back of the camera, and hence to make rapid and easy adjustments to placement or exposure; and the growth of Internet communities. Although developments with electronic flash were unfolding simultaneously with the evolution of flashbulbs, it took some decades before the equipment was of a manageable enough weight and size to appeal to the non-professional user, and before such equipment was affordable. James Bailey claims, however, that by 1948, 'electronic flash units were being manufactured by 36 companies. Popular and professional magazines printed articles and plans for building your own flash.'[68] Such flash units achieve their brief, intense bursts of illumination through sending electric current through tubes with electrodes at opposite ends, and filled with xenon gas—the same technique, essentially, as that used by Harold Edgerton. Since flashlight needs to have both measurable brightness and measurable duration, the accuracy of the latter was greatly improved with the introduction of thyristor units: silicon-controlled rectifiers that stop the flash as soon as the photocell within the unit has received enough light. This technology is the basis for what those of us with built-in flash in our cameras engage today when we take a photograph with flash, and it's found within the speedlights that we fix into the hot shoe on top of the camera.

In the last decade, the gap between the casual picture-taker and the dedicated photographer—whether professional or amateur—has widened again. Flash photography may even be said to be in decline, due to the rapid spread of digital photography, and the concomitant ever-increasing ability of light sensors to capture and record light, even when very little is available. This means that many people are not so quick as in the past to turn on the flash that comes as a built-in part of their point-and-shoot or cell-phone camera, although the Internet is full of advice for those who do—advocating, for example, that one sticks a little bit of paper over the light if it seems to bleach out too much. Yet it is also easy to forget to turn off this flash—witness all those tiny, futile pinpricks in the dark at a live music event or a political rally.

The existence of the Internet has transformed the taking and sharing of photographs. An exhausting 1.8 billion images a day were, it's estimated, uploaded in 2014—that's 657 billion in a year.[69] Put 'flash' into the searchbar on Flickr—a relatively popular photo-sharing site (with about 3.5 million new images uploaded daily), and some 4,113,606 images pop up that have been tagged with this word[70]—pictures taken using flash; pictures of flash equipment, both vintage and new; jagged bolts of lightning (some of them bright against the night sky, some zigzagging down T-shirts); people experimenting with shining speed guns straight in their faces; walls graffitied with the word; men showing just a little strip of leg flesh between sock and kilt; people running very fast; light reflecting off water, off windowpanes, off faces, off rear mirrors in cars, off glass ornaments, off wet road surfaces, off hands put in front of faces, warding off the light. The Internet instantly serves up, that is to say, just about every visual cliché imaginable that involves flash, alongside some admittedly spectacular images.

In addition to the books about flash photography that are still published—which tend to be aimed at the professional, or at the ambitious amateur[71]—to chapters about flash in camera manuals, and to photographic magazines, dedicated websites offer instruction in flash usage at all levels. These may be tied to print magazines (like the site run by *Popular Photography*) or free-standing: either way, paid advertisements are a regular component of the screens on which advice appears, just as press advertisements and the pages at the back of manuals afforded considerable insight into the marketing and presumed use of flash equipment, right back into the nineteenth century. Both instruction and advertisements are melded online with constantly updating consumer reviews, requests for problem solving, and product feedback. All the same, the modern era of flash has produced its own spectacular advertising moments. For the launch of the Nikon D700 camera in 2009, Nikon commissioned the Cheil advertising agency to create an installation in Seoul Sindorim Subway Station, one of the largest subway stations in South Korea, with around 500,000 people passing through it daily. It's also the site of a multiplex electronics shopping mall. A red carpet—the same colour that a superstar might expect to strut down at an awards ceremony—ran along the connecting passageway leading to the Nikon store. It passed a light box containing a life-size image of a phalanx of press photographers, all with their Nikon cameras and speed guns raised for the shot. Each pedestrian that passed by triggered a motion detector, and a barrage of flashguns flared right at them. It wasn't a piece of publicity that anyone could ignore.[72]

Online sites, as well as manuals, provide a good deal of sensible advice for the novice flash photographer. 'Don't make these 7 mistakes with flash', runs a typical header, before enumerating them for the reader:

(1) 'thinking it's not worth using during the day'—and offering a brief outline about how to use fill-flash to highlight what's in the picture's foreground on a sunny day;
(2) 'not diffusing it'—whether by bouncing it off a large surface, like a ceiling or wall, or, if one doesn't possess a tiltable flash, taping a foil-covered piece of card in front of it to direct the light upwards, or shooting through a piece of semi-translucent material—home improvisation is still very much the order of the day here;
(3) forgetting about shutter speed, reminding one that a slow shutter speed can be very effective in capturing an image that combines both sharpness and blur—best done when one has a powerful flash;
(4) 'using when shooting through glass'—in an aquarium, for example—with predictable white-out results;
(5) 'leaving it on auto', and thus firing the flash in situations where it's unwelcome;
(6) 'buying a speedlight flash and only using it on-camera'; and
(7) 'ignoring third party branded flashes'.[73]

Other sites help one avoid lens hood shadow, harsh highlights, using flash with distant subjects, finding that flash kills the atmosphere of a scene, and so on—advice, in these last two cases, that flash photographers have been receiving for more than a century. Other pieces of advice are more occasion-specific: one is firmly advised not to bother shooting with flash (even if one were to be allowed to do so) at a big arena concert.[74] As digital photography guru Scott Kelby claims in one of his helpful print guides, he wrote back to a friend who'd been disappointed in his images,

> So let me get this straight—there were around 275 of these huge 1,000-watt stage lights aiming straight at the performers, but you thought there just needed to be one more? . . . You want to see the color and vibrance of the stage lights, and you want the scene you photograph to look like what it looked like when you were there at the concert. Using flash wipes all that out (besides making the performers angry). And reveals all sorts of distracting things like cables, cords, plugs, duct tape, etc., that would never have been seen under normal stage lighting.[75]

Once again, flash is revealed to be an unmasker of the ordinary, a debunker of illusion. This anecdote also functions, of course, as an example of how little thought people can put into using flash, when there is no expenditure on flashbulbs to take into consideration, and when digital technology allows for the easy taking, and easy deletion, of huge numbers of images.

Whilst the Internet functions as an unprecedented means of disseminating images, of providing information about the availability and quality of flash equipment, and of offering plenty of instruction, it is also an invaluable source for assessing the cultural climate of everyday flash photography. Some of the questions raised are long-standing ones, like the cause of the red-eye effect—the telltale sign of flash in myriads of snapshots—that is, the propensity of flashlight to reflect back from the retina at the back of the eye. Flash is so rapid that one's pupils don't have time to contract and let in less light (unless they've already been prepared by the red-eye reduction feature that is now a familiar feature on cameras with a built-in flash). The redness comes from the rich blood supply in the choroid, the layer of connective tissue at the back of the eye that nourishes the retina. Most cats and dogs have a special reflective layer at the back of their eyes, the tapetum, that helps them to see in the dark, and this accounts for the blue or gold glowing eyes that flash produces in images of them.[76]

Another favourite, and often fiercely debated, issue is the question of where flash is, and is not, allowed in public places. Sometimes its prohibition makes good sense: at a sports arena where it could dazzle a player, for example. Flash is banned on almost all Disney rides and attractions: as 'Doctor Disney' explains, coming up with a set of reasons that make sense in very many other contexts, it ruins them for other guests, rendering the dark of Neverland or Space Mountain thoroughly unmysterious and full of visible machinery; it can trigger migraines and/or epilepsy (hence the warning, too, on many BBC news clips that a report contains flash photography); it can disorient or momentarily alter the vision of a performer.[77] The Internet is full of recommendations on wording for wedding programmes asking people not to use flash during a ceremony: it is seen as a distraction from the solemnity and sanctity of the occasion. Complaints have been made about flash photography in restaurants disturbing a low-lit and intimate atmosphere.[78] As Figure 9.14 shows, wildlife parks warn against disturbing animals at night by using flash.

The ban on flash photography in many museums and art galleries is especially contentious, and gives rise to speculation—some apparently well informed, some less so—about why this may be the case: a vivid example of the Internet's power to spread theories that proliferate like kudzu. Museum attendants, in particular, seem to have enjoyed passing on strange notions: one maintained 'that the light was so bright it could freeze an object, and this sudden cold shock would be damaging to a delicate wooden exhibit'.[79] Whilst certainly this interdiction made sense in an age when flashbulbs still exploded, others (like Carl Grimm, head paintings curator for the DeYoung Museum in San Francisco, who provided his explanation in 2000) have argued that the high-energy wavelengths emitted by a flash will cause a breakdown in the chemical composition of an artwork over time.[80] Martin Evans's research seems to have disproved this belief, showing that there is little scientific evidence to support it. However, he also explores a range of other reasons that have been advanced for prohibiting flash photography in galleries: copyright issues, which sometimes have the effect of causing all photography to be banned; the potential for flashes to trigger security alarm systems (apparently plausible); and, once again, arguments based on the power of flash to cause distraction, breaking into the experience of other visitors.[81] Evans also repeats the

Figure 9.14 Notice asking one not to photograph wild animals with flash. Manuel Antonio National Park, Costa Rica, 2017 (photo: Kate Flint).

frequently heard hypothesis that flash photography is not allowed in galleries because the taking of pictures by visitors will hurt postcard sales in the gallery store—an argument that he pooh-poohs, not least because so many photographs taken by flash in galleries suffer from reflections from glass or varnish.

Reflections, glare, and the obliteration—rather than the revelation—of detail have long been seen as flash's trademark when placed in the hands of an amateur. Vernacular photography started to receive more critical attention in its own right towards the end of the twentieth century, and studies of its place within family histories and memory work, of its materiality, and of the genre of the snapshot itself have helped to establish its centrality to photographic history. Many of the images discussed in this chapter bear out Catherine Zuromskis's contention that 'snapshot photography is an intensely private and personal form of representation, yet as a cultural convention, it is also one of the most public'.[82] As Zuromskis points out, as 'snapshots become ever more ingrained in the American cultural imagination'—this generalization may be extended way beyond America's shores—'it is increasingly difficult to separate the way snapshots are taken, and indeed the very impulse to photograph, from the guiding interests of commerce and the culture industry'.[83] It is also hard to separate them—as her later chapters discuss—from the role that they have played within the work of those who incorporate them within their artistic practice. One might think of the work of Andy Warhol or Nan Goldin—both of whom have used a snapshot aesthetic to suggest intimacy, naturalness, candidness—and who have simultaneously drawn attention to the stilted conventions of pose and occasion that crowd both material and virtual family albums.

Both Warhol and Goldin, too, on occasion incorporated flash's flare into their work, whether one considers Warhol's self-documentation after he was shot by Valerie Solanas in 1968, or the light that shines back from saucepan lids and slick fabrics, dark glasses and leather banquettes and brown paper bags and people's foreheads in Goldin's

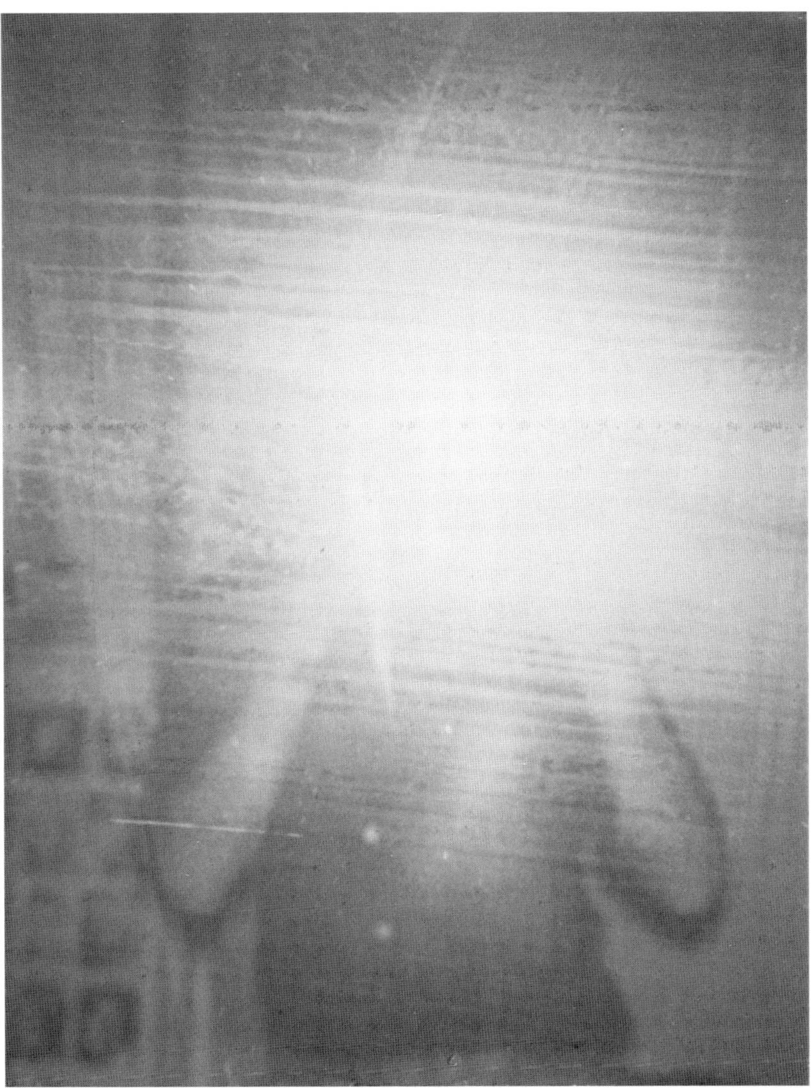

Figure 9.15 Timm Rautert, 'Selbst, im Spiegel/Self in Mirror', 1972. Farbfotografie, Polaroid, auf Karton [colour photograph, Polaroid, on cardboard] 10.8 × 8.5 cm (4.25 × 3.35 in.). Colour in the original. © Timm Rautert, Courtesy Parrotta Contemporary Art.

Ballad of Sexual Dependency and other works in which she recorded the life of herself and friends in Boston and New York in the 1970s and 1980s. As Elisabeth Sussman has put it: 'For Goldin, the gleam of artificial light was a stimulant. She discovered her color in flashes of electricity. Even when photographing in natural light, she often unconsciously replicated the effect of artificial lighting.'[84]

But I want to conclude with two photographers who use flash in a quite different way, deliberately mimicking the amateur photographer's mistake of obliterating faces in a flare of light. German photographer Timm Rautert's time in New York between

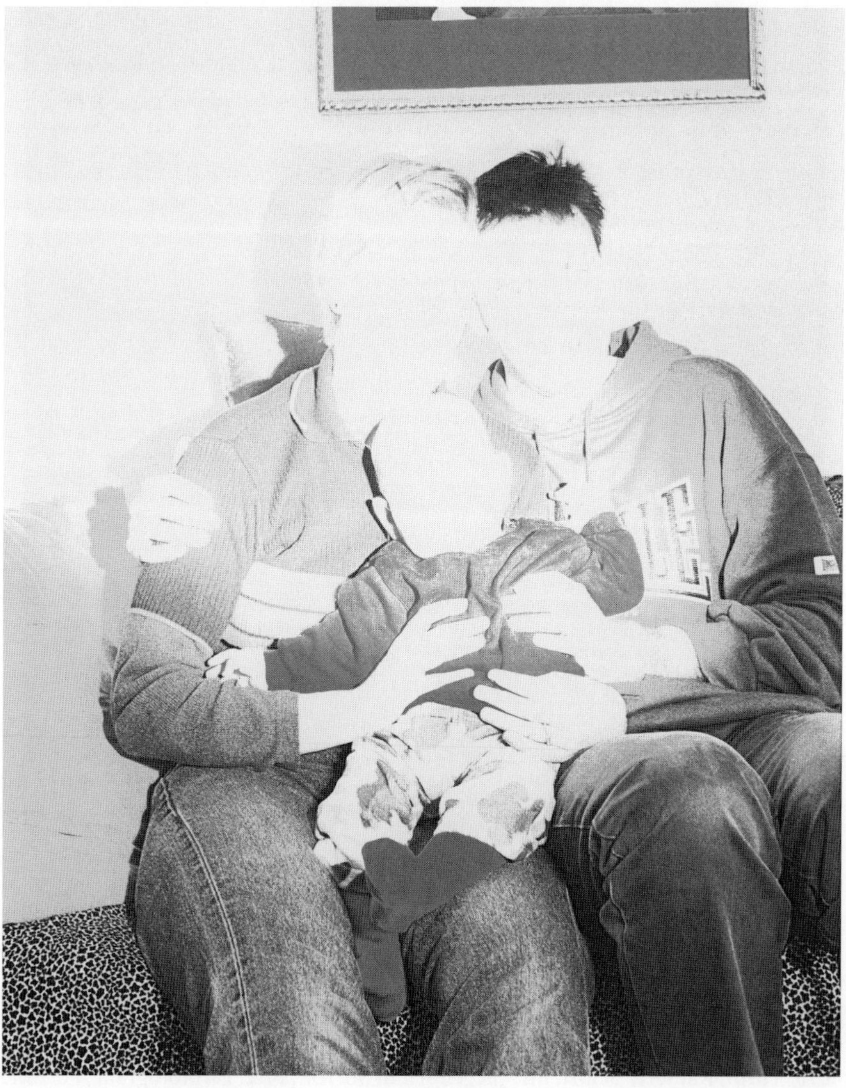

Figure 9.16 Maya Dickerhof, 'family' from the series *Memory*, 2001, original work in colour. Image courtesy of the artist.

1969 and 1970 brought him into contact with Warhol, and he shared Warhol's interest in—among other forms of artificiality—the dehumanizing flash created in photo booths. In his 1972 'Selbst, im Spiegel/Self in Mirror' (Figure 9.15), he sets off the flash so that it completely destroys his reflection in a mirror, the uncanniness of the image reinforced by the faded aquamarine of the Polaroid's colours. The flare is so intense that it leaves deep gouges, striations of light. In a different context, this could be a source of comedy—the self-portrait gone badly, badly wrong. In the hands of someone who knows exactly what they are doing, and what effect will result from them shooting a powerful flash straight into a mirror, it looks like a wilful act of self-destruction, a refusal of identity—or, perhaps, suggesting that as a photographer, one's identity is obscured, irrelevant, subsumed into light's power.[85]

A 2001 image by Swiss photographer Maya Dickerhof, shown in Figure 9.16, makes a somewhat different point. It shows a couple seated on a sofa, holding a small baby between them. It is precisely the kind of happy family grouping that has been assumed to be a prime subject for domestic photography since its early days. Yet Dickerhof is making a point that goes far beyond suggesting that achieving the photograph that one hopes for can sometimes pose a challenge to an inexpert person behind a camera. This image forms part of a series called *Memory*, and that series title makes us reflect, once again, on the relationship between flash photography, time, and memory. It speaks to our inability to recollect a moment except through the mediation of a photograph. That bleaching flash is also the white light of time's passage: it stands for the fading, obliterating effects of memory itself that vernacular photography so desperately seeks to deny.

CHAPTER TEN

Flash's Aesthetics

HOWARD NEMEROV'S 'The Winter Lightning' (1968) is a poem about the violence of revelation.[1] Cold, blue-white light is a means of stripping things bare, of seeing them clearly and dispassionately. The poem opens in a snowstorm, where the lightning splits open the 'sky torn to the bone'. The land 'hard as a stone | Cold, and blue-white' is frozen under a rigid white blanket that reflects back this lightning. The world is shattered with this light 'As though this were the moon's hell'—a negative version of burning fire, but just as cruel.

This lightning is more than a natural light. It is seen as invasive; splintering open the 'drowned world of dark'. Although momentary, like all lightning, Nemerov grants it the same properties as a searchlight, or early street illumination, or security lighting. The theology of this 'high, charged carbon arc | Light of the world' is not that of transcendental epiphany, but of surveillance, of laying bare all secrets.

> So in the camera's glare
> The fortunate and the famed,
> For all their crooked smiles,
> Reveal through their regarded stare
> How all that's publicly acclaimed
> One brutal flash reviles
> For cold despair.

Neither lightning nor camera flash makes any allowance for pretence or disguise. What is revealed is eviscerated of compassion, of humanity. In the final stanza, Nemerov invokes literary critic M. H. Abrams's influential distinction between the mirror and the lamp. The mirror, in Abrams's terms, stands for the pre-Romantic view of writing, which functioned, he maintained, in a mimetic relation to the world—much as photography was usually regarded in the first eight or so decades of its existence, and much as it is popularly still thought of as doing. The lamp, on the other hand—more broadly, a 'light', in Nemerov's poem—was seen by Abrams as the major contribution of Romantic poets and thinkers. It stands for the soul, for individual feeling, for subjective expression. This offers an approach to literary analysis, moreover, that foregrounds the engagement of the author. 'The Winter Lightning' demands that we sever 'the mirror from the light'; that we divorce, that is to say, the objective from the expressive. But the world view of the poet—who may or may not be specifically equated with Nemerov himself—is seen here as a bleak one. So may

> The poet, from his wintry heart
> And in the lightning's second's sight,
> Illuminate this dream
> With a cold art.

There is something verging on the uncanny in this (the pun on 'second's sight'), but at the same time the poet is seen as both honest and dispassionate. The dream that is illuminated seems to be the 'sleeping innocence' that is quietly hidden in 'the drowned world of dark' evoked in the third stanza. Invoking the shocking, cruel, and terrifying clarity of lightning, Nemerov drew on the vocabulary of the camera flash because it gave him the associations that he needed of a light with no compassion. When it is flashed upon the world—from the sky, by the photographer, from the poet—there is, whether literally or metaphorically, no place to hide from its exposure.

As we have seen, flash photography has attracted an increasingly negative set of associations. Initially linked to the sublime grandeur and terror of lightning, it became far more frequently linked to aggression, intrusiveness, and a lack of subtlety. Such

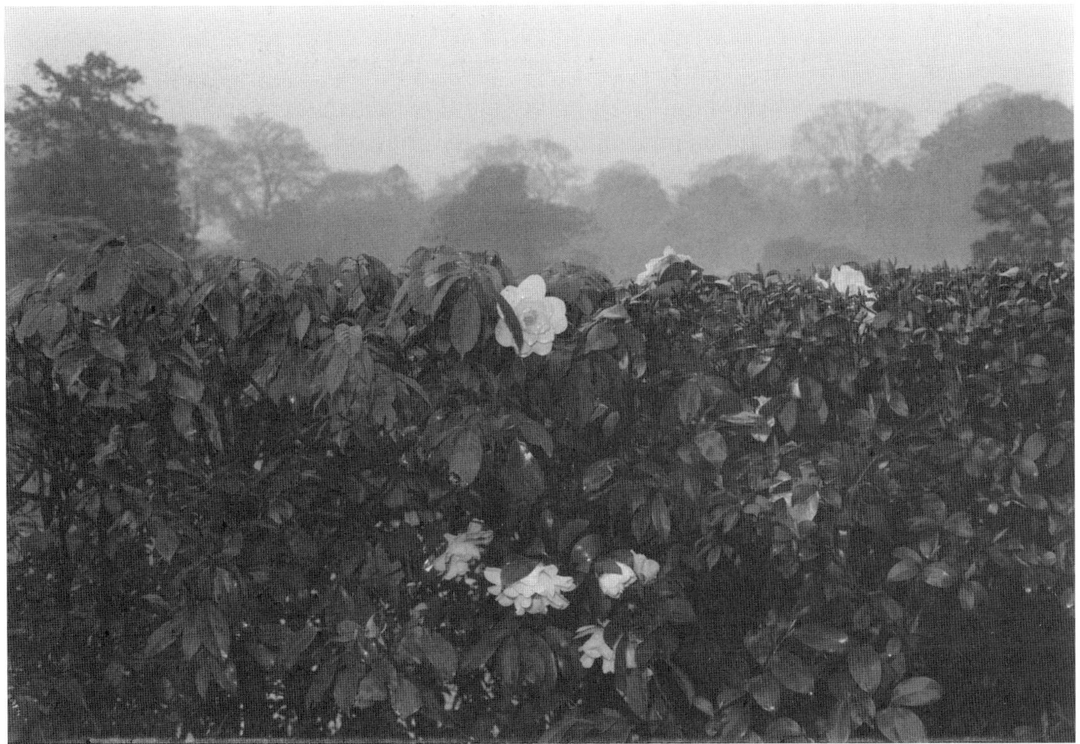

Figure 10.1 Lee Friedlander, 'Kyoto', 1977. © Lee Friedlander, courtesy Fraenkel Gallery, San Francisco.

extreme contrasts may be the work of more than flash itself, of course. The stark Manichaean visual vocabulary may be intensified post-production—in darkroom or Photoshop, and in printing and paper choices—because it serves a desire for dramatic absolutes. What has become submerged in this antagonistic discourse, or in the descriptions and advice surrounding flash's everyday use, is a sense of what is aesthetically distinct in a positive way about its attributes: the power of the thick darkness that it can create in an image; its propensity to create gleam and shine; and—perhaps an unexpected feature—its subtleties. These are properties that may emerge as an accidental felicity when flash is used for purely pragmatic reasons, but my prime concern in this chapter is with those who, recognizing the distinctive qualities that flash creates, deliberately choose to use them. We see subtleties of gradations in grey emerge when flash is used in daylight—as in Lee Friedlander's 1977 image of damp camellias in Kyoto shown in Figure 10.1; or when it provides a component of the available lighting in the electric city of the twentieth century; or when it leads to an intensification of colour within a scene. What is more, a number of contemporary visual artists have sought to push back against the bad press that flash has so often received. They have looked to redeem flash, appropriating its connotations for works that call attention to flash's unique properties. Flash, at last, has become a subject in its own right, and not just a means to an end.

Perhaps no statement about flash photography has been more frequently repeated than Henri Cartier-Bresson's repudiation of it. Cartier-Bresson famously advised the readers of the magazine *Photography* in 1955: 'It's no good jostling or elbowing. And no photographs taken with the aid of flashlight either, if only out of respect of the actual light—even when there isn't any of it. Unless a photographer observes such conditions as these, he may become an intolerably aggressive character.'[2] His dislike of flash showed up at other moments, too. Although, as he admitted in the captions accompanying his film roll negatives that are now in the Fondation Henri Cartier-Bresson in Paris, he had 'a camera I keep in case of flashes', the photographer also noted, after mentioning a shot of accountants in a 'Peiping duck' restaurant, that 'I must say that flash gun is too brutal an instrument to my mind to register such a delicate thing as Peiping duck, as well as shooting a gun is regarded unharmonious during a string quartet'.[3] Cartier-Bresson's statement is customarily interpreted in the light of his general aesthetic principles, in which he strongly promoted the notion that a great photograph was the product of the photographer's trained eye coupled with an impeccable sense of timing. 'To take photographs means to recognize—simultaneously and within a fraction of a second—both the fact itself and the rigorous organization of visually perceived forms that give it meaning. It is putting one's head, one's eye, and one's heart on the same axis.'[4] Blinding oneself through using a flash—however briefly—is anathema to such a process.

There may, however, have been a specific point of origin for Cartier-Bresson's vehemence. Claude Cookman has written about how both the Frenchman (who, together with Robert Capa, had just founded the Magnum photo agency) and Margaret Bourke-White—representing *Life* magazine—were in New Delhi on 30 January 1948, the day that Mahatma Gandhi was assassinated in the middle of the political and religious struggles following the partition of India and Pakistan. The two photographers had very different approaches to their covering of this event. Cartier-Bresson 'mingled inconspicuously with the mourners at the Birla House compound'. Bourke-White's method—just as it had been with poor rural communities in the American South ten years before—was far less discreet. As Cookman tells it,

> Flash had become a contentious issue in Bourke-White's coverage of Gandhi. She had used a flash bulb to make her famous picture of Gandhi by his spinning wheel. Gandhi, who nick-named her 'the torturer', tolerated the technique, but his inner circle never did. They thought flash was disrespectful, and they feared the bright flash would harm his sensitive eyes. Flash became a serious liability for Bourke-White in her coverage of Gandhi's funeral. With her camera concealed, she slipped into the room where his body lay surrounded by grieving relatives, supporters, and government officials. It was about 6.30 p.m., too dark for available light. When she ignited a flash bulb to make her exposure, his followers became enraged by her violation of their privacy and grief. They seized her camera and threatened to destroy it. Hannah Sen intervened, calming the group. After Bourke-White's film was removed and exposed to the light, Mrs. Sen escorted her from the room. She returned the camera with the understanding that Bourke-White would leave Birla House and not return. Not one to give up after one rebuff, she reloaded her camera and tried to re-enter the room to get another picture. Eventually, Bourke-White yielded to Mrs. Sen's pleas to honour her promise and left empty-handed.[5]

Cookman hypothesizes that this discourtesy and aggressiveness played a foundational role in establishing not just Cartier-Bresson's intense dislike of flash, but also the principled terms in which he couched it. The story certainly encapsulates the very worst about flash's intrusive properties, and about the competiveness and rudeness of those who would stop at nothing to snatch their photograph at the most painful and inappropriate moments of other people's lives. A street light provided Cartier-Bresson with all the illumination that he needed for his sombre and dramatic picture of Nehru announcing Gandhi's death.

Others were to follow Cartier-Bresson's lead in making an absolute disavowal of the use of flash for reasons that were both aesthetic and ethical. In Chapter 6, we encountered Roy DeCarava's views on the subject. Likewise, the Brazilian social documentary photographer and photojournalist, Sebastião Salgado—who has been much influenced by Cartier-Bresson—emphatically prefers not to use flash, finding it extraordinarily intrusive. He notes, however, that the advent of digital photography has made it much easier for him to work in poor lighting conditions.[6] Irving Penn, who has worked around the world as an ambulant studio photographer, taking mainly portraits—a great deal of his work has appeared in *Vogue*—prefers to use natural light falling from the north for its 'sweetness and constancy'. It is a cold light, but not flash-cold. Artificial lights of whatever kind are, for Penn, a convenience, but his preference—expressed as an aesthetic choice, above all—is always for a natural source, because of 'that simple three-dimensional clarity, that *absolute existence* that a subject has standing before a camera in a north-light studio'.[7] Flash may bring out details, display the overlooked, display every last facial crease and wrinkle and age spot on the hands. But the implication here is that only natural light is going to manage to convey the pure essence of the person themself.

Nor is an aversion to flash exclusive to certain art photographers. For all of the many manuals that have been devoted to the workings of flash equipment of various types, giving advice to the amateur taking everyday photographs with a point-and-shoot, others take the time to warn them against the flash. Nothing, in fact, makes one look *more* like an amateur than flash's obvious presence, cautions Nick Kelsh, in *How to Photograph Your Life*. 'Turn off the flash and shoot from a higher angle,' he advises, when it comes to taking photographs of a festive table.

> Whenever you are taking a picture near anything that emits light you should be asking yourself, 'How can I use this light to my advantage?' The answer will almost assuredly be more aesthetically pleasing than the flash built into your camera. Actually, just about anything is better than the flash on your camera, including an open refrigerator door. I'm serious.[8]

Even for commercial photographers who make extensive use of flash, its pop-up, on-camera form is to be despised: crude in its undirectable effects, and redolent of a lack of artistry. As Joe McNally puts it in *The Hot Shoe Diaries*—a book that has a great deal of useful advice to offer about shooting with flash, albeit continually couched in language that reads like a parodic ventriloquization of photographic machismo, as though it were written by Carl Hiaasen's Bang Abbott—

> AHH, THE POP-UP FLASH. Let's talk straight, okay? It is the condom of on-camera flash. Use it if ya really gotta, right?... Or if you really, reeeeaaallly don't like somebody, or if you get caught up in a rugby scrum of paparazzi and get knocked over and your SB unit goes tumbling and you roll into the gutter in between the horde and the limo and you look desperately up from that angle as the door opens and out steps Paris and Britney in short skirts (and nothing but short skirts) and you can retire on the stock sales of the next set of frames, then by all means, go for it. Use the damn pop-up.[9]

Even for some art photographers who fully exploited flash's potential for creating strong visual effects, the excitement of using it could pall. Diane Arbus—Howard Nemerov's younger sister—for a while enjoyed not just the capacity that flash had to deliver every last physiognomic individuality—'I began to get terribly hyped on clarity'—but also the very element of surprise that using flash brought with it.

> One of the excitements of strobe at one time was that you were essentially blind at the moment you took the picture. I mean it alters the light enormously and reveals things you don't see. In fact that's what made me really sick of it. I began to miss light like it really is and now I'm trying to get back to some kind of obscurity where at least there's normal obscurity.
>
> Lately I've been struck with how I really love what you can't see in a photograph. An actual physical darkness. And it's very thrilling for me to see darkness again.[10]

Flash photography can, however, itself produce deep darkness. Whatever the nature of the illuminated subject—faces, rooms, the motionless lynx on the shore of a lake depicted in Figure 10.2—it is often surrounded by a dense velvety black. One might well note, in passing, the etymological relationship of 'flash' to 'black'. In *The Story of Black*, John Harvey explains that the English 'black' comes from the Indo-European *bhleg-*, meaning 'to shine, flash or burn', as well as from the Germanic *blakaz*, 'burned'.[11]

This photographic blackness is an absence of light given yet greater resonance through careful printing and choice of paper.[12] These lightless elements carry with them a number of expressive overtones: of silence and mystery and expectation; of concealment and threat; of the promise or dread of a narrative that may unfold or explode; of the unconscious, of desires, of the unspeakable as well as the invisible; or of a peace and stillness that could fade with dawn. Of course, and paradoxically, this is illusory peace, one that has in fact just been shattered by the sudden burst of artificial light that took the image. But a surround of darkness, or the deep obscurity of shadows that are created by

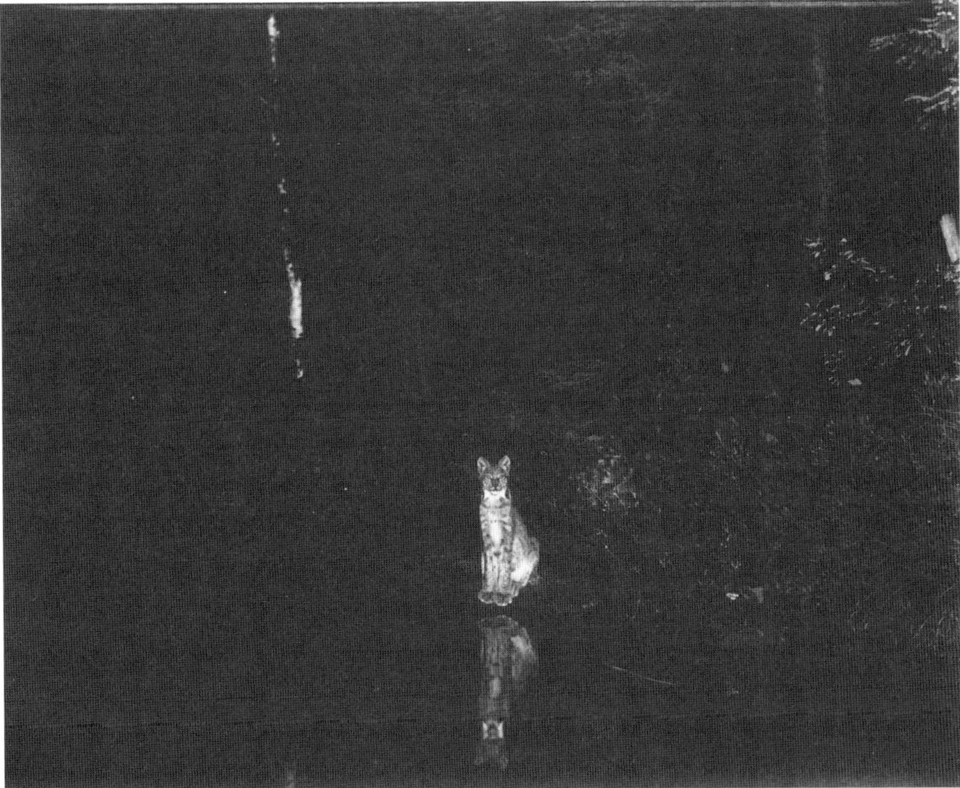

Figure 10.2 George Shiras, 'Lynx, Loon Lake, Ontario, Canada', 1902. Courtesy National Geographic Creative.

the flash itself, distinguishes some of the most dramatic flash photographs. As Noam M. Elcott shows in his important study *Artificial Darkness*, it is, however, important to note the crucial 'physiological distinction between darkness and blackness—between the absence of stimulation and the positive sensation of black'; that is, between the quality of darkness itself and the quality of blackness in the photographic image.[13]

True darkness is imperilled, in the actual world, by increasing amounts of light pollution: by concerns that 'Ecological systems, with their own patterns of nocturnal life', are, compared with those of times past, suffering 'immeasurably. With darkness diminished, opportunities for privacy, intimacy, and self-reflection will grow more scarce.'[14] Such entirely justifiable anxieties may be temporarily allayed if one looks at many flash photographs that have been taken at night, since these restore a sense of deep darkness—another reason, of course, to note the untrustworthiness of flash, making complete, yet artificial darkness out of that which, in reality, glows faintly.

Bright cities have received their fair share of attention in recent years. Sometimes, this is part of a fascination with the social and cultural impact of electricity, whether this is seen in positive or negative terms; sometimes—as discussed in William Sharpe's *New York Nocturne* (2008)—because they produce a certain aesthetic.[15] This is an aesthetic dominated by the interplay of artificial light (of which flash photography is just one type) and human activity on the one hand, and the unseen or unseeable on the other. Argentinian photographer Gabriel Valansi has complicated this further in an image that positions the photographer's flash in front of an aerial map showing Argentina's glowing cities at night—the flash acting to obliterate some of the Province of La Pampa, the country's traditional heartland, but victim to 'the devastation of the countryside by the neoliberal concentration of the metropolis and its satellite cities'.[16]

An earlier urban lightscape is also the source of the expressive, contrastive lighting of that style of film-making that flourished in the late 1940s and the 1950s—what Nicholas Christopher terms 'the teeming, multifarious darkness of film noir'.[17] Its effects frequently depend on the tension created by the sudden burst of light into darkness—an opening door; someone stepping into the pool of light shed by a street lamp; a flare from a gun muzzle. The enclosed spaces of alleyways, rooftops, fire escapes, and the angles of street corners—exactly the kind of urban topography encountered in many of Weegee's contemporary images—combine with the exaggerations of noir style to intensify our feelings of apprehension and claustrophobia.[18] Such lighting effects are themselves very much the product of technological developments within film lighting. Film historian David Bordwell has explained how during the 1910s, the adoption of carbon-arc equipment, such as Kliegl spotlights ('klieg lights'), 'moved American film lighting practice away from a dominant use of diffused, overall illumination towards a concentration on "effects" lighting',[19] although he claims that the so-called Lasky lighting, which created 'extreme contrasts of light and dark'—and was therefore closest in its dramatic impact to the tonal polarization and dark-edged shadows created by flash—was not widely adopted by directors and cinematographers. Rather, by 1920, 'most Hollywood filmmakers had adopted the three-point lighting style, which mixed key and fill, often adding a touch of backlight'.[20]

Within films of suspense, flash itself has been used to great effect, not because of the still images that result from its use, but because of the shock that it creates. The setting need not necessarily be an urban one: deeper rural darkness can add to the creation of tension. The 2010 Uruguayan movie *La casa muda* is a case in point (an American version was made in 2011, *Silent House*). In this extraordinarily creepy film, Laura and her father enter a secluded cottage with the intention of repairing it. To the film's viewer, the signs are decidedly sinister: the windows are boarded up; there is haunting music playing from a couple of radios in different parts of the house. Then she finds the freshly murdered body of her father. Then she finds the doors are locked—before locating a way out, meeting the sceptical and indeed increasingly sinister owner, and entering again. Then Laura's light goes out. She finds an old Polaroid camera on a table, and for a while, the only lighting comes each time that she makes as if to take a photo, and fires the flash. The Polaroid's whine adds to the visual discomfort of these bursts of cold light. What the light discovers are more photographs; what flash's brevity does not give us is the time necessary to interpret them fully. We, like Laura, are given instantaneous impressions—and then darkness snaps back over them. Shot entirely on a hand-held Canon EOS 5D Mark II, this film is technically innovative, shot to look as though it was one eighty-eight-minute real-time take.[21] At the same time, the use of flash ensures that any sense of continuity is disrupted, together with our own security and stability as spectators. 'Real fear in real time', the film's trailer promises: even the wording that appears on screen during this trailer disappears in literal flashes, engendering the same edginess that permeates the movie.[22]

The shocks that *La casa muda* provides the viewer come from rapid, unpredictable alternations of dark and light; from suddenly tilted camera angles and defamiliarized perspectives; from an emphasis on psychological as well as physical darkness. As with other South American directors of horror movies, Gustavo Hernandéz's heritage is not just that of Hollywood, but reaches back to the same filmic origins as does film noir: to German expressionist film, and the work of Fritz Lang and F. W. Murnau, in particular.[23] European émigrés, and the aesthetics that they brought with them, had an enormous impact on American film, to be sure, whilst the diasporic movements of exiles, ideas, and aesthetic influences within Europe made a significant contribution not just to experimenting with forms of representation, but also to bringing different art forms into new dialogue with one another. Coupled with the fact that there was a growing understanding of photography as a mode of artistic practice in its own right, there was a new openness to the idea of flash creating its own particular aesthetic.

Using flashlight to intensify emotional impact in photographs goes back at least as far as the very early years of the twentieth century. The assumption in Riis's images, and in those taken by social investigators more broadly, is that the flash allows the camera to function much like a housing inspector—even if the details that are brought to light by the flash are recorded with a precision and clarity that may never have been available to inspectors themselves, let alone a dwelling's inhabitants. But as well as making visible the material details of dwelling and workplace, the flash did something else besides: it

Figure 10.3 Jack London, 'Picking Oakum at St George's Workhouse', 1902. JLP 466 Alb. 28 #03624. The Huntington Library, San Marino, California.

could create great pools of contrastative and visually impenetrable darkness at the sides of images. Jack London, who much admired Riis's work, took photographs of London's East End to accompany his 1902 *People of the Abyss.* More than with Riis, we see how he deliberately deployed the photographic properties of dark and lightness to create emotional responses. He was well aware of flash's potentially intrusive powers, knowing that it may be necessary, but mocking the revelatory claims of the authorities that use light to disturb people in the surely posed '*Truth*: The Weekly Newspaper' (see Figure 5.5). In 'Picking Oakum at St George's Workhouse' (Figure 10.3), he appears to use both natural *and* artificial light, but the overall effect depends on the patches of Stygian gloom that simultaneously stand for the deep reach of poverty and for the desolation and despair that finds its physical manifestation in the men's postures. And in an outdoor shot, shown in Figure 10.4, the bleaching power of the flash renders the foreground as empty white space, suggestive of a gulf between these men and society. It illuminates the shabby—and ironic—would-be Egyptian exoticism of the winged camel, designed by George John Vulliamy, that supports the bench; and it shows us the sleeping, resting, and insomniac men passing the night upon it. Beyond them? Given

Figure 10.4 Jack London, 'View on Thames Embankment', 1902. JLP 466 Alb. 28 #03594. The Huntington Library, San Marino, California.

the setting of the Thames Embankment, and given the date (1902), it's tempting to see this as an allegorical version of London's river, leading away into the actual and metaphorical 'heart of an immense darkness' that Joseph Conrad's narrator describes, just as much as it is a piece of social exposé.[24] It is a photograph that makes us register the invasiveness of flash, its power to throw light on that which we would not otherwise see—and flash's aesthetic capacities. The surround that has been created through this technology, *because* of its absence of detail, plays a shaping role in our response.

The work of two later photographers helps to show that this aesthetic could be a dramatically nuanced as well as a pragmatic one: one that was in conversation with other art forms, yet without seeking to imitate them as the pictorialist photographers of the late nineteenth and early twentieth century had done. Both the Hungarian/French Brassaï (he used this pseudonym—'from Braşov', the name of his birthplace, in preference to his given name, Gyula Halász) and the German/British Bill Brandt were photographers of the night. Both made their careers away from their native countries: Brassaï moving to Paris in 1924, and Brandt to London in 1933. Brassaï trained in Hungary as a painter and sculptor. He learned his photography in 1929 from fellow Hungarian immigrant André Kertész—Kertész seems to have been very generous with his instruction: although not a big enthusiast when it came to using flash himself, he taught Robert Capa how to use flashbulbs properly when the latter was visiting New York in 1937. Brassaï learned his French through reading Proust. Indeed, Brassaï went on to publish a book on Proust on photography, *Proust in the Power of Photography*, in which he draws attention to the number of actual references to and metaphorical invocations of photography in *A la recherche du temps perdu*; speculates on the analogy 'between Proust's innovative narrative techniques—changes in perspective and optical angle—and those which the universe of photography afforded him';[25] and writes about him as a '"night photographer", recorder of that night "which effaces the objects of everyday life"'. Indeed, he says, for 'the author of the *Search*, memory itself is a sort of night whose shadows swallow up our recollections, but out of which, sometimes, the images of the past loom when a sudden ray of light makes them emerge from the darkness'. He quotes Proust describing a night in blacked-out Paris, during the First World War, when 'the moonlight seemed like a gentle form of magnesium', and his invocation of other forms of flash when it comes to remembering Combray, the village in *A la recherche*:

> And so, for a long time, when, waking in the middle of the night, I remembered Combray, I never envisioned it except in a sort of luminous flash, silhouetted against vague shadows, like those details which a signal-flare or some electric projection illuminate and isolate in a building whose other parts remain plunge in darkness.[26]

Brassaï said that he himself felt an affinity with Proust; that he thought that, if Proust had had a camera in his hands, he would have had a very similar relationship with the city to the one that he himself enjoyed. They both responded to the deep pools of dark in the nocturnal city, and the sudden, dazzling, unexpected illuminations that one encounters within it.

Brassaï made his name when he published *Paris de nuit* in 1931. Many of the images in this volume were made with very long exposures, which showed Paris in an atmospheric foggy haze, punctuated by street lights and car lamps: they established him as a photographer of night. 'Night only suggests things, it doesn't fully reveal them. Night unnerves us, and surprises us with its strangeness; it frees powers within us which were controlled by reason during the day', he wrote.[27] The fiction writer Paul Morand, who provided the preface to *Paris de nuit*, saw Brassaï as presenting the psychology not just of the city, but of the French themselves. He posits a photographic contra-analogy: 'Night is not the negative of day; black surfaces and white are not merely transposed, as on a photographic plate, but another picture altogether emerges at nightfall.' The 'furtive menace' that Brassaï captures in his images is not the Gothic danger fostered by the Romantic tradition, but 'the more authentic menace of the subconscious mind of the French race, the night-side of their daytime perspicacity, all the more copious for being repressed beneath apparent equilibrium'.[28]

As these invocations of the unconscious suggest, Brassaï's modernity was cerebral, rather than technological. He used a large, fixed-lens, 6.5×9-centimetre Voigtländer Bergheil folding camera, mounted on a heavy wooden tripod (and on occasion other

Figure 10.5 Brassaï (Gyula Halász), 'Gisèle at "La Boule Blanche", Montparnasse', ca. 1932. Silver gelatin print. Pl.469. Repro-photo: Michèle Bellot © RMN-Grand Palais / Art Resource, NY.

cameras, like the Rolleiflex, although he was not attracted by the lightweight 35-millimetre Leica). He did his own meticulous darkroom work, concentrating on bringing out the deep darkness in the prints. This perfectionism extended to his use of flash. Despite the fact that his career as a photographer took off at precisely the moment that the flashbulb came into wide use, he deployed an old-fashioned flashgun and powder when he took the interior scenes of bars and brothels and clubs and dances that made him famous (including the image in Figure 10.5)—he thought that the flashbulb gave too harsh a light. An assistant exploded the flash, whilst Brassaï himself talked to his subjects—in a sense collaborating with them, relaxing them. They knew that the exposure would be made; they knew that the blinding and odorous flash would go off, but they could never be exactly sure when: these are images that fuse documentary and performance.[29] The exposures were doubtless startling for other patrons as well. Executing a quite different type of flash-lit work, photographing the sculpture of his friend Picasso in late September 1943, as seen in Figure 10.6, Brassaï noted that he 'sometimes [lit] the scene with magnesium powder. The explosion frightens and amuses Picasso. He nicknames me the "Terrorist" and henceforth adopts that sobriquet to refer to me.'[30]

Figure 10.6 Brassaï (Gyula Halász), '"Man with a Goat" and "Bust of Dora Maar" in the Grand-Augustins', Gelatin-silver print, h. 29.9 cm. Inv. MP1986-33. Copy photo: Franck Raux © RMN-Grand Palais / Art Resource, NY.

Superficially, Bill Brandt's images, particularly of London streets at night, share a good deal in common with Brassaï's nocturnal work: indeed, his *A Night in London* (1938) was inspired by it, and may directly have had its origins in a commission from the Paris-published Arts et Métiers Graphiques, who had produced *Paris de nuit*.[31] Like Brassaï, he was pragmatic rather than dogmatic in his attitude towards flash. In an artist's statement, he asserted his freedom from the current—but prevalent—purist conventions. 'When young photographers come to show me their work', he wrote, 'they often tell me proudly that they follow all the fashionable rules. They never use electric lamps or flashlight; they never crop a picture in the darkroom, but print from an untrimmed negative; they snap their model while walking about the room.' Yet for his part, 'if I think a picture will look better brilliantly lit, I use lights, or even flash. It is the result that counts, no matter how it was achieved... Photographers should follow their own judgment, and not the fads and dictates of others.'[32]

Brandt used a variety of lighting techniques to achieve his night-time scenes. Like Brassaï, he made use of light from street lamps, although he did not often borrow the Frenchman's signature imagery of a street lamp's flare in a moisture-heavy night; he preferred to set up his camera once the lights were turned on, but there was still some natural daylight.[33] He occasionally employed the 'day for night' technique that cinematographers adopted to transform images taken in daylight into ones that looked as though they were shot at night (this was to become a favourite tool of film noir)—as with the sinister-looking 'Policeman in a Dockland Alley'. And, when necessary, he used flash.

Before the war, London—like New York, like Paris—was an electric city. James Bone, editor of the *Manchester Guardian*, wrote in the introduction to *A Night in London* of 'Floodlit attics and towers, oiled roadways shining like enamel under the street lights and headlights, the bright lacquer and shining metals of motorcars, illuminated signs'.[34] Brassaï's and Brandt's images of the modern city show us that when flashbulbs are *not* used, there is, indeed, a good deal of ambient light around. Although a curve of a cobbled passage off the Boulevard de Clichy may head off into the unknown dark, there are lights shining from windows, or illuminating doorways, or, in neon, advertising 'HOTEL'. As Weegee's photographs of New York repeatedly demonstrate, it takes the intensity of the flashbulb (or expert work in a darkroom) to restore deep darkness to the modern city.

When Brandt photographed London under the blackout, the buildings, whether intact or bombed wrecks, appear as an intense black. Flash's presence reasserts itself in his hands in a completely different way during this blackout, however. In 1940 Brandt was commissioned by Hugh Francis, director of the Photographic Division at the Ministry of Information, to make a full record of life in bomb shelters: he went out each night between 4 and 12 November to do this, showing people in Tube stations and wine cellars, church crypts and railway arches, as demonstrated in Figures 10.7 and 10.8. Although there were some electric lights deep in the Tube, Brandt took with him 'Kodak lamp-holders, some photoflood bulbs and enough flex to stretch the full length of Winchester Cathedral'.[35] The flash unit, according to Robert Butts, Brandt's assistant, was placed away from the camera and fired after Brandt had removed the cap from the open shutter of his Rollei. It was an old-fashioned technique, and one that demanded a long exposure, but one that revealed the rows of people sleeping—or trying to sleep, catching the contours of their sausage-like forms as well as bouncing vividly off walls and shiny objects.[36]

Figure 10.7 Bill Brandt, 'An Elephant and Castle platform crowded with shelterers, some resting against the stationary London Transport train, 11 November 1940', 1940. © Imperial War Museums (D 1570).

The contrast of flash's blinding light and the dimly lit shelters comes from the images themselves, of course, but implicit in these works is a quite different set of associations involving obscurity and sudden light. Up in the blackout streets, different sorts of flashes and flares were lighting up the sky, creating contrasts that were full of dread—photographs could be seen week after week in *Picture Post* that set the intense darkness of the blackout against the luminous activity overhead, and the fires set off in the streets. The novelist and firefighter William Sansom wrote of the artificial 'flash and lustre' that 'permutated into many freakish effects—the searchlights above turning to turquoise in

Figure 10.8 Bill Brandt, 'Christ Church, Spitalfields: Two women sleep either side of a small boy', November 1940. © Imperial War Museums (D 1515).

the fireglow, the faces yellow in the gaslight, the perpetual sunset coppered and orange above any black roofscape'. His coloration provides a necessary corrective to the blacks, greys, and whites of very many wartime photographs, although his emphasis on contrasts is telling: But broadly speaking, at an incident there seemed to be two most regular and most penetrating effects—one of the bombed house cold and away from all firelight, and the other warm and garish in the pantomime light of the fire.[37] In February 1944 Stephen Spender witnessed a colossal Luftwaffe raid on London in which the house directly opposite his was hit: he dusted off part of the kitchen table and wrote a first draft of 'Abyss'.[38]

> When the foundations quaked and the pillars shook,
> I trembled, and in the dark I felt the fear
> Of the photograph my skull might take
> Through the eye sockets, in one flashlit instant
> When the crumbling house would obliterate
> Every impression of my sunlit life
> With one impression of black final horror
> Covering me with irrecoverable doom.[39]

If the flash of the camera was not to be used in these blacked-out streets, its cruel light was nonetheless available for poetic appropriation.

For flash photography's deepest dark, we need to look not at the modern city, with its patches and traces and bursts of light, but to the wild—even if the effects that are created are no less artificial. The pioneering wildlife photographer and environmental activist George Shiras used his photographs to raise awareness about the occupants of the natural world, inhabiting their own nocturnal space.[40] If his earliest photography by flashlight was a substitute for hunting with a rifle during the off season, his concern for protecting animals from wholesale slaughter by sportsmen soon took over. He used two main approaches. One, based on a traditional Ojibway hunting technique, involved jack-lighting: lighting a small birchwood fire in a pan on a boat's bow to attract an animal's attention—lynx, moose, snowy owl, deer. Once the creature was intrigued, he opened the shutter and fired the flash. At first, this was a haphazard and risky process. Shiras employed three spirit lamps, and sprayed magnesium powder across their flames using a rubber powder flask. No wonder he was grateful to learn of *blitzpulver*—which caused a ball of fire that he called a 'blowing moon'.[41] Later, he was to introduce and patent (jointly with his assistant John Hammer) a double-flash system, that showed an animal leaping away from the first flash, as we see with the deer in Figure 10.9.

In a 1900 article that was reprinted in the 1921 *National Geographic Magazine* (and then in his two-volume autobiography of 1935, *Hunting Wildlife with Camera and Flashlight*), Shiras described the jack-lighting process of taking flash, presenting it from the point of view of human and animal. It is an account of extremes of illumination and darkness, of beauty and terror.

> Fifteen yards now, the form of the deer appears, and the tension is becoming great. Suddenly there is a click, and a white wave of light breaks out from the bow on the boat—deer, hills, trees—everything stands out for an instant in the white glare of noonday. A dull report, and then a veil of inky darkness descends.
>
> Just a twenty-fifth of a second has elapsed, but it has been long enough to impress the picture of the deer on the plates of the cameras, and long enough to blind for the moment the eyes of both deer and men. Somewhere out in the darkness the deer makes a mighty leap... He is beginning to see a little now, and soon he is heard running, as only a frightened deer can, away from the light that looked so beautiful, but proved to be so terrifying.
>
> What an account he may have for his brothers and sisters of the forest of a thing which he himself would not have believed if he had not seen it with his own eyes[42]

Figure 10.9 George Shiras, 'Deer Leap', 1906. Courtesy National Geographic Creative.

Shiras's second flashlight method worked with the smaller animals who did not come down to drink from the lake: with raccoons and skunk, beavers and mink. These animal selfies were made through what he called 'flashlight trapping': he suspended bait from a black silk thread that when pulled triggered a flash that in turn released the shutter of a camera hidden in the undergrowth, protected by a waterproof casing—this is demonstrated in Figure 10.10. Deer were also photographed using a form of tripwire placed across their path.[43]

To be sure, Shiras had to engage in some careful optical calculations involving distance, focus, and light range, and had to use his knowledge of the animals' habits and habitat. But there was necessarily a huge element of chance involved in the taking of these pictures, which means that when we speak of their aesthetics, we are necessarily describing the aesthetics of flash in terms that remove human agency to a very considerable extent. If the individual image is not predictable, the overall pattern of illumination and darkness is common to each photograph. If taken under a sky far enough from light pollution for tens of thousands of stars to be visible—whether in the United States or in Africa—this sense of distance is obliterated through flash's bright immediacy, and the night in the finished print appears to envelop the animal subject. Yet if each animal is surrounded by the apparently impenetrable darkness to which it can return,

Figure 10.10 George Shiras, 'Flashlight Scene where a raccoon triggers a camera flash', *c.*1902. Courtesy National Geographic Creative.

this is a highly artificial version of nature. The light that falls on each creature individualizes it in a way that no lightning flash would do. That glimmerless night of the photographs is created through flash. As Sonia Voss has put it, these are not images that belong in the nineteenth-century tradition of 'a nostalgic, idealized nature, unspoiled and authentic. They bear the legacy of the confrontation between man and animal that determined their creation.'[44]

In other words, the wild, when photographed by flash, is as artificial a creation as the noir-ish ominous shadows of the urban street. Let us consider just one further area of its use that displays these irresolvable tensions between nature and artificiality. This paradox is necessarily at the heart of all photography of the environment—the presence of the camera that enables the subsequent possession of knowledge, or the enjoyment of beauty, or that provides the spur for environmental awareness and protection is itself not just a human-made and operated intrusion, but also the embodiment of materials and processes with an environmentally damaging history, from its use of heavy metals like mercury and silver to the role that digital cameras play in contributing to electronic waste.

In the case of Antarctica, the climate and winter light conditions could hardly be less hospitable to photography. Herbert Ponting travelled with Captain Scott's ill-fated Terra Nova expedition to Antarctica and the South Pole in 1910–12 as photographer and cinematographer.[45] Night-time photography was challenging—even a breath of wind would scatter the magnesium flash powder, he recalls—and painful. Preparing the flashes to take images of two colleagues, Atkinson and Clissold setting a fish trap 'necessitated the removal of my thick fur mits', rendering his hands without circulation, white and bloodless.[46] Yet he not only obtained images of the expedition members going about their daily tasks, and instructed the physicist and glaciologist Charles Seymour Wright on how to use magnesium wire to take images of frost crystals, he also obtained a spectacular image of the enormous Castle Berg, shown in Figure 10.11, taken 'on a comparatively mild day in June—that is to say when there was only about 50° of frost', using two flashes of 8 grams of powder for the part he wanted fully lighted, and one part for the part he wanted to be more or less in shadow. This was, he boasted, 'probably the only example in existence of a magnificent iceberg photographed by artificial light in the depths of a Polar winter'. This is documentary evidence not just of the iceberg, but of Polar darkness itself, something that can only be *shown* through artificial means as the hulk of whiteness gleams in the long dark of winter (the expedition's meteorologist had to be disabused of the idea that he had just witnessed

Figure 10.11 Herbert Ponting, 'Ice Castle, Antarctica', *c.*1911. © Popperfoto/Getty Images.

Figure 10.12 Frank Hurley, '*Endurance* at night (side view)', *c.*1914–16. Courtesy of the Royal Geographical Society (with IBG).

'three exceedingly brilliant flashes of lightning').[47] Even more striking are the winter pictures taken by the Australian Frank Hurley, photographer with Shackleton's expedition to Antarctica, of the *Endurance* trapped in ice in 1915, like a frozen *Marie Celeste* (Figure 10.12). Here light reflects back off the ship's rigging, and off the boulders and rubble of ice.

Flash creates shine, whether it bounces off snow or skin. We have frequently encountered its inadvertent presence, reflected in window glass or mirror or polished furniture or a celebrity's car. But sometimes shine is quite deliberate. It can help provide a compelling point of illumination that pulls a spectator's sight and imagination into an image. The early twentieth-century German wildlife photographer Carl Georg Schillings assures readers in his Preface that even when his pictures show 'remarkable, extraordinary light effects', like 'the flash-light picture, showing the glowing eyes of the lioness . . . no retouching has been done'.[48] Sometimes, indeed, it is celebratory, deliberate, intentionally electrifying. Krista Thompson's *Shine: The Visual Economy of Light in African Diasporic Aesthetic Practice* offers eloquent testimony to shine's positive qualities, its appropriation within the field of contemporary African diasporic art. She reminds us how Robert Farris Thompson in *Flash of the Spirit*, and Henry J. Drewal and John Mason in *Beads,*

Body, and Soul: Art and Light in the Yoruba Universe, understand light 'in part as representative of the spirit of Africa that remained ignited in the diaspora'.[49] Her concern, however, is not with inward light, but with the bling that shines out from the portraits made by street photographers, and with the searing bright lights fixed to the video cameras that have become fixtures in Jamaica's urban dance halls and clubs. She writes of black public spheres that are distinguished by cultures of seeing and being seen, and of how these cultures are aided by visual technologies. Much of what she says, in relation to staging visibility, in terms of how a body recognizes the experience of these intense lights, and of the importance of privileging the visual effects of conspicuous consumption, is highly pertinent to understanding the contemporary functioning of flash. As she writes,

> Video light and some of the other photographic practices inhabit the representational edge of hypervisibility and invisibility, optical saturation and blindness, presence and absence, blackness and white light. They produce a form of excess, a visual superfluity, that points precisely to the limits of vision or what lies just beyond photographic and visual capture.[50]

Nowhere is the question of shine's positive quality more politically charged than when that shine comes from black skin, and this question is explored not just by Thompson, but also by others who have written about the gleam and glisten of surfaces, and about their relationship to cultural values, to prejudice, to fetishism.[51]

Yet flash's operations do not necessarily illuminate dark skin. As the pair of images that Gordon Parks placed in *Flash Photography* demonstrated (Figures 6.21 and 6.22), a black face may be dulled, its contours muffled—and with film, this could be exacerbated, as we have seen, by the 'Shirley chart', used to calibrate skin tones, and predicated upon Caucasian complexions. In 1971 Caroline Hunter, a young chemist working for the Polaroid company in Cambridge, Massachusetts, came to realize that the firm was doing a significant amount of business in South Africa: something that led to the first campaign for boycotting and disinvesting from that country.[52] One part of this history was the use of Polaroid's ID-2 system to take pictures for the notorious South African passbooks—a system that has a button allowing its operator to boost the flash by 42 per cent, since black skin absorbs light by precisely that amount. Even if the equipment was initially developed for use in the United States when photographing dark skins—for example, for drivers' licences[53]—it clearly signals flash's ability to enable racial repression and discrimination. This is dramatized by its use in Athold Fugard's play *Sizwe Bansi is Dead* (1972), opening and ending in a photographer's studio, and looking at the reality of passbook laws in apartheid South Africa when it comes to both mobility and worker identification. Flashing out on stage, startling and disturbing the audience, the photographer's lighting stands in for the violence and coercion implicit in the system.

Flash's aesthetic effects are not necessarily as dramatic as literalizing dichotomies between dark and light, however. Whilst the saturation of black and the obliteration of background detail have been a theme running through this chapter, saturation of a different kind is to be found when flash is used in conjunction with colour. Instructions for using flash with colour processes are not recent. A writer in the *British Journal of Photography* for October 1910 is excited to explain how the 'use of flashlight powders for colour photography with the Autochrome plates has largely come into vogue of late, this method of illuminations possessing the distinct advantage of providing a light of high actinic intensity, uniform in its character, and capable of ready adjustment according to the quantity of powder used'.[54] But until the 1970s, flash's use with colour was largely confined to amateur photography, the work of some portrait photographers, commercial and advertising photography—as histories of photography routinely note, colour photography was not taken seriously as an art form until the 1970s. Ansel Adams's objections were typical: he felt that colour was distracting; diminishing the skilled photographer's control over the composition and tonality of their scene, and detracting from the importance of delicate (or major) adjustments in the darkroom. Complaining that 'The Creator did not go to art school and natural color, while more gentle and subtle, seldom has what we call aesthetic resonance', he saw a demand for colour as a pandering to popular taste.[55]

Flash brings a depth and an intensity to colour photography—even as the surface effects of flare and shine can be as visible as with black-and-white pictures. This intensification is especially apparent when the ring flash is used, since unlike the images made using top and side-mounted flashguns, virtually no shadows are formed, even if the subject is against a background wall, although it can create a kind of shadowy halo, especially with rounded objects—a face, a breast.[56] The doughnut-shaped ring flash was invented by Lester A. Dine in 1952 for use in dental photography, and fits around the lens. It is ideal for photographing close-ups—again, it caters to the needs of the hobbyist.[57] Its most significant impact has been on fashion photography. It was co-opted by some of the big names of the 1970s, including Guy Bourdin, Helmut Newton, and Chris von Wangenheim, before they tired of it—visual novelty is at a premium in this milieu—and then was rediscovered in the 1990s.[58]

But ring flash has been used by other photographers who appreciate its power to deliver bright, saturated light. The British photographer Martin Parr has long used flash, even when he was working in black and white: for his *Bad Weather* series, largely shot in Yorkshire, he deployed regular flash and an underwater camera, catching thick falling raindrops or wet snow in the flash's light and behind them, a sodden street; a tea towel flapping on a washing line, a deserted park bandstand, pedestrians under umbrellas or holding newspapers or cardboard boxes over their heads (Figure 10.13).

Parr moved to colour around 1982, using a Plaubel camera and flash, having seen some of the new American work of photographers like Joel Meyerowtiz, William Egglestone, and Stephen Shore (and inspired, too, by the bright saturated picture postcards of British photographer John Hinde), and then evolving by the mid-1990s to use a Macro camera with ring flash. Again, he learned from predecessors and contemporaries: Lee Friedlander, who had used ring flash in shooting his series of nudes, and the Japanese photographer Nobuyoshi Araki, who employed it for *The Banquet* (1993), a tribute to his late wife that portrayed the food they shared together during the last months of her life. Araki's volume shifts, in fact, halfway through, from deeply saturated colour images taken using the ring flash to black-and-white photographs, shot at home, using only available light. As Martin Parr and Gerry Badger observe, 'The obvious metaphor

Figure 10.13 Martin Parr, 'Bad Weather, Halifax, Yorkshire, UK, 1975' from *Bad Weather*, December 1978. © Martin Parr/Magnum Photos.

is to suggest that the color was leaving Araki's world, but his intentions are not quite so simple. The retreat from color is a retreat from realism to romanticism.'[59] Parr was influenced, too, by the early work of Chris Killip—Killip's 'Queen's Silver Jubilee celebration, North Shields, Tyneside' (1977) offers a wonderful example of his use of daylight flash—and, especially, by the German Heiner Blum, who used fill flash to shoot when the sun is high. Although this is not a time of day when one traditionally takes photographs, 'why waste that time', Parr asked, 'especially if that's when everything is happening?'[60]

Parr has used flash and natural light to deliberate, contrastive effect, as in his series in the mid-1980s documenting changing patterns of shopping in Salford, making a distinction between the old and the new. He used available light in an old-style business, like Betty's the hairdresser's, but flash inside a large supermarket—in part because he can take pictures with it without customers tripping over his tripod, but with 'the added bonus that the flash can help to express the alienation which is so often a trademark of these large anonymous stores'.[61] But in the work for which he has become best known, he photographs out of doors, using a ring flash.[62]

In many ways, Parr belongs in the long tradition of documentary photographers, recording the everyday life of the British middle and working classes, and bringing out every nuance of class to be found in expressions of national and family pride and in very everyday rituals, from taking afternoon tea to shopping for food or furniture, or celebrating royal milestones, or sunbathing, or sipping a cocktail, or decorating their homes with what some of us might think of as questionable taste, or growing rhubarb. This portrayal of a country—showing both slow evolution and remarkable stasis over nearly forty years (there's little trace in Parr's work of England's more dramatic changes)—is simultaneously affectionate and replete with ridicule—much like British humour. It is a portrayal that brings out the vulnerability of its subjects, even as Parr readily acknowledges that, like any photographer who works in public spaces, there is also an element of exploitation at stake.[63] 'He has photographed', as Val Williams puts it, 'the British awkwardness about themselves (which he shares).' But as she also perceptively notes, his photography is 'uncomfortable' because of the position in which he places his spectators: 'in many ways it brings out the worst in us, makes us scornful or silly, snobbish or cynical'.[64]

Both our discomfort and Parr's mild satire are accentuated by Parr's use of daylight flash. This slightly intensifies colour, making everything just a little bit bolder than in life. Whereas the visual anthropology that the Colliers advocated back in the 1960s, like so much of the FSA work that preceded it, gave a respectful dignity to everyday objects, domestic scenes, and out-of-the-ordinary moments of celebration and festivity, this barely perceptible increased saturation makes even something as everyday as drinking a cup of tea seem suddenly worthy of scrutiny. Parr's flash gives visibility to the ordinary, to be sure, but its slight edge of artificiality defamiliarizes British social practices, bringing out their idiosyncrasies. In Parr's hands, there is a very easy slippage from realism to satire in recording these idiosyncrasies—although he prefers the lighter term 'irony'—and there is certainly criticism, especially of the values of Thatcher's England, of deeply engrained snobbery, and of the endurance of a class system that many in his pictures appear to take, unquestioningly, for granted. This is flash gently, but relentlessly, deployed for polemical ends.

One of the most startling of all colour flash photographs—quite different in its flamboyant artificiality from Parr's work—is the cover that Nick Knight shot for the cover of British *Vogue* for November 1993, featuring Linda Evangelista.[65] Knight is a photographer who works on the edge between fashion and art photography.[66] His reflection on how he uses flash exemplifies a different kind of equilibrium, one between carefully calculated effect and intuition, and one that runs counter to so much photographic emphasis on the importance of the past. 'I always work in the future tense', he comments.

> As a photographer, you never see the moment you're recording. When you press the button, the flash goes off and overstimulates the retina; or you look into the camera, the shutter goes down and it goes black. You're always working in a pre-emptive, intuitive way. The future is where I find myself most of the time, and it's an odd place to be.[67]

This photographic philosophy is deliberately futuristic, celebrating the brash energy signified by flash.

In so much flash photography, the presence of its bleaching flare is inadvertent. But in Knight's cover, as in the portraits with which Chapter 9 concluded, flash has become the subject. For this is a cover *about* flash, about artificiality. 'Glamour is back', the wording proclaims, but there is nothing subtle about this style statement. It features not just a sparkle effect from Knight's ring flash on the blood-red wall behind (an effect repeated on the inside page-spreads), but the elegantly, racily dressed Evangelista herself setting off the flare of a conventional flashgun, blinding the photographer in front of her, and giving herself a large, skewed halo of blazing white light. The conventional object of the photographer's gaze is using the flash to assert her own power and presence.

Flash is deployed for a number of self-referential ends in contemporary photography. Each one of these calls attention to one or more of the major themes discussed in this book—illumination, speed, memory, paparazzi work, violence. Sometimes flash just jokily announces its presence as a necessary tool. And sometimes, photographers look to diminish its pejorative associations, and try to recapture some of its early properties, showing that it can still captivate and astound.

Flash illumination registers most obviously when the photographer deliberately calls attention to the artifice that they are employing—as with Timm Rautert's self-obliteration in 'Selbst, im Spiegel/Self in Mirror' (Figure 9.15) or the flashes that appear in Lee Friedlander's self-portraits. At least one of these, of himself and his son Erik in a motel room in Fort Lee, New Jersey in 1974, serves a very similar purpose to Rautert's self-obliteration. The flash is reflected in a murky round mirror that surely would have shown the photographer badly, anyway; as it is, it contributes to a theme of alienation and dissatisfaction that picks up on the faraway, melancholy look on the boy's face, set low in the frame, and on the downbeat surroundings: a bleak empty wall, and a dull dark sofa. Friedlander has taken numerous self-portraits—his shadow falls across landscapes or people's backs in the street; his face is reflected on top of a mannequin's head in a plate glass window or in a television set on sale; in 'Provincetown, Cape Cod, Massachusetts' (1968) it is only partially visible behind a bare, lit lightbulb. Flash appears very rarely, which means that when it does, we should look carefully for the commentary that it implicitly offers. A couple of images ask what, exactly, is providing light: a firing flash, or a candle, or—again, but keeping company with a flashgun—a light bulb? In one picture, Friedlander holds the flash so that its light bounces off the woodwork, whilst he himself stands in a patch of perfectly adequate sunlight. In one of the many images in which he captures his own image in a car's wing mirror, the bright star of the flash appears in the corner (Figure 10.14). This reminder of artificiality has one looking harder at the scene outside: sure enough, the agave cactus in this corner of a Californian desert is not alive, but is sculpted from galvanized rubber. At the same time, the flash was not used to illuminate this monstrous piece of false vegetation, but lit up the car's interior, giving its manufactured surfaces the same tonal range as outside.

Figure 10.14 Lee Friedlander, 'California', 2008. © Lee Friedlander, courtesy Fraenkel Gallery, San Francisco.

Capitalizing on the associations of flash and speed and the capturing of an instant, Canadian Michael Snow's 'Flash! 20:49, 15/6/2001', shown in Figure 10.15, is a staged image, very much in the style of Jeff Wall. Indeed, in theme it demands a close comparison with Wall's 'A Sudden Gust of Wind (After Hokusai)'. A woman and man sit opposite each other at a restaurant table: as Joanna Lowry has noted, 'the scene has the appearance of a cheap advertisement, or perhaps an image from a technical handbook on amateur photography. There is a compelling banality to the props, and the actors, and the slightly old-fashioned quality of the color print.'[68] Amateurism is strongly signalled, too, in the presence of 'that ugly edge of shadow so common in direct flash pictures' on the wall behind.[69] But the conceit of the picture is that a celebratory moment—an anniversary, a birthday?—has been smashed into by, indeed, a sudden gust of wind, with bread rolls and red wine sent flying: an instant of mild disaster that has been caught by the camera before its impact has had a chance to register on the couple's faces, even as the woman's hair billows out behind her. In its frozen stiltedness, the image parodies the conventions of the vernacular use of flash.

By contrast, Gary Schneider takes portraits using flashlights: not flashlights in the sense of a Speedlite, but in the parallel usage that the word carries, that of a torch. Inspired jointly by Julia Margaret Cameron's portraits, and the long exposure times that

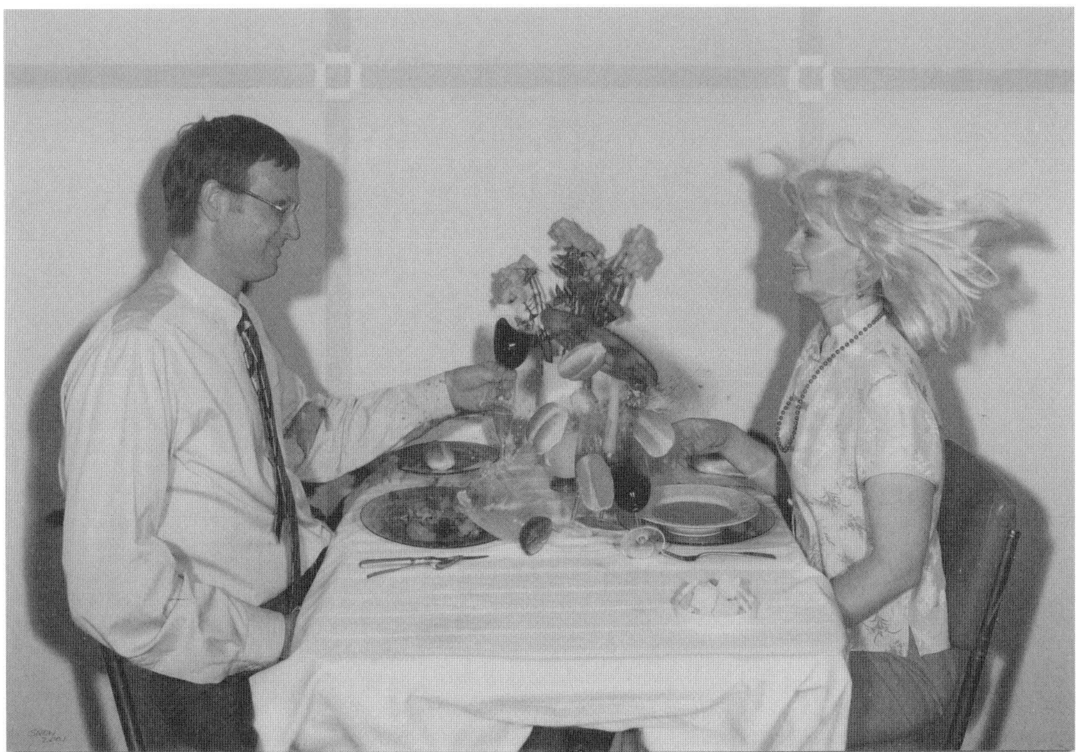

Figure 10.15 Michael Snow, 'Flash! 20:49 15/6/2001', 2001. Laminated colour photo on aluminium. 48 × 72 in. © Michael Snow. Courtesy of the artist and Jack Shainman Gallery, New York.

she needed for her wet-plate process, and by the philosophy of performance artist Vito Acconci, who—as Schneider put it—'used performance as a framework for exploring the event rather than how something looks',[70] he positions the subjects of his ongoing *Heads* series on the floor of his studio with a camera suspended over them, turns out the lights, opens the camera shutter (he uses a Toyo G 8×10-format camera), and for eight or ten minutes, slowly moves the flashlight over their faces, just 3 inches above them. The results, like the head shown in Figure 10.16, are, as he describes them, images that are 'intimate' and 'vulnerable'.[71] They are also other-worldly, with the uncanny pallor of a waxwork or corpse—in part because of the unhealthy gleam that comes off the skin, whether brown or white; and the intense white reflections from eyeballs and glasses. The subjects look damaged, bruised.

These soft-edged portraits indicate a slow play of light. Max Kozloff, focusing only on the end result, rather than considering what is far more significant—the process behind them—unfairly and sneeringly called these images 'the belated spawn of Pictorialism'.[72] They are the complete antitheses of that other series of *Heads* that we encountered in Chapter 1, where Philip Lorca diCorcia caught people unawares in a city street. The fact that Schneider's portraits are, in all their unflattering revelation,

Figure 10.16 Gary Schneider, 'John', 1989. Courtesy the artist.

made with their subjects' full participation is one of the many factors that makes them so uncomfortable to look at. They are the antithesis, too, of fast paparazzi work. Appropriating paparazzi style came remarkably late to art photography: we find it taken up by Andy Warhol in his *Exposures* series (1979), and then by Cindy Sherman in her series *Untitled Film Stills* (1977–80).[73] In 'Untitled Film Still #54', seen in Figure 10.17, Sherman appears caught in the flash's sudden glare, looking somewhere between surreptitious and angry at exposure, somewhere between Marilyn Monroe and Princess Di.

Recent photographers, though, have experimented with using the discarded or unusable work of actual paparazzi (the German Thomas Demand); with following non-glitzy celebrities at a distance (as with French photographer François-Marie Banier's images of Samuel Beckett, taken with a telephoto lens); or, in the case of Swedish Ulf Lundin, following his own family around, paparazzi-style, for a year. But most telling of all, from the point of view of flash photography, is the 2008 series by German artist Viktoria Binschtok, *Flash*. In pale greys and whites, her images, like that reproduced as Figure 10.18, show—very faintly, barely discernible—a celebrity actor walking through a crush of photographers, entering their car. As Quentin Bajac writes, 'when discussing paparazzi photography, the ambiguity of the term "overexposure" applies in its fullest sense. It may refer to a subject who is excessively photographed and

Figure 10.17 Cindy Sherman, 'Untitled Film Still #54', 1980. Gelatin silver print. 8 × 10 in. (20.3 × 25.4 cm) Courtesy of the artist and Metro Pictures, New York.

hyped in the media. It may also allude to a photo that is spoiled by improper exposure techniques. The burst of light from a flash is the instant when the two meanings converge.'[74] These images—themselves originally exhibited in a very dark gallery (Klemm's, Berlin) with carefully directed lighting, so that they seemed to gleam off the walls—are a series of still images made from found video footage shot as paparazzi followed the actor. Their powerful lights flooded the video, making its imaging illegible, yet bringing out the media frenzy, so intensely competitive that it has cannibalized itself through light.[75]

This intense bleaching recalls flash's largest and most deadly form, the flash of the nuclear bomb: the extreme point reached by flashes that accompany potentially lethal activity. Flash bombs were used in America in the early 1930s 'to make a flash of three billion candle power, by the light of which a considerable area of the land below has been photographed from the 'plane', with the photographs being developed and printed in a laboratory built inside the cabin.'[76] In the Second World War, army photographers from both the United Kingdom and the United States used time-fused magnesium—'flashlight bombs'—through which to image the land below them.[77] But the regular explosive materials in a firearm have flashy properties. A 'flash in the pan' is not—as some have asserted—that welcome glimmer of gold in a prospector's sieve, but is a

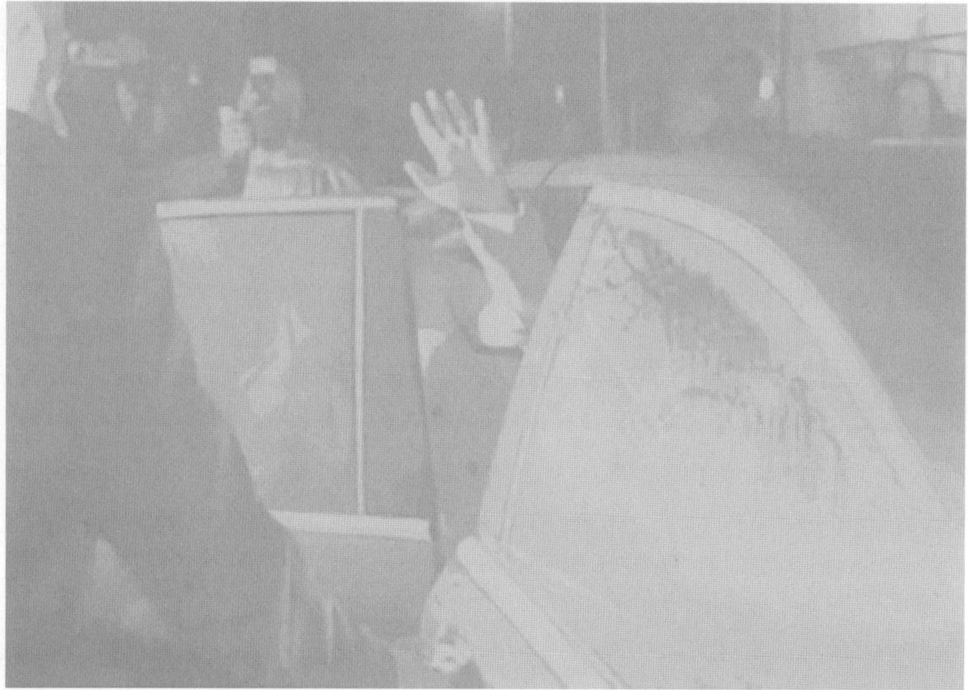

Figure 10.18 Viktoria Binschtok, 'Flash #6', 2008, light-jet-print behind acrylic, framed. 94 × 134 cm.

Edition 3+1 a.p. Courtesy the artist and KLEMM'S, Berlin.

term going back at least to the late seventeenth century when a musket would have a little compartment in which to store gunpowder: the term refers to the gunpowder exploding without a bullet being fired. During the Vietnam War, Mai Nam recollects that, fighting against the French and the Americans,

> We photographers never stopped innovating. When I was taking pictures near the DMZ and the Vinh Linh area in 1968, we even came up with a new form of flash photography to illuminate our fighters and villagers who were living in bomb shelters and tunnels. We emptied gunpowder from rifle cartridges onto a small handheld device and then lit the gunpowder with a match. The burning powder created all the light we needed.[78]

This close relationship of flash photography to actual weaponry is explicitly referenced in British photographer Sarah Pickering's *Celestial Objects* series (2013). Unlike Harold Edgerton, using strobe to stop a bullet, turning its flight into a disconcerting thing of beauty rather than a display of weaponry, Pickering opens her camera shutter and photographs a bullet fired from a revolver in the complete dark, representing the whole of the shooting of the bullet from beginning to end (Figure 10.19). All the light comes from the explosion itself. Pickering is highly alert to the history that connect guns with photography—Marey's photographic rifle, Muybridge's image of chickens scared by a

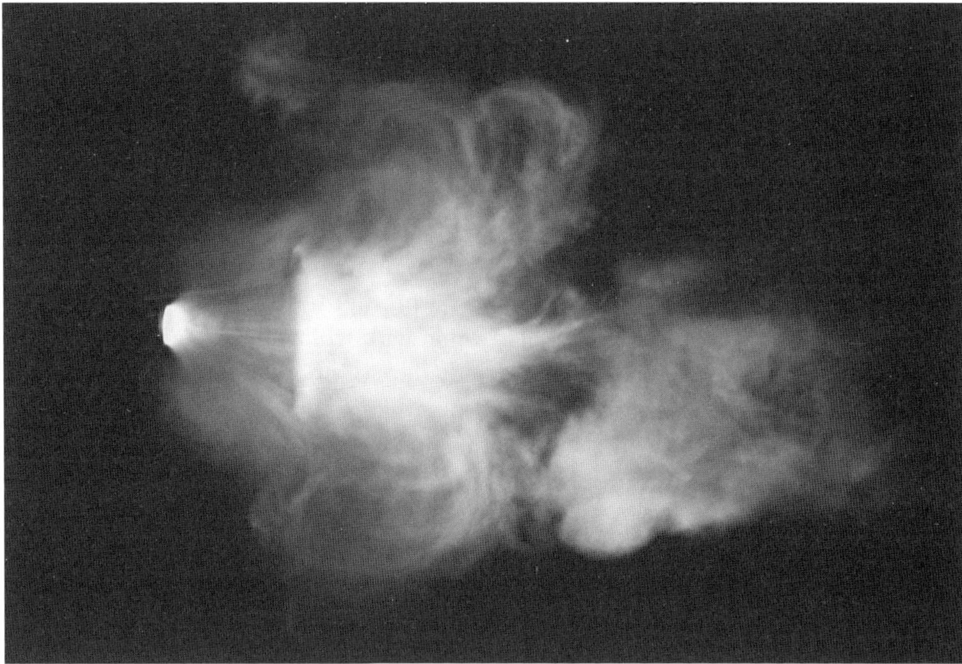

Figure 10.19 Sarah Pickering, 'Muzzle Flash', from the *Celestial Objects* series, 2013. Courtesy the artist.

torpedo; she collects images of pistol flashes. She also cites as a formative influence an episode (Assignment 4) of the British time-travel series *Sapphire and Steel* that aired in 1980, in which guncotton and flash paper are used to ignite old photographs that still have the spirit of the people photographed living within them.[79] Her *Black Hole* employs the effects of a flashing pistol with even more attention to its material repercussions. She places unexposed photo paper in the direct line of fire, and thus records the exposures and punctures that are made by shots. At the same time, of course, the title consciously evokes a whole other register of flashes: the huge explosions that take place deep in space, among far distant galaxies.

Across her whole body of work, Pickering references the idea of unfathomable space; the power and beauty of fire; and explosions and pyrotechnics of all kinds. She is concerned with psychological states of readiness and preparedness—and threat, disruption, the uncontrolled. Conceptually, as well as in her visual registers that incorporate darkness and flame, the blur of light and the white-hot core of gunpowder's ignition, she returns flash photography to the unpredictable and thrilling category of the sublime—even as she juxtaposes this with a different set of contemporary social imperatives that seek after order, organization, and control. Her images leave one in no doubt where her own imaginative sympathies lie.

Flash can, indeed, be magical. We see this in the video made by British artist Sutapa Biswas, *Magnesium Bird* (2004). Filmed in the eighteenth-century walled gardens of

Harewood House, Yorkshire, it commemorates the passing of her father. Small birds, sculpted from magnesium ribbon, are ignited at dusk, and they flare in little balls of fire, like tiny funeral pyres, or apocalyptic wreckage, under a dark and thundery sky. The soundtrack is the haunting cry of the children heard playing in the background, and the song of birds: the last conversation that Biswas had with her father before he died was about the importance of his words, and birdsong.[80] It is a piece about the migration of souls, and the Biswas's literal migration from India to England; about time passing and mourning; a reflective piece in which magnesium ribbon is used not to capture a person or a moment *for* memorialization, but as a prompt to think about evanescence, brightness, darkness, loss. The material burning with white and pale green flames in Biswas's piece implicitly returns us to the early days of photography, and reminds us how flash's properties were initially seen as something approaching the transcendent, the sublime. These are hardly the associations that it typically carries today, when its use is usually synonymous not only with the rapidity with which very many photographs are taken, but also with a mechanistic, soulless approach.

One of the rules that greets visitors who are dropped off at Walter de Maria's remarkable installation in Central New Mexico, the *Lightning Field*, is a prohibition against taking photographs. This is less, I think, an attempt to keep a tight control on copyright than an attempt to ensure a particular mode of aesthetic viewing: one that, like that necessary when viewing other Land Art works—by Robert Smithson, Charles Ross, and James Turrell, for example—makes one reflect upon tiny variations in natural light, upon duration, and on the importance of experiencing the interrelation between art work, human scale, and the scope of a landscape. To spend twenty hours in the company of 400 stainless steel poles arranged in a rectangular 1 mile by 1 kilometre grid, in wild grazing country under huge skies, is to be exposed, indeed, to slow art. This insistence on continuity within space and time, the meditative space that the piece offers for exploring the links between the natural and the creative, the pressure on interiority that the site produces—all are quite antithetical to the moment seized by a camera shutter, let alone by the photographic flash. The lightning that occasionally irradiates the *Lightning Field*—or that can be observed flickering and flaring all around it, at completely unpredictable intervals—drives this point home. For flash is, indeed, very much a presence here: not as a tool of photographic technology, but as something imminent, hoped for, anticipated in the clouds—even if it never arrives to hit, dramatically, the solid pointed tips of the poles.[81]

Flash! has been a history of attempts to appropriate the effects of naturally produced interruptive moments, to claim the illumination and the violence of lightning for both documentary and aesthetic ends. If flash photography retains the power to disturb us today, it is largely because we see it as signifying the invasion of private space, not because it is a manifestation of the external sublime. This applies both to the person who snaps away at a family party, temporarily halting the flow with little sudden shards of light, and, for some, to the street photography of Philip-Lorca diCorcia, singling out individual figures—even their heads—and catching their image unawares by means of a sudden powerful spotlight flash. Its invasive potential continues to be described—at its most extreme—in terms of sexual violation. Araki—who is himself a prolific producer of erotic imagery—remarked of his compatriot Daido Moriyama that he 'once published a series of shocking nudes in *Playboy*. They were all of rapes'. This was not literally true, despite their disturbing nature, but as he goes on to explain,

> The flash from a strobe exposed them, raping them. Moriyama raped them all with his gaze. Photographing women is a gaze that rapes.[82]

But, by and large, photographic flash has lost its novelty. Flash technology, as this book demonstrates, became a finely calibrated instrument for creating and controlling light. Whatever the pragmatic advantages of this, it has been for a long time at the expense of an aesthetics—and a related metaphorical storehouse—that emphasizes not just the sudden, but also the surprising, the unpredictable, and the revelatory. We have become used to the flash of the flashbulb—irritant though it might temporarily be—whilst the flash of a lightning bolt, in all its dangerous unpredictability, remains something that startles, terrifies, and awes us—in other words, something quite different from artificially produced illumination. We are inured to the kind of modernization of the body described by Walter Benjamin: one in which 'abrupt movement . . . has taken the place of the steady movement that used to be required', so that now passing through the world involves 'the individual in a series of shocks and collisions'.[83] All the same, in this mechanized universe the potential of unexpected flash illumination to shock has not quite disappeared from our visual lexicon, at least in the immersive environment of film.

And yet, that raw electrical power is still being deployed by photographers—not as a metaphor, the *blitz* in *blitzlichtpulver*, but in its own right.[84] Floris Neusüss, who has throughout his career experimented with camera-less photography, made some of his *Nachtbilder*—'night photos'—by leaving sheets of photographic paper out at night in thunderstorms. They, as exemplified by Figure 10.20, are spattered with rain marks, bear marks of downpours, but also carry the ghostly marks of leaves—the negative imprint of the exposures made by lightning—as well as streaks left by the flashes of lightning themselves.

In Chapter 4, I wrote of Hiroshi Sugimoto's use of long exposures as a channelling of technological modernity, yet one that he uses in defiance of modernity's emphasis on rapidity and on the chopping up of time. His *Lightning Fields* project deliberately harks back to earlier technological experimentation. Its title also, and obviously, evokes the potential for sublimity inherent in de Maria's installation. Sugimoto has said that his desire to observe the effect of electrical discharges on photographic plates is a form of homage to Benjamin Franklin's experiments with electricity, Michael Faraday's formulation (in 1831) of the law of electromagnetic induction, and Fox Talbot's invention of calotype photography. He wanted, he said, 'to re-create the major discoveries of these scientific pioneers in the darkroom and verify them with my own eyes'.[85] He might well have invoked, as well, nineteenth-century experiments by Étienne-Léopold Trouvelot,

Figure 10.20 Floris Neusüss, 'Gewitterbild, Kassel', 1984. Photogram from the *Nachtbilder* series. 27.16 × 26.77 in. (69 × 68 cm). Courtesy the artist.

which exploited and enjoyed the capriciousness of electricity, and its capacity to produce unpredictable aesthetic results.

As with Neusüss's work, no camera was involved in Sugimoto's *Lightning Fields*. He introduced a Van de Graaff generator into his studio, which fired off 400,000-volt electrical charges that were then captured on film. He used other devices of his own making that discharged electricity; experimented with using film that had itself been electrically charged. The end results, like the image in Figure 10.21, look like streaks of lightning branching off, root-like, from an incandescent spinal core; or like trees, highlighted as bleached trunks and branches in a pitch-dark landscape; or like forms of primeval life, turning and sending out tendrils of new growth in swirling water—Sugimoto, indeed, also employed tanks of saltwater in making some of these images.

In writing about these works, Sugimoto explains that he is paying homage, in his way, to two opposing forces. On the one hand, there is the daily technical challenge that he faces in his darkroom—the 'demonic specters of static electricity that haunt silver halide photography'. On the other, there is the metaphysical threat already lurking in his choice of the words 'demonic specters', and that has him putting up a *Shinto kamidana* altar in this darkroom and praying to it daily for trouble-free developing.

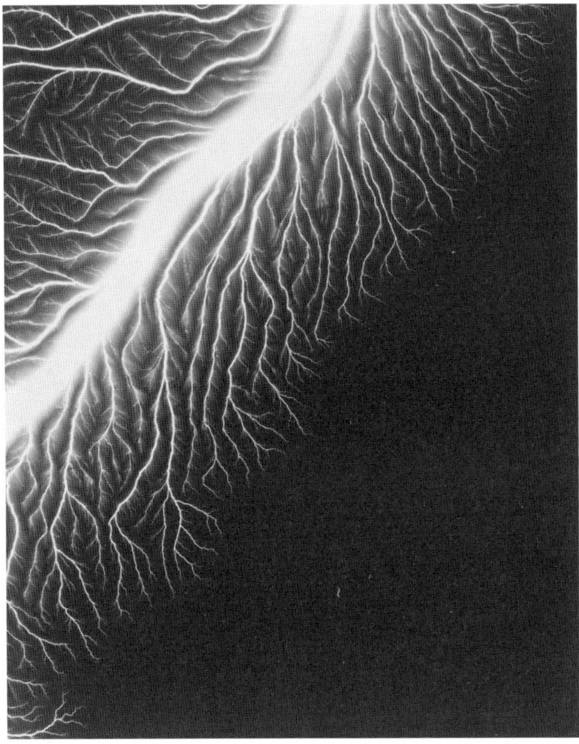

Figure 10.21 Hiroshi Sugimoto, 'Lightning Fields 128', 2009. © Hiroshi Sugimoto, courtesy Fraenkel Gallery, San Francisco.

'An interest in cultural anthropology likewise saw me retracing how ancient people gave mystical readings to arcane natural phenomena, then found ways to cope.' He continues: 'One winter's day, in the midst of a particularly infuriating bout with the demons in the darkroom, I quietly shut my eyes and began chanting mantra to myself. And in a miraculous flash, the demons disappeared.' [86] But they returned. So Sugimoto decided that he would turn them from his demons into his angels, and the *Lightning Fields* were the result.

The cultural history of flash photography involves tracing its technological developments—sometimes overlapping, sometimes commercially competing, sometimes the product of laboratory experimentation, and sometimes the inventions or improvisations of amateurs. To be sure, the practice is frequently irritating or invasive. But as Sugimoto's *Lightning Fields* suggests, sudden and surprising light can still be deployed by the inventive photographer so that we pay close attention to the sense of magic it can awaken. These images show that despite the bad press that flash photography has—at times quite justifiably—received over the century and a half since its invention, something of the original wonder that attended it may still, very effectively, be produced.

ENDNOTES

Prologue

1 Maurice Merleau-Ponty, *Phenomenology of Perception*, trans. Colin Smith (New York: Routledge & Kegan Paul, 1962), 310.
2 Arthur Symons, 'Pastel', *Silhouettes* (London: Elkin Mathews and John Lane, 1892), 13.
3 Arnold Bennett, *The Regent* (London: Methuen & Co., 1913), 116.
4 My underlying approach to the history of flash photography is indebted to the issues outlined by Lisa Gitelman, 'Introduction: Media as Historical Subjects', *Always Already New: Media, History, and the Data of Culture* (Cambridge, MA: MIT Press, 2006), 1–22.
5 William Faulkner, 'All the Dead Pilots', *These Thirteen* (New York: Jonathan Cape and Harrison Smith, 1931), 109.
6 Faulkner, 'All the Dead Pilots', 82.
7 Sam Selvon, *The Lonely Londoners* (1956; London: Penguin Classics, 2006), 98.
8 Ross Macdonald, *The Drowning Pool* (1950; New York: Vintage Books, 1996), 79.
9 Ulrich Baer, 'Photography and Hysteria: Toward a Poetics of Flash', ch. 1 of *Spectral Evidence: The Photography of Trauma* (Cambridge, MA: MIT Press, 2002), 25–60 (an earlier version was published in *Yale Journal of Criticism* 7 (1994), 41–78).
10 Alexander Nemerov, 'Burning Daylight: Remington, Electricity, and Flash Photography', in Nancy K. Anderson (ed.), *Frederic Remington: The Color of Night* (Princeton: Princeton University Press, 2003), 76–95. For Nemerov's interest in artists working at a moment when artificial light was bringing a reconceptualization of darkness, see also his 'The Dark Cat: Arthur Putnam and a Fragment of Night', *American Art* 16/1 (2002), 36–59, esp. 53–6.
11 Marilyn Ivy, 'Dark Enlightenment: Naitō Masatoshi's Flash', in Rosalind C. Morris (ed.), *Photographies East: The Camera and Its Histories in East and Southeast Asia* (Durham, NC: Duke University Press, 2009), 229–57: 230.
12 Katja Müller-Heller and Florian Sprenger (eds.), *Blitzlicht* (Zurich: diaphanes, 2012).

Chapter 1

1 Ralph Waldo Emerson, 'Self-Reliance' (1841), *Essays and Lectures*, ed. Joel Porte (New York: Library of America, 1983), 249.
2 Jonah Lehrer, *Proust Was a Neuroscientist* (New York: Houghton Mifflin, 2008), 7.
3 Friedrich Nietzsche, section 155, *Human, All Too Human: A Book for Free Spirits* (1878), trans. R. J. Hollingdale (Cambridge: Cambridge University Press, 1996), 83.
4 William Henry Fox Talbot, 'Some Account of the Art of Photogenic Drawing' (1839), in Vicki Goldberg (ed.), *Photography in Print: Writings from 1816 to the Present* (Albuquerque, NM: University of New Mexico Press, 1981), 41.
5 [David Brewster], 'Photogenic Drawing, or Drawing by the Agency of Light', *Edinburgh Review* 76 (January 1843), 309–44: 317.

6 [Lady Elizabeth Eastlake] 'Photography', *London Quarterly Review* 101 (April 1857), 442–68: 465.

7 H. J. Rodgers, *Twenty-Three Years Under A Sky-Light, or Life and Experiences of a Photographer* (Hartford: H. J. Rodgers, 1872), 27–8.

8 Julia Margaret Cameron, 'Annals of My Glass House' (1874), in Goldberg (ed.), *Photography in Print*, 181.

9 Amy Levy, *The Romance of a Shop* (1888; Peterborough, Ontario: Broadview Press, 2006), 76.

10 For the history of nineteenth-century photography, see Geoffrey Batchen, *Burning with Desire: The Conception of Photography* (Cambridge, MA: MIT Press, 1997); Steve Edwards, *The Making of English Photography* (University Park, PA: Pennsylvania State University Press, 2006); Mary Warner Marien, *Photography and Its Critics: A Cultural History, 1839–1900* (Cambridge: Cambridge University Press, 1997); Martha Sandweiss (ed.), *Photography in Nineteenth-Century America* (Fort Worth, TX: Amon Carter Museum, Fort Worth and Harry N. Abrams, 1991); Larry J. Schaaf, *Out of the Shadows: Herschel, Talbot & the Invention of Photography* (New Haven: Yale University Press, 1992). Brian Coe, *Cameras: From Daguerreotype to Instant Pictures* (London: Marshall Cavendish Editions, 1978) gives an overview of developments in camera technology. For a history that emphasizes technological processes, see Reese V. Jenkins, *Images and Enterprise: Technology and the American Photographic Industry 1839 to 1925* (Baltimore: Johns Hopkins University Press, 1975).

11 Roland Barthes, *Camera Lucida: Reflections on Photography* (1980), trans. Richard Howard (New York: Hill and Wang, 1981), 88, 96. Rosalind Krauss's gloss on photography's indexicality is perhaps more useful, through the analogues that it offers, than Roland Barthes: she writes that photography 'is an imprint or transfer off the real; it is a photochemically processed trace [or electronically processed, we might say of digital photography] causally connected to that thing in the world to which it refers in a manner parallel to that of fingerprints or footprints or the rings of water that cold glasses leave on tables. The photograph is thus generically distinct from painting or sculpture or drawing. On the family tree of images it is closer to palm prints, death masks, the Shroud of Turin, or the tracks of gulls on beaches... technically and semiologically speaking, drawings and paintings are icons, while photographs are indexes'—and in this consists photography's 'special status with regard to the real'. Rosalind Krauss, 'Tracing Nadar', *October* 5 (Summer 1978), 29–47: 34.

12 Hans Jonas, *The Phenomenon of Life: Toward a Philosophical Biology* (New York: Harper & Row, 1966), 149–50.

13 Chris Otter, *The Victorian Eye: A Political History of Light and Vision in Britain, 1800–1910* (Chicago: University of Chicago Press, 2008), 47.

14 [John A.] Tennant and [H. Snowden] Ward, *Flashlight Portraiture: A Book of Common Sense Information and Practical Methods of Making Portraits by Flashlight at Home or in the Photographic Studio* (New York: Tennant and Ward, 1912), 5.

15 Walter Benjamin, 'Theses on the Philosophy of History' (1940), in *Illuminations*, ed. Hannah Arendt, trans. Harry Zohn (New York: Schocken Books, 1968), 255.

16 Bill Knott, 'Flash', *Poetry* 183/6 (2004), 333.

17 Quoted in Philip Gefter, 'Sex in the Park, and Its Sneaky Spectators', *New York Times*, 23 September 2007.

18 Begun in 1938, these images were eventually gathered together and published in book form in 1966, in a volume entitled *Many are Called*. See Sarah Greenough, *Walker Evans: Subways and Streets* (Washington, DC: National Gallery of Art, 1991), 13–46.

19 'INTERVIEW. Philip-Lorca diCorcia Talks', transcript of Dorian Devens and Philip-Lorca diCorcia in conversation on *The Speakeasy*, WFMU.org, 2003, *ASX*, http://www.americansuburbx.com/2011/09/interview-photographer-philip-lorca-dicorcia-talks-2003.html, accessed 21 May 2012.

20 William Wordsworth, *The Prelude: 1799, 1805, 1850*, ed. M. H. Abrams, Stephen Gill, and Jonathan Wordsworth (New York: W. W. Norton & Co., 1979), vii. 626–9 (1850 version).

21 Georg Simmel, 'The Metropolis and Mental Life' (1903), in Donald L. Levine (ed.), *Georg Simmel on Individuality and Social Forms* (Chicago: University of Chicago Press, 1971), 324–39: 325.

22 Luc Sante, 'The Planet', in Philip-Lorca diCorcia, *Heads* (Göttingen: SteidlBoxPacemacgill, 2001), n.p.

23 For a full and thoughtful discussion of this case, which brings it into relation with what it means to 'people watch' in a city, see Rachel A. Wortman, 'Street Level: Intersections of Art and the Law. Philip-Lorca diCorcia's "Heads" Project and Nussenzweig v. diCorcia', *Gnosis* 10/2 (2010), http://gnovisjournal.org/2010/04/25/street-level-intersections-art-and-law-philip-lorca-dicorcias-heads-project-and-nussenzweig/, accessed 22 May 2012. I am indebted to Wortman for the juxtaposition of Simmel and Sante's different takes on the facial masks that city walkers adopt.

24 Lorraine Daston (ed.), *Biographies of Scientific Objects* (Chicago: University of Chicago Press, 1999), 1.

25 e.g., http://www.photomemorabilia.co.uk/.

26 David Robinson, Stephen Herbert, and Richard Crangle (eds.), *Encyclopedia of the Magic Lantern* (London: Magic Lantern Society, 2001), 174.

27 [Alexander Bain], 'Electrotype and Daguerreotype', *Westminster Review* 34 (September 1840), 434–60: 459. As with the other illustration, of fossil shells, 'When the impression was fixed upon the plate an outline of the image was traced upon it by an engraver in the dotting style: a print was then taken from the plate and transferred to stone, when the shading required was filled in by a lithographic artist' (460).

28 V.C. and Ed., 'Artificial Light for Photographic Purposes', *Photographic News* 3 (14 October 1859), 71.

29 This early history is recounted in Alfred Brothers, *Photography: Its History, Processes, Apparatus, and Materials* (2nd edn., London: Charles Griffin & Co., 1899), 59–62.

30 For the international history of magnesium production, see Ian McNeil (ed.), *An Encyclopedia of the History of Technology* (London: Routledge, 1990), 113–21.

31 For electrical demonstrations in the context of public instruction and amusement, see Iwan Rhys Morus, *Frankenstein's Children: Electricity, Exhibition, and Experiment in Early Nineteenth-Century London* (Princeton: Princeton University Press, 1998).

32 See Chris Howes, *To Photograph Darkness: The History of Underground and Flash Photography* (Carbondale, IL: Southern Illinois University Press, 1989), 45. For Piazzi Smyth's use of magnesium in photographing the pyramids, see H. A. Brück and M. T. Brück, *The Peripatetic Astronomer: The Life of Charles Piazzi Smyth* (Bristol: Adam Hilger, 1988), 95–134.

33 'The Magnesium Flashlight', *Photographic News* 32 (24 February 1888), 119.

34 Unsigned article, 'An American Magnesium Lamp', *British Journal of Photography* 12 (15 December 1865), 638.

35 Editor's note following a letter (dated Cincinatti, 14 July 1866) from Charles Waldack describing his methods, 'Photography in the Mammoth Caves by Magnesium Light', *Philadelphia Photographer* 3 (August 1866), 241–4: 243–4.

36 Unsigned article, 'Photography in the Mammoth Cave at Kentucky', *Photographic News* (30 November 1866), 565. Chris Howes's book continues the story of cave photography, highlighting the work of Max Müller (not the philologist), one of the first to use flash powder underground, who developed an ingenious method of keeping fumes and light away from the lens, and the late nineteenth-century cave explorers, especially in the Causses, who invented the Regnard lamp that would blow magnesium through a flame, thus avoiding the dangers inherent in taking flash powder deep below the surface. As Howes writes elsewhere, 'the determination, inventiveness and quality of results' produced by these pioneers was remarkable. Chris Howes, 'Art of Darkness', *New Scientist* 124 (23–30 December 1989), 13–16: 16.

37 Johannes Gaedicke, 'The Lightning Photographer: A Sketch of the Future', *American Annual of Photography and Photographic Times Almanac* 2 (1887), 97.

38 Jacob Riis, *The Making of an American* (New York: Macmillan Co., 1901), 267.

39 'New Photographic Light', *Sun* (16 October 1887), 8.

40 Riis, *Making of an American*, 273.

41 For Jacob Riis, see Tom Buk-Swienty, *The Other Half: The Life of Jacob Riis and the World of Immigration*, trans. Annette Buk-Swienty (New York: W. W. Norton, 2008); Keith Gandal, *The Virtues of the Vicious: Jacob Riis, Stephen Crane, and the Spectacle of the Slum* (New York: Oxford University Press, 1997); Peter Bacon Hales, *Silver Cities: Photographing American Urbanization 1839–1939* (rev. and expanded edn., Albuquerque, NM: University of New Mexico Press, 2006); Bonnie Yochelson and Daniel Czitrom, *Rediscovering Jacob Riis: Exposure Journalism and Photography in Turn-of-the-Century New York* (New York: New Press, 2007).

42 'Notes and Queries', *Photographic Times and American Photographer* 17 (19 August 1887), 426.

43 Unsigned report of meeting held 13 December 1887, 'The Society of Amateur Photographers of New York', *Photographic Times and American Photographer* 17 (30 December 1887), 673.

44 Riis, *Making of an American*, 268.

45 Unsigned article, 'English Notes', *Anthony's Photographic Bulletin* 19 (11 February 1888), 69.

46 F. J. Mortimer, *Magnesium Light Photography* (London: Dawbarn & Ward, 1906), 12.

47 *Photographic News* (6 February 1891), 112.

48 Alfred Gell, 'The Technology of Enchantment and the Enchantment of Technology', in Jeremy Coote (ed.), *Anthropology, Art, and Aesthetics* (Oxford: Clarendon Press, 1992), 40–63: 42.

49 See note in *Camera Craft* 21 (1914), 611.

50 [The Smith-Victor Co.], *Flashlight Photography* (Chicago: James Smith & Sons, *c.*1912), n.p.

51 Arjun Appadurai, 'Introduction: Commodities and the Politics of Value', in Appadurai (ed.), *The Social Life of Things: Commodities in Cultural Perspective* (Cambridge: Cambridge University Press, 1986), 5.

52 Eastman Co. advertisement for the '"Kodak" Electric Flashlight Outfit', in John J. Curtis, *Flashlight for the Amateur Photographer* (London: British Periodicals Ltd, 1925), n.p.

53 Burt Murphy, *Police and Crime Photography* (New York: Verlan Books, 1960), 61.

54 See Alejandro Martínez, '"A souvenir of undersea landscapes:" Underwater Photography and the Limits of Photographic Visibility, 1890–1910', *História, Ciências, Saúde-Manguinhos* 21/3 (2014), 1–18.

55 http://www.theatlantic.com/video/index/250927/kodaks-swinging-60s-commercial-for-flashcube/, accessed 7 January 2017.

56 T. D. Towers, *Electronics and the Photographer* (London: Focal Press, 1976), 143.

57 Transcription of a video interview with Malick Sidibé by Jerome Sother for www.gwinzegal.com in 2008, published in *LensCulture*, 2016. https://www.lensculture.com/articles/malick-sidibe-interview-with-malick-sidibe, accessed 27 January 2017.

Chapter 2

1 Lady Emmeline Stuart-Wortley, 'Sonnet: A Night Storm at Venice', *Sonnets: Written Chiefly During a Tour Through Holland, Germany, Italy, Turkey, and Hungary* (London: J. Rickerby, 1839), 56.
2 Edmund Burke, *A Philosophical Enquiry into the Origin of Our Ideas of the Sublime and the Beautiful* (1757; Oxford: Oxford University Press, 2009), 73.
3 Stuart-Wortley, *Sonnets*, 56.
4 John Milton, *Paradise Lost* (1667; Oxford: Oxford University Press, 2008), 5.
5 Longinus, *On Literary Excellence, Literary Criticism: Plato to Dryden*, ed. Allan H. Gilbert (Detroit: Wayne State University Press, 1962), 174.
6 John Ruskin, diary entry for 8 May 1841, *The Diaries of John Ruskin*, ed. Joan Evans and J. Howard Whitehouse, 3 vols. (Oxford: Clarendon Press, 1956–9), i. 185.
7 For research on lightning, its causes and effects, see Peter E. Viemester, *The Lightning Book* (New York: Doubleday, 1961).
8 Stuart-Wortley, *Sonnets*, 56.
9 Alfred Tennyson, *In Memoriam*, in *Tennyson: A Selected Edition* (Longmans Annotated English Poets), ed. Christopher Ricks (2nd edn., London: Routledge, 2006), 471.
10 Alexander Bain, *The Senses and the Intellect* (London: Longmans, 1855), 61–2.
11 Walt Whitman, *Leaves of Grass: The Complete Poems* (London: Penguin, 2005), 91.
12 Accounts written by those who have actually been struck by lightning are, of course, very different in this respect. Gretel Ehrlich's memoir, *A Match to the Heart: One Woman's Story of Being Struck by Lightning* (New York: Penguin, 1995) is a notable piece of writing, in which she builds on her near-death experience and researches the effects of lightning strikes upon the body.
13 Mark Twain, *Autobiography of Mark Twain: The Complete and Authoritative Edition*, 3 vols., ed. Harriet E. Smith, Benjamin Griffin, Victor Fischer, Michael B. Frank, Sharon K. Goetz, and Leslie Diane Myrick (Berkeley and Los Angeles: University of California Press, 2010), 89–90.
14 Randall Jarrell, 'Reflections on Wallace Stevens', *Poetry and the Age* (New York: Knopf, 1953), 148.
15 Charles Dickens, *Little Dorrit* (1855–7; Oxford: Oxford University Press, 2008), 565.
16 Percy Bysshe Shelley, 'A Defence of Poetry' (1821), *The Major Works* (Oxford World's Classics) (Oxford: Oxford University Press, 2009), 685. My thanks to Herbert Tucker for this reference.
17 William Wordsworth, *The Prelude* (1805; 1851), *The Prelude: The Four Texts (1798, 1799, 1805, 1850)* (London: Penguin, 1995), 240.
18 Wordsworth, *The Prelude*, 241.
19 Friedrich Nietszche, *Ecce Homo: How One Becomes What One Is* (1888; London: Penguin, 1992), 103.
20 Gerard Manley Hopkins, *The Major Works*, ed. Catherine Phillips (Oxford: Oxford University Prcss, 2009), 128.
21 Gerard Manley Hopkins to Robert Bridges, 4 January 1883, in *Gerard Manley Hopkins: Selected Letters*, ed. Catherine Phillips (Oxford: Clarendon Press, 1990), 176. For further discussion of

this image, see Elizabeth Villeponteaux, 'Flashing Foil and Oozing Oil: Trinitarian Imagery in "God's Grandeur"', *Victorian Poetry* 40/2 (2002), 201–7, which connects the lightning of this sonnet to the Pentecostal flame.

22 Gerard Manley Hopkins, *The Journals and Papers of Gerard Manley Hopkins*, ed. Humphry House and Graham Storey (New York: Oxford University Press, 1990), 195.

23 Jonathan Edwards, 'Images of Divine Things', in *The Works of Jonathan Edwards*, ed. Wallace E. Anderson, 26 vols. (New Haven: Yale University Press, 1977–2009), xi. *Typological Writings* (1993), 59.

24 Hopkins, 'The Wreck of the Deutschland', *Major Works*, 183. For more about Hopkins and lightning, and indeed about his interest in electricity in general, see John Gordon, 'The Electrical Hopkins: A Critical Study of His Best-Known Poems, *The Wreck of the Deutschland* and "The Windhover"', *University of Toronto Quarterly*, 65/3 (1996), 506–22.

25 Hopkins, 'The Shepherd's Brow', *Major Works*, 183.

26 Heraclitus, Fragment 64, *The Presocratic Philosophers: A Critical History with a Selection of Texts*, ed. G. S. Kirk, J. E. Raven, and M. Schofield (2nd edn., Cambridge: Cambridge University Press, 1983), 198.

27 See Jude V. Nixon, '"Death blots black out": Thermodynamics and the Poetry of Gerard Manley Hopkins', *Victorian Poetry* 40/2 (2002), 131–55.

28 Frazer's *Golden Bough* lays out the global reach of this mythology: the reverence offered to trees that have been struck by lightning; the superstitions offered to protect houses from its lethal impact; the way in which its threat could be appropriated as an instrument of power, with one early king of Alba allegedly setting himself up as the equal to Jupiter, constructing 'machines whereby he mimicked the clap of thunder and the flash of lightning', in order to overawe his subjects. James George Frazer, *The Golden Bough: A Study in Magic and Religion: A New Abridgement from the Second and Third Editions* (Oxford: Oxford University Press World's Classics, 1998), 118.

29 Milton, *Paradise Lost*, 243.

30 Mary Shelley, *Frankenstein: or 'The Modern Prometheus'* (1818; Oxford: Oxford University Press, 2008), 24.

31 Shelley, *Frankenstein*, 55.

32 Shelley, *Frankenstein*, 56.

33 Shelley, *Frankenstein*, 56.

34 Herman Melville, 'The Lightning-Rod Man' (1854), *Pierre, Israel Potter, The Piazza Tales, The Confidence-Man, Uncollected Prose, & Billy Budd* (New York: Library of America, 1984), 757. A far better known treatment of lightning by Melville can be found in chapter 119 of *Moby Dick*, 'The Candles'.

35 Melville, 'Lightning-Rod Man', 762.

36 Melville, 'Lightning-Rod Man', 763.

37 Melville, 'Lightning-Rod Man', 756.

38 As Sean Silver persuasively argues in 'The Temporality of Allegory: Melville's "The Lightning-Rod Man"', *Arizona Quarterly* 62/1 (2006), 1–33.

39 Hershel Parker, 'Melville's Salesman Story', *Studies in Short Fiction* 1/2 (1964), 158.

40 Melville, 'Lightning-Rod Man', 756.

41 Elizabeth Gaskell, *The Life of Charlotte Brontë* (1857; London: Penguin, 1998), 252–3.

42 Charlotte Brontë, *Jane Eyre* (1847; Oxford: Oxford University Press, 1980), 108.

43 Brontë, *Jane Eyre*, 245.

44 Walt Whitman, 'Song of Myself' (Fr. XXVIII, ll. 619–23), *The Complete Poems [Walt Whitman]*, ed. Francis Murphy (1975; Harmondsworth: Penguin Books, 1986), 91.

45 'Perhaps it [transgression] is like a flash of lightning in the night which, from the beginning of time, gives a dense and black intensity to the night it denies, which lights up the night from the inside, from top to bottom, and yet owes to the dark the stark clarity of its manifestation, its harrowing and poised singularity.' Michel Foucault, 'A Preface to Transgression' (1963), in *Religion and Culture*, selected and ed. Jeremy Carrette (London: Routledge, 1999), 61.

46 I have written about Eliot's use of the imagery of electricity in this novel, and its relationship to G. H. Lewes's ideas about the nervous system, in 'The Materiality of *Middlemarch*', in Karen Chase (ed.), *Middlemarch in the Twenty-First Century* (Oxford: Oxford University Press, 2006), 65–86.

47 George Eliot, *Middlemarch* (1871–2; Oxford: Oxford University Press, 1998), 760–1.

48 Thomas Hardy, *Desperate Remedies* (1871; London: Penguin, 1998), 137–8.

49 Hardy, *Desperate Remedies*, 138.

50 John Moule does not appear to have been any relation to Hardy's great friend Horace Moule.

51 See Lt.-Col. John H. Janeaway, 'Artificial Illumination for Photographic Purposes', *Photographic Times* 26 (June 1895), 351–7.

52 Advertisement, 'Night Photography', *Photographic News* (28 January 1859), p. ii.

53 See James Sheridan Muspratt, *Chemistry, Theoretical, Practical, and Analytical: As Applied and Relating to the Arts and Manufactures*, 2 vols. (Glasgow: W. Mackenzie, 1857–60), ii. 709. M. Gaudin, experimenting in France with photogen as a means for taking night-time photographs, diffused the glare by covering the floor and walls of the room near the reflector that spread the light with light blue calico. See M. Mc A. Gaudin, 'New Photogen for Obtaining Portraits at Night', *Photographic News* 7 (1863), 572, repr. from *La Lumière*.

54 John Ruskin, *Modern Painters*, IV (1856), in *The Works of John Ruskin*, ed. E. T. Cook and Alexander Wedderburn, 39 vols. (London: George Allen, 1903–12), vi. 82.

55 Unsigned review, 'The Exhibition', *Journal of the Photographic Society* 4 (21 May 1858), 210.

56 Oliver Wendell Holmes, 'The Stereoscope and the Stereograph' (1859), *Soundings from the Atlantic* (Boston: Ticknor and Fields, 1864), 164.

57 This figure was given by a Mr McKie, speaking at a meeting of the Newcastle-on-Tyne and North of England Photographic Society in 1861, and reported in the New York press. Unsigned note, 'Moule's Photogens for Taking Portraits by Artificial Light', *Humphrey's Journal* (August 1861), 96.

58 For more about Hardy's knowledge of contemporary photography and his deployment of it in his writing, see Jennifer Green-Lewis, *Framing the Victorians: Photography and the Culture of Realism* (Ithaca, NY: Cornell University Press, 1996), 77–88, and Arlene M. Jackson, 'Photography as Style and Metaphor in the Art of Thomas Hardy', *Thomas Hardy Annual* 2 (1984), 91–109.

59 See Bill Jay, 'Keraunography: Notes on the Photographic Effects of Lightning as Reported in 19 Century Journals', http://www.billjayonphotography.com/Keraunography.pdf, accessed 13 June 2012.

60 Dr T. L. Phipson, *Familiar Letters on Some Mysteries of Nature and Discoveries in Science* (London: Sampson Low, Marston, Searle, & Rivington, 1876), 213–14.

61 'Human Camera', *Daily Mail* (8 August 1904), from its New York correspondent, 1904. When one considers the readiness with which sensational material such as this was syndicated, it's possible to see how such far-fetched stories could gain wide currency. I have found this

story reprinted in the US in as apparently authoritative a journal as the *American Amateur Photographer* 16 (1904), 442, and as far away as Adelaide (*Advertiser*, 14 September 1904) and Christchurch, NZ (*Star*, 24 September 1904).

62 See Jennifer Tucker, *Nature Exposed: Photography as Eyewitness in Victorian Science* (Baltimore: Johns Hopkins University Press, 2005), esp. ch. 5, 'Acquiring a Scientific Eye', 126–58. See also Harry S. Silcox, *Jennings' Philadelphia: The Life of Philadelphia Photographer William Nicholson Jennings (1860–1946)* (Philadelphia: Brighton Press, 1993).

63 Ralph Abercromby, First Report of the Thunderstorm Committee, 'On the Photographs of Lightning Flashes', *Journal of the Royal Meteorological Society* 14 (1888), 226–34. The Royal Meteorological Society (RMS) had sent out about 200 circulars to photographic societies in Europe and America in June 1887, requesting photographs of lightning, and received about sixty examples, which were exhibited at a meeting of the RMS in March 1888. Jennings's was not the first photograph of lightning: in addition to the daguerreotype mentioned earlier (see Tucker, *Nature Exposed*, 144), a German photographer, prior to 1866, inadvertently captured a streak of lightning emanating from the end of a lance held by a bronze statue of an Amazon vanquishing a serpent—'the first flash of lightning that was ever fixed upon sensitive collodion'. Wilfrid de Fonvielle, *Thunder and Lightning* (*Éclairs et tonnerres*, 1866), trans. T. L. Phipson (New York: Scribner, Armstrong & Co., 1875), 45.

64 A. J. Jarman, 'Photographing by Lightning', *Photographic News* 21 (6 July 1877), 322.

65 De Fonvielle, *Thunder and Lightning*, 208.

66 Unsigned note, 'Photographing by Moonlight', *Photo-Beacon* 10 (1898), 139.

67 For general histories of artificial lighting, see Jane Brox, *Brilliant: The Evolution of Artificial Light* (New York: Houghton Mifflin Harcourt, 1910); Jill Jonnes, *Empires of Light: Edison, Tesla, Westinghouse, and the Race to Electrify the World* (New York: Random House, 2003); and Wolfgang Schivelbusch, *Disenchanted Night: The Industrialization of Light in the Nineteenth Century*, trans. Angela Davies (Berkeley and Los Angeles: University of California Press, 1988). A useful account of a range of methods employed in photographic lighting by the end of the 1870s is given in chapter VII, 'Photography by Artificial Light', in Owen Edlestone Wheeler, *Practical Photography* (London: 'The Bazaar' Office, 1879), 243–9.

68 See Audrey Linkman, *The Victorians: Photographic Portraits* (London: Tauris Parke Books, 1993), 137.

69 Gaedicke, 'Lightning Photographer', 94–5.

70 Hales, *Silver Cities*, 271.

71 Riis, *Making of an American*, 423, 439.

72 Riis, *Making of an American*, 271.

73 Jacob August Riis, *How The Other Half Lives: Studies Among the Tenements of New York* (New York: Charles Scribner's Sons, 1890), 33. Riis attempts to protect himself against accusations of callous irresponsibility. 'Afterward, when I came down to the street I told a friendly policeman of my trouble. For some reason he thought it rather a good joke, and laughed immoderately at my concern lest even then sparks should be burrowing in the rotten wall that might yet break out in flame and destroy the house with all that were in it. "Why, don't you know", he said, "that house is the Dirty Spoon? It caught fire six times last winter, but it wouldn't burn. The dirt was so thick on the walls, it smothered the fire!"'

74 Immanuel Kant, *Critique of the Power of Judgement* (1790, 1793), trans. Paul Guyer and Eric Matthews (Cambridge: Cambridge University Press, 2001), 144.

75 Jean-Jacques Rousseau, *Emile; or, On Education* (1762), trans. Christopher Kelly and Allan Bloom (Dartmouth, MA: University Press of New England, 2010), 80.

76 David E. Nye, *American Technological Sublime* (Cambridge, MA: MIT Press, 1994), 152.
77 Nye, *American Technological Sublime*, 144. See also David E. Nye, *Electrifying America: Social Meanings of New Technology, 1880–1940* (Cambridge, MA: MIT Press, 1990).
78 André Kertesz in conversation with Rupert Martin, 28 October 1982, quoted in Martin, *Floods of Light: Flash Photography 1851–1981* (London: Photographers' Gallery, 1982), 8.
79 Vladimir Nabokov, *Lolita* (1955; New York: Vintage Books, 1989), 10.
80 Susan Sontag, *On Photography* (New York: Picador, 1977), 81.
81 Walter Benjamin, *The Arcades Project*, trans. Howard Eiland and Kevin McLaughlin (Cambridge, MA: Harvard University Press, 1999), 462 [N2a,3].
82 Benjamin, *Arcades Project*, 473 [N9,7]. For a discussion of these passages from Benjamin in the context of modernism's—particularly filmic modernism's—preoccupation with the moment, see Leo Charney, 'In a Moment: Film and the Philosophy of Modernity', in Leo Charney and Vanessa R. Schwartz (eds.), *Cinema and the Invention of Modern Life* (Berkeley and Los Angeles: University of California Press, 1995), 282–5.
83 Eduardo Cadava, *Words of Light: Theses on the Photography of History* (Princeton: Princeton University Press, 1997), 21.
84 Anne Carson, *Autobiography of Red* (New York: Alfred A. Knopf, 1998), 146.
85 Emily Dickinson, *The Complete Poems* (London: Faber and Faber, 1970), 521–2.
86 Ken Kesey, *Sometimes a Great Notion* (1964; New York, Penguin, 2006), 286.
87 I am much indebted to Devin Griffiths for helping me understand the productive powers of incomplete or dysfunctional analogies. See his *The Age of Analogy: Science and Literature Between the Darwins* (Baltimore: Johns Hopkins University Press, 2016).

Chapter 3

1 Levy, *Romance of a Shop*, 84.
2 Levy, *Romance of a Shop*, 84.
3 Levy, *Romance of a Shop*, 86.
4 Levy, *Romance of a Shop*, 86.
5 Levy, *Romance of a Shop*, 87.
6 Levy, *Romance of a Shop*, 87.
7 Levy, *Romance of a Shop*, 86.
8 Levy, *Romance of a Shop*, 87.
9 Geoffrey Batchen, *Forget Me Not: Photography & Remembrance* (New York: Princeton Architectural Press, 2004). For deathbed photography, see also Audrey Linkman, *Photography and Death* (London: Reaktion Books, 2011), and Jay Ruby, *Secure the Shadow: Death and Photography in America* (Cambridge, MA: MIT Press, 1995).
10 Christian Metz, 'Photography and Fetish', *October* 34 (1985), 81–90.
11 See Helen Groth, *Victorian Photography and Literary Nostalgia* (Oxford: Oxford University Press, 2003).
12 William Wordsworth, '"I wandered lonely as a Cloud"' (1802), *Selected Poems*, ed. Stephen Gill (London: Penguin Classics, 2005), 164. Supposedly, the final two lines quoted here, among the most memorable in the poem, were given to Wordsworth by his wife Mary.
13 Nathaniel Parker Willis, *The Convalescent* (New York: Charles Scribner, 1859), 435. The *OED* mistakenly claims that the first use of 'photographic memory' dates from Willis's use of the phrase in *Life, Here and There: Sketches of Society and Adventure at Far-Apart Times and Places* (1850) but it is, in fact, to be found in this later work.

14 John Plumbe (1809–57) opened a string of daguerreotype studios across the eastern US (and in Paris and Liverpool) in the 1840s: he patented a lithographic method of making prints from dageurreotypes.

15 Nathaniel Parker Willis, *Life, Here and There: Or Sketches of Society and Adventure at Far-Apart Times and Places* (New York: Baker and Scribner, 1850), 341.

16 John William Draper, *Human Physiology* (1856; 7th edn., New York: Harper & Brothers, 1878), 269, quoted in Douwe Draaisma, *Metaphors of Memory: A History of Ideas about the Mind* (Cambridge: Cambridge University Press, 2001), 120.

17 Adolf Kussmaul, *Die Störungen der Sprache* (Leipzig: F. C. W. Vogel, 1877), 35; trans. and quoted in Draaisma, *Metaphors of Memory*, 122.

18 Jennifer Green-Lewis, 'Not Fading Away: Photography in the Age of Oblivion', *Nineteenth-Century Contexts* 22 (2001), 559–85: 564.

19 Green-Lewis, 'Not Fading Away', 569.

20 Milan Kundera, *Ignorance* (2000), trans. Linda Asher (New York: HarperCollins, 2002), 121.

21 Francis Galton, *Inquiries into Human Faculty and Its Development* (1883; London: J. M. Dent, 1911), 230.

22 Thomas De Quincey, *Confessions of An English Opium Eater and Other Writings*, ed. Grevel Lindop (Oxford: Oxford University Press, 1988), 144.

23 Marcel Proust, *In Search of Lost Time*, ii. *Within a Budding Grove* (1919), trans. C. K. Scott Moncrieff and Terence Kilmartin, rev. D. J. Enright (New York: Modern Library, 1992), 621–2.

24 Clare Dillon, 'Reinscribing De Quincey's Palimpsest: The Significance of the Palimpsest in Contemporary Literary and Cultural Studies', *Textual Practice* 19 (2005), 243–63: 252.

25 Siegfried Kracauer, 'Photography' (1927), *The Mass Ornament: Weimar Essays*, trans. and ed. Thomas Y. Levin (Cambridge, MA: Harvard University Press, 1995), 50.

26 Kracauer, 'Photography', 51.

27 Frances Power Cobbe, 'The Fallacies of Memory' (1866), *Hours of Work and Play* (Philadelphia: J. B. Lippincott, 1867), 87–116: 104.

28 Edmund Spenser, *The Yale Edition of the Shorter Poems of Edmund Spenser*, ed. William Oram, Einar Bjorvand, and Ronald Bond (New Haven: Yale University Press, 1989), 645.

29 Oscar Rejlander, 'An Apology for Art Photography', *British Journal of Photography* 10 (16 February 1863), 76–8: 76.

30 Given the painting's title, the work has also been read as evoking (despite the child) Charles Dickens's *Hard Times* (1853), in which Stephen Blackpool sits beside his dying wife. See Stephanie Spencer, O. G. *Rejlander: Photography as Art* (Ann Arbor: UMI Research Press, 1981), 82. Another non-composite image shows not only a dresser with empty drawers—all possessions have presumably been sold or pawned—but also some of Rejlander's own photographs tacked to the wall (Slide 30 of 97, http://www.luminous-lint.com/__phv_app.php?/p/Oscar_Gustave__Rejlander/, accessed 16 June 2017).

31 Robin Kelsey, *Photography and the Art of Chance* (Cambridge, MA: Harvard University Press, 2015), 138.

32 Levy, *Romance of a Shop*, 114.

33 Levy, *Romance of a Shop*, 93.

34 'The Magnesium Light', *Photographic News* (20 January 1865), 26.

35 *British Journal of Photography* (10 July 1891), 437. This item was referenced in 'Post-Mortem Photography', *American Journal of Photography* 12 (1891), 350.

36 'Photographing the Dead', repr. from the *Chicago News* in the *Milwaukee Daily Journal* (25 April 1888), 2.

37 Levy, *Romance of a Shop*, 179.
38 Levy, *Romance of a Shop*, 188.
39 Virginia Woolf, *The Voyage Out* (1915; Oxford: Oxford University Press, 2009), 427.
40 Marcel Proust, *Jean Santeuil*, preceded by *Les Plaisirs et les jours*, ed. Pierre Clarac and Yves Sandre (Paris: Bibliothèque de la Pléiade, 1971), 243; *Jean Santeuil*, trans. Gerard Hopkins, pref. André Maurois (London: Penguin Books, 1985), 40.
41 Alan K. Russell, *Rivals of Sherlock Holmes: Forty Six Stories of Crime and Detection from Original Illustrated Magazines* (Secaucus, NJ: Castle Books, 1981), 233.
42 See Ulrich Baer, 'Photography and Hysteria: Toward a Poetics of the Flash', *Spectral Evidence: The Photography of Trauma* (Cambridge, MA: MIT Press, 2002), 25–60. Baer's chapter is eloquent and insightful about the abstract properties of a flash, although with no clear evidence about how long the illumination provided by Charcot's '*lumière oxydrique très brillante*' (39) lasted, it is hard to know how to understand the sudden burst of light that transfixed and froze his patients. This is not to devalue, however, the remarks that Baer makes about the interruptive suddenness created by Charcot's lamp, and about the striking photographs that he includes in this chapter.
43 See Alison Winter, *Memory: Fragments of a Modern History* (Chicago: University of Chicago Press, 2012), 13–32.
44 The most extended and extremely thoughtful treatment of Grant Allen's *Recalled to Life* is by Anne Stiles, *Popular Fiction and Brain Science in the Late Nineteenth Century* (Cambridge: Cambridge University Press, 2012), 85–115. Chris Willis has written on Allen's treatment of divided consciousness in this work and *What's Bred in the Bone* (1891), and sets it in the context of late nineteenth- and early twentieth-century psychological theories. See 'The Detective's *Doppelgänger*: Conflicting States of Female Consciousness in Grant Allen's Detective Fiction', in William Greenslade and Terence Rodgers (eds.), *Grant Allen: Literature and Cultural Politics at the Fin de Siècle* (Farnham: Ashgate, 2005), 150–1. For Allen's life and career, see Peter Morton, *The Busiest Man in England': Grant Allen and the Writing Trade, 1875–1900* (New York: Palgrave, 2005).
45 For these details, and for an account of Marey's career as a whole, I'm indebted to Marta Braun, *Picturing Time: The Work of Etienne-Jules Marey (1830–1904)* (Chicago: University of Chicago Press, 1992), esp. 57.
46 The literature on Muybridge is copious: I've found particularly useful Phillip Prodger, *Time Stands Still: Muybridge and the Instantaneous Photography Movement* (Oxford: Oxford University Press, 2003), and Rebecca Solnit, *River of Shadows: Eadweard Muybridge and the Technological Wild West* (New York: Viking, 2004).
47 Worthington's earlier researches were illustrated by drawings: he used photography exclusively from 1894 onwards to record his results. Worthington's progress in recording the shapes formed by rapidly moving liquids is documented in *The Study of Splashes* (London: Longmans, Green and Co., 1908).
48 Worthington, *Study of Splashes*, 5.
49 Grant Allen, *Recalled to Life* (New York: Henry Holt and Co., 1891), 1.
50 Allen, *Recalled to Life*, 1.
51 Allen, *Recalled to Life*, 2.
52 Allen, *Recalled to Life*, 2–3.
53 Allen, *Recalled to Life*, 4–5.
54 Allen, *Recalled to Life*, 5.

55 Grant Allen, 'A Thinking Machine', *Gentleman's Magazine* 260 (1886), 30–41: 30. As Stiles explains, Allen shared his mechanical, brain-based view of human consciousness with other prominent scientists of his day, including Thomas Henry Huxley, William Kingdon Clifford, and Shadworth Hodgson, *Popular Fiction*, 86. For specific consideration of the analogy between the telegraph and the mind, see Laura Otis, 'The Metaphoric Circuit: Organic and Technological Communication in the Nineteenth Century', *Journal of the History of Ideas* 63/1 (2002), 105–28.

56 Allen, *Recalled to Life*, 21.

57 Allen, *Recalled to Life*, 26. In a later chapter, Allen describes Mr Callingham having taken photographs not just of horses trotting, but also of an athletic meeting—a flat race seen from the front, a high jumper, a hammer thrower—all very Muybridge.

58 Allen, *Recalled to Life*, 26.

59 Allen, *Recalled to Life*, 77.

60 Allen, *Recalled to Life*, 156.

61 Allen, *Recalled to Life*, 158–9.

62 Allen, *Recalled to Life*, 173.

63 Allen, *Recalled to Life*, 204.

64 Allen, *Recalled to Life*, 213.

65 Allen, *Recalled to Life*, 215.

66 Unsigned and untitled review, *American Journal of Photography* 13 (May 1892), 149.

67 Stiles, *Popular Fiction*, 107. All the same, as Stiles points out, Allen's attempt to equate his heroine with a camera mechanism only partly succeeds, because of the affective register of his prose. 'Due to the novel's subtle equation between photographic registration and traumatic shock, the reader is left with a haunting memory of Una's feelings of loss, rather than an objective view of her mental "machinery" at work. No matter how relentlessly Allen compares Una to a photographic apparatus, one cannot help feeling that her intense psychological pain is *not* equivalent to the creaking of a rusty wheel', 90–1.

68 Grant Allen, *Physiological Aesthetics* (New York: D. Appleton and Co., 1877), 200.

69 Vladimir Nabokov, *Speak, Memory: An Autobiography Revisited* (1966; London: Penguin Modern Classics, 2000), 6.

70 Hugo Münsterberg, *The Photoplay: A Psychological Study* (New York: D. Appleton and Company, 1916), 64.

71 Prodger, *Time Stands Still*, 154.

72 For an extensive treatment of the history and function of flashbacks in film, see Maureen Turim, *Flashbacks in Film: Memory & History* (New York: Routledge, 1989).

73 Turim, *Flashbacks*, 4.

74 Epes Winthrop Sargent, *The Technique of the Photoplay* (2nd edn., New York: Moving Picture World, 1913), 14, 16.

75 Catherine Carr, *The Art of Photoplay Writing* (New York: Hannis Jordan Co., 1914), 34. See also Eustace Hale Bell, *The Art of the Photoplay* (New York: G. W. Dillingham, 1913); Arthur Winfield Thomas, *How to Write a Photoplay* (Chicago: Photoplaywrights Association of America, 1914).

76 Captain Leslie T. Peacocke, *Hints on Photoplay Writing* (Chicago: Photoplay Publishing Co., 1916), 141–2.

77 Glenn Erickson has hypothesized that the whole 'flashback' sequence was in fact imposed on a film that 'wasn't working'. See 'It's a Wonderful Life:—or It's a Wonderful Recut?', http://www.dvdtalk.com/dvdsavant/s55wonderful.html, accessed 28 December 2010.

78 Roger Brown and James Kulik, 'Flashbulb Memories', *Cognition* 5 (1977), 73–99. Although Brown and Kulik's methods and conclusions have been much discussed, their terminology has proved enduring. For a comprehensive engagement with these debates, see Eugene Winograd and Ulric Neisser (eds.), *Affect and Accuracy in Recall: Studies of 'Flashbulb' Memories*, Emory Symposia in Cognition (Cambridge: Cambridge University Press, 2006), esp. the concluding essay (written after the 1990 conference at which almost all these papers were first delivered), William F. Brewer, 'The Theoretical and Empirical Status of the Flashbulb Memory Hypothesis', 274–305. For an excellent analysis of the place that controversies around 'flashbulb memories' had in the 'memory wars' of the late 1980s, see Winter, *Memory*, 157–78.

79 Brown and Kulik, 'Flashbulb Memories', 74.

80 Melissa Pierson, *The Place You Love Is Gone* (New York: W. W. Norton, 2006), 29.

81 Ulric Neisser, 'Snapshots or Benchmarks?', in Ulric Neisser and Ira Hyman (eds.), *Memory Observed: Remembering in Natural Contexts* (San Francisco: W. H. Freeman and Co., 1982), 43–8.

82 Charles Fernyhough, *Pieces of Light: How the New Science of Memory Illuminates the Stories We Tell About Our Pasts* (New York: Harper, 2013), 203.

83 Barbie Zeliger, 'The Voice of the Visual in Memory', in K. R. Phillips (ed.), *Framing Public Memory* (Tuscaloosa, AL: University of Alabama Press, 2004), 157–86: 158.

84 Eric Gregory, 'Flash Memory', *Encyclopædia Britannica*. http://www.britannica.com/technology/flash-memory, accessed 18 March 2016.

85 Barthes, *Camera Lucida*, 91.

Chapter 4

1 William Henry Fox Talbot to Michael Faraday, 15 June 1851, *The Correspondence of Michael Faraday*, ed. Frank A. J. L. James, iv (London: Institution of Engineering and Technology, 1999), 310. The reply from Faraday indicated that Fox Talbot very probably used a concave mirror to better focus the bright light. Pierre Bron and Philip L. Condax, in their detailed analysis of this experiment, debunk various of the myths that have grown up surrounding it (such as the belief that the 'printed paper' was a sheet of *The Times*), and suggest that the battery used was most likely the huge, room-sized electrical battery that was located in the basement of the Royal Institution. See Pierre Bron and Philip L. Condax, *The Photographic Flash: A Concise Illustrated History* (Allschwil: Bron Elektronik, 1998), 12–21. Unfortunately, the glass plate used in the experiment has not survived. See also Gail Buckland, *Fox Talbot and the Invention of Photography* (London: Scholar Press, 1980), 107–18.

2 Jacob Riis, *The Children of the Poor* (New York: Charles Scribner's Sons, 1908), 109.

3 Sir Charles Wheatstone, 'An Account of Some Experiments to Measure the Velocity of Electricity and the Duration of Electric Light', *Philosophical Transactions of the Royal Society* (1834), repr. in *The Scientific Papers of Sir Charles Wheatstone* (London: Physical Society, 1879), 95–6.

4 Particularly useful in the discussion of the photography of moving objects in relation to the production of knowledge is Josh Ellenbogen, *Reasoned and Unreasoned Images: The Photography of Bertillon, Galton, and Marey* (University Park, PA: Pennsylvania State University Press, 2012).

5 Philip Brookman, 'Helios: Eadweard Muybridge in a Time of Change', in Brookman, *Eadweard Muybridge* (London: Tate Publishing, 2010), 24.

6 Sue Zemka, *Time and the Moment in Victorian Literature and Society* (Cambridge: Cambridge University Press, 2012), 2.

7 Martha Rosler, in Sarah Thornton, *33 Artists in 3 Acts* (New York: W. W. Norton & Co., 2014), 99.

8 William Prynne, *God No Impostor Nor Deluder* (London: Elizabeth Allde, 1630), 13.

9 Leo Charney, 'In a Moment: Film and the Philosophy of Modernity', in Charney and Vanessa R. Schwartz (eds.), *Cinema and the Invention of Modern Life* (Berkeley and Los Angeles: University of California Press, 1995), 279; Georg Simmel, 'The Metropolis and Mental Life', in *The Sociology of Georg Simmel*, ed. Kurt Wolff, trans. H. H. Gerth (1903; New York: Free Press, 1950), 410.

10 'Experimentelle Studien über das Sehen von Bewegung', *Zeitschrift für Psychologie* 61 (1912), 161–265.

11 Peter O. K. Krehl, *History of Shock Waves, Explosions, and Impact* (New York: Springer, 2009) provides, in an encyclopedic format, a huge amount of information about the use of flash photography in this area of physics. See also Robert S. Cohen and Raymond J. Seeger (eds.), *Ernst Mach: Physicist and Philosopher* (Boston Studies in the Philosophy and History of Science; New York: Springer, 1975), and Christoph Hoffmann, 'Mach-Werke', *Fotogeschichte* 60 (1996), 3–18. As Bron and Condax point out, when chronicling a number of scientists across Europe who worked with spark photography in the late nineteenth and early twentieth centuries, few images and records are apparently extant, and it's more than possible, because of military secrecy, that there were other workers in the field whose contributions they have failed to trace. *Photographic Flash*, 29–34.

12 For a clear description of the process, see 'Photography by the Electric Spark', *Dublin Review* 109 (1891), 420–1. Also see Simon Schaffer, 'A Science Whose Business is Bursting: Soap Bubbles as Commodities in Classical Physics', in Lorraine Daston (ed.), *Things That Talk: Object Lessons from Art and Science* (New York: Zone Books, 2004), 147–92.

13 [C. V. Boys], 'On Electric Spark Photographs; Or, Photography of Flying Bullets, &c. by the Light of the Electric Spark. I', *Nature* 47 (2 March 1893), 415.

14 Walter Benjamin, 'A Short History of Photography' (1931), trans. Stanley Mitchell, *Screen* 13/1 (1972), 5–26: 7. Rosalind Krauss's elaboration of this principle has been particularly influential: see Krauss, *The Optical Unconscious* (Cambridge, MA: MIT Press, 1993).

15 [C. V. Boys], 'On Electric Spark Photographs; Or, Photography of Flying Bullets, &c. by the Light of the Electric Spark. II', *Nature*, 47 (9 March 1893), 446.

16 Boys, 'Electric Spark Photographs I', 415–16. There is no indication as to whether or not Smith or Boys knew of Marey's more successful experiments in photographing a falling cat in 1890.

17 Kelley Wilder, *Photography and Science* (London: Reaktion Books, 2009), 7–8.

18 In the Preface to *Objectivity*, Daston and Galison use Worthington's experiments to provide a paradigmatic distinction between the desired objectivity of a human eye and what is achievable through mechanical means. Lorraine J. Daston and Peter Galison, *Objectivity* (2007; New York: Zone Books, 2010), 11–16: 11.

19 The literature on Edgerton is considerable. See esp. Roger Bruce, *Seeing the Unseen: Dr. Edgerton and the Wonders of Strobe Alley* (Rochester, NY: Publishing Trust of George Eastman House, 1994). Harold Edgerton's own publications are indispensable, especially *Flash! Seeing the Unseen by Ultra High-Speed Photography* (with James R. Killian, 1939; 2nd edn., 1954), in which, notably, a photograph of a golf club hitting a ball is replaced with one of a nuclear explosion; *Electronic Flash, Strobe* (with James R. Killian, 1970); *Moments of Vision* (1979), and *Stopping Time* (conceived by Gus Kayafas, foreword by Edgerton, 1987).

20 Unsigned article, 'Speaking of Pictures…These Culminate 70 Years of High-Speed Photography', *Life* (27 October 1941), 13.
21 See James Elkins, 'Harold Edgerton's Rapatronic Photographs of Atomic Tests', *History of Photography* 28/1 (2004), 74–81.
22 Genevieve Wanucha, 'Remembering "Papa Flash"', *MIT News* (4 January 2013), http://web.mit.edu/newsoffice/2013/remembering-harold-edgerton.html, accessed 28 June 2013.
23 From the PBS special presentation, *Edgerton and his Incredible Seeing Machines*, originally broadcast 15 January 1985.
24 Controversial, that is, because of the show's location in MOMA, and the complaint voiced by some contemporary critics that photography had no business to be displayed in a building that also showed paintings.
25 Geoffrey Batchen, *Each Wild Idea: Writing, Photography, History* (Cambridge, MA: MIT Press, 2001), 125.
26 Quoted Kayafas, *Stopping Time*, 12.
27 Berenice Abbott, whilst best known for her studies of New York streets and buildings, also worked as a science photographer, designing and building her own apparatuses with which to take high-speed photographs. The stroboscopic image of a bouncing golf ball became extremely well known, since it appeared on the cover of a standard physics textbook. For Abbott's science work, see 'Photophysics', ch. 5 in Terri Weissman, *The Realisms of Berenice Abbott* (Berkeley and Los Angeles: University of California Press, 2011), 171–208.
28 Kris Belden-Adams, 'Harold Edgerton and Complications of the "Photographic Instant"', *Frame: a journal of visual and material culture* 1 (spring 2011), 96–107: 107.
29 Charles Sanders Peirce, *Collected Papers of Charles Sanders Peirce*, ed. Charles Hartstone and Paul Weiss (Cambridge, MA: Harvard University Press, 1932), 267. Other uses of the term 'instantaneous photograph' in his writing would suggest that he has the snapshot in mind, rather than a split-second image, but the general principle remains the same.
30 Thierry de Duve, 'Time Exposure and Snapshot: The Photograph as Paradox', *October* 5 (summer 1978), 113–25: 115.
31 David Brewster, 'On the Influence of Successive Impulses of Light Upon the Retina', *London and Edinburgh Philosophical Magazine and Journal of Science* 4 (1834), 241–2. For these references, and for a superb general overview of strobe experimentation into visionary and extreme experiences, I'm indebted to Jimena Canales, '"A Number of Scenes in a Badly Cut Film": Observation in the Age of Strobe', in Lorraine Daston and Elizabeth Lundeck (eds.), *Histories of Scientific Observation* (Chicago: University of Chicago Press, 2011), 230–54.
32 Canales, 'Observation in the Age of Strobe', 232–3.
33 Canales, 'Observation in the Age of Strobe', 237.
34 Aldous Huxley, *The Doors of Perception* and *Heaven and Hell* (1954; 1956; New York, Harper Perennial, 2009), 146.
35 For the history of the government's involvement with LSD testing, and the history of LSD more generally, see Martin A. Lee and Bruce Shlain, *Acid Dreams: The Complete Social History of LSD: The CIA, the Sixties, and Beyond* (rev. edn., New York: Grove Press, 1994).
36 Tom Wolfe, *The Electric Kool-Aid Acid Test* (1968; New York: Bantam Books, 1999), 415.
37 Tim Adams, quoting Tom Wolfe, 'Dances with Wolfe', *The Observer* (19 January 2008), http://www.guardian.co.uk/books/2008/jan/20/fiction.tomwolfe, accessed 4 July 2013.
38 Carol Brightman, *Sweet Chaos: The Grateful Dead's American Adventure* (New York: Gallery Books, 1999), 14.

39 Brightman, *Sweet Chaos*, 36.
40 Brightman, *Sweet Chaos*, 52.
41 Wolfe, *Acid Test*, 192.
42 Wolfe, *Acid Test*, 30.
43 Wolfe, *Acid Test*, 39.
44 Wolfe, *Acid Test*, 127.
45 Wolfe, *Acid Test*, 205.
46 Wolfe, *Acid Test*, 241.
47 John Geiger, *Chapel of Extreme Experience: A Short History of Stroboscopic Light and the Dream Machine* (Brooklyn, NY: Soft Skull Press, 2003), 5. Another significant use of the rapid flash within experimental art—so rapid and continuous that 'flicker' was the preferred term—came with the production in the 1960s of 'flicker' movies. These—classic examples would be Peter Kubelka's *Arnulf Rainer* (1960) and Tony Conrad's *The Flicker* (1966)—showed rapidly oscillating black-and-white frames (for anywhere between four and sixteen or so minutes), which create a strobe effect of illusory colour and lacy patterns. See P. Adams Sitney's classic essay, 'Structural Film', *Film Culture* 47 (Summer 1969), 1–10 (rev. 1970, 1974, and 1979); Nicky Hamlyn, 'Peter Kubelka's *Arnulf Rainer*', in Alexander Graf and Dietrich Scheunemann (eds.), *Avant-Garde Film* (Avant Garde Critical Studies 23; Amsterdam: Rodopi, 2007), 249–60, and Juan A. Suárez, 'Structural Film: Noise', in Karen Beckman and Jean Ma (eds.), *Still Moving: Between Cinema and Photography* (Durham, NC: Duke University Press, 2008), 62–89.
48 Wolfe, *Acid Test*, 241.
49 See further Norman Hathaway and Dan Nadel, *Electrical Banana: Masters of Psychedelic Art* (Bologna: Damiani, 2012); Ken Johnson, *Are You Experienced? How Psychedelic Consciousness Transformed Modern Art* (New York: Prestel, 2011); David Rubin (ed.), *Psychedelic: Optical and Visionary Art since the 1960s* (Cambridge, MA: MIT Press, 2010).
50 Albert Rosenfeld, 'A Remarkable Mind Drug Suddenly Spells Danger: LSD', *Life* 25 (March 1966), 28–33.
51 Wolfe, *Acid Test*, 284.
52 Wolfe, *Acid Test*, 43.
53 Walter Pater, *Studies in the History of the Renaissance* (1873; Oxford: Oxford University Press, 2010), 119–21.
54 'Cioè si tratta di trovare una forma che sia l'espressione di questo nuovo assoluto: *la velocità*, che un vero temperamento modern non può trascurare.' Umberto Boccioni, 'Moto assoluto e moto relative', *Pittura e scultura futuriste*, ed. Zeno Birolli (Milan: SE. Saggi e documenti del novecento, 1997), 91.
55 This was the connotation carried, too, by the 'flash press' of the early 1840s in America—the name coming from the genre-setting *Sunday Flash* (1841–3)—which 'aimed to entertain and enlighten literate sporting men about leisure-time activities and erotic entertainments available in New York'. Patricia Cline Cohen, Timothy J. Gilfoyle, and Helen Lefkowitz Horowitz in association with the American Antiquarian Society, *The Flash Press: Sporting Male Weeklies in 1840s New York* (Chicago: University of Chicago Press, 2008), 1.
56 *The Slang Dictionary, Etymological, Historical, and Anecdotal* (2nd edn., London: Chatto and Windus, 1874), 163–4. For a slightly earlier set of dissolute associations, see Gregory Dart, '"Flash Style": Pierce Egan and Literary London, 1820–1828', *History Workshop Journal* 51 (2001), 181–205.
57 Terry King, 'Coming to Terms with Tightrope Time: Three Decades of Heroes and Villains in the Australian Comic Strip', in Toby Burrows and Grant Stone (eds.), *Comics in Australia*

and New Zealand: The Collections, the Collectors, the Creators (New York: Haworth Press, 1994), 41–56: 42.

58 Grandmaster Flash and David Ritz, *The Adventures of Grandmaster Flash: My Life, My Beats* (New York: Crown Archetype, 2006), 163.

59 http://www.dccomics.com/characters/the-flash, accessed 6 July 2013.

60 Wolfe, *Acid Test*, 114.

61 Westbrook Pegler, quoted in Morton Sontheimer, *Newspaperman: A Book about the Business* (New York: Whittlesey House, 1941), 56.

62 Anne Duran, 'Flash Mobs: Social Influence in the 21st Century', *Social Influence* 1/4 (2006), 301–15: 301.

63 Duran, 'Flash Mobs', 302.

64 http://improveverywhere.com/2006/08/19/slo-mo-home-depot/, accessed 16 June 2017. For Improv Everywhere's 'missions', see Charlie Todd and Alex Scordelis, *Causing a Scene: Extraordinary Pranks in Ordinary Places with Improv Everywhere* (New York: Harper Collins, 2009).

65 See http://improveverywhere.com/2008/01/31/frozen-grand-central/, accessed 6 July 2013.

66 [Rowland E. Prothero], 'The Tales of Rudyard Kipling', *Edinburgh Review* 174 (July 1891), 137.

67 Declan Burke, 'Flash Fiction: "Intense, urgent and a little explosive"', *Irish Times*, 26 October 2011, http://www.irishtimes.com/culture/books/flash-fiction-intense-urgent-and-a-little-explosive-1.631904, accessed 25 March 2016.

68 Alison Wells, 'Why Flash Fiction Will Last', 3 June 2011, http://www.writing.ie/guest-blogs/why-flash-fiction-will-last/, accessed 6 July 2013.

69 A video on David Kohn's website gives a sub-two-minute, time-lapse photography version of the three-day build: http://www.davidkohn.co.uk/projects/selected/flash/, accessed 7 July 2013.

70 In 2011, incidentally, Tom Dixon completed his design for the new restaurant at the Royal Academy, which included long arrays of perforated Etch lamps by way of lighting, looking like expanded, simplified disco balls, and made—where else?—under the auspices of Milan's design project, Flash Factory.

71 Simon Reynolds, *Energy Flash: A Journey Through Rave Music and Dance Culture* (Berkeley: Soft Skull Press, 2012), 39 (quoting Louise Gray), and 112.

72 Tim Lawrence, *Love Saves the Day: A History of American Dance Music Culture* (Durham, NC: Duke University Press, 2004), 36.

73 Martin Amis, *London Fields* (1989; New York: Alfred A. Knopf, 2014), 53.

74 Shinichi Maruyama, artist's statement, http://www.shinichimaruyama.com/statement, accessed 9 July 2013.

75 See Al Miner and Yoav Rinon, *Ori Gersht, History Repeating* (Boston: Museum of Fine Art Publications, 2012).

76 Eliasson's *Model for a Timeless Garden* is best appreciated when seen in motion: http://olafureliasson.net/archive/artwork/WEK100033/model-for-a-timeless-garden, accessed 29 January 2017.

77 Norman Bryson, 'Hiroshi Sugimoto's Metabolic Photography', in Nicole Coolidge Rousmanière and William Jeffett (eds.), *Hiroshi Sugimoto* (Norwich: Sainsbury Centre for Visual Arts, 1997), 31–3: 31.

78 Bryson, 'Sugimoto', 33.

79 Hiroshi Sugimoto, artist's statement on website, http://www.sugimotohiroshi.com/theater.html, accessed 9 July 2013.

80 See e.g. JWD, writing on the gallery website for C4 Contemporary Art, http://www.c4gallery.com/artist/database/hiroshi-sugimoto/movie-theatres-theaters/hiroshi-sugimoto-movie-theatres-theaters.html, accessed 9 July 2013.

81 Peter Hay Halbert, 'The Blank Screens of Hiroshi Sugimoto', in Concha Gómez (ed.), *Sugimoto* (Barcelona: Fundacion la Caixa de Pensiones, 1998), 22–7: 26. Originally published in *Artpress* 196 (November 1994).

82 Hans Belting, *Looking through Duchamp's Door: Art and Perspective in the Work of Duchamp. Sugimoto. Jeff Wall* (Cologne: Walther König, 2010), 92, and see also Belting, 'The Theater of Illusion', in *Hiroshi Sugimoto: Theaters* (New York: Sonnabend Sundell Editions, 2000), 1–7. On the importance of slowness in relation to Sugimoto's theatres, see Lutz Koepnick, *On Slowness: Toward an Aesthetic of the Contemporary* (New York: Columbia University Press, 2014), 58–65.

83 Hiroshi Sugimoto, in interview. Helena Tatay Huici, 'Conversación con Hiroshi Sugimoto/A Conversation with Hiroshi Sugimoto', in Gómez (ed.), *Sugimoto*, 10–2: 16.

Chapter 5

1 Lewis Hine to Elizabeth McCausland, 23 October 1938, *Photo Story: Selected Letters and Photographs of Lewis W. Hine*, ed. Daile Kaplan (Washington, DC: Smithsonian Institution Press, 1992), 127.

2 Unsigned article [Jacob Riis], 'Flashes from the Slums', *New York Sun* (12 February 1888), 10. For Riis and his departures from traditions of writing about slum poverty, see Gandal, *Virtues of the Vicious*, esp. 27–38.

3 Jacob Riis, *The Children of the Poor* (1892; New York: Charles Scribner's Sons, 1908), 41.

4 Riis, *Making of an American*, 423, 439.

5 Lewis Fried, *Makers of the City: Jacob Riis, Lewis Mumford, James T. Farrell, and Paul Goodman* (Amherst, MA: University of Massachusetts Press, 1990), 31.

6 For Riis and his engagement with ideology of the Social Gospel, see Gregory S. Jackson, 'Cultivating Spiritual Sight: Jacob Riis's Virtual-Tour Narrative and the Visual Modernization of Protestant Homiletics', *Representations* 83 (summer 2003), 126–66.

7 Bonnie Yochelson, 'Jacob A, Riis, Photographer "After a Fashion"', in Yochelson and Czitrom, *Rediscovering Jacob Riis*, 147.

8 Maren Stange, *Symbols of Ideal Life: Social Documentary Photography in America* (New York: Cambridge University Press, 1989), 12. For a thorough study of visual journalism between 1866 and 1889—the period that formed the visual culture into which Riis's images were received—see Joshua Brown, *Beyond the Lines: Pictorial Reporting, Everyday Life, and the Crisis of Gilded Age America* (Berkeley and Los Angeles: University of California Press), 2006.

9 Yochelson and Czitrom, *Rediscovering Jacob Riis*, 219–23 discusses Riis's imitators and those who co-opted his images.

10 Unsigned piece, 'Novel Exhibition of Instantaneous Photographs made by Magnesium Flash Light', *Photographic Times and American Photographer* 18 (17 February 1888), 81.

11 Publishers' Preface, Helen Campbell, *Darkness and Daylight, or, Lights and Shadows of New York Life* (New York: A. D. Worthington, 1891), p. ix.

12 For a good recent discussion of the politics of documentary in relation to Riis, see Christopher Carter, *Rhetorical Exposure: Confrontation and Contradiction in US Social Documentary Photography* (Tuscaloosa, AL: University of Alabama Press, 2015), 16–45.

13 Hales, *Silver Cities*, 314–15.

14 Robin Kelsey, *Photography and the Art of Chance* (Cambridge, MA: Belknap Press of Harvard University Press, 2015), 81.

15 I'm building on comments made by Martha Rosler in relation to Lee Friedlander's documentary work, in 'Lee Friedlander, an Exemplary Modern Photographer' (originally published as 'Lee Friedlander's Guarded Strategies', *Artforum* 13/8 (April 1975)), *Decoys and Disruptions: Selected Writings, 1975–2003* (Cambridge, MA: MIT Press, 2004), 113–31: 115.

16 James Elkins, *What Photography Is* (New York: Routledge, 2000), 116–17.

17 William Chapman Sharpe, *New York Nocturne: The City After Dark in Literature, Painting, and Photography* (Princeton: Princeton University Press, 2008), 150.

18 Virginia Woolf, *Three Guineas* (1938), *A Room of One's Own* and *Three Guineas*. (Oxford World's Classics; Oxford: Oxford University Press, 2015), 96.

19 Lewis W. Hine, 'Social Photography: How the Camera May Help in the Social Uplift', in Alexander Johnson (ed.), *Proceedings of the National Conference of Charities and Correction at the Thirty-Sixth Annual Session Held in the City of Buffalo, New York, June 9–16, 1909* (Fort Wayne, IN: Press of Fort Wayne, 1909), 355–9.

20 Kate Sampsell-Willmann, *Lewis Hine as Social Critic* (Jackson, MS: University Press of Mississippi, 2009), 53. In relation to Hine's work, I've also found especially useful Judith Mara Gutman, *Lewis Hine and the American Social Conscience* (New York: Walker, 1967); Alexander Nemerov, *Soulmaker: The Times of Lewis Hine* (Princeton: Princeton University Press, 2016); Maren Stange, 'The Pittsburgh Survey: Lewis Hine and the Establishment of Documentary Style', in *Symbols of Ideal Life: Social Documentary Photography in America* (Cambridge: Cambridge University Press, 1989), 47–87.

21 This is not to say, however, that his captions were always accurate. Peter Seixas, following Jonathan Doherty, makes the point that sometimes Hine wrote captions for different occasions indicating different national origins for the same person. Notably, he often gave the names of his subjects, thereby bestowing individuality rather than typicality. However, as Seixas also shows, this practice was not uncontroversial: Margaret Byington, one of his co-workers on the pioneering Pittsburgh Survey (1908–9), thought that publishing names was a breach of trust and privacy. Peter Seixas, 'Lewis Hine: From "Social" to "Interpretive" Photographer', *American Quarterly* 39/3 (Autumn 1987), 381–409: 389, 386.

22 I here build on the reading given by Judith Mara Gutman, *Lewis W. Hine 1874–1940: Two Perspectives* (New York: Grossman Publishers, 1974), 43.

23 For Jessie Tarbox Beals's experiences at the St Louis World's Fair in 1904, see Laura Wexler, *Tender Violence: Domestic Visions in an Age of U.S. Imperialism* (Chapel Hill, NC: University of North Carolina Press, 2000), 269–90. For Beals more generally, see Alexander Alland, Sr., *Jessie Tarbox Beals: First Woman News Photographer* (New York: Camera/Graphic Press, 1978).

24 This photograph appeared in the *New York American and Journal*, 15 March 1903: the way that the lighting falls certainly suggests that Beals used flash here.

25 Christine Stansell, *American Moderns: Bohemian New York and the Creation of a New Century* (New York: Metropolitan Books, 2000).

26 Martha Grossman, 'America's Bohemia', *McCall's Magazine* (July 1917), 26–7, 82: 26.

27 Quoted in Alland, *Beals*, 76.

28 C. Grand Pierre, *The Little Book of Greenwich Village* (New York: C. Grand Pierre, 1935), 14.

29 Stansell, *American Moderns*, 335.

30 At least, she makes no mention of it in the contents in the boxes of Jessie Tarbox Beals papers held in the Schlesinger Library, Radcliffe Institute, Harvard University, except in advertisements for her portrait studio.

31 Miles Orvell, 'Portrait of the Photographer as a Young Man: John Vachon and the FSA Project', in Townsend Ludington (ed.), *A Modern Mosaic. Art and Modernism in the United States* (Chapel Hill, NC: University of North Carolina Press, 2000), 306–33: 307. There is an extensive literature on photography and the FSA. Among the studies that I have found most useful are Cara A. Finnegan, *Picturing Poverty: Print Culture and FSA Photographs* (Washington, DC: Smithsonian Books, 2003); Finnegan, ch. 4 of *Making Photography Matter: A Viewer's History from the Civil War to the Great Depression* (Urbana, IL: University of Illinois Press, 2015), 125–75; Carl Fleischhauer and Beverly W. Brannan (eds.), *Documenting America, 1935–1943* (Berkeley and Los Angeles: UP of California in association with the Library of Congress, 1988); James Guimond, *American Photography and the American Dream* (Chapel Hill, NC: University of North Carolina Press, 1991); F. Jack Hurley, *Portrait of a Decade: Roy Stryker and the Development of Documentary Photography in the Thirties* (Baton Rouge, LA: Louisiana State University Press, 1972); Gilles Mora and Beverly W. Brannan, *FSA: The American Vision* (New York: Abrams, 2006); Karin Becker Ohrn, *Dorothea Lange and the Documentary Tradition* (Baton Rouge, LA: Louisiana State University Press, 1980); Hank O'Neal, *A Vision Shared: A Classic Portrait of America and Its People, 1935–1943* (New York: St Martin's Press, 1976); David P. Peeler, *Hope Among Us Yet: Social Criticism and Social Solace in Depression America* (Athens, GA: University of Georgia Press, 1987), 58–109; and, reaching beyond the FSA, Pete Daniel, Merry A. Foresta, Maren Stange, and Sally Stein, *Official Images: New Deal Photography* (Washington, DC: Smithsonian Institution Press, 1987; David M. Kennedy, *Freedom from Fear: The American People in Depression and War, 1929–1945* (New York: Oxford University Press, 1999).

32 These images are all now accessible online, at http://www.loc.gov/pictures/collection/fsa/background.html. In total, the collection consists of about 175,000 black-and-white film negatives and transparencies, 1,610 colour transparencies, and around 107,000 black-and-white photographic prints, most of which were made from the negatives and transparencies.

33 Alan Trachtenberg, 'From Image to Story: Reading the File', in Fleischhauer and Brannan (eds.), *Documenting America*, 43–73: 57.

34 James Agee and Walker Evans, *Let Us Now Praise Famous Men* (1941; Boston: Houghton Mifflin Co., 1960), 172. (The image—not in the book—is FSA LC-USF342-T01-008136-A.) James Curtis draws our attention to this reversed mirror in *Mind's Eye, Mind's Truth: FSA Photography Reconsidered* (Philadelphia: Temple University Press, 1989), 38–9.

35 Arthur Rothstein to Roy Stryker, 23 September 1939: Stryker Pares. Quoted in Stephen J. Leonard, *Trials and Triumphs: A Colorado Portrait of the Great Depression* (Boulder, CO: University Press of Colorado, 1993), 130.

36 Roy Stryker to Marion Post Wolcott, 18 May 1939, quoted in Paul Hendrickson, *Looking for the Light: The Hidden Life and Art of Marion Post Wolcott* (New York: Knopf, 1992), 148.

37 John Vachon to Penny Vachon, 29 and 26 October 1938, in Miles Orvell, *John Vachon's America: Photographs and Letters from the Depression to World War Two* (Berkeley and Los Angeles: University of California Press, 2003), 146, 142.

38 John Vachon to Penny Vachon, 5 November 1938, in Orvell, *John Vachon's America*, 151.

39 John Vachon to Penny Vachon, 6 November 1938, in Orvell, *John Vachon's America*, 152. All three shots would seem to have been unacceptable—at least, none resembling them appear in the FSA Archive.

40 John Vachon to Penny Vachon, 12 July 1940, in Orvell, *John Vachon's America*, 165.

41 Sontag, *On Photography*, 6.

42 Roy Stryker, quoted by Linda Gordon, 'Dorothea Lange Photographs the Japanese American Internment', in Linda Gordon and Gary Y. Okihiro (eds.), *Impounded: Dorothea Lange and the Censored Images of Japanese American Internment* (New York: W. W. Norton & Co., 2006), 24. Gordon claims this is from the interview that Richard Doud did with Stryker that is held in the Archives of American Art, Smithsonian Institution; however, I cannot locate it in the Stryker transcript.

43 Richard Doud, Oral History Interview with Ben Shahn, 14 April 1964, Archives of American Art, Smithsonian Institution, https://www.aaa.si.edu/collections/interviews/oral-history-interview-ben-shahn-12760. Shahn did not remain an utter purist, though that angled viewfinder was to cause him some problems with flash. Jack Delano recounted: 'Incidentally, there is a hilarious story about Ben Shahn and this right-angle finder; I don't know whether anybody ever told you, but we all knew about it. When flashbulbs first came into use Ben wouldn't have anything to do with them; they were terrible; this was an invention of the devil, you know; beautiful light is the most wonderful thing, you don't need any of that stuff. But somebody finally convinced him to try it. "After all, there were certain areas in which it might be very useful." So Ben said, "Okay." And they got him a flash attachment for his Leica and he put the flash bulb in, and of course he had this right-angle finder on it, and he pressed the button and the bulb went up right in his face.' Richard Doud, Oral History Interview with Jack and Irene Delano, 12 June 1965, Archives of American Art, Smithsonian Institution, https://www.aaa.si.edu/collections/interviews/oral-history-interview-jack-and-irene-delano-13026.

44 Doud, Oral History Interview with Ben Shahn, 14 April 1964. This position was slightly reframed by Richard Doud two weeks later, when he was interviewing John Vachon. Vachon recounted the prevalent attitude among FSA photographers 'that photographs should never be fake, and that we only take the real thing, we don't doctor things up, make people do what they're really not doing' (Doud, Oral History Interview with John Vachon, 28 April 1964, Archives of American Art, Smithsonian Institution, https://www.aaa.si.edu/collections/interviews/oral-history-interview-john-vachon-11830). This is an approach, he said, that he had carried forward into the work that he did for the news picture magazine *Life*. 'A purist approach, perhaps, to photography then', Doud states.
JOHN VACHON: Is that the word? I don't know.
RICHARD DOUD: I'm not sure that's the right word, but I know Shahn was saying he had this attitude, and he couldn't even reconcile himself to the use of flash. It was almost immoral, he thought, at the time, to use flash, because you were actually photographing things that you would not have seen, you see, and in this sense he was a purist there.'

45 Ben Shahn, 'Interior of strawberry grower's house, Hammond, Louisiana', October 1935, LC-USF33-006176-M3.

46 John Tagg, *The Disciplinary Frame: Photographic Truths and the Capture of Meaning* (Minneapolis: University of Minnesota Press, 2009), 60.

47 John Vachon to Penny Vachon, 28 February 1942, in Orvell, *John Vachon's America*, 192.

48 Vicki Goldberg, *Margaret Bourke-White: A Biography* (New York: Harper & Row, 1986), 192. Stryker had, indeed, used a number of Bourke-White's pictures in a reissue of his 1924 co-authored textbook: Thomas Munro, Roy E. Stryker, and Rexford Guy Tugwell, *American Economic Life and the Means of its Improvement* (3rd edn., New York: Harcourt, Brace and Co., 1930). For Bourke-White, see also Melissa A. McEuen, *Seeing America: Women Photographers Between the Wars* (Lexington, KY: University Press of Kentucky, 2000), 197–249.

49 Robert E. Snyder, 'Erskine Caldwell and Margaret Bourke-White: You Have Seen Their Faces', *Prospects: An Annual of American Cultural Studies*, xi. *Essays* (Cambridge: Cambridge University Press, 1987), 393–405: 393. For an overview of criticism levelled against *You Have Seen Their Faces*, see William Stott, *Documentary Expression and Thirties America* (New York: Oxford University Press, 1973), 59–60, 211–24.

50 'Notes on photographs by Margaret Bourke-White', in Erskine Caldwell and Margaret Bourke-White, *You Have Seen Their Faces* (New York: Viking Press, 1937), 187–90.

51 Goldberg, *Margaret Bourke-White*, 168.

52 Caldwell and Bourke-White, *You Have Seen*, 187.

53 Exminster, at any rate, is the name given in the caption, although I cannot find it in any map or gazeteer for South Carolina.

54 Margaret Bourke-White, *Portrait of Myself* (New York: Simon and Schuster, 1963), 134.

55 Caldwell and Bourke-White, *You Have Seen*, [133].

56 Caldwell and Bourke-White, *You Have Seen*, [135].

57 Caldwell and Bourke-White, *You Have Seen*, 144.

58 Richard Doud, Oral History Interview with Roy Stryker, 13 June 1963, Archives of American Art, Smithsonian Institution, https://www.aaa.si.edu/collections/interviews/oral-history-interview-roy-emerson-stryker-12480.

59 LC-USF 34-56952-D; LC-USF34-057465-E.

60 Paul Hendrickson, *Looking for the Light: The Hidden Life and Art of Marion Post Wolcott* (New York: Knopf, 1992), 76.

61 Although I've found no firm evidence that Post Wolcott and Beals knew each other, they would have moved in the same circles when she was a teenager, after her mother divorced and moved to 'a little apartment on the edge of Greenwich Village and enjoyed the company of creative, talented people'. F. Jack Hurley, *Marion Post Wolcott: A Photographic Journey* (Albuquerque, NM: University of New Mexico Press, 1989), 7. For Post Wolcott, see also McEuen, *Seeing America*, 125–95.

62 These hanging dolls are most clearly seen in Post Wolcott, 'Children in bedroom of their home, Charleston, West Virginia. Their mother has TB. Father works on WPA (Works Progress Administration)', September 1938, LC-USF34-050119-D, which regrettably is not of a high enough quality to be successfully reproduced here.

63 Marion Post Wolcott, 'FSA (Farm Security Administration) borrower's son getting some canned goods for dinner out of the pantry in his home. La Delta Project, Thomastown, Louisiana', June 1940, LC-USF34-054130-D.

64 Lawrence W. Levine makes this point when he argues, 'That the photographs from Stryker's section are filled with these tensions and ambiguities is a clue to their essential soundness as guides for the historian. The argument that only those photographs that depict unrelieved suffering and exploitation can be trusted as accurate portrayals and have anything to say to us has at its core a concept which ultimately subverts the struggle for historical understanding: the notion that things must be one way or the other, and therefore that it is impossible to maintain any semblance of dignity or self-worth or independence in the face of poverty and exploitation.' 'The Historian and the Icon: Photography and the History of the American People in the 1930s and 1940s', in Fleischhauer and Brannan (eds.), *Documenting America*, 15–42: 22.

65 Hendrickson, *Looking for the Light*, 84.

66 [LC-USF34- 052678-D].

67 J. B. Colson, 'Introduction: "There was a job to do": The Photographic Career of Russell Lee', Russell Lee Photograph Collection, Center for American History, University of Texas at

Austin, *Russell Lee Photographs: Images from the Russell Lee Photograph Collection at the Center for American History* (Austin, TX: University of Texas Press, 2007), 11–12.

68 F. Jack Hurley, *Russell Lee, Photographer* (Dobbs Ferry, NY: Morgan & Morgan, 1978), 11.

69 John Szarkowski, Foreword to *Russell Lee Photographs: Images from the Russell Lee Photograph Collection* (Austin, TX: University of Texas Press, 2007), p. x.

70 Notably, a number of these Pie Town images are in colour. Notably, too, the Pie Town inhabitants didn't just cooperate in the making of these photographs; they also took ownership of the results. The images were shown at Pie Town's annual fair in September 1940, and Lee wrote to Stryker: 'The pix you sent out are certainly appreciated by the community. I don't believe that you could ever get a more enthusiastic crowd for an exhibit. I tacked them on the walls for everybody to see. The Farm Bureau is going to keep them intact so they may have a good historical record of what Pie Town looked like in 1940.' Lee to Stryker, 27 September 1940, quoted in J. B. Colson, 'The Art of the Human Document: Russell Lee in New Mexico', in *Far from Main Street: Three Photographers in Depression-era New Mexico. Russell Lee, John Collier, Jack Delano* (Santa Fe, NM: Museum of New Mexico Press, 1994), 8. The town still takes pride in them: a number, blown up, hang on the walls of the Pie-o-Neer café (much recommended for its excellent pies).

71 Russell Lee, quoted in Hurley, *Russell Lee*, 19.

72 Transcript of tape made by John Collier for Roy Stryker, March 1959, Archives of American Art, Smithsonian Institution: 5.

73 Lee Interview I: tapes in Memphis State University Mississippi Valley Archives, quoted in Hurley, *Russell Lee*, 17.

74 Richard Doud, Oral History Interview with Roy Stryker, 13 June 1964, Archives of American Art, Smithsonian Institution, https://www.aaa.si.edu/collections/interviews/oral-history-interview-roy-emerson-stryker-12480.

75 O'Neal, *A Vision Shared*, 287.

76 John Collier, Jr and Malcolm Collier, *Visual Anthropology: Photography as Research Method* (1967; Albuquerque, NM: University of New Mexico Press, 1986), 9.

77 Collier and Collier, *Visual Anthropology*, 9.

78 Collier and Collier, *Visual Anthropology*, 16–17, 13.

79 Collier and Collier, *Visual Anthropology*, 9.

80 The Colliers expressed a strong preference for the use of off-camera flash.

When the flash unit is right on the camera, it is called flat flash, simply because the flash eliminates all shadows. This is fine for investigating murders, but not very revealing in photographing technology and social process. Without shadows we lose all sculptural detail and delineation of planes. Also, as every amateur knows, faces near the camera always appear like floured-faced actors in a minstrel show, whereas people in the near background cannot be seen except as shadows. The only way we can defeat this harshness of lighting is to get the light away from the camera. You can hold the flash reflector in your hand, clamp the light on the wall focusing down at an angle to the subject, or you can flash the light up on the ceiling, if there is one, and *bounce* the light back on the subject. The angle lighting gives hard shadows, but shows good detail in technology. The bounced light gives a more rounded well-modified light over the room area and is less intrusive and more generally useful.

Collier and Collier, *Visual Anthropology*, 228.

81 Collier and Collier, *Visual Anthropology*, 45, 199.

82 Collier and Collier, *Visual Anthropology*, 45.

83 Collier and Collier, *Visual Anthropology*, 16.

84 Richard Doud, *Oral History Interview with Edwin and Louise Rosskam*, 3 August 1965, Archives of American Art, Smithsonian Institution, https://www.aaa.si.edu/collections/interviews/oral-history-interview-edwin-and-louise-rosskam-13112.

85 Jacques Rancière, *Aisthesis: Scenes from the Aesthetic Regime of Art* (2011), trans. Zakir Paul (New York: Verso, 2013), 224.

Chapter 6

1 See Sara Blair, 'Ralph Ellison, Photographer', ch. 3 of *Harlem Crossroads: Black Writers and the Photograph in the Twentieth Century* (Princeton: Princeton University Press, 2007), 112–59, and, more broadly, Lena Hill, *Visualizing Blackness and the Creation of the African American Literary Tradition* (Cambridge: Cambridge University Press, 2014), 180–213.

2 Ralph Ellison, *Invisible Man* (1952; New York: Vintage International, 1995), 6. For metaphors associated with vision in the novel, see Alice Bloch, 'Sight Imagery in "Invisible Man"', *English Journal* 55/8 (November 1966), 1019–1021, 1024.

3 Ellison, *Invisible Man*, 7.

4 Ralph Ellison, 'Introduction to the Thirtieth-Anniversary Edition of *Invisible Man*' (1981), in *The Collected Essays of Ralph Ellison*, ed. John F. Callahan (New York: Modern Library, 2003), 475–89: 482. For discussion of the idea of 'high visibility' as it relates to Ellison's understanding of the term, see Avery Gordon, *Ghostly Matters: Haunting and the Sociological Imagination* (Minneapolis: University of Minnesota Press, 1997), 17. In particular, sociologist Robert E. Park had argued that the Negro's 'high visibility' was the major reason behind white America's racist attitudes. For Park and Ellison, see Daniel Y. Kim, 'Invisible Desires: Homoerotic Racism and Its Homophobic Critique in *Invisible Man*', ch. 1 of *Writing Manhood in Black and Yellow: Ralph Ellison, Frank Chin, and the Literary Politics of Identity* (Stanford, CA: Stanford University Press, 2005), 65–82.

5 Ellison, 'Introduction', 482. To be in 'Macy's window at high noon' was a slang phrase signifying maximum visibility, found, for example, in the film *The Purchase Price* (1932) and in James Jones's novel *From Here to Eternity* (1951): '"I'll kiss your ass in Macy's window at high noon on Sataday if I ever heard of a Smith in Brooklyn"'.

6 Ellison, *Invisible Man*, 3; 'Introduction', 482.

7 Most notably in the photographs taken by Weegee that appeared in the New York *Daily News*'s coverage of these events. It is worth noting, however, that Weegee's images avoid portraying African Americans as violent and dangerous. As Samantha Baskind has pointed out, 'Instead of showing African Americans wreaking havoc, he offers moments before and after the riot.' She argues that 'Weegee's approach to African American subjects indicates that his position as a Jew may have inclined him to champion another oppressed American minority'. 'Weegee's Jewishness', *History of Photography* 34/1 (2010), 60–78: 77, although Eddy Portnoy disputes this ('Weegee and the Two-Bit Nobodies', in Brian Wallis (ed.), *Murder is My Business* (New York: International Center of Photography, 2013), 59). Indeed, referring to another episode of 'trouble' in Harlem, Weegee described 'a mob of black people – quiet, sullen, terrible' in terms that suggest no racial fellow feeling. Rosa Reilly, 'Free-Lance Cameraman', *Popular Photography* (December 1937), 21–3 and 76–9: 77.

8 Ellison, *Invisible Man*, 556.

9 Weegee also borrowed the mannequin/corpse analogy in a 1943 or 1944 image, 'Manhattan Murder', that shows a large crowd, behind police barriers, peering at a desecrated mannequin lit up by flash in the foreground—minus her arms, and wearing only high heels.

10 Ken Gonzales-Day, *Lynching in the West: 1850–1935* (Durham, NC: Duke University Press, 2006), 60.

11 Amy Louise Wood, *Lynching and Spectacle: Witnessing Racial Violence in America, 1890–1940* (Chapel Hill, NC: University of North Carolina Press, 2009), 77.

12 Luc Sante, *Folk Photography: The American Real-Photo Postcard 1905–1930* (Portland, OR: Yeti/Verse Chorus Press, 2009), 17.

13 Dora Apel, 'Lynching Photographs and the Politics of Public Shaming', in Apel and Shawn Michell Smith (eds.), *Lynching Photographs* (Berkeley and Los Angeles: University of California Press, 2007), 43–78: 46.

14 There is a growing literature on lynching photography. In addition to the works cited earlier in this chapter, see James Allen and John Lewis, *Without Sanctuary: Lynching Photography in America* (Santa Fe, NM: Twin Palms Publishers, 2000), and Leigh Raiford, *Imprisoned in a Luminous Glare: Photography and the African American Freedom Struggle* (Chapel Hill, NC: University of North Carolina Press, 2013).

15 This is a succinct version of the argument that has been advanced in relation to colonial anthropologically driven image-making in, say, James Ryan, '"Photographing the Natives"', ch. 5 of *Picturing Empire: Photography and the Visualization of the British Empire* (Chicago: University of Chicago Press, 1997), 140–82.

16 Richard Wright, Preface to *12 Million Black Voices* (1941; New York: Basic Books, 2008), p. xxi. See Maren Stange, '"Not What We Seem": Image and Text in 12 Million Black Voices', in Ulla Haselstein, Berndt Ostendorf, and Peter Schneck (eds.), *Iconographies of Power: The Politics and Poetics of Visual Representation* (Heidelberg: Universitätsverlag Winter, 2003), 173–86; John Rogers Puckett, *Five Photo-Textual Documentaries from The Great Depression* (Ann Arbor: UMI Research Press, 1984), 61–81. For a study of Wright's background in sociology and his preacher-like rhetoric in this volume, see John M. Reilly, 'Richard Wright Preaches the Nation: 12 Million Black Voices', *Black American Literature Forum*, 16/3 (Autumn 1982), 116–19. Wright also planned a photographic documentary about the children of Harlem, and—failing to find a black photographer with the requisite access and knowledge—asked Helen Levitt to execute it. However, this was never realized. Michel Fabre, *The Unfinished Quest of Richard Wright*, trans. Isabel Barzun (New York: William Morrow & Co., 1973), 267.

17 Defining 'blackness' is a nuanced and multilayered undertaking. I employ the word in several ways: to describe skin pigmentation that, when flashlight is thrown on it, absorbs and reflects its light differently from untanned Caucasian skins; as recognizing a self-identification; as acknowledging the responses—identificatory and otherwise—that a person may have when visually encountering another individual, whether face to face or mediated through a representation. I also use it in recognition of its potential to occupy a site of resistance or interrogation within a white-dominated society. At the same time, I acknowledge its shifting historical and transnational significations.

18 See John Vincent Jezierski, *Enterprising Images: The Goodridge Brothers, African American Photographers, 1847–1922* (Detroit: Wayne State University Press, 2000). For the broader history of African American photography, see Deborah Willis, *Reflections in Black: A History of Black Photographers 1840 to the Present* (New York: W. W. Norton & Co., 2000).

19 See Library of Congress, *A Small Nation of People: W. E. B. Du Bois and African American Portraits of Progress*, with essays by David Levering Lewis and Deborah Willis (New York: Amistad/Harper Collins, 2003); Shawn Michelle Smith, '"Looking at One's Self through the Eyes of Others": W. E. B. Du Bois's Photographs for the 1900 Paris Exposition', *African American Review*, 34/4 (winter 2000), 581–99.

20 A succinct history of these quickly expiring magazines is given in the autobiography of *Ebony*'s first editor, Ben Burns, *Nitty Gritty: A White Editor in Black Journalism* (Jackson, MS: University Press of Mississippi, 1996), 28–9. See also Roland E. Wolseley, *The Black Press, U.S.A.* (2nd edn., Ames, IA: Iowa State University Press, 1990), chs. 2 and 4, and esp. Walter C. Daniel, *Black Journals of the United States* (Westport, CT: Greenwood Press, 1982).

21 *Flash!* 'The New Year Forccast' (3 January 1938), 6.

22 Daniel, *Black Journals*, 182.

23 *Flash!* (27 March 1937), 16.

24 *Flash!* (20 March 1937), 16–17.

25 See Morgan Smith and John Smith, *Harlem: The Vision of Morgan and Marvin Smith* (Lexington, KY: University Press of Kentucky, 1997).

26 See National Museum of African American History and Culture, *Picturing the Promise: The Scurlock Studio and Black Washington* (Washington, DC: Smithsonian Books, 2009).

27 For McNeill, see Nicholas A. Natanson, 'Robert McNeill and Black Government Photographers', *History of Photography* 19/1 (1995), 20–31, and Natanson, 'From Sophie's Alley to the White House: Rediscovering the Visions of Pioneering Black Government Photographers', *Prologue Magazine*, special issue on Federal Records and African American History, 29/2 (summer 1997). http://www.archives.gov/publications/prologue/1997/summer/pioneering-photographers.html, accessed 3 December 2015.

28 Nicole R. Fleetwood, *Troubling Vision: Performance, Visuality, and Blackness* (Chicago: University of Chicago Press, 2011), 38.

29 Fleetwood, *Troubling Vision*, 47, quoting an interview, transcribed by Fleetwood, in *One Shot: The Life and Work of Teenie Harris*, written by Joe Seamans, dir. Kenneth Love, San Francisco: California Newsreel, 2003.

30 bell hooks, 'In Our Glory: Photography and Black Life', in *Picturing Us: African American Identity in Photography*, ed. Deborah Willis (New York: New Press, 1995), 48.

31 Quoted in Christopher A. Brooks and Robert Sims, *Roland Hayes: The Legacy of an American Tenor* (Bloomington, IN: Indiana University Press, 2014), 221. I've not been able to find the correct page in the publication they cite.

32 Vera Jackson, quoted in Jeanne Moutoussamy-Ashe, *Viewfinders: Black Women Photographers* (New York: Dodd, Mead & Co., 1986), 87. Jackson herself did photostories with titles like 'The Best Dressed' and 'First Achievements by Blacks' for the *California Eagle*.

33 See Lorna Roth, 'Looking at Shirley, the Ultimate Norm: Colour Balance, Image Technologies, and Cognitive Equity', *Canadian Journal of Communication* 34 (2009), 111–36.

34 *Flash!* (20 March 1937), 5. Derricotte was an attorney and became a member of the District Republican State Committee, according to a brief obituary in *Jet* (12 April 1962), 25.

35 On 'colorism'—that is, 'a type of skin-color bias that involves systematic discrimination against the darker-skinned members of a particular group', see Nina G. Jablonski, *Living Color: The Biological and Social Meaning of Skin Color* (Berkeley and Los Angeles: University of California Press, 2012), esp. 169–81: 172.

36 *Flash!* (10 May 1937), 4.

37 *Ebony* (November 1945), quoted in Paul M. Hirsch, 'An Analysis of *Ebony*: The Magazine and Its Readers', *Journalism Quarterly* 45/2 (Summer 1968), 261–70, 292: 261. See also Maren Stange, '"Photographs Taken in Everyday Life": *Ebony*'s Photojournalistic Discourse', in Todd Vogel (ed.), *The Black Press: New Literary and Historical Essays* (New Brunswick, NJ: Rutgers University Press, 2001), 207–27.

38 *Ebony* (November 1945), quoted in Hirsch, 'An Analysis of *Ebony*', 261.

39 Daniel, *Black Journals*, 160.

40 For the dominance of these categories—together with that of the politician—in black photo-iconography, see Nicole R. Fleetwood, *On Racial Icons: Blackness and the Public Imagination* (New Brunswick, NJ: Rutgers University Press, 2015). *Life*, of course, was well known for its photo-essays that introduced representative families to its readership, especially after the Second World War: see Wendy Kozol, Life's *America: Family and Nation in Postwar Photojournalism* (Philadelphia: Temple University Press, 1994), esp. ch. 1, 'Documenting the Ordinary: Photographic Realism and *LIFE*'s Families'. But when it came to the representation of African American families, *Life* failed to provide the aspirational depictions that could be found in *Flash!* and *Ebony*. *Ebony* was not the only photo-news magazine launched for a black readership: John H. Johnson, of the Johnson Publishing Company, also put out *Hue*, *Jet*, and *Tan*, but *Ebony* remained the leader. See Daniel, *Black Journals*, and Irwin D. Rinder, 'A Sociological Look into the Negro Pictorial', *Phylon Quarterly* 20/2 (1959), 169–77 (which concentrates on *Ebony*).

41 Sara Blair, 'Ellison, Photography, and the Origins of Invisibility', in Ross Posnock (ed.), *The Cambridge Companion to Ralph Ellison* (Cambridge: Cambridge University Press, 2005), 56–81: 57.

42 Mary Alice Sentman, 'Black and White: Disparity in Coverage by Life Magazine from 1937 to 1972', *Journalism Quarterly* 60 (autumn 1983), 501–8: 508.

43 'Bronx Slave Market', *Flash!* (14 February 1938), 8–10.

44 For the history of the Federal Theatre Project, see Laura Browder, *Rousing the Nation: Radical Culture in Depression America* (Amherst, MA: University of Massachusetts Press, 1998); Elizabeth A. Osborne, *Staging the People: Community and Identity in the Federal Theatre Project* (New York: Palgrave Macmillan, 2011); Susan Quinn, *Furious Improvisation: How the WPA and a Cast of Thousands Made High Art out of Desperate Times* (New York: Walker & Co., 2008); Bonnie Nelson Schwartz and the Educational Film Center, *Voices from the Federal Theatre* (Madison: University of Wisconsin Press, 2003; Paul Sporn, *Against Itself: The Federal Theater and Writers' Projects in the Midwest* (Detroit: Wayne State University Press, 1995).

45 *Flash!* (14 June 1937), 25.

46 A similar reappropriation may be found in Ida B. Wells's publication of lynching photographs in her anti-lynching books, their appearance in *Crisis*, the official magazine of the National Association for the Advancement of Colored People, and their reprinting in a range of African American newspapers.

47 Shawn Michelle Smith, 'The Evidence of Lynching Photographs', in Apel and Smith, *Lynching Photographs*, 11–41: 32.

48 Ralph Ellison, 'A Special Message to Subscribers' (1980), in *Collected Essays*, 355.

49 Claudia Rankine, *Citizen* (Minneapolis: Graywolf Press, 2014), 91.

50 Robert McNeill, interview with Nicholas Natanson, 26 June 1989, in Natanson, *The Black Image in the New Deal: The Politics of FSA Photography* (Knoxville, TN: University of Tennessee Press, 1992), 266.

51 Gordon Parks, *Voices in the Mirror: An Autobiography* (New York: Doubleday, 1990), 65.

52 Gordon Parks, *Half Past Autumn: A Retrospective* (Boston: Little, Brown & Co., 1997), 28; *Voices in the Mirror*, 145. Elsewhere, Parks claimed he had read the volume 'many times'. Gordon Parks, *A Choice of Weapons* (New York: Harper and Row, 1965), 244. For more on the FSA/Office of War Information documenting of urban Chicago, see Maren Stange, *Bronzeville: Black Chicago in Pictures, 1941–1943* (New York: New Press, 2003).

53 Richard Wright, *12 Million Black Voices* (1941), introd. David Bradley, foreword by Noel Ignatiev (New York: Basic Books, 2008), 106. A 'kitchenette', in Chicago and New York in the mid-twentieth century, was not a miniature kitchen, but rather a one-room apartment converted from what had formerly been a large house. Each apartment contained one small gas stove and one small sink; toilets were shared by all tenants.

54 'We are with the new tide. We stand at the crossroads. We watch each new procession. The hot wires carry urgent appeals. Print compels us. Voices are speaking. Men are moving! And we shall be with them'. Wright, *12 Million Black Voices*, 147.

55 Stange, *Bronzeville*, p. xxv.

56 Natanson, *Black Image*, 250–1.

57 Martin H. Bush, *The Photographs of Gordon Parks* (Wichita, KS: Wichita State University, 1983), 'A Conversation with Gordon Parks', 13–120: 46.

58 Bush, *Photographs of Gordon Parks*, 69.

59 Bush, *Photographs of Gordon Parks*, 38.

60 After his early conversation with Stryker about Washington's racial bigotry, at which he was given the advice to talk with as many people as possible who had lived in DC all their lives, 'I sat for an hour mulling over his advice and the humiliation I had suffered. It had grown late; the office had emptied and Stryker had left for the day. Only a black charwoman remained but she was mopping the floor in an adjoining office. "Talk to other black people who have spent their lives here", he had said. She was black, and I eased into conversation with her. Hardly an hour had gone by when we finished, but she had taken me through a lifetime of drudgery and despair in that hour. She was turning back to her mopping when I asked, "Would you allow me to photograph you?" "I don't mind." There was a huge American flag hanging from a standard near the wall. I asked her to stand before it, then placed the mop in one hand and the broom in the other. "Now think of what you just told me and look straight into this camera." Eagerly I began clicking the shutter. It was done and I went home to supper. Washington could now have a conversation with her portrait.'

61 Parks, *Voices in the Mirror*, 84.

62 For an excellent reading of Parks's 'Ella Watson and Her Grandchildren', see Philip Brookman, 'Unlocked Doors: Gordon Parks at the Crossroads', in Brookman, *Gordon Parks: Half Past Autumn: A Retrospective* (Boston: Bulfinch Press, Little, Brown and Co., 1997), 346–53: 350.

63 For an insightful treatment of Parks's 'Harlem Gang Leader', see Russell Lord, 'The Making of an Argument', *Gordon Parks: The Making of an Argument* (which accompanied an exhibition mounted in New Orleans and then at the University of Virginia) (Göttingen: Steidl/The Gordon Parks Foundation, 2013), 27–45.

64 Bush, *Gordon Parks*, 92.

65 The unattributed text of this essay was by *Life*'s staff writers, in places drawing on Parks's own account. 'Harlem Gang Leader', *Life* (1 November 1948), 96–106.

66 Parks, *Voices in the Mirror*, 108.

67 Gordon Parks and Michael Torosian, *Harlem: The Artist's Annotations on a City Revisited in Two Classic Photographic Essays*, introduction and interview by Michael Torosian (Toronto: Lumiere Press, 1997), 30. The success—both topical and aesthetic—of this assignment led to Parks becoming a highly regarded staff photographer for *Life* magazine. As he was to say, it opened doors for him, setting him up 'to do stories on the black resurgence, the Muslims, the Black Panthers, Stokely Carmichael, Eldridge Cleaver. Huey Newton, all of them. They knew I was

the only black photographer on *Life* and they knew that I was their only chance for a big voice in a prestigious magazine'—although, as a black man working for 'the great white father, *Life Magazine*', Parks surmised that he was not particularly trusted. Parks and Torosian, *Harlem*, 34. For Parks's career at *Life*, see Erika Doss, 'Visualizing Black America: Gordon Parks at *Life*, 1948–1971', in Doss (ed.), *Looking at* Life *Magazine* (Washington, DC: Smithsonian Institution Press, 2001), 221–41.

68 Bush, *Gordon Parks*, 76.

69 Gordon Parks, *Flash Photography* (New York: Franklin Watts, 1947), 85.

70 National Archives 111-SC-196741.

71 Parks, *Flash Photography*, 28.

72 Parks, *Flash Photography*, 46.

73 Parks, *Flash Photography*, 47.

74 Quoted in Bush, *Gordon Parks*, 42.

75 Sontag, *On Photography*, 7; 14.

76 Ivor Miller, '"If It Hasn't Been One of Color": An Interview with Roy DeCarava', *Callaloo* 13/4 (Autumn, 1990), 847–57; Charles H. Rowell, '"I Have Never Looked Back Since": An Interview with Roy DeCarava', *Callaloo* 3/4 (autumn 1990), 859–71. Unfortunately, permission was not granted to reproduce any of DeCarava's work here.

77 DeCarava, in Miller, '"If It Hasn't Been"', 849.

78 DeCarava, in Miller, '"If It Hasn't Been"', 855.

79 According to Sherry Turner DeCarava, 'Pages from a Notebook', in Peter Galassi (ed.), *Roy DeCarava: A Retrospective* (New York: Museum of Modern Art, 1996), 40–60: 42. She also mentioned the influence of the Mexican muralist painters, especially José Clemente Orozco, J. M. W. Turner, and Thomas Eakins on her husband's treatment of light. He was, of course, originally a painter.

80 Cartier-Bresson's repudiation of flash will be discussed more fully in Chapter 10.

81 Richard Wright, *Native Son* (1940; New York: Harper Perennial Modern Classics, 2005), 201–2.

82 See Maren Stange, 'Illusion Complete Within Itself: Roy DeCarava's Photography', in Townsend Ludington (ed.), *A Modern Mosaic. Art and Modernism in the United States* (Chapel Hill, NC: University of North Carolina Press, 2000), 279–304.

83 Roy DeCarava to Minor White, 21 November 1955, Art Museum, Princeton, quoted in Stange, 'Illusion Complete', 292.

84 Hughes, quoted in Arnold Rampersad, *The Life of Langston Hughes*, ii. *1941–1967, I Dream a World* (Oxford: Oxford University Press, 1988), 244.

85 For Bellocq's work, see John Szarkowski, *Bellocq: Photographs from Storyville, the Red-Light District of New Orleans* (New York: Random House, 1996).

86 Natasha Trethewey, *Bellocq's Ophelia* (Minneapolis: Graywolf Press, 2002), 48.

87 Trethewey, *Bellocq's Ophelia*, 27.

88 Peter Galassi, 'Introduction', in Galassi and Sherry Turner DeCarava, *Roy DeCarava: A Retrospective* (New York: Museum of Modern Art, 1996), 11.

89 DeCarava in Rowell, '"I Have Never Looked Back"', 865.

90 DeCarava in Rowell, '"I Have Never Looked Back"', 868.

91 Teju Cole, 'On Photography', *New York Times Magazine* (22 February 2015), 62–70: 64, 68, 68–70.

92 DeCarava in Miller, '"If It Hasn't Been"', 849.

Chapter 7

1 Unsigned, 'Instantaneous Studies, No. 13: The "Flash" Photograph', *Photographic News* (10 February 1888), 83.

2 Cecil Carnes, *Jimmy Hare News Photographer: Half a Century with a Camera* (New York: Macmillan, 1940), 106.

3 Don M. Paul, 'Supplementary Notes on Professional Flash', in William Mortensen, *Flash in Modern Photography* (San Francisco: Camera Craft Publishing Co., 1950), 192.

4 James Jarché, *People I Have Shot* (London: Methuen, 1934), 5.

5 Francis A. Collins, *The Camera Man* (New York: Century, 1916), 70.

6 George Howard, quoted in Charles F. Briggs and Augustus Maverick, *The Story of the Telegraph; And a History of the Great Atlantic Cable* (New York: Rudd & Carleton, 1858), 97. Transatlantic cable communication was permanently established in 1866.

7 'Accident to a Lady Lion-Tamer', *Illustrated Police News* (11 February 1888), 3.

8 *Photographic Times* 18 (2 November 1888), 519; *Philadelphia Evening Bulletin* (20 October 1888), 524. *Philadelphia Photographer* 25 (1888), 690. As is made clear in an unsigned article, 'Danger of Explosive Magnesium Compounds', *Photographic Times* 18 (3 February 1888), 50–1, magnesium powder was especially volatile when mixed with picric acid.

9 *Photographic Times* 18 (9 November 1888), 531. Information in *Philadelphia Photographer* 25 (1888), 416, suggests that this pistol should properly be used with 'Non-explosive Illuminating Powder', but the device seems to have had a short life, and perhaps was not too reliable.

10 Henry Leffman, 'Flash-Powder Accidents', *Wilson's Photographic Magazine* 49 (1912), 380–2; repr. from the *Journal of the Photographic Society of Philadelphia.*

11 Dr [Ernst] Von Schwartz, *Fire and Explosion Risks*, trans. from the rev. German edn. by Charles T. C. Salter (London: Charles Griffin and Co., 1904), 307–8.

12 William Nesbit, 'High Speed Flashlight Photography', *American Annual of Photography* 30 (1915), 260.

13 Leo Kraft, 'Flashlight Pictures', *American Photography* 15 (1921), 66.

14 James C. Kinkaid, *Press Photography* (London: Chapman and Hall, 1936), 208.

15 Kinkaid, *Press Photography*, 209.

16 *Society Dog Show*, Disney, 1939. https://www.youtube.com/watch?v=_G05ymTKOdk, accessed 29 January 2017.

17 Harry J. Coleman, *Give Us a Little Smile, Baby* (New York: E. P. Dutton & Co, 1943), 72.

18 Edward J. Dean, *Lucky Dean: Reminiscences of a Press Photographer* (London: Robert Hale, 1944), 25.

19 Carnes, *Jimmy Hare*, 107–8.

20 Kenneth Kobre, *Photojournalism: The Professionals' Approach* (5th edn.) (London: Focal Press, 2004), 390.

21 Christopher Lynch, *When Hollywood Landed at Chicago's Midway Airport: The Photos & Stories of Mike Rotunno* (Charleston, SC: History Press, 2012), 35.

22 Stanley Devon, *'Glorious': The Life Story of Stanley Devon* (London: George G. Harrap, 1957), 198. For Devon's career, see also Ruth Boyd, *Stanley Devon: News Photographer* (Twyford: Derek Harrison Publishing, 1995).

23 Sontag, *On Photography*, 14–15. Sontag's typically overstated comment is, as film critic and essayist Phillip Lopate puts it, 'nonsense, but nicely written'. *Notes on Sontag* (Princeton:

Princeton University Press, 2009), 203. For the more general association of photography with violence, see Bill Jay, 'The Photographer as Aggressor', in David Featherstone (ed.), *Observations: Essays on Documentary Photography (Untitled 35)* (Carmel: Friends of Photography, 1984), 7–23.

24 *Picture Snatcher*, dir. Lloyd Bacon, Warner Brothers, 1933.

25 Dashiell Hammett, *Red Harvest* (1929; New York: Vintage Books, 1992), 135.

26 Mortensen, *Flash*, 148.

27 Sammy Schulman, *'Where's Sammy?'*, ed. Robert Considine (New York: Random House, 1943), 41.

28. Schulman, *'Where's Sammy?'*, 42.

29 J. R. Hunt, *Pictorial Journalism* (London: Sir Isaac Pitman & Sons, 1937), 44. See also (and with more technical detail) Laura Vitray, John Mills, Jr, and Roscoe Ellard, *Pictorial Journalism* (New York: McGraw-Hill Book Company, 1939), and Kinkaid, *Press Photography*.

30 John J. Floherty, *Shooting the News: Careers of the Camera Men* (Philadelphia: J. B. Lippincott, 1949), 65.

31 Morton Sontheimer, *Newspaperman: A Book about the Business* (New York: Whittlesey House, 1941), 234.

32 T. Thorne Baker, *The Kingdom of the Camera* (London: G. Bell & Sons., 1934), 1.

33 William Hannigan, 'Making American Images', in Hannigan and Ken Johnston, *Picture Machine: The Rise of American Newspictures* (New York: Harry N. Abrams, 2004), 9.

34 Jack Price, *News Photography* (New York: Round Table Press, 1935), 127.

35 Jarché, *People I Have Shot*, 183.

36 David J. Krajicek, *Scooped! Media Miss Real Story on Crime While Chasing Sleaze Sex and Celebrities* (New York: Columbia University Press, 1998), 93.

37 V. Penelope Pelizzon and Nancy M. West, '"Good Stories" from the Mean Streets: Weegee and Hard-Boiled Autobiography', *Yale Journal of Criticism* 17/1 (2004), 20–50. Ryan Linkof, in his excellent PhD dissertation 'The Public Eye: Celebrity and Photojournalism in the Making of the British Tabloids, 1904–1938', University of Southern California, 2011, offers the important caveat that 'Especially in the case of the memoirs of photographers, one has to be vigilant of the fact that sensational journalistic flourishes and ever-present professional gloating might have clouded the recollection, and limited the efficacy of the document as a historical source'. Linkof, 'Public Eye', 44.

38 Devon, *'Glorious'*, 35, 37.

39 See Carol Squiers, '"And so the moving trigger finger writes": Dead Gangsters and New York Tabloids in the 1930s', in Sandra S. Phillips, Mark Haworth-Booth, and Carol Squiers, *Police Pictures: The Photograph as Evidence* (San Francisco: Chronicle Books, 1997), 40–9. For the rise in sensationalist journalism at this time, see John D. Stevens, *Sensationalism and the New York Press* (New York: Columbia University Press, 1991).

40 Raymond Chandler, *The Big Sleep* (1939; New York: Vintage Crime/Black Lizard, 1988), 33. Filmed as *The Big Sleep* (dir. Howard Hawks), 1946.

41 The Giant Flash Camera was part of a whole arsenal of domestic or quotidian objects transformed into weapons and other useful devices, including a Giant Pepper Shaker, a Giant Umbrella, a Giant Cash Register, a Giant Vacuum Cleaner and—with a nod to the film industry—a Giant Movie Studio Egyptian Statue Prop.

42 G. E. Davis [one of the inventors], Letter to the editor, 'Electricity and Photography', *Photographic Times and American Photographer* 19 (10 May 1889), 236.

43 Rus Arnold, *Flash Photography* (Little Technical Library; Chicago: Ziff-Davis Publishing Company, 1940), 97.

44 Jailed criminals were first photographed in Belgium in 1843–4. The earliest systematic photography of crime scenes was probably that practised by the French photographer Alphonse Bertillon (who also recognized the importance of the anthropometrical standardization of the photographs of individual criminals): for the career of Bertillon, who used both magnesium ribbon and magnesium flash powder to obtain his results, see Pierre Piazza (ed.), *Aux origines de la police scientifique: Alphonse Bertillon, précurseur de la science du crime* (Paris: Karthala, 2011).

45 Paul, in Mortensen, *Flash*, 197.

46 Larry S. Miller and Richard T. McEvoy Jr, *Police Photography* (6th edn., Amsterdam: Elsevier Science, 2010), 67. See e.g. Christopher D. Duncan, *Advanced Crime Scene Photography* (Boca Raton, FL: CRC Press, 2010), and Raul Sutton and Keith Trueman (eds.), *Crime Scene Management: Scene Specific Methods* (New York: Wiley, 2013).

47 See Ben Singer, *Melodrama and Modernity: Early Sensational Cinema and Its Contexts* (New York: Columbia University Press, 2001), 198.

48 Anthony Sharpe, *The Mystery of the Flashlight Print* (London: Aldine Books, 1924), 48.

49 Arthur Ransome, *The Big Six* (London: Jonathan Cape, 1940), 350.

50 Matthew Brower, *Developing Animals: Wildlife and Early American Photography* (Minneapolis: University of Minnesota Press, 2011). Flash photography of wildlife carries its own dangers with it: the creature photographed can equate flash with weapon. Eric Hosking, the renowned bird photographer, was blinded in one eye by a tawny owl that attacked him whilst having its photograph taken by flash. Eric Hosking, *Eric Hosking's Owls* (London: Pelham Books, 1982), 15. The best-known pioneer of such photography was George Shiras, about whom more will be said in Chapter 10. Most probably the book referred to in Sharpe's novel was George Shiras, *The Wild Life of Lake Superior, Past and Present: The Habits of Deer, Moose, Wolves, Beavers, Muskrats, Trout, and Feathered Wood-Folk Studied with Camera and Flashlight* (London: National Geographic Magazine, 1921).

51 Dean, *Lucky Dean*, 60–1.

52 Sontheimer, *Newspaperman*, 234.

53 Schulman, *'Where's Sammy?'*, 12.

54 For a good study of the genre, see Erin A. Smith, *Hard-Boiled: Working-Class Readers and Pulp Magazines* (Philadelphia: Temple University Press, 2000).

55 Coxe also created a somewhat more sanitized photographer/detective in the figure of Kent Murdock. For a full account of Casey, and the different stories and media formats in which he appeared, see J. Randolph Cox and David S. Siegel, *Flashgun Casey, Crime Photographer: From the Pulps to Radio and Beyond* (New York: Bookhunter Press, 2005).

56 Alonso Deen Cole, 'The White Monster' (1945), repr. in Cox and Siegel, *Flashgun Casey*, 131. There are a number of flashbulb sounds available for download (or for listening to online): I recommend http://www.theodoregray.com/PeriodicTable/Samples/054.1/Sample.WAV, accessed 11 February 2016.

57 George Harmon Coxe, *Murder for Two* (New York: Dell, 1943), 22. Karen Harding has to contend with sexism as well as violent criminals in this story: when she later asks Casey's colleague Wade if he could develop some infrared film for her, he patronizingly inquires '"What've you been doing, fooling with blackout bulbs?"', *Murder for Two*, 67.

58 Coxe, *Murder for Two*, 229.

59 George Harmon Coxe, *The Man Who Died Too Soon* (New York: Alfred A. Knopf, 1962), 37.

60 Mark Gabrish Conlan has an episode by episode account of the *Man With a Camera* series on his excellent blog, MovieMagg: http://moviemagg.blogspot.com/2013/04/man-with-camera-abc-tv-1958-1960.html, accessed 12 February 2016. Conlan makes very clear how varied were the show's genres, including adventure and detective drama, social realism, and film noir.

61 This bulb did not produce a very bright flash—indeed, it gave a wink of light—but used in conjunction with ISO 3000 B&W film in a Land Camera, and with the aid of ordinary home lighting, it created very effective images for domestic users. Advertisement, *Ebony* 15/1 (November 1959), 105.

62 Charles Bronson, quoted Brian D'Ambrosio, *Menacing Face Worth Millions: A Life of Charles Bronson* (Minneapolis: Jabberwocky Press, 2014), 83.

63 See Jodi Hauptman, '*FLASH!* The Speed Graphic Camera', *Yale Journal of Criticism* 11/1 (1998), 129–37.

64 Weegee, *Naked City* (New York: Da Capo Press, 1945), 10.

65 Weegee, *Weegee's Secrets of Shooting with Photoflash as Told to Mel Harris* (New York: designers 3, 1953), 5. Weegee probably overstates, judging by the number of (often non-sensational) photographs that he took of New York street scenes; these, however, were often not the ones that he sold for publication.

66 The call for his assistance with the squeegee—used to clean water off prints in the darkroom—apparently gave Weegee his name, although he liked to claim that it referred to his uncanny, Ouija-board-like ability to sense the scene of a crime. His access to police radio wavelengths was probably of more use to him in this respect.

67 Weegee [Arthur Fellig], *Weegee by Weegee* (New York: Ziff-Davis Publishing Company, 1961), 28. Take note of Colin Westerbeck's remark, in the colloquium that appears in the In Focus volume on Weegee, that 'Miles Barth's 1997 book, *Weegee's World*, is very important because he clears up a lot of things. One must understand that in *Weegee by Weegee* the photographer is not completely truthful with the facts about his life.' 'An Elusive Fame: The Photographs of Weegee', in Judith Keller, *Weegee: Photographs from the J. Paul Getty Museum* (Los Angeles: J. Paul Getty Museum, 2005), 91.

68 For *PM* (1940–8), see Paul Milkman, *PM: A New Deal in Journalism, 1940–1948* (New Brunswick, NJ: Rutgers University Press, 1997). Weegee did not express clear political leanings, although he was associated with the left-wing Photo League in the 1930s.

69 Paul, in Mortensen, *Flash*, 200–1.

70 The neo-noir 1992 Universal Studios film *The Public Eye* (dir. Howard Franklin, starring Joe Pesci and Barbara Hershey) is loosely based on Weegee's career (and some of the photographs in the film are by him). It contains a lot of period-flavour flash photography (and exploding flashbulbs).

71 Luc Sante, 'City of Eyes', in Luc Sante, Cynthia Young, Paul Strand, and Ralph Steiner, *Unknown Weegee* (New York: International Center for Photography/Steidl, 2006), 9.

72 Weegee, *Weegee by Weegee*, 37.

73 For Weegee and voyeurism, see esp. David Corey, 'Weegee's Unstaged Coney Island Dramas', *American Art* 5/1–2 (winter–spring 1991), 16–21, and Miles Orvell, 'Weegee's Voyeurism and the Mastery of Urban Disorder', *American Art* 6/1 (winter 1992), 18–41.

74 Miles Barth, 'When Weegee went to Hollywood' (12 November 2011), *Vanity Fair* online edition, http://www.vanityfair.com/hollywood/features/2011/11/naked-hollywood-slideshow-201111#slide=1, accessed 4 February 2012.

75 Weegee, *Weegee by Weegee*, 46–7.

76 Squiers, 'Dead Gangsters', 42–3. See Rosa Reilly, 'Free-Lance Cameraman', *Popular Photography* 1/ 8 (December 1937), 21–3, 76–9.

77 Sharpe, *New York Nocturne*, 300.

78 Weegee, *Weegee's Secrets*, 10.

79 Richard Meyer, 'Learning from Low Culture', in Meyer and Anthony W. Lee, *Weegee and* Naked City (Berkeley and Los Angeles: University of California Press, 2008), 13–61.

80 Orvell, 'Weegee's Voyeurism', 22.

81 Richard Meyer, 'Photography is Elastic: Weegee's Cockeyed View of Hollywood', *American Art* 27/2 (2013), 33–7: 33–4.

82 Weegee, *Weegee by Weegee*, 69.

83 Weegee, *Weegee by Weegee*, 75–6.

84 Patricia Bosworth, *Diane Arbus: A Biography* (New York: Alfred A. Knopf, 1984), 238.

85 Diane Arbus to Alex Eliot, November 1968 [fn. claims 1938], quoted in Sandra S. Phillips, 'The Question of Belief', in San Francisco Museum of Modern Art, *Diane Arbus: Revelations* (New York: Random House, 2003), 57.

86 As Phillips puts it, she was drawn to 'the power of myth as a means of ascribing meaning to everyday existence. In an age and culture that prized rationalism and technology, Arbus was attuned to the ancient, folkloric, or talismanic aspects of contemporary life'. 'Question of Belief', 50.

87 Diane Arbus, from interviews conducted in 1971, in *Diane Arbus* (Millerton, NY: Aperture, 1984), 9.

88 John Szarkowski, *New Documents*. Exhibition wall label, New York, Museum of Modern Art, 1967, cited by Cynthia Young, 'Unknown Weegee', in Sante et al., *Unknown Weegee*, 16.

89 *Naked City*, published in 1945, gave its name to the 1948 semi-documentary film noir directed by Jules Dassin, a movie that falls uneasily into two genres: part police procedural, and part street shots that fulfil the desire of the producer, Mark Hellinger, to have New York itself play a starring role. Weegee himself was hired as a still photographer; certain street scenes were inspired by his work. William Park has convincingly argued, however, that it is also much indebted to Italian realist cinema of the time. *What Is Film Noir?* (Lewisburg, PA: Bucknell University Press, 2011), 60.

90 Weegee, 'Naked Everything', Photographer's Showplace, reproduced in Richard Meyer and Weegee, *Naked Hollywood: Weegee in Los Angeles* (New York: Rizzoli, 2011), 102.

91 Quoted by MacKenzie Stevens, 'Chronology', in Meyer and Weegee, *Naked Hollywood: Weegee in Los Angeles*, 122.

92 Weegee, *Weegee by Weegee*, 127, 131.

93 Helen Gee, *Limelight: A Greenwich Village Photography Gallery and Coffeehouse in the Fifties* (Albuquerque, NM: University of New Mexico Press, 1997), 235.

94 Weegee, *Weegee's Secrets*, 7.

95 Alan Trachtenberg, 'Weegee's City Secrets', *E-rea: Revue électronique d'études sur le monde anglophone* 7/2 (2010), sect. 12. https://erea.revues.org/1168, accessed 10 May 2016.

96 Weegee, *Weegee's Secrets*, 9.

97 Weegee with Roy Ald, *Weegee's Creative Camera* (New York: Vista House, 1959), 90.

98 Then typically, of course, he could undercut this point, too: one of the composite images in *Weegee's Secrets* places a woman riding a bicycle along a tightrope into this scene.

Chapter 8

1 Several contributors to the Graflex.org forum point out that there is some anachronism in some of the flash attachments and bulbs that are visible: http://graflex.org/helpboard/viewtopic.php?t=3486&sid=421e6086bc956d94dd4f67a9ce9ff4a9, accessed 8 April 2016.

2 Paul Martin, *Victorian Snapshot* (London: Country Life, 1939), 40.

3 Bernard Grant, *To the Four Corners: The Memoirs of a News Photographer* (London: Hutchinson & Co., 1933), 231.

4 Linkof, 'Public Eye', 204. He stresses the frequent need for cooperation on the part of an establishment's proprietor.

5 Glenn Harvey and Mark Saunders, *Diana and the Paparazzi* (London: John Blake, 2007), 223.

6 Philip Waller, chapter 8: 'Product Advertising and Self-Advertising', in *Literary Life in Britain 1870–1918* (Oxford: Oxford University Press, 2006), 329–63. The same necessarily applies to theatrical personalities and other entertainment notables.

7 For the manufacture of celebrity, see Linkof, 'Public Eye', Charles L. Ponce de Leon, *Self-Exposure: Human Interest Journalism and the Emergence of Celebrity in America, 1890–1940* (Chapel Hill, NC: University of North Carolina Press, 2002), and Graeme Turner, *Understanding Celebrity* (London: Sage Publications, 2004). Leo Braudy, *The Frenzy of Renown: Fame and Its History* (New York: Vintage, 1997) remains the go-to volume on the overall concept of fame and celebrity.

8 For the creation and promotion of stars through the Hollywood studio system, see Ronald L. Davis, *The Glamour Factory: Inside Hollywood's Big Studio System* (Dallas: Southern Methodist University Press, 1993); Douglas Gomery, *The Hollywood Studio System: A History* (London: British Film Institute, 2005); Ethan Mordden, *The Hollywood System: House Style in the Golden Years of the Movies* (New York: Knopf, 1988); Thomas Schatz, *The Genius of the System: Hollywood Filmmaking in the Studio Era* (Minneapolis: University of Minnesota Press, 2010). Richard deCordova, *Picture Personalities: The Emergence of the Star System in America* (Urbana, IL: University of Illinois Press, 1990) focuses on the promotion of the stars themselves in fan magazines and early movie journalism, and gives a good sense of the many outlets for promotional photography.

9 Peggy Phelan, 'Introduction', in Tim Etchells, *Certain Fragments: Contemporary Performance and Forced Entertainment* (London: Routledge, 1999), 14.

10 Barbara Hodgdon, 'Photography, Theater, Mnemonics; or, Thirteen Ways of Looking at a Still', in W. B. Worthen (ed.), with Peter Holland, *Theorizing Practice: Redefining Theatre History* (Basingstoke: Palgrave Macmillan, 2003), 88–119: 89.

11 For the aesthetics of the film still, see Steven Jacobs, 'The History and Aesthetics of the Classical Film Still', *History of Photography* 34/4 (2010), 373–86, and Thomas Van Parys, 'A Typology of the Publicity Still: Film for Photograph', *History of Photography* 32/1 (2008), 85–92.

12 Hodgdon, 'Photography, Theater, Mnemonics', 97.

13 The catalogue to a large and important exhibition, held at the Centre Pompidou-Metz in Metz, France in 2014, that looked at the history, practices, and associations of the paparazzi, gives a terrific selection of paparazzi images from the 1950s to the present, plus supporting essays, and as well—this was the most important intervention of the exhibition—introduces a range of artists who have appropriated the work of paparazzi as the basis for their own commentary on the practice, on the nature of celebrity, and on the public fascination with paparazzi shots. Clément Chéroux (ed.), *Paparazzi! Photographers, Stars, Artists* (published in French as *Paparazzi! Photographes, stars et artistes*) (Paris: Flammarion, 2014).

14 Carol Squiers, 'Class Struggle: The Invention of Paparazzi Photography and the Death of Diana, Princess of Wales', in Squiers (ed.), *Over Exposed: Essays on Contemporary Photography* (New York: New Press, 1999), 269–304: 271.

15 Peter Howe, *Paparazzi* (New York: Artisan, 2005), 17. Howe's remains the go-to book on the subject. See also Paolo Costantini et al., *Paparazzi* (Florence: Alinari, 1988), and Ron Galella, *The Stories Behind the Pictures: A Guide to the Paparazzi Approach* (Montville, NJ: Ron Galella Ltd, 2014).

16 Rahul Bhatia. 'Why India Has No Paparazzi', *Open* (11 September 2010). http://www.openthemagazine.com/article/india/why-india-has-no-paparazzi, accessed 15 April 2016.

17 Viral Bhayani. 'Page 3 Photographer Viral Bhayani Talks about India's Paparazzi Culture', *Hindustan Times* (18 July 2015), http://www.hindustantimes.com/bollywood/page-3-photographer-viral-bhayani-talks-about-india-s-paparazzi-culture/story-41IYCSrNc7eq7RmyWH5f2O.html, accessed 15 April 2016.

18 Zhu Ping. 'Paparazzi's Immorality over Singer's Death', *China Daily* (19 January 2015), http://www.chinadaily.com.cn/opinion/2015-01/19/content_19344317.htm. accessed 15 April 2016. This incident received some international coverage, as well.

19 Lisa Henderson. 'Access and Consent in Public Photography', in Larry Gross, John Stuart Katz, and Jay Ruby (eds.), *Image Ethics: The Moral Rights of Subjects in Photographs, Film, and Television* (New York: Oxford University Press, 1988), 91–107: 104.

20 Various versions of why Fellini, or his scriptwriter Ennio Flaiano, chose this name are in circulation. Fellini claimed to *Time* magazine that 'Paparazzo…suggests to me a buzzing insect, hovering, darting, stinging', which seems very apt, although Flaiano himself said that the name came from *Sulla riva dello Jonio*, Margherita Guidacci's 1957 translation of George Gissing's travel book *By the Ionian Sea* (1901), where it belongs to a restaurant owner. 'Paparazzo'—a local word for clam—is also a slang word for a camera lens in the Abruzzi dialect spoken by Flaiano. For paparazzi work in Rome at this time see Achille Bonito Oliva, *A Flash of Art: Action Photography in Rome 1953–1973* (Milan: Photology, 2003).

21 Roger Ebert, 'Great Movie: *La Dolce Vita*', http://www.rogerebert.com/reviews/great-movie-la-dolce-vita-1960, accessed 14 April 2016.

22 For Secchiarioli's career, see Diego Mormorio, *Tazio Secchiaroli: Greatest of the Paparazzi* (1998), trans. Alexandra Bonfante-Warren (New York: Harry N. Abrams, 1999).

23 Howe, *Paparazzi*, 59.

24 Felix Hoffmann, 'Posing Reality', in Hoffmann (ed.), *Ron Galella: Paparazzo extraordinaire* (Ostfildern: Hatje Cantz, 2012), 9–15: 15.

25 Over forty years later, Galella revealed that he thought that Brando had slugged him because he had found out about a top-secret affair between the actor and Jackie Onassis. Derek Blasberg, 'Ron Galella on the Paparazzi's Golden Era and Why Marlon Brando Broke His Jaw', *Vanity Fair* (19 November 2015). http://www.vanityfair.com/style/2015/11/ron-galella-photographer-interview, accessed 15 April 2016.

26 Ron Galella, *No Pictures* (Brooklyn, NY: Powerhouse Books, 2008).

27 Allan Sekula, 'Paparazzo Notes', *Photography Against the Grain: Essays and Photo Works 1973–1983* (Halifax, Nova Scotia: Press of the Nova Scotia College of Art and Design, 1984), 23–31: 24, 31. The article first appeared in *Artforum* 13/8 (April 1975).

28 What are *less* visible, however, are the pre-print corrections made to negatives in order to darken and eliminate other elements—like reflections from belts and buckles—that might also have caught the light, leaving the shining emphasis to fall on faces and hands. See Hoffmann, *Ron Galella*, 16–17.

29 As well as the flashgun, the telephoto lens—originally developed by the Germans to spy on the English coast in the 1890s—is invaluable for such work. By the 1930s, it was in widespread use in press photography. See Linkof, 'Public Eye', 175.
30 Howe, *Paparazzi*, 17.
31 Ginette Vincendeau, *Brigitte Bardot* (London: BFI/Palgrave Macmillan, 2013), 100.
32 My thanks to Vanessa Schwartz for bringing this movie to my notice. Her article on glamour photography and the paparazzi culture of the Cannes Film Festival in the early 1960s valuably draws our attention to the 'interdependent relation between the still and the moving image' in the early 1960s, and offers an interesting analysis of a far better known film featuring Bardot's relationship with press photographers, *Le Mépris* (dir. Jean-Luc Godard, 1963). Vanessa R. Schwartz, 'Wide Angle at the Beach', *Études photographiques* (26 November 2010), http://etudesphotographiques.revues.org/3455, accessed 14 January 2016.
33 Harvey and Saunders, *Diana*, 44.
34 Harvey and Saunders, *Diana*, 10.
35 Tina Brown, *The Diana Chronicles* (2007; New York: Anchor Books, 2008), 281, 3.
36 Quoted Brown, *Diana Chronicles*, 442, from an NBC News Bulletin, 31 August 1997.
37 Brown, *Diana Chronicles*, 444, 452. Brown provides a comprehensive assessment of the night of the crash and its aftermath, 441–99.
38 Carl Hiaasen, *Star Island* (New York: Alfred Knopf, 2010), 5.
39 Hiaasen, *Star Island*, 337.
40 Pascal Rostain, in Clément Chéroux et al., 'Hazards of the Trade: Interviews with Paparazzi'. Chéroux, *Paparazzi!*, 35.
41 Advertisement, *The Colonist* (12 July 1859), 2.
42 'Wholesale Flashlight', *Photographic News* 50 (12 January 1906), 34.
43 It should be noted that these decades also witnessed the development of sophisticated forms of less temporary outdoor lighting. General Electric's house journal, the *Magazine of Light* (1930–53), has little to say about flashlights, but is full of articles about landscape and garden illumination.
44 As Michele H. Bogart has shown, photographs were not widely used in advertising prior to the early 1920s, despite the attempts on the part of amateur photography journals, since early in the twentieth century, to promote its use in this respect. The camera, however, was frequently thought of as being *too* factual, whereas 'The painted or drawn illustration could at once evoke the fullness, the totality, of an object perceived and endow it with an aura of lifelikeness, or spirit'. Michele H. Bogart, *Artists, Advertising, and the Borders of Art* (Chicago: University of Chicago Press, 1995), 176.
45 George Wallace Hance, *Commercial Photography of Today* (Cleveland: *Abel's Photographic Weekly*, 1914), 33.
46 'Art and Artists', *Daily Inter Ocean* (4 March 1888), 13.
47 Hance, *Commercial Photography*, 93.
48 In early twentieth-century America, the best-known of these cameras were manufactured by Korona and by Folmer & Schwing.
49 J. B. Schriever, *Commercial, Press, Scientific Photography: Complete Self-Instructing Library of Practical Photography*, ix (Scranton: American School of Art and Photography, 1909), 229–40.
50 Baker, *Kingdom of the Camera*, 203.
51 Unsigned article, 'Herbert Gehr', *American Photo* 12 (September–October 2001), 32.

52 Don Mohler, 'Multiple Flashes in Press Photography', in National Press Photographers Association, *Complete Book of Press Photography* (New York: National Press Photographers Association, 1950), 77.

53 Geoffrey Gilbert, *Photo-Flash in Practice* (London: Focal Press, 1947), 195.

54 'Speaking of Pictures', *Life* (3 August 1942), 15. For the politics of food in the US during the Second World War, see Lizzie Collingham, *The Taste of War: World War II and the Battle for Food* (New York: Penguin, 2012), 415–34.

55 Thomas H. Garver, 'Afterword: O. Winston Link and His Working Method', in O. Winston Link, *Steam Steel and Stars: America's Last Steam Railroad* (New York: Harry N. Abrams, 1987), 139–44: 142. For Link, see also Tony Reevy, *O. Winston Link: Life Along the Line* (New York: Abrams, 2012).

56 'A Town Takes Its Own Picture', *Collier's* (22 September 1951), 34–5. For the history and significance of Levittown, including a discussion of the making of the Big Flash photograph, see Peter Bacon Hales, *Outside the Gates of Eden: The Dream of America from Hiroshima to Now* (Chicago: University of Chicago Press, 2014), 73–111: esp. 105–9.

57 James Bailey, *How to Select & Use Electronic Flash* (Tucson, AZ: HPBooks, 1983), 7.

58 Charles E. Kurtak, 'Photography Has Big Role in Opening of Met', *Burlington (N.C.) Daily Times-News* (13 October 1966), 3D. I deliberately choose a provincial newspaper as my source, to show how widely Big Shot news and images were disseminated: this same piece, written for the Associated Press, could be found syndicated nationwide.

59 *New York Evening News* (12 July 1969), 16.

60 Rochester Institute of Technology, 'The RIT Big Shot: Celebrating More Than a Quarter Century of Painting With Light', http://bigshot.cias.rit.edu/examplepage/, accessed 19 April 2016.

61 For the making of this photograph, see http://bigshot.cias.rit.edu/2014/02/09/rit-big-shot-no-29-high-falls-rochester-new-york/, accessed 19 April 2016.

62 Kodak still maintains a presence in Rochester, however: it has emerged from bankruptcy as a technology company focused on imaging for business.

63 Alfred Hitchcock in an interview with François Truffaut. Truffaut, *Hitchcock* (New York: Simon & Schuster, 1967), 160.

64 Lawrence Howe, 'Through the Looking Glass: Reflexivity, Reciprocality, and Defenestration in Hitchcock's *Rear Window*', *College English* 35/1 (winter 2008), 30.

65 John Belton, 'Introduction', in Belton (ed.), *Alfred Hitchcock's* Rear Window (Cambridge: Cambridge University Press, 2000), 12.

66 In its turn, Woolrich's story is heavily indebted to an unpleasant, and racist, short story by H. G. Wells, 'Through a Window'.

67 Cornell Woolrich, 'Rear Window', first published as 'It Had to be Murder' (1942), in *The Cornell Woolrich Omnibus* (New York: Penguin Books, 1998), 5–36: 25.

68 Woolrich, 'Rear Window', 31.

69 Anthony J. Mazzella, in 'Author, Auteur: Reading *Rear Window* from Woolrich to Hitchcock', mentions in passing this passage as the probable source for the flashbulb moment in the film, but he does not expand further on the story's references to illumination. In Walter Raubicheck and Walter Srebnick (eds.), *Hitchcock's Rereleased Films. From* Rope *to* Vertigo (Detroit: Wayne State University Press, 1991), 74.

70 Woolrich, 'Rear Window', 33.

71 The subjects of other photographs here establish Jeff's identity as a news journalist: a racing-car crash; a fire.

72 This aspect of *Rear Window* is comprehensively and thoughtfully discussed in Robert J. Corber, 'Resisting History: *Rear Window* and the Limits of the Postwar Settlement', *boundary 2* 19/1 (1992), 121–48.

73 '"Biggest Yet" Atom Blast Fired', *Reno Evening Gazette* (22 April 1952), 1. The operation's official name 'Operation Big Horn' resonates appallingly for many reasons.

74 The Pacific War Research Society, *The Day Man Lost: Hiroshima, 6 August 1945* (Tokyo: Kodansha International, 1972), 237, 236.

75 Richard B. Frank, *Downfall: The End of the Imperial Japanese Empire* (New York: Random House, 1999), 264.

76 Joseph Kanon, *Los Alamos* (New York: Broadway Books, 1997), 395.

77 Among the many accounts of this episode in American history, I've found Richard Rhodes, *The Making of the Atomic Bomb* (New York: Simon and Schuster, 1986), to be particularly clear and comprehensive.

78 In fact, the flash of a nuclear bomb is a *double* flash, the flashes too closely spaced to be discernible by the human eye. For a clear explanation of this, see Rhodes, *Making*, 671.

79 Kai Bird and Martin J. Sherwin, *American Prometheus: The Triumph and Tragedy of J. Robert Oppenheimer* (New York: Alfred A. Knopf, 2005), 307, quoting Richard P. Feynman, *Surely You're Joking, Mr Feynman! (Adventures of a Curious Character)* (New York: W. W. Norton, 1997), 134. Bird and Sherwin's book contains a number of first-hand accounts of the Trinity Test. Other accounts can be found at http://www.atomicarchive.com/Docs/Trinity/index.shtml, accessed 19 April 2016.

80 Brigadier General Thomas F. Farrell, in Cynthia C. Kelly (ed.), *The Manhattan Project: The Birth of the Atomic Bomb in the Words of Its Creators, Eyewitnesses, and Historians* (New York: Black Dog and Levanthal, 2007), 296. His account was included in General Leslie R. Groves's Memorandum for the Secretary of War of 18 July 1945.

81 These words come from a speech given by Rabi on 3 January 1946 at the opening session of the Boston Institute for Religious and Social Studies. Quoted by John S. Rigden, *Rabi, Scientist and Citizen*, with a new preface (Cambridge, MA: Harvard University Press, 2000), 156.

82 A notable alternate approach to atomic issues is through black comedy, like Stanley Kubrick's 1964 political satire *Dr Strangelove*. Kubrick's 'technical adviser' on visual issues was none other than Weegee; additionally, Weegee's distinctive Hungarian/NYC accent was apparently the vocal model for Peter Sellers's accent in the film. See Ed Sikov, *Mr Strangelove: A Biography of Peter Sellers* (New York: Hachette Books, 2002), 194–5.

83 Lansing Lamont, *Day of Trinity* (New York: Atheneum, 1965), 210.

84 For a critique of the banality of the libretto, see Ron Rosenbaum, 'The Opera's new Clothes. Why I Walked Out of Doctor Atomic', *Slate* (24 October 2008), http://www.slate.com/articles/life/the_spectator/2008/10/the_operas_new_clothes.html, accessed 25 April 2016.

85 *Doctor Atomic* libretto, quoted in Alex Ross, '*Doctor Atomic*. "Countdown"', *New Yorker* (3 October 2005), http://www.newyorker.com/magazine/2005/10/03/countdown-4, accessed 3 February 2017.

86 Ross, '*Doctor Atomic*'.

87 Ross, '*Doctor Atomic*'.

88 Julia Bryan-Wilson, 'Posing By the Cloud: US Nuclear Test Site Photography in Process', in John O'Brian (ed.), *Camera Atomica* (London: Black Dog Publications, 2015), 107–23.

89 VCE Inc., *How to Photograph an Atomic Bomb* (Santa Clarita, CA: VCE, Inc., 2006), 68. For other important work on photography and nuclear explosions, see Peggy Rosenthal, 'The Nuclear Mushroom Cloud as Cultural Image', *American Literary History* 3/1 (spring 1991), 63–92; Robert

Harman and John Luis Lucaites, 'The Iconic Image of the Mushroom Cloud and the Cold War Nuclear Optic', in Geoffrey Batchen and Jay Prosser (eds.), *Picturing Atrocity: Photography in Crisis* (London: Reaktion Books, 2012), 134–45.

90 Bryan-Wilson, 'Posing by the Cloud', 118.

91 Susan Schuppli, 'Radical Contact Prints', in O'Brian (ed.), *Camera Atomica*, 277–91.

92 Akira Mizuta Lippit, *Atomic Light (Shadow Optics)* (Minneapolis: University of Minnesota Press, 2005), 81–2. Lippit is quoting Willem de Kooning, 'What Abstract Art Means to Me' (1951), in *Collected Writings*, ed. George Scrivani (New York: Hanuman, 1988), 60.

93 Bryan-Wilson, 'Posing by the Cloud', 119.

94 Marguerite Duras, *Hiroshima mon amour* (1959), trans. Richard Seaver (New York: Grove Press, 1961), 15. Film dir. Alain Resnais, 1959.

Chapter 9

1 Such rings were newly fashionable, after the De Beer company's expansion in South Africa enormously increased the supply of diamonds; Tiffany & Co. introduced the 'Tiffany setting' in 1886 which maximized the diamond's brilliance by raising it up from the band's surface, and department store catalogues, such as Sears and Roebucks', started to carry advertisements for diamond engagement rings from the 1890s.

2 Although other associations may come into play. Pierre Bourdieu may be something of an outlier here, but he remarked that flash 'adds to the solemnity of the photographic act and doubles its power of solemnization, evoking the pomp of the official ceremonies with which it is habitually associated', albeit also noticing the camera's presence at celebratory family events. Pierre Bourdieu, *Photography: A Middle-Brow Art*, trans. Shaun Whiteside (1965; Cambridge: Polity Press, 1990), 179, n. 21.

3 *Half a Sixpence*, music and lyrics by David Heneker, first London performance 21 March 1963; film (directed by George Sidney) 1967.

4 More people who fell into this category were to be found in Britain than in the United States, where the majority of technological innovators were those who made their living from photography. This, at any rate, is the conclusion to be drawn from photgraphic journals of the time.

5 For a succinct account of this dichotomy, and the social and industrial conditions that helped to maintain it, see Stephen Knott, *Amateur Craft: History and Theory* (London: Bloomsbury, 2015), p. xiv.

6 Paul Spencer Sternberger, *Between Amateur and Aesthete: The Legitimization of Photography as Art in America, 1880–1900* (Albuquerque, NM: University of New Mexico Press, 2001), p. xi. For the British context, see Grace Seiberling with Carolyn Bloore, *Amateurs, Photography, and the Mid-Victorian Imagination* (Chicago: University of Chicago Press, 1986).

7 P. H. Emerson, *Naturalistic Photography for Students of the Art* (London: Sampson Low, Marston, Searle & Rivington, 1889), 147. He is not entirely consistent on the topic of this new light, however: later, he puts down art critic P. G. Hamerton's critique of photography as unable to bring out the detail to be found in dark subjects by saying 'that probably he does not know that photographs can now be taken at midnight by a *flash of light* in a fraction of a second, and with very fair results, as any one can prove for himself', *Naturalistic Photography*, 283.

8 W. S. Ritch, 'Flashlight Portraiture', *American Amateur Photographer* 15 (June 1903), 278.

9 Robert A. Stebbins, *Amateurs, Professionals, and Serious Leisure* (Montreal: McGill-Queen's University Press, 1992), 6–7. For an illuminating and extensive study of hobbyism in its

American context—albeit one that curiously omits photography—see Steven M. Gelber, *Hobbies: Leisure and the Culture of Work in America* (New York: Columbia University Press, 1999).

10 See Madelyn Moeller, 'Ladies of Leisure: Domestic Photography in the Nineteenth Century', in Kathryn Grover (ed.), *Hard at Play: Leisure in America, 1840–1940* (Amherst, MA: University of Massachusetts Press, 1992), 139–60. Catherine Weed Barnes, herself an active member of the Society of Amateur Photographers of New York (where she claimed to have experienced no discrimination), offers a powerful rebuttal to some of the objections raised against women's membership of photographic societies that also gives a clear picture of the opposition that they could face in 'Why Ladies Should Be Admitted to Membership in Photographic Societies', *American Amateur Photographer* 1 (December 1889), 223–4.

11 For the impact of Kodak's products on popular photography, as traced through the history and evolution of Kodak's advertisements, see Nancy Martha West, *Kodak and the Lens of Nostalgia* (Charlottesville, VA: University of Virginia Press, 2000).

12 There is an extremely useful list of Kodak camera models and prices available at http://www.kodak.com/global/en/consumer/products/techInfo/aa13/aa13.pdf, accessed 5 April 2016.

13 Unsigned article, 'The Present Aspect of Amateur Photography', *American Amateur Photographer* 1 (July 1889), 5.

14 Olla Mason, 'Popularising Kodakery', *Photo-Era Magazine* 56 (February 1926), 68–9.

15 Advertisement, Eastman Kodak Company, 'Flashlight Time', *American Amateur Photographer* 15 (October 1903), p. v.

16 C. Mills, 'Flash-light Photography', *Photographic Times* 30/4 (1 April 1898), 153–5: 155.

17 Heinz K. Henisch and Bridget A. Henisch, *Positive Pleasures: Early Photography and Humor* (University Park, PA: Pennsylvania State University Press, 1998), p. ix.

18 'A Remarkable Invention', *St-Louis Globe-Democrat* (18 October 1887), 7; repr. from the *Philadelphia Evening Telegram*.

19 See Melody Davis, *Women's Views: The Narrative Stereograph in Nineteenth-Century America* (Lebanon, NH: University of New Hampshire Press, 2015).

20 For Austen, see Anne Novotny, *Alice's World: The Life and Photography of an American Original, Alice Austen, 1866–1952* (Old Greenwich, CT: The Chatham Press, 1976).

21 Negative sleeve caption: Alice Austen House, http://aliceausten.org/trude-i, accessed 6 April 2016.

22 Grace Lees-Maffei, 'Introduction: Studying Advice: Historiography, Methodology, Commentary, Bibliography', *Journal of Design History* 16/1 (2003), 1–14: 1.

23 Louis Clarence Bennett, *Flash Lights and How to Take Them* (New York: Louis Clarence Bennett, 1891), 10.

24 Bennett, *Flash Lights*, 31.

25 F. J. Mortimer, *Magnesium Light Photography* (London: Dawbarn & Ward, 1906), 12.

26 D. Grant, *Manual of Photography: With Special Reference to Work in the Tropics* (London: Murray and Evenden, 1914).

27 For the introduction of half-tone printing, and its impact on reading and spectatorial practices, see Gerry Beegan, 'Learning to Read the Halftone', *The Mass Image: A Social History of Photomechanical Reproduction in Victorian London* (Basingstoke: Palgrave Macmillan, 2008), 186–209.

28 F. W. Guerin, *Portraits in Photography by the Aid of Flash* (n.p.: n.pub., 1898), [6]. In his technical notes, we learn that he used a Williams flash lamp with thirty-six cups for powder—something way out of the reach of the average amateur—sold by A. A. and H. T. Anthony, and Luxo flash powder: 52–3. The inclusion of such information perfectly demonstrates

the difficulty of separating out information, advertising, and what we might term product placement.

29 Guerin, *Portraits*, 33.

30 Rus Arnold, *Flash Photography* (Chicago: Ziff-Davis Publishing Company [Little Technical Library], 1940), 15.

31 John J. Curtis, *Flashlight for the Amateur Photographer* (London: British Periodicals Ltd, 1925), 3–4.

32 Mortimer, *Magnesium Light Photography*, 85–6.

33 Wm. S. Ritch, *Amateur Portraiture by Flash-Light* (Rochester, NY: Eastman Kodak Co., 1904), 4–5.

34 H. G. Wells, *The Time Machine* (1895; Oxford: Oxford University Press World's Classics, 2017), 53.

35 C. J. Cutcliffe Hyne, *The Recipe for Diamonds* (London: W. Heinemann, 1894).

36 Alexander Black, *Captain Kodak: A Camera Story* (Boston: Lothrop Publishing Company, 1899), 31.

37 Arnold Bennett, *The Grand Babylon Hotel* (New York: George H. Doran, 1902), 151. Rocco is actually Elihu P. Rucker, from New Jersey—an Italian name was, however, essential to his profession.

38 *Flashlight Photography* (Chicago: James H. Smith & Sons: n.d. [early 1920s]), [7].

39 Curtis, *Flashlight*, 43.

40 Curtis, *Flashlight*, 10.

41 Curtis, *Flashlight*, 29–31.

42 Curtis, *Flashlight*, 12–13.

43 This transformation was very noticeable in other spheres of photography, as well, especially its commercial applications, whether one considers the use of flash in advertising, or in the documentation of products, workplaces, and interior architecture and design.

44 In the US, the German-originating Agfa products were marketed by Ansco, in Binghamton: the two companies merged in 1928. The subsequent commercial history is a complex one, in large part because of the Second World War: the company was the last to be sold to the US in the 1960s as 'enemy assets'.

45 User's manual, *Picture Taking with the Brownie Flash Six-20*, no other details on unpaginated pamphlet: early 1940s. This manual is reproduced, in its entirety, on Mike Butkus's extraordinarily valuable website, a camera manual library (all lovingly scanned and uploaded by him) which contains over 2,000 items, and is an indispensable reference for the appearance and working of cameras and flash units. http://www.butkus.org/chinon/index.html, accessed 8 April 2016.

46 Arnold, *Flash Photography*, 7.

47 'By changing the distance between the flash and the subject illuminated you can get more light or less. Suppose you place the lamp 8 feet from a subject; when you move it so as to cut this distance in half (to 4 feet), you quadruple the effect of its light. Take it twice the distance away, and you cut its power to one fourth, in conformity with the rule that the intensity of light varies inversely with the square of its distance.' Arnold, *Flash Photography*, 12.

48 Arnold, *Flash Photography*, 16.

49 West, *Kodak*, 113. Eastman's words are from Elizabeth Brayer, *George Eastman: A Biography* (Baltimore: Johns Hopkins University Press, 1966), 135.

50 West, *Kodak*, 114.
51 Arnold, *Flash Photography*, 96.
52 Arnold, *Flash Photography*, 7.
53 Arnold, *Flash Photography*, 8.
54 Arnold, *Flash Photography*, 8.
55 The history of advertising brings together a full and complex understanding of changing consumer markets and ideas of taste; visual and typographic styles; theories of signification, allusion, and typifying (both direct and oblique); modes of persuasion; the national and international flows of capital and agency staff; the representation, inclusion, and exclusion of women, men, and racial, differently abled, and other visible minorities, and the targeting of particular groups through particular images or emphases. The literature surrounding it is commensurately huge: I've found especially useful Jackson Lears, *Fables of Abundance: A Cultural History of Advertising in America* (New York: Basic Books, 1994); Winston Fletcher, *Powers of Persuasion: The Inside Story of British Advertsing: 1951–2000* (Oxford: Oxford University Press, 2008); and Juliann Sivulka, *Soap, Sex and Cigarettes: A Cultural History of American Advertising* (Belmont, CA: Wadsworth Publishing Co., 1998).
56 This camera was manufactured by the Federal Manufacturing & Engineering Co. of Brooklyn, NY (best known as a company that made enlargers) from *c.*1947 to 1956. At around $11.99 for camera and flash unit, it was aimed at a family market, and the advertising reflects this.
57 Lancelot Vining, *My Way with the Miniature* (13th edn., London: Focal Press, 1958), 188.
58 Howard Luray, *Your Simple Flash Camera: How to Use It* (San Francisco: Camera Craft Publishing Company, 1953), 1.
59 Advertisement for Polaroid 600 System Photography, *Ebony* (August 1984), 10.
60 Advertisement for the Kodak Colorburst 250 instant camera, *Ebony* (November 1979), 8.
61 Lears, *Fables of Abundance*, 380.
62 Kmart Camera Department advertisement, *Ebony* (April 1983), 21.
63 https://www.youtube.com/watch?v=30KXzBXKZnM, accessed 11 April 2016.
64 Advertisement for Sylvania flashbulb, in such mainstream outlets as *Reader's Digest* and *Life* 44 (21 April 1958), 74.
65 https://archive.org/details/SylvaniaCameraFlash-bulbsCommercial, accessed 11 April 2016.
66 https://www.youtube.com/watch?v=bpjyUQsPiBA, accessed 11 April 2016.
67 http://www.digitaltrends.com/mobile/camera-phone-history/, accessed 9 April 2016.
68 James Bailey, *How to Select & Use Electronic Flash* (Tucson, AZ: HPBooks, 1983), 11. Bailey's book gives a very clear and useful account of the development and workings of the electronic flash.
69 This is according to Mary Meeker's annual Internet Trends Report.
70 At 2.28 p.m. ET on 11 April 2016.
71 For an excellent and highly informative example of the genre, see Tilo Gockel, *Creative Flash Photography: Great Lighting with Small Flashes: 40 Flash Workshops* (Santa Barbara, CA: Rocky Nook, 2014).
72 http://directdaily.blogspot.com/2009/06/nikon-sensory-light-box.html, accessed 9 April 2016.
73 http://www.discoverdigitalphotography.com/2015/dont-make-these-7-mistakes-with-flash/#more-1010, accessed 13 April 2016. Googling 'flash photography tips' or 'flash photography courses' opens up a wealth of information, most of it very helpful (and most of it with advertisements in its margins).

74 All the same, amateur use of flash at concerts has led to at least one extraordinary photograph by a professional photographer, Alfred Wertheimer, who, shooting Elvis Presley from behind during a 1956 concert, captured a flashbulb going off in the crowd that appears like a starburst above his head.

75 Scott Kelby, *The Digital Photography Book*, iii (Berkeley: Peachpit Press, 2009), 172.

76 J. Phillip Pickett, 'Why Do Dogs Get Blue, Not Red, Eyes in Flash Photos?', *Scientific American* (28 October 2002). https://www.scientificamerican.com/article/why-do-dogs-get-blue-not/, accessed 13 April 2016.

77 http://www.doctordisney.com/2013/03/20/doctor-disney-explains-this-is-why-flash-photography-is-not-allowed-on-rides-and-attractions/, accessed 24 March 2016.

78 Nicholas Lander, 'Flash Photography in Restaurants', *Financial Times* (London), 18 October 2013.

79 Cited by Martin H. Evans, 'Amateur Photographers in Art Galleries: Assessing the Harm Done by Flash Photography', http://people.ds.cam.ac.uk/mhe1000/musphoto/flashphoto2.htm, accessed 13 April 2016.

80 Carl Grimm, cited in 'Why Isn't Flash Photography Permitted in Museums?', 29 May 2000, http://www.straightdope.com/columns/read/1783/why-isnt-flash-photography-permitted-in-museums, accessed 13 April 2016.

81 Evans, 'Amateur Photographers'. Photography of any sort in museums has been criticized by some curators, who argue that it stops visitors from engaging fully with the displayed objects themselves.

82 Catherine Zuromskis, *Snapshot Photography: The Lives of Images* (Cambridge, MA: MIT Press, 2013), 8.

83 Zuromskis, *Snapshot Photography*, 9. For the history of snapshot photography, see also Brian Coe and Paul Gates, *The Snapshot Photograph: The Rise of Popular Photography 1888–1939* (London: Ash and Grant, 1977).

84 Elisabeth Sussman, 'In/Of Her Time: Nan Goldin's Photographs', in Nan Goldin, David Armstrong, and Hans Werner Holzwarth (eds.), *Nan Goldin: I'll Be Your Mirror* (New York: Whitney Museum of Art, 1996), 25–44: 31. As Sussman points out, Goldin's style changes in the early 1990s: having been 'a master of nighttime dazzle and found glamour in tacky objects caught in a strobed glare' (41), she shifted to more subtle, natural lighting.

85 Rautert reprised this idea in 'Self-Portrait with Green Wall' (2004), in which his face, in a mirror, is again replaced with the effects of flash. But we see his hands, a little of his torso, the camera—and, more importantly, three-quarters of the image is taken up with a shot of four of his students, painting a high interior wall green prior to an installation. If he has here taken self-effacement literally, it is in order to give prior place to his students, his contribution to an artistic future.

Chapter 10

1 Howard Nemerov, 'The Winter Lightning', *The Winter Lightning: Selected Poems of Howard Nemerov* (London: Rapp & Whiting, 1968), 7–8.

2 Henri Cartier-Bresson, 'The Decisive Moment' (1952), *The Mind's Eye: Writings on Photography and Photographers*, ed. Michael L. Sand (New York: Aperture, 2005), 28.

3 Quoted in Peter Galassi, *Henri Cartier-Bresson: The Modern Century* (New York: Museum of Modern Art, 2010), 68, n. 30.

4 Henri Cartier-Bresson, 'The Mind's Eye' (1976), *Mind's Eye*, 16.

5 Claude Cookman, 'Margaret Bourke-White and Henri Cartier-Bresson: Gandhi's Funeral', *History of Photography* 22/2 (1998), 199–209: 200. My thanks to Nadya Bair for bringing this article to my attention.

6 'Portrait of the Artist: Sebastião Salgado, Photographer', Interview with Laura Barnett, *The Guardian* (28 February 2012), http://www.theguardian.com/culture/2012/feb/28/sebastiao-salgado-photographer, accessed 20 April 2016.

7 Irving Penn, *Worlds in a Small Room* (New York: Grossman Publishers, 1974), 7.

8 Nick Kelsh, *How to Photograph Your Life* (New York: Stewart, Tabori & Chang, 2003), 14, 24, 36.

9 Joe McNally, *The Hot Shoe Diaries: Big Light from Small Flashes* (Berkeley: New Riders, 2009), 162.

10 Edited from interviews given by Diane Arbus in 1971, *Diane Arbus: An Aperture Monograph* (Millerton, NY: Aperture/Museum of Modern Art, 1972), 9. See also Arthur Lubow, *Diane Arbus: Portrait of a Photographer* (New York: HarperCollins, 2016), 409 for Arbus's waning enthusiasm for what she termed '"remorseless frontal" portraits illuminated by flash'.

11 John Harvey, *The Story of Black* (London: Reaktion Books, 2013), 11.

12 No photographic black, of course, is ever *completely* black: a print of the darkest night returns some photons to the eye.

13 Noam M. Elcott, *Artificial Darkness: An Obscure History of Modern Art and Media* (Chicago: University of Chicago Press, 2016), 31.

14 A. Roger Ekirch, *At Day's Close: Night in Times Past* (New York: W. W. Norton, 2005), 339. For night-time and darkness, see also Peter C. Baldwin, *In the Watches of the Night: Life in the Nocturnal City, 1820–1930* (Chicago: University of Chicago Press, 2012); Wolfgang Schivelbusch, *Disenchanted Night: The Industrialization of Light in the Nineteenth Century* (Berkeley and Los Angeles: University of California Press, 1995).

15 William Sharpe, *New York Nocturne: The City After Dark in Art, Literature, and Photography* (Princeton: Princeton University Press, 2008).

16 David William Foster, *Urban Photography in Argentina: Nine Artists of the Post-Dictatorship Era* (Jefferson, NC: McFarland & Co., 2007), 46.

17 Nicholas Christopher, *Somewhere in the Night: Film Noir and the American City* (New York: Free Press, 1997), 1. The literature on film noir is enormous: for description, analysis, and many examples, see Foster Hirsch, *The Dark Side of the Screen: Film Noir*, rev. and updated (Boston: Da Capo Press, 2008)—esp. ch. 1, 'The City at Night', 1–21; Eddie Muller, *Dark City: The Lost World of Film Noir* (New York: St Martin's Griffin, 1998); James Naremore, *More than Night: Film Noir and Its Contexts* (updated and expanded edn., Berkeley and Los Angeles: University of California Press, 2008); Alain Silver et al., *The Film Noir Encyclopedia* (New York: Overlook Press, 2010); Alain Silver and James Ursini, *The Noir Style* (Woodstock, NY: Overlook Press, 1999).

18 For a comparison between Weegee's treatment of topography and the spaces of film noir, see Edward Dimendberg, *Film Noir and the Spaces of Modernity* (Cambridge, MA: Harvard University Press, 2004), 47–85.

19 David Bordwell, Janet Staiger, and Kristin Thompson, *The Classical Hollywood Cinema: Film Style and Mode of Production to 1960* (New York: Columbia University Press, 1985), 223. On the development of film lighting in the US, see John Alton, *Painting with Light* (1949; Berkeley and Los Angeles: University of California Press, 1995); Patrick Keating, *Hollywood Lighting from the Silent Era to Film Noir* (New York: Columbia University Press, 2010), and in Germany, Frances Guerin, *A Culture of Light: Cinema and Technology in 1920s Germany* (Minneapolis: University of Minnesota Press, 2005).

20 Daisuke Miyao, *The Aesthetics of Shadow: Lighting and Japanese Cinema* (Durham, NC: Duke University Press, 2013), 27. Miyao's book offers an excellent study of the material and cultural conditions that affected the lighting of Japanese cinema in the first half of the twentieth century; the means by which various effects of darkness, illumination, and shadow were produced and the associations that they carried. Among these were the dramatic, brutal flashes of swords that were a dominant motif in *jidaigeki*, or period drama films.

21 This particular camera can only shoot up to fifteen minutes at a time, however, so any claim that it was taken all in one go shouldn't be taken completely literally.

22 *La casa muda*, Uruguay, 2010 (dir. Gustavo Henández). My thanks to Dinah Birch, who first told me about this film.

23 For German expressionist cinema, see Lotte H. Eisner, *The Haunted Screen: Expressionism in the German Cinema and the Influence of Max Reinhardt* (1952), trans. Roger Greaves (Berkeley and Los Angeles: University of California Press, 1969).

24 Joseph Conrad, *Heart of Darkness* (1899; London: Penguin Classics, 2007), 96.

25 Brassaï, *Proust in the Power of Photography* (*Marcel Proust sous l'emprise de la photographie*, 1997), trans. Richard Howard (Chicago: University of Chicago Press, 2001), p. xi.

26 Brassaï, *Proust*, 107.

27 Undated page, Gilberte Brassaï Archives, quoted by Annick Lionel-Marie, 'Letting the Eye Be Light', in Alain Sayag and Annick Lionel-Marie, *Brassaï: The Monograph* (Boston: Bulfinch Press, 2000), 151–64: 157.

28 Paul Morand, foreword to *Brassaï: Paris By Night* (*Paris de Nuit*, 1933), trans. Stuart Gilbert (Paris: Arts et Métiers Graphiques, 1993), n.p.

29 This fusion could be found in other aspects of his work: he had friends pose as clients in images of brothels, for example, and he appears himself as an anonymous Parisian exiting a urinal. Likewise, Brandt posed individuals in some of his photographs: for example, his first wife, Eva Boros, appears as a sex worker in night-time Hamburg. However, his first book, *The English at Home* (1936), is far more of a bona fide documentary photo book.

30 Brassaï, *Conversations with Picasso*, trans. Jane Marie Todd (Chicago: University of Chicago Press, 1999), 63. Brassaï notes on the same occasion that when Picasso asked him why he did not use spotlights, he explained that he does not like the 'chopped-up, muddled shadows. I like light from a single source and I soften the shadows by reflecting it off screens'.

31 Paul Delany, *Bill Brandt: A Life* (Palo Alto, CA: Stanford University Press, 2004), 126. For Brandt, see also Sarah Hermanson Meister, *Bill Brandt: Shadow & Light* (New York: Museum of Modern Art, 2013).

32 Bill Brandt, artist statement, www.americansuburbx.com/2011/04/bill-brandt-statement-on-photography.html, accessed 27 August 2017. This site says that the statement is printed in *Camera in London* (1948): however, I have not located it in the copies of this that I have consulted.

33 Bill Brandt, 'Pictures by Night', in L. A . Mannheim, *The Rollei Way: The Rolleiflex and Rolleicord Photographer's Companion* (1951; 9th edn. London: Focal Press, 1970), 177–86: 178.

34 James Bone, 'Introduction' to Bill Brandt, *A Night in London* (London: Country Life, 1938), pp. ii–iii.

35 Brandt, *Camera in London*, 89. There is some ambiguity in this language: the reference could well be to portable lighting units rather than to flash, but both the remainder of the written testimony and the visual evidence of some of the pictures indicate that flash was certainly used.

36 The painter and sculptor Henry Moore, whom Brandt was later to photograph, was similarly sent off, and at the same time, to draw night-time life in the Tube shelters. For a comparison

of their work, see David Ashford, 'Children Asleep in the Underground: The Tube Shelters of Brandt and Moore', *Cambridge Quarterly* 36/4 (2007), 295–316.

37 William Sansom, *The Blitz: Westminster at War* (Oxford: Oxford University Press, 1990), 175. In this context, Paul Virilio's description of the bombing raids as a '*son-et-lumière*, a series of special effects, an atmospheric projection designed to confuse a frightened, blacked-out population' is highly prescient. Paul Virilio, *War and Cinema: The Logistics of Perception*, trans. Patrick Camiller (London: Verso, 1989), 78. For this quotation and the introduction to Sansom's work, I'm indebted to Lara Feigel, '"The savage and austere light of a burning world": The Cinematic Blitz', ch. 6 of *Literature, Cinema and Politics 1930–1945: Reading between the Frames* (Edinburgh: Edinburgh University Press, 2010), 193–231.

38 John Sutherland, *Stephen Spender: A Literary Life* (Oxford: Oxford University Press, 2005), 295–6.

39 Stephen Spender, 'Abyss', *Citizens in War—and After* (London: Harrap, 1945), 52–3; repr. in revised form as 'Rejoice in the Abyss', in Spender, *New Collected Poems*, ed. Michael Brett (London: Faber and Faber, 2004), 243–4.

40 For Shiras, see Jean-Christophe Bailly, *George Shiras: In the Heart of the Dark Night* (Paris: Éditions Xavier Barral, 2015).

41 George Shiras, *Hunting Wildlife with Camera and Flashlight*, 2 vols. (London: National Geographic Society, 1930).

42 Shiras, *The Independent* (7 June 1900), quoted in Shiras, 'The Wild Life of Lake Superior, Past and Present', *National Geographic Magazine* 40 (August 1921), 113–204: 176–7. After they had been 'flashed', deer were often scared off for some time from the area where they had had this disorienting experience.

43 An extensive account of different possible means of taking wildlife photographs, including by various flash methods, and an introduction to contemporary wildlife photographers, is given in William Nesbit, *How To Hunt with the Camera: A Complete Guide to All Forms of Outdoor Photography* (New York: E. P. Dutton, 1926).

44 Sonia Voss, 'George Shiras and the Birth of Wildlife Photography', in Bailly, *George Shiras*, 81–9: 87.

45 Although the majority of these pictures show the black-and-white contrasts of extreme and endless whiteness, or complete dark, Ponting did, however, make a couple of successful Autochrome images on this expedition: he had been furnished with a number of boxes of Autochrome plates by the Lumière company, although these 'were really too old to obtain satisfactory results by the time I had an opportunity of using them on the beautiful afterglow effects we had in the autumn, and they had deteriorated in the slow journey through the heat of the Tropics'. Herbert G. Ponting, *The Great White South or With Scott in the Antarctic* (1921; London: Duckworth & Co., 1923), 118.

46 Ponting, *Great White South*, 122.

47 Ponting, *Great White South*, 137. Another picture of Castle Berg taken by Ponting on 17 September 1911, when there was more natural light, is made impressive through the placement of a dog-sleigh team in front of it in order to indicate its imposing size.

48 C. G. Schillings, *With Flashlight and Rifle: A Record of Hunting Adventures and of Studies in Wild Life in Equatorial East Africa*, trans. Frederic Whyte, 2 vols. (London: Hutchinson & Co., 1906), vol. i, p. xii.

49 Krista Thompson, *Shine: The Visual Economy of Light in African Diasporic Aesthetic Practice* (Durham, NC: Duke University Press, 2015), 44.

50 Thompson, *Shine*, 14.

51 See e.g. Anne Anlin Cheng, *Second Skin: Josephine Baker & the Modern Surface* (New York: Oxford University Press, 2011). Her comment that 'for a brief period in the early twentieth century, before cultural values collapsed back once again into a (shallow) surface and (authentic) interior divide, there was this tensile and delicate moment when these flirtation with the surface led to profound engagements with and reimaginings of the relationship between interiority and exteriority, between essence and covering' (11) is very pertinent to the play on visibility and invisibility in relation not just to skin, but also to the lighting of cityscapes that I have been discussing in this chapter. For the bright shininess of skin, and such photographic practices as 'lighting for whiteness', see Richard Dyer, *White* (London: Routledge, 1997). Robert Mapplethorpe's portraits of black bodies provide a key point of convergence for debates about the fetishizing of their shine.

52 See transcript of 'Polaroid & Apartheid: Inside the Beginnings of the Boycott, Divestment Movement Against South Africa', *Democracy Now* (13 December 2013), https://www.democracynow.org/2013/12/13/polaroid_apartheid_inside_the_beginnings_of, and 'Polaroid and South Africa', http://kora.matrix.msu.edu/files/50/304/32-130-1F7-84-african_activist_archive-a0a8g3-b_12419.pdf, both accessed 2 February 2017.

53 Christopher Bonanos, 'Polaroid and Apartheid', *Polaroidland* (6 April 2013), http://www.polaroidland.net/2013/04/06/polaroid-and-apartheid/, accessed 2 February 2017.

54 Unsigned article, 'Flash-Powders for Autochrome Work', *British Journal of Photography* (7 October 1910), 74–5: 74.

55 Ansel Adams, notes written in 1983. Quoted in James L. Enyeart, 'Quest for Color', in Harry M. Callahan (ed.), *Ansel Adams in Color* (Boston: Little, Brown and Co., 1993), 9–32: 13. All the same, Adams was happy to photograph in colour for the money that he earned from commercial commissions.

56 See Mark Cleghorn, *Portrait Photography: Secrets of Posing and Lighting* (New York: Lark Books, 2004), 86.

57 'The even, shadowless illumination brings out in detail and is perfect for small tabletop objects, models, insects, flowers, coins, stamps and similar objects'; unsigned article, 'Wrap a Ring Light Around', *Popular Mechanics* (February 1971), 84–7 and 198: 84.

58 Russell Hart, 'Ring Cycle', *American Photo* (November–December 1994), 120.

59 Martin Parr and Gerry Badger, *The Photobook: A History* (London: Phaidon Press, 2004), 307.

60 *Parr by Parr: Quentin Bajac meets Martin Parr: Discussions with a Promiscuous Photographer* (Amsterdam: Schildt Publishing, 2010), 36.

61 Martin Parr, quoted in Val Williams, *Martin Parr* (2nd edn., London: Phaidon Press, 2014), 156.

62 For Parr's colour work—black-and-white reproduction can't do justice to my point about saturation—see http://www.martinparr.com/.

63 See Parr's responses to faq on his home page: http://www.martinparr.com/faq, accessed 20 April 2016.

64 Williams, *Parr*, 23, 160.

65 http://www.vogue.co.uk/gallery/nick-knight-in-vogue, accessed 24 February 2017.

66 See Charlotte Cotton, 'Introduction', *Nick Knight* (New York: Harper Collins, 2009), 7–21.

67 Alice Rawsthorn, 'Vision Quest', *T Style Magazine. New York Times* (15 April 2007), http://query.nytimes.com/gst/fullpage.html?res=9A04E1DF153FF936A25757C0A9619C8B63&pagewanted=all, accessed 2 February 2017.

68 Joanna Lowry, 'Modern Time: Revisiting the Tableau', in Jan Baetens, Alexander Streitberger, and Hilde Van Gelder (eds.), *Time and Photography* (Leuven: Leuven University Press, 2010), 47–64: 56.

69 Frank Van Riper, 'Focused Flash for Great Portraits' (first published in the *Washington Post*, 31 January 1997), *Talking Photography: Viewpoints on the Art, Craft and Business* (New York: Allworth Press, 2002), 94–7: 97.

70 Gary Schneider, quoted in Jackie Higgins, *Why It Does Not Have to Be In Focus: Modern Photography Explained* (London: Thames and Hudson, 2013), 27.

71 Gary Schneider, quoted in David Rosenberg, 'The Intimate Results of Photographing Subjects for Eight Minutes Each', 'Behold: The Photo Blog', *Slate* (8 April 2015), http://www.slate.com/blogs/behold/2015/04/08/gary_schneider_the_series_heads_examines_the_performative_aspect_of_making.html, accessed 2 February 2017. For further colour examples of Schneider's work, see http://www.garyschneider.net/index.cfm.

72 Max Kozloff, quoted in Higgins, *Modern Photography Explained*, 27.

73 For art photography's appropriation of paparazzi style, see Quentin Bajac, 'Migrations and Appropriations: Artists and the Paparazzi Aesthetic', Chéroux, *Paparazzi!*, 214–39.

74 Bajac, 'Migrations', 234.

75 See Binschtok's website: https://viktoriabinschtok.wordpress.com/work-3/flash/, accessed 20 April 2016.

76 Baker, *Kingdom of the Camera*, 13.

77 Unsigned article, 'Army Flashlight Bomb Illuminated Objectives for Night Air Pictures', *Life* 9 (11 November 1940), 123.

78 Mai Nam, in Tim Page, *Another Vietnam: Pictures of the War from the Other Side* (Washington, DC: National Geographic, 2002), 52.

79 Sarah Pickering, speaking at 'Beyond Vision: Photography, Art and Science', Conference held at Science Museum, London, 12 September 2015.

80 'Migratory Aesthetics. Sutap Biswas, *Magnesium Bird*, 2004, AHRC Center for Cultural Analysis, Theory & History, University of Leeds. http://www.leeds.ac.uk/cath/ahrc/events/2006/0111/abs/biswas.html, accessed 2 June 2016.

81 For the *Lightning Field* in general, see Kenneth Baker, *The Lightning Field* (New Haven: Yale University Press, 2008), and the more personal and meditative approaches offered by Geoff Dyer, *White Sands: Experiences from the Outside World* (New York: Pantheon Books, 2016), 67–80, and Laura Raicovich, *At the Lightning Field* (Minneapolis: Coffee House Press, 2017).

82 Nobuyoshi Araki, 'The Photo Apparatus Between Man and Woman', in Ivan Vartanian, Akihiro Hatanaka, and Yutaka Kambayashi (eds.), *Setting Sun: Writings by Japanese Photographers* (New York: Aperture, 2006), 145.

83 Walter Benjamin, 'On Some Motifs in Baudelaire', *Illuminations: Essays and Reflections*, ed. Hannah Arendt (New York: Schocken Books, 1968), 155–200: 174–5.

84 This channelling of raw electricity has its own history. Back in 1874, T. L. Phipson wrote about what he saw as the photographic potential of lightning, and recounted a couple of experiments involving its power, including one by a Mr Justice Grove, who 'several years ago…produced certain images similar to those produced by the lightning-flash. He scratched a design with the point of his penknife upon a piece of white paper; he placed it between two plates of polished glass, which were there and then submitted to an electric discharge. On removing the plates, no image was visible upon the glass, but on exposing the latter for a few minutes to the vapour of hydrofluoric acid the impression came out most distinctly.' Dr T. L. Phipson, *Familiar Letters on Some Mysteries of Nature and Discoveries in Science* (London: Sampson Low, Marston, Searle, & Rivington, 1876), 214.

85 Hiroshi Sugimoto, statement on artist's website, http://www.sugimotohiroshi.com/index.html, accessed 2 June 2016. The homage to Fox Talbot is most evident in a concurrent series, in which Sugimoto is creating toned silver-gelatin prints from the pioneer's original negatives.

86 Hiroshi Sugimoto, 'Let There Be Lightning', *Hiroshi Sugimoto: Nature of Light* (Shizuoka, Japan: Izu Photo Museum and Nohara, 2010), 79–85: 79, 81.

BIBLIOGRAPHY

Select Newspapers, Periodicals, and Journals

Amateur Photographer
American Amateur Photographer
American Annual of Photography and Photographic Times Almanac
American Journal of Photography
American Photo
American Photography
Anthony's Photographic Bulletin
British Journal of Photography
Collier's
Daily Mail
Ebony
Edinburgh Review
Humphrey's Journal
Illustrated Police News
Jet
Journal of the Photographic Society of Philadelphia
Life
McCall's Magazine
Magazine of Light
New York Sun
Philadelphia Evening Bulletin
Philadelphia Photographer
Photo-Beacon
Photographic News
Photographic Times
Photographic Times and American Photographer
Popular Mechanics
Popular Photography
Scientific American
Wilson's Photographic Magazine

Printed and Web Sources

Abercromby, Ralph, First Report of the Thunderstorm Committee, 'On the Photographs of Lightning Flashes', *Journal of the Royal Meteorological Society* 14 (1888), 226–34.

Agee, James, and Walker Evans, *Let Us Now Praise Famous Men* (1941; Boston: Houghton Mifflin Co., 1960).

Alland, Alexander, Sr., *Jessie Tarbox Beals: First Woman News Photographer* (New York: Camera/Graphic Press, 1978).

Allen, Grant, *Physiological Aesthetics* (New York: D. Appleton and Co., 1877).

Allen, Grant, 'A Thinking Machine', *Gentleman's Magazine* 260 (1886), 30–41.

Allen, Grant, *Recalled to Life* (New York: Henry Holt and Co., 1891).

Allen, James, and John Lewis, *Without Sanctuary: Lynching Photography in America* (Santa Fe, NM: Twin Palms Publishers, 2000).

Alton, John, *Painting with Light* (1949; Berkeley and Los Angeles: University of California Press, 1995).

Amis, Martin, *London Fields* (1989; New York: Alfred A. Knopf, 2014).

Apel, Dora, and Shawn Michell Smith (eds.), *Lynching Photographs* (Berkeley and Los Angeles: University of California Press, 2007).

Appadurai, Arjun, 'Introduction: Commodities and the Politics of Value', in Appadurai (ed.), *The Social Life of Things: Commodities in Cultural Perspective* (Cambridge: Cambridge University Press, 1986).

Araki, Nobuyoshi, 'The Photo Apparatus Between Man and Woman', in Ivan Vartanian, Akihiro Hatanaka, and Yutaka Kambayashi (eds.), *Setting Sun: Writings by Japanese Photographers* (New York: Aperture, 2006), 143–6.

Arbus, Diane, *Diane Arbus: An Aperture Monograph* (Millerton, NY: Aperture/Museum of Modern Art, 1972).

Arnold, Rus, *Flash Photography* (Little Technical Library; Chicago: Ziff-Davis Publishing Company, 1940).

Ashford, David, 'Children Asleep in the Underground: The Tube Shelters of Brandt and Moore', *Cambridge Quarterly* 36/4 (2007), 295–316.

Baer, Ulrich, *Spectral Evidence: The Photography of Trauma* (Cambridge, MA: MIT Press, 2002).

Bailey, James, *How to Select & Use Electronic Flash* (Tucson: HPBooks, 1983).

Bailly, Jean-Christophe, *George Shiras: In the Heart of the Dark Night* (Paris: Éditions Xavier Barral, 2015).

[Bain, Alexander], 'Electrotype and Daguerreotype', *Westminster Review* 34 (September 1840), 434–60.

Bain, Alexander, *The Senses and the Intellect* (London: Longmans, 1855).

Bajac, Quentin, *Parr by Parr. Quentin Bajac Meets Martin Parr. Discussions with a Promiscuous Photographer* (Amsterdam: Schildt Publishing, 2010).

Baker, Kenneth, *The Lightning Field* (New Haven: Yale University Press, 2008).

Baker, T. Thorne, *The Kingdom of the Camera* (London: G. Bell & Sons, 1934).

Baldwin, C., *In the Watches of the Night: Life in the Nocturnal City, 1820–1930* (Chicago: University of Chicago Press, 2012).

Barthes, Roland, *Camera Lucida: Reflections on Photography* (1980), trans. Richard Howard (New York: Hill and Wang, 1981).

Baskind, Samantha, 'Weegee's Jewishness', *History of Photography* 34/1 (2010): 60–78.

Batchen, Geoffrey, *Burning with Desire: The Conception of Photography* (Cambridge, MA: MIT Press, 1997).

Batchen, Geoffrey, *Each Wild Idea: Writing, Photography, History* (Cambridge, MA: MIT Press, 2001).

Batchen, Geoffrey, *Forget Me Not: Photography & Remembrance* (New York: Princeton Architectural Press, 2004).

Beegan, Gerry, *The Mass Image: A Social History of Photomechanical Reproduction in Victorian London* (Basingstoke: Palgrave Macmillan, 2008).

Belden-Adams, Kris, 'Harold Edgerton and Complications of the "Photographic Instant"', *Frame: a journal of visual and material culture* 1 (spring 2011), 96–107.

Bell, Eustace Hale, *The Art of the Photoplay* (New York: G. W. Dillingham, 1913).

Belting, Hans, 'The Theater of Illusion', in *Hiroshi Sugimoto: Theaters* (New York: Sonnabend Sundell Editions, 2000), 1–7.

Belting, Hans, *Looking through Duchamp's Door: Art and Perspective in the Work of Duchamp. Sugimoto. Jeff Wall* (Köln: Walther König, 2010).

Belton, John (ed.), *Alfred Hitchcock's* Rear Window (Cambridge: Cambridge University Press, 2000).

Benjamin, Walter, *Illuminations*, ed. Hannah Arendt, trans. Harry Zohn (New York: Schocken Books, 1968).

Benjamin, Walter, 'A Short History of Photography' (1931), trans. Stanley Mitchell, *Screen* 13/1 (1972), 5–26.

Benjamin, Walter, *The Arcades Project*, trans. Howard Eiland and Kevin McLaughlin (Cambridge, MA: Harvard University Press, 1999).
Bennett, Arnold, *The Grand Babylon Hotel* (New York: George H. Doran, 1902).
Bennett, Arnold, *The Regent* (London: Methuen & Co., 1913).
Bennett, Louis Clarence, *Flash Lights and How to Take Them* (New York: Louis Clarence Bennett, 1891).
Bird, Kai, and Martin J. Sherwin, *American Prometheus: The Triumph and Tragedy of J. Robert Oppenheimer* (New York: Alfred A. Knopf, 2005).
Black, Alexander, *Captain Kodak: A Camera Story* (Boston: Lothrop Publishing Company, 1899).
Blair, Sara, 'Ellison, Photography, and the Origins of Invisibility', in Ross Posnock (ed.), *The Cambridge Companion to Ralph Ellison* (Cambridge: Cambridge University Press, 2005), 56–81.
Blair, Sara, *Harlem Crossroads: Black Writers and the Photograph in the Twentieth Century* (Princeton: Princeton University Press, 2007).
Bloch, Alice, 'Sight Imagery in "Invisible Man"', *English Journal* 55/8 (November 1966), 1019–21, 1024.
Boccioni, Umberto, 'Moto assoluto e moto relative', in *Pittura e scultura futuriste*, ed. Zeno Birolli (Milan: SE. Saggi e documenti del novecento, 1997).
Bogart, Michele H., *Artists, Advertising, and the Borders of Art* (Chicago: University of Chicago Press, 1995).
Bonanos, Christopher, 'Polaroid and Apartheid', *Polaroidland* (6 April 2013), http://www.polaroidland.net/2013/04/06/polaroid-and-apartheid/.
Bordwell, David, Janet Staiger, and Kristin Thompson, *The Classical Hollywood Cinema: Film Style and Mode of Production to 1960* (New York: Columbia University Press, 1985).
Bosworth, Patricia, *Diane Arbus: A Biography* (New York: Alfred A. Knopf, 1984).
Bourdieu, Pierre, *Photography: A Middle-Brow Art*, trans. Shaun Whiteside (1965; Cambridge, Polity Press, 1990).
Bourke-White, Margaret, *Portrait of Myself* (New York: Simon and Schuster, 1963).
Boyd, Ruth, *Stanley Devon: News Photographer* (Twyford: Derek Harrison Publishing, 1995).
[Boys, C. V.], 'On Electric Spark Photographs; Or, Photography of Flying Bullets, &c. by the Light of the Electric Spark. I', *Nature* 47 (2 March 1893), 415–21.
Brandt, Bill, *A Night in London* (London: Country Life, 1938).
Brassaï, *Paris By Night* (*Paris de Nuit*, 1933), trans. Stuart Gilbert (Paris: Arts et Métiers Graphiques, 1993).
Brassaï, *Conversations with Picasso*, trans. Jane Marie Todd (Chicago: University of Chicago Press, 1999).
Brassaï, *Proust in the Power of Photography* (*Marcel Proust sous l'emprise de la photographie*, 1997), trans. Richard Howard (Chicago: University of Chicago Press, 2001).
Braudy, Leo, *The Frenzy of Renown: Fame and Its History* (New York: Vintage, 1997).
Braun, Marta, *Picturing Time: The Work of Etienne-Jules Marey (1830–1904)* (Chicago: University of Chicago Press, 1992).
Brewster, David, 'On the Influence of Successive Impulses of Light Upon the Retina', *London and Edinburgh Philosophical Magazine and Journal of Science* 4 (1834), 241–2.
[Brewster, David], 'Photogenic Drawing, or Drawing by the Agency of Light', *Edinburgh Review* 76 (January 1843), 309–44.
Briggs, Charles F., and Augustus Maverick, *The Story of the Telegraph; And a History of the Great Atlantic Cable* (New York: Rudd & Carleton, 1858).

Brightman, Carol, *Sweet Chaos: The Grateful Dead's American Adventure* (New York: Gallery Books, 1999).

Bron, Pierre, and Condax, Philip L., *The Photographic Flash: A Concise Illustrated History* (Allschwil: Bron Elektronik, 1998).

Brontë, Charlotte, *Jane Eyre* (1847; Oxford: Oxford University Press, 1980).

Brookman, Philip, *Gordon Parks: Half Past Autumn: A Retrospective* (Boston: Bulfinch Press, Little, Brown and Co., 1997).

Brookman, Philip, 'Helios: Eadweard Muybridge in a Time of Change', in Brookman, *Eadweard Muybridge* (London: Tate Publishing, 2010), 23–109.

Brooks, Christopher A., and Robert Sims, *Roland Hayes: The Legacy of an American Tenor* (Bloomington, IN: Indiana University Press, 2014).

Brothers, Alfred, *Photography: Its History, Processes, Apparatus, and Materials* (2nd edn., London: Charles Griffin & Co., 1899).

Browder, Laura, *Rousing the Nation: Radical Culture in Depression America* (Amherst, MA: University of Massachusetts Press, 1998).

Brower, Matthew, *Developing Animals: Wildlife and Early American Photography* (Minneapolis: University of Minnesota Press, 2011).

Brown, Joshua, *Beyond the Lines: Pictorial Reporting, Everyday Life, and the Crisis of Gilded Age America* (Berkeley and Los Angeles: University of California Press), 2006.

Brown, Roger, and James Kulik, 'Flashbulb Memories', *Cognition* 5 (1977), 73–99.

Brown, Tina, *The Diana Chronicles* (2007; New York: Anchor Books, 2008).

Brox, Jane, *Brilliant: The Evolution of Artificial Light* (New York: Houghton Mifflin Harcourt, 2010).

Bruce, Roger, *Seeing the Unseen: Dr Edgerton and the Wonders of Strobe Alley* (Rochester, NY: The Publishing Trust of George Eastman House, 1994).

Brück, H. A., and M. T. Brück, *The Peripatetic Astronomer: The Life of Charles Piazzi Smyth* (Bristol: Adam Hilger, 1988).

Buckland, Gail, *Fox Talbot and the Invention of Photography* (London: Scholar Press, 1980).

Buk-Swienty, Tom, *The Other Half: The Life of Jacob Riis and the World of Immigration*, trans. Annette Buk-Swienty (New York: W. W. Norton, 2008).

Burke, Declan, 'Flash Fiction: "Intense, urgent and a little explosive"', *Irish Times*, 26 October 2011, http://www.irishtimes.com/culture/books/flash-fiction-intense-urgent-and-a-little-explosive-1.631904.

Burke, Edmund, *A Philosophical Enquiry into the Origin of Our Ideas of the Sublime and the Beautiful* (1757; Oxford: Oxford University Press, 2009).

Burns, Ben, *Nitty Gritty: A White Editor in Black Journalism* (Jackson, MI: University Press of Mississippi, 1996).

Bush, Martin H., *The Photographs of Gordon Parks* (Wichita, KS: Wichita State University, 1983),

Cadava, Eduardo, *Words of Light: Theses on the Photography of History* (Princeton: Princeton University Press, 1997).

Caldwell, Erskine, and Margaret Bourke-White, *You Have Seen Their Faces* (New York: Viking Press, 1937).

Callahan, Harry M. (ed.), *Ansel Adams in Color* (Boston: Little, Brown and Co., 1993).

Cameron, Julia Margaret, 'Annals of My Glass House' (1874), in Vicki Goldberg (ed.), *Photography in Print: Writings from 1816 to the Present* (Albuquerque, NM: University of New Mexico Press, 1981).

Campbell, Helen, *Darkness and Daylight, or, Lights and Shadows of New York Life* (New York: A. D. Worthington, 1891).

Canales, Jimena, '"A Number of Scenes in a Badly Cut Film": Observation in the Age of Strobe', in Lorraine Daston and Elizabeth Lundeck (eds.), *Histories of Scientific Observation* (Chicago: University of Chicago Press, 2011), 230–54.

Carnes, Cecil, *Jimmy Hare News Photographer: Half a Century with a Camera* (New York: Macmillan, 1940).

Carr, Catherine, *The Art of Photoplay Writing* (New York: Hannis Jordan Co., 1914).

Carson, Anne, *Autobiography of Red* (New York: Alfred A. Knopf, 1998).

Carter, Christopher, *Rhetorical Exposure: Confrontation and Contradiction in US Social Documentary Photography* (Tuscaloosa, AL: University of Alabama Press, 2015).

Cartier-Bresson, Henri, *The Mind's Eye: Writings on Photography and Photographers*, ed. Michael L. Sand (New York: Aperture, 2005).

Chandler, Raymond, *The Big Sleep* (1939; New York: Vintage Crime/Black Lizard, 1988).

Charney, Leo, 'In a Moment: Film and the Philosophy of Modernity', in Leo Charney and Vanessa R. Schwartz (eds.), *Cinema and the Invention of Modern Life* (Berkeley and Los Angeles: University of California Press, 1995), 279–96.

Cheng, Anne Anlin, *Second Skin: Josephine Baker & the Modern Surface* (New York: Oxford University Press, 2011).

Chéroux, Clément (ed.), *Paparazzi! Photographers, Stars, Artists* (published in French as *Paparazzi! Photographes, stars et artistes*) (Paris: Flammarion, 2014).

Christopher, Nicholas, *Somewhere in the Night: Film Noir and the American City* (New York: Free Press, 1997).

Cleghorn, Mark, *Portrait Photography: Secrets of Posing and Lighting* (New York: Lark Books, 2004).

Cobbe, Frances Power, 'The Fallacies of Memory' (1866), *Hours of Work and Play* (Philadelphia: J. B. Lippincott, 1867), 87–116.

Coe, Brian, *Cameras: From Daguerreotype to Instant Pictures* (London: Marshall Cavendish Editions, 1978).

Coe, Brian, and Paul Gates, *The Snapshot Photograph: The Rise of Popular Photography 1888–1939* (London: Ash and Grant, 1977).

Cohen, Robert S., and Raymond J. Seeger (eds.), *Ernst Mach: Physicist and Philosopher* (Boston Studies in the Philosophy and History of Science; New York: Springer, 1975).

Cole, Teju, 'On Photography', *New York Times Magazine*, 22 February 2015, 62–70.

Coleman, Harry J., *Give Us a Little Smile, Baby* (New York: E. P. Dutton & Co., 1943).

Collier, John, Jr, and Malcolm Collier, *Visual Anthropology: Photography as Research Method* (1967; Albuquerque, NM: University of New Mexico Press, 1986).

Collingham, Lizzie, *The Taste of War: World War II and the Battle for Food* (New York: Penguin, 2012).

Collins, Francis A., *The Camera Man* (New York: Century, 1916).

Colson, J. B., 'The Art of the Human Document: Russell Lee in New Mexico', in *Far from Main Street: Three Photographers in Depression-era New Mexico. Russell Lee, John Collier, Jack Delano* (Santa Fe, NM: Museum of New Mexico Press, 1994).

Colson, J. B., 'Introduction: "There was a job to do": The Photographic Career of Russell Lee', Russell Lee Photograph Collection, Center for American History, University of Texas at Austin, *Russell Lee Photographs: Images from the Russell Lee Photograph Collection at the Center for American History* (Austin, TX: University of Texas Press, 2007).

Conrad, Joseph, *Heart of Darkness* (1899; London: Penguin Classics, 2007).

Cookman, Claude, 'Margaret Bourke-White and Henri Cartier-Bresson: Gandhi's Funeral', *History of Photography* 22/2 (1998), 199–209.

Corber, Robert J., 'Resisting History: *Rear Window* and the Limits of the Postwar Settlement', *boundary 2* 19/1 (1992), 121–48.

Corey, David, 'Weegee's Unstaged Coney Island Dramas', *American Art* 5/1–2 (winter–spring 1991), 16–21.

Costantini, Paolo, Silvio Fuso, Sandro Mescola, and Italo Zannier (eds.), *Paparazzi* (Florence: Alinari, 1988).

Cotton, Charlotte, 'Introduction', *Nick Knight* (New York: Harper Collins, 2009).

Cox, J. Randolph, and David S. Siegel, *Flashgun Casey, Crime Photographer: From the Pulps to Radio and Beyond* (New York: Bookhunter Press, 2005).

Coxe, George Harmon, *Silent as the Dead* (New York: Knopf, 1941).

Coxe, George Harmon, *Murder for Two* (New York: Dell, 1943).

Coxe, George Harmon, *The Man Who Died Too Soon* (New York: Alfred A. Knopf, 1962).

Curtis, James, *Mind's Eye, Mind's Truth: FSA Photography Reconsidered* (Philadelphia: Temple University Press, 1989).

Curtis, John J., *Flashlight for the Amateur Photographer* (London: British Periodicals Ltd, 1925).

D'Ambrosio, Brian, *Menacing Face Worth Millions: A Life of Charles Bronson* (Minneapolis: Jabberwocky Press, 2014).

Daniel, Pete, Merry A. Foresta, Maren Stange, and Sally Stein, *Official Images: New Deal Photography* (Washington, DC: Smithsonian Institution Press, 1987).

Daniel, Walter, C., *Black Journals of the United States* (Westport, CT: Greenwood Press, 1982).

Dart, Gregory, '"Flash Style": Pierce Egan and Literary London, 1820–1828', *History Workshop Journal* 51 (2001), 181–205.

Daston, Lorraine (ed.), *Biographies of Scientific Objects* (Chicago: University of Chicago Press, 1999).

Daston, Lorraine J., and Peter Galison, *Objectivity* (2007; New York: Zone Books, 2010).

Davis, Melody, *Women's Views: The Narrative Stereograph in Nineteenth-Century America* (Lebanon, NH: University of New Hampshire Press, 2015).

Davis, Ronald L., *The Glamour Factory: Inside Hollywood's Big Studio System* (Dallas: Southern Methodist University Press, 1993).

Dean, Edward J., *Lucky Dean: Reminiscences of a Press Photographer* (London: Robert Hale, 1944).

DeCarava, Sherry Turner, 'Pages from a Notebook', in Peter Galassi (ed.), *Roy DeCarava: A Retrospective* (New York: Museum of Modern Art, 1996), 40–60.

deCordova, Richard, *Picture Personalities: The Emergence of the Star System in America* (Urbana: University of Illinois Press, 1990).

de Duve, Thierry, 'Time Exposure and Snapshot: The Photograph as Paradox', *October* 5 (summer 1978), 113–25.

Delany, Paul, *Bill Brandt: A Life* (Palo Alto, CA: Stanford University Press, 2004).

de Leon, Charles L. Ponce, *Self-Exposure: Human Interest Journalism and the Emergence of Celebrity in America, 1890–1940* (Chapel Hill, NC: University of North Carolina Press, 2002).

De Quincey, Thomas, *Confessions of An English Opium Eater and Other Writings*, ed. Grevel Lindop (Oxford: Oxford University Press, 1988).

Devon, Stanley, *'Glorious': The Life Story of Stanley Devon* (London: George G. Harrap, 1957).

Dickens, Charles, *Little Dorrit* (1855–7; Oxford: Oxford University Press, 2008).

Dickinson, Emily, *The Complete Poems* (London: Faber and Faber, 1970).

Dillon, Clare, 'Reinscribing De Quincey's Palimpsest: The Significance of the Palimpsest in Contemporary Literary and Cultural Studies', *Textual Practice* 19 (2005), 243–63.

Dimendberg, Edward, *Film Noir and the Spaces of Modernity* (Cambridge, MA: Harvard University Press, 2004).

Doss, Erika, 'Visualizing Black America: Gordon Parks at *Life*, 1948–1971', in Doss (ed.), *Looking at* Life *Magazine* (Washington, DC: Smithsonian Institution Press, 2001), 221–41.

Doud, Richard, Oral History Interview with Edwin and Louise Rosskam, 3 August 1965, Archives of American Art, Smithsonian Institution, https://www.aaa.si.edu/collections/interviews/oral-history-interview-edwin-and-louise-rosskam-13112.

Doud, Richard, Oral History Interview with Ben Shahn, 14 April 1964, Archives of American Art, Smithsonian Institution, https://www.aaa.si.edu/collections/interviews/oral-history-interview-ben-shahn-12760.

Doud, Richard, Oral History Interview with Jack and Irene Delano, 12 June 1965, Archives of American Art, Smithsonian Institution, https://www.aaa.si.edu/collections/interviews/oral-history-interview-jack-and-irene-delano-13026.

Doud, Richard, Oral History Interview with John Vachon, 28 April 1964, Archives of American Art, Smithsonian Institution, https://www.aaa.si.edu/collections/interviews/oral-history-interview-john-vachon-11830.

Doud, Richard, Oral History Interview with Roy Stryker, 1963–5, Archives of American Art, Smithsonian Institution, https://www.aaa.si.edu/collections/interviews/oral-history-interview-roy-emerson-stryker-12480.

Draaisma, Douwe, *Metaphors of Memory: A History of Ideas about the Mind* (Cambridge: Cambridge University Press, 2001).

Duncan, Christopher D., *Advanced Crime Scene Photography* (Boca Raton, FL: CRC Press, 2010).

Duran, Anne, 'Flash Mobs: Social Influence in the 21st Century', *Social Influence* 1/4 (2006), 301–15.

Duras, Marguerite, *Hiroshima mon amour* (1959), trans. Richard Seaver (New York: Grove Press, 1961).

Dyer, Geoff, *White Sands: Experiences from the Outside World* (New York: Pantheon Books, 2016).

Dyer, Richard, *White* (London: Routledge, 1997).

[Eastlake, Lady Elizabeth], 'Photography', *London Quarterly Review* 101 (April 1857), 442–68.

Edgerton, Harold, with James R. Killian, *Flash! Seeing the Unseen by Ultra High-Speed Photography* (1939; 2nd edn., Newton, MA: Charles T. Branford, 1954).

Edgerton, Harold, with James R. Killian, *Electronic Flash, Strobe* (New York: McGraw Hill, 1970).

Edgerton, Harold, with James R. Killian, *Moments of Vision: The Stroboscopic Revolution in Photography* (Cambridge, MA: MIT Press, 1979).

Edwards, Jonathan, *The Works of Jonathan Edwards*, ed. Wallace E. Anderson, 26 vols. (New Haven: Yale University Press, 1977–2009).

Edwards, Steve, *The Making of English Photography* (University Park, PA: Pennsylvania State University Press, 2006).

Ehrlich, Gretel, *A Match to the Heart: One Woman's Story of Being Struck by Lightning* (New York: Penguin, 1995).

Eisner, Lotte H., *The Haunted Screen: Expressionism in the German Cinema and the Influence of Max Reinhardt* (1952), trans. Roger Greaves (Berkeley and Los Angeles: University of California Press, 1969).

Ekirch, Roger, *At Day's Close: Night in Times Past* (New York: W. W. Norton, 2005).

Elcott, Noam M., *Artificial Darkness: An Obscure History of Modern Art and Media* (Chicago: University of Chicago Press, 2016).

Eliot, George, *Middlemarch* (1871–2; Oxford: Oxford University Press, 1998).

Elkins, James, *What Photography Is* (New York: Routledge, 2000).

Elkins, James, 'Harold Edgerton's Rapatronic Photographs of Atomic Tests', *History of Photography* 28/1 (2004), 74–81.

Ellenbogen, Josh, *Reasoned and Unreasoned Images: The Photography of Bertillon, Galton, and Marey* (University Park, PA: Pennsylvania State University Press, 2012).

Ellison, Ralph, *Invisible Man* (1952; New York: Vintage International, 1995).
Ellison, Ralph, *The Collected Essays of Ralph Ellison*, ed. John F. Callahan (New York: Modern Library, 2003).
Emerson, P. H., *Naturalistic Photography for Students of the Art* (London: Sampson Low, Marston. Searle & Rivington, 1889).
Emerson, Ralph Waldo, 'Self-Reliance' (1841), in *Essays and Lectures*, ed. Joel Porte (New York: Library of America, 1983).
Fabre, Michel, *The Unfinished Quest of Richard Wright*, trans. Isabel Barzun (New York: William Morrow & Co., 1973).
Faraday, Michael, *The Correspondence of Michael Faraday*, ed. Frank A. J. L. James, vol. iv (London: Institution of Engineering and Technology, 1999).
Faulkner, William, *These Thirteen* (New York: Jonathan Cape and Harrison Smith, 1931).
Feigel, Lara, *Literature, Cinema and Politics 1930–1945: Reading between the Frames* (Edinburgh: Edinburgh University Press, 2010).
Fernyhough, Charles, *Pieces of Light: How the New Science of Memory Illuminates the Stories We Tell About Our Pasts* (New York: Harper, 2013).
Finnegan, Cara A., *Picturing Poverty: Print Culture and FSA Photographs* (Washington, DC: Smithsonian Books, 2003).
Finnegan, Cara A., *Making Photography Matter: A Viewer's History from the Civil War to the Great Depression* (Urbana, IL: University of Illinois Press, 2015).
Flashlight Photography (Chicago: James H. Smith & Sons: n.d. [early 1920s]).
Fleetwood, Nicole R., *Troubling Vision: Performance, Visuality, and Blackness* (Chicago: University of Chicago Press, 2011).
Fleetwood, Nicole R., *On Racial Icons: Blackness and the Public Imagination* (New Brunswick, NJ: Rutgers University Press, 2015).
Fleischhauer, Carl, and Beverly W. Brannan (eds.), *Documenting America, 1935–1943* (Berkeley and Los Angeles: UP of California in association with the Library of Congress, 1988).
Fletcher, Winston, *Powers of Persuasion: The Inside Story of British Advertising: 1951–2000* (Oxford: Oxford University Press, 2008).
Flint, Kate, 'The Materiality of *Middlemarch*', in Karen Chase (ed.), *Middlemarch in the Twenty-First Century* (Oxford: Oxford University Press, 2006), 65–86.
Floherty, John J., *Shooting the News: Careers of the Camera Men* (Philadelphia: J. B. Lippincott, 1949).
Fonvielle, Wilfrid de, *Thunder and Lightning* (*Éclairs et tonnerres*, 1866), trans. T. L. Phipson (New York: Scribner, Armstrong & Co., 1875).
Foster, David William, *Urban Photography in Argentina: Nine Artists of the Post-Dictatorship Era* (Jefferson, NC: McFarland & Co., 2007).
Foucault, Michel, 'A Preface to Transgression' (1963), in *Religion and Culture*, selected and ed. Jeremy Carrette (London: Routledge, 1999).
Frank, Richard B., *Downfall: The End of the Imperial Japanese Empire* (New York: Random House, 1999).
Frazer, James George, *The Golden Bough: A Study in Magic and Religion: A New Abridgement from the Second and Third Editions* (Oxford World's Classics; Oxford: Oxford University Press, 1998).
Fried, Lewis, *Makers of the City: Jacob Riis, Lewis Mumford, James T. Farrell, and Paul Goodman* (Amherst, MA: University of Massachusetts Press, 1990).
Galassi, Peter, *Henri Cartier-Bresson: The Modern Century* (New York: Museum of Modern Art, 2010).
Galassi, Peter, and Sherry Turner DeCarava, *Roy DeCarava: A Retrospective* (New York: Museum of Modern Art, 1996).
Galella, Ron, *No Pictures* (Brooklyn, NY: Powerhouse Books, 2008).

Galella, Ron, *The Stories Behind the Pictures: A Guide to the Paparazzi Approach* (Montville NJ: Ron Galella Ltd, 2014).

Galton, Francis, *Inquiries into Human Faculty and Its Development* (1883; London: J. M. Dent, 1911).

Gandal, Keith, *The Virtues of the Vicious: Jacob Riis, Stephen Crane, and the Spectacle of the Slum* (New York: Oxford University Press, 1997).

Garver, Thomas H., 'Afterword: O. Winston Link and His Working Method', in O. Winston Link, *Steam Steel and Stars: America's Last Steam Railroad* (New York: Harry N. Abrams, 1987).

Gaskell, Elizabeth, *The Life of Charlotte Brontë* (1857; London: Penguin, 1998).

Gee, Helen, *Limelight: A Greenwich Village Photography Gallery and Coffeehouse in the Fifties* (Albuquerque, NM: University of New Mexico Press, 1997).

Gefter, Philip, 'Sex in the Park, and Its Sneaky Spectators,' *New York Times*, 23 September 2007.

Geiger, John, *Chapel of Extreme Experience: A Short History of Stroboscopic Light and the Dream Machine* (Brooklyn, NY: Soft Skull Press, 2003).

Gelber, Steven M., *Hobbies: Leisure and the Culture of Work in America* (New York: Columbia University Press, 1999).

Gell, Alfred, 'The Technology of Enchantment and the Enchantment of Technology', in Jeremy Coote (ed.), *Anthropology, Art, and Aesthetics* (Oxford: Clarendon Press, 1992), 40–63.

Gilbert, Geoffrey, *Photo-Flash in Practice* (London: Focal Press, 1947).

Gitelman, Lisa, *Always Already New: Media, History, and the Data of Culture* (Cambridge, MA: MIT Press, 2006).

Gockel, Tilo, *Creative Flash Photography: Great Lighting with Small Flashes. 40 Flash Workshops* (Santa Barbara, CA: Rocky Nook, 2014).

Goldberg, Vicki, *Margaret Bourke-White: A Biography* (New York: Harper & Row, 1986).

Gomery, Douglas, *The Hollywood Studio System: A History* (London: British Film Institute, 2005).

Gonzales-Day, Ken, *Lynching in the West: 1850–1935* (Durham, NC: Duke University Press, 2006).

Gordon, Avery, *Ghostly Matters: Haunting and the Sociological Imagination* (Minneapolis: University of Minnesota Press, 1997).

Gordon, John, 'The Electrical Hopkins: A Critical Study of His Best-Known Poems, *The Wreck of the Deutschland* and "The Windhover"', *University of Toronto Quarterly* 65/3 (1996), 506–22.

Gordon, Linda, 'Dorothea Lange Photographs the Japanese American Internment', in Linda Gordon and Gary Y. Okihiro (eds.), *Impounded: Dorothea Lange and the Censored Images of Japanese American Internment* (New York: W. W. Norton & Co., 2006).

Grandmaster Flash and David Ritz, *The Adventures of Grandmaster Flash: My Life, My Beats* (New York: Crown Archetype, 2006).

Grant, Bernard, *To the Four Corners: The Memoirs of a News Photographer* (London: Hutchinson & Co., 1933).

Grant, D., *Manual of Photography: With Special Reference to Work in the Tropics* (London: Murray and Evenden, 1914).

Green-Lewis, Jennifer, *Framing the Victorians: Photography and the Culture of Realism* (Ithaca, NY: Cornell University Press, 1996).

Green-Lewis, Jennifer, 'Not Fading Away: Photography in the Age of Oblivion', *Nineteenth-Century Contexts* 22 (2001), 559–85.

Greenough, Sarah, *Walker Evans: Subways and Streets* (Washington, DC: National Gallery of Art, 1991).

Gregory, Eric, 'Flash Memory', *Encyclopædia Britannica*. http://www.britannica.com/technology/flash-memory.

Griffiths, Devin, *The Age of Analogy: Science and Literature Between the Darwins* (Baltimore: Johns Hopkins University Press, 2016).

Gross, Larry, John Stuart Katz, and Jay Ruby (eds.), *Image Ethics: The Moral Rights of Subjects in Photographs, Film, and Television* (New York: Oxford University Press, 1988).

Groth, Helen, *Victorian Photography and Literary Nostalgia* (Oxford: Oxford University Press, 2003).

Guerin, F. W., *Portraits in Photography by the Aid of Flash.* ([n.p.: n.pub.] 1898).

Guerin, Frances, *A Culture of Light: Cinema and Technology in 1920s Germany* (Minneapolis: University of Minnesota Press, 2005).

Guimond, James, *American Photography and the American Dream* (Chapel Hill, NC: University of North Carolina Press, 1991).

Gutman, Judith Mara, *Lewis Hine and the American Social Conscience* (New York: Walker, 1967).

Gutman, Mara, *Lewis W. Hine 1874–1940: Two Perspectives* (New York: Grossman Publishers, 1974).

Hales, Peter Bacon, *Silver Cities: Photographing American Urbanization 1839–1939* (rev. and expanded edn. Albuquerque, NM: University of New Mexico Press, 2006).

Hales, Peter Bacon, *Outside the Gates of Eden: The Dream of America from Hiroshima to Now* (Chicago: University of Chicago Press, 2014).

Halpert, Peter Hay, 'The Blank Screens of Hiroshi Sugimoto', in Concha Gómez (ed.), *Sugimoto* (Barcelona: Fundacion la Caixa de Pensiones, 1998), 22–7.

Hamlyn, Nicky, 'Peter Kubelka's *Arnulf Rainer*', in Alexander Graf and Dietrich Scheunemann (eds.), *Avant-Garde Film (Avant Garde Critical Studies* 23; Amsterdam: Rodopi, 2007), 249–60.

Hammett, Dashiell, *Red Harvest* (1929; New York: Vintage Books, 1992).

Hance, George Wallace, *Commercial Photography of Today* (Cleveland: *Abel's Photographic Weekly*, 1914).

Hannigan, William, and Ken Johnston, *Picture Machine: The Rise of American Newspictures* (New York: Harry N. Abrams, 2004).

Hardy, Thomas, *Desperate Remedies* (1871; London: Penguin, 1998).

Harman, Robert, and John Luis Lucaites, 'The Iconic Image of the Mushroom Cloud and the Cold War Nuclear Optic', in Geoffrey Batchen and Jay Prosser (eds.), *Picturing Atrocity: Photography in Crisis* (London: Reaktion Books, 2012), 134–45.

Harvey, Glenn, and Mark Saunders, *Diana and the Paparazzi* (London: John Blake, 2007).

Harvey, John, *The Story of Black* (London: Reaktion Books, 2013).

Hauptman, Jodi, '*FLASH!* The Speed Graphic Camera', *Yale Journal of Criticism* 11/1 (1998), 129–37.

Hendrickson, Paul, *Looking for the Light: The Hidden Life and Art of Marion Post Wolcott* (New York: Knopf, 1992).

Henisch, Heinz K., and Bridget A. Henisch, *Positive Pleasures: Early Photography and Humor* (University Park, PA: Pennsylvania State University Press, 1998).

Hiassen, Carl, *Star Island* (New York: Alfred Knopf, 2010).

Higgins, Jackie, *Why it Does Not Have to Be In Focus: Modern Photography Explained* (London: Thames and Hudson, 2013).

Hill, Lena, *Visualizing Blackness and the Creation of the African American Literary Tradition* (Cambridge: Cambridge University Press, 2014).

Hine, Lewis, *Photo Story: Selected Letters and Photographs of Lewis W. Hine*, ed. Daile Kaplan (Washington, DC: Smithsonian Institution Press, 1992).

Hine, Lewis W., 'Social Photography; How the Camera May Help in the Social Uplift', in Alexander Johnson (ed.), *Proceedings of the National Conference of Charities and Correction at the Thirty-Sixth Annual Session Held in the City of Buffalo, New York, June 9–16, 1909* (Fort Wayne, IN: Press of Fort Wayne, 1909), 355–9.

Hirsch, Foster, *The Dark Side of the Screen: Film Noir* (1981; rev. and updated, Boston: Da Capo Press, 2008).

Hirsch, Paul M., 'An Analysis of *Ebony*: The Magazine and Its Readers', *Journalism Quarterly* 45/2 (summer 1968), 261–70.

Hodgdon, Barbara, 'Photography, Theater, Mnemonics; or, Thirteen Ways of Looking at a Still', in W. B. Worthen with Peter Holland (eds.), *Theorizing Practice: Redefining Theatre History* (Basingstoke: Palgrave Macmillan, 2003), 88–119.

Hoffmann, Christoph, 'Mach-Werke', *Fotogeschichte* 60 (1996), 3–18.

Hoffmann, Felix (ed.), *Ron Galella: Paparazzo extraordinaire* (Ostfildern: Hatje Cantz, 2012).

Holmes, Oliver Wendell, 'The Stereoscope and the Stereograph' (1859), *Soundings from the Atlantic* (Boston: Ticknor and Fields, 1864).

Hooks, Bell, 'In Our Glory: Photography and Black Life', in Deborah Willis (ed.), *Picturing Us: African American Identity in Photography* (New York: New Press, 1995).

Hopkins, Gerard Manley, *Gerard Manley Hopkins: Selected Letters*, ed. Catherine Phillips (Oxford: Clarendon Press, 1990).

Hopkins, Gerard Manley, *The Journals and Papers of Gerard Manley Hopkins*, ed. Humphry House and Graham Storey (New York: Oxford University Press, 1990).

Hopkins, Gerard Manley, *The Major Works*, ed. Catherine Phillips (Oxford: Oxford University Press, 2009).

Hosking, Eric, *Eric Hosking's Owls* (London: Pelham Books, 1982).

Howe, Lawrence, 'Through the Looking Glass: Reflexivity, Reciprocality, and Defenestration in Hitchcock's *Rear Window*', *College English* 35/1 (winter 2008), 16–37.

Howe, Peter, *Paparazzi* (New York: Artisan, 2005).

Howes, Chris, 'Art of Darkness', *New Scientist* 124 (23–30 December 1989), 13–16.

Howes, Chris, To Photograph Darkness: The History of Underground and Flash Photography (Carbondale: Southern Illinois University Press, 1989).

Hunt, J. R. *Pictorial Journalism* (London: Sir Isaac Pitman & Sons, 1937).

Hurley, F. Jack, *Portrait of a Decade: Roy Stryker and the Development of Documentary Photography in the Thirties* (Baton Rouge, LA: Louisiana State University Press, 1972).

Hurley, F. Jack, *Russell Lee, Photographer* (Dobbs Ferry, NY: Morgan & Morgan, 1978).

Hurley, F. Jack, *Marion Post Wolcott: A Photographic Journey* (Albuquerque, NM: University of New Mexico Press, 1989).

Huxley, Aldous, *The Doors of Perception* and *Heaven and Hell* (1954; 1956; New York, Harper Perennial, 2009).

Hyne, C. J. Cutcliffe, *The Recipe for Diamonds* (London: W. Heinemann, 1894).

Ivy, Marilyn, 'Dark Enlightenment: Naitō Masatoshi's Flash', in Rosalind C. Morris (ed.), *Photographies East: The Camera and Its Histories in East and Southeast Asia* (Durham, NC: Duke University Press, 2009), 229–57.

Jablonski, Nina G., *Living Color: The Biological and Social Meaning of Skin Color* (Berkeley and Los Angeles: University of California Press, 2012).

Jackson, Arlene M., 'Photography as Style and Metaphor in the Art of Thomas Hardy', *Thomas Hardy Annual* 2 (1984), 91–109.

Jackson, Gregory S., 'Cultivating Spiritual Sight: Jacob Riis's Virtual-Tour Narrative and the Visual Modernization of Protestant Homiletics', *Representations* 83 (summer 2003), 126–66.

Jacobs, Steven, 'The History and Aesthetics of the Classical Film Still', *History of Photography* 34/4 (2010), 373–86.

Jarché, James, *People I Have Shot* (London: Methuen, 1934).

Jarrell, Randall, *Poetry and the Age* (New York: Knopf, 1953).

Jay, Bill, 'The Photographer as Aggressor', in David Featherstone (ed.), *Observations: Essays on Documentary Photography (Untitled 35)* (Carmel: Friends of Photography, 1984), 7–23.

Jay, Bill, 'Keraunography: Notes on the photographic effects of lightning as reported in 19 century journals', http://www.billjayonphotography.com/Keraunography.pdf.

Jenkins, Reese V., *Images and Enterprise: Technology and the American Photographic Industry 1839 to 1925* (Baltimore: Johns Hopkins University Press, 1975).

Jezierski, John Vincent, *Enterprising Images: The Goodridge Brothers, African American Photographers, 1847–1922* (Detroit: Wayne State University Press, 2000).

Jonas, Hans, *The Phenomenon of Life: Toward a Philosophical Biology* (New York: Harper & Row, 1966).

Jonnes, Jill, *Empires of Light: Edison, Tesla, Westinghouse, and the Race to Electrify the World* (New York: Random House, 2003).

Kanon, Joseph, *Los Alamos* (New York: Broadway Books, 1997).

Kant, Immanuel, *Critique of the Power of Judgement* (1790, 1793), trans. Paul Guyer and Eric Matthews (Cambridge: Cambridge University Press, 2001).

Kayafas, Gus, *Stopping Time: The Photographs of Harold Edgerton* (New York: H. N. Abrams, 1987).

Keating, Patrick, *Hollywood Lighting from the Silent Era to Film Noir* (New York: Columbia University Press, 2010).

Kelby, Scott, *The Digital Photography Book*, vol. iii (Berkeley: Peachpit Press, 2009).

Keller, Judith, *Weegee: Photographs from the J. Paul Getty Museum* (Los Angeles: J. Paul Getty Museum, 2005).

Kelly, Cynthia C. (ed.), *The Manhattan Project: The Birth of the Atomic Bomb in the Words of Its Creators, Eyewitnesses, and Historians* (New York: Black Dog and Levanthal, 2007).

Kelsey, Robin, *Photography and the Art of Chance* (Cambridge, MA: Harvard University Press, 2015).

Kelsh, Nick, *How to Photograph Your Life* (New York: Stewart, Tabori & Chang, 2003).

Kennedy, David M., *Freedom from Fear: The American People in Depression and War, 1929–1945* (New York: Oxford University Press, 1999).

Kesey, Ken, *Sometimes a Great Notion* (1964; New York: Penguin, 2006).

Kim, Daniel Y., *Writing Manhood in Black and Yellow: Ralph Ellison, Frank Chin, and the Literary Politics of Identity* (Stanford, CA: Stanford University Press, 2005).

King, Terry, 'Coming to Terms with Tightrope Time: Three Decades of Heroes and Villains in the Australian Comic Strip', in Toby Burrows and Grant Stone, *Comics in Australia and New Zealand: The Collections, the Collectors, the Creators* (New York: Haworth Press, 1994), 41–56.

Kinkaid, James C., *Press Photography* (London: Chapman and Hall, 1936).

Kirk, G. S., J. E. Raven, and M. Schofield (eds.), *The Presocratic Philosophers: A Critical History with a Selection of Texts* (Cambridge: Cambridge University Press, 1983).

Knott, Bill, 'Flash', *Poetry* 183/6 (2004), 333.

Knott, Stephen, *Amateur Craft: History and Theory* (London: Bloomsbury, 2015).

Kobre, Kenneth, *Photojournalism: The Professionals' Approach* (5th edn.), vol. i (London: Focal Press, 2004).

Koepnick, Lutz, *On Slowness: Toward an Aesthetic of the Contemporary* (New York: Columbia University Press, 2014).

Kozol, Wendy, Life's *America: Family and Nation in Postwar Photojournalism* (Philadelphia: Temple University Press, 1994).

Kracauer, Siegfried, 'Photography' (1927), in *The Mass Ornament: Weimar Essays*, trans, and ed. Thomas Y. Levin (Cambridge, MA: Harvard University Press, 1995), 47–63.

Krajicek, David J., *Scooped! Media Miss Real Story on Crime While Chasing Sleaze Sex and Celebrities* (New York: Columbia University Press, 1998).

Krauss, Rosalind E., 'Tracing Nadar', *October* 5 (summer 1978), 29–47.
Krauss, Rosalind E., *The Optical Unconscious* (Cambridge, MA: MIT Press, 1993).
Krehl, Peter O. K., *History of Shock Waves, Explosions, and Impact* (New York: Springer, 2009).
Kundera, Milan, *Ignorance* (2000), trans. Linda Asher (New York: HarperCollins, 2002).
Lamont, Lansing, *Day of Trinity* (New York: Atheneum, 1965).
Lawrence, Tim, *Love Saves the Day: A History of American Dance Music Culture* (Durham, NC: Duke University Press, 2004).
Lears, Jackson, *Fables of Abundance: A Cultural History of Advertising in America* (New York: Basic Books, 1994).
Lee, Martin A., and Shlain, Bruce, *Acid Dreams: The Complete Social History of LSD: The CIA, the Sixties, and Beyond* (rev. edn., New York: Grove Press, 1994).
Lees-Maffei, Grace, 'Introduction: Studying Advice: Historiography, Methodology, Commentary, Bibliography', *Journal of Design History* 16/1 (2003), 1–14.
Lehrer, Jonah, *Proust Was a Neuroscientist* (New York: Houghton Mifflin, 2008).
Leonard, Stephen J., *Trials and Triumphs: A Colorado Portrait of the Great Depression* (Boulder, CO: University Press of Colorado, 1993).
Levy, Amy, *The Romance of a Shop* (1888; Peterborough, Ontario: Broadview Press, 2006).
Library of Congress, *A Small Nation of People: W. E. B. Du Bois and African American Portraits of Progress*, with essays by David Levering Lewis and Deborah Willis (New York: Amistad/Harper Collins, 2003).
Linkman, Audrey, *The Victorians: Photographic Portraits* (London: Tauris Parke Books, 1993).
Linkman, Audrey, *Photography and Death* (London: Reaktion Books, 2011).
Linkof, Ryan, 'The Public Eye: Celebrity and Photojournalism in the Making of the British Tabloids, 1904–1938', PhD thesis, University of Southern California, 2011.
Lippit, Akira Mizuta, *Atomic Light (Shadow Optics)* (Minneapolis: University of Minnesota Press, 2005).
Longinus, *On Literary Excellence, Literary Criticism: Plato to Dryden*, ed. Allan H. Gilbert (Detroit, Wayne State University Press, 1962).
Lopate, Phillip, *Notes on Sontag* (Princeton: Princeton University Press, 2009).
Lord, Russell, *Gordon Parks: The Making of an Argument* (Göttingen: Steidl/The Gordon Parks Foundation, 2013).
Lowry, Joanna, 'Modern Time: Revisiting the Tableau', in Jan Baetens, Alexander Streitberger, and Hilde Van Gelder (eds.), *Time and Photography* (Leuven: Leuven University Press, 2010), 47–64.
Lubow, Arthur, *Diane Arbus: Portrait of a Photographer* (New York: HarperCollins, 2016).
Luray, Howard, *Your Simple Flash Camera: How to Use It* (San Francisco: Camera Craft Publishing Company, 1953).
Lynch, Christopher, *When Hollywood Landed at Chicago's Midway Airport: The Photos & Stories of Mike Rotunno* (Charleston, SC: The History Press, 2012).
Macdonald, Ross, *The Drowning Pool* (1950; New York: Vintage Books, 1996).
McEuen, Melissa A., *Seeing America: Women Photographers Between the Wars* (Lexington, KY: University Press of Kentucky, 2000).
McNally, Joe, *The Hot Shoe Diaries: Big Light from Small Flashes* (Berkeley: New Riders, 2009).
McNeil, Ian (ed.), *An Encyclopedia of the History of Technology* (London: Routledge, 1990).
Mannheim, L. A. *The Rollei Way: The Rolleiflex and Rolleicord Photographer's Companion* (1951; 9th edn., London: Focal Press, 1970).
Marien, Mary Warner, *Photography and Its Critics: A Cultural History, 1839–1900* (Cambridge: Cambridge University Press, 1997).

Martin, Paul, *Victorian Snapshot* (London: Country Life, 1939).
Martin, Rupert, *Floods of Light: Flash Photography 1851–1981* (London: Photographers' Gallery, 1982).
Martínez, Alejandro, '"A souvenir of undersea landscapes": Underwater Photography and the Limits of Photographic Visibility, 1890–1910', *História, Ciências, Saúde-Manguinhos* 21/3 (2014), 1–18.
Meister, Sarah Hermanson, *Bill Brandt: Shadow & Light* (New York: Museum of Modern Art, 2013).
Melville, Herman, 'The Lightning-Rod Man' (1854), in *Pierre, Israel Potter, The Piazza Tales, The Confidence-Man, Uncollected Prose, & Billy Budd* (New York: Library of America, 1984).
Merleau-Ponty, Maurice, *Phenomenology of Perception*, trans. Colin Smith (New York: Routledge & Kegan Paul, 1962).
Metz, Christian, 'Photography and Fetish', *October* 34 (1985), 81–90.
Meyer, Richard, 'Photography Is Elastic: Weegee's Cockeyed View of Hollywood', *American Art* 27/2 (2013), 33–7.
Meyer, Richard, and Anthony W. Lee, *Weegee and* Naked City (Berkeley and Los Angeles: University of California Press, 2008).
Meyer, Richard, and Weegee, *Naked Hollywood: Weegee in Los Angeles* (New York: Rizzoli, 2011).
Milkman, Paul, *PM: A New Deal in Journalism, 1940–1948* (New Brunswick, NJ: Rutgers University Press, 1997).
Miller, Ivor, '"If It Hasn't Been One of Color": An Interview with Roy DeCarava', *Callaloo* 13/4 (autumn 1990), 847–57.
Miller, Larry S., and Richard T. McEvoy Jr, *Police Photography* (6th edn., Amsterdam: Elsevier Science, 2010).
Milton, John, *Paradise Lost* (1667; Oxford: Oxford University Press, 2008).
Miner, Al, and Yoav Rinon, *Ori Gersht, History Repeating* (Boston: Museum of Fine Art Publications, 2012).
Miyao, Daisuke, *The Aesthetics of Shadow: Lighting and Japanese Cinema* (Durham, NC: Duke University Press, 2013).
Moeller, Madelyn, 'Ladies of Leisure: Domestic Photography in the Nineteenth Century', in Kathryn Grover (ed.), *Hard at Play: Leisure in America, 1840–1940* (Amherst, MA: University of Massachusetts Press, 1992), 139–60.
Mora, Gilles, and Beverly W. Brannan, *FSA: The American Vision* (New York: Abrams, 2006).
Mordden, Ethan, *The Hollywood System: House Style in the Golden Years of the Movies* (New York: Knopf, 1988).
Mormorio, Diego, *Tazio Secchiaroli: Greatest of the Paparazzi* (1998), trans. Alexandra Bonfante-Warren (New York: Harry N. Abrams, 1999).
Mortensen, William, *Flash in Modern Photography* (San Francisco: Camera Craft Publishing Co., 1950).
Mortimer, F. J., *Magnesium Light Photography* (London: Dawbarn & Ward, 1906).
Morus, Iwan Rhys, *Frankenstein's Children: Electricity, Exhibition, and Experiment in Early Nineteenth-Century London* (Princeton: Princeton University Press, 1998).
Moutoussamy-Ashe, Jeanne, *Viewfinders: Black Women Photographers* (New York: Dodd, Mead & Co., 1986).
Muller, Eddie, *Dark City: The Lost World of Film Noir* (New York: St Martin's Griffin, 1998).
Müller-Heller, Katja, and Florian Sprenger (eds.), *Blitzlicht* (Zurich: diaphanes, 2012).
Munro, Thomas, Roy E. Stryker, and Rexford Guy Tugwell, *American Economic Life and the Means of Its Improvement* (3rd edn., New York: Harcourt, Brace and Co., 1930).
Münsterberg, Hugo, *The Photoplay: A Psychological Study* (New York: D. Appleton and Company, 1916).

Murphy, Burt, *Police and Crime Photography* (New York: Verlan Books, 1960).

Muspratt, James Sheridan, *Chemistry, Theoretical, Practical, and Analytical: As Applied and Relating to the Arts and Manufactures*, 2 vols. (Glasgow: W. Mackenzie, 1857, 1860).

Nabokov, Vladimir, *Lolita* (1955; New York: Vintage Books, 1989).

Nabokov, Vladimir, *Speak, Memory: An Autobiography Revisited* (1966; London: Penguin Modern Classics, 2000).

Naremore, James, *More than Night: Film Noir and Its Contexts* (updated and expanded edn., Berkeley and Los Angeles: University of California Press, 2008).

Natanson, Nicholas, *The Black Image in the New Deal: The Politics of FSA Photography* (Knoxville, TN: University of Tennessee Press, 1992).

Natanson, Nicholas, 'Robert McNeill and Black Government Photographers', *History of Photography* 19/1 (1995), 20–31.

Natanson, Nicholas, 'From Sophie's Alley to the White House: Rediscovering the Visions of Pioneering Black Government Photographers', *Prologue Magazine*, special issue on Federal Records and African American History, 29/2 (summer 1997), http://www.archives.gov/publications/prologue/1997/summer/pioneering-photographers.html.

National Museum of African American History and Culture, *Picturing the Promise: The Scurlock Studio and Black Washington* (Washington, DC: Smithsonian Books, 2009).

National Press Photographers Association, *Complete Book of Press Photography* (New York: National Press Photographers Association, 1950).

Neisser, Ulric, 'Snapshots or Benchmarks?', in Ulric Neisser and Ira Hyman (eds.), *Memory Observed: Remembering in Natural Contexts* (San Francisco: W. H. Freeman and Co., 1982), 43–8.

Nemerov, Alexander, 'The Dark Cat: Arthur Putnam and a Fragment of Night', *American Art* 16/1 (2002), 36–59.

Nemerov, Alexander, 'Burning Daylight: Remington, Electricity, and Flash Photography', in Nancy K. Anderson (ed.), *Frederic Remington: The Color of Night* (Princeton: Princeton University Press, 2003), 76–95.

Nemerov, Alexander, *Soulmaker: The Times of Lewis Hine* (Princeton: Princeton University Press, 2016).

Nemerov, Howard, *The Winter Lightning: Selected Poems of Howard Nemerov* (London: Rapp & Whiting, 1968).

Nesbit, William, *How To Hunt with the Camera: A Complete Guide to all Forms of Outdoor Photography* (New York: E. P. Dutton, 1926).

Nietszche, Friedrich, *Ecce Homo: How One Becomes What One Is* (1888; London: Penguin, 1992).

Nietzsche, Friedrich, *Human, All Too Human: A Book for Free Spirits* (1878), trans. R. J. Hollingdale (Cambridge: Cambridge University Press, 1996).

Nixon, Jude V., '"Death blots black out": Thermodynamics and the Poetry of Gerard Manley Hopkins', *Victorian Poetry* 40/2 (2002), 131–55.

Novotny, Anne, *Alice's World: The Life and Photography of an American Original, Alice Austen, 1866–1952* (Old Greenwich, CT: Chatham Press, 1976).

Nye, David E., *Electrifying America: Social Meanings of New Technology, 1880–1940* (Cambridge, MA: MIT Press, 1990).

Nye, David E., *American Technological Sublime* (Cambridge, MA: MIT Press, 1994).

O'Brian, John (ed.), *Camera Atomica* (London: Black Dog Publications, 2015).

Ohrn, Karin Becker, *Dorothea Lange and the Documentary Tradition* (Baton Rouge, LA: Louisiana State University Press, 1980).

Oliva, Achille Bonito, *A Flash of Art: Action Photography in Rome 1953–1973* (Milan: Photology, 2003).

O'Neal, Hank, *A Vision Shared: A Classic Portrait of America and Its People, 1935–1943* (New York: St Martin's Press, 1976).

Orvell, Miles, 'Weegee's Voyeurism and the Mastery of Urban Disorder', *American Art* 6/1 (winter 1992), 18–41.

Orvell, Miles, 'Portrait of the Photographer as a Young Man: John Vachon and the FSA Project', in Townsend Ludington (ed.), *A Modern Mosaic: Art and Modernism in the United States* (Chapel Hill, NC: University of North Carolina Press, 2000), 306–33.

Orvell, Miles, *John Vachon's America: Photographs and Letters from the Depression to World War Two* (Berkeley and Los Angeles: University of California Press, 2003).

Osborne, Elizabeth A., *Staging the People: Community and Identity in the Federal Theatre Project* (New York: Palgrave Macmillan, 2011).

Otis, Laura, 'The Metaphoric Circuit: Organic and Technological Communication in the Nineteenth Century', *Journal of the History of Ideas* 63/1 (2002), 105–28.

Otter, Chris, *The Victorian Eye: A Political History of Light and Vision in Britain, 1800–1910* (Chicago: University of Chicago Press, 2008).

Pacific War Research Society, *The Day Man Lost: Hiroshima, 6 August 1945* (Tokyo: Kodansha International, 1972).

Page, Tim, *Another Vietnam: Pictures of the War from the Other Side* (Washington, DC: National Geographic, 2002).

Park, William, *What is Film Noir?* (Lewisburg, PA: Bucknell University Press, 2011).

Parker, Parker, 'Melville's Salesman Story', *Studies in Short Fiction* 1/2 (1964), 154–8.

Parks, Gordon, *Flash Photography* (New York: Franklin Watts, 1947).

Parks, Gordon, *A Choice of Weapons* (New York: Harper and Row, 1965).

Parks, Gordon, *Voices in the Mirror: An Autobiography* (New York: Doubleday, 1990).

Parks, Gordon, *Half Past Autumn: A Retrospective* (Boston: Little, Brown & Co., 1997).

Parks, Gordon, and Michael Torosian, *Harlem: The Artist's Annotations on a City Revisited in Two Classic Photographic Essays*, introduction and interview by Michael Torosian (Toronto: Lumiere Press, 1997).

Parr, Martin, and Gerry Badger, *The Photobook: A History*, vol. i (London: Phaidon Press, 2004).

Pater, Walter, *Studies in the History of the Renaissance* (1873; Oxford: Oxford University Press, 2010).

Peacocke, Captain Leslie T., *Hints on Photoplay Writing* (Chicago: Photoplay Publishing Co., 1916).

Peeler, David P., *Hope Among Us Yet: Social Criticism and Social Solace in Depression America* (Athens, GA: University of Georgia Press, 1987).

Peirce, Charles Sanders, *Collected Papers of Charles Sanders Peirce*, ed. Charles Hartstone and Paul Weiss (Cambridge, MA: Harvard University Press, 1932).

Pelizzon, V. Penelope, and Nancy M. West, '"Good Stories" from the Mean Streets: Weegee and Hard-Boiled Autobiography', *Yale Journal of Criticism* 17/1 (2004), 20–50.

Penn, Irving, *Worlds in a Small Room* (New York: Grossman Publishers, 1974).

Phelan, Peggy, 'Introduction', in Tim Etchells, *Certain Fragments: Contemporary Performance and Forced Entertainment* (London: Routledge, 1999).

Phipson, Dr T. L., *Familiar Letters on Some Mysteries of Nature and Discoveries in Science* (London: Sampson Low, Marston, Searle, & Rivington, 1876).

Piazza, Pierre (ed.), *Aux origines de la police scientifique: Alphonse Bertillon, précurseur de la science du crime* (Paris: Karthala, 2011).

Pierre, C. Grand, *The Little Book of Greenwich Village* (New York: C. Grand Pierre, 1935).

Pierson, Melissa, *The Place You Love is Gone* (New York: W. W. Norton, 2006).

'Polaroid & Apartheid: Inside the Beginnings of the Boycott, Divestment Movement Against South Africa', *Democracy Now*, 13 December 2013, https://www.democracynow.org/2013/12/13/polaroid_apartheid_inside_the_beginnings_of.

'Polaroid and South Africa', http://kora.matrix.msu.edu/files/50/304/32-130-1F7-84-african_activist_archive-a0a8g3-b_12419.pdf.

Ponting, Herbert G., *The Great White South or With Scott in the Antarctic* (1921; London: Duckworth & Co., 1923).

Price, Jack, *News Photography* (New York: Round Table Press, 1935).

Prodger, Phillip, *Time Stands Still: Muybridge and the Instantaneous Photography Movement* (Oxford: Oxford University Press, 2003).

Proust, Marcel, *Jean Santeuil*, preceded by *Les Plaisirs et les jours*, ed. Pierre Clarac and Yves Sandre (Paris: Bibliothèque de la Pléiade, 1971).

Proust, Marcel, *Jean Santeuil*, trans. Gerard Hopkins, with a preface by André Maurois (London: Penguin Books, 1985).

Proust, Marcel, *In Search of Lost Time*, ii. *Within a Budding Grove* (1919), trans. C. K. Scott Moncrieff and Terence Kilmartin, rev. D. J. Enright (New York: Modern Library, 1992).

Puckett, John Rogers, *Five Photo-Textual Documentaries from the Great Depression* (Ann Arbor: UMI Research Press, 1984).

Quinn, Susan, *Furious Improvisation: How the WPA and a Cast of Thousands Made High Art out of Desperate Times* (New York: Walker & Co., 2008).

Raicovich, Laura, *At the Lightning Field* (Minneapolis: Coffee House Press, 2017).

Raiford, Leigh, *Imprisoned in a Luminous Glare: Photography and the African American Freedom Struggle* (Chapel Hill, NC: University of North Carolina Press, 2013).

Rampersad, Arnold, *The Life of Langston Hughes*, ii. *1941–1967: I Dream a World* (Oxford: Oxford University Press, 1988).

Rancière, Jacques, *Aisthesis: Scenes from the Aesthetic Regime of Art* (2011), trans. Zakir Paul (New York: Verso, 2013).

Rankine, Claudia, *Citizen* (Minneapolis: Graywolf Press, 2014).

Ransome, Arthur, *The Big Six* (London: Jonathan Cape, 1940).

Raubicheck, Walter, and Srebnick, Walter, *Hitchcock's Rereleased Films: From* Rope *to* Vertigo (Detroit: Wayne State University Press, 1991).

Rawsthorn, Alice, 'Vision Quest', *T Style Magazine. New York Times*, 15 April 2007, http://query.nytimes.com/gst/fullpage.html?res=9A04E1DF153FF936A25757C0A9619C8B63&pagewanted=all.

Reevy, Tony, *O. Winston Link: Life Along the Line* (New York: Abrams, 2012).

Reilly, John M., 'Richard Wright Preaches the Nation: 12 Million Black Voices', *Black American Literature Forum* 16/3 (autumn 1982), 116–19.

Reynolds, Simon, *Energy Flash: A Journey Through Rave Music and Dance Culture* (Berkeley: Soft Skull Press, 2012).

Rhodes, Richard, *The Making of the Atomic Bomb* (New York: Simon and Schuster, 1986).

Rigden, John S., *Rabi, Scientist and Citizen*, with a new preface (Cambridge, MA: Harvard University Press, 2000).

Riis, Jacob August, *How The Other Half Lives: Studies Among the Tenements of New York* (New York: Charles Scribner's Sons, 1890).

Riis, Jacob August, *The Making of an American* (1892; New York: Macmillan Co., 1901).

Riis, Jacob, *The Children of the Poor* (New York: Charles Scribner's Sons, 1908).

Rinder, Irwin D., 'A Sociological Look into the Negro Pictorial', *Phylon Quarterly* 20/2 (1959), 169–77.

Ritch, Wm. S., *Amateur Portraiture by Flash-Light* (Rochester, NY: Eastman Kodak Co., 1904).

Robinson, David, Stephen Herbert, and Richard Crangle (eds.), *Encyclopedia of the Magic Lantern* (London: Magic Lantern Society, 2001).

Rodgers, H. J., *Twenty-Three Years Under A Sky-Light, or Life and Experiences of a Photographer* (Hartford: H. J. Rodgers, 1872).

Rodgers, Terence, *Grant Allen: Literature and Cultural Politics at the Fin de Siècle* (Farnham: Ashgate, 2005).

Rosenberg, David, 'The Intimate Results of Photographing Subjects for Eight Minutes Each', 'Behold: The Photo Blog', *Slate*, 8 April 2015, http://www.slate.com/blogs/behold/2015/04/08/gary_schneider_the_series_heads_examines_the_performative_aspect_of_making.html.

Rosenfeld, Albert, 'A Remarkable Mind Drug Suddenly Spells Danger: LSD', *Life*, 25 March 1966, 28–33.

Rosenthal, Peggy, 'The Nuclear Mushroom Cloud as Cultural Image', *American Literary History* 3/1 (Spring 1991), 63–92.

Rosler, Martha, 'Lee Friedlander, an Exemplary Modern Photographer', *Decoys and Disruptions: Selected Writings, 1975–2003* (Cambridge, MA: MIT Press, 2004).

Ross, Ross, '*Doctor Atomic*: "Countdown"', *New Yorker*, 3 October 2005, http://www.newyorker.com/magazine/2005/10/03/countdown-4.

Roth, Lorna, 'Looking at Shirley, the Ultimate Norm: Colour Balance, Image Technologies, and Cognitive Equity', *Canadian Journal of Communication* 34 (2009), 111–36.

Rousmanière, Nicole Coolidge, and William Jeffett (eds.), *Hiroshi Sugimoto* (Norwich: Sainsbury Centre for Visual Arts, 1997).

Rousseau, Jean-Jacques, *Emile; or, On Education* (1762), trans. Christopher Kelly and Allan Bloom (Dartmouth, MA: University Press of New England, 2010).

Rowell, Charles H., '"I Have Never Looked Back Since": An Interview with Roy DeCarava', *Callaloo* 3/4 (autumn 1990), 859–71.

Ruby, Jay, *Secure the Shadow: Death and Photography in America* (Cambridge, MA: MIT Press, 1995).

Ruskin, John, *The Works of John Ruskin*, ed. E. T. Cook and Alexander Wedderburn, 39 vols. (London: George Allen, 1903–12).

Ruskin, John, *The Diaries of John Ruskin*, ed. Joan Evans and J. Howard Whitehouse, 3 vols. (Oxford: Clarendon Press, 1956–9).

Russell, Alan K., *Rivals of Sherlock Holmes: Forty Six Stories of Crime and Detection from Original Illustrated Magazines* (Secaucus, NJ: Castle Books, 1981).

Ryan, James, *Picturing Empire: Photography and the Visualization of the British Empire* (Chicago: University of Chicago Press, 1997).

Sampsell-Willmann, Kate, *Lewis Hine as Social Critic* (Jackson, MS: University Press of Mississippi, 2009).

Sandweiss, Martha (ed.), *Photography in Nineteenth-Century America* (Fort Worth, TX: Amon Carter Museum, Fort Worth and Harry N. Abrams, 1991).

San Francisco Museum of Modern Art, *Diane Arbus: Revelations* (New York: Random House, 2003).

Sansom, William, *The Blitz: Westminster at War* (Oxford: Oxford University Press, 1990).

Sante, Luc, 'The Planet', in Philip-Lorca diCorcia, *Heads* (Göttingen: SteidlBoxPacemacgill, 2001).

Sante, Luc, *Folk Photography: The American Real-Photo Postcard 1905–1930* (Portland, OR: Yeti/Verse Chorus Press, 2009).

Sante, Luc, Cynthia Young, Paul Strand, and Ralph Steiner, *Unknown Weegee* (New York: International Center for Photography/Steidl, 2006).

Sargent, Epes Winthrop, *The Technique of the Photoplay* (2nd edn., New York: Moving Picture World, 1913).

Sayag, Alain, and Annick Lionel-Marie, *Brassaï: The Monograph* (Boston: Bulfinch Press, 2000).

Schaaf, Larry J., *Out of the Shadows: Herschel, Talbot & the Invention of Photography* (New Haven: Yale University Press, 1992).

Schaffer, Simon, 'A Science Whose Business is Bursting: Soap Bubbles as Commodities in Classical Physics', in Lorraine Daston (ed.), *Things That Talk: Object Lessons from Art and Science* (New York: Zone Books, 2004), 147–92.

Schatz, Thomas, *The Genius of the System: Hollywood Filmmaking in the Studio Era* (Minneapolis: University of Minnesota Press, 2010).

Schillings, C. G., With Flashlight and Rifle: A Record of Hunting Adventures and of Studies in Wild Life in Equatorial East Africa, trans. Frederic Whyte, 2 vols. (London: Hutchinson & Co., 1906).

Schivelbusch, Wolfgang, *Disenchanted Night: The Industrialization of Light in the Nineteenth Century*, trans. Angela Davies (Berkeley and Los Angeles: University of California Press, 1988).

Schriever, J. B., *Commercial, Press, Scientific Photography: Complete Self-Instructing Library of Practical Photography*, vol. ix (Scranton: American School of Art and Photography, 1909).

Schulman, Sammy, *'Where's Sammy?'*, ed. Robert Considine (New York: Random House, 1943).

Schwartz, Bonnie Nelson, and the Educational Film Center, *Voices from the Federal Theatre* (Madison: University of Wisconsin Press, 2003).

Schwartz, Vanessa R., 'Wide Angle at the Beach', *Études photographiques* 26 (Nov. 2010), http://etudesphotographiques.revues.org/3455.

Seiberling, Grace, with Carolyn Bloore, *Amateurs, Photography, and the Mid-Victorian Imagination* (Chicago: University of Chicago Press, 1986).

Seixas, Peter, 'Lewis Hine: From "Social" to "Interpretive" Photographer', *American Quarterly* 39/3 (autumn 1987), 381–409.

Sekula, Allan, *Photography Against the Grain: Essays and Photo Works 1973–1983* (Halifax, Nova Scotia: Press of the Nova Scotia College of Art and Design, 1984).

Selvon, Sam, *The Lonely Londoners* (1956; London: Penguin Classics, 2006).

Sentman, Mary Alice, 'Black and White: Disparity in Coverage By Life Magazine from 1937 to 1972', *Journalism Quarterly* 60 (autumn 1983), 501–8.

Sharpe, Anthony, *The Mystery of the Flashlight Print* (London: Aldine Books, 1924).

Sharpe, William Chapman, *New York Nocturne. The City After Dark in Literature, Painting, and Photography* (Princeton: Princeton University Press, 2008).

Shelley, Mary, *Frankenstein: or 'The Modern Prometheus'* (1818; Oxford: Oxford University Press, 2008).

Shelley, Percy Bysshe, *The Major Works* (Oxford World's Classics; Oxford: Oxford University Press, 2009).

Shiras, George, *Hunting Wild Life with Camera and Flashlight*, 2 vols. (London: National Geographic Society, 1930).

Shiras, George, *The Wild Life of Lake Superior, Past and Present: The Habits of Deer, Moose, Wolves, Beavers, Muskrats, Trout, and Feathered Wood-Folk Studied with Camera and Flashlight* (London: National Geographic Magazine, 1921), 113–204.

Sikov, Ed, *Mr Strangelove: A Biography of Peter Sellers* (New York: Hachette Books, 2002).

Silcox, Harry S., *Jennings' Philadelphia: The Life of Philadelphia Photographer William Nicholson Jennings (1860–1946)* (Philadelphia: Brighton Press, 1993).

Silver, Sean, 'The Temporality of Allegory: Melville's "The Lightning-Rod Man"', *Arizona Quarterly* 62/1 (2006), 1–33.

Simmel, Georg, 'The Metropolis and Mental Life' (1903), in *Georg Simmel on Individuality and Social Forms*, ed. Donald L. Levine (Chicago: University of Chicago Press, 1971), 324–39.

Singer, Ben, *Melodrama and Modernity: Early Sensational Cinema and Its Contexts* (New York: Columbia University Press, 2001).

Sitney, P. Adams, 'Structural Film', *Film Culture* 47 (summer 1969), 1–10.

Sivulka, Juliann, *Soap, Sex and Cigarettes: A Cultural History of American Advertising* (Belmont, CA: Wadsworth Publishing Co., 1998).

The Slang Dictionary, Etymological, Historical, and Anecdotal (2nd edn., London: Chatto and Windus, 1874).

Smith, Erin A., *Hard-Boiled: Working-Class Readers and Pulp Magazines* (Philadelphia: Temple University Press, 2000).

Smith, Morgan, and John Smith, *Harlem: The Vision of Morgan and Marvin Smith* (Lexington, KY: University Press of Kentucky, 1997).

Smith, Shawn Michelle, '"Looking at One's Self through the Eyes of Others": W. E. B. Du Bois's Photographs for the 1900 Paris Exposition', *African American Review* 34/4 (winter 2000), 581–99.

[The Smith-Victor Co.], *Flashlight Photography* (Chicago: James Smith & Sons, *c.*1912).

Snyder, Robert E., 'Erskine Caldwell and Margaret Bourke-White: You Have Seen Their Faces', *Prospects: An Annual of American Cultural Studies* 11. *Essays* (Cambridge: Cambridge University Press, 1987).

Solnit, Rebecca, *River of Shadows: Eadweard Muybridge and the Technological Wild West* (New York: Viking, 2004).

Sontag, Susan, *On Photography* (New York: Picador, 1977).

Sontheimer, Morton, *Newspaperman: A Book about the Business* (New York: Whittlesey House, 1941).

Spencer, Stephanie, *O. G. Rejlander: Photography as Art* (Ann Arbor: UMI Research Press, 1981).

Spender, Stephen, *Citizens in War—and After* (London: Harrap, 1945).

Sporn, Paul, *Against Itself: The Federal Theater and Writers' Projects in the Midwest* (Detroit: Wayne State University Press, 1995).

Squiers, Carol, '"And so the moving trigger finger writes": Dead Gangsters and New York Tabloids in the 1930s', in Sandra S. Phillips, Mark Haworth-Booth, and Carol Squiers, *Police Pictures: The Photograph as Evidence* (San Francisco: Chronicle Books, 1997), 40–9.

Squiers, Carol, *Over Exposed: Essays on Contemporary Photography* (New York: The New Press, 1999).

Stange, Maren, *Symbols of Ideal Life: Social Documentary Photography in America* (New York: Cambridge University Press, 1989).

Stange, Maren, 'Illusion Complete Within Itself: Roy DeCarava's Photography', in Townsend Ludington (ed.), *A Modern Mosaic: Art and Modernism in the United States* (Chapel Hill, NC: University of North Carolina Press, 2000), 279–304.

Stange, Maren, '"Photographs Taken in Everyday Life": *Ebony*'s Photojournalistic Discourse', in Todd Vogel (ed.), *The Black Press: New Literary and Historical Essays* (New Brunswick, NJ: Rutgers University Press, 2001), 207–27.

Stange, Maren, *Bronzeville: Black Chicago in Pictures, 1941–1943* (New York: The New Press, 2003).

Stange, Maren, '"Not What We Seem": Image and Text in 12 Million Black Voices', in Ulla Haselstein, Berndt Ostendorf, and Peter Schneck (eds.), *Iconographies of Power: The Politics and Poetics of Visual Representation* (Heidelberg: Universitätsverlag Winter, 2003), 173–86.

Stansell, Christine, *American Moderns: Bohemian New York and the Creation of a New Century* (New York: Metropolitan Books, 2000).

Stebbins, Robert A., *Amateurs, Professionals, and Serious Leisure* (Montreal: McGill-Queen's University Press, 1992).

Sternberger, Paul Spencer, *Between Amateur and Aesthete: The Legitimization of Photography as Art in America, 1880–1900* (Albuquerque, NM: University of New Mexico Press, 2001).

Stevens, John D., *Sensationalism and the New York Press* (New York: Columbia University Press, 1991).

Stiles, Anne, *Popular Fiction and Brain Science in the Late Nineteenth Century* (Cambridge: Cambridge University Press, 2012).

Stott, William, *Documentary Expression and Thirties America* (New York: Oxford University Press, 1973).

Stuart-Wortley, Lady Emmeline, '*Sonnets: Written Chiefly During a Tour Through Holland, Germany, Italy, Turkey, and Hungary* (London: J. Rickerby, 1839).

Sussman, Elisabeth, 'In/Of Her Time: Nan Goldin's Photographs', in Nan Goldin, David Armstrong, and Hans Werner Holzwarth (eds.), *Nan Goldin: I'll Be Your Mirror* (New York: Whitney Museum of Art, 1996), 25–44.

Sutherland, John, *Stephen Spender: A Literary Life* (Oxford: Oxford University Press, 2005).

Sutton, Raul, and Keith Trueman, *Crime Scene Management: Scene Specific Methods* (New York: Wiley, 2013).

Symons, Arthur, *Silhouettes* (London: Elkin Mathews and John Lane, 1892).

Szarkowski, John, *Bellocq: Photographs from Storyville, the Red-Light District of New Orleans* (New York: Random House, 1996).

Szarkowski, John, Foreword to *Russell Lee Photographs: Images from the Russell Lee Photograph Collection* (Austin, TX: University of Texas Press, 2007).

Tagg, John, *The Disciplinary Frame: Photographic Truths and the Capture of Meaning* (Minneapolis: University of Minnesota Press, 2009).

Talbot, William Henry Fox, 'Some Account of the Art of Photogenic Drawing' (1839), in Vicki Goldberg (ed.), *Photography in Print: Writings from 1816 to the Present* (Albuquerque, NM: University of New Mexico Press, 1981).

Tennant, [John A.], and [H. Snowden] Ward, *Flashlight Portraiture: A Book of Common Sense Information and Practical Methods of Making Portraits by Flashlight at Home or in the Photographic Studio* (New York: Tennant and Ward, 1912).

Tennyson, Alfred, *In Memoriam*, in *Tennyson: A Selected Edition* (Longmans Annotated English Poets), ed. Christopher Ricks (2nd edn., London: Routledge, 2006).

Thomas, Arthur Winfield, *How to Write a Photoplay* (Chicago: The Photoplaywrights Association of America, 1914).

Thompson, Krista, *Shine: The Visual Economy of Light in African Diasporic Aesthetic Practice* (Durham, NC: Duke University Press, 2015).

Thornton, Sarah, *33 Artists in 3 Acts* (New York: W. W. Norton & Co., 2014).

Todd, Charlie, and Alex Scordelis, *Causing a Scene: Extraordinary Pranks in Ordinary Places with Improv Everywhere* (New York: Harper Collins, 2009).

Towers, T. D., *Electronics and the Photographer* (London: Focal Press, 1976).

Trachtenberg, Alan, 'Weegee's City Secrets', *E-rea: Revue électronique d'études sur le monde anglophone* 7/2 (2010), sect. 12, https://erea.revues.org/1168.

Trethewey, Natasha, *Bellocq's Ophelia* (Minneapolis: Graywolf Press, 2002).

Truffaut, François, *Hitchcock* (New York: Simon & Schuster, 1967).

Tucker, Jennifer, *Nature Exposed: Photography as Eyewitness in Victorian Science* (Baltimore: Johns Hopkins University Press, 2005).

Turim, Maureen, *Flashbacks in Film: Memory & History* (New York: Routledge, 1989).

Turner, Graeme, *Understanding Celebrity* (London: Sage Publications, 2004).

Twain, Mark, *Autobiography of Mark Twain: The Complete and Authoritative Edition*, 3 vols., ed. Harriet E. Smith, Benjamin Griffin, Victor Fischer, Michael B. Frank, Sharon K. Goetz, and Leslie Diane Myrick (Berkeley and Los Angeles: University of California Press, 2010).

Van Parys, Thomas, 'A Typology of the Publicity Still: Film for Photograph', *History of Photography* 32/1 (2008), 85–92.

Van Riper, Frank, *Talking Photography: Viewpoints on the Art, Craft and Business* (New York: Allworth Press, 2002).

VCE Inc., *How to Photograph an Atomic Bomb* (Santa Clarita, CA: VCE Inc., 2006).

Viemester, Peter E., *The Lightning Book* (New York: Doubleday, 1961).

Villeponteaux, Elizabeth, 'Flashing Foil and Oozing Oil: Trinitarian Imagery in "God's Grandeur"', *Victorian Poetry* 40/2 (2002), 201–7.

Vincendeau, Ginette, *Brigitte Bardot* (London: Palgrave Macmillan, 2013).

Vining, Lancelot, *My Way with the Miniature* (13th edn., London: Focal Press, 1958).

Vitray, Laura, John Mills, Jr, and Roscoe Ellard, *Pictorial Journalism* (New York: McGraw-Hill Book Company, 1939).

Von Schwartz, Dr [Ernst], *Fire and Explosion Risks*, trans. from rev. German edn. by Charles T. C. Salter (London: Charles Griffin and Co., 1904).

Waller, Philip, *Literary Life in Britain 1870–1918* (Oxford: Oxford University Press, 2006).

Wallis, Brian (ed.), *Murder Is My Business* (New York: International Center of Photography, 2013).

Wanucha, Genevieve, 'Remembering "Papa Flash"', *MIT News*, 4 January 2013, http://web.mit.edu/newsoffice/2013/remembering-harold-edgerton.html.

Weegee, *Naked City* (New York: Da Capo Press, 1945).

Weegee, *Weegee's Secrets of Shooting with Photoflash as told to Mel Harris* (New York: designers 3, 1953).

Weegee, with Roy Ald, *Weegee's Creative Camera* (New York: Vista House, 1959).

Weissman, Terri, *The Realisms of Berenice Abbott* (Berkeley and Los Angeles: University of California Press, 2011).

Wells, Alison, 'Why Flash Fiction Will Last', 3 June 2011, http://www.writing.ie/guest-blogs/why-flash-fiction-will-last/.

Wells, H. G., *The Time Machine* (1895; Oxford: Oxford University Press World's Classics, 2017).

West, Nancy Martha, *Kodak and the Lens of Nostalgia* (Charlottesville: University of Virginia Press, 2000).

Wexler, Laura, *Tender Violence: Domestic Visions in an Age of U.S. Imperialism* (Chapel Hill, NC: University of North Carolina Press, 2000).

Wheatstone, Sir Charles, 'An Account of Some Experiments to Measure the Velocity of Electricity and the Duration of Electric Light', *Philosophical Transactions of the Royal Society* (1834); repr. in *The Scientific Papers of Sir Charles Wheatstone* (London: Physical Society, 1879), 95–6.

Whitman, Walt, *The Complete Poems [Walt Whitman]*, ed. Francis Murphy (1975; Harmondsworth: Penguin Books, 1986).

Wilder, Kelley, *Photography and Science* (London: Reaktion Books, 2009).

Williams, Val, *Martin Parr* (2nd edn., London: Phaidon Press, 2014).

Willis, Chris, 'The Detective's *Doppelgänger*: Conflicting States of Female Consciousness in Grant Allen's Detective Fiction', in William Greenslade and Peter Morton (eds.), *'The Busiest Man in England': Grant Allen and the Writing Trade, 1875–1900* (New York: Palgrave, 2005), 143–53.

Willis, Deborah, *Reflections in Black: A History of Black Photographers 1840 to the Present* (New York: W. W. Norton & Co., 2000).

Willis, Nathaniel Parker, *Life, Here and There: Or Sketches of Society and Adventure at Far-Apart Times and Places* (New York: Baker and Scribner, 1850).

Willis, Nathaniel Parker, *The Convalescent* (New York: Charles Scribner, 1859).

Winograd, Eugene, and Ulric Neisser (eds.), *Affect and Accuracy in Recall: Studies of 'Flashbulb' Memories*, Emory Symposia in Cognition (Cambridge: Cambridge University Press, 2006).

Winter, Alison, *Memory: Fragments of a Modern History* (Chicago: University of Chicago Press, 2012).

Wolfe, Tom, *The Electric Kool-Aid Acid Test* (1968; New York: Bantam Books, 1999).

Wolseley, Roland E., *The Black Press, U.S.A.* (2nd edn., Ames: Iowa State University Press, 1990).

Wood, Amy Louise, *Lynching and Spectacle: Witnessing Racial Violence in America, 1890–1940* (Chapel Hill, NC: University of North Carolina Press, 2009).

Woolf, Virginia, *The Voyage Out* (1915; Oxford: Oxford University Press World's Classics, 2009).

Woolf, Virginia, *Three Guineas* (1938), in *A Room of One's Own* and *Three Guineas* (Oxford: Oxford University Press World's Classics, 2015).

Woolrich, Cornell, 'Rear Window', *The Cornell Woolrich Omnibus* (New York: Penguin Books, 1998), 5–36.

Wordsworth, William, *The Prelude: 1799, 1805, 1850*, ed. M. H. Abrams, Stephen Gill, and Jonathan Wordsworth (New York: W. W. Norton & Co., 1979).

Wordsworth, William, *Selected Poems*, ed. Stephen Gill (London: Penguin Classics, 2005).

Worthington, Arthur Mason, *The Study of Splashes* (London: Longmans, Green and Co., 1908).

Wortman, Rachel A., 'Street Level: Intersections of Art and the Law. Philip-Lorca diCorcia's "Heads" Project and Nussenzweig v. diCorcia', *Gnosis* 10/2 (2010), http://gnovisjournal.org/2010/04/25/street-level-intersections-art-and-law-philip-lorca-dicorcias-heads-project-and-nussenzweig/, accessed 22 May 2012.

Wright, Richard, *Native Son* (1940; New York: Harper Perennial Modern Classics, 2005).

Wright, Richard, *12 Million Black Voices* (1941), introduction by David Bradley, foreword by Noel Ignatiev (New York: Basic Books, 2008).

Yochelson, Bonnie, and Daniel Czitrom, *Rediscovering Jacob Riis: Exposure Journalism and Photography in Turn-of-the-Century New York* (New York: The New Press, 2007).

Zeliger, Barbie, 'The Voice of the Visual in Memory', in K. R. Phillips (ed.), *Framing Public Memory* (Tuscaloosa, AL: University of Alabama Press, 2004), 157–86.

Zemka, Sue, *Time and the Moment in Victorian Literature and Society* (Cambridge: Cambridge University Press, 2012).

Zuromskis, Catherine, *Snapshot Photography: The Lives of Images* (Cambridge, MA: MIT Press, 2013).

INDEX

Image locations are in **bold**